ELEVENTH EDITION

CANADIAN ENTREPRENEURSHIP AND SMALL BUSINESS MANAGEMENT

D. Wesley Balderson
UNIVERSITY OF LETHBRIDGE

Dr. Peter Mombourquette
MOUNT SAINT VINCENT UNIVERSITY

Mc Graw Hill

Canadian Entrepreneurship & Small Business Management
Eleventh Edition

ISBN-13: 978-1-260-06590-9
ISBN-10: 1-26-006590-1

1 2 3 4 5 6 7 8 9 0 M 24 23 22 21 20

Printed and bound in Canada.

Product Director: *Rhondda Mcnabb*
Portfolio Manager: *Amy Clarke-Spencley & Mark Grzeskowiak*
Marketing Manager: *Emily Park*
Content Developer: *Peter Gleason*
Portfolio Associate: *Christine Albert*
Supervising Editor: *Jack Whelan*
Photo/Permissions Researcher: *Indu Arora*
Copy Editor/Proofreader: *Margaret Henderson*
Plant Production Coordinator: *Joelle McIntyre*
Manufacturing Production Coordinator: *Jason Stubner*
Cover Design: *Lightbox Visual Communications Inc.*
Cover Image: © *KreativeKolors/Shutterstock*
Page Layout: *SPi Global*
Printer: *Marquis*

Dedication

To my wonderful son Jack. You have helped me more that you will ever be able to understand. I love you always.

Peter Mombourquette

Brief Contents

Contents

Preface

Canadian Entrepreneurship & Small Business Management, eleventh edition, is the result of many years of teaching entrepreneurship business classes at the college and university levels; of starting and managing several successful small businesses; of working closely with numerous owners of small businesses in a consulting role; and, of course, of having experience with all the previous successful editions. This edition builds on the changes in the previous edition, with an increased emphasis on being current, generating and maintaining student interest in the subject matter, and improving academic rigour. All changes were made while staying true to the book's vision of being easy to follow and absorbing.

To accomplish these sometimes diverse aims, the text draws on theory from the fields of entrepreneurship, small business management, and the major functional areas of business, including management, marketing, accounting, and finance. The text supports theory with hundreds of real-life business examples featured in boxes and opening profiles. These features have been carefully selected to reflect the diversity of Canada and include a mix of both young, inspiring entrepreneurs and experienced, high-profile business owners. In addition, many boxes have become cases with thought-provoking discussion questions to generate student interest in the subject matter. The chapters now include over 500 additional in-text examples about current business owners, trends in small business, and emerging topics in entrepreneurship.

The book is supported by numerous end-of-chapter cases that illustrate the small business management concepts discussed in the text. These concepts are stated at the beginning of each case in the Instructor's Manual to aid in teaching. Each case proceeds in a logical order from start-up of the business, through management of the existing business, and finally to planning for the future.

WHAT'S NEW IN THIS EDITION

The eleventh edition introduces several improvements to the previous editions based on professor and student feedback. Specifically, this edition includes the following:

Chapter 1: The Role of Entrepreneurship and Small Business in Canada

- Enhanced discussion of the benefits of studying small business and entrepreneurship
- Enhanced discussion of young and immigrant entrepreneurs, including exciting examples and in-chapter cases
- Additional facts and figures on Canadian entrepreneurship and why young people would benefit from starting a business.
- New and revised in-chapter cases and examples on:
  - New chapter opening Small Business Profile: Jay Dingwall, Famous Folks
  - New in-chapter case: Peace by Chocolate started by the Hadhad family, Syrian refugees to Canada
  - New in-chapter case: Chic Marie, a Canadian online clothing rental business
  - Young Canadian social entrepreneurs
  - Ryan Holmes & HootSuite.com

Chapter 2: The Small Business Decision

- Enhanced discussion of the advantages and disadvantages of entrepreneurship, including the inclusion of many new and exciting examples to support the theory in the text.
- Enhanced discussion on the small business decision.
- New and revised in-chapter cases on:
  - New chapter opening Small Business Profile: Xavier Peich and Gabriel Alberola, SmartHalo
  - New in-chapter case: Tulip, an online company that is hoping to transform and save retail, as well as its founder Ali Asaria
  - New in-chapter case: Poppy & Peonies, a direct sales handbag company
  - Updated case on Mompreneurs

Chapter 3: Evaluation of a Business Opportunity

- New and enhanced information on idea generation
- Enhanced information on opportunity assessment
- Discussion and in-chapter case on replacing traditional market research with crowdfunding.
- New and revised in-chapter cases and examples:
  - New chapter opening Small Business Profile: David Tao and Jayden Li, Tapplock
  - New in-chapter case: fantasy sports and fan-controlled football
  - New case on replacing market research with crowdfunding
  - Updated case on Gord Dickie and his web company goalline.ca

Chapter 4: Organizing a Business—The Business Plan

- New information on the importance of business planning
- Discussion and in-chapter case on the Lean Start-up
- New and revised in-chapter cases and examples:
  - New chapter opening Small Business Profile: Michele Romanow, young serial entrepreneur and her latest business Clearbanc, a FinTech company
  - Lean Startup and the advantages and disadvantages
  - Alyssa Furtado and Ratehub, an online company that assists people in finding competitive mortgage and insurance rates
  - Updates on Notable.ca and its planning strategy
  - Shockbox, a concussion sensor for hockey and football helmets

Chapter 5: Buying a Business and Franchising

- Enhanced discussion on buying a business and franchising as a means of becoming an entrepreneur
- New and expanded information on evaluating franchise opportunities
- New and revised in-chapter cases and examples:
  - New in-chapter case: Chris Guillemet and Boris Martin and Velofix, the mobile bicycle-repair franchise they started and are expanding globally after only a few short years in business
  - New in-chapter case: Carmelo Marsala and Spray-Net, the innovative home-painting company that he is franchising across Canada
  - Trends in franchising
  - Unhappyfranchisee.com and A&W restaurants

Chapter 6: Financing the Small Business

- New information on sources of financing and types of financing used by small business
- New information on crowdfunding, including how to create a successful crowdfunding campaign, and how to avoid common mistakes
- New information on angel investors and angel organizations
- Significantly increased coverage of bootstrap financing
- Introduction of FinTech, financial companies that operate online to compete with banks. We look at what it means to small business when FinTech companies are offering financing and services at lower costs
- New information on government programs aimed at youth startups
- Significantly increased the number of in-chapter examples of young entrepreneurs and how they successfully raised money
- New and revised in-chapter cases and examples on:
  - Creating a successful crowdfunding campaign
  - Next steps after a successful crowdfunding campaign
  - Qasim Mohammad's choice to use bootstrap financing for his customer advocacy business
  - The willingness of the chartered banks to lend money to entrepreneurs
  - FinTech and entrepreneurs

Chapter 7: Marketing Management

- Enhancements to the sections on market planning
- Increased coverage of customer profiles, target marketing, and customer-relationship management.

- New and revised in-chapter cases and examples on:
  - Spin Master and their success using innovative marketing and public relations
  - New case on Indigenous entrepreneur Mark Marsolais Nahwegahbow and his company Birch Bark Coffee
  - Updates to the case on Leonard Asper and target marketing

Chapter 8: Managing the Marketing Mix

- Enhanced coverage of all aspects of the marketing mix
- Introduced the concept and included discussion of "influencers" in marketing for small businesses
- Increased the amount of information on promotions for small business, beginning with an emphasis on traditional marketing and extending to Internet and digital marketing
- Expanded information on direct selling or peer-to-peer sales
- New information on the use of digital marketing and marketing using social media
- Increased coverage of Facebook, YouTube, Instagram, and Pinterest in marketing a business, including the use of Snapchat and dating apps such as Tinder
- New information on using mobile devices to market a business
- New information and examples on guerrilla marketing and public relations
- Introduced many new in-text examples of successful entrepreneurs and their marketing ideas
- New and revised in-chapter cases and examples on:
  - New chapter opening Small Business Profile: Christian Lunny and Aaron Wojnowski who have created a very successful music app, Musi, with virtually no investment of money
  - New in-chapter case: Indigenous entrepreneur Patrice Mousseau and her business, Satya
  - New case on social media guerrilla marketing
  - New information on impact of appearing on *Dragons' Den* for small business owners

Chapter 9: Financial Management

- New information on bootstrap financing
- New in-text examples supporting the theories discussed in the text
- New and revised in-chapter cases on:
  - New in-chapter case: bootstrapping as young entrepreneurs with limited resources grow their candy business
  - New in-chapter case: Glow Promotions and the importance of controlling costs and managing finances

Chapter 10: Operations Management

- New information on how entrepreneurs can use bootstrapping techniques in operation management
- New information on creating retail locations that are both functional and attractive, with brand new information on window displays
- New in-chapter case: Robin Godin, his family business Godin Guitars, and their manufacturing process
- New in-text examples

Chapter 11: Human Resources Management

- New information on the pending labour crisis in Canada and its impact on small business owners
- Enhanced information on human resources planning
- New information on the use of social media and human resources management
- New information on company culture, as well as leadership, and its importance in building a successful company
- New and revised in-chapter cases on:
  - New chapter opening Small Business Profile: Jason Tafler, founder of Unyte, a company that focuses on helping people reach their health goals through meditation
  - New in-chapter case: Chris and Rebecca Troelstra and their company AvenueHQ, which offers flexible work schedules and a strong company culture in their efforts to recruit employees and build a successful organization
  - New in-chapter case: Mandy Rennehan and her company Freschco's employee screening, orientation, and culture
  - New in-chapter case: entrepreneur Nikolai Bratkovski and the importance of hiring properly, and creating a winning team of employees and a successful organizational culture

- Use of LinkedIn and employee recruitment
- Purdy's Chocolates and building employee loyalty
- New information in the in-chapter case of bringing pets to work as a motivational strategy

Chapter 12: Management Help: Mentors, Boards of Advisors or Directors, and Tax Assistance

- New information on mentors and their importance to young entrepreneurs
- New information on boards of directors and boards of advisors
- New information on establishing boards and maintaining relationships
- New and revised in-chapter cases on:
  - New chapter opening Small Business Profile: Devon Brooks and her new company Sphere, which connects coaches/mentors with people
  - Updated in-chapter case on establishing a board of advisors
  - Updated case: Victoria Sopik and Jennifer Nashmi of Kids & Company

Chapter 13: Managing Growth

- New information on the importance of growth in small and medium-sized businesses
- Enhanced information on growth strategies and planning for growth
  - New chapter opening Small Business Profile: Chris Webb and Victoria Foulger and their business, Pavia, an illustration of how growth can allow entrepreneurs to run a more sustainable business
  - Updated information on BeyondtheRack.com, a Canadian flash retailer that enjoyed significant growth but was plagued with problems associated with growth
  - Updated information on Enviro Paving, a company seeking growth by franchising–the company repaves driveways with recycled rubber

Chapter 14: Managing the Transfer of the Business

- New information and statistics on succession planning and family-owned businesses in Canada
- New information on creating a successful succession plan
- New information on successfully selling a business
- New and revised in-chapter cases on:
  - New chapter opening Small Business Profile: Dani Reiss and Canada Goose, illustrating the progression of a company from a family business to one pursuing an exit strategy to facilitate growth
  - Updated information on harvesting strategies

This text remains appropriate for any entrepreneurship or small business management class at the college or university undergraduate or graduate level. It can also be adapted easily to continuing education classes for those who are thinking about or are currently involved in running their own businesses. In many cases, the text would also be a useful resource book for practitioners outside the classroom setting.

CHAPTER STRUCTURE OF *CANADIAN ENTREPRENEURSHIP & SMALL BUSINESS MANAGEMENT*

Canadian Entrepreneurship & Small Business Management is divided into four parts. Each part covers an essential aspect of starting or managing a small business.

Part 1 provides background information essential to the decision to undertake small business ownership. Chapter 1 reviews the characteristics of small business and its contribution to Canadian society. Chapter 2 covers areas required for a personal evaluation of their suitability for small business ownership. Chapter 3 presents a systematic procedure for determining whether a small business opportunity is feasible. It includes numerous sources of information essential in carrying out a feasibility analysis.

The three chapters in Part 2 discuss important aspects of starting or obtaining a business. Chapters 4, 5, and 6 review the three methods of establishing a small business. Chapter 4 discusses organizing the small business from scratch, including a special emphasis on the preparation of the business plan. Chapter 5 covers both buying a business and franchising as options for small business ownership.

Chapter 6 discusses financing concerns in starting the business and includes a listing of sources of financing for entrepreneurs.

Part 3 includes six chapters that discuss the fundamental management practices used in operating the already established business. Chapters 7, 8, 9, 10, and 11 cover in detail the small business applications in marketing, finance, internal operations, and personnel management. Chapter 12 focuses on establishing and managing relationships with outside advisors, such as mentors and boards, along with a discussion of tax considerations for the small business owner-manager.

Part 4 discusses the future and long-term aspects of small business. Chapter 13 deals with the principles underlying effective growth management. Chapter 14 discusses methods of terminating or transferring the ownership of the enterprise, with a special emphasis on family businesses.

FEATURES OF THIS BOOK

Every chapter opens with a list of **Learning Objectives,** which clearly identify the key topics of each chapter and what the student should take away from the discussion.

LEARNING OBJECTIVES

By the end of this chapter, you should be able to:

LO1 Recognize the importance of the marketing mix.

LO2 Explain how products and services are created.

LO3 Explain the differences in marketing to consumers and marketing to businesses.

LO4 Discuss three methods of price setting.

LO5 Identify the major steps in a promotion campaign.

LO6 Compare and contrast different promotional tools.

The **Small Business Profiles** that open every chapter are real-life examples and real-person profiles, the epitome of applied learning.

SMALL BUSINESS PROFILE

XAVIER PEICH & GABRIEL ALBEROLA *SMARTHALO*

Ideas for successful businesses can come from anywhere. Some ideas can come from a deliberate search, where an entrepreneur is looking for the next great business idea. Other times ideas can come from personal experiences—both good and bad. Xavier Peich notes that he came up with the idea for SmartHalo, a bicycle accessory that turns any bike into a smart bike, after a particular run of bad luck riding his bicycle around Montreal. Peich says he was trying to use his phone to navigate through the city streets and the phone slipped out of his hands breaking the screen. A short time later his bike was stolen. Peich, who was looking for a business to pursue with his long-time friend Gabriel Alberola thought their had to be a simple solution to some of the many problems bikers face in navigating city streets. Together the pair formed the company CycleLabs and developed the concept of SmartHalo which they affectionally describe as a bike companion.

SmartHalo, which attaches to the handlebars of any bike, marries together several features cyclists are looking for including a GPS, alarm system, fitness app, messaging notification system and a headlight which switches itself off when the bike it not in use. The SmartHalo accessory also comes with a protected locking system so it cannot be stolen. SmartHalo attachment works in conjunction with the user's phone and the SmartHalo app to provide bikers with an improved biking experience.

SmartHalo's design and ease of use has led it to championed by such influential publishers as *Times, Forbes, Fortune,* and CBC. The Halo uses Bluetooth technology to link your phone's GPS to the attachment. A rider simply uses their phone's GPS to select a desired location and the Halo becomes operational illustrating the correct path using lights that are easy to see and follow. If the rider misses a turn the Halo flashed red indicating the need for a U-turn. The GPS alone has been described as a significant improvement over using your phone as a GPS. In addition to the GPS feature, the SmartHalo offers cyclists a variety of desired features that are easy to use. The SmartHalo can act as a compass, allowing riders to select their own route to a desired destination; has a light that automatically turns on as the sun sets and shuts off when the cyclist stops biking; will sound an alarm if someone is attempting to steal the bike; serve as a fitness tracker, allowing riders to track their progress as they peddle; and act as an assistant by notifying riders to incoming calls and messages.

Photo courtesy of SmartHalo

Peich and Alberola with their concept in hand then did what may aspiring entrepreneurs are doing today, they opted to skip traditional market research, and bring their product directly to consumers using the crowd-funding site Kickstarter. They initially were hoping to raise $67,000 in pre-orders for SmartHalo but exceeded that goal on day one and raised almost $540,000 over the course of their month-long Kickstarter campaign. The large influx of cash and pre-orders proved that the concept was a viable product and the pair started to work on building their business. The SmartHalo founders partnered with other companies to manufacture SmartHalo including Osedea, a mobile app developer, Mapbox, a GPS mapping company, and Optech, a design optics lab. Roughly 18 months after their Kickstarter campaign started, SmartHalo was being shipped to eager consumers.

CycleLabs continues to push SmartHalo and now has the product available in all Apple stores in North America and Europe. Consumers can also purchase the accessory at Best Buy and Amazon. The company is currently working on alternate maps to allow cyclists to maximize their riding experience and considering expanding the attachment to work as a guide for tourists.

The **Small Business Beginnings** and **Small Business in Action** boxes contain current, real-world examples of small business and entrepreneurship successes and challenges and discuss relevant issues related to the chapter topic. Many boxes have been expanded to include **Discussion Questions.**

SMALL BUSINESS BEGINNINGS 1-2

PEACE BY CHOCOLATE

The Hadhad family were well-known chocolatiers in their native Syria. Under father Assam Hadhad's leadership, they had a factory in Damascus, Syria, and were shipping their unique chocolates all over the Middle East when war broke out in their country. With their factory and most of Damascus destroyed, the family fled to a Lebanese refugee camp. They lived at the camp for three years until qualifying to come to Canada.

Once they arrived in Canada in 2016, the family moved to the small community of Antigonish, Nova Scotia, where community leaders had fund-raised to sponsor the Hadhad's immigration. To welcome the Hadhads to Canada, they were invited to a potluck and Assam made some of his chocolates in their new home. The chocolates were the hit of the gathering and soon afterwards the Hadhads started to sell their chocolates at local farmer's markets. Sales grew quickly and soon the family wanted to open a retail location. A short time later, 60 members of the community came together to build the Hadhads a small shed that would serve as the first store front. Tariq Hadhad, Assam's son and current CEO of the family company, says the community rallied around the family and the support from the local people was incredible.

As sales grew, so did news about the company. Soon people across Canada were talking about the Syrian family's entrepreneurial skills and their chocolates. Prime Minister Justin Trudeau spoke about the Hadhads at the United Nations, and the company was featured in dozens of news stories. The Hadhads also wanted to give back, ever thankful that Canada welcomed them into their country. While still starting their new company, the company donated money to Fort McMurray charities after the fire in 2016, and the company produced some specialty chocolate bars to celebrate and embrace Pride.

As their sales continued to grow, the Hadhads began looking to expand. They worked out an agreement with Sobeys, who had an empty building in the town: Sobeys would supply the building and Peace by Chocolates would supply Sobeys with chocolates. With the new factory in place, Peace by Chocolate required more help; they hired 10 employees in 2017 and employed 45 by 2019. Antigonish mayor Laurie Boucher says the Hadhads have been an inspiration to the small rural community. Boucher says that Hadhads have given people hope that entrepreneurship can work in rural parts of Nova Scotia.

Still looking to give back, the Hadhads have recently committed to hiring 50 refugees by 2022 and mentoring 10 refugee startups. As of 2019, Peace by Chocolate is available in over 400 Canadian locations with online sales throughout the world.

Discussion Questions

1. The Hadhad family has been quite successful in public relations (PR). The business has been featured in numerous articles and on television. What are some of the advantages of this type of marketing? Do you think the business will be able to maintain this positive PR long term? Why or why not?
2. What do you think would be some of the advantages and disadvantages associated with starting a business in rural Nova Scotia, specifically Antigonish, which has a population of approximately 4300 people.
3. Do you think Peace by Chocolate should be considered a social enterprise? Why or why not?

SMALL BUSINESS IN ACTION 1-2

YOUNG CANADIAN SOCIAL ENTREPRENEURS

More younger Canadians are turning toward social entrepreneurship as a way to make a difference in society and earn a living. For example, Greg Overholt, founder of Toronto-based **Students Offering Support**, or SOS, recruits volunteers to set up on-campus tutoring sessions for groups of students rather than traditional one-to-one tutoring. This lowers tutoring costs: students pay on average $10 to $20 for help compared with the $50 to $75 charged by for-profit tutors for a similar session. Overholt's company retains a small portion of the fee and uses the rest of the money to send volunteers on two-week outreach trips to build education projects in developing nations. The company's motto is "Raise money to raise roofs through raising marks." To date, the company has recruited more than 10,000 tutor volunteers, who have helped more than 100,000 students and raised $2.5 million for projects throughout the world.

Chris Janssen saw an opportunity to give back when he left Canada to teach in Rwanda. Janssen noticed that groups of African students were often huddled together sharing a single textbook. Knowing that there are tens of thousands of used textbooks in Canada, Janssen and his business partner, Tom Hartford, started **Textbooks for Change**. Textbooks for Change collects textbooks in Canada and sends them to post-secondary libraries in East Africa after they fit a list of partnership criteria. It also raises money by selling used books at low cost to students across North America, and it recycles textbooks that would normally end up in landfills. The company boasts that 50 percent of the textbooks they collect are redistributed to post-secondary libraries in East Africa, 30 percent are sold at affordable prices, and 20 percent are recycled efficiently. To date, Janssen's company has donated 300,000 textbooks, distributed over $250,000 in donations/micro-loans, and recycled/redistributed over 300,000 textbooks as well. After making Textbooks for Change sustainable, Janssen has moved to Kenya to work on his second social enterprise called eLengo, which focuses on digital education in the agriculture sector.

Chris Janssen founded Textbooks for Change, a social enterprise that collects used textbooks to provide affordable educational material for students around the world.

Photo courtesy of Chris Janssen, Textbooks for Change

Discussion Questions

1. How would you define social entrepreneurship? Do you think there is a difference between social entrepreneurs and regular entrepreneurs? Why or why not?
2. Can entrepreneurs consider themselves social entrepreneurs if they retain all the profits from their business?
3. Either in groups or individually, list some ideas for a social enterprise. If time permits, discuss the marketing mix for one social enterprise, including the product or service you will sell, how you will promote the business, the price you will charge, and where the business will be located.

Figures and **tables** are included to illustrate relevant ideas and concepts.

FIGURE 2-2 Characteristics of Entrepreneurs

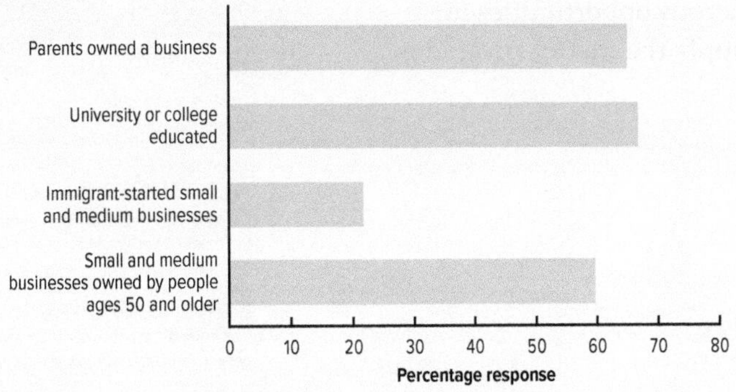

TABLE 6-1 Start-Up Cost Schedule

ITEM	COST	SOURCE
Land and buildings	No cost—leased	If purchased, a similar business or quotes from suppliers
Equipment	$ 34,000	Other similar businesses or quotes from suppliers
Initial inventory	70,000	Other similar businesses or quotes from suppliers Use the formula Inventory = Projected sales/ Inventory turnover (300,000/4.3)
Wages (first two months)	6,000	Other similar businesses or current wage rates
Utilities and telephone		
First deposit	100	Quotes from provider
First two months	680	Quotes from provider
Rent (deposit)	500	Quotes from lessor
First two months	3,000	Quotes from lessor
Advertising agency/media	960	Quotes from advertising agency or media
Insurance (prepaid)	975	Quotes from insurer
Licences and permits	200	Quotes from municipal agency
Other prepaids	285	Other similar businesses
Contingency	3,300	
Total start-up requirements	**$120,000**	

Each chapter contains a **Learning Objectives Summary** that clearly reinforces the learning objectives covered in the chapter.

LEARNING OBJECTIVES SUMMARY

LO1 **A key element in the marketing plan is establishing the correct marketing mix. A good marketing mix will create value and long-term relationships with target customers and distinguish a business from its competitors.**

LO2 **Product development involves idea generation, product testing, and ultimately, if successful, commercialization.**

LO3 **Consumer marketing involves less detail and a shorter buying cycle compared with business marketing.**

LO4 **The three methods of setting price are cost-based, demand-based, and competition-based pricing.**

LO5 **Within a marketing plan, businesses usually have a promotional plan that includes objectives, information about target markets and an understanding of their needs, a theme, strategies and tools, messages, budgets, the timing of implementation, and a method of evaluation.**

The **Time to Take Action, Discussion Questions,** and **Experiential Exercises,** appearing at the end of every chapter, allow students to use applied and lateral thinking and to come up with unique solutions to typical small business issues.

DISCUSSION QUESTIONS

1. Briefly explain the ways of entering a market. List examples that fit these methods other than those mentioned in the text.
2. J&J Inc. is thinking of developing a new coin laundry. The firm first needs to do some market research to determine the demand for the product. What kind of information should it collect?
3. Why is it important to make adjustments in market potential and market share figures?
4. For a small business of your choice, show how you would evaluate nonquantitative factors, such as goals, experience, lifestyle, and content of work.
5. Discuss the difficulties of preparing a feasibility analysis for an e-commerce business.

The end-of-part **Cases,** as well as the end-of-text **Supplementary Cases,** provide numerous opportunities for students to apply the theory covered in the text.

CASES FOR PART 3

Derocher's Market	Taylor Construction Company
Home Smart Hardware Store	The Barrow Bracket
Martha's Designs	Threadz
Sadie's Country n' Western Store	Garner Men's Wear
Dale's Sport Pursuit	Boomerang Bouncers Entertainment
Susie's Fashions	

DEROCHER'S MARKET

Derocher's Market opened a new store in Québec City in January 2019. Although the firm has been in business for three generations, the neighbourhood in which the original store stood had become shabby, and many of its loyal clientele had moved to the suburbs. The present owner, Claude Derocher, decided to follow the population move. The new store is located next to a several other small independent businesses near more than 70 four-storey apartment buildings that house more than 400 families. Many more apartment buildings are under construction, as well as three- and four-bedroom single-family homes in several nearby housing developments. The nearest competition is located approximately three kilometres northeast of the present shopping centre.

The **Comprehensive Case** runs throughout the text and has been updated for the eleventh edition. Following a typical small business person's progress and challenges, this case allows students to build on the concepts as the course progresses.

COMPREHENSIVE CASE DAN KIM: PART 3

Dan is quite proud of his business plan and realizes that he has learned a lot in preparing it. He also realizes, however, that for the business to get off the ground, he needs to raise additional money. Suzie will only let Dan use $20,000 of their savings for the venture, but Dan is of the opinion that this will at least help them get started. Once the business is up and running, additional funds will be generated through sales of the Ladder Helper.

Dan has also decided that he would rather establish the manufacturing facility from scratch rather than lease or purchase an existing facility. This way he can arrange the building as it suits him, and he will not have to spend money to retrofit. In addition, Dan lives on an acreage which he inherited and he already owns enough property on which to construct the building. He estimates that constructing a small building of 2000 square feet will cost

AWARD-WINNING TECHNOLOGY

McGraw-Hill connect®

McGraw-Hill Connect® is an award-winning digital teaching and learning solution that empowers students to achieve better outcomes and enables instructors to improve efficiency with course management. Within Connect, students have access to SmartBook®, McGraw-Hill's adaptive learning and reading resource. SmartBook prompts students with questions based on the material they are studying. By assessing individual answers, SmartBook learns what each student knows and identifies which topics they need to practice, giving each student a personalized learning experience and path to success.

Connect's key features also include analytics and reporting, simple assignment management, smart grading, the opportunity to post your own resources, and the Connect Instructor Library, a repository for additional resources to improve student engagement in and out of the classroom.

Instructor Resources for Canadian Entrepreneurship and Small Business Management, 11e

- Instructor's Manual
- Test Bank
- Microsoft® PowerPoint® Presentations

Manager's HotSeat Videos

This resource allows students to watch real managers apply their years of experience to management and organizational behaviour issues. Students assume the role of the manager as they watch the video and then answer multiple-choice questions following the segment. The Manager's HotSeat Videos are ideal for group or classroom discussions.

Application-Based Activities

The Connect Application-Based Activities are highly interactive and automatically graded application- and analysis-based exercises wherein students immerse themselves in a business and marketing environment, analyze the situation, and apply their knowledge of small business and marketing strategies. Students progress from understanding basic concepts to assessing and solving complex real-world scenarios.

McGraw Hill connect®

Effective. Efficient. Easy to Use.

McGraw-Hill Connect is an award-winning digital teaching and learning solution that empowers students to achieve better outcomes and enables instructors to improve course-management efficiency.

Personalized & Adaptive Learning

Connect's integrated SmartBook helps students study more efficiently, highlighting where in the text to focus and asking review questions to give each student a personalized learning experience and path to success.

High-Quality Course Material

Our trusted solutions are designed to help students actively engage in course content and develop critical higher-level thinking skills, while offering you the flexibility to tailor your course to meet your needs.

Analytics & Reporting

Monitor progress and improve focus with Connect's visual and actionable dashboards. Reporting features empower instructors and students with real-time performance analytics.

Seamless Integration

Link your Learning Management System with Connect for single sign-on and gradebook synchronization, with all-in-one ease for you and your students.

Impact of Connect on Pass Rates

Without Connect | With Connect

SMARTBOOK®

NEW SmartBook 2.0 builds on our market-leading adaptive technology with enhanced capabilities and a streamlined interface that deliver a more usable, accessible and mobile learning experience for both students and instructors.

Available on mobile smart devices – with both online and offline access – the ReadAnywhere app lets students study anywhere, anytime.

SUPPORT AT EVERY STEP

McGraw-Hill ensures you are supported every step of the way. From course design and set up, to instructor training, LMS integration and ongoing support, your Digital Success Consultant is there to make your course as effective as possible.

Learn more about Connect at mheducation.ca

ACKNOWLEDGEMENTS

Many people contributed to *Canadian Entrepreneurship & Small Business Management,* eleventh edition. I am as always particularly grateful to my beautiful wife who serves as an editor, an idea generator, and a friend. I also could not do anything in life without the love and support of my children Jack, April, and Will–you mean the world to me. I am, of course, indebted to the wonderful people at McGraw-Hill, who I have worked with for 20 years. I especially want to thank Amy Clarke-Spencley and Peter Gleason. Reviewers and users of the previous editions also provided valuable suggestions. Thanks to our digital author, Michael Madore, who has been instrumental in the preparation of supplementary resources for the book. We acknowledge and thank David Newhouse, Professor and Director, Chanie Wenjack School for Indigenous Studies, Trent University, for his review of all indigenous content in this edition.

I also want to thank Wes Balderson and Professor Jim Clark, University of Lethbridge, who authored some of the cases.

I also thank the many authors and entrepreneurs who granted us permission to use figure, tables, profiles, and article excerpts to illustrate the text concepts.

Dr. Peter Mombourquette

PART 1

THE DECISION TO START A BUSINESS

The decision to start your own business is a difficult one. It often involves leaving secure employment to face an uncertain financial future. Such a decision can have far-reaching effects on the physical, emotional, and financial aspects of your life. To provide a better understanding of the implications and preparation for this decision, Part 1 discusses three topics.

Chapter 1 reviews the role of small business in Canadian society. It examines current trends and the probable future environment for small business.

Chapter 2 describes the characteristics of successful and unsuccessful small businesses, and the personal characteristics that most successful entrepreneurs have. The chapter also reviews the potential advantages and disadvantages of operating your own business. Understanding this information can help you make an informed small business career decision.

Once an individual understands the relative merits of starting a small business and feels suited to such a career, he or she can do several things in pursuit of the best business opportunity. Generally, a person needs to gather a considerable amount of information to evaluate business opportunities. Chapter 3 presents ideas that can improve information collection and analysis skills for this purpose.

CHAPTER 1

THE ROLE OF ENTREPRENEURSHIP AND SMALL BUSINESS IN CANADA

LEARNING OBJECTIVES

By the end of this chapter, you should be able to:

LO1 Discuss the level of interest and activity in the small business sector.

LO2 Evaluate common methods of defining small business and explain why a definition is important.

LO3 Summarize the current extent of entrepreneurship and small business in Canada.

LO4 Describe the benefits a healthy small business sector can offer society.

LO5 Explain the probable future environment for entrepreneurship and the small business community.

SMALL BUSINESS PROFILE

JAY DINGWALL *Famous Folks*

Photos courtesy of Famous Folks

Jay Dingwall recalls walking the streets of Toronto and becoming frustrated. He had just completed his Masters degree in Business Administration in Florida and, rather than return to his native Nova Scotia, he decided to move to Toronto and pursue his ambition to work for a marketing agency. Unfortunately, he was not having much success in landing a job. Dingwall had some work experience, two degrees, and spent considerable time playing competitive sports, which he thought would illustrate to others he was a strong team player. Yet his couldn't find a job working in the field he wanted; some firms said he was overqualified, while others didn't offer much in the way of an explanation. Dingwall, who is originally from the working-class community of Cape Breton, decided if he couldn't find a job with an agency, he would start his own. He says part of his resilience came from growing up in place where people didn't quit.

At the time, celebrities and other well-known people were becoming aware of their online brand, and he decided to create a firm that would help celebrities profit from their online and personal brands, so he named his company Famous Folks.

Dingwall knew he needed help with design for his firm and reached out to Ryan Joseph, a fellow Cape Bretoner who was working in Halifax, Nova Scotia. Dingwall said it was the best decision he ever made. Not only did Joseph think the same way he did about branding, but he was also creative and exceptionally hard working. A short time later the pair became partners.

The partners started looking for clients and noticed Pizzatown, a Halifax landmark, was in need of a branding redesign. With no contract in hand, Dingwall and Joseph created a new brand for the firm and met with the owner. A short time later, they received a contract—their first—and Famous Folks was officially started. They began to develop a niche in creating powerful brands both on- and offline.

Dingwall says the start-up stage for Famous Folks was more educational and far outweighed what he learned in school. But, he noted, starting up is hard: the entrepreneur must hunt and gather clients and there are many ups and downs. For example, shortly after landing the Pizzatown deal, Famous Folks signed its first larger client in Toronto, the owner of several high-end car dealerships specializing in Porsche and Audi cars. Dingwall was sure their business was really moving in the right direction. Then, the economic crash of 2008 struck. With the economy in a tailspin, no one was buying high-end cars, and with the decline in the economy came the end of the contract.

Dealing with the ups and downs of the business environment is part of being an entrepreneur, Dingwall notes. Rather than quit in 2008 when other small and even large firms closed, he and his partner persevered, slowly building their business over time. Because he and Joseph believed in their shared vision of creating a boutique entrepreneurial firm, this is exactly what they have established. Dingwall says his firm has roughly 15 full-time employees who like to work for Famous Folks as they can multitask and take on entrepreneurial-type roles. Employees and both owners really get their hands dirty on each and every project, and are able to learn from one another. Being small and engaged, the co-owners and the rest of the team are able to invest time in getting to know

[continued]

[continued]

clients and their business. The deep knowledge gained is empowering, and it enables Famous Folks to create powerful branding and marketing messages, and to position materials in the appropriate forms.

Dingwall says that being an entrepreneur, especially a young entrepreneur, is both challenging and educational. He notes that the advantage of starting a business right out of school, as he did, is people are willing to help young people get started. In the end, he says, entrepreneurship will grow your confidence and overall business knowledge.

FAMOUS FOLKS
famousfolks.ca

INTRODUCTION TO ENTREPRENEURSHIP AND WHY STUDENTS WILL WANT TO STUDY THE SUBJECT

This chapter provides an overview of the importance of and trends toward small business. The terms *entrepreneurship* and *small business ownership* will be used interchangeably throughout the chapter. Entrepreneurs typically start small businesses, but sometimes they establish larger enterprises. At the same time, many small business owners may not be considered very entrepreneurial. The differences between entrepreneurs and small business owners or managers will be discussed in detail in **Chapter 2**. In addition, the distinction between the entrepreneur and the small business is often difficult to make because the owner-manager and the business are frequently very much intertwined. This relationship between entrepreneur and business will also be discussed in the next chapter.

You may be asking yourself, "Why should I study entrepreneurship?" Perhaps you are interested in owning a business or are curious about why some businesses succeed and others fail. Entrepreneurship is an exciting field and studying small business has many benefits:

- Students who study entrepreneurship are more likely to start a business.
- Students who enroll in entrepreneurship courses earn more money.
- Students who enroll in entrepreneurship courses learn about important topics such as business planning, managing growth, and family businesses.
- Students who study entrepreneurship develop critical thinking and problem-solving skills.
- Because of trends in the workforce, such as outsourcing and subcontracting, many would-be employees end up working for themselves. People who study entrepreneurship are more likely to succeed in today's workforce.
- Ninety-nine percent of businesses in Canada are considered small or medium-sized enterprises (SMEs), so even if you never become an entrepreneur, you are likely to work in a small firm.[1] Studying entrepreneurship will provide you with the knowledge and skills to be successful in small companies.
- Research indicates that students enjoy learning about entrepreneurship.

In an opinion piece for *The Globe and Mail,* Bruce Rothney, CEO and Country Head of Barclays Canada, says that young people need exposure to entrepreneurship and risk taking if they are to be successful in the changing economy. Rothney is not alone in this belief, but he offers pointed advice to young people that entrepreneurship can build resilience and knowledge leading to long-term business success.[2] Jay Dingwall, who is featured in the

Small Business Profile that opens this chapter, agrees: he says he learned more about business being an entrepreneur than he learned in school.[3]

To better understand entrepreneurship and small business, it is important to consider the nature and development of the subject, particularly as it pertains to Canada.

NATURE AND DEVELOPMENT OF ENTREPRENEURSHIP IN CANADA LO1

Since the mid-1970s, there has been a reawakening of interest in entrepreneurship and business ownership in Canada, the United States, and abroad. After World War II, the philosophy in many circles was that bigger was better in both business and government. As a result, for several years, government increased in size, and the climate for big business improved.

The critics of "bigness," however, have gathered support because big government and big business have failed to provide the expected panacea for society's economic problems. The result has been that more people and more governments are looking to small business to provide a catalyst for their stagnant economies and to enable faster economic growth. As John Naisbitt stated in *Global Paradox,* "The entrepreneur is the most important player in the building of the global economy, so much so that big companies are decentralizing and reconstituting themselves as networks of entrepreneurs. Huge companies must break up to become confederations of small, autonomous, entrepreneurial companies if they are to survive."[4]

In a survey conducted by Ernst and Young, eight out of ten influential North Americans indicated that they believe entrepreneurialism will define twenty-first-century business.[5] For example. Arlene Dickinson, angel investor, owner of **Venture Communications** and star of CBC's *Dragons' Den,* says that entrepreneurs are the most important element of the Canadian economy and build our country's social and cultural makeup.[6] Growth in entrepreneurial interest and behaviour is evident in Canada. Approximately 500,000 people start a business each year in Canada, and interest among Canadians about entrepreneurship is growing.[7] For example, a recent **RBC** survey found that 54 percent of Canadians said they have thought about starting their own business. Additionally, 56 percent of Canadians are already acting entrepreneurial whether it be making money from a project (28 percent), taking on side jobs (20 percent) or testing out new business ideas (8 percent).[8] Additionally young people are especially interested in entrepreneurship as 46 percent of university students envision themselves starting a business after they graduate.[9] The international Global Entrepreneurship Monitor places Canada second in the world, behind only the United States, in entrepreneurship activity.[10] Additionally, Canada has been consistently recognized for having one of the highest levels of entrepreneurial activity in innovation-driven economies and in early-Stage Entrepreneurial Activity, according to Global Entrepreneurship Monitor guidelines.[11] By any measure, the trend toward improved entrepreneurial attitude, self-employment growth, and small business formation is positive in Canada. Starting a business is now seen as a preferred occupational alternative for many Canadians, and self-employed people make up over 15 percent of the labour force (**Figure 1-1**).

This growth in entrepreneurial attitudes, along with the significant growth in self-employment and small business formations, illustrates that entrepreneurship is firmly established in Canada. Except for a brief slowing of this growth from 1999 to 2002 and from 2008 to 2010, the growth of small businesses has consistently surpassed that of larger organizations and the economy as a whole.[12] As a result, the importance of the small business sector of Canadian society is now more widely acknowledged than ever.

What has fuelled this growth? Throughout this text, we will use many examples of entrepreneurs to illustrate why an increasing number of people are establishing their own businesses. The dream of starting small and developing a successful business, such as that of Jay Dingwall, who was featured in the **Small Business Profile**, or brothers Jesse, Luke, and Mason Hambly who invented the Pressa Bottle, a water bottle that allows users to infuse healthy fruit into their water (see **Small Business in Action 1-1**), is shared by many. However, many individuals have become successful entrepreneurs because of the downsizing of larger organizations. A survey found that 22 percent of small businesses are started for this reason.[13] For example, Ted Nugent, a Vancouver computer games developer, started Genius Factor Games when he was laid off from a gaming company. He was

FIGURE 1-1 **Self-Employed as a Percentage of the Labour Force**

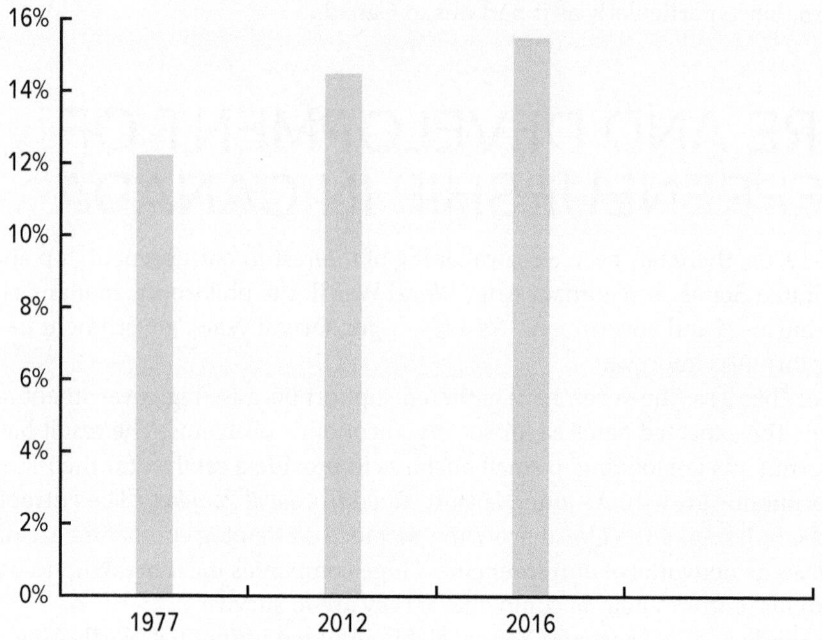

able to use his experience and his interest in being his own boss to launch his first product: *Gravity Well.* Nugent described the product as a cross between pinball and mini-golf.[14] Genius Factor Games went on to launch several games for smartphones and mobile devices, and developed *Heart Hero,* a game that teaches people how to administer CPR, for the Canadian Heart and Stroke Foundation.

SMALL BUSINESS IN ACTION 1-1

CROWDFUNDING HELPS BROTHERS BUILD A BETTER WATER BOTTLE

Brothers Jesse, Luke, and Mason Hambly from Elora, Ontario, are the creators of **Pressa Bottle**, a water-bottle infuser that allows users to press fruit and vegetables into their water for a refreshing and healthy drink.

Jesse Hambly says he came up with the idea for the product when he noticed that many of his friends were infusing their water bottles with fruits and vegetables yet were unhappy with the results. Friends complained both about the taste of the water and their inability to properly release healthy nutrients into their drinks. The three brothers decided to try current water-bottle infusers themselves and were unhappy with the results. Given the trend in society towards the consumption of more water and the desire to encourage people to drink healthier, the brothers decided they could create a better water infuser and a business. Rather than start building expensive prototypes, the trio accessed a 3D printer and within a week created their first working Pressa Bottle.

While the brothers admit the first bottle may not have been aesthetically pleasing, they did have a working prototype that would infuse juice into water to capture the full

Jesse, Luke and Mason Hambly used Kickstarter to raise $40,000, which helped them commercialize their Pressa Bottle.

Photo courtesy of Pressa Bottle

taste of the fruits and/or vegetables. They worked on the design until they were happy with the look and feel. Then, they brought the prototype to Conestoga and Georgian College for some entrepreneurship consulting; they eventually worked with the Accelerator Centre in Waterloo, Ontario.

Desperate to know what people thought about the bottle, the brothers brought it to a variety of public events asking people to try it and to provide feedback. Based on that feedback, the business partners felt they had the desired design and that the product met its promise of delivering fresh, infused juice into a traditional water bottle.

Photo courtesy of Pressa Bottle

With the finished product in hand, the brothers opted to pre-sell the water bottle on the crowdfunding site Kickstarter. Kickstarter allows supporters of a business idea an opportunity to pre-purchase products, usually at a discount, prior to the product being manufactured. With a catchy Kickstarter campaign that included a focus on local public relations, the brothers managed to pre-sell $40,000 worth of Pressa bottles and could begin manufacturing. A short time later, a website was launched, and initial monthly sales eclipsed $35,000 a month. The Pressa Bottle, which delivers Pressed Water as the brothers like to say, is now for sale on Amazon and Indigo websites as well as retail locations. The brothers hope to earn in excess of $500,000 in sales in their first year of business.

Discussion Questions

1. Do you think the Pressa Bottle will continue to be a successful product? Why or why not?
2. What do you think are some of the advantages and disadvantages of crowdfunding?
3. Visit the Kickstarter website and report back to the class on some of the best ideas that are being pitched. What are the terms associated with the ideas? Would you personally donate or invest money using crowdfunding?

During the recession from 2008 to 2010, many companies downsized, and many college and university graduates who were unable to secure employment started their own businesses. For example, David McDonald of Halifax started his own landscaping business after he could not find work when he graduated from **Mount Saint Vincent University** with a bachelor of business administration degree. McDonald used his business skills to determine there was a market for environmentally friendly landscaping and offered lawn care using organic products and push mowers. Others chose to leave secure employment and strike out on their own because of a natural interest or a desire for a challenge.

While some people are drawn to starting a business from scratch to make money or are pushed into entrepreneurship when they cannot find a job, others are attracted to entrepreneurship as a means to make a living and help solve some of society's problems. This trend of earning money and helping society has given rise to the term "social entrepreneurship." A social entrepreneur is a person who applies the skills of entrepreneurship, such as risk taking, problem solving, and business planning, to create social change. Social entrepreneurs not only strive to make money but also work toward making the world a sustainable community. For example, Dr. Gavin Armstrong, founder and CEO of **Lucky Iron Fish Enterprise (LIFE)**, a Guelph-based social enterprise developed a solution to iron deficiency, one of the world's largest nutrient challenges, which can cause anemia, cognitive deficiencies, and fatigue. Armstrong says people with iron deficiency usually have to take supplements which are difficult to digest and expensive. Armstrong says people need a simple solution and his iron fish which can be placed in boiling water can fortify meals with healthy iron. His company sells the iron fishes globally and for every one sold he donates an iron fish to a family in need. To date the company has donated 45,000 iron fish helping 250,000 people.[15]

Dr. Gavin Armstrong's social enterprise, Lucky Iron Fish, sells an affordable and safe solution to iron deficiency. Consumers simply drop the iron fish into boiling water or liquid-based meals to infuse their meals or drinking water with the needed supplement.

Jesse Winter/Toronto Star via Getty Images

Other examples of social entrepreneurship include Indigenous entrepreneur Jenn Harper founder of **Cheekbone Beauty Cosmetics Inc.** Harper's company which specializes in making and selling lip gloss, donates 10 percent of all profits to First Nations Child and Family Caring Society of Canada.[16] **Small Business in Action 1-2** for more examples of young social entrepreneurs. Canadian philanthropist, and eBay's first employee and eventual CEO, Jeff Skoll believes so much in the idea of social enterprise and social entrepreneurship that he created the **Skoll Foundation** to invest in social entrepreneurs. The Foundation is the world's largest organization dedicated to social entrepreneurship and makes annual grants of $40 million to social entrepreneurs and social organizations throughout the world. Skoll thinks that many of society's complex problems need to be addressed with innovative solutions.[17] Who better to develop these solutions than entrepreneurs? Entrepreneurs are known for their hard work, problem-solving skills, and innovativeness, which is needed in today's society. Social entrepreneurs are usually ambitious people who value helping society over making a profit and are driven to produce results.

SMALL BUSINESS IN ACTION 1-2

YOUNG CANADIAN SOCIAL ENTREPRENEURS

More younger Canadians are turning toward social entrepreneurship as a way to make a difference in society and earn a living. For example, Greg Overholt, founder of Toronto-based **Students Offering Support**, or SOS, recruits volunteers to set up on-campus tutoring sessions for groups of students rather than traditional one-to-one tutoring. This lowers tutoring costs: students pay on average $10 to $20 for help compared with the $50 to $75 charged by for-profit tutors for a similar session. Overholt's company retains a small portion of the fee and uses the rest of the money to send volunteers on two-week outreach trips to build education projects in developing nations. The company's motto is "Raise money to raise roofs through raising marks." To date, the company has recruited more than 10,000 tutor volunteers, who have helped more than 100,000 students and raised $2.5 million for projects throughout the world.

Chris Janssen saw an opportunity to give back when he left Canada to teach in Rwanda. Janssen noticed that groups of African students were often huddled together sharing a single textbook. Knowing that there are tens of thousands of used textbooks in Canada, Janssen and his business partner, Tom Hartford, started **Textbooks for Change**. Textbooks for Change collects textbooks in Canada and sends them to post-secondary libraries in East Africa after they fit a list of partnership criteria. It also raises money by selling used books at low cost to students across North America, and it recycles textbooks that would normally end up in landfills. The company boasts that 50 percent of the textbooks they collect are redistributed to post-secondary libraries in East Africa, 30 percent are sold at affordable prices, and 20 percent are recycled efficiently. To date, Janssen's company has donated 300,000 textbooks, distributed over $250,000 in donations/micro-loans, and recycled/redistributed over 300,000 textbooks as well. After making Textbooks for Change sustainable, Janssen has moved to Kenya to work on his second social enterprise called eLengo, which focuses on digital education in the agriculture sector.

Chris Janssen founded Textbooks for Change, a social enterprise that collects used textbooks to provide affordable educational material for students around the world.

Photo courtesy of Chris Janssen, Textbooks for Change

Discussion Questions

1. How would you define social entrepreneurship? Do you think there is a difference between social entrepreneurs and regular entrepreneurs? Why or why not?
2. Can entrepreneurs consider themselves social entrepreneurs if they retain all the profits from their business?
3. Either in groups or individually, list some ideas for a social enterprise. If time permits, discuss the marketing mix for one social enterprise, including the product or service you will sell, how you will promote the business, the price you will charge, and where the business will be located.

Recently, governments have been promoting social enterprise at the national and provincial levels, and several provinces, such as Nova Scotia, have developed strategies to assist social entrepreneurs. Prominent Canadian social enterprise organizations the **Social Enterprise Council of Canada**, and the **Canadian Social Enterprise Foundation**. Additionally, a school for social entrepreneurs has been started in Ontario, the **School for Social Entrepreneurs**, whose mission is "to empower communities by developing community leaders and transformational social ventures that produce tangible, visible, meaningful, and positive impact."[18]

The information and examples discussed so far provide evidence of the growth of small business and how entrepreneurs, such as Jay Dingwall, Jesse Hambly, and Greg Overholt, can overcome hurdles to be successful. A detailed discussion of the evidence for small business growth follows.

INCREASES IN THE NUMBER OF BUSINESS ESTABLISHMENTS

Considerable research has been done to determine the number of new businesses established each year. This has proved a difficult, if not impossible, task because of the many different types of businesses and the varied methods of estimating business start-ups. Some indicators of business start-ups that researchers have used include tax returns, new employer registrations, phone hookups, new incorporations, and business registrations.[19]

Figure 1-2 shows the number of small businesses in Canada in 2017. Small businesses with few employees constitute the majority of all businesses with employees, but small businesses with no employees make up an even larger number. In addition, the number of businesses with fewer than 50 employees has increased substantially over the past decade. Similar trends for the United States show even more increases in small business formations than in Canada.[20] Statistics Canada has estimated that 97.9 percent of all existing businesses have fewer than 100 employees, 73.4 percent have fewer than 10 employees, and 53.8 percent have from one to four employees.[21] By 2018, small businesses employ 10.7 million people or 89.6 percent of all private sector employees.[22]

FIGURE 1-2 **Number of Businesses by Firm Size, 2017**

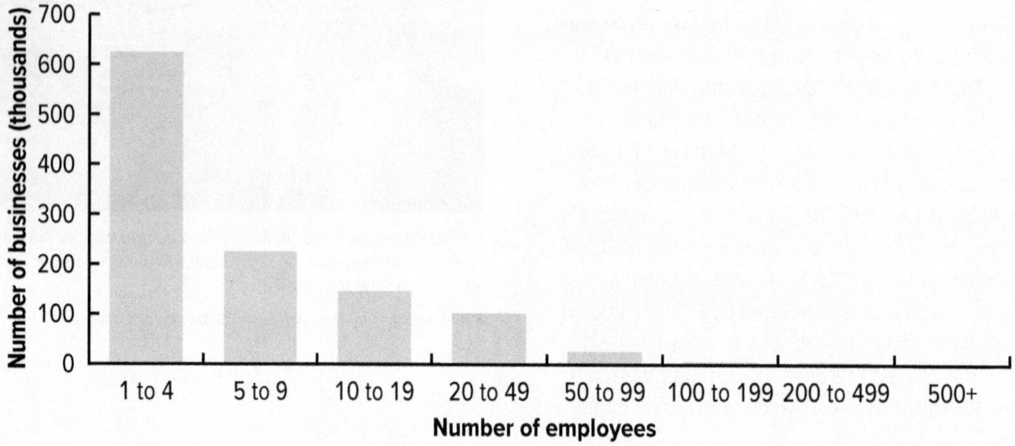

INCREASES IN THE NUMBER OF EMPLOYEES OF SMALL BUSINESSES

The number of Canadians employed by small and medium-sized businesses has grown substantially in recent years and has been estimated at slightly over eight million.[23] In addition, there has been a marked shift in new job creation from a reliance on big firms and projects to small firms and entrepreneurs. The federal department of Business and Industry indicates that 85.3 percent of new net jobs were created by small and medium businesses from 2013 to 2017.[24]

INCREASES IN GOVERNMENT INTEREST AND PROGRAMS

Politicians recognize the importance of small business to a healthy economy and are beginning to offer various financial and non-financial programs to assist the small business owner. Recently both the federal and provincial governments have been working to reduce the amount of red tape or bureaucracy small business owners have to manage.[25] The Department of Innovation, Science and Economic Development Canada (formerly Industry Canada) administers and works with Canadians to coordinate programs designed to aid small business at the federal level. Likewise, all the provinces and territories have departments that perform the same function for small businesses within their jurisdictions. **Appendix 3A** lists some of these agencies. In addition, Canada Revenue Agency provides a number of tax breaks to entrepreneurs and investors who lend money to small and growing firms.

INCREASES IN THE NUMBER OF SMALL BUSINESS–RELATED COURSES AT COLLEGES AND UNIVERSITIES

The level of interest in small business–related courses at Canadian colleges and universities has risen dramatically in the past few years. The trend of increasing the number of entrepreneurship courses in business schools appears to be continuing.[26] Traditionally, such courses were housed in management and commerce faculties and attracted only students of those faculties. However, as a result of the growing general interest in small business, many nonbusiness majors now take these courses. In addition, entrepreneurship courses have become increasingly common in arts and science programs throughout the country. This growth has been attributed to a number of factors, including a strong likelihood that these students, particularly those studying fine arts and engineering, may one day become entrepreneurs. As such, many schools have added entrepreneurship courses as a matter of practicality. Demand has also been fuelled by arts and science students who see studying entrepreneurship as a way to link career development to their chosen field of study. Entrepreneurship courses are also becoming common at high schools throughout Canada, and some entrepreneurial topics are being discussed in classrooms before high school.

Entrepreneurship can begin early, even with school-age children.
Blend Images/Shutterstock.com

INCREASES IN ENTREPRENEURIAL ACTIVITIES KNOWN AS INTRAPRENEURSHIP IN LARGE BUSINESSES

Intrapreneurship can be defined as entrepreneurship within an existing organization. Intrapreneurs are employees who use entrepreneurial skills to solve problems or create additional revenue streams for a company. The Global Entrepreneurship Monitor, which studies entrepreneurship activity throughout the world, has concluded that Canada ranks second in employee entrepreneurial activity which is a measure of intrapreneurship.[27] For example, Ali Asaria was acting as an intrapreneur when he created the mobile game *Brick Breaker* for **BlackBerry**. Many large, successful companies have developed or altered their organizations to promote creativity, entrepreneurship, and individual initiative.[28] These businesses have realized considerable productivity gains by encouraging this type of intrapreneurship. For example, **3M Canada** encourages employees to act intrapreneurially and will give them time away from their traditional jobs if it believes the employee's ideas could lead to costs savings or additional revenue. In their extensive study of successful large companies, which resulted in the best-selling book *In Search of Excellence,* Thomas Peters and Robert Waterman found that one common characteristic of these organizations was their formal encouragement of entrepreneurship within and among departments. These companies were quick to recognize increases in productivity and innovativeness by rewarding employees who engaged in such entrepreneurial behaviour.[29] Canadian companies such as Bombardier and CGI Group have incorporated these practices into their organizations. Other large companies have struggled with the implementation of intrapreneurship because of their size and bureaucratic structure. This difficulty also exists within spin-off entrepreneurial divisions of the main company.[30] This will be discussed further in **Chapter 2**.

INCREASES IN THE POLITICAL POWER OF SMALL BUSINESS

The small business community is a significant economic force in Canadian society. Several organizations are currently attempting to advance the small business cause through lobbying efforts and educational programs. The largest and most visible organization is the Canadian Federation of Independent Business (CFIB), which boasts a membership of more than 110,000. Current concerns of CFIB members include lowering tax rates, improving government regulations, and creating a stronger business environment.[31] Lobbying has resulted in many government programs and some legislation beneficial to small business. Many industry associations made up primarily of small businesses are also very active in lobbying activities and have influenced the directions of government initiatives.

IMPROVEMENT IN THE IMAGE OF SMALL BUSINESS

Small business owners and entrepreneurs are viewed very positively today. The benefits of entrepreneurship are being proclaimed by universities and colleges, governments, and corporations. Entrepreneurship careers are considered to be honourable and, in some cases, prestigious pursuits. For example, Global Entrepreneurship Monitor reported that Canada leads all G7 economic nations in the perception that entrepreneurship is a good career choice (65.6 percent). The report considers three factors when assessing a countries attitudes towards entrepreneurship including whether people consider entrepreneurship as a good career choice, if entrepreneurs have a high status in society, and positive media coverage of entrepreneurs. Canada ranked well above the average compared to other innovation-driven economies in all three categories: good career choice (66 percent vs 57 percent), high status (78 percent vs 70 percent), and positive media coverage (77 percent vs 62 percent).[32]

As discussed above, increased coverage of entrepreneurship in the media has been a significant influence on the public's positive attitude toward it. The media have played a powerful role by engaging in discussions about the impact of entrepreneurship on society, highlighting entrepreneurial successes, and offering entrepreneurs and potential entrepreneurs advice as well as stories on emerging trends. *The Globe and Mail, National Post,* and *Canadian Business* all regularly publish content both in print and online highlighting entrepreneurial success stories and offer advice to current and aspiring entrepreneurs.

Television networks are increasingly offering shows that celebrate the achievements of entrepreneurs and promote business ownership. For example, CBC's hit series ***Dragons' Den*** has entrepreneurs presenting their business ideas to a panel of wealthy investors known as the Dragons. Entrepreneurs who appear on the show are hoping to get the Dragons to invest money and time into their business for a share of future profits. Entrepreneurs on the show also benefit from airtime on CBC, and estimates are that businesses appearing on the program see sales increase by 30 percent after an episode airs.[33] Although the show has its share of critics, as some do not care for the personalities of the Dragons, most people agree that *Dragons' Den* has positively promoted entrepreneurship as a career.

WHAT IS SMALL BUSINESS? LO2

What size of business qualifies as a small business? This question is not easy to answer because the organizations and agencies concerned with small businesses use different definitions. It is essential, however, to understand some of the common characteristics of these definitions to better appreciate what constitutes a small business.

COMPARISON AND EVALUATION

To compare the performance of a small business with that of other small businesses, it is necessary to understand the sizes and characteristics used by data collection and dissemination agencies, such as Statistics Canada and Dun and Bradstreet. Ensuring that firms are relatively the same size allows a more meaningful monitoring of sales levels, performance, and productivity in relation to other similar firms in the industry. Currently, Statistics Canada publishes operating data for incorporated and unincorporated businesses with average net sales of $1 million or less.

GOVERNMENT PROGRAMS

Knowing how various government departments define a small business enables an entrepreneur to take advantage of the tax incentives and other government assistance programs designed for small business. Examples of differences in definitions among government agencies are given below.

LENDING PROGRAMS

A small business owner needs to know the size of business that lenders require in their lending programs to take advantage of favourable small business provisions. Programs are available to small businesses from the Business Development Bank of Canada (BDC), provincial or territorial government lending agencies, and chartered banks. Therefore, it is important to understand the criteria commonly used to distinguish a small business from a large one. At least four criteria are used.

1. Number of Employees.

Innovation, Science and Economic Development Canada specifies a small business as one that employs fewer than 100 people in a manufacturing industry and fewer than 50 employees in a non-manufacturing industry. The Ministry for Small Business and Tourism also uses the guideline of 50 employees, while the **BDC** considers a business that employs fewer than 75 people to be eligible for some of its consulting services. Other organizations, such as the Canadian Bankers Association, classify a company as small if it qualifies for a loan authorization of less than $250,000. Micro-businesses are businesses that employ fewer than five employees, while businesses employing fewer than 500 are classed as SMEs (small and medium-sized enterprises).[34]

2. Total Revenue.

Although the limits vary by industry, total revenue is a common basis for defining small business. The Ministry of Small Business and Tourism uses $2 million in revenue as a benchmark. The Canadian Small Business Financing Act applies to firms with revenues of less than $10 million. The Small Business Administration in the United States uses business specific revenue guidelines in determining the size of a business with the amount varying greatly by industry. For example, a carpet and upholstery business will be classified as small as long as revenue does not exceed $5.5 million while a men's clothing store will be classified as small up to $11 million in revenue.[35]

3. Profits.

Canada Revenue Agency uses operating profits as a guideline to define which businesses qualify for the small business deduction. This special deduction allows a reduced tax rate (the small business deduction is discussed in detail later in the text). This limit is presently set at a net operating profit of $500,000.[36]

4. Type of Management-Ownership Structure.

Another criterion used to define small business is the degree to which the owner is also the day-to-day manager of the business. With some exceptions, the majority of small business owners are also the managers.[37] Because the guidelines differ among industries and agencies, the Committee for Economic Development in the United States uses a slightly different and less specific approach in defining small business. Its definition states that if any two of the following characteristics exist, the business may be classified as a small business:

1. Independent management (i.e., the owner is the manager)
2. Owner-supplied capital
3. Local area of operations
4. Relatively small size within its industry

It is no easy task to define the size limits of small business. The definition used depends on the purpose and the agency or program concerned.

CURRENT STATE OF SMALL BUSINESS IN CANADA LO3

Although the size and extent of small business in Canada depends on the definition used, a review of the data compiled by Statistics Canada and Innovation, Science and Economic Development Canada illustrates that small business is a significant part of the Canadian economy. Some interesting facts about the importance of small business include:

- 99.8 percent of business in Canada can be classified as small or medium enterprises; that is, they have fewer than 500 employees.
- 97.9 percent of all businesses operating in Canada employ fewer than 100 employees, while 73.4 percent of all businesses have fewer than 10 employees.
- 48 percent of the labour force or slightly over five million people are employed in small business.
- 50.2 percent of gross domestic product (GDP) is provided by small business.
- 41.9 percent of exports were from small businesses, accounting for $202 billion in sales.
- 83.5 percent of net job creation is from small business from 2013 to 2017.
- 100,000 new small businesses are started annually.[38]

YOUNG ENTREPRENEURS

In addition to the large general increases in the number of small businesses in recent years, more small businesses are being started by young people. Interest in entrepreneurship, particularly among young people, is growing, and almost 50 percent of university students in Canada believe they will one day become entrepreneurs. The Global Entrepreneurship Monitor recently competed a study on youth entrepreneurship in Canada and found the data supports the assertion that young Canadians have a very positive perception of entrepreneurs and entrepreneurship as a career option.[39] Examples of young Canadian entrepreneurs include Bryan McCrea and Evan Willoughby who, at age 29, started **3twenty Modular**, a Saskatoon-based company that converts steel shipping containers into temporary offices and housing for the booming resource industry.[40] The modular units come with heat and plumbing and replace tents or flimsy wood structures. The pair cannot keep up with the demand for their product and have expanded their manufacturing space ten times since the company's inception. Similarly, Rebecca Cotter of Toronto is experiencing success in her business **Water-on-Wheels**, or WOW. Cotter started the mobile water station business at age 27 after becoming disgusted with the number of plastic bottles in garbage cans at special events. Her company allows people to fill reusable water containers for free, and she charges event partners for her service. Event planners like the turnkey solution WOW provides with its own cooling system, tents, and staff—all of which results in lower clean-up costs when an event ends.[41]

As youth unemployment remains high, starting their own business is an attractive career option for many younger Canadians. A cost-of-living sample shown in **Small Business Beginnings 1-1** outlines why starting a business is an ideal option for recent graduates. Further, a recent survey of Canada's fastest-growing small businesses indicated that the average age of the owners was about 40.[42] Organizations such **Enactus** have been formed in Canada to provide networking and information for these young entrepreneurs. In addition, government and private organizations have recognized the importance of young entrepreneurs in lending programs offered by the Business Development Bank of Canada (BDC) as well as **Futurpreneur**. Annual awards are also made to top Canadian youth entrepreneurs by the BDC.

Young entrepreneurs Bryan McCrea and Evan Willoughby created 3twenty Modular, an innovative, prefab design solution for permanent commercial, institutional and retail developments. Their company is now the industry leader in the country.
Photo courtesy of 3twenty Modular

SMALL BUSINESS BEGINNINGS 1-1

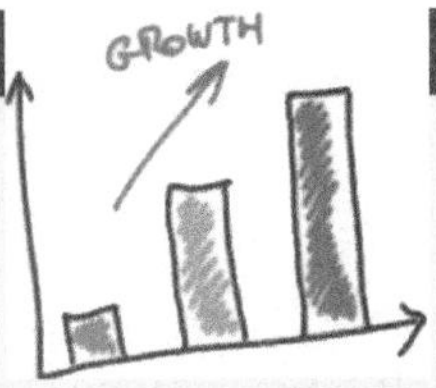

WHY STUDENTS AND RECENT GRADUATES SHOULD START A BUSINESS

Amanda MacDonald was thrilled. She had just received her teaching licence in New Brunswick and landed a job. Her starting salary was $50,000 a year, and she was excited to be earning a great paycheque doing the job she loved. With her new income, MacDonald thought that her worries about money were over. Unfortunately, a short time later, she started to wonder if she could afford to maintain her apartment on her salary and was considering selling her car. MacDonald was quickly learning that $50,000 a year was not that much money after all.

Here is MacDonald's monthly cash flow statement:

MacDonald's monthly take-home pay $2,500

Less MacDonald's monthly expenses:

Rent	$600
Car and insurance	$400
Gas	$150
Food	$400
Phone/cable/Internet	$200
Student loans	$150
Entertainment	$100
Clothing	$100

This left MacDonald with only $400 a month for other expenses and no money for savings, and she could not imagine saving enough for a down payment on a condo she wanted to buy. Furthermore, she was disappointed that she had only $100 a month for entertainment. Rather than take a part-time job to supplement her income, MacDonald started a small business teaching four-year-olds to read.

[continued]

[continued]

MacDonald works at her own business on Saturday and Sunday mornings and is making an extra $300 a week or $1200 a month. Rather than being concerned about money problems, she is saving for a dream vacation and considering buying a house. What MacDonald has learned is the secret that many Canadians already know: if you can find a way to supplement your income, even by a small amount, it can make a big difference in your lifestyle. You can go from living in an apartment to owning a house or a condo, driving a new car versus driving an old car, and saving money versus living paycheque to paycheque.

SENIOR ENTREPRENEURS

Recently, more senior citizens have become entrepreneurs in Canada. Older entrepreneurs are currently the fastest-growing segment in the small business sector, and long-term demographic trends indicate that they will become an even more significant part of the economy in the future. In addition, a large number of older Canadians are strongly considering working in some capacity after they retire.[43] For example, Corin and Brian Mullins founded HapiFoods Group Inc., a firm based in British Columbia that is best known for its breakfast cereal **Holy Crap**. The retired couple came up with their idea for a healthy breakfast cereal after Brian developed food allergies and sensitivities. The cereal was originally sold at farmers' markets, netting the couple approximately $60,000. A trip to CBC's *Dragons' Den* quickly accelerated growth for the business, and the day after their segment aired they had $1.5 million in sales and reached over $5 million within a year.[44] Unlike the Mullins, many older entrepreneurs share a unique characteristic in business in that they do not want their businesses to grow. They are content to have a business that will provide some income but also allow them to maintain a balanced lifestyle.

FEMALE ENTREPRENEURS

Self-employment among women has increased rapidly in recent years. From 1976 to 2018, the number of self-employed women tripled, from 311,600 to 1,079,000 accounting for 37 percent of all self employed people.[45] While the likelihood of being self-employed has grown considerably for both men and women over the past 20 years, the rate of growth has been stronger for women. Statistics Canada found that 47 percent of small and medium-sized businesses in the country have some degree of female ownership, with 16 percent majority-owned by women.[46] In addition, a great number of women are also aspiring entrepreneurs: a recent survey found that 85 percent of women are interested in starting a business.[47] Another study found that 27 percent of female managers in corporate settings intend to leave their employer to start their own businesses. Reasons cited are dissatisfaction and frustrations with their current employment.[48] Increasingly, female entrepreneurs are well educated (24 percent have a university education), and many are over age 55.[49] Many of the examples and profiles in this text describe the significant contributions of female entrepreneurs in Canada. See **Figure 1-3** for summary facts on female entrepreneurs.

This growth in female entrepreneurship is not limited to North America; a Global Economic Entrepreneurship study found that over 40 percent of entrepreneurs starting new businesses were female.[50] Organizations such as Women Entrepreneurs of Canada (WEC) and Women Presidents Organization (WPO) have increased the political power and networking opportunities for female entrepreneurs.

The majority of self-employed women in 2018 worked in the service sector (83 percent); female owners are less likely to participate in international business and are slightly less innovative than men. The backgrounds of male and female entrepreneurs tend to be similar, but women have a tendency to start their businesses later in life. Women are also more likely to work at their businesses on a part-time basis compared to men and, as a result, work fewer hours. Statistics Canada reports that roughly 40 percent of women run their businesses part-time compared with less than 15 percent of men. While some women are running part-time businesses, many more are like Marie-Philip Simard, founder of Chic Marie, working full time at managing growing companies. She is featured in **Small Business in Action 1-3** in this section.

FIGURE 1-3 **Facts about Female Entrepreneurs**

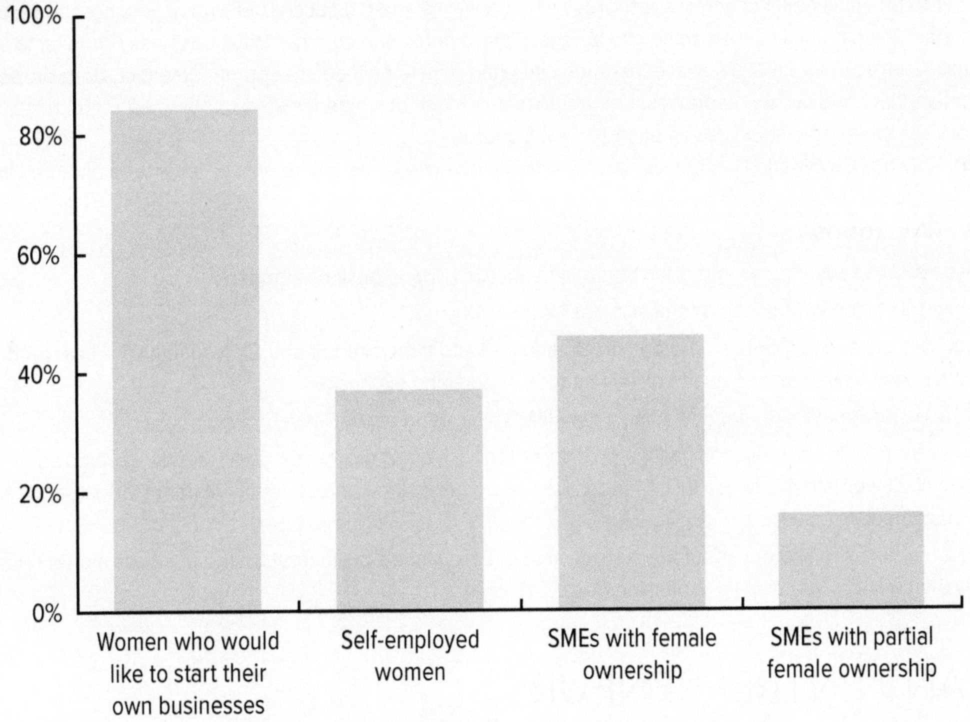

SMALL BUSINESS IN ACTION 1-3

FASHIONING AN ONLINE BUSINESS

Montrealer Marie-Philip Simard says the idea for **Chic Marie** resulted from a conversation with colleagues at her law firm and her desire to be an entrepreneur. Simard says she was bored at work and was discussing with some other women how much they spend on clothes a year and was surprised by the amount. She decided to conduct some research and discovered that North American women buy 64 new pieces of clothing a year but only regularly wear 22 items. The result is two thirds of new clothing sits unworn in a closet. Simard thought that there must be a better alternative for women who want to update their wardrobe without buying so many new items. From this idea, Chic Marie was born. Chic Marie is an online women's clothing rental business. Each month women received nine new items which they can integrate into their wardrobe and when the month is over, they ship them back. Simard says her company will dry clean the clothes and then send them off to next customer. Of course, if women love an item, they can purchase it from Chic Marie at a discount based on its rental history.

Simard says she originally thought customers would mainly be corporate clients, but the business serves all demographics. She says corporate clients can opt for the $95-a-month membership for their business attire. The $65-a-month membership supplies non-corporate attire, a more casual line of clothes perfect for going out with friends, on a date, or other social activities. In addition, Chic Marie has embraced the use of Artificial Intelligence or AI with their Scarlett app. Scarlett uses knowledge it gathers from a customer's past rental and purchase history as well as their social media activity to create clothing packages for clients, thus ensuring customer satisfaction.

Chic Marie has grown quickly, reaching $500,000 in revenue in year one with expectations to reach $4 million in sales in year two. Such rapid growth does come with a few hurdles. The company needed to expand the number of designers they work with to access clothes and needed money to purchase inventory. In 2018, the company worked with 40 designers but planned to grow the number to well over 100 within the year. Simard has also had to raise money from investors. She says she

[continued]

[continued]

left her well-paid job as a corporate lawyer and moved back in with her parents to save money, but rapid expansion has put pressure on her to bring in capital to acquire resources to grow. While she did successfully raise funding, she recalls being a woman in the start-up world has caused some challenges. Simard notes she sent her initial business proposal to investors and only one actually replied. As a bit of a social experiment, she had a male colleague send off the exact same proposal to the same investors and he received six responses. She notes that the lack of women in start-ups, especially tech start-ups, does impact her ability to raise capital but it is something she will overcome.

Simard currently has Chic Marie in expansion mode with an increase in marketing activity in Ontario and the United States.

Discussion Questions

1. What are some of the advantages and disadvantages of the Chic Marie business model?
2. Do you think Chic Marie will be a long-term success? Why or why not?
3. Simard is quickly expanding her business both in Ontario and into the United States. Do you think this is a good idea? Why or why not? What are some advantages and disadvantages of pursuing expansion?
4. Were you surprised Simard experienced some initial difficult in raising capital? Why or why not?
5. There are many monthly subscription services. Working either in a small group or independently, develop some products you think would fit well into this subscription model. Be sure to justify the choices, identify target markets, and how you would appeal to customers.
6. Use Internet resources to find out about the current state of Chic Marie's business. Has the business model remained the same? Has the company reached its expansion goals?

IMMIGRANT ENTREPRENEURS

A large number of Canadian entrepreneurs are immigrants to Canada or have parents who were immigrants. Close to one in five of the self-employed in Canada today are immigrants, almost double the rate observed in the 1980s. Examples include the Hadhad family who started Peace by Chocolate, profiled in the **Small Business Beginnings 1-2**, in Antigonish, Nova Scotia, after fleeing Syria in 2016. The family started selling chocolates out of a shed, and within a few months were employing 10 people. Today, Peace by Chocolate is being sold throughout North America and has grown to 45 employees.[51] Other examples include Frank Stronach, one of Canada's most successful entrepreneurs, who came to Canada in his early 20s. He started a small Toronto machine shop, where he logged such long hours that he often slept on a cot rather than go home. Stronach grew this small machine shop into Magna International, a global supplier of automobile parts, and accumulated a net worth of $1.2 billion.[52] Well-known entrepreneurs Arlene Dickinson and Robert Herjavec, both of whom have become famous on CBC's *Dragons' Den* as investors and successful entrepreneurs, are also immigrants. Dickinson has made her fortune in the communications industry, while Herjavec's success came mostly in information technology (IT). Both share a similar story: they came to Canada as children, and their families had very little. Dickinson, who emigrated from South Africa, recalls that her parents arrived in Canada with $50 to support a family of five, while Herjavec's family emigrated from Croatia, arriving in Canada with $20. Many immigrants become entrepreneurs because they speak little English or French and lack the networks to find traditional employment. In addition, many immigrant communities in large Canadian cities offer support for would-be entrepreneurs, including advice, start-up funds, and access to established networks.

SMALL BUSINESS BEGINNINGS 1-2

PEACE BY CHOCOLATE

The Hadhad family were well-known chocolatiers in their native Syria. Under father Assam Hadhad's leadership, they had a factory in Damascus, Syria, and were shipping their unique chocolates all over the Middle East when war broke out in their country. With their factory and most of Damascus destroyed, the family fled to a Lebanese refugee camp. They lived at the camp for three years until qualifying to come to Canada.

Once they arrived in Canada in 2016, the family moved to the small community of Antigonish, Nova Scotia, where community leaders had fund-raised to sponsor the Hadhad's immigration. To welcome the Hadhads to Canada, they were invited to a potluck and Assam made some of his chocolates in their new home. The chocolates were the hit of the gathering and soon afterwards the Hadhads started to sell their chocolates at local farmer's markets. Sales grew quickly and soon the family wanted to open a retail location. A short time later, 60 members of the community came together to build the Hadhads a small shed that would serve as the first store front. Tariq Hadhad, Assam's son and current CEO of the family company, says the community rallied around the family and the support from the local people was incredible.

As sales grew, so did news about the company. Soon people across Canada were talking about the Syrian family's entrepreneurial skills and their chocolates. Prime Minister Justin Trudeau spoke about the Hadhads at the United Nations, and the company was featured in dozens of news stories. The Hadhads also wanted to give back, ever thankful that Canada welcomed them into their country. While still starting their new company, the company donated money to Fort McMurray charities after the fire in 2016, and the company produced some specialty chocolate bars to celebrate and embrace Pride.

As their sales continued to grow, the Hadhads began looking to expand. They worked out an agreement with Sobeys, who had an empty building in the town: Sobeys would supply the building and Peace by Chocolates would supply Sobeys with chocolates. With the new factory in place, Peace by Chocolate required more help; they hired 10 employees in 2017 and employed 45 by 2019. Antigonish mayor Laurie Boucher says the Hadhads have been an inspiration to the small rural community. Boucher says that Hadhads have given people hope that entrepreneurship can work in rural parts of Nova Scotia.

Still looking to give back, the Hadhads have recently committed to hiring 50 refugees by 2022 and mentoring 10 refugee startups. As of 2019, Peace by Chocolate is available in over 400 Canadian locations with online sales throughout the world.

Discussion Questions

1. The Hadhad family has been quite successful in public relations (PR). The business has been featured in numerous articles and on television. What are some of the advantages of this type of marketing? Do you think the business will be able to maintain this positive PR long term? Why or why not?
2. What do you think would be some of the advantages and disadvantages associated with starting a business in rural Nova Scotia, specifically Antigonish, which has a population of approximately 4300 people.
3. Do you think Peace by Chocolate should be considered a social enterprise? Why or why not?

ENTREPRENEURIAL ACTIVITY BY INDUSTRY

As in other countries, Canadian small business activity is more dominant in sectors that are not capital intensive, such as the service industry. Statistics Canada has found that 99 percent of Canadian SMEs would be classified as service or service related businesses. For example, Cameron Ritchie from Fredericton started Homewurk while still attending high school. The company which specializes in connecting students with odd jobs in New Brunswick was recognized in 2018 as Canada's young entrepreneur of the year by Startup Canada.[53]

ENTREPRENEURIAL ACTIVITY BY REGION

Although small businesses exist in all areas of Canada, some regions seem to be more fertile areas for growth. **Figure 1-4** shows that the economies of all provinces and Yukon are dominated by small businesses with one to four employees. Among the provinces, Manitoba has the lowest percentage of businesses with fewer than five employees, while Alberta has the highest. Small businesses with fewer than ten employees make up more than 70 percent of the total share, while businesses with fewer than 100 employees represent more than 90 percent of the total businesses in every province and territory. Alberta and Ontario have seen the most rapid growth in self-employment over the past decade, and this trend is expected to continue.[54]

FIGURE 1-4 **Number of Small Businesses by Province and Territory, December 2017**

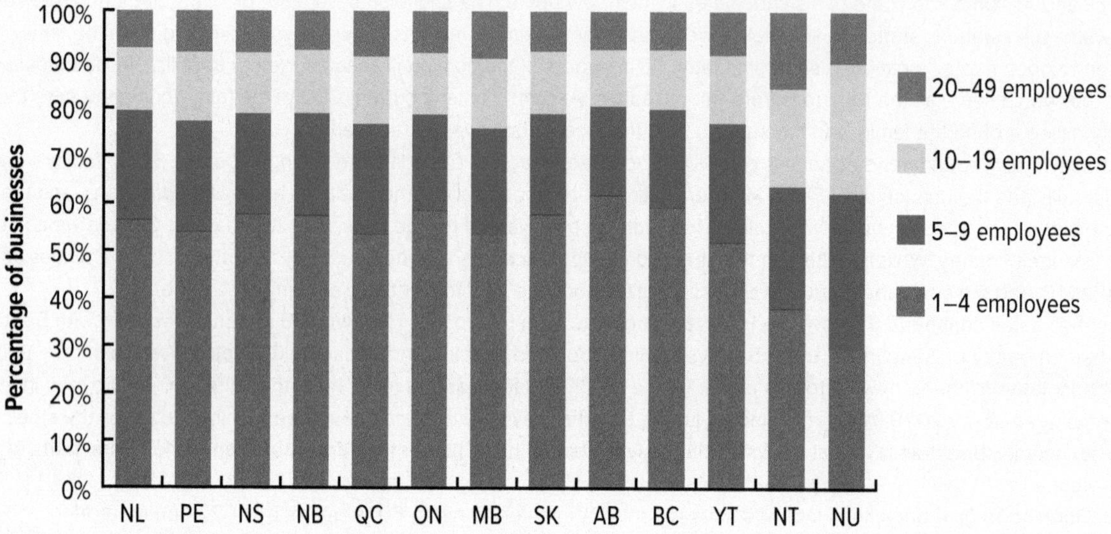

Source: Statistics Canada, Business Register, December 2017, http://www.ic.gc.ca/eic/site/061.nsf/eng/h_03090.html#table5 (Table 5).

CONTRIBUTIONS OF SMALL BUSINESS LO4

The size of the small business sector is not the only reason that it is important to Canada. The following sections discuss other significant benefits of small business to Canadian society.

LABOUR INTENSITY

Small businesses are generally more labour intensive than large companies. This means they typically employ more people to produce a certain level of output than a larger business does. In this era of concern about employment levels, it is not surprising that current government policy includes incentives to promote the establishment of small businesses.

INNOVATIONS AND INVENTIONS

Individuals in small businesses have been responsible for a majority of the inventions and innovations that society benefits from today. Small firms produce approximately 58.3 percent of innovations.[55] Among important twentieth-century innovations by Canadian small firms are the smartphone, insulin, the snowmobile, the pacemaker, the washing machine, the IMAX movie system, and the television. Potential innovations being developed by Canadian entrepreneurs include a portable Zamboni for backyard rinks, an underwater communications system, a one-handed ice cube tray, and a spacecraft docking system. The tech industry is another are small Canadian companies have found success, as we discuss in **Small Business in Action 1-4**. Even innovations within larger companies are often made by individuals who are rewarded for their entrepreneurial creativity. Studies show that small businesses have six "innovation enablers" that make them more likely than large corporations to innovate.[56] These are personal passion, customer connection, flexibility, experimentation, resource limitations, and information sharing. Recent studies show that small and medium-sized businesses do, in fact, invest more money in research and development as a proportion of their revenue compared with large firms.[57]

SMALL BUSINESS IN ACTION 1-4

INNOVATION IN NEW BUSINESS—A SOCIAL MEDIA SUCCESS STORY

Canadian entrepreneur Ryan Holmes, founder and CEO of Hootsuite, a social media dashboard, saw the value of his company climb from $6 million in 2010 to $1 billion today.

Simon Dawson/Bloomberg via Getty Images

Ryan Holmes, CEO of Vancouver-based HootSuite (hootsuite.com), a social media dashboard, is hoping his innovative company will grow into an Internet giant. Founded in 2008, Holmes' social media dashboard allows companies to manage multiple social media campaigns from one central website. Essentially, HootSuite allows companies to send messages to a variety of social media sites, including Twitter, Facebook, LinkedIn, and Pinterest from one central location. HootSuite can also be used with YouTube, Instagram, MailChimp, Reddit, Storify, Tumblr, and Vimeo. The business offers some of its services for free but charges a premium if a company wants to post information to more than five sites. In addition, HootSuite bills clients for its social media analytical tools, which provide companies with insight as to what consumers are saying about both their social media campaigns and the company in general. Businesses like sending messages to multiple sites using HootSuite because it saves them time and money. Over 15 million large and small businesses are using HootSuite, and the company boasts that both the Prime Minister's Office and the U.S. President's Office, as well as more than 80 of the Fortune 100 companies, are using its services. Holmes has seen a rapid appreciation of the firm's value: HootSuite was estimated to be worth $6 million in 2010, $500 million in 2013, and more than $1 billion in its most recent round of financing.

Discussion Questions

1. What are some of the advantages and disadvantages of using a product like HootSuite for your company?
2. Given that many consumers are becoming increasingly concerned about privacy rights, do you think HootSuite or companies that use its social media tracking tools could be subject to public backlash against monitoring social media use and activities?
3. If time permits, visit HootSuite's website, and try the free tools. Report back to the class if the tools worked as you expected. Prepare a summary of the features HootSuite can offer businesses.

PRODUCTIVITY AND PROFITABILITY

During the twentieth century, the conventional wisdom was that the larger the organization, the greater was the opportunity to be more productive and profitable. As a result, both business and government have tended to increase in size. However, the validity of this thinking has been questioned in recent years and shown to be empirically weak.

Large businesses are also recognizing the gains in productivity associated with smallness. Of the eight attributes of success listed by Peters and Waterman in their study of successful corporations, no fewer than six are commonly found in small businesses:[58]

1. Bias for Action.

These organizations have found that a preference for doing something—anything, rather than sending an idea through endless cycles of analyses and committee reports—encourages new ideas and creativity. This principle seems typical of most successful businesses.

2. Staying Close to the Customer.

Small businesses learn about customer preferences and cater to them. They are generally closer to and have more contact with the customer. Larger organizations spend considerable amounts of money to maintain this closeness.

3. Autonomy and Entrepreneurship.

Breaking the corporation into small companies and encouraging each unit to think independently and competitively has become a strategy of many large businesses.

4. Productivity through People.

Creating the awareness in all employees that their best efforts are essential and that they will share in the rewards of the company's success is a major goal of profitable companies. In small businesses, owner and employees typically share in the rewards of success and the disappointments of failure.

5. Hands On—Value Driven.

Many organizations insist that executives keep in touch with the firm's essential business and promote a strong corporate culture. A popular method of management, known as management by walking around, testifies to the realization that management needs to be familiar with the firm's employees and the operation of the business. The successful owner-manager follows this principle faithfully.

6. Simple Form—Lean Staff.

Few administrative layers, with few people at the upper levels, is characteristic of many successful businesses. In many small businesses, employees have direct access to the owner-manager. This arrangement increases the flexibility of the organization and improves employee morale.

FLEXIBILITY

Small businesses are generally able to respond more quickly than large businesses to changes in the economy, government policies, and competition. For example, Kelsey Ramsden, owner-operator of **Belvedere Place Development**, based in British Columbia, and one of *Profit* magazine's Top Women Entrepreneurs, reinvented her business when the economy went into the most recent recession. At that time, almost all Ramsden's clients came from government sources, and the number of competitors doubled almost overnight. Competitors were desperate for work and they were driving down the price of government contracts. Rather than compete, Ramsden expanded the company into private sector work, which resulted in a three-year growth rate of 804 percent.[59]

Many markets can be served by only small businesses because the areas are too small or too localized for large companies to serve profitably. This situation alone presents countless opportunities for entrepreneurs. For example, Ingonish in Cape Breton sits on the world famous **Cabot Trail**, a vacation destination that draws thousands of visitors each year with its majestic coastal drive, national parks, and golf courses. Yet the tourism operators are not large businesses or national chains, as the region, even with strong tourist numbers, is too small to support big firms.

CANADIAN OWNERSHIP

The percentage of Canadian ownership, a major concern of economic nationalists in Canada, tends to be much higher in small business than in large business.[60] Of businesses operating in Canada with less than $2 million in sales, less than 1 percent are foreign owned.

SMALL BUSINESS HEALTH AS A LINK TO ECONOMIC GROWTH

Considerable evidence exists that economies that provide the most encouragement for entrepreneurship and small business have experienced the highest growth rates since the 1950s.[61] Recognition of this fact by many centrally planned economies has resulted in more encouragement of entrepreneurship, with the associated potential of rewards for those engaged in this type of productive activity.[62] This recognition may also have contributed to the dramatic changes that have occurred in these countries in recent years. One key finding of the second annual study by Global Entrepreneurship Monitor, which examines new and growing business in 21 countries, was that a country has a better chance of achieving economic well-being if it supports entrepreneurial activities.[63]

SOCIAL CONTRIBUTIONS

Small business owners often have a long-term interest in the communities in which their businesses operate. As a result, they contribute to those communities in nonbusiness ways to a greater extent than an employee of a large corporation might do. In a recent survey conducted by 76 percent of entrepreneurs think they have a moral obligation to give back to their communities through philanthropic endeavours. When asked about the amount their business contributed to social causes in the last year, entrepreneurs reported they donated an average of 9.3 percent of revenues, including cash donations, in-kind donations, and employee time.[64] Some entrepreneurs, such as Kalen Emsley, David Luba, and Derrick Emsley, are using their philanthropic donations as part of their overall marketing strategy. The three young business partners are co-owners of Ten Tree Apparel, an environmentally friendly clothing brand that plants ten trees for every item it sells. The company's website, tentree.ca, maintains an active count of the trees the company has planted to date and highlights the business' ongoing success. The business was recently featured on CBC's *Dragons' Den,* where the entrepreneurs won accolades for being one of the top ten presentations in the history of the show.[65]

Kalen Emsley, David Luba, and Derrick Emsley are using donations as part of their marketing strategy. Their company donates ten trees for every product you purchase. Consumers love the concept, and the trio's business is growing more quickly than they could have imagined.

Photo courtesy of Ten Tree

SMALL BUSINESS AND THE FUTURE LO5

An important question for present and future entrepreneurs and policymakers is, What effects will changes in our society have on the small business community? As mentioned at the beginning of this chapter, the 1970s and 1980s were a period of entrepreneurial revolution. Moreover, the late 1990s through the 2000s determined that changes were in fact permanent adjustments to the Canadian business environment.[66] Essentially, entrepreneurship has become engrained as part of Canada's society. Now as we progress through this decade from 2010 to 2020, interest and demand for entrepreneurship appears to be growing. Several developing trends have potentially positive implications for entrepreneurs, if entrepreneurs' actions in response are the result of insight, research, and careful planning. Some of the more significant factors that will affect the future of small business are discussed briefly in the following sections.

The world is now undergoing a period of rapid change, and this is expected to continue. Businesses carry out their activities very differently today than they will ten years from now. Flexibility will likely continue to be a competitive strength for the entrepreneur. Changes in technology, the Internet and mobile technology, consumer demographics and buying patterns, the competitive aspects of markets, the economy, the political climate, and the social climate will likely be significant factors.

TECHNOLOGY

Technology has revolutionized the activities of both small and large businesses. Ted Glendening, Vice President of Corporate Development at Nortek, says technology has allowed smaller businesses to compete on an equal footing with their large counterparts.[67] Computers allow the entrepreneur to manage large amounts of information as effectively as a larger business. Such advances have created significant small business opportunities. Financial management and accounting, marketing research and planning, promotion, and consulting are areas in which small businesses, many of them home-based, have succeeded.

New technology has also allowed small businesses to obtain subcontracts for many services from larger businesses and government organizations that are unable to or choose not to carry out these activities themselves. Despite these potential opportunities, however, small businesses must be prepared to embrace new technology or face the possibility of obsolescence and lack of competitiveness.

Increased performance in the areas of customer service, marketing, and manufacturing, and improved communications are all benefits an entrepreneur can achieve through the use of technology.

THE INTERNET AND MOBILE TECHNOLOGY

The Internet and mobile technologies, such as cloud computing, smartphones, and tablets, have forever changed how businesses operate and have levelled the playing field between large and small firms. Small businesses can now serve global markets once out of reach, create professional marketing and social networking campaigns, and communicate with stakeholders at a fraction of what it used to cost. An article in the *National Post* sums this up when the author notes, "The Web has lowered the bar for people with skills and ideas. People don't need a development team or a big budget; they just need a good idea and a laptop."[68] For example, Mike McDerment of Toronto-based **FreshBooks**, an online accounting company aimed at servicing small businesses, when he was 23 years old. FreshBooks has 24 million customers spread throughout the globe, all of whom pay approximately $19.95 a month for its accounting services. The Internet has also provided entrepreneurs with opportunities that did not exist in the past. For example, Vincent Cheung started **ShapeCollage Inc.**, an online application that allows users to arrange their photos into a collage in a variety of shapes. Cheung's software has been downloaded over a million times, and he recently won the Ontario Entrepreneur of the Year award.

CONSUMER DEMOGRAPHICS

Demographics plays a significant role in shaping the types of businesses entrepreneurs start. If there are large segments of the population in a certain age category to which a business caters, then the likelihood of success increases as a result. Of particular interest to most businesses are the baby boomers, those born between 1946 and 1964, and their children, known as the "echo generation" or "millennial generation," who were born between 1980 and 2000. Entrepreneurs are interested in these two groups because of their large size and spending habits. Baby boomers are the second-largest segment of the population, composing close to two-thirds of the Canadian population, and remain the most significant demographic group due to their buying power. Baby boomers are known to be materialistic and interested in health care, fitness, and travel. The millennial generation is also an attractive market for business owners and the largest in Canada. This generation is well educated and interested in the environment, social causes, and technology. This group has started to get married, buy homes, and have families. Millennials are interested in career coaching, investing, travel, and the betterment of their children. Since this group is having fewer children than their parents did, and having them later in life, they are willing to spend more money and time on their development. For example, Shaindy Alexander, owner of Toronto-based **Momma Goose Products**, produces a premium line of teethers made from organic cotton and untreated maple wood among other items. Alexander, who now sells her teethers in 13 countries, says, "Millennials will invest in quality and in products that are healthier for their children."[69]

COMPETITIVE ASPECTS OF MARKETS

Two major occurrences in recent years have affected the already intensely competitive environment that most small businesses face. The first is the worldwide movement to global markets, augmented by recent developments in Europe. The second is big business' response to the growth of the small business sector.

Global Markets.

The world is currently experiencing a major shift to the globalization of markets. The erosion of domestic and international market boundaries means that smaller businesses should have increased opportunities to source, produce, and deliver to international markets. As a result, many small businesses will eventually include an international aspect in their operations. The signing of the North American Free Trade Agreement was a major occurrence for Canadian businesses because it gave them access to more than 380 million consumers in the United States and Mexico.[70] The agreement eliminated tariffs, offered Canadian companies much greater and surer access to markets in Mexico and the United States,[71] and disallowed prohibition of most services.[72] NAFTA is in the process of being updated and replaced by the new USMCA agreement. While not ratified at the time of writing this text, the agreement appears to further open up trade between the nations in greater depth and detail. For example, once the agreement is ratified, online companies will be able to sell upwards of $150 across borders with no duties. While the news may not be good for brick-and-mortar retailers, it could be a boon to Canadian small businesses selling products to the over 300 million American consumers.[73]

Other events which have led to trade liberalization include the defeat of communism in the Eastern European bloc countries, which created new opportunities for entrepreneurs. Consumers in these countries have an insatiable appetite for Western products and services. As remaining barriers and purchasing power problems are overcome, these areas will offer huge untapped markets.

Another development that has affected Canadian entrepreneurs is the European Union (EU). The EU is the largest single common market, with a $18.8 trillion economy and 508.2 million consumers. The EU allows for free trade between member nations and uses protective tariffs to keep out goods from non-member countries. Although Canada is not a member of the EU, in 2016 the federal government agreed to participate in a free trade agreement called the Comprehensive Economic and Trade Agreement; it came into force in 2017. As a result of this agreement, Canadian business owners have access to a large market that would likely be interested in many Canadian products and services. And in 2016, Canada agreed to participate in the Trans Pacific Partnership Agreement. The agreement includes twelve countries and four continents, and would give Canadian businesses access to 800 million potential customers.[74]

The market with perhaps the most potential for Canadian entrepreneurs in the future is in Southeast Asia in countries such as India, and, most notably, China. China's population of more than one billion alone represents a massive market. These areas are also increasingly receptive to Western goods and services.

Large Business Response.

Small businesses have always had difficulty competing with large businesses, particularly for such things as capital, raw materials, and labour. This situation is not expected to change appreciably in some industries. Financing problems continue to plague small businesses. Despite new programs, influence over suppliers by large businesses is strong, and wage rates paid by larger organizations and government are often too high for the smaller business to meet.

In addition to the difficulty of matching wage rates, labour shortages continue. This will increase the competition for competent employees even more. Small businesses will need to find ways to retain top employees through non-financial methods. One survey of small business owners indicated that close to half see labour shortages as a major concern for small business.[75]

One positive and often overlooked aspect is that many large businesses and government agencies are increasingly downsizing and subcontracting (outsourcing) the purchase of products and services to small business. It is estimated that close to one-half of small businesses become established through outsourcing with another business.[76] Many small businesses are also joining together through such means as industry associations in an attempt to be more competitive. Such a collaborative relationship, however, often runs against the grain of the entrepreneur's independent nature.

Large businesses in some industries have recently adopted strategies employed by smaller businesses to recoup lost market share. The adoption of entrepreneurial programs in product development (intrapreneurship), the increased attention to customer service, and the addition of some small business operating policies have enhanced the growth and success of smaller enterprises.

THE ECONOMY

The performance of many small businesses is directly related to the Canadian economy. For the better part of the last decade, the Canadian economy has been experiencing steady growth along with the global economy. The growth has benefited the small business sector because, as people have more disposable income, they are more likely to be employed and more likely to make purchases. In 2019, the Canadian economy appears to be slowing due to weaker oil prices, higher borrowing costs, and a decline in global trade.[77] One positive result of the decline was the fall in the value of the Canadian dollar, making goods manufactured in Canada cheaper in the rest of the world. During slow periods and downtime, small companies increase their focus on innovation to a greater degree than large businesses do.[78] Learn how one company took advantage of a change in the economy in **Small Business in Action 1-5**. However, certain economic occurrences affect many small businesses negatively by adding to increased costs and decreased customer traffic for some of Canada's key industries and industrial areas.

SMALL BUSINESS IN ACTION 1-5

ECONOMIC DOWNTURN PRESENTS OPPORTUNITIES

While many businesses suffer significantly when a recession or downturn in the economy occurs, **Warren Industries Ltd.** is an exception. Warren is an automobile parts manufacturer located in Concord, Ontario, that is predicting a three-fold increase in sales contracts over the next three years and a doubling of its staff over the next four. The secret, according to David Freedman, president and CEO, is that a couple of years before the recession, they began developing a strategy to make the company more resilient and adaptable to change. They became more aggressive in obtaining business rather than sitting back, cutting costs, and waiting until the tough times passed. The company bolstered its engineering staff so that it could develop more of its own products and move up the value chain rather than rely on outsourcing as it had done in the past. It became more aggressive in negotiating with hungry suppliers. The result has transformed Warren into a tier 1 supplier that develops innovative and highly engineered products that it can now sell directly to customers.

Felix Alim/E+/Getty Images

Discussion Questions

1. Why do you think some companies fail to plan for a downturn in the economy?
2. Do you think it is ethical for businesses to negotiate deep price cuts from suppliers? Why or why not?
3. What ongoing actions do you think an entrepreneur should engage in to sustain a business for the long term?

THE POLITICAL CLIMATE

Over the last decade, the political climate for small business ownership seemed to be improving. This was evidenced by attempts to reduce the burdens of paperwork and provide tax incentives to small businesses. For example, the Canadian government has prioritized cutting red tape and reforming regulations under its 2019 Red Tape Reduction Action Plan. Under the plan, red tape will be reduced and regulations will be reviewed taking into account their impact on small business.[79] According to the Global Entrepreneurship Monitor, entrepreneurship is fostered as governments reduce state involvement in economic activities and instead promote entrepreneurship at the cultural level.[80] The World Bank states that out of 190 countries, Canada ranks third in ease of starting a new business.[81]

The federal government has attempted to encourage entrepreneurship with incentives for immigrant entrepreneurs to enter the country. Special visas are provided for immigrants who invest in small business. These entrepreneurs have injected considerable capital into the Canadian economy.

Although there is considerable interest in government circles in reducing government involvement in business and encouraging entrepreneurial activity,[82] most small business proponents are still waiting for significant action to take place.[83] A recent report by the Canadian Federation of Independent Business (CFIB) states that small businesses are especially hard hit by regulation, as it takes time and money away from other more productive activities. This also puts them at a competitive disadvantage with respect to larger businesses that can afford individuals or whole departments devoted to regulatory compliance.[84] Small businesses state repeatedly that some of the major concerns about the business environment are high taxes, regulations, and paper work burdens imposed by government, and ineffective government programs.[85] A recent study by CFIB estimates that Canadian businesses spend $36.2 billion per year to comply with regulations imposed by government.[86] Continued collective lobbying efforts through organizations, such as CFIB, are required to achieve a political environment more conducive to the establishment and successful operation of small businesses.

THE SOCIAL CLIMATE

Society tends to look favourably on small business and entrepreneurial activities as a legitimate way to make a living. An Angus Reid survey indicated that entrepreneurs have the highest level of respect from Canadians, edging out doctors, police officers, and teachers.[87] As discussed earlier, the Global Entrepreneurship Monitor reports that Canadians view entrepreneurs very favourably and think quite highly of entrepreneurship as a career option. More and more college and university graduates are beginning their careers by starting their own businesses, joining the ranks of the many people who left the once secure confines of large business to strike out on their own. Although this trend is expected to continue, adequate preparation and planning will increasingly be required to achieve success following this route. In addition, a structural shift has occurred in Canada to a strong culture of individualism and self-betterment that has resulted in a more accepted and positive attitude toward the small business sector.[88]

The onus is now on entrepreneurs as prospective owner-managers to sharpen their skills in this competitive and rapidly changing society. An owner-manager in today's world cannot survive on guesswork. Numerous programs, courses, and types of assistance are available to allow the owner-manager to acquire this training. The remaining chapters in this book cover the critical areas a prospective owner-manager should be familiar with in starting and operating a successful small business.

LEARNING OBJECTIVES SUMMARY

LO1 **The entrepreneurial revolution is evidenced by the growing numbers of business establishments, employees in small businesses, government small business programs, college and university small business classes, and entrepreneurial activities of large companies.**

LO2 **Although defining a small business is difficult, having a definition is important when comparing and evaluating small businesses, as well as when taking advantage of various lending and assistance programs. Some common criteria for defining small businesses are gross sales, number of employees, profitability, and type of management structure.**

LO3 **Small business accounts for 98 percent of all businesses, 30 percent of gross domestic product, and 48 percent of the labour force in Canada.**

LO4 **Small businesses can provide jobs, innovations, high productivity, flexibility, a higher proportion of Canadian ownership, and more contributions to society.**

LO5 **The climate for starting a small business should continue to be strong despite some competitive disadvantages.**

TIME TO TAKE ACTION

If you are reading this book, it is most likely because you have some interest in entrepreneurship. We hope this chapter has convinced you that entrepreneurship can be a rewarding career choice and something you can achieve. If you want to start down the entrepreneurial path, or have to write a business plan for a course you are taking, completing some of the following steps will help you with your goal.

On a notepad or using your smartphone, start to jot down ideas about a business you may want to start.

Watch some TV shows such as *Dragons' Den* to see some small business ideas and to get some insight into what investors may be looking for in a successful business.

Talk to some entrepreneurs. Do not make it an official interview, but ask them out for coffee and find out why they started a business. What suggestions do they have for aspiring entrepreneurs? Run some of your business ideas by them, and find out what they think.

DISCUSSION QUESTIONS

1. Why do you think entrepreneurial activity has increased? Do you think this trend will continue? Why or why not?
2. What excites or interests you about being an entrepreneur? What are your major concerns?
3. Under what conditions would the various definitions of small business be more appropriate (e.g., the level of profit may be used by Canada Revenue Agency to determine the small business tax rate)?
4. What is meant by the statement "small business is the backbone of the Canadian economic system"? Give evidence to support this statement.
5. The computer-consulting business is becoming more and more fragmented. In data processing, for example, there are hardware versus software consultants, batch versus time-sharing service bureaus, and mainframe versus microcomputer specialists. What effect does this type of industry fragmentation have on the small business community?

EXPERIENTIAL EXERCISES

1. Form groups of two to three, and start a small business or mini-venture that will run for four to six hours. There are only four rules:
   a. The business has to be legal
   b. No lotteries
   c. Maximum investment of $1
   d. Businesses must cease operations at day's end.

   After completing the project, write a reflection stating what you did, whether you made a profit, and what you learned. You may also present this information to the class.
2. Ask three small business owners about their projections for the future of small business. What problems and opportunities do they foresee?
3. Using Internet resources, find out how different Canadian organizations define social enterprise. After preparing a summary report on your findings, draft your own definition of the term.
4. Write a short essay discussing your views on the future of small business given current trends in society *and* in your geographic area.

CHAPTER 2

THE SMALL BUSINESS DECISION

LEARNING OBJECTIVES

By the end of this chapter, you should be able to:

LO1 Summarize the advantages and disadvantages of business ownership as a starting point in making the small business decision.

LO2 List the personal and organizational attributes of a successful small business owner.

LO3 Explain the reasons some businesses succeed and others fail.

LO4 Identify the differences between an entrepreneur and a manager.

LO5 Describe entrepreneurial development in large businesses.

SMALL BUSINESS PROFILE

XAVIER PEICH & GABRIEL ALBEROLA *SMARTHALO*

Ideas for successful businesses can come from anywhere. Some ideas can come from a deliberate search, where an entrepreneur is looking for the next great business idea. Other times ideas can come from personal experiences—both good and bad. Xavier Peich notes that he came up with the idea for SmartHalo, a bicycle accessory that turns any bike into a smart bike, after a particular run of bad luck riding his bicycle around Montreal. Peich says he was trying to use his phone to navigate through the city streets and the phone slipped out of his hands breaking the screen. A short time later his bike was stolen. Peich, who was looking for a business to pursue with his long-time friend Gabriel Alberola thought their had to be a simple solution to some of the many problems bikers face in navigating city streets. Together the pair formed the company CycleLabs and developed the concept of SmartHalo which they affectionally describe as a bike companion.

SmartHalo, which attaches to the handlebars of any bike, marries together several features cyclists are looking for including a GPS, alarm system, fitness app, messaging notification system and a headlight which switches itself off when the bike it not in use. The SmartHalo accessory also comes with a protected locking system so it cannot be stolen. SmartHalo attachment works in conjunction with the user's phone and the SmartHalo app to provide bikers with an improved biking experience.

SmartHalo's design and ease of use has led it to championed by such influential publishers as *Times, Forbes, Fortune,* and CBC. The Halo uses Bluetooth technology to link your phone's GPS to the attachment. A rider simply uses their phone's GPS to select a desired location and the Halo becomes operational illustrating the correct path using lights that are easy to see and follow. If the rider misses a turn the Halo flashed red indicating the need for a U-turn. The GPS alone has been described as a significant improvement over using your phone as a GPS. In addition to the GPS feature, the SmartHalo offers cyclists a variety of desired features that are easy to use. The SmartHalo can act as a compass, allowing riders to select their own route to a desired destination; has a light that automatically turns on as the sun sets and

Photo courtesy of SmartHalo

shuts off when the cyclist stops biking; will sound an alarm if someone is attempting to steal the bike; serve as a fitness tracker, allowing riders to track their progress as they peddle; and act as an assistant by notifying riders to incoming calls and messages.

Peich and Alberola with their concept in hand then did what may aspiring entrepreneurs are doing today, they opted to skip traditional market research, and bring their product directly to consumers using the crowd-funding site Kickstarter. They initially were hoping to raise $67,000 in pre-orders for SmartHalo but exceeded that goal on day one and raised almost $540,000 over the course of their month-long Kickstarter campaign. The large influx of cash and preorders proved that the concept was a viable product and the pair started to work on building their business. The SmartHalo founders partnered with other companies to manufacture SmartHalo including Osedea, a mobile app developer, Mapbox, a GPS mapping company, and Optech, a design optics lab. Roughly 18 months after their Kickstarter campaign started, SmartHalo was being shipped to eager consumers.

CycleLabs continues to push SmartHalo and now has the product available in all Apple stores in North America and Europe. Consumers can also purchase the accessory at Best Buy and Amazon. The company is currently working on alternate maps to allow cyclists to maximize their riding experience and considering expanding the attachment to work as a guide for tourists.

SMARTHALO
smarthalo.bike/

THE SMALL BUSINESS DECISION: PERSONAL EVALUATION

LO1

An important but often difficult part of making the small business decision is to separate this decision into two parts: personal considerations and those related to the business or the opportunity. Each will be discussed in this chapter. In contemplating whether to start their own businesses, individuals are well advised to consider the potential consequences of such a move, both for themselves and for their families and friends. Failure to do this can lead to disillusionment, frustration, and an unsuccessful attempt to capitalize on a viable business opportunity. Frequently, the entrepreneur finds that the reasons for continuing in a small business are different from the reasons for start-up. Therefore, a good way to begin this evaluation is to learn the potential advantages and disadvantages of starting and operating your own business. In addition, understanding the personality characteristics and abilities required of an entrepreneur, as well as making an honest self-appraisal of your own suitability, is essential in making an intelligent small business decision.

ADVANTAGES OF SMALL BUSINESS OWNERSHIP

Running your own business offers some unique advantages over being an employee. Numerous small business owners cite the following advantages.

Independence.

Often, independence is the primary reason for going into business for yourself. This includes the freedom to make your own decisions without having to ask a superior. One study of successful entrepreneurs indicated that the majority started their businesses to "control their own lives" or to "be their own boss."[1] Kenzie MacDonald left his job as vice-president at Colliers International, a global commercial real estate firm, to start his own company in Halifax. MacDonald stated that the main reason for leaving his job was a strong desire to be his own boss: "I wanted to be in charge, to do things the way I wanted to do them. . . . When you work as an employee for years, you're always answering to someone. . . . It's nice to be able to make all the decisions, to be in control."[2] Young Toronto entrepreneur Bill Hennessey, owner of RoyalPak, a cleaning-products manufacturer, and Oxford Beach, an events planning company, echoes MacDonald's comments about independence: "As an entrepreneur, you control your own destiny. I work the hours I want to work, and I take vacations when I want to take vacations."[3] Motherhood offers entrepreneurial opportunities that may offer work-life balance, as discussed in **Small Business in Action 2-1**. In a recent TD Bank survey, 95 percent of entrepreneurs cited being their own boss and independence as the main reasons they like being an entrepreneur. Additionally, Statistics Canada has cited the desire for independence as the main motivator for starting a business. Entrepreneurs should realize, however, that even though they own their businesses, they must still answer to customers, suppliers, key employees, and creditors. Increased independence allows many entrepreneurs to better balance work and family commitments. A study by CIBC World Markets found this to be important to 79 percent of entrepreneurs.[4]

Young entrepreneurs like Bill Hennessey love the independence entrepreneurship provides.

Photo courtesy of Bill Hennessey, RoyalPak Inc.

More Personal Contact with People.

Running a small business usually means making contact with a large number of people, including customers, suppliers, and employees. Those who enjoy and are skilled at working with people find such interactions the most rewarding aspect of their businesses.

Skill Development.

Abilities in many functional areas of management are necessary to run a small business and can be developed during the process. Often, possessing such skills makes an individual more sought after in larger organizations. Today, many progressive and innovative organizations look for employees who have had small business experience. For example, David Reynolds of Halifax, while attending Mount Saint Vincent University, founded Quicksnap, a plastic clip that eliminates the need to tie shoelaces. Reynolds, who eventually sold the company after a successful appearance on CBC's *Dragons' Den,* says the skills and knowledge he gained by running a company helped him find a job after he graduated: "After I graduated, I had experience running and growing a business and a track record in sales. Several companies wanted to hire me because they knew I could sell, and they liked that I had acted entrepreneurially when I was in university."

Potential Financial Rewards.

The higher risk associated with operating a small business offers the possibility of a higher financial return. As the old saying goes, "you cannot get rich working for someone else." Owning a business provides entrepreneurs with unlimited earnings potential—something that is attractive to many. For example, Ryan Smolkin, owner of **Smoke's Poutinerie**, one of Canada's fastest-growing franchises had started two businesses before he was 25 years old. Smolkin made so much money from the sale of his branding company, Amoeba, that he retired! But he soon developed the entrepreneurial itch again and started his growing restaurant franchise. Other people are starting entrepreneurial ventures to supplement traditional income. In a recent RBC poll on Canadian Entrepreneurship, of the roughly 54 percent of Canadians with entrepreneurial intentions, 56 percent of them have already started earning money entrepreneurially. Most often these businesses are in areas the person is passionate about, such as a hobby or a recreational activity (28 percent), and they are testing a business idea (8 percent).[5] For example, Jeremy Hannan of Toronto was passionate about snorkelling, so he started CobraMask to supplement his income as a wood finisher. Hannan noticed that traditional snorkelling masks often resulted in water flowing into the breathing apparatus and non-traditional masks that solved the problem were quite expensive. So Hannan created CobraMask, a full-face, premium snorkelling mask at a non-premium price. With year one sales in excess of $100,000, Hannan has more than supplemented his income and is considering running his new business full time.[6]

Jeremy Hannan started CobraMask to supplement his income. His idea for a more effective and affordable mask has led to Hannan becoming a full-time entrepreneur.

Photo courtesy of CobraMask

Challenge.

Many people start small businesses for the challenge as well as the feeling of personal accomplishment. A study of Canadian entrepreneurs' perceptions of the ideal workplace indicated that work offering a challenge is most important.[7] And an Angus Reid poll of entrepreneurs indicated that the most common reason for starting a business was "the appeal of doing something interesting and challenging."[8] For example, Heidi Fortes, founder of the chic cannabis accessory company **Accoutrements**, says that she enjoys entrepreneurship and all the challenges that come with running her own business and, although there can be ups and downs, entrepreneurship is a rush and rewarding.[9] Ronald Richardson, co-founder of **Benbria Corp.**, a software company based in Kanata, Ontario, echoes Fortes and notes the rewards, challenges, and learning opportunities outweigh the risks of entrepreneurship.[10] In fact, some people leave larger companies because their positions lack the opportunities and challenges a small business can offer. Fortes left a successful sales career to pursue her entrepreneurial dream. Other examples include Tonia Jahsha, from Ancaster, Ontario, founder of the social selling company **Steeped Tea**. Jahsha left her high-paying job in electronics to start selling loose tea at parties and eventually adopted the social selling or direct sales model. In a few short years, Steeped Tea has grown to have 9000 consultants who sell their products at parties and social gatherings, and Jahsha has been recognized as one of Canada's leading female entrepreneurs.[11]

Enjoyment.

Most successful entrepreneurs enjoy what they do. As mentioned above, entrepreneurs tend to get their best ideas from their hobbies, activities they are passionate about.[12] When we researched this text and read countless interviews with entrepreneurs, both successful and unsuccessful entrepreneurs told us they loved being their own boss. Research indicates that 90 percent of entrepreneurs would start their business again, and in a national survey conducted by TD Bank, two-thirds of business owners described themselves as very happy. For example, Traci Costa from Richmond, British Columbia, founder of Peekaboo Beans, a children's clothing company producing trendy clothes that allow children to play freely, says she loves being an entrepreneur. She confirms that starting her own business was the best decision she has ever made.[13] Costa's words are echoed by entrepreneur Betsy Hiebert, founder of Winnipeg-based, My Care Necessities, who has created an easy-to-use journal that allows seniors to keep track of their health care. Hiebert says she loves owning her own business, even with all its challenges, and how the various projects associated with being a business owner stretch her to grow.[14] The Entrepreneurial Research Consortium found that one of the top motivators for starting a business was having a passion for the field.[15] This factor explains, in part, why financial rewards are not necessarily the prime motivation for establishing a business.

SMALL BUSINESS IN ACTION 2-1

MOMPRENEURS

Mompreneurs, such as Sarah Davis, have started businesses to achieve work–life balance. While some mompreneurs stay small, others, like Davis, have grown multi-million–dollar companies.

AP photo/Lenny Ignelzi/CP Photo

Some women are attracted to entrepreneurship as a way to achieve work–life balance. For example, many mothers have started their own businesses so they could be personally in charge of their own work schedule, which allows them to spend more time with their families. In fact, mother entrepreneurs have become so common that they have become known in the mainstream media as "mompreneurs." *Mompreneur* is defined as a female business owner who is actively balancing the role of mom and the role of entrepreneur. Sometimes when people hear the term "mompreneur," they imagine a mother operating a very small business, but this is not always the case, and many mompreneurs are managing growing businesses. For example, Maria Locker is the founder and CEO of **Mompreneur Showcase Group Inc.**, a company that operates *MOMpreneur Magazine*, which is dedicated to assisting other mompreneurs in running successful companies in Canada. Other examples include Sarah Davis, owner of **FashionPhile.com**, an online site that sells used high-end purses and bags. Davis, who originally started the company by selling her own branded clothing on eBay, discovered that high-end accessories such as handbags held their value so well that used items were selling at close to retail prices. Davis' company, which guarantees its products are authentic, had sales in excess of $57 million last year.

Discussion Questions

1. Given the challenges associated with starting and running a business, do you think being a mompreneur allows for more work–life balance compared with traditional work or part-time employment?
2. What do you think are some of the advantages and disadvantages of being a mompreneur?
3. What do you think are some business ideas that would allow work and life balance?

DISADVANTAGES OF SMALL BUSINESS OWNERSHIP

Although there are many advantages to owning and operating a small business, there are several often overlooked disadvantages. We will discuss some of these next.

Risk.

The failure rate of small businesses is very high. One of the key reasons for Canadians' hesitancy to start a small business is the risk of failure.[16] In Canada, about 85 percent of small to medium-sized businesses survive the first year, 70 percent make it through year two, and 50 percent last more than five years. There are many potential reasons for these failures, but the major causes appear to be inexperience and unbalanced management.

Stress.

Studies show that small business owners have high stress levels, a high incidence of heart disease, and a high rate of divorce owing to the increased pressures of managing their businesses.[17] Many sources of stress are due to the individual nature of entrepreneurship, where the business owner ultimately makes final decisions and is responsible for the success or failure of the company. For example, Josh Horowitz, owner of **Sell My Stuff Canada**, a Toronto-based company that specializes in content or estate sales, says that while he loves being his own boss, he does feel the pressure of being responsible: "There's no one higher up," he says. "You're the last line of defence when a tough question comes up. It's a quick learning curve."[18] Colin McDonald, co-founder of **Clearwater**, a Halifax firm he grew from a small business to a publicly traded company, echoes Horowitz's comments: "Being your own boss is stressful. When we were a small company, I would look around the room and think that I had to make sure there was enough money to pay everyone at the end of the week. I still think that from time to time."[19] In owning a business, it is difficult, if not impossible, to confine concerns about the business to the workplace. Typically, these pressures will affect the entrepreneur's personal life and family situation as well.

Limited Financial Rewards.

Although the possibility of high earnings exists, relatively few small business owners become extremely wealthy. The financial rewards are often very meagre, especially during the first few years. A Royal Bank of Canada survey found that while 42 percent of new entrepreneurs expected their income to be higher after starting their business, only 34 percent of them achieved this.[20] Even businesses that grow rapidly are not necessarily as profitable as you might think. The Canadian Federation of Independent Business reports that although a few small business owners do very well financially, the majority earn less than the average paid employee.[21] Statistics Canada found that the median income of self-employed individuals was 91.4 percent of the median income of paid employees[22] and that employees of small businesses earned only 85 percent of the income of employees in large businesses.[23] Heidi Fortes, owner of the company Accoutrements discussed above, says you can essentially become broke running your own business. She says it's a particularly large adjustment for people who leave paid employment. Fortes notes entrepreneurs should be prepared to invest all their profits back into their business, especially early on.[24] Entrepreneurs find ways to invest in their small business ideas, as discussed in **Small Business in Action 2-2**.

Young entrepreneur Brandon Turner, who quit being self-employed to join the fast-growing company **BiggerPockets**, notes that one of the reasons he left self-employment was that he could make more money as a paid employee. This extra income allows him to invest in creating long-term wealth and taking vacation time. Turner says, "While most of the world would simply buy a larger house, a nicer car and better wardrobe, I've been sinking this cash into several other more productive avenues, including more real estate investments, paying off debt and going on some relaxing vacations. Simply put: I'm leveraging this job to create even greater wealth in my future." [25]

Need for Many Abilities.

Acquiring all the necessary skills, such as accounting, finance, marketing, and personnel management, is a difficult task that many owner-managers never master. This is particularly true for the countless businesses that start out very small. In these situations, entrepreneurs generally cannot afford to hire people with specialized expertise. Failure to acquire these skills, either personally or through recruitment, can seriously hinder the growth of the business.[26]

SMALL BUSINESS IN ACTION 2-2

TAKING THE PLUNGE

On the surface, it seemed that Ali Asaria was content in his lucrative job as a software engineer at BlackBerry), where he was best known for designing the game *Brick Breaker*, which was the most successful mobile game of its time. However, Asaria wanted to be an entrepreneur, so he subsequently quit his job to start his own company **Well.ca**, an online health, beauty, and baby store. Asaria says he left BlackBerry out of frustration that his work benefited the company but not necessarily him. "I got to the point where I just couldn't work for someone else. I think it's great for some people, but it wasn't right for me," he says.

Asaria, who initially raised $10,000 in capital to start Well.ca, later sold his car and Toronto home to raise additional funds for the business. While Asaria had some experience building online stores for other companies, he knew little about the health and beauty industry. Luckily for Asaria, who had to move in with his father after the sale of his house, he had identified an area in Canada which was being significantly underserved with little competition. Consumers had a strong demand for ordering personal care items, such as adult diapers, condoms, and other products, online and having them delivered the next day. Asaria pushed sales by using a variety of unconventional marketing campaigns, such as placing billboards next to the Toronto Subway stops promoting products some people would normally not want to buy in public. Well.ca urged people to purchase products now, in public, on their mobile phones.

Asaria, who was clearly bitten by the entrepreneurial bug, stepped down as CEO of Well.ca in 2015 to focus on his new startup, **Tulip**. Asaria founded Tulip to help traditional brick-and-mortar stores compete against online companies such as Amazon. Just as with Well.ca, he was lacking in industry experience, but he believed his mobile app could help struggling retailers compete. Tulip's app exploits the one big advantage Asaria thinks traditional retailers have: sales associates. Tulip's app enables sales associates to use their smartphone to access customer and product data to better serve in-store customers. For example, if a customer visits Toys 'R' Us, an early Tulip adopter, looking for a stroller, the sales associate can quickly learn about the advantages of each type of stroller allowing them to better serve the customer, access inventory information, check the customer out, view customer shopping habits and even provide consumers with competitor prices.

The impact of the Tulip app, which is available on a subscription service, includes increases in store sales and order sizes, repeat customers, and customer satisfaction. As a result, many retailers, including Indigo, Michael Kors, Coach, and Chanel, have adopted the product. Some business analysts are not convinced brick-and-mortar stores can be saved and hesitate about predicting Tulip's potential for long-term success. Skeptics point out that the earliest Tulip adopter, the American arm of Toys 'R' Us, went bankrupt, and that, generally, the customer service experience, even with Tulip, is heavily reliant on having motivated and trained in-store sales associates, which can be difficult to find and maintain. Asaria, of course, disagrees and has successfully raised $52 million to further expand Tulip globally.

Asaria founded Well.ca and Tulip to avoid traditional employment and to assist consumers and retailers; he has recently announced that 80 percent of his Tulip shares, valued at roughly $30 million, have been pledged to a charitable trust controlled by his employees. He notes that successful startups can further income inequality and the creation of the trust will avoid Tulip from contributing to the problem.

Discussion Questions

1. What are some of the reasons that Asaria's businesses have succeeded?
2. Asaria has managed to raise millions for Well.ca prior to stepping down as CEO and ultimately selling the company. He has since raised in excess of $51 million for Tulip. Would you have invested money in Well.ca and Tulip? Why or why not?
3. Asaria hopes to grow Tulip into a $100-billion company? Do you think he will be successful? Why or why not?
4. What do you think are some of the advantages and disadvantages of Asaria pledging 80 percent of his shares in Tulip to an employee-controlled trust?

People Conflicts.

Because owning a small business tends to require more contact with people, the potential arises for more conflicts with employees, suppliers, and customers. This factor could turn what is often thought of as an advantage into both a disadvantage and a frustration.

Time Demands.

Almost all small businesses require long hours of work, at least initially. Owner-managers of small businesses often have a longer workday than if they were working for someone else. On average, the self-employed person worked 39.1 hours per week in 2016 compared with 36.1 hours for employees.[27] Even more striking is the large difference in those who usually worked over 50 hours per week, a recent survey found that, 30.3 percent of self-employed persons worked over 50 hours compared with less than 4.1 percent of employees.[28] This is confirmed by entrepreneurs like Natalie Dusome, from Penetanguishene, Ontario, founder of **Poppy & Peonies**, a highly successful direct sales handbag company, notes that when she left a well-paying job as head designer for Aldo to become an entrepreneur, she worked non-stop on almost no sleep for two years.[29] But her hard work has paid off: her company recently reported $1.1 million in sales and a significant expansion plan.[30] Ambareen Musa, founder and CEO of **Souqalmal**, the leading Middle East financial website that enables consumers to compare financial products and solutions, says there is no such thing as working nine to five when you're an entrepreneur, and employee benefits, such as maternity leave, really don't exist: "There's no such thing as a 9-to-5 schedule for the company founder and no holiday when he or she can take a complete break from work . . . and when it comes to maternity leave, forget it. When my second child was born this past summer, I took one week off."[31]

Young entrepreneur Ambareen Musa, founder of Souqalmal, likes being an entrepreneur but asserts that people have to realize it is not a nine-to-five job.

Photo courtesy of Ambareen Musa

In a national survey of owners of small and medium-sized businesses, *Profit* magazine found that entrepreneurs worked on average 54 hours a week.[32] The Entrepreneurial Research Consortium found that the main reason entrepreneurs voluntarily stopped operating their own business was that they were working too hard.[33] **Figure 2-1** illustrates that long hours are part of owning a small business, particularly in the early years of its existence. Another study of 650 small businesses in the service and retail sector found that the most frequently mentioned advice to potential entrepreneurs was to "be prepared to work hard and put in long hours."[34]

FIGURE 2-1 **Percentage Distribution of Usual Weekly Hours Worked by Employees and the Self-Employed, 1991, 2001, and 2011**

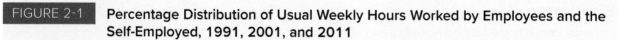

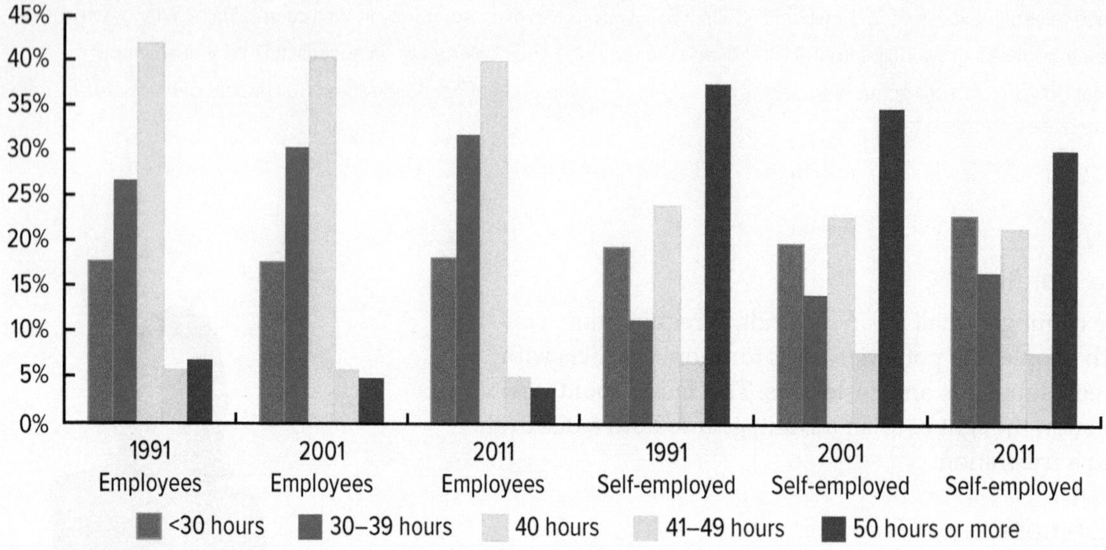

Source: Statistics Canada, *Labour Force Survey*, April 2012.

DEMOGRAPHIC CHARACTERISTICS OF ENTREPRENEURS

LO2

Although entrepreneurs come from all demographic backgrounds, some conditions seem to be correlated with entrepreneurial activity. Entrepreneurs are more likely to come from families in which parents set high standards for their children's performance, encouraged habits of self-reliance, and avoided being strict disciplinarians.[35] A recent significant trend is that the greatest growth of small business start-ups comes from those who have postsecondary education.[36] Statistics Canada reports that the education level of entrepreneurs has improved significantly in recent years.[37] The percentage of self-employed workers who have university degrees increased by 33 percent from 2000 to 2008.[38] Several recent reports have found that entrepreneurs are more likely to have a degree, with 53 percent of business owners having studied at university.[39] In addition, entrepreneurs tend to be children of parents who owned their own businesses. Some of the relevant demographic characteristics of entrepreneurs are shown in **Figure 2-2**.

PERSONALITY CHARACTERISTICS REQUIRED BY SUCCESSFUL ENTREPRENEURS

What are the personality traits of the successful owner-manager? In his book *Peak Performers*, Charles A. Garfield estimates that 70 percent of the 1500 peak performers he studied were entrepreneurs. These individuals exhibited some common characteristics that confirmed the results of previous studies.

In discussing the following characteristics, note that Canadian entrepreneurs have many different traits and come from diverse backgrounds. Very few entrepreneurs, if any, possess all the traits discussed, but many possess at least a few of them. However, even possessing such characteristics does not guarantee success in small business.

FIGURE 2-2 **Characteristics of Entrepreneurs**

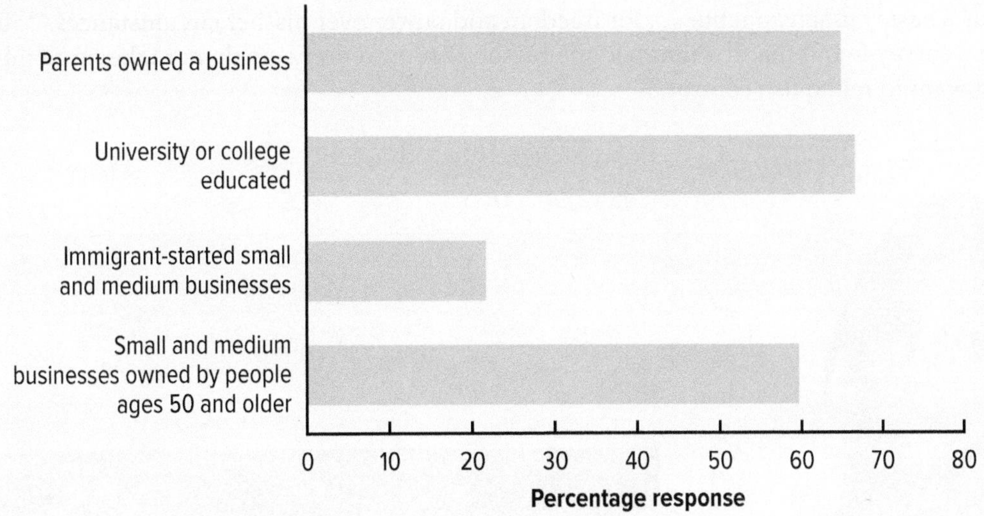

Individuals contemplating small business ownership would do well to evaluate their own suitability to operate a small business by noting the following personality characteristics. Keep in mind, however, that being an entrepreneur is less about being a type of individual and more about possessing an attitude of pursuing opportunity.

Achievement Orientation.

Those who place a high value on achievement, competition, aggressiveness, and hard work may be ideal owner-managers. Such people tend to be disciplined goal setters and have a bias for action. For example, Andrew Doyle, co-founder of 2nd Act Innovations, later Oris 4, a data storage company that enables firms to search through all their data for useful information, wants to build a billion-dollar company in Atlantic Canada. Since having opened an office in Silicon Valley, Doyle has demonstrated that he has the drive and ambition shared by many entrepreneurs. Doyle, who was previously president of the marketing company Extreme Group, talked about his love of starting a new company, comparing it to playing offense in sports and trying to stay one step ahead of the competition. Business owners also tend to possess above-average focus and drive, as well as the initiative to make things happen. Because they are hard workers, they generally strive to maintain good health to sustain this high level of energy. As Terence Corcoran, writer for the *National Post* states, "The entrepreneur is the driving force, the mover, the hero who sees opportunity, who grasps the importance of the product, knows when to assume risks, and, in the end, accumulates the largest fortunes."[40]

Risk Taking.

As previously mentioned, the very nature of small business suggests that entrepreneurs are risk takers, although they often do not think of themselves as such. Evidence shows, however, that successful entrepreneurs usually do take calculated risks. Brett Wilson, former star of CBC's *Dragons' Den,* states that a willingness to take smart risks is a key to entrepreneurial success.[41] John A. McCluskey, Ernst and Young Ontario Entrepreneur of the Year award winner and president of **Alamos Gold Inc.**, was recognized for his willingness to take calculated risks to grow his business. Colleen McMorrow of Ernst and Young had this to say about McCluskey, who transformed his company from virtually no employees to 500 paid workers and one of the largest gold producers in three different countries: "John risked everything when founding Alamos Gold Inc. at the bottom of a 20-year gold bear market and amid significant macroeconomic issues. But the risk paid off."[42] When he started the company, McMorrow took a calculated risk that gold prices would improve.

Independence, Self-Confidence, and Self-Assurance.

Entrepreneurs tend to resent authority and want to take credit or blame for their own actions. Karl Vesper, a well-known spokesperson for entrepreneurship, states in his book *New Venture Strategies* that "the entrepreneur . . . has a basic human appetite . . . for freedom and power over his/her circumstances."[43] In fact, an American Express survey found that the number one reason that entrepreneurs do not take more time off is because they do not want to relinquish control.[44]

Lisa Patel says watching her parents run and manage numerous companies inspired her to be an entrepreneur.
Photo courtesy of Lisa Patel, Property Princess

Other characteristics of successful small business ownership strongly correlated with independence are self-confidence and self-assurance. Often these traits are acquired through parents who were also small business owners. A recent study found that 50 percent of Canadian entrepreneurs' parents owned businesses. For example, Lisa Patel, owner of the **Property Princess** team, an Ontario-based real estate company, credits watching her parents start and sell 18 businesses as her inspiration to become an entrepreneur: "Growing up I knew I'd own my own business," she says. "My parents raised four children, and each of us worked in the family businesses. They taught us that ambitious people can have what they want in life."[45]

Innovativeness.

Successful entrepreneurs tend to be creative and willing to try new ideas. They are not afraid to evaluate an idea in a nontraditional way and to ask questions such as, "why not?" They also tend to experiment and test their ideas. Such entrepreneurs are sensitive to new trends in society arising from the ways consumers experience products and to potential opportunities that result from these trends. For example, Mike Gettis and Rajen

Ruparell from Calgary founded Endy in 2015, an online bed-in-a-box company offering comfortable beds shipped to your door for roughly one-third the cost of a traditional mattress. Gettis says the company's concept of buying a bed online and receiving it in a few days was innovative and unique.[46] Only three years later Gettis and Ruparell sold the company to Sleep Country Canada for almost $89 million.[47]

The North American trend of car sharing prompted Wilson Wood to found Ottawa's **Vrtucar**. Wood, who admits to not actually liking cars, was more than happy to build a profitable company around the growing trend. Interestingly, one of the major reasons given by Canadian entrepreneurs for starting their own businesses was that they had found an attractive market niche and wanted to pursue it.[48] For example, Derrick Fung, former owner of Richmond Hill–based Tunezy.com, was well aware that many new musicians were using the Internet to gain fans and yet failing to capitalize or make money from the attention. Tunezy allowed independent musicians to earn money by providing fans with online concerts. Fung made money by selling advertising and customer information from these events and sharing the revenue with the musicians.[49] Tunezy did so well that it was noticed by the publicly traded firm SFX Entertainment, which purchased the company from Fung. Fung has since co-founded **Drop**, an app that allows people to link their credit and debit cards to earn points, which then can be redeemed for rewards. Drop has just reached one million users, been recognized as one of the top 25 start-ups of 2019 by LinkedIn and the company has announced they have raised $21 million for further expansion.[50]

Mike Gettis and Rajen Ruparell co-founded Endy in 2015; the company sold mattresses in boxes. Three years later they sold the company for roughly $89 million.
Photo courtesy of Endy

Strong Verbal and Numerical Skills.

Successful small business owners are able to communicate their thoughts well. One study of 264 Canadian entrepreneurial companies found that communication skills were judged to be the most important contributor to the success of entrepreneurs.[51] In a BDC article discussing key skills for entrepreneurs, Rony Israel, a business consultant with over 30 years' experience, says ongoing communication, especially with employees, in both good and bad times, is essential for entrepreneurial success.[52] Additionally, numerical skills can help entrepreneurs solve problems that arise in operating a small business. Whether or not they have a high level of formal education, successful entrepreneurs have usually acquired the necessary skills and knowledge from various sources. Increasingly, however, the educational background of Canadian entrepreneurs has been improving. The CIBC Economic Analysis division found that the majority of the owners of small business start-ups had at least some postsecondary education.[53] Statistics Canada has also found that the growth in the number of self-employed persons with graduate degrees was higher than for other educational levels.[54]

Selling Skills.

Most successful entrepreneurs have above-average marketing and selling skills. Selling skills are not only helpful in promoting the business to customers but are also essential for obtaining debt or equity capital, securing suppliers, and maintaining employee loyalty. Saeed El-Darahali, founder of Halifax-based **Simplycast**, a specialized digital marketing company, says sales and marketing skills are essential to growing a business. They are also very valuable in establishing networking contacts or sources of assistance for the operations. Lisa Patel, previously discussed, says, "Business today is all about connections. Networking is a long-term process and the key is to establish relationships. If you don't connect, it doesn't work."[55] Successful entrepreneurs tend to handle rejection well, realizing that when they are told no, they cannot take it personally.

Problem-Solving Abilities.

Entrepreneurs identify problems quickly and respond with effective solutions. Typically, they rank above average at sorting through irrelevant details and getting to the heart of a problem. For example, Brian Chesky and Joe Gebbia founded Airbnb when they discovered two problems in one area: first, the consistently high rent in New York City that left many, themselves included, struggling; second, the limited hotel space NYC. In solving these two problems, Airbnb was born.[56] Entrepreneurs are also more likely to delegate, refuse to accept defeat, are willing to experiment, are creative, and think long term.[57] One such entrepreneur's story is found in **Small Business Beginnings 2-1**. Some of the most successful companies created in the past two decades, such as Shopify, Hootsuite, Uber, and Glassdoor, have resulted from entrepreneurial problem solving.[58]

Strategic Planning.

Successful small business owners tend to excel at setting business objectives and developing different ways of achieving them. They adapt to change easily and know their industries and products thoroughly. A recent BDC survey of Canadian entrepreneurs found that successful businesses were much more likely to have a strategic plan.[59] For example, Janet MacMillan, owner of Halifax-based **MTL Communications Group**, a communications and public relations firm, states that planning has been key to her company's long-term success: "Companies, especially businesses in ever-changing fields such as communications, have to anticipate changes in the marketplace and be ready to respond accordingly."[60]

Perseverance.

Because of the difficulties in starting and operating a small business, successful entrepreneurs tend to have perseverance. They do not quit amid adversity. Jim Treliving, owner of **Boston Pizza**, could not find the money to purchase his first store. Rather than give up, Treliving convinced his friends to lend him half the money to buy the business and then he convinced the original owner to lend him the other half. Treliving went on to build Boston Pizza into the most successful Italian franchise in Canada. On a smaller scale, Eryn Green and Tamar Wagman, founders of Sweetpea Baby Food, had difficulty raising funds from traditional sources. The pair eventually wrote a business plan that they pitched to their family and friends for the opportunity to invest in their business. The partners eventually raised $150,000, which was enough to kick-start their successful company. One study found that successful entrepreneurs "average 3.8 failures before the final success."[61] Business owners tend to view these failures as part of their entrepreneurial education and point out that many millionaires failed several times before becoming successful. Successful business owners also tend to have greater self-discipline, as they often forgo paying themselves or taking vacations in the early months of the business.

To assess the suitability of their personalities for starting a small business, entrepreneurs should evaluate their own capabilities in the areas just described. Completing a checklist from the large number of checklists that are available allows for a quantitative evaluation of these characteristics. A simple example of one such checklist appears in **Table 2-1**. Links to longer, more comprehensive checklists and tests can be found in **Appendix 2A**.

TABLE 2-1 **Characteristics Checklist**

1. If the statement is only rarely or slightly descriptive of your behaviour, score 1.
2. If the statement is applicable under some circumstances but only partially true, score 2.
3. If the statement describes you perfectly, score 3.

	Statement	Score
1.	I relish competing with others.	______
2.	I compete intensely to win regardless of the rewards.	______
3.	I compete with some caution but will often bluff.	______
4.	I do not hesitate to take a calculated risk for future gain.	______
5.	I do a job so effectively that I get a feeling of accomplishment.	______
6.	I want to be tops in whatever I elect to do.	______
7.	I am not bound by tradition.	______
8.	I am inclined to forge ahead and discuss later.	______
9.	Reward or praise means less to me than a job well done.	______
10.	I usually go my own way regardless of others' opinions.	______
11.	I find it difficult to admit error or defeat.	______
12.	I am a self-starter—I need little urging from others.	______
13.	I am not easily discouraged.	______
14.	I work out my own answers to problems.	______
15.	I am inquisitive.	______
16.	I am not patient with interference from others.	______
17.	I have an aversion to taking orders from others.	______
18.	I can take criticism without feeling hurt.	______
19.	I insist on seeing a job through to the finish.	______
20.	I expect associates to work as hard as I do.	______
21.	I read to improve my knowledge in all business activities.	______

A score of 63 is perfect; 52 to 62 is good; 42 to 51 is fair; and under 42 is poor. Obviously scoring high here is not a guarantee of becoming a successful small business owner, because many other personal qualities must also be rated. But it should encourage you to pursue the matter further.

SMALL BUSINESS BEGINNINGS 2-1

SOCIAL SELLING

Natalie Dusome of Penetanguishene, Ontario, displayed both risk taking and perseverance when she started her handbag company, **Poppy & Peonies**. Her company's handbags provide women with affordable, stylish, and multifunctional purses. What sets them apart is that they contain inserts that allow the bags to be converted into a variety of different styles for use on different occasions. For example, larger purses or diaper bags come with inserts allowing women to convert the original bag into a smaller cross-body bag, a handbag, or a clutch.

Dusome says that starting her own business involved a great deal of risk, as she left a secure job at Aldo to become an entrepreneur where she worked non-stop for the first two years. She says her love of the handbag industry coupled with her determination and passion enabled her to succeed.

Along with her multifunctional handbags, Dusome also differentiates Poppy & Peonies with her sales strategy. Her purses are not sold in stores but are only available online, and through her direct-sales or social-selling model. Dusome says her

[continued]

[continued]

strategy is simple: find women, whom she calls influencers, and empower them to be entrepreneurs who can sell her handbags at parties and social events. She says the ideal target for her purses are busy women like herself. Her brand ambassadors, the influencers, create fun and relaxed social events, where they can display and sell her bags while giving friends and potential customers a break from their busy schedules. Dusome's strategy is clearly paying off as she has recently reported sales in excess of $1.1 million with $250,000 in net profit.

Discussion Questions

1. What do you think are some of the advantages and disadvantages of social or direct selling?
2. Develop a list of business ideas you think would be successful using the direct sales model. Your idea should include a product(s) and some justification why social selling would work.
3. Use Internet resources to discover other social selling businesses. Identify some opportunities you think have significant potential and present them to class. Be sure to include the product(s), what support the company offers, and, if possible, the commission structure.

THE SMALL BUSINESS DECISION: ORGANIZATIONAL EVALUATION LO3

It is important not only to evaluate your personal capabilities to operate a small business successfully but also to investigate why some businesses succeed and others fail. The following discussion reviews what some businesses do right and what others do wrong. The potential small business owner should incorporate the things successful businesses do right and avoid the mistakes other businesses have made.

SMALL BUSINESS SUCCESSES

Despite the high risk associated with starting a small business, many small businesses operate successfully. Numerous examples of these successes appear throughout this book. These examples illustrate many of the characteristics of successful businesses and their owners. The characteristics discussed next are compiled from reviews of successful small businesses.

Alertness to Change.

Small businesses that are flexible and plan ahead are able to adapt to changing environmental conditions more quickly and, in many cases, more effectively than larger businesses. Vancouver's Ryan Holmes, who is mentioned throughout this text, founded **Hootsuite**, one of the global leaders in social media management. Holmes first started a company that built websites called Invoke. While running Invoke, he discovered that many customers were looking to make better use of social media, so Holmes created Hootsuite. Today Hootsuite has over 16 million users and the company is worth over $1 billion.[62]

Successful computer software companies are also good examples of companies that can embrace change. Specific examples include Ben Baldwin and Jamie Schneiderman, past owners of **ClearFit**, a Toronto-based software company that makes applicant screening software. After engaging in discussion with clients, the pair realized that an industry trend of ramping up sophistication in systems was pushing many small clients away. As a result, the partners re-thought their strategy and better aligned their software with their clients' needs.[63] The computer industry changes very rapidly, and the new needs that emerge offer many opportunities for small business. Albert Iannantuono, owner of **Tri-Media**, has managed to remain successful through the re-invention of his company by jumping into new technologies. Iannantuono says, "I call [re-invention] an evolution. What we are today is not what you're going to be tomorrow."[64]

Ability to Attract and Hold Competent Employees.

Small businesses tend to be labour intensive. Thus, the value of employees cannot be overstated. Small businesses face increasing competition from large firms and even government in attracting and holding good employees. A recent survey of Canadian entrepreneurs found that attracting good employees is a challenge for 43 percent of small and medium-sized businesses in Canada. Entrepreneurs who have mastered employee recruitment and retention are generally more successful. Many of the owner-managers profiled in this text have retained their good employees by using creative personnel management techniques. For example, **Schleese**, an Ontario manufacturer of custom saddles, uses flex-time as a way to attract and retain employees. Employees at the company can work longer hours and bank them to use against Fridays or to attend family events or other appointments. Since implementing the strategy, the company reports it has experienced very little turnover.[65] In 2018, **Raintree Capital Inc.** one of the fastest-growing companies in Canada, used a similar approach. The company allows employees to pick their daily start and end times, and provides employees with a great deal of flexibility in their schedules. CEO Nick Fournier says employees can select whatever hours best suit their lives.[66] Other entrepreneurs, such as Edward Quilty, founder of **Aquatic Informatics Inc.**, a high-growth, Vancouver-based company that specializes in software that monitors water data, recommends entrepreneurs try to hire the best people because "even if you are seen as a tech company, you are really a people company." Quilty states that one way to attract and retain top employees is to have a compelling mission, a culture of transparency and continuous learning, and to decentralize decision making. [67]

Some entrepreneurs, like founder of Aquatic Informatics Inc. Edward Quilty, motivate employees by giving them a share of ownership in the company.

Photo courtesy of Aquatic Informatics Inc.

Staying Close to the Consumer.

Business owners who have a good knowledge of consumers' wants and needs and are able to incorporate them within the operations of their companies tend to be more successful. This skill involves constant monitoring of and responding to the market. For example, Jason McCann, co-founder and CEO of VARIDESK®, the workspace innovation company dedicated to creating environments that elevate people, says he learned about the importance of customer feedback from Amazon. He notes that Amazon, which is the top retailer in the world, takes consumer feedback and engagement quite seriously, and uses the information to create better products and services. McCann says that when he brought his first product, a sit-desk to market, he asked for customer feedback and made 22 design tweaks as a result. McCann urges companies to solicit feedback and not wait to hear from customers. With social media and other forms of communication readily available, entrepreneurs can quickly access valuable consumer knowledge.[68] Andrew Warner, founder of **Mixergy**, an online business that specializes in educating people about entrepreneurship and providing them with mentors, states that one of his biggest regrets was not reaching out to customers sooner for feedback. When he started to engage with his customers, he discovered that the information they offered could help him in create a better product.[69]

Jason McCann, co-founder and CEO of VARIDESK®, encourages entrepreneurs to listen to their customers to be successful. McCann argues that if Amazon, the top retailer in the world, is engaging with customers, then everyone should.

Photo courtesy of Varidesk

Thoroughness with Operating Details.

Successful businesses have a very detailed and highly controlled operating plan, whether in the plant or out in the market. Goals, reports, evaluations, and adjustments are made constantly. **College Pro Painters**' success can be attributed to the very thorough operating plan the founder, Greig Clark, set up while testing the business concept. Many successful entrepreneurs subscribe to the "management by walking around" technique, with which they remain on top of operations details.

Ability to Obtain Needed Capital.

A potential constraint on the operation and growth of any business is a lack of funds. Even if a businesses is destined to succeed, they may experience some difficulty in raising money. As evidenced throughout this text, successful entrepreneurs sometimes have to make sacrifices and be persistent in raising the start-up and growth money necessary to succeed. Nima Ashtari's story is a good example. He is co-founder of **X-Matik Inc.**, a Toronto-based company which created LaneCruise, an after-market, semi-autonomous attachment for cars for universal self-driving. Ashtari reveals that he sold his house and used his personal savings to fund his company, although he eventually managed to raised $350,000 from investors and sold beta kits to further fund the development of his product. Ashtari hopes to launch LaneCruise across North America in late 2019, thus allowing anyone to transform their car into an autonomously driven automobile.[70]

Most entrepreneurs will say that there is not a shortage of capital in Canada for good ideas.

Money is available to young Canadian entrepreneurs who have good ideas, such as Eric Migicovsky, who raised over $10 million using crowdfunding to build his Pebble smartwatch, and Jordan Satok, whom you can read about in **Small Business in Action 2-3**).

SMALL BUSINESS IN ACTION 2-3

YOUNG ENTREPRENEUR APPEARS TO POSSESS ALL THE KEYS TO SUCCESS

Eighteen-year-old Jordan Satok appears to have mastered most, if not all, of the keys to entrepreneurial success discussed above. Satok founded AppHero an interactive iPhone and iPad app bearing the company's name. AppHero assists people in identifying which apps are best for them based on their online habits. The app also works with Facebook, as AppHero tracks usage, likes, dislikes, and so forth, and identifies the apps that users will most likely will appreciate. The software allows users to view the apps their friends use and to share the apps they use with their friends. Satok, who also owned the company App of the Day, managed to raise $1.8 million in start-up money for his firm. Satok believed his product is better than traditional ways of finding apps, which include online searches, because these rely on the consumer's knowledge to enter key words. Satok says, "people don't know what they don't know." Satok further states that his app will recommend many apps that users may like but are not aware of.

Satok soon discovered that a rather large competitor, **Apple**, was also operating in this marketplace and was engaging in some rather tough business practices. Apple was essentially blocking companies like AppHero out of its App store and making it difficult for them to operate. Around the same time, Satok also recognized that more and more consumers were finding apps via online ads on social media websites. So when **Fuse Powered**, a Toronto-based firm, offered to purchase App Hero, Satok agreed. The result is that Fuse Powered now uses Satok's system of collecting and managing people's social media interests and recommending apps via online advertising. While the financial terms of the deal were not made public, Satok notes that all his initial investors were quite happy with the terms of the sale.

Eighteen-year-old Jordan Satok has already managed to raise close to $2 million for his company, AppHero. AppHero helps people find apps that will be useful to them.

Vince Talotta/Getty Images

Discussion Questions

1. Review the keys to entrepreneurial success. Does Satok possess most of these characteristics?
2. Do you think AppHero was a strong product? Why or why not?
3. Are you surprised by Apple's behaviour toward its competitors? Why or why not? Was its behaviour ethical?
4. Were you surprised that an 18-year-old was able to raise $1.8 million for a business? What do you think made the app attractive to investors? What do you think are some of the challenges of trying to raise money while still in high school?
5. Satok now works for Fuse Powered. Do you think entrepreneurs can easily switch to the role of employees? Why or why not?
6. Mobile business offers entrepreneurs incredible opportunities. List and, if time permits, develop an explanation of some mobile-based businesses you may want to start. For example, for a similar project, an Acadia University student developed a beer appreciation app that he is now selling.

Effective Handling of Government Laws, Rules, and Regulations.

Owners of successful small businesses keep abreast of legislation and programs that may affect their operations. They realize that ignorance of certain regulations can cost their organizations not only in a direct financial sense but, perhaps more importantly, also in terms of a tarnished reputation or a missed opportunity.

SMALL BUSINESS FAILURES

Despite the considerable appeal of operating your own business, it can also be disappointing if adequate preparations are not made. This section discusses some of the causes of small business failure. It is hoped that prospective entrepreneurs will avoid making the same mistakes as they start their own businesses. Readers should also recognize that businesses start and cease to exist continually. It is a natural occurrence in the business community for businesses to exit the marketplace and new businesses to appear. As mentioned in **Chapter 1**, the Canadian economy sees an increase of approximately 100,000 businesses a year, which traditionally outnumbers the number of small businesses that exit the marketplace.

Often, when we hear about business failure, we think bankruptcy, but very few business closings actually end in bankruptcy. The reality is that, on average, 11,000 businesses declare bankruptcy in Canada each year. More businesses simply cease to exist, some are bought out by competitors, and others just close. For example, The Book Room, Canada's self-proclaimed oldest book store, located in Halifax, had been in operation for 169 years before closing. The store that survived two world wars, the Great Depression, and a massive fire could not compete with online retailers, and its owner decided to close rather than suffer any more financial losses. Often customers and area residents are surprised when a business closes, as they fail to see it as part of a normal business life cycle. For example, it would have been doubtful that Canadians in the 1970s and 1980s would have predicted the end of Sears, which closed its doors in Canada in 2018.

Why do so many new businesses fail? Although a variety of problems can cause businesses to fail, including external shock, a downturn in the economy, or an entrepreneur's lack of management experience, another problem causes the demise of many companies—the failure of the entrepreneur to identify and deal with problems quickly. Often business owners ignore or do not see problems until it is too late. Thus it is important that entrepreneurs become aware of problems so that they develop effective solutions.

Factors That Cause Businesses to Fail.

While various studies indicate there are numerous reasons a business can fail, most of them can be classified as external shocks or management problems.

External Shocks.

Statistics Canada estimates that roughly 68 percent of businesses fail because of some type of external shock. These commonly include a downturn in the economy, changes in the economy such as in interest or currency rates, new competition or substitute product, loss of customers, loss of suppliers, and change in laws or regulations. For example, there has been some concerns raised by Ontario restaurant owners that the newly imposed minimum wage hikes may force some businesses to close. Carl Scammell, owner of Smokin' Tony's BBQ in Guelph, says the higher wages are the reason he was forced to close his restaurant as the higher labour costs made the business unprofitable.[71] Other restaurant owners have tried to manage the rise in minimum wage by lowering ingredient costs, reducing employee hours and eliminating items with low profit margins from their menus. For example, Lil' Baci's, a Toronto-based restaurant, originally removed 16 low-margin items from its offerings to offset the increase in minimum wage. Even with those changes in place, the restaurant announced they were closing in 2018 due to higher costs.[72]

Management Problems.

Management problems usually revolve around issues such as starting a business without raising enough funds, being unable to raise additional capital, failing to control costs, having problems attracting or retaining employees, growing too quickly, and planning poorly for expansion. Additionally, some entrepreneurs will also suffer from burnout associated with working too many hours.

If entrepreneurs are paying attention to their business plan and carefully monitoring the firm's financial progress, they may notice warning signs that their business may be in trouble. Such signs include a failure to achieve objectives in the firm's business plan, a decrease in sales, an inability to pay some bills, and so forth. When this happens, an entrepreneur should take immediate action to solve the problem. Entrepreneurs should spend some time identifying the major problem at hand and engaging in some corrective actions. Often business owners who are struggling to survive will have to re-draft business plans, cut costs, raise additional funds—sometimes by selling excess products at a discount—and engage in discussions with lenders. If business owners take the necessary steps, they may prevent the closure of their business and the business may in fact thrive.

A study of failing Canadian small businesses sheds further light on the specific types of management weaknesses that exist (**Table 2-2**).

TABLE 2-2 Common Failure Factors for a Small Business

1. Poor or nonexistent management information systems (inventory and accounts receivable control)
2. Poor controls on management expenses
3. Overreliance on a few key customers
4. Lack of financial skill (cash flow and profitability management)
5. Company is overleveraged (high debt), and debt is not being reduced
6. Poor cash flow management
7. Company management does not ask for help

ENTREPRENEURSHIP AND SMALL BUSINESS MANAGEMENT LO4

So far, we've used the terms "entrepreneurship" and "small business management" interchangeably. However, considerable confusion exists about these two terms, the types of skills they describe, and the type of training required to develop such skills. This section distinguishes between these terms. Understanding this distinction can be valuable in establishing and maintaining a business. Although they differ, both entrepreneurial and managerial skills may be necessary at different stages of the business's life cycle. This is the primary reason that both types of skills and traits were discussed together earlier in this chapter.

ENTREPRENEURIAL SKILLS

Entrepreneurial skills are required to start or expand a business. The specific traits that describe entrepreneurship are creativity, flexibility, innovativeness, risk taking, and independence. Entrepreneurs who have a high tolerance for ambiguity and change tend to think and plan with a long-term perspective. Entrepreneurs are generally idea oriented.

Those who start their own businesses are known as *founders* of the business, and there are two types. The first, sometimes called the *artisan* entrepreneur, has expertise in the technical or operations side of the business. They may have invented the product and tend to be passionate about it and confident of its success. The second is the *promoter,* who identifies a product or service they feel has potential and teams up with the founder to assist with initial financing or marketing expertise. Many small businesses are established following this pattern.

MANAGERIAL SKILLS

The skills of a manager are useful in maintaining and solidifying the existing product, service, or business. The effective manager knows how to develop strategy, set organizational goals, and develop methods for achieving those goals. Managers require skill and knowledge in several functional areas of a business, including finance, marketing, personnel, network development, research, teamwork development, and operations. Such skills are most valuable after the business has been established.

As can be seen, although the entrepreneur's and the manager's skills differ, they are, nevertheless, essential for the long-run success of the business. Entrepreneurial skills help get the business started, while managerial skills help ensure that the business continues to operate successfully. Entrepreneurial skills may be essential once again to promote the growth of the business. **Table 2-3** summarizes the distinction between entrepreneurial and managerial skills and the situations to which they apply.

TABLE 2-3 **Small Business Skills**

TYPE	CHARACTERISTICS	APPROPRIATE SITUATIONS
Entrepreneurial	Creativity and innovativeness Independence Risk taking Being idea oriented	Generating ideas or solutions to problems Starting new business Expanding or adding new products
Managerial	Ability to develop strategy and goal setting Preferring to know outcomes of actions or activities Being a team player Ability to work through others Having skills in finance, marketing, personnel, operations	Reaching performance objectives Maintaining control of operations

A major problem associated with small business is that individuals who have strengths in both areas are rare. Because most small businesses are started and operated by the same person, skills or characteristics that the person might lack must be found in others who are hired or otherwise acquired. Failure to do so may doom the venture. A study by the Harvard Business School found that only one-tenth of 1 percent of the ideas patented and listed in the *Patent Gazette* had actually made money or could be considered successful.[73] This suggests that many of the businesses established to develop these ideas may have lacked the necessary managerial skills. **Part 2** of this text discusses essential considerations in starting a business (the entrepreneurial side). These chapters refer to the individual as the entrepreneur. **Part 3** covers the managerial skills required for the established enterprise (the management side). It refers to the individual as the owner-manager or the small business manager.

ENTREPRENEURIAL SUCCESS IN LARGE BUSINESSES

LO5

Many individuals may possess the characteristics and desire to be an entrepreneur but find themselves part of an already established company or organization. In addition, many larger organizations realize that to remain competitive, they need to adopt some of the entrepreneurial traits discussed in **Chapter 1** and what was referred to as intrapreneurial activity. **Table 2-4** compares traditional managers to entrepreneurs and intrapreneurs.

TABLE 2-4 Comparison of Traditional Managers to Entrepreneurs and Intrapreneurs

	TRADITIONAL MANAGERS	ENTREPRENEURS	INTRAPRENEURS
Primary motives	Promotion and other traditional corporate rewards, such as office, staff, and power	Independence, opportunity to create, and money	Independence and ability to advance, gain corporate rewards
Time orientation	Short term—meeting quotas and budgets, weekly, monthly, quarterly, and the annual planning horizon	Survival and achieving 5- to 10-year growth of business	Between entrepreneurial and traditional managers, depending on urgency to meet self-imposed and corporate timetable
Activity	Delegation and supervision more than direct involvement	Direct involvement	Direct involvement more than delegation
Risk	Careful	Moderate risk takers	Moderate risk takers
Status	Concerned about status symbols	Not concerned about status symbols	Not concerned about traditional status symbols—desire independence
Failure and mistakes	Try to avoid mistakes and surprises	Deal with mistakes and failures	Attempt to hide risky projects from view until ready
Decisions	Usually agree with those in upper management positions	Follow dream with decisions	Able to get others to agree to help achieve dream
Who serves	Others	Self and customers	Self, customers, and sponsors
Family history	Family members worked for large organizations	Entrepreneurial small business, professional, or farm background	Entrepreneurial small-business, professional, or farm background
Relationship with others	Hierarchy as basic relationship	Transactions and deal making as basic relationship	Transactions within hierarchy

Because attempts by large organizations to incorporate intrapreneurialism are not always successful, the following suggestions have been made to increase the chances of success.[74] These were first developed by management consultant Gifford Pinchot and have been referred to as the "Ten Commandments for Intrapreneur Success."[75] Many large companies have followed these "commandments" to successfully develop and manage products and organizations.

Ten Commandments for Intrapreneur Success

1. Do any job needed to make your project work, regardless of your job description.
2. Share credit wisely.
3. Remember, it is easier to ask for forgiveness than to ask for permission.
4. Come to work each day willing to be fired.
5. Ask for advice before asking for resources.
6. Follow your intuition about people; build a team of the best.
7. Build a quiet coalition for your idea; early publicity triggers the corporate immune system.
8. Never bet on a race unless you are running in it.
9. Be true to your goals, but be realistic about ways to achieve them.
10. Honour your sponsor.

LEARNING OBJECTIVES SUMMARY

LO1 Owning a small business can have many advantages and disadvantages. Some of the most common advantages are frequent contacts with people, independence, skill development in many areas, potential financial rewards, challenge, and enjoyment. The possible disadvantages include high risk, higher stress levels, the need for many abilities, conflicts with people, limited financial rewards, and time demands.

LO2 Certain personality characteristics are associated with a successful owner-manager. These include an achievement orientation, risk taking, independence, self-confidence and self-assurance, innovativeness, strong verbal and numerical skills, problem-solving abilities, strategic planning ability, and perseverance.

LO3 The major causes of business failure are generally related to management problems and external shocks. Businesses that identify problems and try to resolve them are more likely to survive.

LO4 Entrepreneurs are creative, independent, and idea oriented, whereas managers possess strengths in solving problems, working with others, and developing strategies.

LO5 Large businesses must develop intrapreneurship activity to retain employees who would otherwise leave to start their own businesses.

TIME TO TAKE ACTION

In this chapter, you have learned about some of the advantages and disadvantages of entrepreneurship, the keys to entrepreneurial success, how to avoid business failure, and the difference between entrepreneurship and small business.

After reading this chapter, you should start to consider some of the ideas you have for a business. Write down these ideas, and begin conducting research on any potential changes or innovations in and around your product or service. Can you identify any types of niches that you may want to explore?

At this point, you may want to present some of your ideas to entrepreneurs or former business owners. Ask them what they think about your idea. What did they say was good about your idea? What suggestions did they make for improvement? Remember, networking is a key to business success, and by engaging in this exercise, you are building these networks.

You may want to begin attending some entrepreneurship events, such as guest lectures or discussions in your community. Talk to like-minded entrepreneurs at these events, and see what they see as potential good ideas for businesses.

DISCUSSION QUESTIONS

1. What are the advantages and disadvantages of small business ownership?
2. Which characteristic of successful small business owners do you think is the most important? Why?
3. How do managerial skills differ from entrepreneurial skills? When would an entrepreneur's skills be more useful than a manager's? Why?
4. Select a successful small business, and discuss the reasons for its success, drawing on the success characteristics outlined in the text.
5. What are the most common reasons for small business failure?

EXPERIENTIAL EXERCISES

1. Investigate a local business that has recently failed. Using Internet sources and other research methods, identify why the business ceased to exist.
2. Interview a local small business owner about what he or she feels are the advantages and disadvantages of small business ownership.
3. Interview a local entrepreneur, and attempt to identify his or her entrepreneurial characteristics and leadership style.
4. Select a successful small business, and discuss the reasons for its success, drawing on the success characteristics outlined in the text.

APPENDIX 2A

ENTREPRENEUR SUITABILITY CHECKLISTS AND TESTS

Entrepreneurial Self-Assessment, Business Development Bank of Canada
bdc.ca/EN/articles-tools/entrepreneur-toolkit/business-assessments/Pages/self-assessment-test-your-entrepreneurial-potential.aspx

Entrepreneurship Psychometric test
psychometrictest.org.uk/entrepreneur-test/

Canada One—Assessing Your Business Readiness
canadaone.com/tools/assessments/self_assessment.html

Larry Myler, "Want to Be an Entrepreneur? Take This Test to See If You're Ready," *Forbes*
forbes.com/sites/larrymyler/2012/09/19/want-to-be-an-entrepreneur-take-this-test-to-see-if-youre-ready/

EVALUATION OF A BUSINESS OPPORTUNITY

LEARNING OBJECTIVES

By the end of this chapter, you should be able to:

LO1 List the four stages of the entrepreneurial process.

LO2 Identify the sources of ideas for new ventures.

LO3 Summarize the qualitative aspects of evaluating business opportunities.

LO4 Describe the methods by which an entrepreneur can enter a market with a product or service.

LO5 Recognize the ways that an entrepreneur can develop a strategic competitive advantage.

LO6 Examine the types of information available to assist in the quantitative analysis of selecting a small business and illustrate how that information can be used.

LO7 Identify a systematic way to quantitatively assess an industry and evaluate the financial feasibility of a specific small business opportunity.

SMALL BUSINESS PROFILE

DAVID TAO & MICHAEL WANG *Tapplock*

How many people have lost a key to a lock, or couldn't remember the combination? While there is not any accurate statistics, David Tao of Toronto co-founder and CTO of Tapplock would bet the number is pretty high. Tao, who co-founded his company with partner Michael Wang while studying at Queens University says he became frustrated with losing keys to padlocks and forgetting combination lock numbers which resulted in him cutting locks on more than one gym locker. As Tao was growing agitated cutting open his gym locker, he remembered that Apple had just released an iPhone allowing for finger print access and the idea for Tapplock was born.

Photo courtesy of Tapplock

Tao and Wang started working on the idea full time after graduation and opted to pre-sell the product on the crowdfunding site Indiegogo. The pair envisioned pre-sales as a way to evaluate viability of the product. The entrepreneurs set an initial goal of raising US$50,000 pre-selling Tapplock one, a heavy-duty lock and Tapplock lite, a lighter model, which people can use on the go for taking to the gym, on bikes and so forth. The crowdfunding campaign was an overwhelming success and the partners pre-sold 5000 locks raising over US$330,000.

After their initial crowdfunding success Tao and Wang had to start building the product. They reached out to factories in China to manufacture the lock and started to work on ensuring they could create a satisfactory design. During design stage the partners solicited feedback from their crowd-funding backers to ensure the product met consumer satisfaction. Along the way, the entrepreneurs learned that commercially developing Tapplock was more difficult than they initially thought. Not only did they significantly underestimate the development costs causing them to raise additional funds they had to overcome issues with the battery life and manage a shortage of key components. The co-founders also had to manage the expectations of their crowd-funding backers some of whom were becoming increasingly impatient with the longer than anticipated manufacturing process.

Tao and Wang persevered and brought the Tapplock one to market in 2017 with the Tapplock lite shipping in 2019. The completed product allows users to open the lock using either their fingerprints, Bluetooth or Morse code by tapping unique combinations on the power button.

Tapplock also allows users to share access remotely by sending a one-time, permanent or temporary invitation which they can use to open the lock through their smartphone.

Consumers love the product and sales are expected to exceed $5 million in year one. Next up, the entrepreneurs are expanding into the enterprise smart access control industry.

TAPPLOCK
tapplock.com

ENTREPRENEURIAL PROCESS LO1

The process of starting a new venture can be referred to as the *entrepreneurial process*. The process involves four specific stages: (1) identification and evaluation of an opportunity, (2) development of a business plan, (3) determination of the resources required, and (4) management of the business. Although the stages proceed sequentially, no one stage is dealt with in isolation or completed before work on the next stage begins. For example, some elements of evaluating an opportunity complement elements of business planning. We will deal with ideas and opportunity evaluation in this chapter and look at business planning and the other elements in the entrepreneurial process in subsequent chapters.

IDEAS

All businesses start with one thing–an idea. Without ideas there would be no businesses or entrepreneurship. In this chapter, we want to encourage students and entrepreneurs to see all the ideas that surround them. Since many traditional employers ask employees to think creatively and develop new concepts, this chapter should be helpful to both those who do not have any intentions of starting a business in the near term and those who wish to start a business of their own soon. Studying about idea generation should be enjoyable. You are looking for ideas, both big and small. Most entrepreneurs and innovators agree that looking for innovative ideas is a fun learning experience. For example, serial entrepreneur Michele Romanow from CBC's *Dragons' Den,* founder of Clearbanc, and the Small Business Profile in **Chapter 4**, says she spends hours thinking about and investigating new business ideas. Romanow says this process enables her to know more about a variety of businesses, which benefits her both professionally and personally.

Students should try to develop as many ideas as possible when using the techniques below. Do not worry if they appear to be impossible to create, sound silly or insignificant–many great ideas seemed like that originally. Think about bottled water, smartphones, and fitness monitors such as **Fitbit**. Would any of these ideas would have sounded practical or even possible 50 years ago?

SOURCES OF NEW IDEAS LO2

Some of the more frequently used sources of ideas include past or current occupations, hobbies, personal experiences, observation of consumers, existing products and services, and deliberate searches for ideas. Distribution channels and federal government sources are discussed later in the chapter.

Occupations.

Work experience, whether current or prior, is the most common source of new business ideas. It is estimated that over 80 percent of new businesses are based on an entrepreneur's current or previous job, as shown in **Small Business in Action 3-1**. Since entrepreneurs have the greatest chance of being successful if they start a business in which they have some past experience, it makes sense to seize opportunities from your work experience. For example, Marty Algire and Corey Velan of Montreal were working in the computer security industry and were aware of the many viruses and malware causing problems for computer owners. Rather than create an online, downloadable product, the partners put their virus removal software on a USB stick that can be

Marty Algire and Corey Velan were aware of all the security problems that plague personal computers, so they developed the FixMeStick, a plug-in USB solution for security issues.

Photo courtesy of FixMeStick Technologies Inc.

plugged into a computer. The benefits of a USB stick is that it works when a computer's operating system is off, so viruses cannot hide or fight back. Using their knowledge and experience, and creating a product customers want has resulted in **FixMeStick** surpassing $20 million in sales.[1] As mentioned in **Chapter 2**, another example of an entrepreneur creating a company based on work experience is Ryan Holmes, founder of Hootsuite, one of the global leaders in social media management. Holmes was working in the computer business, running his own company creating websites, when he became of aware of the growing opportunity to help businesses manage their social media interactions.[2]

SMALL BUSINESS IN ACTION 3-1

CANADA DRIVES: CHANGING HOW CANADIANS SHOP FOR CARS

Hopefully you never have to hear, "We are sorry, but your credit application was turned down." Whether you are buying furniture, a computer, a car, or a house these words can be agonizing to not only the potential customer but also the salesperson, who maybe as invested in the deal as their client.

Cody Green realized people do indeed hear these words shortly after starting a job at a Hyundai dealership in West Edmonton when he was fresh out of university. Unfortunately, for both the potential customer, the salesperson, and the dealership, customers often only hear they are not eligible for financing after picking out their desired car. Green thought the purchase process was broken and customers should know what types of cars and financing they could successfully acquire prior to test driving and selecting a car. He first tested his theory by flipping the sales process with his clients. When potential customers came to the dealership he worked at, he first obtained financing approval, then had them view and test drive cars they were eligible to purchase. His sales soared as a result. With proof of concept in hand, Green left the dealership, and started **Canada Drives**, a company specializing in matching car buyers with car dealers.

The Canada Drives process is simple: a potential car purchaser visits the company website and select what types of cars they might be interested in buying, they enter some credit information on the site, and they are matched with a dealership in their area who can meet both their car and financing needs. When the customer visits the dealership, they feel empowered. The customer knows the type of car for which they have been approved, that they have financing, and even what they will pay monthly. Car dealerships are more than happy to pay Canada Drives for delivering clients.

Green says that most of his original clients were under-banked, meaning traditional lenders would not extend them credit due to low credit scores. Now, with ever passing year, more and more people who reach car-buying age grew up relying on the Internet for almost everything including shopping for high ticket items such as cars and being approved for credit. As a result, his company is now servicing a variety of clients.

Since the advent of the company, Canada Drives has been on a significant growth trajectory. In 2016 they were recognized as the Fastest Growing Company in Canada; and from 2016 to 2018, the company was recognized in Deloitte's Fast 50 Program, which celebrates world-class achievement by Canadian technology companies. Canada Drives, which is based out of Vancouver, has expanded to both the United States and the United Kingdom, and has added additional financial products such as personal loans and credit cards.

Discussion Questions

1. Would you use a site like Canada Drives? Why or why not?
2. Many of Green's customers are still considered under-banked. As such, some of them will pay very high interest rates on any car they purchase. Do you think it's ethical to assist people in obtaining a car with interest rates that many would call excessive?
3. Think about your past experiences. Can you identify any opportunities for a business. List your ideas and then select the best three to share with your peers.

Hobbies.

Getting an idea from a hobby ties back to the notion of starting a company in an area in which you have previous knowledge. You enjoy your hobby, so perhaps working in that industry will provide similar enjoyment. Sometimes starting a business based on a hobby can be as simple as a comic book collector starting a comic book website or an avid hiker starting a backpacking business. For example, Toronto's Alyssa Jagan loved making crafts and especially enjoyed creating her own slime. At just 16 years old, she decided to post some of her videos online using Instagram and, much to her surprise, her videos went viral. Today she has over 846,000 Instagram followers (@craftyslimecreator), she posts daily videos and interacts with her fans, sells slime online, and has released two slime-oriented books.[3]

Personal Experience.

One of the best ways to develop a new idea is to reflect on past experiences and think about consumer habits and demands. For example, Alexander Peters and Rohan Mahimker, who founded **Prodigy**, a Burlington, Ontario, game-based online learning company in their fourth year at the University of Waterloo, wanted to combine math with video games. The pair recalled their own childhoods playing Pokémon-style games and learning math by completing worksheets. Peters and Mahimker were confident that blending math and interesting video games would be a successful combination. Parents would want their children to learn additional math and children would love playing an interactive video game. The partners' concept has proven to be true as Prodigy currently has 30 million global users.[4] Arif Bhanji of Toronto offers a similar example of creating a business idea through reflection on experience. Bhanji was trying to find a service shop to put snow tires on his car and, when he couldn't find any tire service centres with openings, Bhanji hired someone from Kijji to come to his house and complete the service. As he watched the mechanic quickly change his tires he thought that there was clearly a need for car-repair services at consumers home or work. A short time later he partnered with his friends Khallil Mangali and Zain Manji to start **Fiix**, an online company that matches mechanics with customers. Consumers book service appointments online using the Fiix website or one of their social media sites, such as Facebook or Twitter, and a mechanic shows up at the scheduled time with a coffee in hand for the customer and completes the service. Other examples include Marco Longley from Richmond, British Columbia, who created The Heft, an ergonomic attachment which enables people to shovel snow more effectively without causing back pain. Longley, who was involved in a serious accident, was struggling to use a shovel when he came up with the idea. To date, Longley has sold over 350,000 units in Canada and is now selling the product throughout the world.[5]

Observations.

Entrepreneurs should continually pay close attention to potential customers. This attention can take the form of informally observing consumers to identify gaps in the marketplace, monitoring potential ideas and needs, or formally arranging for consumers to have an opportunity to express their opinions. One of the best methods of finding business ideas is to simply observe your current environment. Often, the best ideas come from day-to-day activities. For example, Jay Gould, founder of **NY Fries**, a Canadian fast-food company that can be found in almost every mall coast to coast, recalls loving french fries as he was growing up—as did everyone else whether they admitted it or not! People especially love french fries from food trucks that focused on their production, so the idea of a specialized french fry store made perfect sense to him. Then, when he discovered a restaurant selling what he would describe as the perfect fry in New York City, he returned to Canada and built a company around the idea. Gould says entrepreneurs should not be distracted when others criticize their ideas: "The one thing all my ideas had in common is that everyone I told about them thought they were dumb. That includes my bankers, my lawyers and accountants."[6]

Existing Products and Services.

Potential entrepreneurs should monitor and evaluate existing products and services on the market. Frequently this analysis uncovers ways to improve on these offerings that may result in a new product or service with more market appeal. As proof, look to Carl Mercier and Tami Zuckerman from Toronto who created **VarageSale**, an online classified site similar to Kijiji and Craigslist. VarageSale differentiates itself by approving the identity of buyers and sellers before they can participate on the site and ensuring people use their real names. This offers visitors a sense of security and results in a community swap-meet feel.[7] VarageSale has grown quickly and now has millions of users. Sequoia Capital and Light Speed Venture Partners recently invested $34 million in the firm.[8]

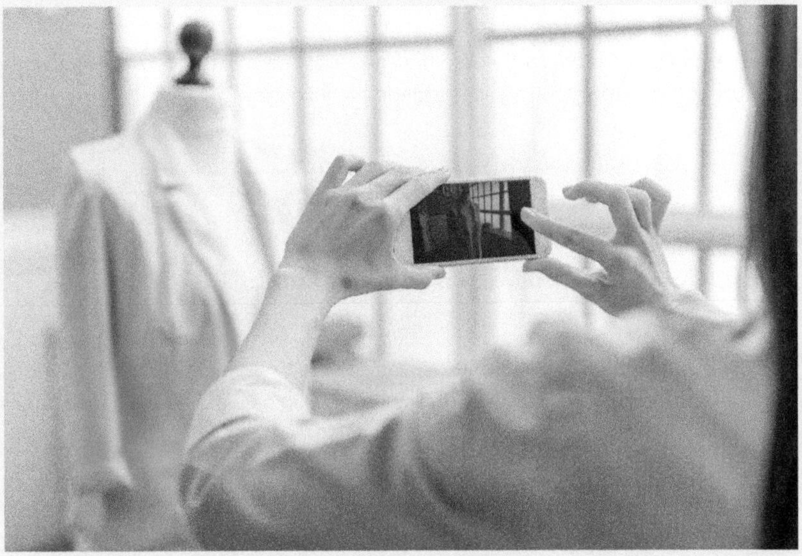
VarageSale has quickly accumulated millions of users and raised $34 million from investors. The online classified site has people verify their name and location through Facebook before registering.

George Rudy/Shutterstock.com

Oded Shenkar, a business expert who studies businesses that imitate other businesses, argues that one important skill for entrepreneurs is the ability to copy other ideas. Shenkar notes that while many aspiring entrepreneurs think they have to come up with a truly original idea to be successful, this does not have to be the case.[9] For example, entrepreneur Eric Pateman, founder of **Edible Canada**, an organizer of culinary trips and tours, got the idea for the firm when he was travelling in France and discovered **Edible Paris**. Pateman says that borrowing an idea to start a business is just fine: "I don't have a problem with that at all. You don't need to reinvent the wheel. You just need to make it your own."[10] Discover sources for entrepreneurial ideas in **Small Business in Action 3-2**.

SMALL BUSINESS IN ACTION 3-2

CONSUMER TRENDS

Entrepreneurs should pay attention to consumer trends. Duplicating an existing trend or designing a product to meet a trend in consumers' lifestyles can be extremely profitable. Some methods of looking for trends include paying attention to what is happening in the mainstream media. For example, CBC's ***Dragons' Den*** frequently discusses new products and trends that entrepreneurs could build a company around. The show's website provides visitors with a great deal of information on the businesses that have been on the show, including old episodes. Other opportunities to view the latest trends include various print and online media sources, such as the following:

- ***Wired*** magazine focuses on news about innovative concepts.
- **Small Business Trends** discusses the latest trends affecting small and medium-sized businesses, including business ideas.
- **Josh Spear** highlights truly original products.
- **Trend Watching** uses trend watchers around the globe to find emerging trends.
- **Springwise** has 15,000 trend watchers posting the latest business ideas for both products and services.

Other entrepreneurs are relying on social media sites, such as **Pinterest**, **Digg**, **Instagram**, and **Facebook**, to identify new and emerging trends.

Another source of new ideas is crowdfunding sites. As discussed throughout this text, crowdfunding sites allow average citizens to support or invest in businesses. Some sites allow consumers to pre-purchase products thus providing entrepreneurs

[continued]

[continued]

with much-needed capital to manufacture products, while other sites allow people to directly invest in the business by acquiring a small equity share. The most popular crowdfunding sites include the following:

Indiegogo

Go Fund Me

Kickstarter

Equity Net

Onevest

Discussion Questions

1. Do you think entrepreneurs can identify business opportunities by visiting media sites such as the ones mentioned above?
2. Many businesses have become quite successful by taking an idea from someone else and making it their own. If you observe a great business opportunity on *Dragons' Den* or see an idea for a product on Indiegogo.com, do you think it is ethical to simply duplicate the idea under a new business name? Why or why not? What if a student talks about an idea she has in class? Would it be ethical for you to start a business based on your peer's idea?
3. Visit some of the trend and crowdfunding sites mentioned above individually or in small groups. Report back to the class on some ideas you found that have the most business potential. What ideas were you surprised by? Did you think any ideas were really bad?
4. What do you think are some of the advantages and disadvantages of using social media sites to discover trends? What social media sites would you recommend to trend watchers?

Deliberate Searches.

Entrepreneurs deliberately searching for an idea may attempt to create products, discuss ideas with friends and family, search through specific publications, and attend presentations and conferences. For example, Deland Jessop engaged in a deliberate search when he co-founded his company Counting Sheep Coffee. Jessop says his wife loves coffee but cannot even drink decaf in the afternoon or she will not sleep at night. Jessop says he turned his kitchen into a lab and tried to create a coffee that would allow people to relax. Jessop ended up combining decaf coffee with valerian root, a natural sleep aid. On its own, valerian root tastes awful; but the coffee masks the taste and the resulting drink provides a relaxing way to fall asleep.[11]

Entrepreneurs may also engage in formal idea-generation methods, such as focus groups or brainstorming.

Focus Groups.

In a focus group, a moderator leads a group of people through an open, in-depth discussion rather than simply asking questions to solicit participant responses. For example, one company interested in the women's slipper market received its new product concept for a "warm and comfortable slipper that fits like an old shoe" from a focus group of 12 women from various socioeconomic backgrounds in the Boston area. In addition to generating new ideas, the focus group is an excellent method for initially screening ideas and concepts. The Internet has also made the practice of holding focus groups both less expensive and more convenient. Business owners and potential entrepreneurs can now bring people from diverse backgrounds together online, saving time and money and getting input from an increased number of participants.

Brainstorming.

Brainstorming allows people to be more creative by meeting with others and participating in organized group experiences where the goal is to produce new business ideas or solve problems. Both aspiring entrepreneurs and existing businesses use brainstorming to develop ideas. For example, **Crelogix Credit Group Inc.**, a firm based in British Columbia, which provides lending to consumers in a number of niche markets, uses online brainstorming to generate ideas. The firm makes use of Chatter, an online social media tool, where employees post ideas and information for new products. Crelogix's CEO, Karl Sigerist, credits Chatter with the development of loans for families to hire elementary school tutors for their children.

ASSESSMENT OF BUSINESS OPPORTUNITIES

An idea is just that—an idea. It may be something that can be turned into a profitable business, or it could just be something interesting. An opportunity is much more; it is an idea that if managed correctly can result in a successful new business. Before writing a full business plan, entrepreneurs engage in an opportunity assessment process to determine if their idea has merit. Opportunity assessment consists of a qualitative assessment and a detailed analysis, including quantitative measures. After completing a full assessment of an idea, entrepreneurs then decide whether to proceed with writing a business plan.

SMALL BUSINESS IN ACTION 3-3

FAN-CONTROLLED FOOTBALL: YOU'RE THE GM AND COACH

Sports fans love many things about the sports they watch. They love to cheer for their favourite team, they love to eat and drink while they watch the games, and, perhaps most of all, they love to argue about how they would coach or manage their team differently. Questioning a coach's decision has actually led to the creation of the term *armchair quarterback*, referring to fans who think they can do a better job selecting plays and managing their team than paid professionals.

Ray Austin, Sohrob Farudi, and Vivek Jain wanted to give fans a chance to see if this were true. The trio—who love football, fantasy sports, and video games—have created the **Fan-Controlled Football League**. The owners describe the concept as a real-life version of the video game *Madden*. The Fan-Controlled Football league, which started play in 2019, consists of eight teams who play in a production studio rather than a stadium. The league will allow fans to select the team's name, logo, coach, and roster. Most importantly, once the game starts, fans will select the all the plays the teams run. Rather than airing games on national television, the games will air on **Twitch**, a subsidiary of Amazon that streams video game events and other sports. Twitch has 120 million users and has offered the company 70 percent of subscription fees from fans who sign up to watch their team play, as well as a 50-50 split on advertising revenue along with other incentives.

Prior to starting their full-fledged league, the partners bought a team in the Indoor Football League to pilot the concept. Not only did fans have input on the team name, roster, and coach selection—completed via vote after an online interview process on YouTube—fans even selected the city where the team would play: Salt Lake City was chosen over Oklahoma. With fan support, the Salt Lake City Eagles were born. The Eagles played a full year of Indoor Football League with the fans calling all the plays. While the team finished with 5 wins and 11 losses, the fans overachieved managing the Eagles offence, which was third overall, and the team tied for second in passing yards.

With a successful pilot, the owners have taken a huge next step and, as of this writing, plan to launch their league in 2019. As with any venture, the founders need start-up money. The company has to raise $7 million to get the league up and running, and the company founders are working tirelessly to raise the necessary funds.

Discussion Questions

1. What do you think are some of the advantages and disadvantages of the business concept?
2. With any new venture, creating revenue streams will be vital to the company's long term success. Think about social media, sports, and other related industries. Develop a list five to ten ways in which the league could earn additional revenue.
3. Do you think the business will be successful? Why or why not? Would you invest in the company if given the opportunity?

QUALITATIVE ASSESSMENT LO3

A qualitative assessment looks at non-quantitative factors to determine if the idea for a business aligns with an individual's goals and expectations. The major factors considered in a qualitative assessment are as follows.

GOALS

Individuals should examine their personal goals regarding income earned from the business. The question to address: How well will the type of business I choose allow me to achieve not only my financial goals but also my occupational status goals?

CONTENT OF WORK

Individuals should assess their suitability for the business' working conditions. Questions to be addressed: What type of work will the business involve? Will the business require hard physical work or considerable contact with people?

LIFESTYLE

Remember that most small businesses take much more time to operate than the owner anticipates before start-up. Consider these questions: What type of lifestyle will the business allow? Will the hours be long or concentrated in the evenings or on weekends? Will the business allow family members to be involved?

CAPABILITIES

In addition to the personal characteristics needed to run a small business that were discussed in **Chapter 2**, at least two other capabilities are required.

The first requirement is good health. As mentioned earlier, managing a small business usually involves long hours and is often physically and mentally stressful. Good physical health and stamina, as well as the ability to withstand high levels of stress, are essential.

The second requirement is expertise in the fundamentals of management, including administration, marketing, and finance. Although numerous courses can provide valuable training, many successful small business managers have acquired expertise in these areas through self-education. For example, Ryan Smolkin, owner of Smoke's Poutinerie, a Canadian poutine franchise, says one of the reasons his company has been so successful is he understands marketing and branding. While he did not know much about actually running a restaurant, he had strong business skills that have enabled him to build his company across Canada.

EXPERIENCE

Potential entrepreneurs may want to consider starting businesses in areas where they have experience either through work or as volunteers. Lack of experience and unbalanced experience are two major causes of business failure. One of the best preparations prospective small business operators can make is to acquire knowledge of the type of business or industry they plan to enter. For example, Jill Strong of Halifax-based **Wildflower Clothing** worked part-time in retail before starting her own store. Strong credits this experience with helping her successfully own and operate an independent clothing store for over 13 years.

OPPORTUNITY ASSESSMENT

A full opportunity assessment can be done either after completing a qualitative assessment or at the same time. A full assessment requires the entrepreneur answer the questions listed below. Remember, while this may seem like a lot of work, research indicates entrepreneurs who conduct full evaluations of business ideas are more likely to be successful.

Entrepreneurs will normally want to be able to discuss the following:

1. What product or service will the business provide? How will the business offer value to customers?
2. How will you enter the market? What will your competitive advantage be?

3. Who will the customers be? Why will they buy from you?
4. Assess the industry and environments your business will be operating in: What is the state of the economy? What are the economic trends? Who will your competitors be? What advantages and disadvantages do they have? What are the key success factors?
5. How will you market your product or service? What will your marketing mix look like?
6. Where will you get your major supplies? What will your costs be? Will suppliers sell to a new firm? What terms are offered?
7. What will your start-up costs be? Where will you get the money? Project your income over the next three years.

After answering the questions, entrepreneurs should have a good sense whether the idea they are assessing is just that, an idea, or something much more valuable, an opportunity. Small business owners know that market entry, competitive advantage, and information are particularly important to starting a successful venture, and these will be discussed in more detail next. This will be followed by information that will help you calculate important financial statements.

EVALUATING HOW TO BREAK INTO THE MARKET LO4

An entrepreneur can enter a market in three ways. The first is to offer a totally new product to the market. This involves "inventing" a product that meets a need that is not being fulfilled. Thousands of successful products have resulted from someone's dissatisfaction with the lack of a product. For example, Canadian Ron Foxcroft invented the first pea-less whistle, the Fox 40, after becoming dissatisfied with a malfunctioning pea-whistle: "I always had a problem with whistles. They have a cork pea in them, and when you blow a pea-whistle really hard, nothing comes out. When they're frozen or wet or get some dirt inside, they lose their efficiency." Not only did Foxcroft manage to invent a new whistle, but he also successfully built the idea into a company. **Fox 40** produces whistles for almost every major sporting league and the Olympics.[12]

Sometimes entrepreneurs can enter the market selling fad or novelty types of products. The needs these types of products satisfy are often emotional or subjective rather than rational. For example, Adil Hooda and Kyle Fitzgerald of Calgary have made money by taking advantage of consumer trends. The business partners first started an ugly Christmas sweaters company called Holiday Rejects, which took advantage of the ugly Christmas sweater fad. A short time later, the pair noticed zombies were growing in popularity and started a **Zombie Survivor** run to profit from the zombie craze.

A second approach is to offer an existing product to a different market or industry. Tim Kimber, founder of **PlaSmart** Toys, is an example of someone using this business strategy. Kimber discovered plastic cars that could be propelled using hand motions were popular in several global markets. He brought the car to North America, renamed it Plasma Car, and built a successful company around the product. Kalpana Daugherty has a similar story. While travelling in China, she noticed vendors at the market grilling food yet none of the food was sticking to their pans. Shortly after returning to Canada, she looked for material on pans at a variety of stores and could not find it anywhere. Rather than give up on finding the pans, she researched what they were made of, acquired the North American rights to the product, and started **UNSTICK**. The pans are now available throughout Canada and were even included in celebrity gift bags at the 2017 Oscars and 2016 Emmy Award Shows.[13] Another form of this approach is to offer an existing product or service in the same geographic market but to a different age or income group or to use the product for a different purpose.

The third way to enter the market is to offer a product or service similar to those already existing in the same market. In this case, the prospective small business owner attempts to obtain some competitive advantage over the existing products or businesses in the industry to maintain viability. For example, Michael Kay founded Toronto-based Alexa Translations, a company that offers translation services and stands out by focusing on quality. **Alexa Translations**, which operates in a growing and fragmented market, uses only translators who have degrees in translation or are certified, and they must have experience with the subject matter they are working with. Kay says the company's fees are higher than average, but they stand out from the crowd by focusing on quality service.[14]

Other times the market is large and or growing enough to accommodate an additional business, or the level of satisfaction with existing businesses or products in the industry is low. For example, one of the authors of this text, Peter Mombourquette, noticed a growing market for specialized cross-training for young athletes. As a result, he formed a company called Halifax Explosion, which offers younger athletes high-level hockey, soccer, and martial arts training. Other examples of this type of entry into the market include establishing a retail store that stocks brand-name and conventional merchandise, and manufacturing a product in a way that it can be sold at a lower price.

The Plasma Car was sold in several countries throughout the world under various names. It was not until Tim Kimber acquired the North American rights to distribute the product that sales soared.

Hixson/Dreamstime.com/GetStock.com

DEVELOPING A STRATEGIC COMPETITIVE ADVANTAGE LO5

An important part of being successful with a start-up business is selecting an industry, a business, or a part of a business that will provide a competitive advantage. A competitive advantage exists when a firm has a product or service that is viewed as better than those of its competitors. More will be discussed about the specifics of developing the competitive advantage in the next chapter, as part of preparing the business plan. However, an entrepreneur can save valuable time and energy by identifying the most appropriate area in which to develop that advantage by selecting (1) the right industry, (2) the right business, and (3) the right aspect of the business to focus on. A brief discussion of each follows.

THE RIGHT INDUSTRY

Some industries tend to be conducive to small business success and may provide a competitive advantage over larger businesses:

- *Businesses or industries in which the owner's personal attention to daily operations is essential to success.* In a service business, for example, the expertise of the owner-manager is a major factor in generating revenue.
- *Businesses in which owner contact with employees is important to the motivation of staff and the quality of work done.* Specialized or custom-made manufacturing processes or service businesses and other businesses in which employees have direct contact with customers fit into this category. As evident in the example above, Alexa Translations is building a competitive advantage by offering superior service to clients.
- *Markets in which demand is small or local, making large businesses generally reluctant to pursue them.* For example, many shuttle services have sprung up in rural parts of the country in recent years. These services offer transportation to and from rural communities to larger urban centres.
- *Industries that require flexibility.* These include industries with high growth rates, erratic demand, or perishable products. For example, there has been high growth in businesses that appeal to parents of young children who are seeking to maximize their personal development. Many specialized tutoring companies, dance and music instruction, and sports training businesses have started small and been quite successful.
- *Businesses that are more labour intensive and less capital intensive.* Because of the above points, a business that relies heavily on people rather than machines to provide its product or service may be easier to manage if it is small. For example, many specialized businesses have remained quite small. **Simply Sweet** is a Montréal bakery that has managed to be successful baking specialized wedding and occasion cakes. The amount of labour and expertise involved has served as barriers to larger businesses.
- *Industries that receive considerable encouragement from the government in the form of financial, tax, and counselling assistance.* Much of this assistance is directed at smaller businesses in the manufacturing, processing, exporting, and tourism industries. Such industries represent potential opportunities for small businesses.

While these specific industries tend to offer competitive advantages to small business, readers should realize they are not essential to small business success. Many entrepreneurs have started small and medium-sized businesses using technology to level the playing field between themselves and competitors. Technology such as the Internet has allowed many firms to compete on an International scale while maintaining some of the advantages of staying small. For example, Jad Saliba has built a successful software company, **Magnet Forensics**, based in Waterloo, Ontario, into a fast-growing firm. Saliba, a former police officer, used to spend hours reading through computer files and social networks of suspects to look for evidence and thought there had to be a better way to search for clues. He eventually built an Internet Evidence Finder (IEF), working part time at home–the product is now being used by the RCMP, FBI, CIA, and U.S. Homeland Security.

THE RIGHT BUSINESS

To identify a business that may provide a greater chance of success as a small business, the entrepreneur should be aware of those areas that are predicted to grow rapidly in the future. The following are some of the top Canadian business areas for the future as reported by *Canadian Business* magazine:

- Health care
- Services for small business
- Mobile business
- Services that appeal to parents
- Green products and services
- Online businesses

THE RIGHT ASPECT OF THE BUSINESS

Once the industry and type of business are selected, the entrepreneur should decide which aspect(s) of the business to focus on to ensure the company performs better than the competition. Natural advantages for the small business typically are flexibility, innovation, customer service, and product quality. A detailed example of these attributes are shared in **Small Business in Action 3-4**. Aspects such as price, selection, and location may also provide a competitive advantage, although they are typically more difficult for small businesses to achieve. The entrepreneur should be aware of the aspect of the business that is the most important to the consumer and attempt to develop superiority in that relative to competitors. A related decision is to determine the scale of operations (size and scope) that the entrepreneur will attempt to establish.

The results of the analysis in this chapter will allow the entrepreneur to formalize the strategy into the initial development of the business model, which is a critical part of the business plan. The business model is the framework for creating economic, social, and other forms of value. The business model includes a broad range of core aspects of the business, including purpose, offerings, strategies, infrastructure, organizational structure, trading practices, and operational processes and policies. The business model is the method of doing business by which an organization can sustain itself by specifying where it is positioned in the value chain. Considerable research should be carried out to finalize the business model and then develop the comprehensive business plan (see **Chapter 4**).

SMALL BUSINESS IN ACTION 3-4

WEB SUCCESS

When Gord Dickie was growing up he dreamed about being a professional hockey player. While this dream did not come true, he did manage to combine his love of sports and his IT skills to build North America's leading sports-administration company—**Goalline**.

Goalline, located in Halifax, provides amateur sports teams and leagues with website administration, registration, and statistics. Dickie, who played university varsity hockey, noticed after graduation that there was an opportunity to administer websites for amateur sports teams throughout North America. Goalline's original premise was to provide teams and organizations with a consistent and professional site, allow for online registration, and track player statistics. At the time, many amateur sports teams were struggling with creating a web presence, and Dickie offered them a turnkey package that met their needs. Dickie felt Goalline would be able to offer quality service in a growing market. Goalline originally targeted minor hockey teams throughout North America and quickly became the web-hosting site of choice for hockey teams and organizations.

The company began aggressively expanding into other sports, including soccer and baseball, ramping up its online advertising sales and working in partnership with Pac Rim Hospitality to develop an online team travel booking service called Team Travel Centre.

Goalline's strategies were successful, as Dickie managed sites for 1,200 sports organizations and 60,000 teams, and year-over-year revenue doubled. Online advertising efforts also been paid off, as online ads accounted for roughly one-third of Goalline's revenue. Dickie said, "We have 20 million page views a month, and while it took us some time to demonstrate we had a base of web users, the strategy is working."

Dickie believed Goalline's latest offering, booking team travel through their site had tremendous growth potential. TTC would allow teams to book hotels, cars, and make other arrangements through one point of contact. For example, rather than have a team call several hotels to compare group rates, TTC will be able to check rates at several hotels electronically and allow team managers to make entire travel arrangements from one central site.

After introducing TTC, and the sustained growth of the company, Dickie opted to sell the firm to Blue Star Sports in 2016.

Discussion Questions

1. Review the information in this chapter on market entry and competitive advantage. How did Dickie choose to enter the market, and how did he achieve a competitive advantage?
2. Goalline's original business was web hosting for sports teams, specifically hockey teams. The company eventually expanded into several other businesses. Do you think this was a good strategy for the company? Why or why not?
3. Why do you think Goalline began aggressively looking for other revenue streams?
4. What do you see the primary advantages of a service such as TTC to consumers?

COLLECTING INFORMATION LO6

The key to making a wise decision regarding which industry to enter and the type of business to start is the gathering and analysis of information. The more relevant the information, the less uncertainty about the results of this decision. One study showed that the overwhelming majority of small business owners do no formal marketing research, although many do informal, unsystematic information gathering.[15] Studies indicate that research carried out by small firms is only 1.35 percent of value added, much lower than in large businesses.[16] Failure to do adequate or appropriate market research is frequently cited as one of the most commons reason for small business failure.[17]

Some reasons entrepreneurs commonly give for not researching and investigating a business are that it is too time consuming, too expensive, too complicated, and irrelevant. Although each of these claims has some substance, some simple, inexpensive, but effective methods of collecting and analyzing data are available to the entrepreneur. Carey Smith, founder of Big Ass Solutions, a company which specializes in large commercial ceiling fans, says that completing research may take a little bit of time and cost some money, but the work is less costly and time consuming than creating something that fails.[18]

SOURCES OF INFORMATION

The first thing entrepreneurs should be aware of is the many sources of information available to assist them in their investigations. Two general types of information can help prospective small business owners select the right small business—secondary data and primary data. Secondary data consist of data previously published by another organization. Primary data are collected by the entrepreneur. The following sections discuss both types of information in detail. After understanding the details around secondary and primary data, learn about the internet's impact on information gathering in **Small Business in Action 3-5**.

SMALL BUSINESS IN ACTION 3-5

THE INTERNET'S IMPACT ON COLLECTING INFORMATION

Developer Robert Fung wanted to know what type of retail establishments local residents wanted in the new 8000 square feet of space he had recently built in New Westminster, British Columbia. Rather than turning to traditional market research, Fung opted to use Facebook, Twitter, and blogs to ask residents what types of establishments they wanted in their community. The response, according to Fung, was quick and informative, providing insight into what type of retail community residents wanted.

Mike Brcic often uses social media to get input from consumers on potential promotional campaigns by asking them to select the photo he should use in an ad. Brcic is getting strong results.

Photo courtesy of Mike Brcic

While Fung's use of social networks is interesting, it is certainly not groundbreaking, as more entrepreneurs are turning toward the Internet to get consumer opinions on various topics instead of relying on traditional market research. For example, Mike Brcic, owner and operator of Toronto-based **Sacred Rides Mountain Bike Adventures**, was designing a new poster campaign and was not sure which picture he should use. Rather than using traditional means of collecting data such as presenting various pictures to focus groups and listening to their opinions, Brcic decided to post some pictures on Facebook and informed his followers he was going to crowdsource his new poster. This meant that followers would select the new poster picture for his company by selecting "like" on Facebook or commenting on the images.

[continued]

[continued]

Photo courtesy of Mike Brcic

Other examples of firms using the Internet to collect information are plentiful. For example, rather than paying market research firms to conduct surveys, many businesses are using online survey tools, such as **SurveyMonkey**, to create and conduct online surveys with consumers. Small firms are using crowdfunding sites, as already discussed, as a means to test market products, and other businesses are using online focus groups and observing customer reviews and comments on such sites as Yelp and Facebook, all with the goal of collecting meaningful information at a low cost.

Some market research experts point out there are problems with entrepreneurs relying on the Internet and their own judgment in collecting data. Luke Zukowski, co-owner of **Reveal Research**, a firm that specializes in small business research, says many entrepreneurs lack the knowledge to use online tools to collect information. Furthermore, Zukowski notes that not all consumers are online, so relying solely on online sites could lead to businesses making the wrong conclusion. Other experts disagree with Zukowski, stating online data are easier and cheaper to access than traditional data, and almost all Canadians are, in fact, online.

Discussion Questions

1. What do you think are some of the advantages and disadvantages of entrepreneurs using online information to assess an opportunity?
2. Do you think Robert Fung and Mike Brcic obtained enough information online to make the correct business decision for their companies? Why or why not?
3. A lot of business owners are spending countless hours reading and, in many cases, responding to online reviews about their companies. Do you think reading and responding to online reviews is a good business strategy? Why or why not?
4. If you were going to start a travel company catering to university students, how would you use the Internet to evaluate the opportunity? How could you use social media and online information to improve your marketing mix?

Secondary Data.

Secondary data take the form of reports, studies, and statistics that another organization or individual has already compiled. A great deal of secondary data is available to the entrepreneur, and collecting is usually inexpensive. A major problem, however, is finding information relevant to a particular situation. The secondary data available may be too general or may not apply to the type of business being established. Some reports may be out of date and will need to be adjusted to make them useful. Such data can be updated by projecting past trends.

Secondary information is inexpensive, which makes it very attractive to the prospective small business owner. Much of the secondary information available in Canada is provided by the federal and provincial or territorial governments. However, valuable secondary information is also available from private and semi-private sources. **Appendix 3A** presents a listing of those sources most relevant for small businesses. **Table 3-1** gives an example of using secondary data to begin the feasibility analysis for a business. This example uses Statistics Canada reports to estimate the market potential for a bookstore in Toronto.

TABLE 3-1 **Assessing the Market Feasibility of Opening a Bookstore in Toronto by Using Secondary Data**

Problem	To estimate the size of the market for a bookstore in Toronto		
Step 1:	Determine the population in Toronto Population of Metropolitan Area of Toronto (Source: Metro Toronto Information)	=	5,500,000
Step 2:	Determine the number of families in Toronto 5,500,000 divided by 3 (average size of families in Ontario) (Source: Statistics Canada Census information)	=	1,833,000
Step 3:	Estimate total bookstore sales for Toronto 1,833,000 × $300 (average household expenditures on books and magazines) (Source: Average Household Expenditures, Market Research Handbook)	=	$549,000,000

This shows that a total of $549,000,000 could be expected to be spent in the Toronto area in bookstores.

In addition to obtaining published secondary information, entrepreneurs can consult several agencies for counselling in both starting a business and managing ongoing operations. The most inexpensive and often most valuable source is the counselling provided to entrepreneurs by federal and provincial or territorial governments. The Business Development Bank of Canada can provide start-up counselling and analysis of an existing business.

Most provincial and territorial governments also employ consultants to assist the small business. Many of these agencies provide start-up and business plan preparation assistance similar to that offered by the federal government.

Another potentially valuable source of assistance comes from universities and colleges. Many universities have student consulting programs designed to help small business owners. Using the expertise of graduating or graduate students, these programs can assist in preparing feasibility analyses or evaluating a business problem for a minimal fee, usually the cost of materials used. Some businesses, such as Laval-based **Ergoresearch**, a manufacturer of orthotics and orthopaedic products that help people manage pain, are partnering with faculty and students to develop new business ideas. Sylvain Boucher, president and CEO, says partnering with universities makes sense, as they can provide firms with new business ideas or further develop ideas that are in progress. Boucher also notes that various government programs, such as the **National Research Council** and the **Natural Sciences and Engineering Research Council of Canada**, often cover much of the cost. "Partnering on research is a great way for an entrepreneurial company to innovate, because you can really leverage your money," says Boucher. "For every dollar you invest in a project, government programs may invest two or three times that."[19]

Other helpful counselling sources are lawyers, accountants, and bankers. Some of these sources may be more expensive than government services, however. Numerous consulting firms also specialize in small business operations. Innovation, Science and Economic Development Canada has found that small businesses that use professional advisors experience sales of 76 percent more than those that do not.[20]

Informal sources of valuable information for the entrepreneur that are gaining popularity are social networking sites, such as LinkedIn, Facebook, and blogs. Networking with other entrepreneurs on these sites can be an excellent source of ideas and information. Similarly, many cities hold entrepreneur forums and speaker series, such as entrepreneur igniter meetings.

In addition to the types of assistance just described, another concept appears to promise considerable help in establishing new enterprises: the incubation or accelerator centre. The centres consists of an organization—usually a municipal or provincial or territorial agency—that provides essential services for new small businesses, either free or at minimal cost. Office space, secretarial services, computer capabilities, and financial and business counselling are examples of these services. For example, **Innovate Calgary** is a business incubation centre dedicated to helping researchers, entrepreneurs, and businesses within the advanced technology sector. The centre offers entrepreneurs access to more than 50 years of combined experience supporting the technology community and was recognized as Canada's top incubation centre, third in North America, and sixth in the world.[21] A Statistics Canada study found support for using incubation centres, concluding that 80 percent of businesses nurtured by incubators were still operating after five years.[22]

More than 7500 incubators currently operate worldwide with over 500 operating in North America.[23] In Canada, more than 150 business incubation and accelerator centres operate across the country.[24] For a complete listing, visit **The Definitive Guide to Canadian Accelerators and Incubators**. Business incubators allow the small business community to work, individually or collectively, through the chamber of commerce and with municipal (city or town) governments, provincial or territorial governments, universities, and colleges. Statistics show that businesses receiving assistance from incubator centres have a 30 percent greater chance of success after five years over those who do not use them.[25]

Primary Data.

Primary data are collected through your own research. Although usually more costly to obtain than secondary data, these can be more relevant to your business and more current. Primary research is essential if secondary sources do not provide the information required for the feasibility analysis. It may also be beneficial to supplement the information obtained from secondary sources. Despite these advantages, small business owners have traditionally hesitated to do much primary research because of their lack of knowledge about how to do it and its relatively high cost. The Internet and social networking sites have gone a long way in reducing the costs associated with collecting information, but some entrepreneurs still cite cost as a deterrent.

Some research methods, however, are not complicated and can be of great value to the entrepreneur in evaluating the feasibility of a potential business opportunity. Three general methods that can be used to collect information through primary research are observation, surveys, and test marketing.

1. Observation.

Observation involves monitoring the who, what, where, when, and how relating to market conditions. For the small business, this method might involve observing auto and pedestrian traffic levels or customer reactions to a product, service, or promotion. It may also entail simply observing sales or expenditure levels. The Internet has allowed entrepreneurs to engage in online observation of consumers for a fraction of the cost. Businesses that once monitored customer reaction to a product or service can visit review sites, such as Yelp or TripAdvisor, to learn what customers are saying about their products. They can also monitor Facebook, Twitter, Instagram, and so forth, to review customer feedback on various aspects of their marketing mix, including products and promotions. The observation method, especially traditional observation, may be fairly expensive, as it requires that time be spent monitoring events as they occur. Another limitation of observation research is that it allows the small business owner to only infer the reasons people respond in certain ways. There is no two-way interaction with the subject of the research that might shed light on such motivations.

2. Surveys.

To obtain more detailed information from potential consumers and to better understand their motivations for purchasing a product or service, a small business owner can carry out a survey. The entrepreneur should clearly define the objectives of the research before questionnaire construction and ensure that each question addresses one of the objectives. Usually, it is not possible to survey each potential customer or the total market; therefore, only a part of the market is surveyed. It is essential, however, that the responses obtained be representative of the total market. **Table 3-2** illustrates a simple but accurate method for determining a representative sample for a research project for a small business. Such a survey might give the entrepreneur a general indication of the extent of demand for a new business. Of course, more detailed research should be carried out before a decision to start the business is made. Many businesses have failed because the owners acted on their own feelings or the opinions of a few acquaintances. In some cases, these responses do not represent the opinions of the total market.

TABLE 3-2 **Calculating a Representative Survey Sample for a Small Business**

Step 1: Use the following chart to determine the number of surveys that should be completed to achieve a 95 percent confidence level at 0.05 degree of precision.

POPULATION SIZE	SAMPLE SIZE
50	44
100	80
500	222
1,000	286
5,000	375
10,000	385
100,000 and over	400

Step 2: Choose the respondents. If a phone survey is being conducted, there are two ways to choose the respondents. The first is to use the phone book and choose every *n*th individual. The second is to use a random number generator to come up with the phone numbers. Both of these methods have advantages and disadvantages, but both allow the surveyor to obtain a representative sample.

Occasionally, through design or necessity (e.g., limited funds), a non-representative group of people is surveyed as part of the primary research project. This could involve surveying only experts or knowledgeable people in an industry rather than an equal cross-section of consumers. This method is also often used in surveying shopping mall customers. The most obvious drawback is that the findings may not be representative of the total market.

Three types of surveys are used to collect market information: mail surveys, telephone surveys, and personal interviews.

Mail and Internet Surveys

These surveys are most appropriate in the following cases:

- A small amount of information is required.
- Questions can be answered with yes–no or check-the-box answers, or brief responses.
- A picture of the product is required.

One problem with mail and Internet surveys is their poor response rate—typically well under 50 percent—and the lack of control over who fills out the questionnaire. The preparer also needs to make sure that the survey is not too long or too complicated.

Telephone Surveys

Telephone surveying has become the most popular survey method in recent years, most likely because of its low cost and quick response time. However, it is even more restricted than a mail survey in the amount and detail of information the entrepreneur can obtain. The telephone interviewer should follow a survey guide to ensure consistency. A phone survey might give the entrepreneur an indication of the acceptance of the concept, but further research and analysis is required before a decision can be made.

Personal Interviews

The most expensive type of survey is the personal interview. Although this method generally costs more and requires greater expertise, it is the best approach for obtaining more detailed information and opinion-oriented responses. Since the number of people surveyed typically is smaller than in mail or phone surveys, this method is more suitable for interviewing knowledgeable people in an industry as opposed to surveying a cross-section of potential consumers. This type of research is known as *customer-focused interviews.* Personal interviews may involve surveying one individual at a time or, as many companies do, surveying several people together in a *focus group.* The personal interview may be used for purposes such as testing a new product concept or advertisement or evaluating a company's image.

Entrepreneurs are often unsure about what types of questions to use in a survey. Some areas in which information should be obtained are the following:

- Respondents' reactions to the product or service
- The price respondents are willing to pay for the product or service
- Respondents' willingness to purchase the product or service (answers to such questions are often overly positive and should be adjusted downward by as much as 20 percent)
- Frequency of purchase
- Level of satisfaction with the current product or service
- Demographic characteristics of the respondents

3. Test Marketing.

Test marketing involves an attempt to simulate an actual market situation. For an inventor, it may mean letting a number of people try a new product and then finding out their reactions. For a business, it may mean marketing a product on a limited basis and observing sales levels or surveying to find out the level of satisfaction with the product or service. This method is fairly costly in that the product must be developed and marketed, albeit on a limited basis. The main advantage of experimental research, or test marketing, is that it measures what people actually do, not just what they say they will do, concerning the product.

Small businesses have successfully used this method when taking prototype products to trade shows, exhibitions, or potential customers to assess acceptance. The Internet, in particular crowdfunding sites, have enabled many small business owners to test market products with wide audiences for a fraction of the traditional cost. Some successful entrepreneurs see the benefits of crowdfunding, as discussed in **Small Business in Action 3-6**.

SMALL BUSINESS IN ACTION 3-6

SHOULD CROWDFUNDING REPLACE MARKET RESEARCH?

Michele Romanow, of *Dragons' Den* fame and featured in the **Small Business Profile** of Chapter 4, argues that entrepreneurs really don't need to do market research. In fact, she says, they don't even need a product. Romanow encourages entrepreneurs to skip time-consuming market research and product development, and instead use crowdfunding to see if consumers will buy their concept. After all, why should entrepreneurs waste money building products, or time on research, when all they need is one prototype and a home-made video they can display on Kickstarter? Other crowdfunding advocates agree with Romanow, including the popular Arikovani Blog, which states that crowdfunding will quickly allow entrepreneurs to gain feedback on their ideas and to test if there is a market for their product.

Of course, not everyone agrees with Romanow. Tim Metz, founder of Saent, a hardware product funded though the crowdfunding site Indiegogo, argues that entrepreneurs shouldn't rush to crowdfunding sites, noting some, including himself, bring products to crowdfunding before they have all the details worked out. Charlie Gentles, who writes for *The Startup* agrees with Metz. He says that successful crowdfunding is not that easy: only one in three crowdfunding campaigns work, and you must invest time to generate a successful campaign.

There are other problems associated with bringing a concept to crowdfunding too soon. With many crowdfunding sites, such as Kickstarter and Indiegogo, entrepreneurs are pre-selling products. However, the crowdfunding sites stipulate these are not pre-sales, but rather rewards for backers who are assisting the entrepreneur or creator in bringing a project to life. It is clear from reading backers' posts and feedback that many supporters think they are pre-ordering a product. Now imagine an entrepreneur has placed a product on a crowdfunding site prior to determining the full manufacturing costs or, worse yet, how to actually manufacture the product. The result could be backers who never receive their rewards or entrepreneurs who are selling products below costs.

David Tao and Jayden Li, featured in the **Small Business Profile** of this chapter, have experienced both the pros and cons of crowdfunding. The pair successfully raised over $300,000 to construct Tapplock, a lock that can be opened using a person's fingerprints. Unfortunately for the entrepreneurs, the manufacturing process was longer and costlier than they imagined and, as evident on the Indiegogo site, they have struggled to meet all their pre-sale commitments. Many initial backers grew quite impatient with the entrepreneurs and how long it took them to successfully commercialize their idea; some accused them of stealing their money. This charge became more rampant when Tapplocks started being sold elsewhere prior to the product being shipped to consumers who pre-bought the lock on Indiegogo. Tapplock founders explained they had to sell the product as they had spent all the money, they initially raised on Indiegogo on product development. Without the new sales they wouldn't have had the capital to fulfill the Indiegogo pre-orders.

What was likely adding to Tao and Li's woes is that many consumers who supported Tapplock didn't see the receipt of a lock as a reward for helping the entrepreneurs fulfill their goals. Most consumers simply thought they were pre-buying locks, and some clearly lacking an understanding of the risk involved in investing.

Discussion Questions

1. What are some of the advantages and disadvantages of using crowdfunding instead of market research?
2. Most, if not all, crowdfunding sites offer backers or consumers little to no protection if entrepreneurs fail to deliver on their promises. The sites make money off the backers by charging a percentage of money raised. Do you think this is ethical? Why or why not?
3. Do you think Tapplock should have pre-sold their lock prior to fully understanding their manufacturing process and costs? Why or why not?
4. Do you think Tapplock should have sold their locks on sites such as Amazon prior to fulfilling all their pre-orders from Indiegogo? Why or why not?

As discussed in **Chapter 1**, crowdfunding sites enable entrepreneurs to illustrate what a potential product may look like without having a finalized product ready for market. Consumers are often asked to comment on the product, and in many cases, companies can pre-sell finished products before manufacturing them. This prepurchase provides entrepreneurs with a real sense of the market potential for their business. Perhaps the most famous use of crowdfunding is the Pebble watch example discussed in **Chapter 1**, where the entrepreneur presold over $10 million worth of smartwatches in a short period of time on Kickstarter. Another example is Ben Grynol's use of the crowdfunding site **Indiegogo** to determine if his concept of a new cane called Top & Derby would sell. The cane quickly racked up over $14,000 in pre-orders and illustrated to Grynol that a market did exist.[26] Grynol's company, Winnipeg's **Top & Derby**, then had several months to produce the canes before shipping them to customers. Test marketing is especially appropriate where little capital investment is required, such as with a small service business or online marketing to other businesses and consumers.

The proper collection of secondary and primary data can be invaluable to entrepreneurs when they assess business opportunities. It can provide a base of data that, if analyzed correctly, may allow for the capitalization of a successful opportunity or the avoidance of a disaster. The types of market research just described require an investment in time and money, but many successful entrepreneurs are convinced research is a worthwhile investment.

Although owner-managers often use these information collection methods before starting their businesses, they can and should use them on an ongoing basis after the businesses have been established to stay abreast of changes in market conditions. Many successfully established businesses become complacent and, as a result, eventually fail because they lose touch with consumers or market conditions. To avoid this, small businesses should set aside the time and money required to regularly collect and use relevant market information. **Chapter 7** discusses this subject further.

QUANTITATIVE ASSESSMENT OF BUSINESS OPPORTUNITIES LO7

After the entrepreneur has collected the relevant information about the market, the next step is to use this information as quantitatively as possible to assess the financial feasibility of the proposed venture. The purpose of this assessment is to determine whether the business will earn the income the entrepreneur desires. The financial feasibility analysis as described in this section is most appropriate for starting a new business from scratch, but much of it could be applied to the purchase of an existing business or the operation of a franchise.

PREPARING THE FEASIBILITY ANALYSIS

The first step in doing a feasibility analysis for a small business is to prepare a sales or revenue forecast. This is a very important estimate, as it will become the foundation for the projected income and cash flow statements, which will ultimately indicate the feasibility of the venture. **Small Business Beginnings 3-1** is an example of why this step is so important for a small business.

SMALL BUSINESS BEGINNINGS 3-1

CRAZY PLATES

When Crazy Plates frozen meals flopped, their inventors started over, but this time they used a recipe. Crazy Plates had high expectations, with the meals being an extension of two of the most successful Canadian cookbooks ever—*Crazy Plates* and *Looneyspoons*, written by Janet and Greta Podleski. The team behind the meals also included David Chilton, author of *The Wealthy Barber*.

Chilton and his team had made the all-too-familiar error of creating a product for themselves rather than for the researched market: "Almost all of them [the problems] came about because we didn't research our market," says Chilton. The meal kit could feed a family of four or five for about $14. However, research could have told them that 85 percent of frozen food is marketed to feed two people for less than $10. The packaging was also a problem because the boxes contained too much visual clutter and had no wax coating, making them look cheap and fragile.

The team decided to start again and, using market research, reformulated the meals and redesigned the packaging. Chilton also created a 24-page business plan that outlined what exactly went wrong. After only a year, the sales of Crazy Plates were up 400 percent over those of the old product. "The real lesson is you can't replace solid research with pure instinct," says Chilton. Crazy Plates continues to be a successful company by marketing numerous products worldwide.

There are two methods of forecasting sales. Both secondary and primary information may be required to follow either method. The first is the build-up method in which the entrepreneur identifies each target market and estimates potential daily sales to each. This estimate may be obtained by observing similar businesses or from industry experts, suppliers, or government sources. The daily sales estimate is then projected to find an annual amount.

The second method of sales forecasting is referred to as the *breakdown method.* The entrepreneur may not be as familiar with the specific target market and so begins with the total population and breaks down this large market by eliminating demographic or buyer markets that would be less likely to purchase. **Figure 3-1** later in the chapter includes an example of a breakdown method of sales forecasting by using secondary information only.

The procedure and example that follow are more similar to the breakdown method of sales forecasting than to the build-up method. Keep in mind that the following and accompanying examples are simplified. Difficulty in obtaining relevant data and rapidly changing market conditions can increase the uncertainty of the result.

Three steps are required to estimate the financial feasibility of a proposed business venture. The first step is to determine potential revenue (demand) for the total market. The second is to estimate the share of total market revenue that the new business might obtain. The third is to subtract the associated expenses from the revenue estimate to arrive at a projected estimated net income for the prospective business. A more detailed explanation of the steps in calculating a feasibility analysis is presented next. A detailed example of such an analysis is given in **Figure 3-1** later in the chapter. In carrying out the feasibility analysis, remember to be conservative with all estimates.

STEP 1: CALCULATE MARKET POTENTIAL

The purpose of step 1 is to arrive at a dollar or unit sales estimate for the total market. It may involve three substeps:

1. *Determine the market area and its population.* Delineate the geographic area or target market the business will serve. This can be done by obtaining a map and marking off the size of the market. Then estimate the population (numbers) within that market that might conceivably purchase the type of product or service to be offered. This process yields an estimate of the size of the target market.
2. *Obtain revenue (sales) statistics for this market area for the product type or service.* Usually, federal, provincial or territorial, or municipal governments have this information for many standard types of products or businesses. For example, Statistics Canada publishes retail expenditure and manufacturing data for many products and services. If total revenue or sales figures are not available for the proposed type of business or product but per capita or per family expenditures are, simply multiply this figure by the population estimate obtained in substep 1 (population of market × per capita expenditures).

   If the product or service is new and no secondary data are available, use secondary data about a similar product. If there is no similar product, primary research–in the form of a survey, for example–may be used to assess consumer acceptance of the concept. If the results indicate that a certain percentage of the market shows a purchase interest, multiply that percentage by the size of the market to obtain the market potential estimate.

   Many entrepreneurs have started Internet businesses. Obtaining an estimate of market potential for this type of business may be difficult because many markets are untested and hard to define. Some methods, however, can be helpful in determining the size of the market for an Internet business. Data are emerging that indicate Internet usage for various types of products and services. This information can be used to help attain market revenue estimates as described above, although the geography for the market size may be more difficult to estimate. **Table 3-3** provides an example.

TABLE 3-3 **Calculating a Representative Survey Sample for a Small Business**

Background: An entrepreneur wants to estimate the market potential for a website that provides information and booking services for the 60 ski areas in British Columbia.

Step 1: Using the Internet, the B.C. Skiers Profile 2003–04, and Ski Market Study 2007 were located. These studies indicated that 4.5 million skiers visited ski areas in British Columbia annually.

Step 2: Using the Internet, it was found that the Travel Activities and Motivation Study (Government of Ontario) indicates that 78 percent of U.S. and Canadian skiers and snowboarders used the Internet for research, and 36 percent of those used the Internet to book their latest trip.

Step 3: Using the information collected in steps one and two above, make the following estimate:

$$4,500,000 \times 78\% \times 36\% = 1.26 \text{ million}$$

The market potential estimate is 1.26 million customers. Adjustments should then be made to this estimate to update the data by using skiing trends and to reconcile natural and British Columbia skiing differences. However, the estimate provides a good starting point for the analysis.

3. *Adjust the market potential total as necessary.* If a small business owner is able to obtain actual revenue statistics for the market, usually the only adjustment needed is to update the data. As mentioned previously, secondary data are typically a year or two out of date. A simple way to update sales and expenditure data is to increase the amount of sales by the annual rate of inflation for the years involved. This might also include a forecast of trends that will affect demand in the future. Such trends could be included in the estimate.

   If national averages of per capita expenditures are used, make adjustments for local shopping patterns. A common adjustment is for those living in the market area who purchase outside the market, and vice versa. For example, if it is estimated that 20 percent of the market buys the product or service outside the market area, reduce the market potential by 20 percent.

   Projections should include one-year and five-year estimates to reflect trends that may exist in the industry. Projections should also include trends with respect to growth of the competition that might affect future market share.

STEP 2: CALCULATE MARKET SHARE

The purpose of this step is to estimate the percentage of the total market potential the proposed business will obtain. Because the method of calculating market share differs significantly, depending on the type of business, market share calculations for retail, manufacturing, and service firms are illustrated separately.

Remember that the market share calculations as described below are preliminary estimates only. They serve as a simple starting point from which significant adjustments must be made. Some of the required adjustments may be difficult to arrive at because of a lack of current information and their possible subjective nature. Collecting the information to make these adjustments typically requires primary information with qualified sources, such as industry experts and personal experience. The amount of the required adjustment may also be difficult to establish. However, arriving at a quantitative and objective initial market share percentage and recognizing that appropriate adjustments are necessary will lend confidence to the entrepreneur and credibility to the outside observer.

Retail Firm.

1. *Estimate the total amount of selling space in the market devoted to the merchandise the new business will sell (usually in square feet or square metres).* This involves taking an inventory of space of competing stores (specialty and department stores) devoted to this product. This estimate may be obtained informally by observation or by asking the owners. In some areas, secondary information about retail selling space may be available through a municipal or city government department.
2. *Estimate the size of the proposed store (in square feet or square metres).* It is likely that the entrepreneur will have a good idea of the size of the proposed store. The actual size, of course, may depend on the availability of outlets.
3. *Calculate the market share based on selling space.* Integrate the information collected in steps 1 and 2 in the following formula:

$$\frac{\text{Proposed store selling space}}{\text{Total market selling space (including proposed store)}} = \text{Percentage market share}$$

4. *Make adjustments to reflect any competitor strengths and weaknesses regarding the proposed store.* Typical adjustments might include the following:
   a. Decrease the percentage share if the competition has a better location, is larger, or has considerable customer loyalty. Also, decrease the percentage because the proposed store is new and will take time to build customer loyalty.
   b. Increase the percentage share if the proposed store will offer unique products, services, location, advertising, or other advantages over the competition.

   The amount of the adjustments may be arbitrary and somewhat subjective, but typically they are fractions of a percentage of the market share.

5. *Multiply the revised market share percentage by the market potential estimate obtained in step 1.* The result is a dollar revenue estimate for the proposed business for the first year of operations. By applying market trends to this figure, a one- to five-year estimate can be obtained, if required.

Manufacturing Firm.

1. *Estimate the total productive capacity in the market for the product to be manufactured.* Typically, this will be calculated in units, but it may be in dollars. This will involve estimating the production size of competitors (both domestic and foreign).

   If the product is a new innovation and no competition exists, market share is the same as the market potential calculated previously.
2. *Estimate the productive capacity of the proposed manufacturing plant.*
3. *Calculate the market share based on productive capacity.* Integrate the information obtained in steps 1 and 2 into the following formula:

$$\frac{\text{Production capacity of proposed business}}{\begin{array}{c}\text{Total production capacity}\\ \text{(including proposed business)}\end{array}} = \text{Percentage of market share}$$

4. *Make adjustments to reflect competitive strengths and weaknesses that the proposed plant may possess.* The market share percentage estimated in step 3 will likely need to be adjusted. Determine the strengths and weaknesses of competitors, and compare them with the proposed business. Primary research is often required to obtain this type of information.

   Generally, a higher market share can be obtained in industries in which competitors are smaller, the product can be differentiated from competitors' products, and primary research shows a particular level of dissatisfaction with existing products.

   Market share will tend to be smaller if the industry is made up of a few large and powerful competitors that hold key contracts, or where consumer satisfaction with the existing product is determined to be high.

   Even though the existing market may look formidable, some sectors of the economy look favourably on purchases from small businesses. The federal government, for example, is a very large potential purchaser that should not be overlooked. These types of markets are discussed in **Chapter 7**. For a manufacturing firm, success at obtaining key contracts may provide the certainty required to calculate the market share and bypass some of these calculations.
5. *Multiply the estimated market share percentage by the market potential estimate obtained in step 1.* This figure projects estimated dollar sales for the first year of operations. As in the retail example, industry trends can assist in estimating this figure for more than one year.

Service Firm.

1. *Estimate the total capacity of the service available in the market area.* The base used to calculate capacity will vary, depending on the type of service being offered. For example, restaurant capacity may be measured by number of seats, tables, or square footage; motel capacity by number of rooms; and beauty salon capacity by number of employees or number of workstations. It is important to determine which base most accurately reflects the service capacity. Obtain this estimate by observing existing businesses or talking to owners.
2. *Estimate the service capacity of the proposed business.* This involves projecting the size of the proposed business in terms of service capacity.
3. *Calculate market share based on the capacity base.* Integrate the information obtained in steps 1 and 2 into the following formula:

$$\frac{\text{Proposed business service capacity}}{\begin{array}{c}\text{Total production capacity}\\ \text{(including proposed business}\\ \text{service capacity)}\end{array}} = \text{Percentage of market share}$$

4. *Make adjustments similar to those made for a retail store.* The adjustments in the service industry tend to be more significant than in retailing. The opportunity to differentiate from competitors in the service industry is much greater than in retailing, which tends to deal with more standardized products. Therefore, the percentage adjustments may be larger for service industry market share calculations.
5. *Multiply the estimated market share percentage by the market potential estimate obtained in step 1.* This figure projects estimated dollar sales for the first year of operations. As in the retail example, industry trends can assist in estimating this figure for more than one year.

STEP 3: CALCULATE NET INCOME AND CASH FLOW

1. *Using the market share revenue figure obtained in step 2 as the starting point, calculate the expenses expected to be incurred for the business.* Obtain most of these figures by checking with suppliers and other similar businesses. However, some secondary sources, such as those provided by Statistics Canada, provide typical operating statements for many types of small businesses. Often these statements express expenses as a percentage of revenue and thus can be easily adapted to the proposed business. Some of the more important required expenses are as follows:
   - Cost of goods sold and gross profit percentages—these can be obtained from secondary data but should be confirmed with suppliers.
   - Cash operating expenses, such as rent, wages, utilities, repairs, advertising, and insurance—these expenses can also be obtained from secondary sources but should be verified by checking with vendors of these services, because they may differ for the market area of the proposed business.
   - Interest and depreciation—a list of the costs of capital items (i.e., building and equipment) and total start-up costs needs to be made so that yearly depreciation and interest expenses can be calculated. **Chapter 6** presents information on determining start-up costs and the subsequent interest calculation.

     Remember that only the portion of these assets estimated to be used during that period should be included as the depreciation expenses. Using these start-up costs as a basis, determine an estimate of the amount of debt and annual interest costs using current rates.
2. *Subtract expenses from revenue to determine the projected net income from the proposed business in the first year and subsequent years, if required.* Once a projected income figure is calculated, the prospective entrepreneur is in a position to evaluate and compare this result with other types of available investments. Compare return (income) as a percentage of investment (funds put into the venture) with other types of businesses or safe uses of money, such as the return obtained by placing the funds with a bank. The rate of return of the business should be higher than bank interest, however, to compensate for the risk factor that accompanies a new business.

   It is conceivable—and not uncommon—that the projected income for the new business will be negative, at least in the first few years of operation. Usually, the entrepreneur is taking a long-term view of the business, and thus long-term projections may be required to evaluate financial feasibility. In addition to a net income projection, many feasibility analyses include a projected cash flow statement. This document is of particular interest to potential lenders and investors. The cash flow simply describes the cash in minus the cash out on a chronological basis. Usually cash flow statements are shown monthly (see **Chapter 6**).

   A quantitative financial feasibility analysis for a retail pharmacy is presented in **Figure 3-1**. This example illustrates the steps described in the preceding sections.

FIGURE 3-1 **Feasibility Analysis for a Pharmacy in Lethbridge, Alberta (approximately 300 square metres)**

Step 1: Calculate Market Potential

1. *Market area.* The market area is the population of Lethbridge, Alberta, plus outlying regions. This region includes towns within a 100-kilometre radius of Lethbridge. The population of this total market area is about 200,000. (Source: City of Lethbridge estimate.)
2. *Sales for market area.* The per capita sales for pharmacies in the market area can be determined through two sources. First, the actual sales figures may be published and available from the municipality. Second, if that information is not available, find the per capita sales by taking Canadian or provincial sales of pharmacies divided by the respective population. This information is available from Statistics Canada.

$$\frac{\text{Pharmacy sales for Alberta (2009)}}{\text{Population Alberta (2009)}} = \text{Per capita pharmacy sales}$$

$$\frac{\$31{,}400{,}000}{3{,}650{,}000} = \$860$$

Once per capita sales have been determined, this number can be applied to the market area population.

$$\begin{aligned}
\text{Lethbridge} &= \text{Population} \times \text{Per capita sales} \\
&= 85{,}000 \times \$860 \\
&= \$73{,}100{,}000 \\
\text{Outlying area} &= \text{Population} \times \text{Per capita sales} \\
&= (200{,}000 - 85{,}000) \times \$860 \\
&= (\text{Total market} - \text{Lethbridge}) \\
&= 115{,}000 \times \$860 \\
&= \$98{,}900{,}000
\end{aligned}$$

Since only 30 percent of people in the outlying area made their purchases in Lethbridge (primary research), multiply this figure by 0.3:

$$\begin{aligned}
\$98{,}900{,}000 \times 0.3 &= \$29{,}670{,}000 \\
\text{Total market potential} &= \$73{,}100{,}000 + \$29{,}670{,}000 \\
&= \$102{,}770{,}000 \text{ (rounded to \$100,000,000)}
\end{aligned}$$

3. *Adjustments.* Typical adjustments might include updating secondary information regarding population and purchases by applying past trends.

Step 2: Calculate Market Share

1. *Estimate selling space in market.* There are a total of 45 pharmacies and pharmacy departments in Lethbridge, with a total estimated size of 17,000 square metres. (Primary research collected by observation.)
2. *Size of proposed store.* The size of the proposed pharmacy is 300 square metres.
3. Calculation of market share. Percentage share of the market:

$$\frac{\text{Proposed store selling space}}{\text{Total market selling space (including proposed store)}} = \frac{300\ \text{m}^2}{17{,}000\ \text{m}^2 + 300\ \text{m}^2} = 1.7\%$$

[continued]

4. *Adjustments.* The percentage of market share would probably have to be decreased slightly, because the proposed pharmacy is new and would not have built up clientele and the reputation of an existing store.

   Based on the above factors, market share has been adjusted to 1.5 percent.

5. *Multiply market share percentage by the market potential.*

Market share × Market potential = Estimated market share

1.5% × $100,000,000 = $1,500,000

Therefore, market share is approximately $1,500,000.

Step 3: Calculation of Net Income and Cash Flow

NEW PHARMACY

PROJECTED INCOME STATEMENT

FOR THE PERIOD ENDED DECEMBER 2009

		% OF SALES	SOURCE OF INFORMATION
Sales	$1,500,000	100.0	From calculation in step 2
Less: Cost of goods sold	1,080,000	72.0	Dun and Bradstreet Key Business Ratios (2007)
Gross margin	420,000	28.0	
Expenses: Manager's salary	80,000		Primary information (talked to owners)
Employee wages (Schedule 1)	200,000		Schedule 1, primary information
Fringe benefits	5,000	0.75	Statistics Canada operating results for pharmacies (2007)
Rent	50,000		Primary information (talked to owners)
Utilities and telephone	20,000		Primary information (talked to owners)
Accounting, legal, taxes, and licence	6,500		Primary information (checked with agencies)
Insurance	6,500		Primary information (checked with agencies)
Repairs and maintenance	6,500	0.65	Stats Canada (operating results, etc.)
Advertising	6,500	0.65	Stats Canada (operating results, etc.)
Depreciation (Schedule 2)	24,000		Schedule 2
Interest, exchange, and bank charges	7,500		Schedule 3
Office and store supplies	5,000	0.5	Stats Canada (operating results, etc.)
Contingency	5,000	0.5	Stats Canada (operating results, etc.)
Total expenses	432,500		
Net income (loss) before tax	(12,500)		

Schedule 1 (obtained through primary research)

Employee wages	
1 Full-time pharmacist	80,000
1 Part-time pharmacist	40,000
1 Full-time cashier @ $20,000	20,000
2 Part-time cashiers @ $10,000	20,000
1 Bookkeeper	20,000
2 Marker/ receiver/ delivery persons	20,000
Total	$ 200,000

Schedule 2 Depreciation Schedule

Equipment cost = $150,000 Capital cost allowance (CCA) = 20% (obtained from Master Tax Guide)

YEAR	UNDEPRECIATED AMOUNT	×	CCA	=	DEPRECIATION
2009	$150,000	×	0.20	=	$30,000
2010	120,000	×	0.20	=	24,000
2011	96,000	×	0.20	=	19,200
2012	76,800	×	0.20	=	15,360
2013	61,440	×	0.20	=	12,288

The above process is continued until the entire item is depreciated.

Schedule 3

Interest schedule

Amount borrowed = $100,000

Interest rate = 5%

Interest 2009 = 100,000 × 5%	=	$5,000
Estimated bank and service charges	=	$ 500
Debit machine lease	=	$2,000
Total		$7,500

Another potentially important part of the feasibility analysis, particularly for the manufacturing firm, is to estimate the level of production and sales required to break even financially. A detailed discussion of break-even analysis is included in **Chapter 9**. After the feasibility analysis is completed, the prospective entrepreneur should have enough information to decide whether to pursue a particular business opportunity. The areas covered up to this point can be used to make this decision. **Table 3-4** presents a checklist for personal and opportunity evaluation.

TABLE 3-4 **Self-Assessment for a Small Business Opportunity**

Personality:	Do I possess most of the personality characteristics of successful entrepreneurs introduced in **Chapter 2**?
Nature:	Does this business opportunity meet my occupational and lifestyle goals and interests?
Abilities:	Do I have the expertise in the fundamentals (financial, marketing, personnel, production) needed to manage this business opportunity? If I do not, am I able and willing to acquire or hire such expertise?
Experience:	Do I have experience with the business or industry? If not, am I able and willing to obtain it or find someone who can help me get started?
Financial base:	Do I currently have, or can I obtain, the necessary funds to finance the venture?
Feasibility:	Does the financial feasibility of the business opportunity meet my expectations and financial goals?

LEARNING OBJECTIVES SUMMARY

LO1 **The process of starting a new venture can be referred to as the entrepreneurial process. The process involves four specific stages: (1) identification and evaluation of an opportunity, (2) development of a business plan, (3) determination of the resources required, and (4) management of the business.**

LO2 **All businesses start with an idea. Some of the more frequently used sources of ideas are past or current occupations, hobbies, personal experiences, observation of consumers, existing products and services, and deliberate searches for ideas.**

LO3 **Before deciding which small business opportunity to pursue, entrepreneurs must consider some nonquantitative factors, such as their goals, the content of the work, the lifestyle the business offers, and their capabilities and experience.**

LO4 **There are three ways to enter a market with a new product or service. The first method is to offer a completely new product. The second is to offer an existing product to a different market or industry. The third is to offer a product or service similar to those that already exist in the same market.**

LO5 **An entrepreneur can develop a competitive advantage by choosing the right industry to enter, the right kind of business to pursue, and the right aspect of the business to focus on.**

LO6 **Two general types of information are available to help a potential small business owner select a business opportunity. The first and most inexpensive method is to collect secondary data about a potential market. Many government documents and other sources can provide valuable secondary data. When little current secondary data are available, prospective small business owners can collect primary data to help determine the feasibility of their businesses. Primary data are collected through the entrepreneur's own research. Although usually more costly than secondary data, these can be more current and relevant to the analysis. Three general methods of doing primary research are observation, surveys, and test marketing. Surveying is usually the most effective method for a small business.**

LO7 **There are three steps in estimating the financial feasibility of a proposed business venture. The first step is to determine potential revenues for the total market. The second step is to estimate the proposed business share of that total market. The third step is to subtract the associated expenses from the revenue estimate to determine an estimated net income for the prospective business.**

TIME TO TAKE ACTION

In this chapter, you learned about idea generation and opportunity assessment.

If you have not done so already, prepare a list of ideas that you may want to develop into a business plan.

Start to narrow the list of ideas by reviewing your qualitative goals. Then start to review each idea by answering some of the questions identified in this chapter around opportunity assessment.

After narrowing your list to one or two ideas, complete a full opportunity assessment of the idea. If you can, access both primary and secondary research.

DISCUSSION QUESTIONS

1. Briefly explain the ways of entering a market. List examples that fit these methods other than those mentioned in the text.
2. J&J Inc. is thinking of developing a new coin laundry. The firm first needs to do some market research to determine the demand for the product. What kind of information should it collect?

3. Why is it important to make adjustments in market potential and market share figures?
4. For a small business of your choice, show how you would evaluate nonquantitative factors, such as goals, experience, lifestyle, and content of work.
5. Discuss the difficulties of preparing a feasibility analysis for an e-commerce business.

EXPERIENTIAL EXERCISES

1. Form groups and brainstorm ideas that you could turn into a business. Select two or three ideas as a group and develop the marketing mix for the idea along with some justification why the business will be successful (competitive advantage). Present the ideas to the class.
2. Design a simple mail-in questionnaire to assess demand for a carpet-cleaning business in your city.
3. Contact an entrepreneur of your choice and ask what the person feels is their competitive advantage.

COMPREHENSIVE CASE DAN KIM: PART 1

Dan Kim has worked for a carpentry company building homes in Hamilton, Ontario, for the past five years. Although he has moved up in the organization to be a project manager, he is becoming increasingly frustrated with the negative aspects of working for a small company with little room for advancement. Dan has suggested to the business owner that he should consider expanding, perhaps consider moving into commercial construction, and that Dan himself could handle more duties under his proposed expansion plans. Dan has even offered to become a partner in the business or eventually buy the company from the owner. The owner, who is nearing retirement age, prefers to maintain the business as it is. He recognizes Dan as ambitious, dependable, and hardworking, but he has little desire to grow his company at this stage in his life.

Dan, while making a good wage, is certain that he could make more money if he worked on his own. Having grown up with parents who owned their own restaurant, he also fondly remembers the freedom that his father had in taking time off to attend Dan's hockey games and to take family trips. His father's restaurant had been successful and had grown to the point where he added four additional locations and eventually sold them all for a significant profit. Dan is not certain he wants to work for someone else for the rest of his life, nor is he even certain he wants to be a carpenter. Dan has recently started to think about ideas to start his own business and has been searching the Internet late into the evening for information on the latest trends in the construction and housing industries. Dan is certain that his experience and hands-on ability will help him identify an opportunity he could turn into a company, and he has started making notes on his iPhone about various business ideas he has during the day.

After spending six months thinking about various ideas for a business, Dan believes he has found one that would work. After watching extension ladders wobble, lean, and sometimes move, Dan thought there had to be a better way to increase their stability without having someone stand and hold a ladder all day. Dan spent the next few months building various prototypes that would solve this problem, and he finally developed a set of rails that could be easily attached to extension ladders to make them more stable and increase their safety. The rails are made of lightweight aluminum, bent so that they attach to a ladder through the holes of the ladder rungs. Dan was thrilled with his invention, which he intends to call the Ladder Helper. He is sure that the product will especially appeal to those in the construction industry and to homeowners. He is confident that he can produce enough ladder rails in his garage out of lightweight aluminum (the same material that ladders are made from) with metal cutters and benders to launch a viable business.

Dan brought the Ladder Helper to work and showed it to his boss. His boss thought it was an interesting invention but stated he did not think people would buy them. This reaction concerned Dan, and while he was excited about the product's potential, he decided to post some information about the concept on several crowdsourcing sites and on his Facebook page asking for input. While most respondents agreed the idea was a good one, many entrepreneurs stated that Dan would never be able to produce enough of the ladders himself to meet demand. Others suggested that rather than trying to make the extension, he should bring his concept to some of the larger ladder manufacturers and see if they would buy the idea from them. At this point, Dan was satisfied he had done enough research to determine the idea was a good one, and he believed people would buy the product. Although he appreciated all the advice he received online, he wanted to be the one to build the ladders, and he was not interested in selling the idea. After all, if he sold the idea, he would just be back working at the same company again, albeit with a little more money in his pocket.

Dan is more determined than ever to start his own business. He feels that his invention has great potential. He discusses the possibility of becoming an entrepreneur with his wife, Suzie. Suzie is somewhat apprehensive about the idea, because she and Dan both have good jobs and have accumulated some savings. Furthermore, Suzie is concerned that Dan has not done enough work to assess if the idea is good enough for Dan to quit his job and start a business. She states that Dan's only real market research was online and from friends, family, and other entrepreneurs and they would, of course, be encouraging. She would prefer if Dan engaged in more traditional market research or tried to pre-sell some of his ladders on a crowdsourcing site. Dan is confident that he has collected enough information to determine there is a market for the product, and given that he is uncertain how he will ultimately sell the Ladder Helper, he is unsure if he is ready to commit to a crowdfunding campaign. While Suzie says she has reservations, she agrees that Dan should at least do some additional research on the feasibility of the product. Dan has learned by reading blog posts from successful entrepreneurs that he needs to collect some information to find out whether the Ladder Helper can provide a large enough income so he can quit his job and make a living at it.

Dan feels that the primary market for the Ladder Helper is construction and home renovation companies. He also wonders whether homeowners will buy the Ladder Helper. This market would likely purchase ladders at their local hardware stores, such as Canadian Tire, Home Depot, or Home Hardware. Dan believes that while the Ladder Helper would have global appeal, he should likely focus his business on Canada in the near term but be prepared to quickly expand into the United States. Dan is also starting to realize that he will likely have to lease a facility to manufacture in large quantities. Dan thinks that he should start small by attempting to market the product initially in the Hamilton area.

He uses the Statistics Canada website and goes to the local library to obtain some data for construction, population, households, and expenditures for Canada and for Hamilton. The information that he collected is found in **Table 1-A**.

TABLE 1-A Dan's Market Research

	CANADA	ONTARIO	HAMILTON
Population	31,413,990	11,410,046	662,401
Households	11,552,010	4,302,710	260,968
Household expenditures (Hardware tools per annum)	$ 1,655	$ 1,928	$ 1,848

Dan is not quite sure what to do with this information or what additional information he needs. He is aware that the company he works for has 20 ladders and employs 100 people, so he estimates that one ladder is purchased per five employees in a construction or roofing company. Dan estimates that one out of 10 households would buy an aluminum ladder for such things as painting, cleaning the gutters, roof repairs, satellite dish adjustments, and putting up holiday lights. He thinks that at least 30 percent of these ladder owners will be interested in the Ladder Helper. It costs Dan about $10 to make the standard Ladder Helper, and he estimates that he could sell them for about $40. A breakdown of his costs is shown in **Table 1-B**. He feels that he could surely get 5 percent of the market. If so, he would be a rich man.

Questions

1. If Dan came to you asking for advice about whether to pursue this idea, what advice would you provide?
2. What aspects of Dan's background and personality traits are suited to owning his own business? What aspects might hinder his success?
3. Briefly discuss aspects of the product and business that may contribute to or hinder its success.
4. What positive things has Dan done in investigating the new business?
5. What additional information should Dan obtain before completing his feasibility analysis?
6. With the information provided, prepare a feasibility analysis for the homeowner market.
7. What other information would make this calculation more accurate?

TABLE 1-B Manufacturing Expenses for the Ladder Helper

Metal	$7 per unit
Labour	$2 per unit
Overhead	$1 per unit

CASES FOR PART 1

Petite Shop (A) Big D's Painting Company
Petite Shop (B) April's Micro-Business Mobile Marketing Company

PETITE SHOP (A)

Alice Wood is concerned. She has worked in a women's clothing store for several years after graduating from high school and is now considering opening a store of her own. Her investigations have yielded considerable secondary information, but she is not sure how to go about estimating the potential for another women's clothing store in the city of Jacakes. Jacakes is a city of 86,100 surrounded by a large trading area. It currently has 17 clothing stores and five department stores that retail women's clothing. During the past few years, Alice has been saving her money and learning all she could so that her Petite Shop women's wear store will be a success.

In anticipation of starting her own store, Alice enrolled in a small business management course at a local college. The instructor stressed the importance of market research and mentioned several sources of secondary information that could assist in determining market potential for a new business. Alice obtained the reports she felt were relevant to her prospective business from the Provincial Department of Small Business, Statistics Canada, and the city hall in Jacakes. This information is presented in **Tables 1** and **2**.

Alice now has this information, however she is not sure how to proceed.

TABLE 1 Selected Data for the City Jacakes

Population	86,100
Number of families	29,200
Per capita income	$ 25,000
Retail sales	$737,700,000
Per family expenditure on women's clothing	$ 1,600

TABLE 2 Estimated Retail Space for Selected Retail Establishments (in square feet) City of Jacakes

Food stores	1,200,000
Apparel stores:	
Men's clothing stores	145,000
Women's clothing stores	180,000
Hardware stores	600,000
Department stores	1,650,000

She does not want to retail all kinds of ladies' clothing, but plans to cater to the "petite" woman who wears dress sizes 3 to 9. Alice herself is petite (at 5 feet or 1.5 metres tall), and she feels she understands the difficulties women of her size have in shopping for clothing. From her retailing experience, she estimates that about 60 percent of all clothing sales are in women's clothing, and 20 percent of all women fit in the size 3 to 9 category. She arrived at her decision to select a store directed at the petite woman after she visited all 17 clothing stores in Jacakes and the clothing departments of the city's five department stores. She estimates that only about 10 percent of clothing stores' stock is sized 3 to 9, and the five department stores devote only about 6,500 square feet of selling space to this size range. She believes a small shop of about 1,000 square feet could provide a much better selection to this market than those outlets presently provide.

Questions

1. Using the information provided, prepare an estimate of the market potential for the target market at which Alice Wood is aiming.
2. What portion of this market potential could Alice expect for Petite Shop's market share?
3. What non-quantitative considerations should be brought into this analysis?

PETITE SHOP (B)

Now that Alice Wood has a better idea of the market potential and market share for her proposed retail store, she wants to be satisfied that the Petite Shop will be successful and provide an adequate return on the $45,000 she has saved over the last few years to invest.

Rather than conduct an actual survey on the viability of her business, Alice starts to engage with her social network on Instagram about whether she should open her Petite Shop. While Alice's friends are supportive, she doesn't think she has had enough feedback, so she creates new Facebook, Twitter, and Pinterest accounts to share information about her potential store. Alice spends some time every day talking to her friends and people she has met online, and most people support her idea. However, she has become a bit concerned that some of her friends have suggested she should consider selling online or on eBay as the business would require less cash investment to start and could involve less risk. While Alice agrees that more and more shopping is occurring online, she is convinced there is still room for a bricks-and-mortar Petite Shop.

Alice now begins investigating the typical costs she would incur in operating the store. Alice thinks she can operate her new store with one other full-time person and some part-time help at an estimated monthly cost of $4,000. In looking at potential rental costs, she came across a retail outlet for lease on a busy street in the central business district of Jacakes that seems ideal for the Petite Shop. She learns that the site leases for $20 per square foot, with no royalty payments except $2,550 per year to cover municipal taxes. The estimated utility expenses the owner provided were $300 per month, and the insurance for the retail shoe store that had previously been located there was $2,500 per year. Alice has also spoken to a local entrepreneur who has agreed to build her a website that will work well on mobile devices for $3,000. The hosting costs for the site would be $35 a year.

Although Alice is excited about the potential of this site, she estimates she will need to spend approximately $20,000 for leasehold improvements, of which $12,000 will be depreciable items (20 percent). When obtaining the secondary information from Jacakes City Hall, she learned that the business licences will be $100. Alice estimates all miscellaneous expenses, such as stationery, bad debt expense, credit expense, and telephone, to be about $5,000 per year. These figures are based on her experience at the store where she currently works.

Alice knows she will have to raise some additional money to purchase inventory. She visited her local bank and found out that the interest rate for a business loan was 10 percent, but the bank would only lend her the money if she could pledge personal assets against the loan. She also learned that any potential lender would expect to see a completed income statement and a more-thorough proposal. The bank officer mentioned that, in addition to leasehold improvements, she would need one-fourth of the year's cash expenses as operating funds. Although a bit surprised at the bank's reaction, Alice is determined to prepare such a proposal. She knows the new store will need to be promoted but does not know how much she should spend on advertising. The banker suggested the average for ladies' clothing stores was about 2 percent of sales and gave her a copy of a recent Dun and Bradstreet financial ratio sheet to assist her (**Table 1**). Alice also thinks that the industry is changing and perhaps the banker is stuck in the past. While she thinks she may need to spend some money on advertising she thinks social media and word of mouth might be sufficient.

Alice now finds herself in the same dilemma she was in when determining market potential and market share. She has a lot of information but is not sure how to use it.

TABLE 1 Key Business Ratios, Canada—Corporations

LINE OF BUSINESS CLOTHING, WOMEN'S	
(Number of concerns reporting)	(2,323)
Cost of goods sold	58.4%
Gross margin	41.6
Current assets to current debt	1.4
Profits on sales	2.7
Profits on tangible net worth	15.6
Sales to tangible net worth	5.9
Sales to inventory	5.7
Fixed assets to tangible net worth	63.6
Current debt to tangible net worth	127.6
Total debt to tangible net worth	177.3

Questions

1. Using the information presented in Petite Shop (A) and this case, prepare an estimated income statement and return on investment calculation for the Petite Shop's first year of operation.
2. What are some of the potential advantages and disadvantages of using social media to determine the potential for success for Alice's store compared to more formal market research?
3. What areas has Alice overlooked in her investigation?
4. If Alice does not raise money from a bank, what are some alternate sources of funds?
5. Do you think Alice should open up an actual store or sell online instead? Why?
6. Do you think Alice will have to spend as much money on advertising as her banker suggests? Why or why not?
7. Given your analysis, what would you recommend to Alice?

BIG D'S PAINTING COMPANY

Dave Valdon lives in Maple Ridge, British Columbia, and is contemplating starting his own painting business. Having worked for a national painting franchise during his summers while attending college, Dave feels that he has the experience and skills necessary to be successful with this venture. Because he knows the area, he would like to establish the business in Maple Ridge and the surrounding communities of Pitt Meadows, Port Coquitlam, and Coquitlam. He will concentrate on providing professional and high-quality residential painting services. He intends to base the business out of his home and to set up a home office, as his work will be done at the site of the homeowner. In addition, Dave has been told that part of his home expenses (utilities, rent, insurance, etc.) can be deductible business expenses if he does this.

Although Dave is pretty sure that a viable opportunity exists, he knows that he should prepare an estimate of income for the first year of operations. From his industry experience, he estimates that an average painting job for a residential project is about $2,500. His main concern is whether he will be able to obtain enough of these projects to make this a financially viable business. To that end, he has collected some information from outside sources as well as from his experience working in the industry. This information is found in **Table 1**.

TABLE 1 HOMES IN THE MARKET AREA

Maple Ridge	19,865
Pitt Meadows	3,496
Port Coquitlam	27,134
Coquitlam	15,828

Dave feels that 33 percent of all homeowners initiate painting projects each year in his area. He is not sure how to verify this percentage, however.

Dave estimates there are 100 painting companies in his intended market area. He feels that all will be his competition. He has also made the following estimates concerning his operating expenses for his first year.

Wages (himself and 1 other employee)	$80,000
Utilities/phone	1,500
Licence/accounting/insurance	3,000
Vehicle expense	3,000
Advertising	4,000
Equipment/supplies	5,000
Rent	2,500
Contingency	1,000
Total	$80,000

Questions

1. Using the information provided, prepare an estimate of total market revenue and Dave's share of market revenue for the first year of operations.
2. What adjustments should Dave make to the above information to be more accurate with total market revenue?
3. What adjustments or additions should be made to the information to be more accurate with the market share and projected income statement for the first year of operations?

APRIL'S MICRO-BUSINESS MOBILE MARKETING COMPANY

April Autumn MacDonald needs to make a decision to either start her new small business venture or return to university to pursue a graduate education. She really likes the idea for her new business. It plays into her skills and education in her just-completed undergraduate degree. April really needs to firm up her numbers to make sure that this venture has a great chance of being feasible and earning her a nice living. Her decision needs to be made within the next few weeks.

April is 23 years old and has a degree in business with a minor in information technology. Over the course of her degree she took many courses in website design and invested a lot of time learning about mobile marketing. As a result, she knows she is very skilled in creating, designing, and producing websites that work well on mobile devices as well as traditional computers. She also thinks she knows a fair bit about social media after having taken courses and being fairly active on Instagram. While going to school, April also completed co-operative education and spent her last co-op term working for a digital branding company.

While working at the company she noticed most of the local marketing and website design companies were going after existing successful businesses as clients and very few companies (20 percent) were reaching out to micro-businesses or startups. April thinks there may be a niche in this area which she could exploit. She is considering contacting some of the other local marketing company owners via their Twitter accounts to ask their advice and to see if they would meet with her but she is leery they may steal her idea.

The prospects of this business really excite April as she likes the idea of being her own boss, although she is somewhat afraid of the risk of starting her own business. She has determined some of the other costs to starting this business.

Rent in a local business incubator (April thinks she may be able to work from home).	$400/month
Internet and phone	$300/month
Insurance	$800/year
Supplies	$100/month
Marketing	$200/month
Desks, chairs, etc.	$500
April's wage	$3,000/month

April decided to gather further intelligence on her competition in this business. She noticed that there were roughly 10 companies locally who could provide such a service to businesses and another 30 freelance workers who occasionally service the same market. She estimates that freelancers spend roughly 70 percent of their time subcontracting themselves out to to the larger companies and only 30 percent of their time working for business from the local community

As April ponders her decision to open this business, she feels she needs more information to make a correct decision. She has very little money to start this business. She knows she would have to borrow from family and friends as it is unlikely a bank would lend her money given she has no assets of any substance. As she talks over this idea with her aunt who is a successful entrepreneur, they look at the numbers from Statistics Canada and learn that there are roughly 15,000 business in the Halifax area where April lives and roughly 55 percent of them have fewer than five employees. She has also learned that there are approximately another 2,500 businesses that are strictly owner operated. Of these businesses, she estimates that only 50 percent of them have a web page, and that only 33 percent of those companies have websites that work well on mobile devices.

April tries to find out information on new business startups, but it has proven to be somewhat challenging. Many firms start with just an owner-operator and, given the nature of being a sole proprietor, this information may not be collected by anyone. April works with the local Chamber of Commerce and estimates that a 1,000 new firms start in the area each year. Of the 1,000, April speculates 50 to 75 percent will create a web page; however, most will do it themselves or try to find someone who has enough knowledge to create one for free.

April and her aunt also spend sometime investigating what small firms spend on website design, but they have limited success. Additionally, there is no formal information on what micro- and new businesses spend on social media. April contacted some local micro-businesses and discovered that most spend on average $5,000 a year on marketing and almost all of them do all their own social media posts. Of the 15 business owners she spoke to, most of them felt they lacked the knowledge and experience to use social media effectively.

April is a bit frustrated. She recalled when she enrolled in a small business class in her degree program that she was given clear formulas for calculating market potential and market share. Now that she is in the "real world," April is learning that statistical information does not exist for every business. Based on all of the information she has gathered, April has determined what services she would be willing to offer. She would create and maintain websites for $3,000 a year. She is also willing to create or manage social media posts for small and new businesses. She believes she could charge $100 a month for such a service.

Questions

1. What other information could April look for in determining the viability of her business idea? How could she obtain this information?
2. Do you think April should be concerned about discussing her business idea with potential competitors via Twitter? Why or why not?
3. What are some of the advantages for April in staring her business? Some of the disadvantages?
4. What would you recommend April do? Why?

SMALL BUSINESS REFERENCE BOOKS AND SOURCES OF INFORMATION

Entrepreneurial Toolkit, Business Development Bank of Canada, 204 Richmond Street West, Toronto, Ontario, M5V 1V6. bdc.ca/en/articles-tools/entrepreneur-toolkit/pages/default.aspx

Canadian Federation of Independent Business, Willowdale, Ontario. Has several publications and statistics on small business. cfib.ca

Canadian Industrial Innovation Centre, Waterloo, Ontario. Provides assessment of new product, service, or process ideas by marketing experts and engineers. innovationcentre.ca

CIBC Small Business Planning, Canadian Imperial Bank of Commerce. Provides a business planning workbook to assist in development of the business plan. cibc.com/ca/small-business/article-tools/small-business-guide.html

Compusearch Micromarketing Data and Systems. Provides information on population segments by lifestyle, 1000 product categories, and locations of 650,000 businesses. For a free database catalogue, call 1-800-268-DATA.

The Financial Post Canadian Markets, Maclean Hunter Ltd., 777 Bay Street, Toronto, Ontario, M5W 1A7. This book provides complete demographics for Canadian urban markets. It looks at 500 municipalities across Canada with populations greater than 5000. It includes data on demographics; income; manufacturing activity; television, radio, and newspaper statistics; other economic statistics; average and annual growth rates of the population; and future population projections.

Government of Canada–Canada Business Network–contains startup information from Federal and Provincial governments. canadabusiness.ca/eng/

Handbook of Canadian Consumer Markets, The Conference Board of Canada, Suite 100, 25 McArthur Road, Ottawa, Ontario, K1L 6R3. This book includes data on provincial, rural, marital populations, and so on;

employment; income; expenditures; production and distribution; and pricing. conferenceboard.ca

Small Business Banking, TD Canada Trust. tdcanada trust.com/products-services/small-business/small business-index.jsp

Index to Federal Programs and Services, Service Canada, Ottawa, Canada. servicecanada.gc.ca or Service Canada Programs and Services www.esdc.gc.ca/en/service_canada/programs.page

Innovation, Science and Economic Development Canada provides several services for small businesses across the country. The business service centres contain publications, videos, and computer databases and networking sources, as well as counselling personnel. ic.gc.ca

Key Business Ratios, Dun and Bradstreet Canada Ltd., P.O. Box 423, Station A, Toronto, Ontario. Contains key business ratios for more than 800 different types of businesses. Also, the U.S. affiliate of Dun and Bradstreet publishes "typical" balance sheets, income statements, and "common-size" financial figures. dnb.ca

Kryszak, Wayne D. *The Small Business Index,* Grolier, Inc., Sherman Turnpike, Danbury, Connecticut, U.S.A. 06816. This book is an index to American and Canadian books, pamphlets, and periodicals that contain information on starting and running a small business.

What You Need to Know When Starting a Small Business, Royal Bank of Canada. This series of books offers guidance on starting and running a business. Topics covered include Growing Your Business, Starting a Business, and Business Succession Planning. https://www.rbcroyalbank.com/business/advice/starting-a-business.html

Managing for Success Series, The Institute for Small Business Inc., 1051 Clinton Street, Buffalo, New York, U.S.A. This series contains 16 self-tutorials in business procedure written expressly for the independent business owner. It discusses important business topics such as financing, a do-it-yourself marketing plan, planning and budgeting, and advertising and sales promotion. It provides illustrative case studies, detailed examples, and workbook and checklist pages that let you work out your business details along the lines given in the text.

Advice for Starting or Buying a Business, Business Development Bank of Canada, Management Services, P.O. Box 6021, Montréal, Québec, H3C 3C3. The BDC offers advice to starting and running a small business. The web pages provide information on areas such as strategy and planning; marketing, sales and export; money and finance; recruiting and managing employees; and buying a franchise. The Business Development Bank also templates and business guides as well as an online Learning Centre where new entrepreneurs can learn at their own pace. Areas of study include Money and Finance, Operations, and Business Strategy and Planning. bdc.ca/en/articles-tools/start-buy-business/pages/default.aspx

Periodicals and trade magazines particular to the type of business involved. For example, one would consult *Restaurateur* if opening a new restaurant. These magazines often provide typical start-up and operating costs for a business. In addition, there are several general small business periodicals such as *Entrepreneur, Venture,* and *INC.,* which provide valuable ideas on starting a business.

Provincial and territorial small business departments. These offices can be very useful for those who operate or plan to open a small business. They provide information on sources of financing for small business. In Alberta, for example, government publishes pamphlets on many aspects of running a small business, as well as kind-of-business files (KOB), which contain data on 100 types of small businesses, such as financial ratios, market trends, and so on.

Small Business Resources, Bank of Montreal. Resources and links covering starting and growing your business as well as various management topics. bmo.com/main/business

Small Business Publications, Business and Industry Canada. Provides a variety of reports on aspects affecting Canada's small and medium business enterprises. 235 Queen Street, Room 505A, Industry Canada, Ottawa, K1A 0H5. http://www.ic.gc.ca/eic/site/061.nsf/eng/home Also find archived issues of Small Business Quarterly, a quick and easy-to-read snapshot of recent performance of Canada's small business sector. publications.gc.ca/site/eng/285131/publication.html

Small Business Source Book, John Ganly, Diane Seialtana, and Andrea Pedolsky, editors. Gale Research Company, Book Tower, Detroit, Michigan, U.S.A. 48226. This book was designed as a first step toward finding information for anyone who is considering starting a small business. The book lists 100 companies and associations, sources of supply, statistical sources, trade periodicals, franchises, educational programs, trade shows, and conventions.

Statistics Canada, Head Office, R. H. Coats Building, Tunney's Pasture, Ottawa, Ontario, K1A OT6. www.statcan.gc.ca/eng/start

1. *Census data.* This can be obtained from local city halls. Census data provides information on population growth rates, income, level of schooling, and other facts. Census tracts for large centres can also be obtained from Statistics Canada.
2. *Family expenditure in Canada.* This report provides information on family expenditures in Canada for a very detailed list of items.
3. *Operating results.* This report presents typical expenses, cost of goods sold, inventory, and net profit as a percentage of sales for many types of businesses. It presents results for both incorporated and unincorporated businesses and gives both mean and median results. Data are provided by both level of sales and province or territory.
4. *Market Research Handbook.* This book presents data on selected economic indicators, government revenue, expenditures and employment, merchandising and services, population characteristics, personal income, and expenditures.
5. *Small business profiles.* These provide complete financial operating reports from many small businesses.

TD Small Business Tools & Resources, Toronto Dominion Bank. Includes links to financial, federal and provincial, and business websites to help you start and grow your business. https://www.td.com/ca/en/business-banking/how-to/small-business/tools-and-resources/

SUGGESTED PERIODICALS FOR SMALL BUSINESS

Entrepreneur
Entrepreneur Media, Inc
18061 Fitch
Irvine, CA 92614
entrepreneur.com

INC.
Bernard Goldhirsh, Publisher
38 Commercial Wharf
Boston, MA 02110
inc.com

Journal of Small Business and Entrepreneurship
Faculty of Administration
University of Regina
Regina, SK S4S 0A2
jsbednet.com

Canadian Business
Rogers Publishing Limited
Toronto, ON
canadianbusiness.com

Business Development Bank of Canada
BDC Building
5 Place Ville Marie
Suite 400
Montreal, QC H3B 5E7
bdc.ca

The Balance - Small Business
P.O. Box 1684 Station Main
Holland Landing, ON L9N 1P2
thebalancesmb.com

Success
Lang Communications
230 Park Avenue
New York, NY 10169
successmagazine.com

ONLINE SOURCES OF ASSISTANCE FOR SMALL BUSINESSES

Atlantic Canada Opportunities Agency—acoa.ca—business opportunities and information for the Atlantic region

The Balance - Small Business—https://www.thebalancesmb.com/small-business-info-4161643—a comprehensive small business website on e-commerce startups

Bank of Montreal Entrepreneur Site—bmo.com/home/small-business/banking/resources—provides information on management aspects of running a small business and interaction with other entrepreneurs

Business Development Bank Information Site–bdc.ca/en/pages/home.aspx

B.C. Ministry of Jobs, Trade and Technology–gov.bc.ca/tted–provides guides for planning a business through to functional management of the ongoing business

Canada One–canadaone.com–provides useful business tools to start, run, and grow a successful small business

Canadian Business Magazine–canadianbusiness.com–articles and newsletters for entrepreneurs

Canadian Chamber of Commerce–chamber.ca–information on public policy on business issues

Canadian Federation of Independent Business–cfib.ca

Canadian Industry Statistics–https://www.ic.gc.ca/app/scr/app/cis/search-recherche?lang=eng–statistics for various types of small businesses

CANSIM Main Base Series Directory–index to latest census–5.statcan.gc.ca/cansim/home-accueil?lang=eng?

Census Program–12.statcan.ca/english/census

Employment & Social Development Canada – https://www.canada.ca/en/employment-social-development/campaigns/adult-learning.html –human resources and skill development.

Entrepreneur–Entrepreneur.com–general information about small business

The Essential Guide to Direct Mail–https://www.canadapost.ca/cpc/en/business.page–Canada Post's assistance for small business to reach customers

Export Development Corporation–edc.ca–provides information about exporting

Federal Tax Services and Information–https://www.canada.ca/en/services/taxes.html–provides information on your responsibilities regarding customs, income tax, GST/HST, and so on

Free Management Library–managementhelp.org

Futurpreneur Canada–futurpreneur.ca/en/

Government of Canada–Canadabusiness.ca–access to all government services to start a small business

Information for Canadian Small Businesses–cra-arc.gc.ca/E/pub/tg/rc4070–federal government website to help small businesses

Inc. Magazine–Inc.com

SCC–scc.ca, https://www.scc.ca/en/publications–information about standards provided by Standards Council of Canada

Small-Office and Home-Office Business Links–options for insurance, technology solutions, and more soho.ca

Statistics Canada–https://www150.statcan.gc.ca/n1/dai-quo/index-eng.htm–up-to-date information releases by Statistics Canada, particularly *The Daily*

Trade Commissioner Service website–tradecommissioner.gc.ca–assistance for small business in identifying markets, contacts, and so on

U.S. Small Business Advancement National Centre–sites.google.com/a/uca.edu/sbanc/home–research, training, consulting, and information library

Western Economic Diversification Canada–wd-deo.gc.ca–business opportunities and information for the Western region; also to assess suitability for exporting see tradestart.ca, which is funded by Western Economic Diversification Canada

ORGANIZATIONS AND TRADE ASSOCIATIONS THAT ASSIST ENTREPRENEURS

Business Development Bank of Canada (BDC)
BDC Building
5 Place Ville Marie, Suite 400
Montreal, PQ H3B 5E7
bdc.ca

The Definitive Guide to Canadian Accelerators and Incubators, Fundica
https://www.fundica.com/blog/646c8004aab609c7/The_Definitive_Guide_To_Canadian_Accelerators_and_Incubators.html

Family Enterprise Exchange
https://family-enterprise-xchange.com/

Canadian Association of Women Executives and Entrepreneurs
cawee.net

Canadian Chamber of Commerce
120 Adelaide Street West, Suite 2109
Toronto, ON M5H 1T1
chamber.ca

Canadian Council for Small Business and Entrepreneurship
204 Richmond Street West, 5th Floor
Toronto, ON M5V 1V6
ccsbe.org

Canadian Federation of Independent Business
4141 Yonge Street, Suite 401
Willowdale, ON M2P 2A6
cfib.ca

Canadian Franchise Association
cfa.ca

Canadian Innovation Centre
innovationcentre.ca

Canadian Venture Capital Association
cvca.ca

Directory of Associations in Canada
1-800-387-2689 ext. 4397
Encyclopedia of Associations
proquest.com/

Entrepreneurship and Small Business Office
235 Queen Street
Ottawa, ON K1A 0A5

Association of Home-Based Businesses
https://virtualvideoweb.org/usa-home-businesses

National Small Business Institute
1070 West Broadway, Suite 310
Vancouver, BC V6H 1E7
smallbusinessinstitute.org

Small Business Network
52 Sheppard Avenue West
Willowdale, ON M2N 1M2
businessknowhow.net

Women's Enterprise Centre
womensenterprise.ca

PART 2

PREPARING FOR SMALL BUSINESS OWNERSHIP

Once the entrepreneur has assessed an opportunity, the next important consideration is selecting from among three methods of assuming ownership of the business: organizing the business from scratch, buying an existing business, or signing a franchise contract. Chapters 4 and 5 provide information to help evaluate each of these methods. Just as important is the final start-up consideration: obtaining financing. Chapter 6 discusses the critical factors the entrepreneur should consider in obtaining the financing needed to establish and operate the venture.

ORGANIZING A BUSINESS—THE BUSINESS PLAN

LEARNING OBJECTIVES

By the end of this chapter, you should be able to:

LO1 Describe the advantages and disadvantages of organizing a business from scratch compared with purchasing a business or becoming a franchisee.

LO2 Discuss the importance of formulating and following a business organizational plan.

LO3 List the essential components of a small business plan.

SMALL BUSINESS PROFILE

MICHELE ROMANOW *Clearbanc*

"Don't call me sweetie."

In perhaps one of the best TV moments in CBC's *Dragon's Den* history, Michele Romanow, the youngest Dragon ever on the show let the other investors know she was a confident, successful entrepreneur who would not be pushed around. The exchange came as Jim Treliving, owner of Boston Pizza, attempted to interrupt Michele as she was addressing entrepreneurs who were pitching their business.

Michael Nagle/Bloomberg via Getty Images

Those familiar with Romanow's entrepreneurial journey wouldn't be surprised by the exchange. Romanow is well known for her grit, determination, and perseverance that has enabled her to successfully co-found five businesses before the age of 30 and be selected the 2018 Canadian Angel Investor of the Year, as well as become the only Canadian on *Forbes* magazine's prestigious "Millennial on a Mission" list.

Romanow started her first business, The Tea Room, a zero-consumer-waste coffee shop, as she earned her engineering degree and MBA at Queen's. Along the way, Romanow met and formed a business partnership with two other students, Anatoliy Melnichuk and Ryan Marien, and the trio began looking for the next big business opportunity. Together, the partners would spend hours researching different businesses and discovered that the caviar market was being under-supplied due to over-fishing of sturgeon. Romanow proceeded to spend her vacations meeting sturgeon researchers and, after graduating, drove to Evendale, New Brunswick, one of the few places in the world with a wild sturgeon fishery. Romanow recalls waiting outside of a fisherman's home for ten hours hoping to hire him for their new enterprise. The business partners did hire a fisherman and taught themselves how to process fish, make caviar, and sell their products to high-end restaurants. Unfortunately for the partners, the 2008 recession started and export laws changed, spelling the end of the startup.

Romanow moved back to Ontario and started working for Sears. While there, she noticed the surge in daily-deal sites and mentioned it to her partners; a short time later Buytopia was born. Buytopia, while late to the daily-deal business, managed to secure some national accounts with Sears, Cirque du Soleil, and Staples, therefore gaining a strong foothold in the market. The company also went on an aggressive acquisition spree buying six other deal-of-the-day companies to become one of the largest players in a shrinking Canadian market. While running Buytopia, the trio came up with their next idea, SnapSaves, an app that would allow consumers to earn money by scanning their receipts and sending them to the manufacturers. At the height of the app's popularity, it was exceeding one million downloads a week and every major packaged goods company in Canada was participating.

While raising money in Silicon Valley, Romanow and her partners were approached by Groupon, who ended up purchasing the company. Groupon would re-brand the business as Snap and Romanow would spend the next year and a half working for the tech giant in Chicago.

Upon her return to Canada, Romanow co-founded Clearbanc with Andrew D'Souza and the pair managed to raise in excess of $100 million since founding the company in 2015. Clearbanc provides capital for web-based businesses based on the company's data not on the entrepreneur's credit scores. Clearbanc will allow entrepreneurs to receive advances on receivables and, in perhaps one of the most innovative financing offers available, the company will provide money to firms to purchase web-based advertisements; and Clearbanc and the company will share the profits.

[continued]

[continued]

As of 2018, Clearbanc states that they have provided over 500 firms with over $100 million in marketing capital. Romanow's advice to entrepreneurs is simple: start now, its never a perfect time to start and every great innovation is a result of hundreds of start-up experiments.

CLEARBANC
clearbanc.com

GETTING STARTED: ESTABLISHING THE BUSINESS

LO1

After the entrepreneur has assessed the feasibility of a business opportunity and found it to be favourable, the next step is to select the method of establishing the business. There are essentially three methods from which to choose. The first is to organize a business from scratch, the second is to purchase an existing business, and the third is to become a franchisee. This chapter discusses the essential steps in organizing a business from scratch and details the steps in creating a business plan. **Chapter 5** deals with purchasing an existing business and franchising. Although the topics covered in Chapter 5 are treated separately, a business plan resulting from the strategy development business model and feasibility analysis as discussed in **Chapter 3** should be employed regardless of which method is chosen.

Students should also recognize that business planning is an essential business skill. Whether you start your own company or work as an employee, the ability to write a business plan will assist you in your career aspirations. For entrepreneurs, writing a business plan is essential for raising money and managing the day-to-day operations of their company.

Organizing a business from scratch gives an entrepreneur greater independence in the establishment and operation of the business, but it also poses more risk (**Table 4-1**). For example, if you are starting a home-care business for seniors in your area, you will have to create your own marketing and staffing plans, find customers, and create your own operations systems. If you buy an existing business, or a franchise such as **Nurse Next Door**, then some of these things are already established.

TABLE 4-1 Independence versus Risk

	ORGANIZING	BUYING	FRANCHISING
Level of independence	Higher	Medium to high	Lower
Level of risk	Higher	Medium	Lower
Chance of survival	20%	70%	90%

The option to organize from scratch is often chosen by entrepreneurs who want the satisfaction of creating a business and adding their personal touch to all its aspects. It may also be the preferred route when few suitable businesses are for sale or there is little chance of obtaining a franchise for the market area. Another motive for starting from scratch includes limited financial resources—entrepreneurs can sometimes start a business for a lot less money when compared with other forms of entering a market. A survey of small business owners by Statistics Canada indicates that about two-thirds of them started their business from scratch.[1] In making this decision, the entrepreneur should be aware of the advantages of organizing the business from scratch and the potential drawbacks.

ADVANTAGES OF ORGANIZING A SMALL BUSINESS FROM SCRATCH

This option offers several advantages. First, the small business owner has the opportunity to define the nature of the business, the competitive environment in which the business will operate, the appropriate market, and the size and extent of operations. For example, Angie Stocklin, co-founder of **One Click**, an online eyeglass retailer, says that establishing her own mission was important to her long-term success.[2]

Second, the owner can obtain the exact types of physical facilities they prefer: building, equipment, and location. Buildings and equipment can be precisely tailored to meet requirements. The owner can also choose the most appropriate location for the market, a very important competitive tool in retailing.

Third, the owner can obtain fresh inventory tailored to the target market. Thus, the risk of products becoming obsolete or difficult to turn over is minimized.

Fourth, the owner can personally select and train employees for the business rather than having to rely on the existing personnel of an established business.

Fifth, the owner can develop his or her own information systems, such as the methods used for bookkeeping and for evaluating the operation. The owner also can take advantage of the latest technology in equipment and materials.

Finally, starting a business from scratch can be less costly. Owners can choose to operate out of their home, start with little cash, and grow the business when they choose. For example, Brian Scudamore, founder of **1-800-Got-Junk?**, started his business with a truck and a plan to professionalize garbage pick-up. Scudamore, who eventually grew the company into the largest home garbage–removal service in North America, had very little in the way of start-up costs. If he had been going to buy an existing business, he would likely have had to pay for its assets, customer lists, and income. Buying a franchise likely would have been even more money. Now, buying Scudamore's 1-800-Got-Junk? franchise costs owners approximately $90,000 to $150,000 to start.[3]

Brian Scudamore started a junk-removal business as an unemployed student with one truck. He has grown the company to be the largest home junk-removal service in Canada and the United States.

The Canadian Press/Jeremy Hainsworth

DISADVANTAGES OF ORGANIZING A SMALL BUSINESS FROM SCRATCH

Starting your own business also carries substantial risks. First, the owner lacks historical information on which to base future plans. This can be a drawback if the owner has uncertainties regarding market demand, supplies, and operations. It is also generally more difficult to obtain financing if projections are based on estimates rather than on the extension of trends from existing operations.

Second, the advantage of personally assembling physical facilities can become a liability because of the time required. In some industrial situations in which prompt establishment is critical, purchasing a business or signing a franchise contract may be more advisable.

Third, a new business always has start-up problems or bugs that have to be worked out.

Fourth, establishing outside relationships with financial institutions, suppliers, and other key professionals is often time consuming. For example, new small businesses typically are not granted trade credit initially, whereas an existing business or franchise has far less difficulty. The savings in interest costs can be substantial.

Finally, the owner faces the risk that there will be insufficient demand for the product or service. Even if a feasibility analysis is carried out before business startup, some uncertainty regarding the extent of the market may remain.

THE SMALL BUSINESS PLAN LO2

Regardless of whether an entrepreneur starts the business from scratch, buys an existing business, or signs a franchise contract, a business plan is essential. Research data point to the crucial need for entrepreneurs to formulate business plans. Business plans assist entrepreneurs in a number of ways, such as helping them to understand the business and markets, raise capital, organize their business, and establish short- and long-term goals. Toronto's Lauren Friese, founder of **TalentEgg Inc.**, Canada's most popular job site for recent grads, says writing a business plan forced her to understand her industry and markets, and increased the probability of her success.[4]

A business plan is a vital tool for entrepreneurs—a blueprint to be referred to repeatedly to keep business growth on course.[5] For example, Garrett Neiman, founder of **CollegeSpring**, a company that specializes in helping students from low-income backgrounds prepare for tests, notes that business plans are helpful in crafting realistic three- to five-year plans. Neiman states business plans outline the activities that need to take place, which is essential if you are looking to expand.[6] Kent Groves, founder of Maritime Trading Co., says that for a business plan to work, people must use it not only to get initial financing but also to assist them in running their business. He says that his company constantly checks his business plan to see if their projections are on track and adjusts accordingly. Gary Kaye, partner in Ernst & Young's Assurance and Advisory Business Services in Ontario, says that street smarts and gut feel are not enough to run a company. He says that to be successful, entrepreneurs must plan where they are going and how they will get there. He compares business planning to a road map for entrepreneurial success.[7] For an overview comparison of the lean startup method with business planning, see **Small Business in Action 4-1**.

The use of business plans by Canadian entrepreneurs is increasing. A study of 100 successful Canadian small business owners found that 53 percent used full-scale plans—91 percent had a time frame, and 98 percent were written down. Only 4 percent of Canadian entrepreneurs did not prepare a business plan.[8]

Business plans have both internal and external purposes. For example, when **QHR Technologies**, an Edmonton-based medical billing company, went through a business planning process with the Business Development Centre, the company developed a new plan that included internal measures to improve productivity as well as a means to deal with increased competition from the external environment.[9]

Internally, the business plan provides a blueprint for the business that can help maintain a focus essential to success. The plan can help the entrepreneur in a business start-up and serve as a reference document to assist in the management of the ongoing business. A business plan can also help the entrepreneur by providing a vehicle to evaluate the performance of the operation over time. Business plans should contain both short-term and long-term or growth components for the business. A business plan may also serve an external purpose in that lenders and investors generally require one before lending or investing capital in the venture.

Business plans should be developed for several other reasons: a business plan provides a sense of direction for the business, a test of the idea's viability, assistance in achieving financing, and a clear-cut implementation plan. Stever Robbins, a venture coach, sums up the importance of a business plan this way: a business plan is a tool for understanding how a business operates. You understand how everything connects, how to monitor progress, and to hold yourself accountable.[10]

Successful entrepreneurs also know that business plans need updating if they are going to assist in running a business. Because few things go as perfectly as planned, when an entrepreneur revises their goals and markets, their business plan will need updating also. Julian Brass, founder and CEO of **Notable Life**, an online lifestyle magazine for young professionals, sums up this sentiment when he notes that almost every entrepreneur starts out with a business plan, but the plan almost always has to be revised to suit real market conditions.[11] His comments were echoed by Jeremy Koenig then co-owner of **I Promise Performance**, a Halifax-based healthy lifestyle consultant, who stated, "You can have a plan, but things are going to change. You can't stick to your plan if the market is telling you something different.[12] Writing a plan gives you a starting point, once the business is running, you make changes as the market changes."[13]

The format and emphasis of the business plan vary depending on the user. A plan prepared for a lender should emphasize the entrepreneur's security or collateral position and the cash flow statement. It should show how the loan will be serviced in addition to the other areas. A plan prepared for a potential investor generally requires more detail to compensate for greater risk, including a thorough description of the manager's or management team's capabilities with emphasis on the projected rate of return. A venture capitalist will be interested in knowing the above items and how to liquidate ownership interest in a few years. (More is said about venture capital firms in **Chapter 6**.)

SMALL BUSINESS IN ACTION 4-1

THE LEAN STARTUP VS. BUSINESS PLANNING

The lean startup is a relatively new entrepreneurial process that is changing the way some entrepreneurs are viewing traditional business plans.

The concept is simple, if 75 percent of startups fail, then why spend so much time planning? Entrepreneurs should experiment and get customer feedback as quickly as possible rather than spend time forecasting financial statements or planning next year's marketing. Entrepreneurs using the lean start-up follow three basic principles:

1. Rather than create an elaborate business plan, entrepreneurs draft a short summary about how their product or service can create value.
2. The summary is brought to consumers in a process referred to as *customer development,* gaining feedback on the marketing mix, including customer acquisition.
3. The entrepreneur engages in agile development, that is, building the product concurrently to obtaining customer feedback.

Dropbox and Zappos are succesful companies which have used the Lean Start-up approach.

© Alexander Hermans | Dreamstime.com

[continued]

[continued]

As the entrepreneur is engaging in the process, they are trying to create a product or solution as quickly as possible as well as arranging financial backing. If consumers do not like the product or suggest alternate uses, then the entrepreneur is supposed to pivot and make some changes or corrections. The result is the entrepreneur is able to bring their product to market quickly with the help of consumer feedback.

While the lean startup concept does have its supporters, it also has its detractors. First, many business analysts confirm the concept is not always appropriate for traditional small businesses. The potential business may struggle to get accurate feedback on unfinished products or ideas. Furthermore, some critics point out that some of society's larger problems cannot be solved in a day and that truly great ideas often develop over time. The method also could eliminate good ideas as there is no clear method of deciding when an idea should be removed or eliminated. Finally, research has indicated that the selection of an appropriate business strategy is much more important than speed to market.

Perhaps there is a happy medium for both methods. The lean startup method appears appropriate for developing ideas and getting some feedback. But when the ideas start to take shape, entrepreneurs may want to consider formal business planning with more traditional market research.

Discussion Questions

1. What do you think are some of the advantages and disadvantages of the lean startup method? Please be sure to expand your answer beyond the reasons cited in the case.
2. Students should attempt to replicate the lean startup method. Students should quickly develop an idea and share it with classmates. Students should then report to their peers about the quality of feedback, the quantity and if they would change their concept based on feedback.
3. Use Internet resources to search out companies who have engaged in the lean startup. There are an abundance of successes and failures? Report back to class on your search and what you discovered. Based on your research are you convinced that the lean startup is better than traditional business planning? Why or why not?

WRITING THE PLAN

The business plan should be prepared by the entrepreneur, although it often makes sense to consult with others in its preparation. Sean Wise, entrepreneurship professor, author, and consultant who specializes in helping entrepreneurs find financing, states, "Entrepreneurs should write their own plans. By writing their plans they will gain from the process, they will ask themselves many of the same questions investors would ask them . . . entrepreneurs must go through the writing and investigation process to understand their business."[14] Some aspiring business owners will hire a consultant to write the business plan for them, but this is not advisable. As stated above by Wise, by drafting the business plan, an entrepreneur really gains a firsthand understanding of the opportunity and will have to answer important questions. Additionally, when entrepreneurs draft their business plan, they can make changes to their business model. For example, Tracy MacKinnon dreamed of opening a high-end wedding store in a small town in Nova Scotia. After starting out to write her business plan, she realized the market was not large enough for a premium dress store and further discovered there was a gap in decorating for weddings and other events. Rather than create a new wedding boutique, MacKinnon now runs a profitable decorating and party rental company. She says that if she had not written a business plan that forced her to investigate her idea, she likely would have opened the bridal store and failed.[15]

Writing a business plan can take a significant investment of time. Many aspiring business owners and students look at the different sections and wonder where to start and when, or if, they can possibly finish. Perhaps one of the best ways to deal with this issue is to develop a plan for writing your business plan. The plan should include timelines and break the larger sections of the business plan into smaller, more manageable tasks.

Remember that a business plan starts with a number of headings and what you are doing is filling in the headings and analyzing information. Entrepreneurs will find this process will go a lot easier if they work on one small piece at a time and maintain separate files for each section. The best advice is to start with the marketing plan, because this is the most important section, and go from there. See the excerpt from a sample marketing plan in **Table 4-2**.

TABLE 4-2 Excerpt from Sample Marketing Plan

TOPIC	INFORMATION NEEDED/ACTION REQUIRED	DUE DATE
2. Executive Summary	Make sure it is written for investors; highlight key concepts and sustainable advantage.	December 1, 2020
3. Industry Analysis	Review completed analysis with peers in a similar industry.	September 1, 2021
3a. Future outlooks and trends	Assess the economy and culture in the area; check for any pending legal restrictions; interview potential customers; read trade journals; interview suppliers; make sure to collect Statistics Canada information, and talk to local regional development agent.	July 1, 2021
3b. Analysis of competitors	Determine who the competitors are, determine their marketing mix, interview their customers and suppliers, and assign strengths and weaknesses.	July 1, 2021

COMPONENTS OF THE PLAN LO3

Although each user of the plan may require a different format or emphasis, the components of a comprehensive plan are as follows:

1. Introductory page
2. Executive Summary
3. Industry Analysis
   A. Future outlooks and trends
   B. Analysis of competitors
   C. Market segmentation
   D. Industry and market forecasts
4. Description of Venture
   A. Products and services
   B. Size of the business
   C. Background of the entrepreneur
5. Production Plan
   A. Manufacturing process
   B. Physical plant
   C. Machinery and equipment
   D. Names of suppliers
6. Operational Plan
   A. Description of operations
   B. Flow of goods and services
   C. Technology use
7. Marketing Plan
   A. Target markets and customer profile
   B. Marketing mix (product, price, promotion, place)
   C. Forecasts

8. Organizational Plan
   A. Form of ownership
   B. Identification of partners
   C. Description of management team
   D. Personnel plans, including organizational chart, staffing plans, and so forth
9. Assessment of Risk
   A. Weakness of the business
   B. New technologies
   C. Contingency plans
10. Financial Plans
   A. Pro forma income and cash flow statements
   B. Pro forma balance sheet
   C. Break-even analysis
   D. Sources and application of funds
11. Appendix (contains back-up material)
   A. Letters from customers and suppliers
   B. Market research data
   C. Additional information

Often an entrepreneur will not need this level of comprehension and will opt for a more condensed plan. The general components of a condensed plan are below.

- Prepare a table of contents.
- Prepare a synopsis of the plan in an executive summary and background statement. This should include a mission statement indicating in general what type of business it is and what it is going to do.
- Describe the management team.
- Establish business objectives.
- Plan the marketing approach.
- Describe the selection of the location.
- Determine the physical facilities.
- Plan the financing.
- Plan the personnel.
- Investigate the legal requirements.
- Assess the risk.

The rest of the chapter presents a brief overview of this condensed plan, but readers should be aware that many topics will be further developed throughout the book. For example, while this chapter briefly discusses target markets and customer profiles, **Chapter 7** deals with this in much more depth. And the chapters in **Part 3** discuss the operating aspects of these areas in detail and should be consulted before preparing a business plan.

Appendix 4A at the end of this chapter presents a checklist for a small business plan, and **Appendix 4B** shows two actual business plans following this format. In addition to the business plan outline provided in the appendix, several other business plan templates are available online. Website addresses to some plans including those provided by the BDC and several banks can be found in **Appendix 3A**. Note that a business plan may also be critical when purchasing a business, obtaining a franchise, acquiring financing, and performing other essential activities of the business. The format of the business, however, may vary, depending on whom the plan is intended for.

PREPARE A TABLE OF CONTENTS

A table of contents is mainly for the benefit of outside users of the business plan. It provides an overview of what is included and quick access to various parts of the plan.

PREPARE A SYNOPSIS OF THE PLAN IN AN EXECUTIVE SUMMARY AND BACKGROUND STATEMENT

The executive summary, written at the conclusion of the preparation of the business plan, provides a short summary of the highlights for the reader. Depending on the length of the business plan, the executive summary can be anywhere from one to four pages in length and should stimulate the interest of the reader, especially if the entrepreneur is using the business plan to raise money. The executive summary should sell the business to investors and sell the entrepreneur. This is a very important section of the business plan and should not be taken lightly, as some investors use the summary to determine if the entire business plan is worth reading. For example, Colin MacDonald, co-founder of Clearwater, a national seafood company, is often presented with business plans from aspiring entrepreneurs looking to raise funds. MacDonald states he sees hundreds of business plans a month and often does not get past the executive summary. Generally, the executive summary should address a number of issues or questions that anyone picking up the written plan for the first time would want to know:

- What is the business?
- How will it make money?
- How is this business unique?
- Why will you be successful?
- What advantages does the business have?
- Who are your customers, and why is this segment attractive?
- Who are the individuals starting the business, and why should investors believe in them?
- How much money will you make?
- What are your long-term exit strategies?

DESCRIBE THE MANAGEMENT TEAM

This section should describe the background of the entrepreneur and the management team. For the smaller business, it may simply include a résumé. The qualifications, experience, and education of the owner-manager are important aspects. For example, Kevin O'Leary, one of Canada's—if not North America's—most famous investors who formerly starred in CBC's *Dragons' Den* and now is seen on ABC's *Shark Tank,* says he wants to invest in business owners who have relevant experience in the industry in which they hope to start a business.

ESTABLISH BUSINESS OBJECTIVES

Have clearly thought-out and formally written objectives for the business. The objectives identify goals to be met to achieve the mission and vision of the enterprise. The mission of the business indicates in a general, long-term way what the business is and what it intends to do. A mission statement should guide the firm through long-term decision making. Chris Bart, a management guru, notes that 24 years of studying business has led him to conclude that successful companies must be able to articulate their mission statement and that their mission should reflect what the firm stands for. A vision statement is the ultimate goal for a company; a mission statement is about how a company plans on reaching their vision. Bart states that successful mission statements should focus on customers and staff, provide guidance and inspiration to stakeholders, and assist in the allocation of resources.[16]

After creating mission and vision statements, an entrepreneur will focus on creating goals or objectives. To be effective, an objective must be specific. Specific and quantitative objectives allow meaningful evaluation of the business's performance. Objectives can be set in the following areas for the initial year and for a few years following start-up:

- *Business size.* This includes the size of the physical facilities, financial commitments, and number of employees.
- *Production levels.* The plan should include the number of products, product lines, and unit production anticipated.
- *Performance levels.* Sales, market share, and profit level should all be estimated and may form part of the plan.

PLAN THE MARKETING APPROACH

The next step in the business plan is to develop a marketing plan. Considerable information regarding the calculation of market potential and market share, both essential parts of the marketing plan, is provided in **Chapter 3**. The research and analysis carried out in the previous chapter resulted from an evaluation of the industry. In addition, the business plan should include the growth trends of the industry, the degree of confidence in predicting such trends, the strength and potential entry of new competitors, and a clear statement of the unique position the business is expecting to have within the industry based on the business model. A deeper discussion of industry analysis occurs in **Chapter 7**. The following additional key aspects of a marketing plan should be investigated before starting the business.

Have a Clear Concept of the Target Market.

It is important that the prospective small business owner have a clear idea of who the target customer is and have a well-developed customer profile (as exemplified in **Small Business in Action 4-2**). This profile should include such demographic information as age, income, occupation, and social class, as well as certain personality and lifestyle characteristics.

After determining the target market, the owner can perform the steps discussed in **Chapter 3**: determining market area, market area population, market potential, and market share. Sometimes this information can be obtained by using secondary data alone, but often primary research will be required. **Chapter 7** illustrates a more detailed target market profile.

SMALL BUSINESS IN ACTION 4-2

YOUNG. PROFESSIONAL. CONNECTED.

As Julian Brass was getting ready to start NotableTV, an online site focusing on trendy events and people in Toronto, he spoke the following words, "Every entrepreneur needs to start with a business plan, and like when you're seeking advice and mentorship, it's an ongoing process. You can say, 'This is a golden plan and we're going to be rich in a year,' but often times when you hit the market things are very different than what you perceived before starting out. It's then that you have to return to the drawing board and tweak some things and go from there." Brass notes that one way to stay on target is to picture where you want the business to be in five years and work backward. The ultimate goal will provide a path but how you get there might change. The business plan ensures you know where you are trying to go.

NotableTV did launch, and true to its original vision, much of the focus was on video content, and the only market covered was Toronto. The site attracted much fanfare in the Toronto area, as it quickly became popular among its target group of young, aspiring professionals. While the site, according to Brass, was making money, he became aware that a company of this nature, focusing solely on one city, even Canada's largest, had limited growth potential and other large Canadian markets were becoming ripe for expansion. Additionally, Brass recognized that although video was indeed important to his site, a large segment of the market wanted high-quality written content as well. Brass states, "People in Canada didn't know what '.tv' even was because it had just come out in Silicon Valley, so I had to pivot. There were a bunch of pivots until I got to Notable.ca. Along the way, it constantly evolved." True to his word, Brass revisited his business plan and relaunched NotableTV as a national company with the new name, Notable.ca, and with both video and written content. He also expanded his markets to include Canada's largest cities, Montréal, Calgary, and Vancouver.

Along with the expansion, Brass created **Notable Awards** in Ontario, Québec, and British Columbia/Alberta, with an annual awards dinner and party honouring what Brass describes as the best and brightest millennials and young entrepreneurs in Canada. The finalists, who are chosen by a secret panel of judges, use fan voting on the website as one element of the selection component, resulting in increased traffic for Brass' business. Although some critics contend the awards were created just to increase traffic to Notable.ca, Brass maintains that the awards are another way to recognize the notable people he is already recognizing on his site. His followers seem to agree: the award shows have all been sellouts, including in 2015 when 400 people gathered in Montréal to see P.K. Subban receive a Notable award for his work with the Montréal Children's Hospital.

The website has evolved to become **Notable Life** and attracts 1.5 million visitors a month; it features news and information about notable entrepreneurs, celebrities, events, and restaurants. In addition, and staying somewhat true to its original premise, the site provides links to a vast amount of video content covering everything from trendy events to inspirational lectures. Brass has also incorporated social media into the site with links to Facebook, Twitter, Instagram, and YouTube.

Brass' strategy of national expansion appears to be paying off, as the national launch coincided with the announcement that Lexus and Grey Goose had signed on to advertise on the site. The company's site, which features the tagline "Young. Professional. Connected." is appealing to businesses looking to tap into Notable's target market of successful 25- to 45-year-olds who are interested in what is notable.

Discussion Questions

1. Do you think Brass should have started with a national site, or was he correct in originally focusing on the Toronto market? Why?
2. Why would advertisers want to promote their products on Notable Life's site? What are the advantages and disadvantages?
3. While Notable Life does focuses mostly on Toronto, it does offer some articles about Montréal, Calgary, and Vancouver. Would the Toronto-centric information negatively impact the number of visitors from other regions of the country? Why or why not?
4. Given the small size of many of Canada's cities, should Notable Life focus on becoming a national site, or should it continue to focus on its niche of large urban areas?
5. Instead of branching out to other Canadian cities, would it be a better strategy to expand to larger American urban markets? Why or why not?
6. Visit the Notable Life site, and note the company's strengths and weaknesses. What recommendation would you make to the company's owner, Julian Brass?

Understand the Target Market's Needs, Wants, and Purchasing Habits.

Understanding the target market's needs, wants, and purchasing habits is essential in formulating a marketing strategy. Answers to the following questions may prove valuable:

- Where do, or where will, the target customers purchase the product or service?
- When do, or when will, they purchase it?
- What product or service attributes influence the purchase decision?
- In what quantities will purchases be made?
- Most important, why do customers, or why will they, purchase the product or service?

Once again, the answers to some of these questions may be obtained by using secondary data, but primary research may be required.

Be Aware of Any Uncontrollable Factors That Might Affect the Marketing of the Product or Service.

Several factors external to the business can affect the marketing plan and should be investigated, including those discussed next.

Existing or Pending Legislation Relevant to the Business.

New laws relating to marketing practices, such as advertising, pricing, and manufacturing can have a significant impact on the business and cannot be ignored. This information may be obtained from an office of the federal government or the equivalent provincial or territorial agency.

State of the Economy in the Market.

The prospective small business owner should investigate whether the economy is in a recovery or recessionary period. This trend also can influence the effectiveness of the marketing plan. Statistics Canada and private reports can provide this information.

Extent and Strategies of the Competition.

The entrepreneur should attempt to evaluate the competition and look for competitive strengths in the prospective business. A study found that 33 percent of Canadian entrepreneurs omit this important aspect from their business plans.[17]

Cultural Norms of the Market.

The entrepreneur should ensure that the new business conforms to the social and cultural norms of the market. This is especially important for exporters and for companies moving into new markets (see **Small Business in Action 4-3**). An important aspect in today's business world relates to ethics and social responsibility. This should be an essential part of the business plan and subsequent policies. The business should have a code of ethics covering all operational functions of the business, ensuring honest and ethical behaviour. This code of ethics should be clearly communicated to employees, documented, monitored, enforced, and regularly reviewed. Studies have shown that organizations that display a clear commitment to ethical conduct consistently outperform companies that do not.[18]

SMALL BUSINESS IN ACTION 4-3

OWNERS OF SHOCKBOX HELMET SENSOR APPEAR TO HAVE THE PERFECT PLAN

Impakt Protective was founded in 2010 when co-owner Scott Clark's son was injured in a hockey game. Clark asked his son if he was alright and his son said yes. So his son went back to play the game. It was not until later that night the boy started showing signs of a concussion. The very next day, Clark and his friend Danny Crossman started working on a helmet sensor that would measure the impact of a collision on a player's head to help in determining if further medical attention is warranted.

A short time later, the pair developed Shockbox, a sensor that attaches to helmets and can measure impact and display the results on a smartphone. If a player gets hit in the head, Shockbox will tell the parents, coach, or trainer whether the impact occurred on the front, back, or side and will display the g-force associated with the hit. If the g-force exceeds 50g, Shockbox will display a yellow warning, and if the force exceeds 90g, then the sensor displays an orange signal, which means the player should receive further medical attention. While co-founder Crossman says there is no precise science to determine the g-force that causes a concussion, they used 50g based on research in Junior Hockey. Crossman says, "There is no magic threshold on concussions. Just a certain amount of research and information. A normal hit in the junior or college level shows 96 percent of impacts are below 50g. You have to draw a line in the sand somewhere in order to get a quantitative measure."

When the device was introduced to the market the entrepreneurs thought they had a solid business plan. Clearly a market exists among athletes, parents, sports associations, and insurance companies, who are all interested in preventing head injuries, in particular untreated concussions. Furthermore, they felt the market was large and reachable, and there was what appeared to be a great deal of demand for the product.

Yet when the helmet sensor was commercialized it was met with strong resistance from two surprising sources. Helmet manufacturers warned consumers that adding Shockbox would void any warranty on the helmet. Even though Shockbox weighed only an ounce and was tested by the University of Pittsburgh Medical Center and found to have no negative impact on helmets. Even after Impakt offered to cover the warranty for any helmets damaged due to the device the manufacturers maintained their anti-Shockbox campaign. The other resistance came from coaches who were not overly happy that players may miss playing time due to a diagnosis by Shockbox.

With slow sales, Crossman reached out to competitor i1 Biometrics, who was manufacturing mouth guards that detected concussion, and a friendly takeover was negotiated. While i1 Biometrics, now known as **Athlete Intelligence**, still sold Shockbox, they moved forward with their plan to introduce a new helmet attachment called the Cue. The Cue would be the size of two quarters and offer coaches important player data, such as acceleration and deceleration speeds, as well as monitoring hits to the head. Athlete Intelligence is confident the data will not only be useful for coaches, but also turn them into advocates for the product.

Discussion Questions

1. Do you think Shockbox will ultimately be successful? Why or why not?
2. Review the major aspects of the marketing plan cited in the chapter and answer the following questions: Who will be the target market for the product? How should they promote Shockbox?
3. Given the price tag of $180 for one sensor, do you think parents or sports teams will be willing to pay this much for a product that does not prevent concussions?
4. In groups or as individuals, draft an executive summary for Shockbox that could be used in a business plan. Present this to the class.
5. Athlete Intelligence planned to sell the Cue for roughly $99. Will this make the product more appealing to consumers? Why or why not? Visit the company's current website to see if they were able to stay true to their plan.
6. Are you surprised helmet manufacturers engaged in an education campaign against Shockbox? Why or why not? Do you think their actions were ethical?

Another cultural trend that small businesses should consider addressing relates to environmental issues. As concern for the environment increases, there is mounting evidence that environmental efficiency of organizations leads to reduced waste and operating costs. Although large capital expenditures has been a key concern for small businesses adopting environmental policies, a recent study found that small businesses could become involved in such things as recycling of materials and energy conservation without incurring significant costs.[19]

New Technology That Might Affect the Business.

Regularly review and monitor new technology, as it can represent either opportunities for the business or detrimental competitor strategies. Trade magazines and competitor strategies are good sources of information concerning new technology.

Plan the Marketing Program.

After collecting the above information, the entrepreneur can formulate a marketing program. The essential aspects of the marketing program are as follows:

- *The product or service.* This includes such information as how the product or service is developed, sources of material, and level of quality, variety, and packaging.
- *The distribution system.* This includes determining the path the product or service will take to reach the consumer or ultimate user and may involve selection of wholesalers and retailers.
- *Promotion.* This involves decisions regarding promotion budgets, advertising versus personal selling, and the development of appropriate communications.
- *Pricing.* The development of pricing policies, including the calculation of specific price levels, should be planned. These elements of the marketing program are discussed in more detail in **Chapter 7**.

DESCRIBE THE SELECTION OF THE LOCATION

The next component of a business plan is selecting the location for the business. In setting up a new business, the prospective owner needs to determine the trading area or city in which to locate. Then the owner selects the specific site within the trading area. Internet services such as Google Maps may be helpful in identifying and selecting suitable locations.

The Trading Area.

Several criteria are commonly used to select the trading area. Choosing the general trading area is often more critical for manufacturers than for retailers or service firms, whereas the selection of a specific site within the trade area is generally more important for retailers. The following information is valuable in selecting the trading area.

Economic Base.

Information on population, employment levels, income levels, retail sales, and house values within the trading area may be needed. These elements help small manufacturers determine the availability of employees and expected pay scales. For retail and service firms, they indicate the potential for future sales. The entrepreneur should also examine the trends relating to these key indicators. Most of this information may be obtained from secondary data, such as the government sources listed in **Appendix 3A**.

Attitude of Trading Area toward New Businesses.

Many communities are eager to attract new industry and offer various kinds of incentives for new businesses. Although this benefit is usually more important for manufacturers, any small business owner should contact the local city administration or chamber of commerce regarding incentives. Often these agencies are aware of specific types of businesses their communities need.

Competition.

Competitive firms in a trading area should be noted. A retail or service firm with a fixed geographic market should evaluate various trading areas on the basis of saturation levels for the type of outlet it will establish. There are many methods of calculating the saturation index. A method commonly used in the retailing industry is to divide retail sales of all competitors by the selling space of the trading area:

$$\text{Saturation} = \frac{\text{Competing retail sales}}{\text{Competing retail space}}$$

The saturation index can be compared with other trading areas or industry norms. The higher the index, the more attractive is the opportunity. The statistics needed to compute a saturation index can be obtained from city and provincial or territorial licence and tax records, Statistics Canada reference books, or personal visits.

Costs.

Obviously a key consideration in selecting a trading area is the cost of land and buildings. Another is the cost of required services and expenses once the business is operating. These include such items as utilities, business taxes, and insurance.

The trading area decision can be quantified to allow evaluation among several alternatives.

The Site.

After selecting the trading area, the prospective owner should investigate the following items in selecting the specific site.

Accessibility.

For the manufacturer, this means accessibility of transportation services for incoming supplies and materials as well as ease of shipping the finished product. It might also include the site's accessibility to necessary services, employees of the business, and protection services, such as the fire department.

For the retailer, proximity to major arteries and transit lines and availability of parking is important to ensure maximum customer traffic. Assessing traffic patterns, both pedestrian and vehicular, may be critical to success, especially for retailers of certain types of merchandise (**Chapter 7** further discusses the location considerations for retail goods.) Often the chamber of commerce can provide information on traffic flows.

Site Costs.

The costs of sites within a community usually vary considerably. Generally, the higher-traffic areas are more expensive to buy or lease. The entrepreneur should also investigate other possible costs, such as utilities, taxes, and licences.

Restrictions.

When evaluating a site, any restrictive ordinances, such as zoning by-laws, should be investigated. Such restrictions may hinder current operations and future expansion.

Site History.

The prospective owner should find out whether the site has had several tenants or owners over the years. If this is the case, investigate the reasons for the turnover before proceeding to purchase or lease the site.

Proximity to Other Businesses.

Will the surrounding businesses have a positive or negative influence on the business? Levels of competitiveness and complementarity are two significant factors. **Table 4-3** gives examples of the positive and negative effects of these factors for both noncompetitive and competitive businesses.

TABLE 4-3 Influence of Neighbouring Businesses

POSITIVE INFLUENCE FROM NEIGHBOURING BUSINESSES	NEGATIVE INFLUENCE FROM NEIGHBOURING BUSINESSES
Complementary—for example, a pharmacy by a doctor's office	Uncomplementary—businesses such as a mortuary, tavern, or factory
Competitive—could be positive for shopping goods, such as clothing, automobiles, and motels	Competitive—for non-shopping goods, such as convenience stores

Physical Characteristics.

Size, frontal footage, external facade, contour, and shape are all important considerations in site selection. The business should blend in with surrounding businesses, but it should also be distinctive.

The Buy-or-Lease Decision.

In selecting the specific site, a major consideration is whether to own or lease the premises. Because ownership is generally more expensive, most small businesses find that to reduce the already high risk at the initial stages, leasing is the more attractive option. The small business owner should investigate several factors before signing a lease contract.

Cost of the Lease.

The owner-manager should investigate the cost of the lease, how the rent is calculated, when the payments are due, and what taxes and utilities apply. Most leases are calculated on a per-square-foot basis. In retailing, a percentage of gross sales is often added to the cost of the lease in the form of royalties.

Length of the Lease.

Questions concerning the length of the lease include these: For what length of time will the contract be in place? Is there a provision for renewal at the end of that time? How much notice is required for renewal, termination, or rent increase?

Restrictions.

Potential restrictions on the use of the property should be investigated. Can the site be subleased to someone else? Does anyone have the right to use a part of the property? Are there certain services or products that cannot be sold or manufactured at the site?

Repairs and Leasehold Improvements.

Who is responsible for any repairs and improvements required? When the lease expires, who will own such improvements?

Insurance Coverage.

What insurance does the lessor have on the property? What about liability insurance coverage? What insurance coverage will be required by the lessee?

Running the Business from Home.

The final important consideration in site selection is the possibility of operating the business from home. The accessibility of computer and mobile technology means almost any business can be started and managed from an entrepreneur's home at a significant cost savings over an office or retail space. In his article "The Non-Risk Taker's Guide to Successful Entrepreneurship," Paul Weber, CEO of Entrepreneur Advertising Group, noted that starting at home can save money and allow the entrepreneur to grow the business over time.[20] As mentioned throughout this text, many of Canada's most successful ventures started from the entrepreneur's home. For example, Ottawa-based Shopify is a company that helps other businesses create online storefronts and currently is worth almost $30 billion dollars; it was founded by Tobi Lütke as a home-based business in 2006.[21]

Some situations are particularly suitable for a home-based business. First, if the business is started on a part-time basis, as many are, the costs associated with establishing a home office are minimal. For example, Sunday Steinkirchner, co-founder of **B&B Rare Books** in Manhattan, started the business part time from a home office. She says running a home-based business allowed her to keep her expenses to a minimum and, outside of paying the rent on their apartment, maintaining a website, and merchant service fees, there were no other expenses.[22]

Second, the lower costs associated with starting a business at home reduce the financial risks of a venture that may already carry a high degree of risk. Thus, a home office can serve as a temporary office until the business is more firmly established. Steinkirchner eventually grew her business to the point where she could comfortably establish a storefront.

Third, a home office is suitable for many businesses for which location is of little importance. Many online, service, and even some small manufacturing businesses fit in this category. And finally, locating the business in the home offers several tax-related advantages. **Chapter 12** gives more details on these.

Tobi Lütke founded Shopify as a home-based business when he became unsatisfied with the online storefront software available to him while trying to sell snowboards.

© Ilia Burdun | Dreamstime.com

DETERMINE THE PHYSICAL FACILITIES

In preparing the feasibility analysis outlined in **Chapter 3**, the entrepreneur should have prepared already a detailed estimate of the total capital needed to acquire the building, equipment, furniture, fixtures, and possibly initial inventory. The size of investment in buildings and equipment is typically larger for a manufacturing firm, while the investment in inventory tends to be larger for the retail firm.

Before constructing buildings and purchasing equipment, investigate the relevant building codes and construction standards and obtain required permits.

In addition to these capital requirements and standards, a plan should be made of the operation's flow within the business. This includes such factors as purchasing, inventory control, the production process, the interior layout, and distribution of the finished product. **Chapter 10** discusses all these items in detail.

Insurance.

Small businesses face several risks. **Table 4-4** illustrates four ways that an entrepreneur can deal with risk. The entrepreneur should analyze the extent of such risks and determine whether they threaten the existence of the company. Generally, entrepreneurs transfer risk by buying insurance when the loss would be serious. Insurance coverage for such risks should be purchased before the start of the business.

TABLE 4-4 **Ways to Manage Risk**

METHOD	TYPE OF RISK
Self-insurance	Cover losses out of cash flow (asset values small)
Prevention	Burglar alarms, inspections, education, hiring practices
Avoidance of risk	Leasing, incorporation
Transfer of risk	Purchasing insurance (asset values large)

Types of Insurance.

Common insurable risks for a small business include the following:

- *Loss or damage of property.* This type of coverage protects the business in the case of fire, theft, and similar occurrences.
- *Business interruption.* If one of the above problems occurs, this type of insurance protects the earning power lost because of the occurrence for a short time.
- *Liability and disability.* This coverage includes bodily injury to employees or customers and could include liability coverage for company officials, such as members of the board of directors.
- *Life insurance.* This insurance is usually bought in the form of a group insurance plan or, occasionally, as key employee life insurance. Partners of a business may also want to purchase life insurance for the other partners.

Insurance Decisions.

The entrepreneur faces three insurance-related decisions:

1. What kind of insurance to purchase,
2. How much coverage to take out,
3. From whom to purchase the insurance.

In making these decisions, understanding the following general rules commonly used in the insurance industry is helpful. The first and most important rule is not to risk more than you can afford to lose. In other words, if the prospective loss will put the business into bankruptcy or serious financial difficulty, take out insurance.

Usually the probability of these losses occurring is low, and the associated insurance premiums are also low. The maximum sustainable loss will, of course, vary across firms and times in a particular business.

A second rule of insurance management is not to risk a lot for a little. In implementing this second rule, the premium should be related to the potential loss and treated as savings or costs. For this reason, it is usually advisable to purchase the largest deductible the business can afford. This can result in substantial premium savings.

The third rule is that insurance should be taken out only when absolutely necessary. Insurance always costs more than the expected value of a loss because the premium must also include the insurer's administration and selling costs, plus profit. Thus insurance is economically feasible only when the probability of loss is low and the severity of a potential loss is high. Therefore, in the opposite situation, the best approach may be to take preventive measures and build these losses into the cost or expense structure of the business.

The fourth rule is to buy adequate coverage. The reason is that all property insurance contracts contain a co-insurance clause. The co-insurance clause states that if the amount of insurance purchased on the property is less than some stated percentage (usually 80 percent), the insured will share all partial losses up to the face value of the policy. The purpose of co-insurance is to encourage the small business owner to buy adequate insurance coverage for the business.

The last insurance purchasing rule involves adequately investigating both the insurance company and the agent. Choosing an insurance company with financial stability, satisfactory claims service, and competitive premiums is important, and the selection of the agent may be even more critical. The agent should have a thorough knowledge of insurance, be located where he or she can provide prompt service on claims and inquiries, and possess a genuine interest in clients' needs. Question the agent regarding the claim settlement procedures, cancellation procedures, and premium rates. Many insurance companies now have special policies tailored to small businesses.

Care should be taken to ensure that coverage is current. As replacement costs rise, the level of coverage should increase. Most insurance companies now automatically adjust policies for inflation.

PLAN THE FINANCING

Four major financial aspects of the new business should be planned in advance of opening.

Establish Capital Requirements and Make Feasibility Projections.

As indicated previously, calculations of capital requirements and feasibility projections are made when preparing a feasibility analysis. The results of these calculations form an integral part of the projected income statement for at least the first year of operations and in some cases five years into the future. Although making financial projections involves considerable uncertainty, using average industry financial benchmarks and ratios can increase the reliability of these estimates. These benchmarks and ratios are available through Statistics Canada, Innovation, Science and Economic Development Canada, Dun and Bradstreet, and some provincial or territorial government economic development departments. The website addresses for these are found in **Appendix 3A**, and further explanation of the use of these numbers is made in **Chapter 9** dealing with financial management. In conjunction with the income statement projection, enough information would have likely been obtained to prepare a projected balance sheet and cash flow statement. Although these statements are described fully in Chapter 9, **Table 6-2** in Chapter 6 shows the format of a cash flow statement that would be required in a business plan. It may be advisable for the entrepreneur to enlist the services of an accountant in completing these financial statements. Proper preparation of this financial data is key to obtaining funding from investors and lenders.

Determine Sources of Funding.

The projections discussed above provide an estimate of the funds required to get started and to operate the business. After calculating the required funds, the owner will need to determine a balance between his or her own funds (equity) and borrowed funds (debt). Because raising funds is such a critical area for the small business, **Chapter 6** is devoted entirely to the types of funds required, sources of funding for the small business, and methods of evaluating those sources. Sufficient start-up funding is of critical importance to a new small business.

Plan the Accounting and Bookkeeping Systems.

An essential part of any business is record keeping. Bookkeeping is the recording and classifying of the internal and external transactions of the business. This may be an area that requires professional advice. **Chapter 9** reviews the types of financial records kept and the different types of bookkeeping systems used by small businesses.

Determine Financial Evaluation Measures.

One area crucial to the success of the small business is the financial evaluation of operations. To perform this evaluation, the owner should determine the key indicators of the financial health of the business. These indicators include profit margins, return on investment, and inventory turnover. The owner should also set up a system of regular monitoring and reporting of these areas. This system may also require professional assistance to establish and is discussed in detail in **Chapter 9**.

PLAN THE PERSONNEL

Chapter 11 discusses the operating details of personnel administration for a small business. The following are the major considerations in organizing for the management of personnel.

Administrative Structure.

This involves setting up the responsibility and reporting procedure for all employees of the business. If there are only two owners, the administrative structure takes the form of a clear division of responsibilities. A business with several employees might require an organizational chart.

Employee Recruitment and Training.

Determine the plan for hiring, training, and managing those who will work in the business.

Personnel Policies.

Explicitly state and formally prepare operating policies affecting employees before the business begins operations.

INVESTIGATE THE LEGAL REQUIREMENTS

A small business can be significantly affected by the legal environment in which it operates. Considerable legislation in Canada applies to the ongoing management of the business. Typical areas covered are advertising and promotion, credit, sales contracts, pricing, distribution channels, personnel, record keeping, and financial relationships. Legislation pertaining to each of these aspects of managing the ongoing business is covered in later chapters.

This section discusses the legal requirements relating to the establishment of the business that should be included in the business plan. Some of the most important aspects are selecting the legal structure, investigating which licences are required, and filing for patent protection if necessary. The legal information provided here and in later chapters is not intended to replace the advice and direction of a lawyer but merely to provide a background against which the entrepreneur can work with such professionals more knowledgeably. Care should be taken in the selection of a lawyer. References from business acquaintances or a lawyer referral service could ensure that you enlist the services of a lawyer who has small business experience and expertise.

Legal Structure.

The owner must decide under which legal structure the business will operate. Five types of legal structures can be used (read about how one company evolved through three of them in **Small Business in Action 4-4**). **Table 4-8** (later in this chapter) compares the most common legal structures for small and medium-sized businesses.

SMALL BUSINESS IN ACTION 4-4

QUICKSNAP: THE EVER-CHANGING OWNERSHIP STRUCTURE

When David Reynolds of Halifax, Nova Scotia, started university, he had no idea what he wanted to do with his life. Reynolds says, "I went to university with no real plan or ambition to do anything. I went to university because it's what all my friends were doing." A short time after enrolling at Mount Saint Vincent University, Reynolds attended a lecture on entrepreneurship, and, as part of a class assignment, he had to create and run a small business for a day. Reynolds immediately fell in love with the concept of entrepreneurship. He notes, "I loved the thought of being my own boss. I was always inventing little things, but it never really occurred to me that I could create a company from one of my ideas. That class lecture and the small assignment showed me I could."

Reynolds then knew he wanted to be an entrepreneur but did not have a business idea. A short time later, while waiting impatiently for his friend to tie his shoes, Reynolds had a light bulb moment. He states, "People hate tying their shoes. What if they didn't have to do this? What if there was a way to clip the laces together?" A short time later QuickSnap, a shoe-fastening device, was born. When the company first started, it was structured as a sole proprietorship; as Reynolds quips, "It was just me and my idea." Reynolds says the advantage of being a sole proprietor allowed him to work when he wanted to work, an important aspect as he was a full-time student. Reynolds soon realized that starting a company, especially a manufacturing business, was a lot of work, and he brought in his friend and his brother as partners. The partners brought in some additional capital and, more importantly, some extra help in getting the business off the ground. Together they shared the work and combined their strengths. Reynolds says that forming a partnership was cheaper and easier than forming a corporation: "We drafted a partnership agreement, we all signed it, and we became partners." Together the three managed to bring the product to market, albeit in a small way, in local sporting goods stores.

Reynolds felt that the business needed some additional marketing dollars and soon started pursuing outside investors. He pitched his business idea to a variety of banks and traditional lenders and managed to sell his concept to fellow student Riad Byne, who was attending Mount Saint Vincent University after completing military duty in Afghanistan. Reynolds notes, "At this time, I knew that we needed a formal structure, and the business went through the process of incorporating. We needed the advantages of a private corporation, we needed to be able to issue shares to investors, ensure that everyone involved in the ownership group had limited liability, and so forth."

The business partners eventually brought their idea to the mainstream media, pitching the product on CBC's *Dragons' Den*, where they successfully brokered a deal for $125,000 investment in return for 50 percent ownership in the company. While Reynolds is no longer the CEO, something he attributes to giving up too much ownership control too early to outside investors, he does say he has done well on his investment in the business and is pleased to report that Quicksnap landed several large deals after *Dragons' Den*, including Walmart and Sport Chek.

Discussion Questions

1. Based on the information in the case, what are some of the advantages and disadvantages of the three major forms of business (sole proprietorship, partnership, and corporation)?
2. What do you think are some of the potential markets for Quicksnap? How would you promote the product?
3. Were you surprised to learn the entrepreneurs agreed to give up 50 percent ownership of their business for $125,000? Why or why not?
4. Would you have sold off shares in your business like Reynolds, who was trying to grow his business quickly, or would you prefer the slow-growth method where you maintain 100 percent ownership of your company? Why?

1. Sole Proprietorship.

In a sole proprietorship, the business is owned by a single individual. The proprietor has perfect freedom of operation; when business decisions are made or when actions are taken, it is not necessary to get anyone else's consent. Similarly, all profits are the property of the owner and need not be shared with anyone else. There are, however, certain disadvantages to the one-owner organization. Limited personal assets, for example, do not encourage lenders and cannot always provide the capital needed to meet the needs of the business. But perhaps the biggest disadvantage is the proprietor's personal liability for business debts; in case of business failure, the owner's home, automobile, stocks, cash, and other personal assets may be seized by creditors to satisfy the debts of the business. Registration with the provincial or territorial government is normally required and can help protect the name of the business. **Table 4-5** lists the advantages and disadvantages of a sole proprietorship.

TABLE 4-5	Advantages and Disadvantages of a Sole Proprietorship
ADVANTAGES	**DISADVANTAGES**
1. Simple and inexpensive to start	1. Unlimited liability
2. Offers individual control over operations, profits, and so on	2. Often more difficult to obtain financing
3. Fewer forms and reports to fill out	3. The personal tax rate may be higher than the corporate rate
4. Some tax advantages	4. The business terminates on owner's death

2. Partnership.

In most ways, partnerships are similar to sole proprietorships except that partnerships include two or more people. Partnerships typically provide increased resources and complementary abilities. As such, some business experts consider partnerships an effective strategy to lessen risk when starting a company. *Canadian Business*' report on the fastest-growing firms in Canada in 2018 found that 31 percent of the companies were run by two or more partners.[23] For example, Michele Romanow, featured in the **Small Business Profile** of this chapter, partnered with Anatoliy Melnichuk and Ryan Marien for most of her early businesses, including Buytopia and Snap Saves. Romanow says Marien helped the partners initially get over their fear of hearing the word "no." The trio also opted not to divide tasks and decision making but to tackle major issues together using a simple rule: if two of them voted one way, then the decision was final. Melnichuk says anyone overhearing their discussions might have thought they were having brutal arguments when, in fact, the partners were just passionate.[24]

Partnerships can also allow people to share the heavy workload that is involved in running a company. Shane Graham, Karl Moussa, and brothers Aaron Hardy and David Hardy founded **Golf Without Limits**, a company based in Waterloo, Ontario, that operates an interactive indoor golf centre. The partnership works because they share a similar vision of franchising their concept, and they divide the workload: Graham runs the centre, Moussa looks after client services, Dave manages the physical facilities, and Aaron oversees marketing and finance. Another positive partnership is discussed in **Small Business Beginnings 4-1**.

SMALL BUSINESS BEGINNINGS 4-1

POSITIVE PARTNERSHIP

In the realm of small business, partnerships often go awry. However Jason Cunningham and Derek Brock have found that their partnership in establishing **Jugo Juice**, a successful Calgary-based juice-bar chain, has made life easier for both of them. Cunningham and Brock had both been managers for the Starbucks franchise when they decided to leave the company to start Jugo Juice as a franchise in 1999. Brock indicates that their personalities and skill sets complement each another: "Jason is the more serious one and I'm more friendly." They also say that having a partner to take over when one is not having any luck can be a distinct advantage. When the dynamics behind one personality fail, the other can step in. They have found that the partnership can more effectively manage staff and create and maintain business relationships. They have also found that the partnership provides increased flexibility to get away from the business knowing there is someone to take over. "It definitely helps to get some feedback instead of making a solo decision," says Cunningham. These partners seem to work well together and share the same values and vision for the company. This relationship has led to a successful business with over 100 franchises in operation today.

One major drawback of partnerships is the increased possibility of conflict. Of course conflict is not always a bad thing says Rajen Ruparell, co-founder of Endy, Canada's leader in online mattress sales. Ruparell says all his close partnerships resulted in some conflict as a result of passion and intensity, which usually lead to long-term success.[25] A recent study found that fewer than 20 percent of partnerships last past the five-year mark. It is therefore essential to have a conflict-resolution strategy worked into a partnership agreement and perhaps a buyout clause, in which one partner can purchase the business from the other. Nik Grgic and Karl Gannon, co-CEOs of Western Canada-based **FourQuest Energy**, one of the fastest-growing companies in Canada, offers the following advice to business partners: (1) make sure you get along; (2) play to your strengths; (3) leave time to brainstorm; and (4) share the pain when things are not going well.[26]

Rajen Ruparell, co-founder of Endy, says conflict among passionate partners can actually lead to long-term success.

Photo courtesy of Endy

Table 4-6 summarizes the advantages and disadvantages of partnerships. There are two kinds of partnerships a small business might use:

1. *Limited partnership.* In a limited partnership, one or more partners obtain limited liability in exchange for not taking an active part in the day-to-day management of the business or acting on behalf of the company. These partners, often called *silent partners,* usually provide only the financial investment as their part of the ownership interest. Small businesses are increasingly using this form of ownership because silent partners constitute an important source of equity funding. In addition, limited partnerships offer some tax advantages for the silent partner while retaining the positive aspects of sole proprietorship for the entrepreneur.

TABLE 4-6 Advantages and Disadvantages of a Partnership

ADVANTAGES	DISADVANTAGES
1. Simple and inexpensive to start	1. Unlimited liability
2. Pooling of financial and skill resources	2. Death of a partner terminates the partnership unless a provision to the contrary is specified in the partnership agreement
3. Tax advantages (i.e., income splitting)	3. Greater possibility for disagreements (buy-sell agreements should be drawn up in the event that a partner wants to leave the business)

2. *General partnership.* When the partners share in the management or control of the business, it is referred to in legal terms as a *general partnership.* The most obvious advantage to this form of organization over the proprietorship form is that added capital is made available by combining the assets of the partners, and money is usually easier to borrow because the partners share debts. Similarly, the personal abilities of the partners are complemented, and they may succeed together when neither could alone. However, each

partner by law is equally responsible for all the debts of the partnership, regardless of the amount of capital contributed and regardless of any agreement among them to the contrary. Also, any one partner can bind the entire partnership in a business arrangement, even if it is contrary to the wishes or judgment of the majority. The general partnership has other disadvantages as well, such as the termination of the business by the death or withdrawal of any one of the partners and the inability of a partner to sell or assign his or her interest in the partnership without the consent of all other partners. However, both of these conditions or eventualities can be circumvented by appropriate provisions in a written partnership agreement, which should be prepared with the consultation of a lawyer. Although not legally required to form a general partnership, such an agreement is nonetheless advisable, even among relatives and close friends (see **Small Business in Action 4-5**). At a minimum, it should specify the following:

1. Duration of the partnership.
2. Administrative responsibilities and authority of each partner.
3. Withdrawals and salaries of the partners.
4. Provision for the arbitration of policy disputes among the partners.
5. Provisions for the withdrawal of partners or the admission of additional partners.
6. Amount of capital invested by each partner.
7. Division of profit or loss. (Regardless of the amount of capital invested, general partners must share profit or loss equally unless there is an agreement among the partners to the contrary.)
8. Distribution of assets in the event of dissolution. (As in the case of profits or losses, this distribution must be on an equal basis unless otherwise agreed on in writing.)
9. Settlements in the event of death or disability of a partner. This might include a buy-sell agreement funded with business life insurance in amounts equal to the interest of each partner; thus the surviving partner(s) would be assured of full title to the business, and the deceased partner's estate would be assured of receiving the full value of his or her share of the business. In the absence of such an agreement, the business might well be forced into liquidation to satisfy the demands of the deceased partner's estate.

In a general partnership, unlimited liability applies to all partners.

SMALL BUSINESS IN ACTION 4-5

SHOULD PARTNERS HAVE A SHOTGUN?

"Should partners have a shotgun?" Perhaps the question makes you think of the Old West or organized crime movies, but the term *shotgun* has a very different meaning in partnership agreements.

Essentially, the term is used to describe a clause where one business partner can make a cash offer for the other partner's share of the business. The person being offered the money for their share of the business is usually left with only two choices: (1) accept the offer and take the money or (2) match the partner's offer and assume the partner's share of the business.

People's opinions of shotgun clauses in partnerships differ. Some argue that they are useful tools that allow for a quick end to a partnership that is no longer working. Furthermore, the cash offer is usually at a premium because the person making the offer risks getting removed from the business if he or she makes a low offer. Others argue that shotgun clauses are often used too quickly when other dispute resolutions could be used to save partnerships, that

Elnur/Shutterstock.com

[continued]

[continued]

shotguns favour the partner with the most resources, and that executing a shotgun clause normally ends any personal relationships among partners. For example, when partners Michel Boucher and Chuck Buchanan had a falling out over future plans for their company **Flightexec**, based in London, Ontario, Boucher exercised the partner's shotgun clause. The ten-year partnership which saw the pair take Flightexec out of receivership to a company with over $20 million in sales quickly ended. Buchanan admits that the use of the shotgun clause left him unsettled.

Discussion Questions

1. If you were to ever join a partnership, would you want to have a shotgun clause? Why or why not?
2. What are some of the advantages and disadvantages of a shotgun clause?
3. What alternatives would you suggest to using a shotgun clause?
4. Would you ever enter into a partnership with someone if they had previously used a shotgun clause to terminate a partnership? Why or why not?

3. Corporation.

The corporation, or limited company, is becoming an increasingly popular form for structuring a small business. Innovation, Science and Economic Development Canada reports that more than 40 percent of all self-employed businesses with paid help and 24 percent of small business without paid help in Canada were incorporated in 2008.[27] Moreover, Statistics Canada reports that incorporated companies grew at an annual rate of 3.9 percent compared with 1 percent for unincorporated businesses.[28] The corporation is a legal entity that is separate and distinct from the shareholders of the business. The chief advantages of the corporation are (1) continuity in existence, (2) easy transferability of ownership interest, and (3) limited liability of shareholders. The corporation is long-lived, being able to continue in existence up to the time limit granted in its charter, which may even be granted in perpetuity. In contrast, other forms of organization may cease abruptly with the death of the proprietor or a partner. Ownership in a corporation is easily transferred merely by the sale or exchange of stock; permission of other shareholders is not required. Care should be taken in drafting a shareholder agreement to facilitate the smooth transition of the ownership of the company in the event that a key owner leaves the business. Legal liability of owners or shareholders for suits for personal injury or other activities connected with operating the business is limited to the amount of funds invested in the business. The corporate form of business organization is also more attractive for raising equity capital because capital can be more readily obtained from many more sources and because of the legal limited liability of corporate shareholders.

A corporation has certain disadvantages, however. Its activities are limited to those specifically granted in its charter. Similarly, its geographic area of operations is limited to the province or territory granting its charter until permission is secured from each of the other provinces or territories in which it desires to operate; this means that additional filing fees must be paid and additional legal requirements observed. The corporation must make numerous reports for taxation and other purposes in each jurisdiction in which it does business; not only has federal and provincial or territorial regulation of corporations been increasing for some time, but the paperwork required also increases greatly as the corporation grows in size.

The day-to-day operations of a corporation are handled by a manager who is appointed by and reports to a board of directors. The board of directors is elected by the shareholders. Often in very small businesses, the manager, director, and major shareholder are the same person. Many small businesses have found it valuable to enlist the services of lawyers, accountants, and other noncompeting business people to serve on their boards of directors.

The vast majority of incorporated small businesses are private companies. For a business to qualify as a private company, the following conditions must exist:

- The right to transfer shares is restricted, usually requiring the approval of the board of directors.
- The number of shareholders is limited to 50. The company cannot sell new shares publicly.

Table 4-7 summarizes the advantages and disadvantages of a corporation.

TABLE 4-7 Advantages and Disadvantages of a Corporation

ADVANTAGES	DISADVANTAGES
1. The continuity of the business exists even if the owner dies.	1. The cost to incorporate generally ranges from $800 to $1,200.
2. The owners have limited liability.	2. There is a greater reporting requirement by government.
3. The business may have a manager with professional training or expertise.	3. Flexibility may be reduced because of the binding provisions of the corporate charter.
4. It is easier to raise funds because lenders and equity investors usually look more favourably on incorporated companies.	4. Losses cannot be deducted from other personal income of the owner.
5. The corporate tax rate on small businesses can be lower than the personal rate.	5. Lenders often require a personal guarantee, negating the advantage of limited liability.
6. Incorporation can assist in establishing commercial credibility.	
7. Liability insurance may be less expensive.	

Steps in Incorporation.

Most entrepreneurs regard incorporation as a very complex process that requires a lawyer's assistance. Although it is advisable for a small business to enlist the services of a lawyer to assist in incorporating the business, some entrepreneurs with relatively uncomplicated businesses have incorporated their businesses successfully on their own. Recently, incorporation software has been developed to help entrepreneurs with self-incorporation. Incorporating a business involves four steps:

1. *Selection of a name for the business.* This name must be submitted to and approved by the provincial or territorial government department that handles incorporation. The selection can be facilitated by doing a computer search to ensure that no similar names are currently being used.
2. *Development of the share structure, directors, restrictions on share transfers, and so on.* The owner must determine the number of shares to authorize, the number of shares to issue, the number of directors, the timing of meetings, and approvals required for shares to be bought or sold.
3. *A description of company operations.* This section describes what the business can and cannot do.
4. *Acquisition of the necessary supplies.* This includes such items as the corporate stamp, the minute book, and the necessary journals and ledgers.

Table 4-8 offers a comparison of the most common legal structures of small and medium-sized businesses.

TABLE 4-8 Factors of Three Forms of Business Formation

FACTORS	PROPRIETORSHIP	PARTNERSHIP	CORPORATION
Ownership	Individual	No limit on number of partners; must be at least one general partner	No limit on number of shareholders
Liability of owners	Individual liable for business liabilities	In general partnership, individuals all liable for business liabilities; in limited partnership, partners are liable for amount of capital contribution	Amount of capital contribution is limit of shareholder liability; in closely held corporations, owners may have to become personally liable for some debts

[continued]

[continued]

TABLE 4-8 *Continued*

FACTORS	PROPRIETORSHIP	PARTNERSHIP	CORPORATION
Costs of starting business	None other than filing fees for trade name	Partnership agreement, legal costs, and minor filing fees for trade name; limited partnership requires more comprehensive agreement, hence higher cost	Created only by statute; articles of incorporation, filing fees, taxes, and fees for provinces and territories in which corporation registers to do business
Continuity of business	Death dissolves the business	Death or withdrawal of one partner terminates partnership unless partnership agreement stipulates otherwise; in limited partnership, death or withdrawal of one limited partner has no effect on continuity	Greatest form of continuity; death or withdrawal of owner(s) will not affect legal existence of business
Transferability of interest	Complete freedom to sell or transfer any part of business	General partner can transfer interest only with consent of all other general partners; terms for transferring interest in limited partnerships outlined in the partnership agreement	Public corporations allow for flexible transfer on open exchanges; closely held corporations usually stipulate rules that govern the transfer of shares
Capital requirements	Capital raised only by loan or increased contribution by proprietor	Loans or new contributions by partners require change in partnership agreement	Public corporations may raise capital by selling stock or bonds or borrowing debt; closely held corporations may sell shares or acquire debt, but the shareholders often must personally guarantee debt
Management control	Proprietor makes all decisions and can act immediately	All partners have equal control and majority rules; in limited partnership, only general partners have management control of business	Majority shareholders have most control from legal point of view; day-to-day control in hands of management who may or may not be major shareholders
Distribution of profits and losses	Proprietor responsible and receives all profits and losses	Depends on partnership agreement and investment by partners	Shareholders can share in profits by receipt of dividends; will often depend on shareholders' agreement
Attractiveness for raising capital	Depends on capability of proprietor and success of business	Depends on capability of partners and success of business	With limited liability for owners, more attractive as an investment opportunity

4. Co-operative.

The co-operative is used infrequently by small businesses although with the growing trend in social entrepreneurship, which was discussed in previous chapters, this may start to change. One example of a small and growing co-operative is **Just Us! Coffee Roasters Co-op**, located in Nova Scotia. The company was started by several friends who wanted to make a difference in how coffee was sold and purchased and help farmers in developing countries. The owners say, "We called ourselves Just Us! because we were just a small group of friends who had very little in the way of business experience or resources but really believed we could do our bit for social 'justice.'" The co-op's roasted coffee recently won the award for the best Fair Trade product in Canada, and the co-op has enjoyed significant growth while staying true to its mission: "People and the planet before profits."[29] In most respects, the strengths and weaknesses of a co-operative are similar to those of a corporation (as we saw in **Table 4-7**). The distinguishing feature is that in a co-operative (which needs a minimum of six members) each member has only one vote, whereas in a corporation each voting share has a vote.

Just Us! Coffee Roasters Co-op

Just Us! Coffee Roasters Co-op has enjoyed significant growth while operating as a co-operative in Nova Scotia. Visit the company website to read about their beginnings and recent successes.

Photo and logo courtesy of Just Us! Coffee Roasters

5. Joint Ventures.

A joint venture is an agreement between one or more sole proprietors, partnerships, or corporations to participate in a business venture. Although similar to a partnership in many ways, this form of business allows for individual ownership of assets in the venture. Items such as capital cost allowance can be used by either party, depending on the need. Other advantages and disadvantages are similar to those in a partnership (shown in **Table 4-6**).

Licences and Taxes.

Before starting a business, the prospective owner should investigate the required licences and the taxes that may be payable to the government. Licences and taxes can be levied by federal, provincial or territorial, and municipal governments, and these requirements differ among industries. The following are the most common licences and taxes that apply to the small business.

Federal Government.

1. *Income tax.* The income tax is a tax on both companies and individuals earning income from a business operating in Canada. The rates vary by province or territory and by industry (see **Chapter 12**). Although the income tax payments are made to the federal government, part of this amount is transferred to the province or territory in which the business earns income. Some provinces and territories now collect their own business income tax.
2. *Goods and services tax.* The goods and services tax (GST) is a value-added tax levied on many sellers of goods and services by the federal government. The tax, which currently is 7 percent of the sale price, is collected from the purchaser by the seller and remitted to the government quarterly based on earnings and industry. Although the GST has met with considerable resistance from business and consumers, it has been an effective method for increasing government revenues. Certain exemptions from the GST, relating to the size of the business and type of merchandise sold, are available. Small business owners should consult Canada Revenue Agency for the information about how the GST applies to their business and for information about obtaining a GST remittance number.
3. *Excise tax.* The excise tax is an extra tax imposed on certain goods sold in Canada. Payment is made by the manufacturer and is a hidden component in the cost of purchasing those goods.

Provincial or Territorial Government.

1. *Income tax.* A percentage of federal income tax payable is assessed by the provinces and territories. Some (Ontario, Québec, and Alberta) collect this tax. In other provinces and territories, the federal government collects the tax and remits a portion to the province or territory.
2. *Licences.* Many types of businesses require a provincial or territorial licence to operate. Some of these businesses may also require bonding.
3. *Sales tax.* Most provinces and territories levy retail sales taxes on tangible products sold or imported. This tax is collected by the retailer from the purchaser at the time of the sale and remitted to the government in much the same manner as the goods and services tax. Many businesses have found the administration of the sales tax more difficult since the introduction of the HST/GST.

Municipal Government.

1. *Licences.* Municipalities (cities) are authorized to license all businesses operating within their boundaries.
2. *Property taxes.* Municipalities are also authorized to levy property taxes on the real estate on which a business operates.
3. *Business taxes.* Other taxes levied on businesses by a municipality might be for water use or other services.

Intellectual Property Protection.

As many entrepreneurs create new products or processes, a critical measure for ensuring their success is to secure legal protection. This protection could be required for a patent, trademark, industrial design, or copyright. Copyrights are for literary, artistic, musical, and dramatic works. Industrial designs include shapes, patterns, or ornamentation of an industrially produced object. Trademarks are words, symbols, or slogans that represent origins of goods and services. A patent, the most commonly obtained protection for a small business, is a right granted by the government to an inventor to exclude others from making, using, or selling the invention in Canada for 17 years.

It is important for the inventor to record the date of the invention and file for the patent as soon as possible. Registration of a patent may be made through the Office of Consumer Affairs or the Commissioner of Patents. Other helpful information about intellectual property protection can be obtained through the **Canadian Intellectual Property Office**. In Canada, if the patent has been used publicly or sold within the previous two years, it may not be granted. A patent agent or lawyer can provide valuable assistance in the patenting process and may be essential if infringement on the patent occurs later. Careful screening to ensure that the invention is new, useful, and a result of inventive ingenuity is used in the patent approval.

Two steps are required to register a patent:

1. Conduct a search at the patent office to ensure that the idea is not already registered.
2. File an application, the formal request for the patent, which includes a description of the idea.

A patent application may take from one to three years to receive an approval. Nearly 29,000 patent applications are received each year in Canada, and approximately 24,000 are approved. A listing of patents is available for public perusal at most public libraries and online through the **Canadian Intellectual Property Office database**. Similar procedures for obtaining patents are followed in registering trademarks, industrial designs, and copyrights. Applications for these items are also obtained through the Office of Consumer Affairs or the Commissioner of Patents.

ASSESS THE RISK

Every new venture will be faced with some potential hazards, given the particular industry and competitive environment. It is important that the entrepreneur make an *assessment of risk* in the following manner. First, the entrepreneur should indicate the potential risks to the new venture. Next should be a discussion of what might happen if these risks become reality. Finally, the entrepreneur should discuss the strategy that will be employed to either prevent, minimize, or respond to the risks should they occur. Major risks for a new venture could result from a competitor's reaction; weaknesses in the marketing, production, or management team; changes in government policies; and new advances in technology that might render the new product obsolete.

One way to identify risk in an industry or a marketplace is to use Michael Porter's Five Forces model. The model assesses risk and the nature of competition in a number of important categories. These categories include the following:

- *Rivalry among competitors:* This deals with the strength and intensity of rivalry between competitors. Are competitors pursuing a price penetration strategy or a profit maximization strategy? How do the competitors react to new competition? For example, one entrepreneur decided to start manufacturing Styrofoam plates and cups for the Québec and Atlantic Canada markets. He thought that since there were only two competitors in the industry who also manufactured a number of other products, they would not deal aggressively with a new entrant who could only take a small portion of their market share. Unfortunately, he did not pay enough attention to past history; previously another entrepreneur tried a similar strategy only to see the competitors drop their prices dramatically to force the new entrant out of business. Shortly after introducing his products to the market, both competitors started selling their plates and cups below cost and forced him out of business.
- *Threat of new entrants:* How easy is it to enter the marketplace? What financial and knowledge barriers exist? If your business thrives, how quickly can someone else jump in and compete in the same niche?
- *Supplier power:* How dependent would you be on suppliers? How far are suppliers from your operation? What would you do if you were to lose important suppliers or if a supplier started competing against you?
- *Buyer power:* How dependent are you on your buyers? For example, if you start a book publishing company, you will be very dependent on Amazon. How many buyers are there? What position are they in to negotiate discounts? How far away from your buyers are you?
- *Threat of substitutions:* Are there readily available substitute products in the marketplace? What is the pricing strategy for the substitutes? Is there a chance of consumers demanding a substitute product?

USING AND IMPLEMENTING THE BUSINESS PLAN

The business plan is designed to guide the entrepreneur through the first year of operations. It is important that the implementation of the strategy contain control points to ascertain progress and to initiate contingency plans if necessary. Some of the controls needed in manufacturing, marketing, financing, and the organization are discussed in subsequent chapters. Most important to the entrepreneur is that the business plan not end up in a drawer somewhere once the financing has been attained and the business launched.

MEASURING PLAN PROGRESS

During the introductory phases of the start-up, the entrepreneur should determine the points at which decisions should be made about whether the goals or objectives are on schedule. Typically, the business plan projections will be made on a 12-month schedule. However, many successful entrepreneurs know they cannot wait 12 months to see whether the plan has been successfully achieved. Instead, on a frequent basis (i.e., the beginning of each month), the entrepreneur should check the profit and loss statement, cash flow projections, and information on inventory, production, quality, sales, collection of accounts receivable, and disbursements for the previous month. This feedback should be simple but should provide the business owner with current information in time to correct any major deviations from the goals and objectives outlined. Roger Pierce, co-founder of Toronto-based **BizLaunch**, a company that trains entrepreneurs in business startups, notes, "Measures, especially ones that relate to your customers, are crucial. The more detailed information that you have about your business, particularly your customers, may determine if you succeed or fail."[30] Knowledge is, as they say, power. A brief description of each of these control elements is given below:

- *Inventory control.* By controlling inventory, the firm can ensure maximum service to the customer. The faster the firm gets back its investment in raw materials and finished goods, the faster that capital can be reinvested to meet additional customer needs.
- *Production control.* Compare the cost figures estimated in the business plan with day-to-day operation costs. This will help to control machine time, worker hours, process time, delay time, and downtime cost.
- *Quality control.* This will depend on the type of production system but is designed to make sure that the product performs satisfactorily.
- *Sales control.* Information on units, dollars, specific products sold, price of sales, meeting of delivery dates, and credit terms is useful to get a good perspective of the sales of the new venture. In addition, an effective collection system for accounts receivable should be set up to avoid aging of accounts and bad debts.
- *Disbursements.* The new venture should also control the amount of money paid out. All bills should be reviewed to determine how much is being disbursed and for what purpose.

UPDATING THE PLAN

The most effective business plan is outdated on the day it is finished. The very next day brings changes in the market, economy, and customer base. Successful entrepreneurs know that they cannot update their business plans every day, but they should continually monitor them, making small adjustments and notes as needed. At the very minimum, plans should receive significant updates twice a year, although many entrepreneurs do so on a quarterly basis (Expansion plans offer another opportunity to revisit the business plan, as illustrated in **Small Business in Action 4-6**.) Of particular importance is the need to update the marketing plan as the year unfolds. Many key goals and strategies are encompassed in this section of the business plan, and they need to be reviewed and controlled throughout the year. As noted earlier, by Julian Brass founder of Notable, "You can say, 'This is a golden plan and we're going to be rich in a year,' but often times when you hit the market things are very different than what you perceived before starting out. It's then that you have to return to the drawing board and tweak some things and go from there."[31]

SMALL BUSINESS IN ACTION 4-6

BUSINESS PLAN: THE FOUNDATION OF BUSINESS EXPANSION

Alyssa Furtado, of Toronto, co-founder of **Ratehub**, describes herself as a comparison shopper. She says she cannot imagine buying a hotel room without using Expedia or booking a flight without comparing prices using Kayak. Furtado says it was her preference for comparison shopping that prompted her to start Ratehub in 2010, when she noticed there were no websites offering Canadians comparison pricing for financial products. Furtado says that Canadians were overpaying for banking products as they could not easily compare mortgage rates, credit cards, or interest payments on saving accounts. With this in mind, Ratehub.ca was born.

Ratehub initially earned money in two ways, or as Furtado describes it, they were a double-sided platform. The company initially made money through advertising, including the use of banner ads, and receiving a marketing fee from brokers, banks, and financial institutions when a customer filled out a mortgage or credit card application. Furtado says her company can earn $100 for each credit card application and $200 for a mortgage application.

Then in 2015 Ratehub decided to expand and start their own mortgage brokerage company to service some of consumers visiting the site. Furtado says it was a big risk; it meant the firm was going from one that was primarily in the business of selling leads to brokers to becoming a competitive, in-house brokerage. While the potential for profits was significant—Ratehub could earn four times the money acting as a broker compared to selling their leads—expansion would come with significant risk.

There was potential to lose some or even all their current brokers, who were responsible for most of the company's revenue, if they stopped working with Ratehub. In fact, when Ratehub's plans became public, their largest customer, representing roughly 50 percent of their revenue, informed Furtado they would stop doing business with Ratehub the second they opened their own brokerage. But Furtado pressed on with her expansion plans and her revenue soared. Even with filling some of the mortgage leads in-house rather than selling them to brokers, Ratehub's popularity as Canada's number one online mortgage comparison site allowed her to keep all but one client.

With this successful expansion, Ratehub added comparison information on credit cards and other financial products. Ratehub reported 2016 revenue of $8 million. The company saw revenue soar in 2017 and 2018, with annual growth in the 100 percent range and are planning to reach $100 million by 2021.

A large part of Furtado's growth depends on her new expansion plans, which include offering insurance product comparisons on Ratehub. She describes the current insurance market as cumbersome: consumers must submit significant personal information, often in person, to a salesperson or a broker prior to seeing any rates. Furtado thinks the addition of insurance comparisons to RateHub will fuel revenue growth by tapping into the lucrative insurance advertising and referral business.

Even with Ratehub's current success, there are some skeptics who believe the tradition of Canadians trusting banks much more than consumers do in other countries will continue. The skeptics say Canadians do not engage in as much comparison shopping as consumers elsewhere, thus limiting Ratehub's potential pool of customers. Canadians also do not traditionally do comparison shopping for insurance products, normally purchasing these from trusted brokers, making them less inclined to submit personal applications online in this market also.

Ratehub does have its supporters though, including Boston's Elephant Partners, a venture capital company who invested $12 million into the firm. Elephant Partners no doubt saw that there was very little competition in Canada for Ratehub and likely thought the growing, tech-savvy, millennial population would not be as brand loyal to banks and insurance brokers as their parents.

Discussion Questions

1. Many consumers see Ratehub as a consumer-friendly site offering comparison pricing on financial products. Do you think consumers would think Ratehub is acting ethically by also operating their own brokerage? Why or why not?
2. If you were a broker who worked with Ratehub for five years purchasing leads from the company, would you think Ratehub was acting ethically by starting their own in-house brokerage and keeping some of the leads for themselves? Why or why not?
3. Ratehub has updated their business plan numerous times since the company was founded in 2010. What are some of the advantages and disadvantage with their changing strategy?
4. Visit Ratehub's website. What do you see are some of the website's strengths and weaknesses?
5. Would you have invested money in Ratehub? Why or why not?

LEARNING OBJECTIVES SUMMARY

LO1 **Organizing your own business has several advantages and disadvantages. The advantages of having a hand in determining the type of business, equipment, employees, inventory, and market are balanced against the disadvantages of uncertainty concerning demand, unforeseen problems, and the time required to establish the business. While buying a franchise or other business brings much more certainty, many decisions are not made by the entrepreneur.**

LO2 **A business plan provides a sense of direction for the business, determines the viability, assists in obtaining financing, and helps the owner to evaluate progress.**

LO3 **The basic steps in preparing a business plan are preparing a table of contents and providing a synopsis of the plan in an executive summary and background statement (best done when the plan is complete), setting the overall mission of the business, establishing business objectives, planning the marketing approach, selecting the location, determining the physical facilities, planning the financing, planning the personnel, investigating the legal requirements, and assessing the risk.**

TIME TO TAKE ACTION

If you have completed a thorough opportunity assessment, then you have narrowed down your idea and have thought about who your customers may be. Start to examine these potential customers—speak to them, and if possible, visit where they shop. Some entrepreneurs find it useful to interview potential customers. (This is recommended in **Chapter 7** on marketing.)

Get to know the people in the industry that you are considering entering, including your competition, suppliers, distributors, and so forth. Start to speak to as many people as possible. Examine any opportunities for partnerships or alliances.

Review your competitive advantage. Does it still make sense in light of any new facts? Discuss your competitive advantage with your mentors. Expand your mentors to include potential suppliers of money.

Start to write your business plan! If you have completed your opportunity analysis section, then you should have already conducted some research on your industry, customers, and competitive analysis. If you have not completed it, then this may serve as a good starting point.

DISCUSSION QUESTIONS

1. Given the difficulties in accurately predicting the future, is a business plan useful?
2. What takes a business plan from good to excellent?
3. Would the entrepreneur be better off spending more time selling his or her product rather than investing so much time in writing a business plan?
4. If a business plan is to be used to raise capital, then why would the entrepreneur want to advertise the firm's major risks by detailing them in the business plan?
5. What is the purpose of the business plan if the audience is (a) the entrepreneur, (b) an investor, and (c) a key supplier? How might the plan be adapted for these different audiences? Or do you believe that it is better to simply have one business plan that serves all audiences?
6. What do you think are some of the advantages of buying a business or a franchise compared with starting a business from scratch?
7. You are thinking of opening up a small business consulting company. What uncontrollable factors might affect your decision? Explain.

EXPERIENTIAL EXERCISES

1. Using Internet resources, find a business that is for sale. Compare the costs of buying the business to starting the business from scratch. What do you think is a better choice? Why?
2. The saturation index is useful to a prospective small business owner in selecting a trading area, such as a drugstore within an existing store.
   a. Using the information in the following table, which trading area would you recommend to the prospective owner?

LOCATION	1	2	3
Number of customers for the store	100,000	50,000	25,000
Average purchase per customer	$5	$7	$9
Total square footage of the drugstore (including the proposed store)	20,000	15,000	10,000

b. If you excluded the proposed store (3,000 square feet), which area would you select?

c. Which index of saturation is more accurate—the calculation with the proposed store square footage or the calculation without it? Why?

3. Which variables are important in site location for a pharmacy?
4. Interview a small business owner about the details of his or her start-up plan. Find out what aspects were omitted from the plan that should have been included.
5. Choose a specific type of small business and obtain advice from an insurance agent on the types of insurance needed and the precise costs. Write a short report on your findings.
6. Visit the Canadian Intellectual Property Office website to find out the requirements for registering a patent.
7. Contact local chartered bankers and entrepreneurs about coming to class to listen to the various business ideas that students have. Students should prepare two ideas each and pitch the concept in less than one minute to the visitors. Each visitor should then be given three to five minutes to provide feedback. If the class is large, this can be done in small groups on an informal basis. Assign one entrepreneur and one commercial banker to a group of five to eight students, and have them complete the activity within the group.
8. In groups or individually, write and present a written business plan.
9. In groups or individually, write and prepare a small written business plan for a charitable event that you can run for 5 to 15 days. Run the event and assess the following:
   - Did planning help?
   - Did you follow the business plan? Why or why not?
   - Was the event a success?
   - Did you meet the goals described in the business plan?

APPENDIX 4A

CHECKLIST FOR A SMALL BUSINESS PLAN

INTRODUCTION

1. Have a table of contents, executive summary, and description of the management team been prepared?

BUSINESS OBJECTIVES

1. Have specific business objectives been set? At the end of one or five years, what will the size of the business be in gross sales? In production level? In number of employees? In market share? In profit?

MARKET APPROACH

1. Who is the target market in terms of occupation? Income level? Education? Lifestyle?
2. What is the target market's purchasing behaviour for this product or similar products? Where are purchases made? When are purchases made? What quantities are purchased?
3. Why does the target market purchase this product or similar products? Which characteristics are preferred? What other factors influence the purchase?

4. What external constraints will affect the business? Existing or pending legislation? State of the economy? Competition? Social or cultural trends? New technology?
5. Which product characteristics will be developed? Quality level? Amount of depth? Type of packaging? Patent protection? Extent of warranty protection? Level of service?
6. How will the product get to the consumer? What channel of distribution will be used? Length of the channel? Intensity of channel distributors? Legal arrangement within the channel? Type of physical transportation?
7. How will the product be promoted? What are the promotional objectives? Which media will be used? How much will be spent on production? Who is the target of the promotion? What is the promotional theme? What is the timetable for the promotion?
8. What price levels will be set for the product? Which pricing policies will be instituted? What factors will influence pricing? How important is price to the target market?

LOCATION

1. Has the location been selected?
2. In what trading area or community will the business be established? What is its economic base? Its attitude toward new businesses? Its saturation level in terms of competing businesses? Its costs?
3. What specific site will be selected? Is it accessible to suppliers, employees, and the target market? What is the site cost? What restrictions on site use exist? What is the history of the site? What are the neighbouring businesses? What are the physical characteristics of the site?

PHYSICAL FACILITIES

1. Have the physical facilities been determined?
2. What building, equipment, and start-up supplies will be needed? What are the costs? What are the depreciation rates of the fixed assets? Which building codes or standards are relevant? Which permits are required? What insurance is required?
3. How will the physical facilities be organized? Is the production process efficient and safe? Has the interior layout been carefully planned? Is the exterior facade attractive?
4. How will inventories be managed? What initial inventory is required? How will inventory levels be monitored? How will inventory be valued? What method will be used to order inventory?

FINANCIAL

1. Has a financial plan for the business been made?
2. What are the financial requirements of the business? What are the start-up costs? Ongoing operating costs? What are projected sales, expenses, income, and cash flow?
3. Which sources of funding will be used? How much equity? How much debt? Which sources will be used? Private? Commercial? Government?
4. What bookkeeping system will be instituted?
5. How will the financial information be used? Which accounts will be evaluated? How often? By whom?

PERSONNEL

1. Has a personnel plan been developed?
2. What is the administrative structure? Is there an organizational chart? A responsibility and reporting procedure? Have job descriptions and specifications been developed?
3. Have personnel policies been developed? What are the hours of work? Pay levels? Employee benefits? Conditions and standards of employment? Grievance procedures?
4. How will the business recruit employees? Where will employees be found? How will they be screened? What guidelines will be used in selection? How will employees be trained?

LEGAL REQUIREMENTS

1. Have legal requirements been investigated?
2. Has the legal structure for the business been determined?
3. Have the relevant licences and taxes been researched?
4. Has patent protection been obtained, if necessary?

APPENDIX 4B

SAMPLE BUSINESS PLANS

BUSINESS PLAN 1—RETAIL STOCKING STORE, THE SOCK HOP

TABLE OF CONTENTS

EXECUTIVE SUMMARY AND BACKGROUND

The Sock Hop is a store totally devoted to socks. The product is in the medium price range, and emphasis is on variety and quality. The Sock Hop will be located in the Hillcrest Mall, Sunnyvale, Alberta, which is close to the downtown core. The mall, which opened in August 1998, has a variety of products and services. It contains beauty salons, shoe repair shops, movie theatres, one anchor store (Sport Chek), jewellery stores, men's apparel, ladies apparel, children's stores, toy stores, a food fair, and many other specialty stores.

The majority of the customers of The Sock Hop will be between the ages of 15 and 64, both male and female. The 2019 city census estimates that there are 68,376 people between the ages of 15 and 64.

The feasibility analysis shows that The Sock Hop could be a viable business within five years if it becomes well-known and builds a clientele.

DESCRIPTION OF THE MANAGEMENT TEAM

The owner-manager of The Sock Hop is Sharon Stockwell. She holds a management degree from the University of Lethbridge and has eight years of full- and part-time experience working in the retail clothing industry. She has prepared this business plan to assist in the start-up of this venture.

BUSINESS OBJECTIVES

The Sock Hop's business plan consists of a number of objectives. The first objective relates to opportunity costs for the owner-manager. The owner would like to obtain returns that would exceed that of a salary received through alternative employment and the cost of capital on her equity investment in the business. Therefore,

$$\text{Salary at The Sock Hop (\$24,000)} + \text{Additional profits} > \text{Salary if working for someone else} + \text{Cost of capital on equity}$$

It should be noted that the cost of capital on equity investment is included because had the person placed her life savings in a savings account, it would have been earning a stated interest amount. Thus, for the owner-manager to remain in the business, the total tangible benefits derived from the business must be greater than they would have been without the business. This objective should be met in approximately five years.

The second objective is based on performance. Market share should increase from the present adjusted 22 percent to 33 percent within five years (medium-term goal). It is hoped that as the business grows, it will have a loyal following of customers along with a good business reputation to overcome some of the weaknesses.

As a result, the sales and profits should also increase. The sales per square foot should increase from the present estimate of $278/sq. ft. As a way to increase overall profit, a minor objective is to increase the efficiency in selling the merchandise.

A third objective is a five-year long-term goal for future expansion. By the year 2027, the owner hopes to be able to work out a system to franchise The Sock Hop in Western Canada. By then, the bugs should be worked out of the system and a franchising plan can be established. This is dependent on the Sunnyvale prototype store being successful.

A fourth (short-term) objective involves the method of financing the business. The owner-manager of The Sock Hop will not be the sole contributor of equity capital to the business. However, she wants to retain as much independence and control as possible while spreading the risk. Thus, even when equity capital is obtained, the owner-manager will retain in excess of 51 percent of the control, and there will be an option for the owner-manager to buy out other equity investors.

MARKET APPROACH

Description of the Target Market.

The geographic market area for The Sock Hop is Sunnyvale. However, this must be further defined into a demographic target market, since a consumer-oriented marketing strategy is to be adopted by The Sock Hop.

For The Sock Hop, the target will be anybody between the ages of 15 and 64 who lives in Sunnyvale. Income level, occupation, social class, and education are basically irrelevant for this necessary product.

The fact that this target market will be interested in quality socks at a moderate price is important. Furthermore, The Sock Hop is targeted at those who are looking for variety and fashion in socks. In addition, a good part of inventory will be devoted to high-quality socks, catering to the business community.

Uncontrollable Factors.

There are four uncontrollable factors that the small business owner must understand. The owner must gather information about these uncontrollable factors, predict or monitor trends, and adjust the internal operations to them.

Economy.

At this point, the economy in Sunnyvale is positive. The type of merchandise that The Sock Hop is selling tends to be recession proof. Because socks are not a high-cost item, the market should remain steady. The economic environment will be continually monitored, however, with respect to its effect on this business.

Competition.

There are several stores in Sunnyvale that sell socks. Many of these stores have built up their reputation and convenient location as strengths. Reputation is one of The Sock Hop's weaknesses. However, its main strength is greater variety, particularly in fashion socks.

The Sock Hop plans to monitor the competition closely through primary observation and by reviewing industry reports on a regular basis. Competitor reactions to its entrance into the market will also be noted.

Legal Restrictions.

The specific legal restrictions are discussed in the legal section of this paper. Keeping abreast of new and existing laws that affect retailers and the sock industry is important. Talking to intermediaries in the industry and reading association magazines and newspapers are effective ways to monitor legal effects.

Social/Cultural Trends.

Since The Sock Hop has decided to adopt a consumer-oriented marketing strategy, it is imperative that new trends be monitored. Because the product is very fad-oriented at times, trends are going to be vital, especially to the portion of the target market that is young and attracted by the fashion stock. To keep up with these trends, industry and fashion magazines, social statistics, and government reports will be of particular help. Furthermore, observing the competition and the general surroundings will help to keep The Sock Hop management up to date on lifestyle trends, demographic changes, and purchase patterns.

Marketing Strategy.

Product.

The product strategy for The Sock Hop involves offering a product that can be differentiated from the competition and that will ensure a reasonable profit, anticipating the market's changes in preference and continuing product innovations.

The product will be differentiated by being more fashion-oriented. There will be more variety, greater selection, and better services offered at The Sock Hop than are found with competitors. The customer will be able to choose socks from both the fashion stock and the basic stock. There will be a full money-back guarantee to complete this total package offered to the customer—a package that will sway the consumer's choice toward The Sock Hop.

Distribution.

It is an advantage that The Sock Hop is located close to other stores that carry socks, since it facilitates comparison. The Sock Hop is small and new and thus will have some disadvantages compared with chain stores.
For this reason, it would be best for The Sock Hop to take part in a buying group. There are a lot of sock stores in Calgary and Edmonton, and many are operated as small businesses. The Sock Hop intends to investigate joining a buying group. In this way, it can obtain volume discounts, pass the savings on to customers, and thus

remain competitive. Purchasing with a buying group will help keep a lower inventory, as slow-moving items can be purchased in minimum quantities.

In addition, The Sock Hop will use a more direct channel for purchasing, in accordance with the belief that the fewer the number of intermediaries, the higher the profit margin available to the retailer. It will use a manufacturer/supplier in Canada, if one with a good reputation for quality and dependability exists. The Sock Hop will avoid foreign suppliers, if possible, since it is The Sock Hop's policy to buy Canadian.

Pricing.

Price is not the means of differentiating The Sock Hop from the competition. The Sock Hop is competing on the basis of selection, quality, service, and specialization.

Sales will be held at various times of the year to improve overall profit, to promote certain items, to counter competition, to dispose of excess inventory of inactive stock, and to improve cash flow. However, in the long term, pricing based on the full cost will be used. The economic situation, competition, market demand, and price sensitivity of the customers also have to be taken into account when establishing a markup percentage.

Promotion.

The objective here is to inform, persuade, and remind the target market. Five percent of sales has been devoted to advertising for the first year. This is in spite of the fact that the Dun and Bradstreet average for small businesses for advertising is 1.5 percent. Extra advertising support is needed in the first year of business because sales will not be large compared with those of other clothing stores, and the public needs to be informed about The Sock Hop and its total offering. In the next four years, advertising will be reduced to 3 percent of sales, but it will still be above the Dun and Bradstreet average.

A variety of advertising methods will be used. The normal outlets, such as newspapers, radio, television, and the Yellow Pages will be used. A door-to-door flyer campaign will be considered, as Sunnyvale is relatively small. For television and radio, The Sock Hop hopes to be involved in any promotional efforts in conjunction with the Hillcrest Mall.

At the start of the business, various contests can be held to get ideas on new designs for socks, which will help renew the product life cycle. In addition, sponsoring sock hops at the local high schools will improve public relations. This will be especially advantageous, since the younger, fashion-conscious portion of the target market is high school youth. Moreover, a lot of these youngsters are innovators and thus have the power to influence a major portion of the target market.

Finally, price promotions can be used in busy months, such as January, when clearances are usually held, during August and September, when it is back-to-school time, and during November.

LOCATION

Trading Area.

Economic Base.

The City of Sunnyvale's economy is strongly based on agriculture. The agricultural economy is supported by the food processing, packaging, distilling, and brewing industries. The city has good road and rail connections to various markets and to producers, and these have been important in maintaining Sunnyvale's economic position. In addition, Sunnyvale is in a prominent position in its region, and growth is expected in the area.

Competition.

In terms of general retail and service competition in the trading area, there are 36 major retail/service clusters in Sunnyvale, and they have been evaluated at a total of 3,479,000 square feet of retail and service space in addition to the square footage covered by Hillcrest Mall. The 3,479,000 square feet are allocated in the trading areas as follows:

2,650,000 sq. ft.	in the city of Sunnyvale
829,000 sq. ft.	in the surrounding area, which composes the trading area
3,479,000 sq. ft.	

Attitudes of the Trading Area toward Having a New Business.

The mall has increased the trading area and has shown a positive attitude toward development of the area. Sunnyvale is moving ahead, and as a result, most of the community is anxious for new businesses.

Specific Site.

Accessibility.

Hillcrest Mall is centrally located in the city of Sunnyvale, north of the central business district. There are major roads on all sides with good connections to the city. Careful consideration to traffic flows was given by the city before construction of the mall took place. Sunnyvale is also well served by the major highway system serving southern Alberta. Therefore, vehicular traffic is facilitated both in and around Sunnyvale. The transit system facilitates customers who do not own vehicles. There is a major transit station downtown within walking distance of the mall. A proposal to move the station north of Belcourt Gardens has also been considered, which would bring this station to the street facing this mall. In addition, bus routes include the mall.

Thus, all customers will have good access to the site, which is fairly visible from the major thoroughfares (Moodie Drive, Crowchild Parkway, First Avenue).

Site Costs.

The specific site costs (information obtained from Hillcrest Mall administration and the city of Sunnyvale) include the following:

Rent	\$20–\$30/sq. ft. per year (\$30 × 400 sq. ft. = \$12,000 per year)
Utilities	\$5–\$10/sq. ft. per year (\$10 × 400 sq. ft. = \$4,000 per year)
Business taxes	4.2% of fair rental value [4.2% × (400 × 30)] = \$504
City business licence	\$53 per year
Business Revitalization Zone fees	\$3.78 per month–\$45.36 per year (0.75% of business tax)
Insurance	\$87.39 per year

The total site and operational costs add to \$16,689.75.

Total rent of The Sock Hop will be \$12,000 per year. In addition, the mall offices generally set a break-even point for the store, and once this point is reached by the store, a royalty of 5 to 8 percent of sales in excess of the break-even point is charged in addition to the normal rent.

The typical term of this lease is between five and ten years. Since this aspect of the lease is negotiable, an attempt should be made to have the term reduced. In addition, advance rent of two months is required by the mall administration. In terms of recharges, the total cost of utilities, electricity, and upkeep of the common area is \$4000 (\$10.00 × 400 sq. ft.).

Insurance for The Sock Hop covers the business contents, such as merchandise, fixtures, furniture, and equipment. The insurance also applies to the actual business loss sustained by the owner and the expenses incurred to resume normal business operations. Thus, the insurance provides coverage when the damage caused by an insured peril results in the interruption of business. The money and securities are also covered against loss by robbery, safe burglary, and theft from a night depository in a bank or from the custodian. The insurance further covers liability for bodily injury and property damage claims arising out of the maintenance and use of premises.

Total insurance per year is equal to

$$\$3.70 \times \frac{\$23{,}618.77}{\$1000} = \$87.39$$

It should be noted that the mall administration insures the common area. (The various taxes and licences will be covered in the final section of this business plan.)

Proximity to Other Businesses.

Hillcrest Mall has many products and services. This is advantageous in that it will generate customer traffic essential to the success of the business. Socks are defined as a shopping good, which means that consumers will usually shop around and compare before making the final purchase decision. Therefore, locating the store close to competing businesses (see **Table 1**) will allow consumers will be able to compare and choose the superior product. The Sock Hop offers good quality socks at a reasonable price, which, when compared with other stores, will draw a loyal following.

TABLE 1 Selling Space in the Market

STORE	NUMBER OF STORES	TOTAL SQUARE FEET (000s)
Safeway	3	22
Walmart	4	484
Ricki's	2	11
Le Chateau	2	11
Winners	1	54
Giant Tiger	1	75
Shoppers Drug Mart	1	32
Tip Top	3	32
Moores	2	22
Sport Chek	1	32
Mariposa	3	11
Error factor	00	237
Total		1,023

Furthermore, other stores will be selling complementary articles of clothing (shoes, pants), which will generate customer traffic for The Sock Hop by creating a need for socks. Other than the businesses in Hillcrest Mall, there are no other stores offering socks in the immediate vicinity of the site.

PHYSICAL FACILITIES

Start-Up Costs.

The start-up costs for a retail store are made up of two things—capital assets and inventory. The following is a detailed breakdown of the physical items required to furnish the store. (This list was obtained from Roll-It Catalogue, Staples, and National Signs.)

ITEM	NO.	EACH	TOTAL VALUE
Furniture and Fixtures			
Multimerchandiser (1.2 m × 1.4 m)	6	$ 507.00	$3042.00
End frame pegboard (1.2 m × 1.6 m)	4	146.65	587.00
Miscellaneous hardware (pegs)	1	1000.00	1000.00
Used bargain bunk	1	200.00	200.00
Counter	1	500.00	500.00
Sign	1	500.00	500.00
Filing cabinet (4-drawer, legal-sized 60-cm deep)	1	190.00	190.00
Desk (76 cm × 1.5 m, steel)	1	250.00	250.00
Swivel chair	1	50.00	50.00

Equipment (obtained from Cypress Business Equipment, AGT Business Office, Office Depot, General Fasteners)			
Software (Bedford)	1	$ 300.00	$ 300.00
Computer and printer	1	2000.00	2000.00
Cash register	1	1200.00	1200.00
Telephone installation	1	40.00	40.00
Adding machine	1	75.00	75.00
Pricing gun	1	80.00	80.00
Vacuum cleaner	1	280.00	$ 280.00
Total			$10,294.00

Initially The Sock Hop will invest about 15 percent of projected sales in inventory. This is standard.

Inventory = Sales × 15%

$13,324.70 = $88,831.33 × 15%

Layout.

In the case of The Sock Hop, the layout is designed to display the merchandise effectively. Although browsing is somewhat encouraged by the multi-merchandisers, there is not enough selling space to encourage a lot of creativity in layout (see **Figure 1**).

FIGURE 1 **Selling Space**

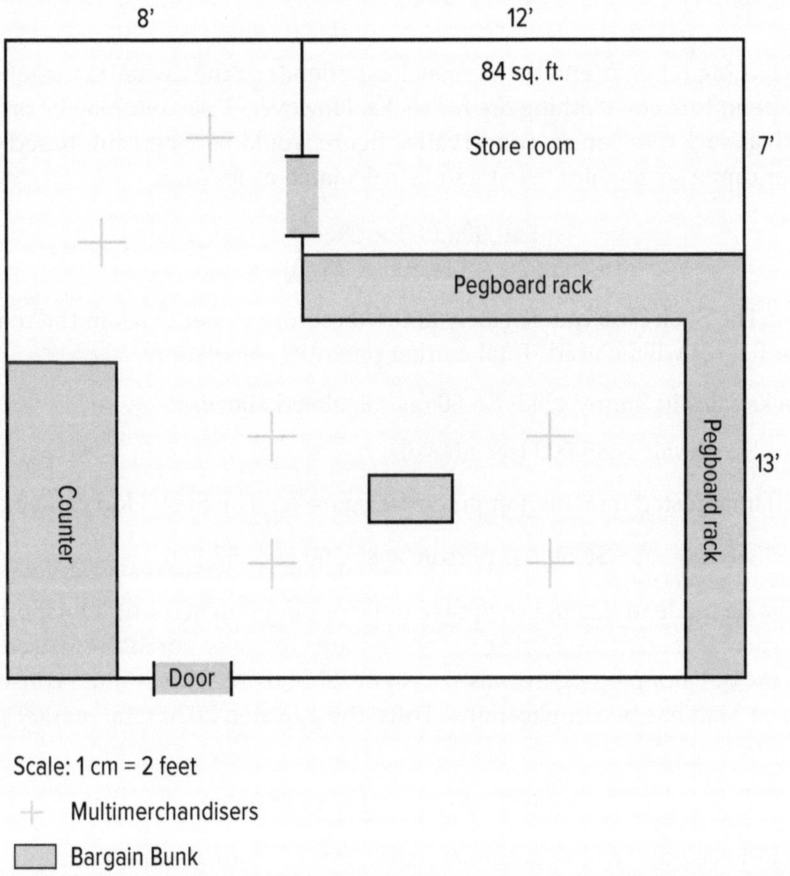

FINANCIAL

Feasibility Analysis.

Target Market and Trade Area.

Geographically, the trade area for Sunnyvale is delineated. The competitive influence of retail and service facilities in the city of Calgary limit the extension of the trade area to 70 kilometres to the north. To the east, competitive retail facilities in the city of Medicine Hat limit the trade area to 95 kilometres. In the south, the trade area extends some 80 kilometres to the Canada–United States border. The trade area to the west extends 130 kilometres from Sunnyvale. Here, it is primarily limited by the distance and driving times and is bounded by the Alberta–British Columbia border. The study by Larry Smith and Associates Ltd. indicates that Hillcrest Mall expects to derive the majority of its sales volume (80 to 95 percent) from this area. The remaining 5 to 20 percent of market support normally reflects customer shopping derived from visitors, tourists, or people working in Sunnyvale but not residing in the delineated trade area.

Market Potential.

- Total 2019 Sunnyvale retail apparel and accessories estimated sales were \$32,260,000 (City of Sunnyvale Economic Development). At an inflation rate of 4 percent per year (Alberta Retail and Service Trade Statistics), the retail sales for 2020 will be

$$\$32,260,000 \times (1.04)^5 = \$40,000,000$$

- The 2020 population of Sunnyvale is 85,000 (city statistics).
- The 2020 population for the trade area excluding Sunnyvale is 11,500 (city statistics).
- The amount of the regional population that shops for socks in Sunnyvale was estimated by clothing retailers to be 33 percent.
- It is estimated by clothing retailers and the personal experience of the owner-manager that between 3 and 5 percent of the expenditures on clothing are for socks. However, 3 percent may be on the high side for a low-price item such as socks, so a more conservative figure would be 2 percent. Based on these figures, the 2020 Sunnyvale per capita socks sales figure can be calculated as follows:

$$\frac{\$40,000,000 \times 2\%}{[85,000 + (11,500 \times 33\%)]} = \$6.50$$

The market area for The Sock Hop can be safely defined as Sunnyvale. Thus, in the remaining calculations, Sunnyvale population figures will be used. Total market potential calculations

- 2020 per capita socks sales in Sunnyvale is \$6.50 (as calculated above).
- 2020 population for Sunnyvale is 85,000 (see above).

Therefore, the 2020 unadjusted total market potential figure for The Sock Hop can be calculated as follows:

$$\$6.50 \text{ per person} \times 85,000 = \$552,500$$

An adjustment must be made to this figure to take outshopping into account. Outshopping is the result of a consumer in a particular market area going to another area to make purchases. Based on interviews with store managers, the outshopping figure was said to be 20 percent. This is quite conservative, since the presence of Hillcrest Mall has two implications. Thus, the adjusted 2020 total market potential for Sunnyvale will be

$$\$552,500 \times 0.80 = \$442,000$$

This figure is the most accurate market potential figure. It takes into account inflation, outshopping buying habits (figure determined by primary research), and 2020 population figures.

Market Share.

No statistics were available on the amount of retail space devoted to socks. Therefore, estimates were obtained through primary research. The proposed store will have an area of 400 square feet, with 300 square feet devoted to selling space. Based on these figures, the unadjusted market share of The Sock Hop should be the following:

$$\frac{320 \text{ sq. ft.}}{872 \text{ sq. ft.} + 320 \text{ sq. ft.}} = 26.8\%$$

This figure represents the unadjusted market share available to The Sock Hop. To adjust the figure, the strengths and weaknesses of the various aspects of the business must be considered.

The major weakness of The Sock Hop is that it is a new store. It does not have a loyal customer following, has no reputation, and has plenty of established competition. In addition, this specialty store will more than likely have higher prices than some of the discount department stores selling socks.

The major strength of The Sock Hop is its location. It is going to be located in a newer major shopping mall, Hillcrest Mall. The customer traffic in the mall is above average. The store is in an attractive setting with good exposure. Furthermore, there is a vast amount of parking space available for the satisfaction of the consumers. The Sock Hop provides a variety of socks in one location that is convenient and pleasant for consumers. Another area of strength is the growing trading area. The outlook is very positive for the Sunnyvale economy, and this can only aid The Sock Hop.

Based on this analysis, the adjusted market share can be said to be a very conservative 20 percent. This is based on present conditions. In the future, the owner-manager hopes that this percentage will increase as the business becomes more established.

Projected Income.

The projected income statements for the next five business years are in **Table 2**. The figures have been derived through primary and secondary research. The revenue figure was calculated by multiplying the adjusted market potential and the adjusted market share figures together:

$$\$442{,}000 \times 20\% = \$88{,}400.00$$

TABLE 2 Projected Income Statement for Five Years (in dollars)

	2020	2021	2022	2023	2024
Sales	$ 88,400	$133,248	$173,222	$207,866	$228,654
Cost of goods sold	43,984	66,624	86,611	103,933	114,327
Gross margin	44,416	66,624	86,611	103,933	114,327
Less expenses					
Rent	12,000	12,000	12,000	12,000	12,000
Staff wages	16,800	17,268	17,911	18,579	19,274
Owner's salary	24,000	24,000	24,000	24,000	24,000
Employee benefits	3,960	4,007	4,071	4,138	4,207
Advertising	4,442	3,997	5,197	6,236	6,860
Licences and taxes					
Business licence	53	53	53	53	53
Business tax—4.2% of rent	504	504	504	504	504
BRZ fees	45	48	48	48	48
Credit card discounts	213	360	433	520	572
Repairs and maintenance	711	1,066	1,386	1,663	1,829

[continued]

[continued]

Utilities and occupancy costs	4,000	4,000	4,000	4,000	4,000
Professional fees	622	933	1,213	1,455	1,601
Office and store supplies	888	1,332	1,732	2,079	2,287
Telephone—Rent	115	120	124	129	135
Estimated toll charges	600	624	649	675	702
Insurance	87	91	95	98	102
Interest expense	2,593	1,594	1,396	398	199
Depreciation	2,059	2,059	2,059	2,059	2,059
Other expenses	1,777	2,665	3,464	4,157	4,573
Total expenses	74,269	75,521	79,135	81,591	83,805
Net income (before income taxes)	(29,853)	(8,897)	7,476	22,342	30,522
Income taxes	0		0		1,500
	4,468				6,104
Income after income taxes	$(28,653)	$ 7,697)	$ 5,776	$ 16,674	$ 23,218

Financing.

This section pertains to the financing plan for The Sock Hop. Business start-up costs are needed to determine the financing needed. These costs are made up of the following:

CASE program	$ 400.00
Inventory	13,324.77
Incorporation fees	1,000.00
Physical facilities	10,294.00
Rent (last 2 months of lease + 1 month rent)	3,000.00
Total	$28,018.77

Most lenders require the borrower to prepare a financing proposal. This will provide answers to questions the lender will have about the owner and about the proposed business. For the lenders to know how a loan will be repaid, they need to look at income and cash flow projections for evidence of earnings that will support the loan. These are shown in **Tables 2** and **3**.

TABLE 3 **Projected Cash Flow for Five Years (in dollars)**

	2020	2021	2022	2023	2024	TOTALS
Cash in						
Net income	$(29,853)	$(8,897)	$7,476	$22,342	$30,522	$18,138
Add non-cash items:						
Depreciation	2,059	2,059	2,059	2,059	2,059	10,294
Cash flows from operations	(27,794)	(6,838)	9,535	24,401	32,581	28,432
Equity contribution	35,000	15,000				50,000
Loan receipts —Operating	13,325					13,325
—BDC	7,500					7,500
Total cash inflows	28,031	8,162	9,535	24,401	32,581	99,257

Cash out						
Loan repayments—Operating	0	6,662	6,663	0	0	13,325
—BDC	0	1,500	1,500	1,500	1,500	6,000
Return of equity	0	0	0	20,000	30,000	50,000
Start-up costs						
Legal	1,000					1,000
CASE counselling	400					400
Furniture and fixtures	10,294					10,294
Inventory	13,325					13,325
Two months' advance rent	2,000					2,000
Total cash outflows	27,019	8,162	8,163	21,500	31,500	96,344
Net cash flows	$ 1,012	$ (0)	$1,372	$ 2,901	$ 1,081	$ 2,913

Sources of Financing.

The Business Development Bank of Canada (BDC) offers term loans to allow small business owners to acquire fixed assets, such as land, buildings, machinery, and equipment. The loans are offered at floating rates or at fixed rates. BDC may also provide assistance through its Advisory Services, a counselling service offered exclusively to small and medium-sized businesses. These services offer experienced counsellors who advise the small business owner on any aspect of business.

The interest rate for the loan is approximately 8 percent with a minimum repayment period of four years.

The term of the amount borrowed must match the actual lifetime of what is being financed. Thus, the inventory portion will be financed by an operating loan with a term of two years. This will be financing from a chartered bank. It should be noted that although $13,325 is being borrowed for this purpose, a lesser amount will be needed. This is because The Sock Hop will endeavour to finance a good portion of inventory from suppliers who, because of competition in the industry, are willing to market their products through new outlets. The remaining $7500 will be borrowed from BDC on a term of five years. The equity investment will thus be $7500.

Accounting System.

Rather than employ a bookkeeper, the manager of the business will record on a computer all transactions that occur every day. Bedford accounting software will be used, which is priced at less than $300 (quote from computer dealer). The computer and a suitable printer priced at $2000 will also be used.

Bedford accounting software is a fully integrated package for the small business. It is easy to use and very user friendly. It consists of the general ledger, payroll, receivables, payables, and inventory modules that are all posted, as applicable, through single entries. It is very versatile and easily adaptable to small business needs. It produces full audit trails and a number of other management information reports. The vendors have a good track record of maintenance and support. Computing magazines, such as *PC Magazine* and *InfoWorld,* have given good reviews to this software.

The services of a public accountant (CPA or CGA) will be used for annual reviews, for tax advice, and on special occasions when necessary. The business will follow Generally Accepted Accounting Principles in maintaining the financial records.

Credit Policy.

The Sock Hop does not intend to allow any credit to customers, since it is not a practice in the industry. It does not intend to start a trend in this area, as the volume per customer would not justify it. However, it will accept all major credit cards (VISA, MasterCard, American Express, etc.) and bank debit cards. With this facility to customers, there would be no need to extend direct credit, which, in any case, would entail taking some risk on the part of The Sock Hop.

Financial Evaluation.

Monthly financial statements will be prepared and reviewed by the owner-manager in an effort to monitor and evaluate progress. Several financial ratios will be calculated and compared with similar businesses and with previous performance.

PERSONNEL

Administrative Structure.

Since The Sock Hop is not a big store, initially the number of staff employed will be limited and part time.

Store hours for The Sock Hop will be as follows:

Monday to Wednesday, 9:30 a.m.–5:30 p.m.

Thursday and Friday, 9:30 a.m.–9:00 p.m.

Saturday, 9:30 a.m.–5:30 p.m.

Thus, the basic salary and wage expenses will be

Store manager	$24,000.00
1 part-time clerk	13,440.00
1 seasonal part-time clerk	3,360.00
Total salary and wage	$40,800.00

With this staffing plan in mind, the organizational chart will be as follows:

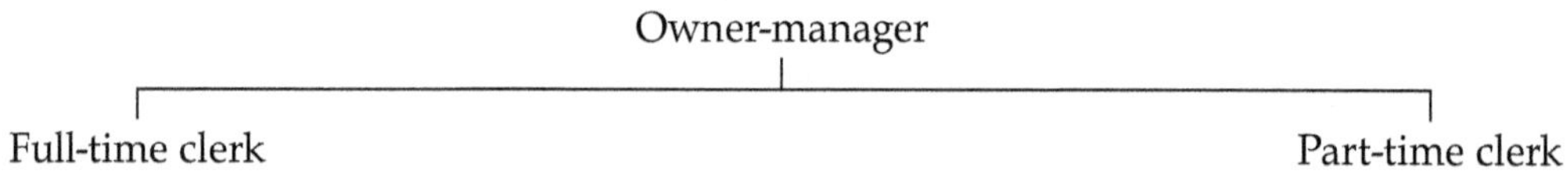

Employee Recruitment and Training.

Job Descriptions.

A typical job description is as follows:

Duties: Greets and helps customers, keeps shelves organized and stocked, rings up sales and bags items, opens and closes store when manager is away, cleans counters, and vacuums

Responsible to: Store owner-manager

Requirements: Must have previous sales experience, be available to work nights and weekends, be able to use a cash register, be able to learn store procedures

Personal: Must be friendly, appropriately dressed and groomed, punctual, and reliable

Recruitment.

The channels of recruitment used by The Sock Hop will include write-ins (applicants), walk-ins, advertising, and postings in educational institutions. Job application forms will be used to collect information about recruits. These application forms will attempt to gather information pertaining to personal data, employment status, education, skills, work history, memberships, awards, hobbies, and references.

Evaluation.

The first three months of employment are a period of observation for the employee and for the owner-manager. The employee will receive professional sales training and will be taught the basics of The Sock Hop store procedures.

Beginning at the end of week three of employment, the owner-manager will initiate a coaching discussion. The employee's job performance will be evaluated, and discussions will be held to help the employee understand the job. In addition, any questions the employee has will be answered.

Training.

Training will be carried out by the owner-manager in three general areas. First, the employee will be provided with information about the business and its philosophy and goals. Second, the employee will receive training about the merchandise, including such things as the material they are made of, washing instructions, and so on. The third area of training involves the teaching of specific selling skills—such things as approaching the customer, presenting the merchandise, closing the sale, and using suggestion selling.

Policies.

The following policies will be followed by The Sock Hop employees:

- An employee is assigned an identification number consisting of four digits to be used for all cash register operations.
- Work schedules will be posted at least one week in advance.
- Scheduling conflicts are to be reported to the manager as soon as possible.
- The wages for the part-time clerk will total $13,440 for year one plus a 2 percent commission on sales.
- The wages for seasonal part-time clerks will total $3360 plus a 2 percent commission on sales.
- An employee who has completed six full months of continuous service by June 30 will be entitled to one week's vacation during the summer vacation period.
- Any employee who has completed one full year of continuous service with the company by June 30 will be entitled to two weeks or 4 percent of earnings as vacation pay (whichever is greater).
- Employees who have completed less than six months service with the company by June 30 must be paid 4 percent of their gross earnings from the date of hire until the last pay period in June.
- All full-time employees must receive vacation pay in the last pay period before leaving for their vacations.
- The employee will be expected to have a professional appearance. This includes proper grooming, clean and pressed clothing (no jeans), name tags, clean and proper footwear, and above all else, a smiling, pleasant attitude.
- The Sock Hop emphasizes customer satisfaction. Therefore, the employee should ask all customers to retain their sales receipts. The Sock Hop will provide a full cash refund or merchandise exchanges on all returns with receipts.
- All staff will be entitled to a 20 percent discount on purchases from The Sock Hop.
- All purchases by staff members must be handled by the owner-manager. At no time is the staff member to key in their own purchases. These purchases are to be conducted during breaks or at the end of shifts.
- The phone is to be answered promptly, giving the store name and the employee's name. It is important that the employee be cheerful, helpful, and courteous.
- Personal calls are to be kept to an absolute minimum.
- The employee should practise the following prevention activities: (1) approach and greet all customers promptly and never leave the sales floor without coverage, and (2) be aware of customers carrying merchandise from one location to another.

LEGAL REQUIREMENTS

The Sock Hop will be an incorporated business. This decision was made after looking at the relative pros and cons of incorporation. The main reason for incorporating is the limited liability of shareholders. Thus, the owner is protected should the business fail. By incorporating, the owner is not risking her savings; she is only liable for the amount invested in the business.

Regulations.

Since The Sock Hop is a retail store, the regulations that apply to it are those common to any regular small business in Sunnyvale. The municipal government requires that the small business owner hold a business licence ($53 per year). In addition, the city requires building and electrical inspections after renovations have been made. Municipal taxes include a business tax of about $504 per year and a Business Revitalization Zone (BRZ) fee of $45.36 per year, since the mall is within the BRZ. In addition, the small business is required to pay various taxes. The federal and provincial government require the filing of yearly income tax returns. The federal GST will need to be collected on sales and remitted to the federal government. Provincial sales tax is not charged in Alberta.

BUSINESS PLAN 2—QUALITY CUTS

TABLE OF CONTENTS

EXECUTIVE SUMMARY AND BACKGROUND

Quality Cuts is a new beauty salon located in the city of Lethbridge, Alberta. It operates from the College Value Mall in south Lethbridge, employs five full-time hairdressers, and is managed by Sue Holland. Quality Cuts provides haircuts, styles, perms, and colour, as well as hair products supplied by well-known manufacturers. It also provides cosmetic and manicuring services. Quality Cuts attempts to target the middle-aged to older women in the Lethbridge area, which is currently the most rapidly growing part of the market. Quality Cuts uses a computer database to build knowledge of customers and improve customer service. The feasibility analysis and business plan projections show that Quality Cuts will be a viable entry to the beauty salon market.

DESCRIPTION OF MANAGEMENT TEAM

Quality Cuts is owned and operated by Sue Holland. She has her hairdressing certification from the Alberta School of Hair and Beauty Design and has worked as a hairdresser for ten years in the Lethbridge area. Before leaving her current employment to plan the establishment of Quality Cuts, Sue was supervising four other hairdressers. Sue is assisted in the financial and computer management aspects of the business by her husband, who is a chartered accountant. Preliminary consultations indicate that a high percentage of Sue's current clients will continue with her in the new business.

BUSINESS OBJECTIVES

The objectives for Quality Cuts are as follows: The first objective is to have a positive cash flow for the first year of operations. Cash flows consist of receipts and payments attributed to operating, investing, and financing activities. As can be seen from the cash flow statement, it is estimated that there will be a positive net cash inflow for each of the four sectors of the first year of operations.

A second objective deals with the prices charged to the customers. The prices will be competitive with other salons. Each hairdresser will have some input into prices charged for his or her clients to ensure that pricing is competitive.

A third objective is to achieve a market share of at least 3 percent by the end of the first year of operation, moving up to 5 percent within five years.

MARKET APPROACH

Description of Target Market.

The target market geographically consists of the city of Lethbridge and some of the surrounding trade area. Lethbridge is an agricultural service centre with a high market draw for many smaller communities within a 48-kilometre radius.

The demographic characteristics include middle-aged to older women in the middle- to higher-income classes. Approximately 80 percent of Sue Holland's current clients fall into this range. The location of Quality Cuts is ideal for this market because the College Value Mall is adjacent to some very large seniors' apartment buildings and upscale housing projects. It is located on the south end of Lethbridge where new housing developments are being built. The purchase characteristics for this market include concern over quality and service in a clean and friendly atmosphere.

Uncontrollable Factors.

Two uncontrollable factors would most affect Quality Cuts. The competition is the first. There are currently 35 other beauty salons or shops in the city employing 150 hairdressers/stylists. Because this is a personal service industry, customer patronage is determined to a large extent by the quality of the service provider and the level of confidence the client has in the hairdresser. Quality Cuts has determined that it will attain a competitive edge through careful hiring and training of its employees. Proximity of competitors may be a secondary factor to customer patronage, and Quality Cuts is the only beauty salon in the College Mall, which should be an advantage.

The second relevant uncontrollable factor is the social/cultural factor. Concern with looks is a major trend in North America. This suggests a continued and growing use of beauty salons. In addition, the Lethbridge market is an aging one. Both of these should be a positive influence on Quality Cuts' performance.

Product.

The product that makes up a beauty salon comprises three distinct parts: hair service, manicures and cosmetic work, and hair products. The hair service side is by far the most important, as it includes such things as haircuts, styles, perms, and colours. This will make up 80 to 90 percent of the entire revenue of the beauty salon. Selling hair products and providing cosmetic and manicure services, although less important, are still vital as they may serve as a draw for passing consumers. The products include such things as gels, shampoos, conditioners, moisturants, hair-repair treatments, protectors, sculpting lotions, and hairsprays. These types of products are available to the consumer in pharmacies but the quality of the professional products that are only found at beauty shops makes them attractive, even if the price is slightly higher. The brands that will be stocked include Paul Mitchell, Matrix, Lanza, Zotos, and Mahdeen. Because hair grooming is a service, Quality Cuts emphasizes superior customer service with its clients. Frequent follow-up communications with consumers is maintained through computer tracking and database programs.

Pricing.

Prices are set close to competitors' prices during the first year to ensure the transfer of existing clients with their hairdresser. Price will eventually rise to 5 percent to 10 percent above the competitors' as the clientele of the business stabilizes. This, in turn, is in harmony with the image Quality Cuts wants to project. Markup on the products is 50 percent of retail selling price.

Promotion.

Advertising takes place at approximately the average for hair salons in Alberta. This amount is 1.9 percent of sales, or approximately $2836 for the first year of operations.

In addition to this amount in the first year, extra "opening" advertising will be conducted for the first month. This is to get the name of the business out to the public and to let the hairdressers' old clients know where their hairdressers have moved. The cost of this opening advertising is an additional $500, making the total advertising budget for the first year $3336.

This advertising will take a couple of forms. First, the Yellow Pages is a must, as it is an easy way for the public to see where salons are located. There are currently seven pages full of advertising just for beauty salons, with the average large advertisement occupying approximately 26 square centimetres.

The entertainment section within the Friday edition of the *Lethbridge Herald* is also a favourite place for beauty salon advertising.

Business cards and extensive use of single-sheet advertising will also be used. These printed sheets of paper, containing information and possible coupons to attract new customers, will be slid under the doors of apartments in neighbouring buildings. As mentioned previously, a sophisticated tracking system is set up on computer to monitor customers' purchases and improve customer service efforts.

Distribution.

There are four main suppliers that Quality Cuts deals with, three from Calgary and one from Lethbridge:

Emerald Beauty Supplies (Lethbridge)

Monarch Messenger Beauty Supplies (Calgary)

Consolidated Beauty Supplies (Calgary)

Obsco Beauty Supplies (Calgary)

All these distributors can supply within two days. Quality Cuts will attempt to take advantage of quantity and cash discounts where possible.

LOCATION

Trading Area.

Lethbridge has a fairly stable population into which many older people from the surrounding areas retire. The socioeconomic level of the community is above average. Both of these factors will have a positive effect on Quality Cuts' performance.

Specific Site.

Quality Cuts is located in the College Mall in the southeast corner of the city, in the space where North West Trust was before it moved to a different place in the mall.

Accessibility.

This location has access from within the mall and private access from outside. It also allows for a neon sign on the outside of the mall to help attract customers. Traffic flow should be quite high, as Walmart is not too far away.

Site Costs.

ITEM	COST ($)	
Rent	18.50	per square foot (includes property tax)
Utilities	3,000	per year (plus $150 deposit)
Telephone	540	per year
Insurance	605	per year
Business taxes	420	per year
Licences/permits	113	per year

Proximity to Other Businesses.

There are no other beauty shops within the mall, but there are many businesses that draw traffic and would be complementary to Quality Cuts.

Physical Characteristics of the Site.

The store size is 1200 square feet. It has the front opening into the mall and a side door open to the outside.

PHYSICAL FACILITIES

Equipment, fixtures, and supplies are an integral part of the business, and a list of these items is included below. The costs have been obtained from prospective suppliers.

ITEM	COST ($)
9 hydraulic chairs	4,500
9 styling stations	2,997
10 hair dryers	2,490
10 dryer chairs	1,480
4 shampoo chairs	592
4 sinks	1,476
9 mirrors	1,350
washing machine	650
dryer	450
2 neon signs	3,000
4 lounge chairs	400
computer system	2,000
air exchanger	5,000
reception desk	300
layout additions	3,000
shelving	500
miscellaneous supplies (includes start-up product)	6,000

Layout.

The layout of the shop is shown in Figure 1. The layout diagram shows that the shop consists of three areas. The first is the reception area, which houses the reception desk, the shelves of products, the coat rack, and the waiting chairs. The second contains the hair salon itself, with the nine stations, four sinks, 10 dryer stations, and coffee area. The third section is at the back of the location and includes a bathroom, washer/dryer area, and an 18 foot by 18 foot office/lunchroom/storage area.

FIGURE 1 **Shop Layout**

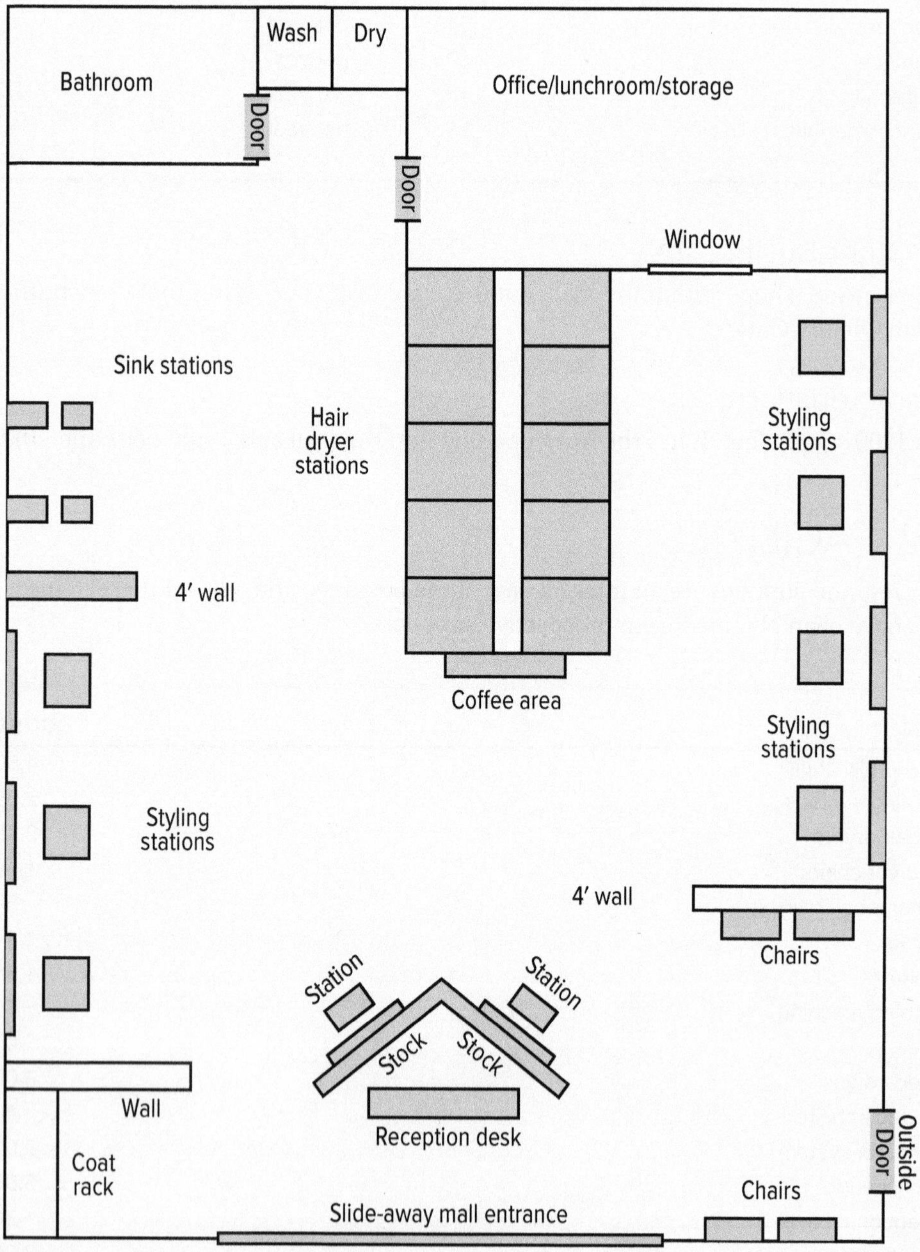

Actual size = 30 feet by 40 feet; Scale: 1 inch = 5 feet

The salon is set up in a way to accomplish three goals: to use the space, to be convenient for the patron, and to be pleasing to the eye. The image projected is one of cleanliness and class, as appropriate for the target market.

FINANCIAL

Feasibility.

Market Potential.

The estimate of average family expenditure on hair grooming for Alberta in 2020 was $375. It is also estimated that 45.5 percent of this amount is for women's hair grooming. Using a percentage of 50 percent should be conservative as Quality Cuts' revenue will also include sales of hair care products and cosmetic/manicuring services, as well as some haircuts to male customers. The population for the target market includes approximately 20,000 households (source: City of Lethbridge). Market potential estimate is as follows:

Households × household expenditures × percent of expenditures for target market = 22,000 × 375 × 0.50 = $4,125,000

Market Share.

The number of beauty salons and hairdressers/stylists in the market area were obtained through calls to all the shops, a total of 35 shops and 150 hairdressers/stylists. An estimate of Quality Cuts proposed market share is shown below:

$$= \frac{6 \text{ hairdressers / stylists (Sue + 5 employees)}}{6 + 150}$$

$$= \frac{6}{150}$$

$$= 3.8\%$$

This share should be decreased to 3.6 percent because the business is new and will take some time to build sales. The start-up delay should not be significant, however, because all five hairdresser/stylists are currently working in the market area and will bring the majority of their clients to the new business.

$$\text{Projected share in revenue} = \text{market share} \times \text{market potential}$$
$$= 3.6\% \times \$4{,}125{,}000 = \$148{,}500$$

Projected Income.

Below are the projected income statements for the first five years of operation. Revenue figures from above are used as the basis behind this information. Amounts and sources of expenses are as follows:

Cost of goods sold	10% (Statistics Canada Small Business and Special Surveys Division, confirmed by primary research)
Wages and salaries	53.5% of sales (Alberta Business Profile, *Barber & Beauty Shops*)
Depreciation	See schedule for calculation
Repairs and maintenance	0.8% of sales (Alberta Business Profile, *Barber & Beauty Shops*)
Utilities	$3000 per year, 5% increase yearly (Primary information from College Mall management)
Phone	$540 per year, 5% increase yearly (Primary information from phone company)
Rent	$10 per sq. foot flat rate for first 2 years, $11 for years 3 and 4, $12 for year 5. $8.50 per sq. foot variable rate, 5% increase yearly (Primary information from College Mall management)
Interest expense	See table for calculation
Legal fees	0.7% of sales (Alberta Business Profile, *Barber & Beauty Shops*)
Advertising	1.9% of sales (Alberta Business Profile, *Barber & Beauty Shops*)
Insurance	See legal section for details
Licences/permits	See legal section for details
Business taxes	$0.35 per sq. foot (City of Lethbridge Taxation Department)
Other expenses	1% of sales (Statistics Canada Small Business and Special Surveys Division)

The projected income for Quality Cuts is as follows:

	YEAR 1	YEAR 2	YEAR 3	YEAR 4	YEAR 5
Sales	$148,500	$156,702	$164,537	$172,764	$181,402
Cost of goods sold	14,850	15,670	16,454	17,276	18,140
Gross margin	$133,650	$141,032	$148,083	$155,488	$163,262
Expenses:					
Wages and salaries	$ 79,448	$ 83,836	$ 88,027	$ 92,429	$ 97,050
Depreciation	1,749	1,749	1,749	1,749	1,749
Repairs and maintenance	1,188	1,254	1,316	1,382	1,451
Utilities	3,000	3,150	3,308	3,473	3,647
Phone	540	567	595	625	656
Rent	22,200	22,710	24,444	25,008	26,796
Interest expense	1,894	1,056	829	578	303
Legal fees	1,040	1,097	1,152	1,209	1,270
Advertising	2,822	2,977	3,126	3,283	3,447
Insurance	605	635	667	700	735
Licences/permits	113	113	113	113	113
Business taxes	420	420	420	420	420
Other expenses	1,485	1,567	1,645	1,728	1,814
Total expenses	$116,504	$121,131	$127,391	$132,697	$139,451
Net income	$ 17,146	$ 19,901	$ 20,692	$ 22,791	$ 23,811

DEPRECIATION SCHEDULE

			YEARS			
ASSETS	CAPITAL COST	LIFE (YEARS)	1–5	6–10	11–15	16–20
Equipment:						
Hydraulic chairs (9)	$ 4,500	20	$1,125	$1,125	$1,125	$1,125
Workstations (9)	2,997	20	749	749	749	749
Hair dryers (10)	2,490	20	623	623	623	623
Dryer chairs (10)	1,480	20	370	370	370	370
Shampoo chairs (4)	592	20	148	148	148	148
Sinks (4)	1,476	20	369	369	369	369
Washing machine	650	10	325	325		
Dryer	450	10	225	225		
Computer system	2,000	5	2,000			
Air exchanger	5,000	20	1,250	1,250	1,250	1,250
Fixtures and furniture:						
Shelves	500	20	125	125	125	125
Neon signs (2)	3,000	20	750	750	750	750
Lounge chairs (4)	400	10	200	200		
Mirrors (9)	1,350	20	338	338	338	338
Reception desk	300	10	150	150		
Total			$8,747	$6,747	$5,847	$5,847

Financing.

Start-up costs are as follows:

ITEM	COST	SOURCE
Initial equipment and fixtures	$30,185	See Physical Facilities section
Miscellaneous supplies and product (includes opening inventory)	6,000	See Physical Facilities section
Rent (one month)	1,850	See Location section
Utility deposit	150	See Location section
Business licences and permits	113	See Legal section
Legal fees	754	See Legal section
Advertising and promotion (first month)	500	See Promotion section
Insurance (first quarter)	151	See Legal section
Total start-up costs	$39,703	

A cash flow statement has also been calculated to determine the cash situation that might arise during the first year of operations. This is shown below:

QUARTER ENDING	MAR 31	JUNE 30	SEPT 30	DEC 31
CASH INFLOWS:				
Sales	$ 29,848	$37,310	$37,310	$ 44,772
Bank loan	37,000	0	0	0
Equity investment	5,000	0	0	0
Mall payback	25,000	0	0	0
TOTAL CASH INFLOW	$ 96,848	$37,310	$37,310	$ 44,772
CASH OUTFLOWS:				
Equipment and supplies	$ 36,185	$ 0	$ 0	$ 0
Inventory	2,985	3,731	3,731	4,477
Wages and salaries	15,969	19,961	19,961	23,953
Advertising	1,334	834	834	834
Licences/permits	113	0	0	0
Business taxes	0	0	0	420
Insurance expense	151	151	151	151
Interest expense	925	323	323	323
Legal fees	209	261	261	313
Rent	5,550	5,550	5,550	5,550
Repairs and maintenance	239	298	298	358
Utilities	900	750	750	750
Telephone	135	135	135	135
Loan repayment	24,075	788	788	788
Other expenses	$ 298	$ 373	$ 373	$ 448
TOTAL CASH OUTFLOW	$ 89,068	$33,155	$33,155	$ 38,500
NET CASH INFLOW	$ 7,780	$ 4,155	$ 4,155	$ 6,272

Sue requires approximately $40,000 to finance Quality Cuts. She intends to invest $10,000 of her own money and borrow $30,000 from RBC. Current interest rates are 8 percent and the term of the loan is five years. The loan repayment schedule is shown below:

YEAR	PAYMENT	PRINCIPAL	INTEREST	BALANCE
1	$28,333	$25,933	$2,400	$4,067
2	1,340	1,014	326	3,053
3	1,260	1,015	245	2,038
4	1,180	1,016	164	1,022
5	1,104	1,022	82	0

Bookkeeping/Accounting System.

The computer system that is purchased will take care of all aspects of a beauty salon, including the financial aspects. The ACCPAC Sage 300 software program for small businesses will be used to monitor and evaluate performance. Monthly financial statements will be prepared and reviewed by Sue and her husband.

The credit policy for the shop is quite simple: cash, cheque, or charge. No credit is granted, except for clients in very good standing and then only with Sue's approval. Cheques are accepted with identification for unknown customers. Also, major credit cards, such as Visa and MasterCard, and bank debit cards are accepted.

PERSONNEL

Quality Cuts will begin operations with five hairdressers and Sue Holland as owner-manager. The organizational chart for the staff is shown below:

MANAGER (owner/operator)

hairdresser | hairdresser | hairdresser | hairdresser | hairdresser

The salon hours follow those of the mall: 9:30 a.m.–5:30 p.m. Monday to Wednesday and Saturday; 9:30 a.m.–9:00 p.m. Thursday and Friday. It is not open on Sundays and will not extend its hours during the holiday season.

Hairdressers work on commission, so the estimate of wages paid out over a year makes up a percentage of total sales. As stated earlier in this plan, secondary data suggest that this percentage averages 53.5 percent of total sales in Alberta, which is used to calculate the wages and salaries paid out over the first year of $79,844.

Hairdressers work 16 to 24 hours per week. This is in accordance with industry averages as most hairdressers/stylists prefer to work part time. A work schedule is drawn up at least one week in advance and accommodates client preference for certain hairdressers/stylists.

Employee Recruitment and Training.

Skill training is limited in this field of work as hairdressers have to attend a qualified beauty school and earn their certificate. However, Quality Cuts devotes extra effort to stressing to each employee the importance of customer service and projecting the right image. Explanation of company procedures and the commission payment plan will also be a part of the training.

Recruitment stresses that the workers project the image that the beauty salon itself projects. Sue has already made contact with three hairdressers/stylists who fit the Quality Cuts image and have agreed to work for her. Interviews will be held to select the remaining employees. This should lead to the hiring of those who work well with the customers and other hairdressers.

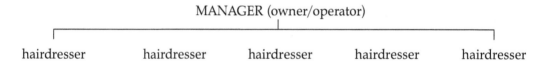

Policies.

The following policies will be in effect at Quality Cuts:

1. Employees must appear neat and clean.
2. No smoking is allowed in the customer area of the shop.
3. The approved uniform top must be worn at all times.
4. No food or drink is allowed in the customer area.
5. Employees will receive a 20 percent discount on all hair-care products.
6. The customer is always right.

Evaluation.

Employees' performance will be evaluated monthly on the basis of revenues generated, referrals, sales of hair-care products, customer complaints, and progress toward employee objectives. As mentioned previously, employees' pay will be based partly on commissions from appointments and other sales.

LEGAL

Legal Structure.

Quality Cuts will operate as a sole proprietorship. This will allow Sue to maintain flexibility and control of operations in the first few years.

Licensing.

The licences necessary to operate this business are as follows:

Development application	$ 31.00
Occupancy permit	20.00
Business licence	62.00
Total licensing costs	$113.00

Insurance.

Insurance is a legal necessity for this business. The breakdown of insurance is as follows:

Commercial general insurance (covering stock and building)	$190.00
Money and security insurance	75.00
Employee dishonesty bond	150.00
Malpractice insurance	190.00
Total insurance (for the first year)	$605.00

CHAPTER 5

BUYING A BUSINESS AND FRANCHISING

LEARNING OBJECTIVES

By the end of this chapter, you should be able to:

LO1 Describe the advantages and disadvantages of purchasing an ongoing business compared with the other methods of small business ownership.

LO2 Identify the sources of businesses that are for sale.

LO3 Explain how to evaluate a business that is for sale.

LO4 Describe the methods used in determining the price to pay for a business.

LO5 Explain the significance of franchising in the Canadian economy.

LO6 Explain the types of franchises available for small business.

LO7 List the relative strengths and weaknesses of franchising as a method of starting a small business.

LO8 Explain how to evaluate a franchise opportunity.

LO9 Explain how to organize a franchising system.

SMALL BUSINESS PROFILE

ANNE CAMPBELL *NovaScotian Crystal*

As the saying goes, the second time's the charm, but you can likely forgive Anne Campbell if she changes the words slightly to "second time is crystal." Campbell recently purchased NovaScotian Crystal, Canada's only mouth-blown crystal, from receivership. Campbell, who was originally involved with starting the company in Halifax, saw an opportunity to buy the company's assets and rescue the business from closing. "I've always had a passion for the business, and when I heard about what was happening, I wondered if there might be a place for me here. I think it's a great brand and it's a great business, and I wanted to see it carry on."

Photo courtesy of NovaScotian Crystal

NS Crystal has a long history in the province and in Canada. The company was founded over 20 years ago as craftsmen from Ireland established the business with the goal of maintaining the traditional mouth-blown process while creating a premium Canadian branded crystal. While enjoying periods of success, the company experienced hard times in 2008 and again in 2013. During the financial crisis of 2008, previous owner Rod McCulloch placed the firm into receivership to protect it from its creditors while he negotiated a repayment plan. McCulloch, who had invested and lost over $1 million in the business, settled his firm's debts when creditors agreed to accept shares in the company instead of payment. Given that the alternative was likely closing the business down, creditors no doubt saw this as a way to give the business time to recover with the hopes of eventually receiving some payment. In 2013, the business went back into receivership, owing creditors slightly less than $2 million. McCulloch cited the lack of efficient manufacturing along with the burden of managing a large debt as two factors contributing to the company's financial problems.

So why would Campbell buy a company that was failing? Common reasons cited by entrepreneurs for purchasing a struggling business are that they believe the company's financial situation can improve or that they can add needed capital to push the business forward. Campbell believed she could do both. As past owner Rod McCulloch stated, the firm was in desperate need of a second furnace to increase efficiency and production during busy times. Unfortunately for McCulloch, while they did add the furnace, the learning curve for the new equipment was steeper than he thought, and the business did not get to benefit from its purchase. According to McCulloch, "What we didn't have then was a second blowing operation; we believe we're on the verge of getting it there. We just didn't quite make it. So I think the learning has been done and that someone coming in should be able to pick up from that point forward." McCulloch further stated the company had a great brand and a loyal following, but he had been unable to produce crystal at low prices—something that the new furnace could change.

Campbell also hopes to add some capital to the business and will benefit from not having to take over the unsecured debt of the company. While the terms of the sale are private, Campbell has stated she will not be assuming the debt as part of her purchase. As stated above, a major challenge for McCulloch was managing his high debt load, especially during the slow sales months of January through April. Even though sales were slow, the company had to meet its debt obligations and continue to pay all of its fixed costs, including wages, as it had to manufacture 12 months a year, even though most revenue only came in for six. McCulloch says, "From January through June, because we are a production facility, the money keeps going out the door. We don't cut back in our expenses the way a normal retail store would, for example. So we've got the production side, and yet there's no money coming in. So we really need a lot of cash to fund the operation through the first six months of the year so that we can then collect all that money back in the last six months of the year.

[continued]

[continued]

And we just got to the point where we didn't have enough and I didn't have any more to put in." While Campbell will likely have to continue with this boom-and-bust cycle of sales, she will be doing so without dealing with the company's debt.

Campbell is quite optimistic the company will continue to grow. She notes that the firm has a great brand and a strong web presence, and she hopes to increase both online and corporate sales. Campbell says the new furnace has enabled Nova Scotian Crystal to produce larger and more expensive items as well as increase production overall, and this will help grow revenue in the future.

NOVASCOTIAN CRYSTAL
novascotiancrystal.com

PURCHASING AN EXISTING BUSINESS LO1

An alternative to organizing a business from the ground up is to purchase an existing business. Many entrepreneurs prefer this method of becoming small business owners.

ADVANTAGES OF PURCHASING

The following are some reasons that buying a business may be an attractive alternative.

1. Reduction of Risk.

The most significant advantage is that the acquired firm has an established image and track record. If the firm has been profitable, the entrepreneur would need only to continue its current strategy to be successful with the existing customer base (see **Small Business in Action 5-1**). When compared with starting a business from scratch, buying a business is often preferred because the entrepreneur will have actual knowledge that a market exists and of the amount of revenue that can be expected. Alison Anderson, CEO and founder of **Succession Matching**, an online company that matches buyers and sellers of businesses, says buying a business can be much less risky for cash flow because there are already existing customers.[1]

SMALL BUSINESS IN ACTION 5-1

ROCKY MOUNTAIN SOAP COMPANY INC.

When Karina Birch and Cameron Baty purchased **Rocky Mountain Soap Company**, the company, located in Canmore, Alberta, just beside the beautiful Rocky Mountains, had been in existence for five years and had established a small niche in the natural handmade soap products market, with gross sales of $90,000 annually.

Although the business was successful before the purchase, Birch and Baty realized that there was potential to substantially expand the business after they attended a trade show in the United States. They saw a growing market that was virtually untapped by Canadian manufacturers and that had not been recognized by the previous owners of the company.

The pair bought the business and set plans in motion to expand all phases of the business. Taking the business to the next level required updating their processes, buying specialized equipment, and learning to become more efficient with the staff they had. A key to the successful purchase and growth strategy involved carrying out extensive research with similar companies in the United States. By doing this, they were able to find out what these companies were doing in the areas of manufacturing, marketing, and distribution.

The pair also started to expand their retail locations and now have 13 locations in Canada. Much like their products, their stores focus on providing a natural environment, and Birch has recently started to remodel all the stores so they are toxin free. Birch notes that natural was not trendy when they first started, but being an early mover certainly helped them succeed.

Baty and Birch's efforts have led to growth and success for the company, which is now the largest manufacturer of handmade soaps in Canada. Revenues are over $11 million annually. The product line has expanded to 27 scents that are marketed through the eight company-owned stores, as well as the Internet, and sold to approximately 700 suppliers. Rocky Mountain Soap Co. products have been featured in many magazines, such as *Chatelaine*, *Western Living*, and *Fashion*. The owners also take an interest in the community and in a close relationship with their customers by sponsoring community events and maintaining an extensive customer database.

Discussion Questions

1. Why was the acquisition of Rocky Mountain Soap Company Inc. such a success?
2. What are the advantages of buying a successful company compared with buying a company that may be struggling?
3. Use Internet resources to find out the current state of Rocky Mountain Soap Company. What are the company's major strengths, weaknesses, opportunities, and threats?

Karina Birch (pictured here) and Cameron Baty purchased Rocky Mountain Soap Company and expanded the business by taking advantage of opportunities they saw in the marketplace.

Photo courtesy of Rocky Mountain Soap Company

2. Reduction in Start-Up Time.

Since an ongoing business already has employees, a location, and products, it will take much less time to acquire the business than to start a venture from scratch. For example, if a furniture store feels the cost of transport is too high and it would be a good complementary business to own, it would take much less time to purchase a shipping company than start one from scratch.

3. Financing.

Finding financing dollars to buy an existing successful business is easier than finding money to start a company from scratch. Since the entrepreneur is buying an existing company, those who would potentially finance the deal will know if the business is profitable and will be able to calculate a rate of return on their investment. It may be challenging, however, to find financing to purchase a struggling business.

4. Location.

Customers are already familiar with the location.

5. Established Marketing Structure.

An acquired firm has its existing channel and sales structure. Known suppliers, wholesalers, retailers, and manufacturers' reps are important assets to an entrepreneur. Additionally, the business may have already established credit terms with suppliers, something that is often difficult for new businesses to initiate. With this structure already in place, the entrepreneur can concentrate on improving or expanding the acquired business.

6. Cost.

The actual cost of acquiring a business can be lower than other methods of expansion or starting from scratch.

7. Existing Employees.

The employees of an existing business can be an important asset to the acquisition process. They know how to run the business and can help ensure that the business will continue in its successful mode. They already have established relationships with customers, suppliers, and channel members and can reassure these groups when a new owner takes over the business.

8. More Opportunity to Be Creative.

Because the entrepreneur does not have to be concerned with finding suppliers, channel members, hiring new employees, or creating customer awareness, more time can be spent assessing opportunities to expand or strengthen the existing business and tap into potential synergies between the business and its environment. For example, Indigenous entrepreneur Lee Arden Lewis left her job in sales and purchased **Jackson's Falls Country Inn** in Prince Edward Country, Ontario. With the Inn already in existence, Lewis opted to get creative in marketing her business in a competitive niche. To distinguish the Inn, Lewis created a bridge to her Mohawk heritage by decorating rooms with local Iroquois and Mohawk art.[2]

Lee Arden Lewis purchased Jackson's Falls Country Inn and decided to distinguish the business by incorporating aspects of her Mohawk heritage.

Photo courtesy of Lee Arden Lewis

9. Reduced Number of Competitors.

By buying an ongoing business, the entrepreneur can reduce the number of competitors operating in a market. For example, if there are five industrial cleaning companies in your area and an entrepreneur starts a new business from scratch, he will have five competitors and perhaps a sixth of the market share. But if he buys one of the existing businesses, he will have only four competitors and perhaps a fifth of the market share. For example, Darren Throop, owner of **eOne**, a Toronto-based distributor of independent movies and TV shows, became the largest player in Canada when the company acquired its major competitor, Alliance Films. Throop states, "By buying Alliance, we took out our main competitor in our two primary markets."[3] Acquisition consultant Will Fischtein notes that this is a good time to take over a rival because financing rates are low and thousands of baby boomer business owners are looking to sell their companies.[4] Another example is offered in **Small Business in Action 5-2**.

SMALL BUSINESS IN ACTION 5-2

TAKEOVER HELPS COMPANY MEET ITS TARGET

Mel Mogil's Toronto-based company **California Innovations** was a successful manufacturer of coolers, freezer bags, diaper bags, and lunch bags, with sales in more than 25 countries. However, they were prevented from being the market leader because of stiff competition from the Chicago company Arctic Zone, which had the giant Target Store account in the United States tied up. Repeated attempts to break into this market had failed. However, in 2004, Mogil learned that Arctic Zone might be up for sale, and even though he had never participated in a takeover, he immediately pursued the opportunity. Mogil states he was nervous about the acquisition but saw benefits, such as economics of scale, an expansion of product line and the addition of new customers. Mogil also notes a driving force of the acquisition was a fear that another competitor might buy the company and become a stronger force in the market: "I don't know how true that was [a rival buying Arctic Zone], but it was a motivating factor."

The acquisition took place along with the large contract with Target, and it has propelled the new company into a market leadership position. Yet the purchase wasn't seamless. Mogil notes that he had to manage a combined staff, that some customers took a while to warm up to purchasing different branded products from one company, and sales staff required additional training. Eventually Mogil opted to continue with the corporate name California Innovations but to use the **Arctic Zone** website as the main site for product sales. Sales increased 22 percent in the first year, and increased enthusiasm was evident with employees as they saw the company growing and progressing. Being the market leader has also led to more credibility with off-shore manufacturers and new customers.

Discussion Questions

1. What are some of the questions Mogil should have asked before buying the business?
2. Given the complexity of integrating one business into another, would you have recommended Mogil pursue this strategy? Why or why not?
3. What are some of the advantages of the acquisition?
4. How would Mogil achieve additional economies of scale by purchasing Arctic Zone?

DISADVANTAGES OF PURCHASING

A prospective purchaser should also be aware of the potential disadvantages of purchasing a business. Many of these problems concern the condition of the assets and other aspects of the business.

1. Marginal Success Record.

Most ventures that are for sale have an erratic, marginally successful, or even unprofitable track record. It is essential to review the records and meet with important constituents to assess the business' future potential. For example, if the store layout is poor, this factor can be rectified; but if the location is poor, the entrepreneur might do better using some other expansion method. Merging two businesses also comes with a host of complicated issues: Will the cultures of the firms work together? Will the new business drain capital and time from the ongoing business? Don Lenz, a Toronto-based consultant, points out that 50 percent of business buyouts result in failure.[5]

2. Physical Facilities.

The building and equipment may be old, obsolete, or below current standards. In addition, they may not be completely paid for or may have charges or liens against them. If the prospective buyer is unfamiliar with how to evaluate the condition of such facilities, he or she should enlist the services of a professional appraiser.

3. Personnel.

The business' employees may be incompetent or unmotivated. They may also resist the new ownership and reduce their productivity or even quit once the transfer of ownership is completed. The potential buyer is well advised to visit with current employees to ascertain their attitudes toward change.

4. Inventory.

The inventory may be obsolete or hard to sell. This factor may be especially critical in a retail store or a high-technology firm. The age of inventory can often be determined through internal records or by price-tag coding.

5. Accounts Receivable.

The outstanding accounts may be uncollectible or at least costly and time consuming to collect. An evaluation of the length of time these accounts have been outstanding can be helpful in evaluating this potential problem.

6. Financial Condition.

The financial health of the business may be deteriorating or less positive than it appears in the financial statements. Always conduct an in-depth evaluation of the firm's financial condition before purchase.

7. Market and Key Customers.

The market for the business' product or service may be deteriorating, or a strong new competitor may be about to enter the market. In addition, factors such as the economic state, interest rates, or government policy could adversely affect the market. Some firms are reliant on one or two key customers for the majority of their revenue. The prospective purchaser will want to ensure the status of these customers before buying the business.

8. Overvaluing.

It is possible that the actual purchase price is inflated because of the established image, customer base, channel members, or suppliers. If the entrepreneur has to pay too much for a business, the return on investment will be unacceptable. It is important to look at the investment required in purchasing a business and at the potential profit and establish a reasonable payback to justify the investment.

9. Paying Too Much for Goodwill.

Many businesses that are for sale include some element of goodwill in the sale price. Goodwill is essentially the favourable reputation the business has established under the tenure of the previous owner. Often the seller overestimates the goodwill associated with the business. A good general rule suggested by some financial advisors is that no more than 20 percent of the selling price should be allocated for goodwill. Other small business experts go a step further and claim that you should not spend any money on goodwill when buying a business. For example, Jeanne Lawrence bought what she thought was a successful clothing store in Winnipeg. But when she took over the store, she was inundated with complaints from current and past customers. Within two years, she lost most of her clientele because of the actions of the previous owner.

Many of the above potential problems associated with buying a business can be uncovered through a detailed investigation of the operations of the business before purchase. Some of the key evaluation areas are discussed later in this chapter.

SOURCES OF BUSINESSES FOR SALE LO2

Where can the entrepreneur who has decided to purchase a business find out which businesses are for sale? The following are common sources.

INTERNET

Numerous ads for businesses for sale can be found on the Internet, including such sites as Kijiji, online newspaper classified ads, and a host of other websites. The **Canadian Real Estate Association**, provides a separate tab for its commercial properties and businesses for sale. Entrepreneurs looking to purchase a business can likely find many opportunities by using **Google** or **Bing** search engines.

GOVERNMENT DEPARTMENTS

The small business or industry department in most provinces and territories is usually aware of businesses for sale. They may also know of communities that want to attract a particular type of business.

TRADE JOURNALS

Trade journals frequently carry listings of businesses that are for sale in that industry. This may be a more effective source than more general classified ads.

REAL ESTATE BROKERS

Many entrepreneurs purchase their businesses with the assistance of a broker whose job is to get buyers and sellers together and help negotiate the sale. If the prospective purchaser knows a certain broker fairly well, they might request that the broker be on the lookout for the type of business desired. Brokers are aware of most businesses that are, or soon will be, for sale and some brokers even specialize in businesses. Toronto-based consultant Ken Smith says that brokers can be particularly helpful when entering a new market in which an entrepreneur may lack business contacts. While there is a cost of using a broker, generally the seller will pay the commission out of the purchase price.[6]

OTHER PROFESSIONALS

Other professionals, such as lawyers, accountants, business appraisers, and bankers, often know of businesses for sale. Some prospective purchasers have found excellent opportunities by sending these professionals letters requesting information about businesses for sale. In addition, organizations such as chambers of commerce may offer match-up services. One example is the **Canadian Investment Network**.

WORD OF MOUTH

In their association with business people, entrepreneurs often learn about business opportunities through word of mouth. For example, Jim Iredale was a frequent customer of Warehouse Hobbies, a Winnipeg-based hobby store. During one visit, he was chatting with the owner who was looking to sell the business. In the conversation, the owner offered to sell the store to Iredale. A short time later, Iredale purchased the business because of his personal interest in the hobby business. Toby Chu, president and CEO of Vancouver-based **CIBT Education Group**, a private college, takes a direct approach to purchasing businesses. Chu uses the Internet to find prospective companies he may want to purchase and investigates their reputation, brand, and financial performance. If he is happy with what he learns, he contacts the company to see if he can buy the business.[7]

EVALUATING A BUSINESS FOR SALE LO3

A wise purchase decision may require considerable investigation. The prospective buyer should look into several key areas of a business before making a decision to purchase.

INDUSTRY ANALYSIS

The entrepreneur should be well informed about the industry in which the business operates. Ideally, this information should come from an extensive background or experience in that industry. Some specific areas to investigate are discussed below.

Sales and Profit Trends of the Industry.

One or more of the following areas could be significant in determining the future success of the proposed purchase. As a result, each should be thoroughly investigated unless the buyer has considerable experience in the industry:

- The degree of competition, the number of competitors entering or leaving the industry, and the nature of competitors' strategies

- The state of the economy in the market area and the extent to which changes in the economy affect the industry
- Legal restrictions currently affecting the operations of the business as well as relevant pending legislation or political pressure
- Social concerns that may adversely affect the industry in the future

THE PREVIOUS OWNER

The entrepreneur should ask the following questions about the owner of the business:

- Why is the owner selling the business? The often-advertised reason, "because of poor health," may refer to financial rather than physical health.
- Is the owner a well-known and respected member of the community? Has this reputation contributed significantly to the success of the business? Will this success continue once that individual is no longer associated with the business?
- Will the previous owner be available—temporarily, at least—to provide assistance and advice to the new owner? This help can be invaluable, especially to a purchaser who lacks experience in the industry or market. For example, Doug Robbins, president of Hamilton-based **Robbinex Inc.**, a business brokerage and consulting company, says in an ideal situation, the owner will remain involved as a full-time employee for a short time following the sale of the firm. He or she will then gradually reduce involvement over time. Robbins actually recommends that a management contract be signed where the seller has to provide strategic advice for a period up to five years.[8]
- Is the owner willing to finance the purchase by spreading it over a number of years? This may be helpful to the purchaser and advantageous to the seller for tax purposes.
- What will the previous owner do after he or she sells the business? To guard against the previous owner starting a similar business in the same market area, the purchaser might insist that a noncompete clause be included in the sales agreement. For example, Dave Millier, former CEO of Toronto-based Sentry Metrics, has been involved in numerous acquisitions and shares that he once overlooked signs that the seller was not going to honour the noncompete clause in the sale of his firm. Miller eventually lost 70 percent of the purchased company's clients when the previous owner started a similar business.[9] Interestingly Miller's company was recently acquired by the **Herjavec Group**, owned by Robert Herjavec, who was on CBC's *Dragons' Den* and is currently on ABC's *Shark Tank.* Herjavec acquired Sentry to access their IT capabilities and their $7.5 million in annual sales.[10]

FINANCIAL CONDITION OF THE BUSINESS

The financial condition of a prospective business is perhaps the most important area to evaluate. Care should be taken in evaluating the financial statements and assessing their validity. As an example, Dominique Brown bought **Chocolats Favoris**, a chocolate chain, which he has grown from three stores in Quebec to 42 stores in select provinces. Brown asserts that due diligence is an important part of any purchase. He says he not only thought about the financial health of the company, but also considered where the company could be in five years and in ten years.[11]

Validity of Financial Statements.

Since accountants can use a variety of methods in increasing or decreasing the net income of a business, an entrepreneur should attempt to validate as much of the reported information as possible. Entrepreneurs should ask for audited financial statements. In many cases, most small and medium-sized businesses will not have audited statements and would usually be unwilling to undertake the costs associated with producing them. Instead, entrepreneurs can ask to see income tax receipts, sales receipts, and any other financial records that are available. If the seller of the business is not willing to provide any of this information, the entrepreneur should complete a very thorough evaluation of the business before buying it. One entrepreneur recounts that he considered buying a takeout restaurant when he was informed that the business, located in a busy waterfront location, was quite profitable. When he asked to see the financial records for the company, he was handed a one-page income statement for the previous year. The seller became upset when the interested entrepreneur asked to see further financial statements and proof that the business was, indeed, profitable. The entrepreneur refused to buy the business and a short time later watched the seller close it. Small business consultant Don Letz says prospective buyers should pay attention to the condition of the financial records and how long it takes sellers to respond to questions. Letz states if a seller appears to be scrambling to find key information it may be a sign that the firm is poorly managed.[12]

Financial Performance of the Business.

To judge the financial performance of the business, the entrepreneur will want to see income statements, balance sheets, and cash flow statements. If possible, entrepreneurs should see or complete their own calculations on liquidity, productivity, and profitability debt ratios. These ratios should be compared with industry benchmarks, when available, to determine if the business is in good financial shape. Entrepreneurs should look for other clues to determine the financial health of the business. They should consider trends in profits, costs, revenue, and so forth. Ideally, the business has been experiencing growth in revenue and profits. After seeing these documents, entrepreneurs will very quickly be able to determine their potential return on investment and often decide whether they should investigate the business further.

Naturally, the buyer would hope the business is strong financially and profitable in its operations. In some situations, however, a business may be a good purchase even if it is unprofitable or has a negative reputation at the time of evaluation (see **Small Business in Action 5-3**). Such situations might include the following:

- The current owner is incompetent or lacks knowledge about the industry, and the purchaser has the competence and knowledge to turn the business around.
- The industry is, or will shortly be, in a growth position that might improve the firm's profitability or resale value.
- The major contributor to the firm's unprofitability is lack of capital leading to high interest costs, and the purchaser has the needed capital to inject into the business.

SMALL BUSINESS IN ACTION 5-3

WILL NOVASCOTIAN CRYSTAL BE SAVED?

As discussed in this chapter's **Small Business Profile**, Anne Campbell acquired NovaScotian Crystal (NS Crystal), Canada's only mouth-blown crystal company, in 2013. Campbell hoped that a new furnace and an injection of capital would turn the business around. Although the terms and conditions of the sale are private, Campbell bought the company out of receivership. Receivership is a form of credit protection for businesses enabling them to keep operating while they negotiate a settlement with their creditors. In this case, NS Crystal owed roughly $1.7 million to investors, lenders, and suppliers. As part of the sale, Campbell indicated she did not assume any of that liability and would operate the company without having to meet those debt obligations. Interestingly, that was the

Photo courtesy of NovaScotian Crystal

[continued]

[continued]

second time NS Crystal has gone into receivership in the past five years. The first time, most creditors were not paid and took shares in the company in lieu of money. These creditors, much like the creditors owed when Campbell took over, would be lucky to get any of their money back as a result of her purchase. When she purchased NS Crystal, Campbell was optimistic that the business would succeed and she would be able to grow the fine crystal company, which employed 46 people at the time, and whose retail store is a tourist attraction on the Halifax waterfront.

Discussion Questions

1. Reread the opening **Small Business Profile**. Based on this information and the material above, do you think Campbell would be able to turn the business around? Why or why not?
2. Based on the information in the chapter, would you have purchased the business? Why or why not? What are some of the negative and positive characteristics of the business from a purchaser's standpoint?
3. Do you think it is ethical for Campbell to take over the operations of the business in a deal that likely saw unsecured creditors and investors left with next to nothing, in terms of payment? Why or why not?
4. Given NS Crystal is both a local employer and a tourist attraction, should the government have stepped in and provided the business with some financial assistance? Why or why not? Note that some government agencies are listed as creditors of the firm, but the amounts would not be classified as significant.
5. What are the key success factors for the company moving forward?

CONDITION OF THE ASSETS

Several business assets may require thorough inspection and possibly, for non-liquid assets, an appraisal by an independent appraiser. The fee for this service is generally reasonable and may be well worth it. Assets to value in this manner are discussed below.

Liquid Assets (Cash and Investments).

An important question to a prospective purchaser concerns how easily the liquid assets can be converted to cash. There may be special terms or conditions with respect to these assets, such as the period on a term deposit.

Accounts Receivable.

Have accounts receivable been aged? How many may be uncollectible? (Accounts receivable aging is discussed in detail in **Chapter 9**.) Enlisting the services of a professional accountant may be well worth the cost.

Inventory.

Is any inventory old, obsolete, or damaged? A detailed evaluation of inventory should be done by someone with knowledge and experience in this area.

Building and Equipment.

Are the buildings and equipment old or obsolete? Are they comparable to competitors' facilities? Are there any liens against them?

Systems and Processes.

Examine the accounting and reporting systems in the business. Are they efficient, accurate, and timely? Are they compatible with your own system? What will be the cost of changing the system, if necessary?

Real Estate.

What are the land taxes and service costs? If the premises are leased, is the lease transferable? What are the terms and conditions of the lease? Has the location experienced a high turnover of businesses in the past?

Goodwill.

What value does the owner place on goodwill? Goodwill is the intangible value of such things as reputation, past experience, expertise, and prominence in the industry or community. Is this value realistic and reasonable? As discussed earlier in this chapter, goodwill costs should not exceed 20 percent of the cost of the assets, even for well-established businesses. Further assistance to evaluate the value of the assets and even the value of the entire business may be obtained by enlisting the services of a qualified chartered business evaluator.

QUALITY OF PERSONNEL

The prospective purchaser should evaluate the efficiency of the business' personnel. How do they compare with employees in other similar businesses? An important factor is personnel reaction to the new owner after the purchase. It may be wise for the buyer to meet with key personnel to better evaluate their reaction to the sale of the business. What is the staff turnover? Peter Byrne, CEO of Edmonton-based **Andersons Liquor**, says he looks at the staff of all the firms he is buying. Not only is Byrne looking for talent he can use to help manage the business, but he is also looking for managerial gaps. He says many small business owners have limited experience in larger operations, and he often needs to recruit external people to help in managing the acquired companies. The strategy appears to be working, as Byrne has acquired 38 businesses, and sales have grown by $40 million over the past eight years.[13]

EXTERNAL RELATIONSHIPS—SUPPLIERS AND CUSTOMERS

The investigation should include a review of those organizations or agencies currently essential to the operations of the business. Will these relationships continue, and if so, under what terms or conditions? Some organizations to contact include suppliers, financial institutions, and key customers. For example, Dave Millier, who was discussed earlier in the chapter, states he requests a customer list of any firm he is considering acquiring and then meets with some of the customers. Millier uses these meetings as part of his assessment of the firm, as he notes that a company that has strong customer relations is an indication of good management and employees.[14]

CONDITION OF THE RECORDS

Other records to review are credit files, personnel files, sales reports, contracts, and customer lists. These items can be valuable to the operations of the business and should be included with the business when it is purchased.

Appendix 5A at the conclusion of this chapter presents a comprehensive checklist of considerations in purchasing a business.

DETERMINING THE PRICE OR VALUE OF A BUSINESS LO4

If the preceding evaluation of the business shows positive results and the prospective purchaser decides to buy the business, they must make a decision concerning the price to pay for it. Is the asking price reasonable? Should a lower counter-offer be made? Several methods can be used to arrive at a price for a business.

There are four approaches to valuing a business. The first is by market value. The second relies heavily on asset value. The third uses the earnings potential of the business as a basis for determining value. The fourth uses a combination of asset value and earnings potential. Each method can help the entrepreneur make a general estimate of the purchase price. Keep in mind, however, that the buyer, the seller, or the business may possess unique characteristics that cannot be incorporated into a formula. Such situations will require adjustments to a formula-determined price. More detailed coverage of the financial terms used in price determination is found in **Chapter 9**.

MARKET VALUE

In a free market, the right price is the one on which the purchaser and seller agree or, in other words, where demand and supply meet. When applied to a business purchase, this price is called the *market value*. To use the market value method effectively, the prospective purchaser must collect data on the market values of many similar businesses. In many markets, the number of sales transactions of similar businesses is fairly small; thus, little data may be available. In such cases, other methods of valuation will be more useful.

ASSET VALUE

There are two approaches to valuing a business by using value of assets as a base: book value and replacement value.

Book Value.

The book value method lists the business at the net balance sheet value of its assets minus the value of its liabilities (**Chapter 9** provides the fundamentals of balance sheet assets and liabilities). This method generally understates the value of the business by a significant amount. For this reason, the book value price may form a lower limit to determining the price of the business.

Replacement Value.

The replacement value method lists the replacement cost of the assets at their value. Because the assets of an existing business typically are not new, the replacement value method tends to overstate the value of the business. When coupled with the liability side of the balance sheet, the replacement cost method may result in an upper limit for the price to pay for the business.

EARNINGS VALUE

The prospective purchaser is interested not only in asset value but also in how the business will perform in the future. Therefore, earnings potential is another factor to be taken into account in setting the price of a business. Dr. David Clough, Assistant Professor at the University of British Columbia, says earnings-based methods are the most common way to determine the price of a business, especially for businesses with steady cash flows. Dr. Clough says a multiple of three to seven times net income is usually used to establish a price.[15]

It is also important to use average earnings in calculating earnings potential rather than just the most recent year's net income figure. When using average earnings, extraordinary items that have affected income should be deleted to make the estimate a true average. This is called *normalizing earnings*. Many analysts will use the previous five years' average of earnings. If earnings appear to be unstable from year to year, a weighted-average calculation might be used. The determination of average earnings by using the weighted-average approach is shown in **Table 5-1**. This method gives a greater weight to the most recent year's earnings in arriving at average earnings.

TABLE 5-1 **Calculating Weighted-Average Earnings for a Business**

	AVERAGE EARNINGS	WEIGHTED-AVERAGE EARNINGS (EARNINGS × WEIGHTS FACTOR)				
Last year	$ 5,000	5,000	×	5	=	25,000
Two years ago	4,000	4,000	×	4	=	16,000
Three years ago	7,000	7,000	×	3	=	21,000
Four years ago	10,000	10,000	×	2	=	20,000
Five years ago	$14,000	14,000	×	1	=	14,000
	$40,000			15		96,000
	Average Earnings 40,000/5 = 8000			Weighted Average Earnings 96,000/15 = 6,400		

Two specific methods of estimating the purchase value of the business use earnings as a base.

Capitalization of Earnings Method.

The capitalization of earnings method is commonly used to arrive at a quick estimate of the price of a business. The capitalized value is found by dividing average earnings of the business by a specified rate of return expressed as a decimal. This specified rate of return figure can be obtained by using bank interest (a risk factor of a few percentage points should be added) or another required rate of return percentage for the investment. It can also be obtained by using average return on tangible net worth statistics from such sources as Dun and Bradstreet and Statistics Canada. Generally, capitalization rates are 12 to 20 percent for well-established businesses and 25 to 50 percent for a new unproven business.[16] **Figure 5-1** illustrates the capitalization of earnings formula.

FIGURE 5-1 **Capitalization of Earnings Formula**

$$\frac{\text{Average earnings}}{\text{Predetermined interest rate or rate of return required for investment}} = \text{Capitalized value}$$

Table 5-2 illustrates a calculation of capitalized earnings value using industry averages. This method measures the firm's ability to earn profits in relation to the capital invested. For example, for a book and stationery store, it will take $45,450 paid for the business to earn $10,000 after taxes if the store were run at the median level.

TABLE 5-2 **Capitalized Earnings Value**

LINE OF BUSINESS	NET PROFITS TO TANGIBLE NET WORTH AS A PERCENTAGE*	CAPITALIZED EARNINGS VALUE†
Retail		
Book and stationery stores	22.0	$ 45,450
Clothing, men's	12.9	77,520
Clothing, women's	12.8	78,125
Drugstores	20.7	48,310
Food stores	10.8	92,595
Gasoline service stations	23.1	43,290
Hardware	14.5	68,965
Jewellery store	8.3	120,480
Manufacturers		
Appliances, small	18.4	54,350
Bakery products	17.8	56,180
Machine shops	19.7	50,760
Meat products	11.8	84,745
Sash, door, and millwork plants	29.0	34,480
Soft drinks	34.9	28,655
Sporting goods and toys	11.0	90,910

[continued]

[continued]

Construction		
Building contractors	23.3	42,920
Services		
Hotels	15.5	64,515
Agriculture, forestry, and fishing		
Agriculture	12.2	81,965

* Tangible net worth is net worth less intangibles, that is, copyrights, goodwill, trademarks, and patents. This figure can be found in Dun and Bradstreet, Key Business Ratios.

† Represents the investment or tangible net worth required to earn $10,000 in profits after taxes, assuming the firm is operating at median level, calculated in the following manner: $ 10,000/Net profit to tangible net worth as percentage = Capitalized earning value.

Times Earnings Method.

The times earnings method arbitrarily multiplies average earnings by a number, usually between 1 and 10, based on past sales and industry experience, to arrive at the price for the business. This is often called the *price-earnings ratio.* Small businesses are usually sold at between four and five times earnings, according to the U.S. Small Business Administration, although recently some Internet companies have sold at much higher multiples. This number can vary significantly for very small businesses. Therefore, the advice of an experienced business broker or accountant valuator should be sought.

COMBINATION METHODS

Because both the asset value and the earnings value are important components of the true value of the business, some methods attempt to combine both values to estimate an appropriate price. Two combination methods can be used to arrive at such a price. The first is an analytical approach, and the second is a method based on historical transactions or experience in the industry. Each will be discussed briefly.

Analytical Method.

The analytical method combines three factors to arrive at the value for the business: adjusted net worth, past earnings, and future earnings.

To obtain adjusted net worth, take the market value of tangible assets, subtract liabilities, and then add goodwill. If the business' assets are worth $220,000 with liabilities of $60,000 and goodwill of $40,000, then the adjusted net worth is $220,000 – $60,000 + $40,000 = $200,000.

To arrive at a value for past earnings, these earnings (net income) are capitalized by multiplying earnings by a number usually between 5 and 10. If the firm is judged to be very solid, the factor used should be closer to 10, and if considerable risk exists, a factor of 5 would be more appropriate. If average past earnings are $40,000 and a capitalization rate of 8 is used, the earnings value is $320,000.

A future earnings value is established by discounting future earnings of the business. This is done by applying a discount factor to current earnings. Such factors reflect the fact that future earnings flows are worth more today than they will be in the future. If the business earns $40,000 today and a discount factor of 10 percent is applied, the future earnings flow make the business worth $400,000 today.

To combine the above factors into one value reasonable for the business requires experience, judgment, and insight. For example, if the business has considerable assets, more emphasis should be given to the net worth method, whereas if the business is a service business, the earnings methods will be given more prominence in the combination. In the above examples, if a 50 percent emphasis is used for assets and 25 percent for each of the earnings factors is used, the combined value for this business would be

$$(\$200{,}000 \times 0.50) + (\$320{,}000 \times 0.25) + (\$400{,}000 \times 0.25) = \$280{,}000$$

Historical Method.

The historical method uses historical experience in determining relevant indicators of the components of the value of a business. As mentioned previously, determining the price of a business by using a formula may provide a good estimate of a business's worth, but the unique characteristics of each situation may alter the price offered and paid for the business.

THE PURCHASE TRANSACTION

The entrepreneur should enlist the services of professionals, such as lawyers and accountants, to assist in the purchase decision. Once a purchase price and other terms and conditions have been agreed on, the buyer should have a lawyer draw up the purchase agreement and close the transaction. This helps ensure that clear title to the business is transferred and post-purchase difficulties are minimized (see **Small Business Beginnings 5-1** for more about post-purchase activities). The purchase agreement should cover the following areas:

- The purchase price, including principal and interest amounts.
- Payment dates—when and to whom payments are to be made.
- A detailed list of all assets to be included in the purchase. It may be advisable to purchase the assets of the business rather than the business itself. By doing this, the purchaser may avoid potential negative intangibles associated with the business.
- Conditions of the purchase—what nonfinancial requirements, if any, are part of the purchase (many purchase contracts are signed subject to the purchaser obtaining suitable financing).
- Provisions for noncompliance with conditions, including penalties for breaches of the contract.
- Collateral or security pledged in the transaction (if the seller is financing the sale).

SMALL BUSINESS BEGINNINGS 5-1

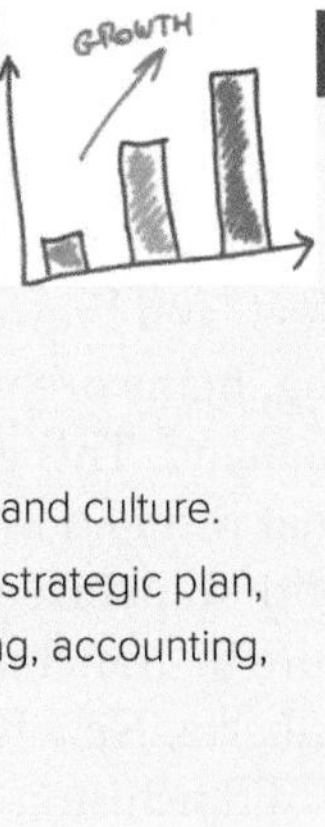

STEPS IN SUCCESSFULLY ACQUIRING A BUSINESS

You bought the company—now what? That is the situation that many entrepreneurs face after deciding to purchase a business. To ensure that the transaction goes as smoothly as possible, entrepreneurs should take the following steps:

1. *Develop an acquisition plan* that covers such aspects as managing people, marketing, relationships, software, and culture.
2. *Make changes quickly.* If an entrepreneur is going to change personnel, alter the marketing mix, or modify the strategic plan, do it as soon as possible. It is important that main operations, such as procurement, production, sales, marketing, accounting, human resources, and information systems, occur as soon as the deal is signed.
3. *Be open and honest* about your intentions for the company.

NEGOTIATING THE DEAL

In purchasing a business, the first formal step is to make the offer to purchase. The offer may be made directly by the buyer or through a realtor or a lawyer. In either case, the offer to purchase should be made only after consulting a lawyer and an accountant. As part of the negotiating strategy, the potential buyer should have calculated (preferably financially) the maximum amount he or she can offer for the business by using one or more of the methods previously cited. This value is generally somewhat higher than the original purchase offer. As negotiations continue, the purchase price or other aspects of the agreement may have to be altered.

Rather than settling on a firm price, buyers are increasingly turning to performance-based guarantees whereby they not only agree to pay a certain price if sales or profits reach certain levels but also set a floor price that applies if targets are not met.[17]

Once the purchase price has been agreed on, the transaction is usually closed, and legal transfer of title to the business takes place. Typically, this is carried out by both the buyer's and the seller's lawyers. The purchaser should exercise caution if the seller's lawyer is to close the deal. The buyer's lawyer should be permitted to review the details of the transaction in this case.

The buyer is normally required to make a deposit of 5 to 10 percent of the purchase price as a show of good faith. This amount should be minimized at least until the seller has met the conditions of the agreement.[18]

HISTORY AND BACKGROUND OF FRANCHISING

LO5

Franchising is becoming an increasingly popular method of establishing and operating a small business. Many entrepreneurs find the opportunity to operate their own business with slightly less risk an attractive option. Others enter franchising out of necessity, having lost jobs with larger organizations. Franchising now occurs in most industries and is experiencing rapid growth in the service sector.

Franchising has been successful not only for entrepreneurs. Many large organizations also recognize that this method of doing business benefits their operations.

From the franchisor's point of view, franchising provides a source of capital and a stable and motivated workforce, usually leading to higher performance. Mac Voisin, co-founder of the successful **M&M Food Market**, says that franchising allows the franchisor to expand quickly as the franchisee provides the capital for growth and serves as a motivated manager with a vested interest in the business.[19] For the franchisee, it offers a turnkey operation with valuable assistance from the franchisor. For example, Gabriel Toupin, a Spray-Net franchisee says that purchasing a Spray-Net franchise allowed him to become his own boss but with a system that was already created and tested. Spray-Net enables its franchisees to paint non-wood finishes with its secret formula allowing for a permanent finish and the franchise will be discussed later in this chapter.

Although the concept has been around for decades, franchising has experienced its most rapid growth in North America only since the 1950s. It began with the automobile manufacturers, oil companies, soft drink bottlers, and breweries, and has since spread to many different industries throughout the world. Through franchising, many organizations with a proven concept or product were able to expand much more rapidly to meet demand. This growth was so rapid that toward the end of the 1960s, several problems developed in the industry that resulted in the formation of franchisee associations and the passage of legislation to protect the rights of both franchisees and franchisors. Currently, several provinces are looking at requiring greater financial disclosure by franchisors to better protect potential franchisees.[20] Six Canadian provinces, Manitoba, Ontario, Alberta, New Brunswick, British Columbia, and Prince Edward Island, have passed such legislation.[21]

Franchising has become an important factor in the Canadian economy. According to research provided by Franchise 101, franchise businesses account for 45 percent of retail sales and there are roughly 76,000 franchise units in the country. These franchises employ approximately 1.86 million people, and account for one out of every five consumer dollars spent.[22] Estimates are that the impact of franchising on retail sales will continue to grow and may reach as high as 60 percent of sales in the future.[23] CFA statistics show growth in franchising from coast to coast in this country.[24] Canada has the second-largest franchising industry after the United States.[25] Canadian franchises are also eyeing global expansion much more aggressively in recent years. For example, **Driverseat** is looking to expand its vehicle chauffeur business globally and is aggressively pursuing both U.S. expansion and considering master franchises in Peru, Australia, and South Korea. A master franchise would allow one entrepreneur the ability to sell to other franchisees throughout a region. Co-founder Brian Bazely says his franchise is attractive because it is home based, scalable, and has low start-up costs.[26]
See **Figure 5-2**. for other information on Canadian franchises.

FIGURE 5-2

Franchising Fast Facts

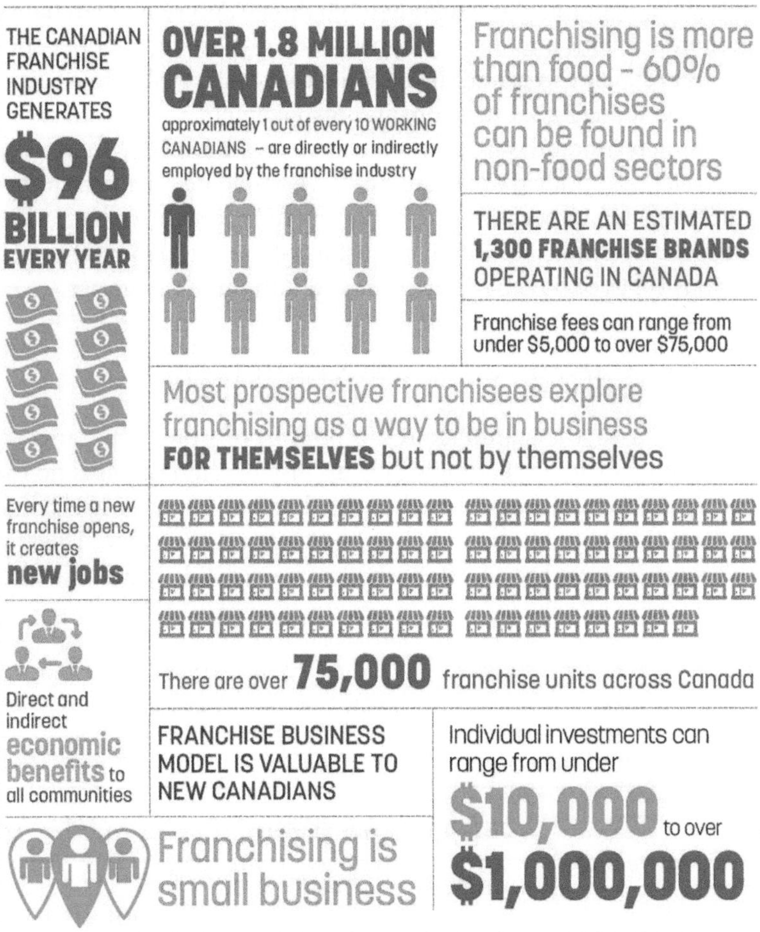

Canadian Franchise Association

Franchises exist in almost all industries today. A major reason for the large recent increase in the number of franchises is expansion into the service sector, which is the fastest-growing sector in the Canadian economy.

WHAT IS FRANCHISING? LO6

Franchising is a system for selectively distributing goods or services through outlets owned by the franchisee. A common definition for a franchise arrangement is a patent or trademark licence entitling the holder to market particular products or services under a brand or trademark according to prearranged terms or conditions. In addition to products and services, the franchise may consist of or may include a system or method of providing the product or service. Today, many applications of this definition translate into a broad range of franchising relationships. The brand identification is an important aspect of this form of distribution. It consists of standardization throughout the system. The various outlets in the system are similar in class of trade, merchandise carried, or services rendered, and other factors that have a bearing on joint merchandising and management through common policies. Also, all outlets in a franchise system are identified as members of the system. They operate under a common name or insignia, and the establishments often have a distinctive appearance common to all members of the system. This standardization is ensured and controlled by the terms of the franchise contract.

A franchise system is therefore a voluntary chain, that is, a chain of individually owned businesses. Franchising, in fact, has been the salvation of many independent wholesale and retail merchants in the face of increasing competition from corporate chains and discount operations. By joining a jobber-sponsored voluntary chain, for example, an independent retailer can get all the benefits that are available to a corporate chain store: central buying and assistance in merchandising, promotion, and management.

The franchising or licensing technique is more often used today, however, when a company comes up with an idea for a product or service and finds that it does not have adequate resources to market its own idea. By licensing prospective entrepreneurs to perform the marketing function for it, the franchising company is able to achieve rapid expansion at relatively low cost, with a substantial part of the investment being contributed by the franchise holder. The various types of franchises are grouped into three categories.

MANUFACTURER-DIRECTED FRANCHISE

In manufacturer-directed franchises, the manufacturer (producer) of a product grants a dealer the right to sell the product. This right, which tends to be geographically exclusive, often requires no initial fee. (See **Table 5-3** for further details of this type of franchising.) Manufacturer-directed franchising is common in such industries as automobile sales, gasoline distributorships, and farm implement dealerships. This type of franchising is successful only when the manufacturer has an established name, a solid reputation, and considerable consumer loyalty.

TABLE 5-3 Types of Franchises

	DETAILS OF AGREEMENT			EXAMPLES	
TITLE	**METHOD OF FRANCHISING**	**FRANCHISOR PROVIDES**	**FRANCHISEE PROVIDES**	**INDUSTRY**	**COMPANY**
Manufacturer	Franchisee has right to sell product	Product sales support	Selling function	Automobile	Ford GMC
		Exclusive territory	Facilities	Oil companies	ESSO Petro Canada
Wholesaler-retailer	Franchisee owns equity in supplier company and purchases product from the franchise	Product and other technical assistance and service	– Selling function – Buys equity – Board of directors	Retail grocery Hardware	Associated Grocers Home Hardware
Franchising company	Franchisee buys the right to sell service or product	– Method of operations – Training – Location, building, etc. – Financing – Proven name – Advertising	– Fee – Royalties – Compliance with conditions of contract	Fast food Auto rental	McDonald's Tim Hortons Avis Budget Hertz

WHOLESALER-RETAILER–DIRECTED FRANCHISE

In a wholesaler-retailer–directed arrangement, one member of the distribution channel such as the wholesaler or retailer initiates the organization of the franchise. The primary purpose of such an organization generally is to centralize many managerial and operational functions and take advantage of volume buying for a group of sellers. As with the manufacturer-owned franchise, there is usually no initial fee, but an equity investment in the franchise may be required. **Table 5-3** illustrates some of the other operating details for this type of franchise and the industries in which it is prevalent.

FRANCHISING COMPANY

This type of franchise usually involves a company (the master licensor) that sells a product or service in exchange for an initial predetermined fee and an ongoing royalty. The franchisee gains the right to sell under the franchisor's name and receives the franchisor's assistance and managerial expertise. Franchising companies are commonly found in the retail and service industries. In recent years, many companies using this method of franchising to expand their operations have experienced rapid growth. See **Table 5-3** for further details of the franchising company arrangement.

ADVANTAGES OF FRANCHISING LO7

Compared with the other two methods of starting a small business (buying and organizing), franchising offers many specific advantages.

PROVEN MARKET FOR THE PRODUCT OR SERVICE

Except for newly established franchises, a known market and instant brand recognition for the franchisor's product or service exists. Information about the performance of existing franchises is normally supplied or can be obtained by the franchisee. Such a track record makes it much easier to make projections for future operations. For example, successful franchises, such as Tim Hortons, Boston Pizza, and Subway, can usually provide reliable estimates for franchise sales based on market size and other conditions. (Read about another successful franchise in **Small Business in Action 5-4**.) For entrepreneurs this is very valuable knowledge, as it will help them in making a decision to invest in the business.

The instant pulling power of the product also greatly helps the small business owner shorten the duration of the initial stage of the business, when the market is being developed and resulting revenues are low. A study by the University of Toronto showed that franchised businesses had higher sales per outlet than independents in almost all types of businesses.[27] Another study of franchisors found that during the last recession, franchised outlets were less affected than non-franchised outlets.[28]

SERVICES THE FRANCHISOR MAY PROVIDE

A franchising company typically provides many valuable services to a franchisee. A description of franchisor services follows.

Selection of Location.

Assistance in selecting the location can be very important, especially if location is critical to the success of the business, such as in retailing and often in the service industry. Often a franchisor has considerable site selection expertise that can be used in establishing the business. Additionally, landlords are more likely to provide entrepreneurs with prime locations if the franchisor guarantees the lease to the landlord.

Purchase or Construction of Site, Buildings, and Equipment.

The franchisor's experience and financial resources in this area may mean considerable savings of time and money. In addition to providing expertise, the franchisor may even purchase or construct the facilities for the franchisee. For example, **Tim Hortons** takes full responsibility for the construction and development of its stores, and its franchise agreement actually prohibits franchisees from developing or constructing locations.[29]

Provision of Financing.

Some franchisors will provide financing for franchisees, and their association often helps the franchisee obtain financing. For example, some banks allow favourable interest rates on franchisee loans because of a franchisee's association with a well-known franchisor.

Standardized Methods of Operating.

Standardized operating procedures and manuals are often part of the services the franchisor provides in the areas of cost accounting, control systems, and customer service standards. Such methods can result in considerable savings for the small business. For example, **Boston Pizza** franchise owners are trained in a system that produces the lowest food costs in the industry. As a result, Boston Pizza franchisees enjoy food costs of 25 percent; this compares quite favourably to the industry average of 38 percent.[30]

Advertising.

Most franchisors will provide national advertising that may benefit the franchisee. Such a level of promotion may be difficult and costly for the franchisee to develop unassisted. For example, Tim Hortons spends millions every year supporting its brand by advertising its products and restaurants.

Purchasing Advantages.

Because the franchising company purchases large volumes of inventories for its franchisees, it can pass the resulting cost savings on to franchisees on purchases made from the franchisor.

Training.

Most franchisors provide training to new franchisees, which may be provided in a variety of forms: an instruction manual, site visits, and/or training at a franchisor's facility. Previous to opening any Boston Pizza franchise, head office sends nine trainers to assist the staff and the franchisee.[31] **Cora**, a Québec-based breakfast and lunch franchise that has been expanding throughout Canada, provides a five-week training program that includes one week of theoretical training and four weeks in-store practice in one of their corporate training facilities. The company's founder, Cora Tsouflidou, says they use these facilities to provide potential franchisees with insight into how busy a restaurant can be and everything that it takes to make it successful.[32] Other examples include **McDonald's** franchisees, who receive training at Hamburger University in Illinois and can even receive a bachelor's degree in Hamburgerology! Because of the extra training provided, franchising (as opposed to buying or organizing) is often more suited to someone who lacks experience in the industry. Recently, knowledge-based businesses such as consulting and research have experienced rapid growth in franchising. The capital investment to get established in these businesses is typically low and flexibility is high.

SMALL BUSINESS IN ACTION 5-4

BOOSTER JUICE—A CANADIAN FRANCHISE SUCCESS STORY

Dale Wishewan grew up wanting to be a baseball player. After completing his degree in mechanical engineering at Portland State University, which he attended on a baseball scholarship, he founded **Booster Juice** with a partner, John Amack. Wishewan felt that there was a market for a healthy alternative to traditional fast food. Booster Juice provides a menu of juices and smoothies consisting of such nutritional ingredients as natural fruits, wheat grass, and Acai berry. Booster Juice's mission statement is "To provide customers with an incredible, healthy alternative to fast food that's great tasting, convenient, and nutritious, making it perfectly suited for today's active lifestyle." The first Booster Juice outlet was opened in Sherwood Park, Alberta, in 1999. Since then, the concept has grown with the help of a well-developed franchise system.

Growth was rapid with 15 outlets added in the first year and 35 in the next. In 2002, however, Wishewan decided to reduce expansion to ensure that the business was on firm footing: "We consciously slowed down after our second year, wanting to be sure our concept grew into something solid," he reported. Wishewan and his management team spent about a year ironing out various kinks in the business plan. He secured better deals with food distributors and improved quality control by hiring permanent staff to visit each franchise on a regular basis. Wishewan understands that successful franchising is all about systems, and Booster Juice provides good training and support for franchisees. This includes hands-on training as well as assistance in the marketing, legal, logistics, and real estate aspects of the franchise. To decrease competition, Booster Juice bought out two smaller smoothie chains. Today, Booster Juice has 400 outlets operating across Canada.

Booster juice has used franchising to become the largest juice and smoothie company in Canada.

© Shane Shaw/iStockPhoto

Booster Juice has also expanded internationally, with several outlets in the U.S. as well as successful franchises in Saudi Arabia and planned entrances into the United Kingdom and China. Expanding internationally has been a challenge, however. Wishewan indicates that it is a big hurdle to find suitable overseas partners: "It is challenging to qualify an individual franchisee in Canada, but it is 10 times as important to choose the right master franchisor in another country." Booster Juice is now Canada's premium juice and smoothie franchise and plans call for the addition of 40 to 50 new locations each year.

Discussion Questions

1. What do you think are some of the strengths and weaknesses of the Booster Juice franchise?
2. Do you think Booster Juice grew too fast in the early years? What are the disadvantages to rapid growth from a franchisor–franchisee perspective?
3. The company originally started out serving fresh fruit, but has since moved to frozen produce to control costs. Do you think this is a good idea? Why or why not?

Ongoing Support.

In addition to initial training many franchises provide ongoing services and support to franchisees. This support can include follow-up training, assistance in managing the business, and, in some cases, help in the day-to-day operations. For example, both Vancouver-based franchise **1-800-Got-Junk?**, a junk removal business, and **Nurse Next Door**, a home-care company, offer call centre support for franchisees. The support enables owners to focus on generating sales and not on answering the phone. Nurse Next Door's call centre, which is open 24 hours a day and staffed by professional agents, saves franchisees an estimated 240 hours of work a month.[33] Both the above-mentioned Boston Pizza and Cora provide ongoing training and support. For example, Cora has corporate managers visit on a weekly basis, and if a store shows signs of financial trouble, corporate consultants are brought in to help manage costs and, if the need arises, to invest in additional local advertising.[34]

Because of these advantages, a franchisee's chance of success in the business is higher than with the other two methods of starting a small business. The franchising industry advertises a failure rate of only 4 to 8 percent, which is much lower than the rate for non-franchised businesses.[35] Some claim, however, that this low failure rate is greatly exaggerated by franchising companies. In the United States and Canada, an increasing number of franchisees are complaining—sometimes in court—about the problems incurred when signing a franchise contract.

POTENTIAL DISADVANTAGES OF FRANCHISING

Because of the advantages just discussed, many individuals have signed franchise contracts. However, some have suffered disillusionment and failure a short while later. The level of franchise litigation is growing. Often franchisees misinterpret the franchise agreement concerning such things as use of advertising funds, restrictions, and services provided by the franchisor. In other cases, the franchisor has acted inappropriately, leading to a dispute. It is critical that the prospective franchisee be aware of the difficulties that can arise when entering the world of franchising. Several areas of potential conflict are discussed in this section. Often, as in the case with a 2011 class-action lawsuit by franchisee owners of **Edible Arrangements**, a North American company that sells fruit bouquets, there is more than one complaint. In this specific case, franchise owners claimed Edible Arrangements made several decisions–such as forcing them to stay open for longer hours, implementing new software systems, and raising supply prices–that increased the costs of operating their stores. The franchisees further stated that the corporation started an online competitor, dippedfruit.com, which competed against the bricks-and-mortar stores.[36] The franchisee should have a clear understanding of how disputes will be resolved in the event that they occur. The following are some of the more common dangers.

LACK OF INDEPENDENCE

In signing a franchise contract, the franchisee can expect to receive a certain amount of assistance from the franchisor. The franchisor will monitor the business, however, to ensure that the conditions of the contract are being met. This condition restricts the franchisee's freedom and independence.

COST OF THE FRANCHISE

Most franchises have a price that often consists of an initial fee and ongoing royalties based on operations. To enter most franchise organizations, individuals have to accumulate a certain amount of capital either to pay the fee or to provide the facilities and the associated set-up costs.

UNFULFILLED PROMISES

Most franchising companies indicate they will provide such services as training and advertising. In some cases, however, this assistance does not materialize or is inadequate.

RESTRICTIONS ON THE CONTRACT

The franchise agreement may contain some restrictions that inhibit the franchisee's freedom. Such restrictions are discussed below.

Product or Service Offered.

The franchisee may not be allowed to offer for sale any products not procured by the franchisor.

Line Forcing.

The franchisee may be required to offer the franchisor's complete line of products for sale, even if some are not profitable in the franchisee's market area.

Termination.

The franchisee may not be able to terminate the franchise contract without incurring a penalty. The franchisee may also be prohibited from selling the business or passing it on to family members.

Remodelling Clauses.

Many franchise agreements force the franchise owner to update the facilities often at a significant cost to the franchisee. Boston Pizza forces franchisees to update their stores every seven years at a cost of approximately $800,000.[37]

SATURATION OF THE MARKET

In some industries, franchising companies have allowed oversaturation to occur in a particular geographic market. For example, David Joseph, an outspoken former owner of a Kumon franchise, a North American franchise that assists children in math and reading, has posted his concerns about Kumon on **UnhappyFranchisee.com**. Joseph, who eventually sold his franchise, cited oversaturation as an ongoing concern stating that Kumon had embraced a major expansion plan, and he suddenly found new stores in close proximity to his franchise.[38] Saturation in established markets is a growing problem in North America. Careful examination of the franchise contract should be made to ensure that this does not occur. This puts financial pressure on those franchisees operating within that market. In some cases, oversaturation has occurred when franchisees failed to understand their rights to protect their territory in their franchise agreement. Sometimes, franchisees get what is known as "right of first refusal." What this means is that if someone else wants to build a franchise near the original franchisee, the owner of the first franchise can purchase the proposed location instead. If they decline the location for any reason, including lack of financing or their franchise is not succeeding, anyone else can open a second franchise. An upset former Robin's Donuts franchise owner describes how he got out of the franchise business at a loss when the chain opened up seven stores in his area in a short time frame. When asked if he could have prevented this in any way he says, "No, the only thing I could have done was bought them all myself." John Sotos, a franchise lawyer in Toronto, thinks that companies such as **Subway** have expanded so much that they are putting franchisees at risk. If a franchisor has a large initial fee and no royalties, its major concern may be the selling of franchises rather than their ongoing success. Such franchises seem particularly vulnerable to over-saturation.[39]

LACK OF SECURITY

A franchisor may elect not to renew a franchise contract once it has expired or may terminate the contract before its expiry if the franchisee has violated the terms or conditions. Many franchising companies operate company-owned outlets as well as franchised outlets. The number of company-owned outlets is only about 18 percent of total franchise outlets, but recent figures show slight increases in this percentage.[40] Some argue that franchising companies take over the outlets after the franchisees have successfully established them. This practice has led to some lawsuits between franchisors and franchisees. For example, Timothy's Coffees of the World Inc. was recently successfully sued by a franchisee in Ontario for failure to renew the franchise agreement. Other examples include a group of Pizza Pizza franchisees who successfully sued Pizza Pizza for interference in store operations and wrongful termination of franchise agreements without cause. In one of the more infamous franchisor-franchisee disputes, Subway corporate employees went into a franchisee's store overnight, changed the locks on the door, and hired a security guard to keep the franchise owner out of the store because he had failed to make a $4600 royalty payment.[41]

COST OF MERCHANDISE

The cost of merchandise purchased from the franchisor may exceed the price the franchisee can obtain elsewhere. However, the contract may require the franchisee to purchase solely from the franchisor. For example, two well-known Canadian franchisors, **Pet Valu Canada** and **Quiznos**, have been involved in legal disputes with franchisees who claim they are either overpaying for supplies or are not getting access to expected volume rebates.[42] The Quiznos suit became a class-action suit that was settled in 2015 at an estimated cost of $100 million to the franchisor. [43]

EFFECTIVENESS OF PROMOTIONS

Most franchisors provide promotion and advertising for their franchisees. In some situations, however, the promotion is not effective for the franchisee's market and may be time consuming and costly for the franchisee to participate in. Often a franchisee does not want to participate in these programs but is required by the contract to do so. For example, a Wendy's franchisee expressed frustration with the franchisor's marketing fee. This is a fee that he had to pay every month as his contribution to Wendy's national and provincial marketing programs. At the time, his store was operating in a French-language community and Wendy's was not advertising in French.

EXAGGERATION OF FINANCIAL SUCCESS

Most franchising companies provide promotional literature for prospective franchisees. This information generally contains financial statements for the typical franchisee. In some cases, these estimates have been overly optimistic and the actual results for the franchisee are disappointing. For example, a **Mr. Sub** franchisee successfully sued the franchisor after the courts found, in part, that the franchisor provided financial statements that were misleading. The judge ordered the franchisor to return the owner's initial investment along with damages.[44] The Unhappy Franchisee website has also targeted Liberty Tax Franchisor as another company with questionable claims. Liberty Tax had been promoting their franchise as one with low risk and high returns, and it claimed to have created hundreds of millionaires. Writers for Unhappy Franchisee note that while the claim may not be illegal it is highly questionable given the long list of complaints against the company from current and previous franchise owners about poor financial results. Early in 2019, Tim Hortons was named in a new lawsuit (**Small Business in Action 5-5** offers information on earlier lawsuits against that corporation). Tim-Minn Inc., owned and operated by Canadian Paul Durigon, had agreed to lead an aggressive franchise expansion plan in Minnesota opening 280 stores in a state where none existed. Durigon, who has only opened 14 stores, is suing the chain stating that they misled him on the potential for success and overcharged him for supplies.[45]

While most would consider Tim Hortons a successful franchisor, they have faced legal challenges, including several class-action lawsuits from upset franchisees.

DIFFICULTY IN SETTLING DISPUTES

One problem for franchisees is they may have very little recourse when it comes to settling disputes. Often the franchisor has drafted a franchise agreement that protects its own interests foremost. In addition, while franchisees can pursue legal action, they often do not have the same legal and financial resources the franchisor has. The result is the franchisor is often better prepared to win disputes. As discussed above, only six Canadian provinces have franchise legislation, and although they all offer franchisees some type of protection if they have been defrauded, there is not a great deal of protection for other grievances. The time it takes to settle a dispute can also be problematic for franchisees. Given that franchisees may want to quickly settle a dispute because they need money or a decision on a difficult question, a franchisor with more resources can often be much more patient. For example, a number of Midas Canada franchisees filed a cooperative class action suit against their franchisor Midas Canada. The franchisees' original complaints against Midas dated from a unilateral change in the franchise agreement by the franchisor in 2003. While the franchisees did eventually reach a settlement with Midas they did not receive any funds until 2014—11 years later![46]

SMALL BUSINESS IN ACTION 5-5

TIM HORTONS FRANCHISEES VS. THE FRANCHISOR

In 2010, a group of Tim Hortons franchisees failed in their attempt to sue the franchisor for $2 billion in a class action lawsuit. The franchisees were upset that Tim Hortons had forced them to stop baking fresh doughnuts in their stores and instead required them to use shipped frozen products, which they warmed-up or finished baking. Tim Hortons' late co-founder Ron Joyce said he did not like the taste of the new doughnuts and it flew in the face of the company's motto, "Always Fresh."

What likely upset the franchisees even more than deviating from the "Always Fresh" model is the cost of the frozen doughnuts is more than double the cost of baking doughnuts in stores—something that was at the heart of the lawsuit. The franchisees claimed that forcing them to sell frozen doughnuts was eating into their profits. Franchisees further claimed that Tim Hortons was setting the price of some lunch items, such as soups and some sandwiches, so low—sometimes below cost—that they were losing money on the sale of goods. The low prices were seen as particularly problematic because franchisees still had to pay Tim Hortons a royalty on sales, creating a larger loss. In responding to the lawsuit, Tim Hortons stated that its franchise agreement allowed it to stipulate the costs of supplies and determine the selling price of its products.

The Ontario court found in favour of Tim Hortons, the franchisor, stating franchisees have a right to earn a reasonable return, and their coffee sales, which have significant markup, allow them to do so. The court further noted franchisees do not get to make money on all items they sell and they should be willing to sell some items below cost in return for the right to sell Tim Hortons branded coffee.

Franchise-owners, undaunted by the failure, brought two new lawsuits forward against the company in 2017. This lawsuit was spearheaded by the Great White North Franchise Association, an alliance of Tim Hortons franchisees from across Canada. The Association alleged that Tim Hortons had improperly used its national advertising money and was seeking $500 million in damages. The second lawsuit, which was seeking $1.5 billion in damages claimed Tim Hortons was not allowing franchisees who joined the Association opportunities to purchase future stores and was planning on buying their franchises back from the store owners. As of 2019, it appears that Tim Hortons is close to settling this suit.

A group of Tim Hortons franchisees unsuccessfully tried to sue the company after Tim Hortons forced them to sell frozen doughnuts. Franchisees were upset that the doughnuts were double the cost of the ones produced fresh in stores.

Niloo/Shutterstock.com

Discussion Questions

1. Were you surprised that the judge agreed with the franchisor in the first case?
2. Do you think it's fair that Tim Hortons, the franchisor, is setting the price of menu items below cost and then taking a royalty on the sale of these items, furthering the franchisees' loss?
3. While many Tim Hortons franchisees are no doubt quite successful, the ones that are struggling would have been negatively affected by the change in doughnut prices. What, if anything, could Tim Hortons do to help these franchisees?
4. Based on what you have read in this case, would the information deter you from buying a Tim Hortons franchise? Why or why not?

FINDING A FRANCHISE

Entrepreneurs searching for a franchise opportunity can use the same opportunity search techniques discussed in previous chapters. They can evaluate franchises that they come into contact with during their daily activities, conduct a search, and seek advice from business contacts, colleagues, and friends. As part of a search, entrepreneurs may use the Internet to search for ideas, buy magazines that discuss franchising, and attend franchise shows. Some helpful directories include *The Franchise Canada Directory*. **Small Business in Action 5-6** below provides details about one unique franchise opportunity and **Table 5-4** lists the hot trends in franchising.

TABLE 5-4 Hot Trends in Franchising – Five Year Growth

1. Maid Service – 129% growth in five years
2. Real Estate – 111% growth in five years.
3. Educational Products & Services – 91% growth in five years
4. Accounting/Tax Services – 60% growth in five years
5. Health and Fitness/Nutrition – 35% growth in five years

Source: "2019 Franchising Trends Report," CFA, accessed August 11, 2019, https://www.cfa.ca/franchisecanada/2019-franchising-trends-report/. Used with permission.

The entrepreneur will usually shortlist some franchises and contact the company for a promotional kit. Most companies will provide the entrepreneur with basic information and ask the entrepreneur to fill out an application form (often found on the company's website) that must be approved before receiving additional documents. The application form usually asks for the entrepreneur's work, financials, and education histories. If the company feels the entrepreneur is a good candidate for a franchise, then it will send a full information kit.

After the entrepreneur receives the information, she should evaluate the documents and ask the franchisor for any clarification that is required. Note that just because an entrepreneur decides to buy a franchise it does not mean that the franchisor will sell one. The franchisor may engage in a lengthy evaluation of the entrepreneur and decide that he or she is not a suitable franchisee in its business. For example, Second Cup and Robin's Donuts, both successful Canadian franchises, have potential franchisees take personality tests to determine whether candidates will be a good fit in the franchise system. **Table 5-5** lists some of the new and growing franchises of 2019.

TABLE 5-5 New and Growing Franchises of 2019 and the Investment Required

1.	uBreakiFix	\$60K–\$225K
2.	velofix	\$169K–\$203K
3.	Fyzical Therapy & Balance Centers	\$139K–399K
4.	Crunch Fitness Canada	\$386K–\$1.6M
5.	Level UP Learning Centers	\$96.5-252K
6.	Rockin' Jump	\$1.4M–\$2.9M
7.	Tommy Guns	\$450K–plus
8.	Holy Falafel	\$125K–\$375K
9.	Goliath Tech Inc.	\$73K–\$176K
10.	Experimac	\$142K–\$321K

SMALL BUSINESS IN ACTION 5-6

VELOFIX, A MOBILE FRANCHISE PURSUING HIGH GROWTH

Cyclists Chris Guillemet and Boris Martin of Vancouver say that one thing people lack is time. Time to work and, more importantly, time to ride bicycles and enjoy life. With this concept in mind, the Vancouver-based partners founded **Velofix**, a franchised mobile bicycle-service business.

The concept is rather simple: bike owners can either phone Velofix or use their app to book a bicycle-repair service. At the confirmed time, a bright red van pulls up and the service repair person, who is usually the owner-operator, performs the repairs. Customers love the convenience and the franchise owner loves the roughly 60 percent gross margins they earn while a running their own business.

Establishing a new franchise business such as Velofix is not always easy. Persuading potential franchisees to invest in a new franchise concept can be challenging as potential clients often think there is little brand value in a newly established franchise. Potential investors often wonder if they could save the franchise fee and ongoing royalties and just start their own independent firm.

What Velofix offers is a unique concept, mobile bike repair, and a well-developed, back-end support system. Support includes cloud-based scheduling software that allows customers to book services; a route optimizer for the van; and a daily planner for the owner-operator, who can take along the necessary parts based on the scheduled services. Velofix has also signed partnerships with roughly 50 online bicycle sellers where the company will deliver and, if needed, build and properly size new bikes. For all of this, franchise owners pay Velofix a $25,000 franchise fee, an eight percent royalty on gross revenue, and invest approximately $45,000 to $50,000 in their vans.

Since the company's inception in 2013, franchise sales have taken off. The company now has over 100 franchisees, including many in the Southern United States where people can bike more due to the favourable weather. Velofix's plans for the future include quickly growing to 450 franchisees and expanding outside of North America.

Discussion Questions

1. Do you think Velofix offers potential franchisee owners enough advantages over starting their own independent mobile bicycle-repair services to justify the franchisee fee and the ongoing royalty? Why or why not?
2. Why do you think Velofix is hoping to grow so quickly? What are some of the advantages and disadvantages of a high-growth strategy?
3. Velofix currently has very few competitors. Given the relatively low cost of starting a rival franchised business, would you invest in Velofix as a franchisee? Why or why not?
4. Velofix has taken a service that has traditionally been performed in repair shops and made it mobile. Develop a list of other businesses (products or services) which could move from a brick-and-mortar location to the mobile world. Share the list with your classmates.

EVALUATION OF A FRANCHISE OPPORTUNITY LO8

In view of the potential disadvantages discussed earlier, it is critical to make a thorough investigation of the prospective franchise before signing the contract. Several key areas should be examined in evaluating a franchise. Thorough investigation of the franchisor, the product or service, the franchise contract, and the market should be carried out.

Franchising involves many risks to an entrepreneur. Although we often read or hear about the success of Tim Hortons or Canadian Tire, for every one of these successes, there are many failures. Franchising, like any other venture, is not for the passive person. It requires effort and long hours, as any business does, since duties such as hiring, scheduling, buying, accounting, and so on, are still the franchisee's responsibility.

Not every franchise is right for every entrepreneur. They must evaluate the franchise alternatives to decide which one is most appropriate. A number of factors should be assessed before making the final decision.

1. UNPROVEN VERSUS PROVEN FRANCHISE

There are some trade-offs in investing in a proven or an unproven franchise business. Whereas an unproven franchise will be a less-expensive investment, the lower investment is offset by more risk. In an unproven franchise, the franchisor is likely to make mistakes as the business grows. These mistakes could inevitably lead to failure. Constant reorganization of a new franchise can result in confusion and mismanagement. Yet a new and unproven franchise can offer more excitement and challenge and can lead to significant opportunities for large profits should the business grow rapidly. A proven franchise offers lower risk but requires more financial investment. For example, Nurse Next Door, a relatively new, Vancouver-based franchise operating in the home health-care market, is pursuing a high-growth strategy and striving to expand across Canada and into the

United States. Currently, almost all the locations have been open for less than five years, the exception being two model stores in Vancouver and Kamloops. Although this franchise may represent a great opportunity for an entrepreneur to own a growing franchise with relatively low start-up costs, they must also realize that Nurse Next Door will not be able to provide substantial information (e.g., long-term sales figures, profit statements) on other franchisees, because many have been open for a short time.

2. FINANCIAL STABILITY OF FRANCHISE

The purchase of a franchise should entail an assessment of the financial stability of the franchisor. A potential franchisee should find answers to the following questions:

- How many franchises are in the organization?
- How successful is each of the members of the franchise organization?
- Are most of the profits of the franchise a function of fees from the sale of franchises or from royalties based on profits of franchisees?
- Does the franchisor have management expertise in production, finance, and marketing?

Some of the above information can be obtained from profit-and-loss statements of the franchise organization. Face-to-face contact with the franchisor can also indicate the success of the organization. It is also worthwhile to contact some of the franchisees directly to determine their success and to identify any problems that have occurred. If financial information of the franchisor is unavailable, the entrepreneur may purchase a financial rating from a source such as Dun and Bradstreet. Generally, the following are good external sources of information:

- Franchise associations
- Other franchisees
- Government (especially provinces or territories with franchise legislation)
- Accountants and lawyers
- Libraries
- Franchise directories and journals
- Business exhibitions

3. POTENTIAL MARKET FOR THE NEW FRANCHISE

It is important for the entrepreneur to evaluate the market that the franchise will attract. A starting point is evaluating the traffic flow and demographics of the residents from a map of the area. Traffic flow information may be observed by visiting the area. Direction of traffic flow, ease of entry to the business, and the amount of traffic (pedestrian and automobile) can be estimated by observation. The demographics of the area can be determined from census data, which can be obtained from local libraries or the town hall. It can also be advantageous to locate competitors on the map to determine their potential effect on the franchise business. Marketing research in the market area is helpful. Attitudes about and interest in the new business can be assessed in the market research. In some instances, the franchisor will conduct a market study as a selling point to the franchisee.

4. PROFIT POTENTIAL FOR A NEW FRANCHISE

As in any start-up business, it is important to develop pro forma income and cash flow statements. The franchisor should provide projections in order to calculate the needed information. The entrepreneur will also want to consider the start-up money required, the terms for any royalty payments, and sources and costs of supplies.

5. TERRITORIAL PROTECTION

Does the franchise offer any territorial protection? As previously discussed some franchisors will only offer "right of first refusal" protection, which means that a franchisee owner is given the chance to open up another franchise in their territory. If the original franchisee does not want to or cannot for any reason, then the franchisor can open another business or sell the rights to another franchisee. Entrepreneurs should try to find franchises that grant them exclusive regions—but they should also realize that the number of franchisors that do this is shrinking.

6. TRAINING AND OPERATIONS ASSISTANCE

Most, if not all, franchises offer some type of training and operations procedures. Entrepreneurs should be looking for comprehensive, documented training that occurs both prior to and after opening the business. Good training programs are easy to follow and have accompanying metrics. In addition, the franchise should provide ongoing operations assistance and managerial controls. Entrepreneurs should seek franchises that offer operating profits superior to their benchmarks. This will indicate that the company's operating systems are providing the franchisee with value.

7. CONTRACT LENGTH AND RENEWAL, AND TERMINATION TERMS

The duration of franchise agreements can vary significantly. Some franchise agreements offer terms of less than five years, while others offer 20-year-plus terms. Entrepreneurs should look for franchises that offer terms of at least ten years, with a 20-year term being more acceptable. Additionally, entrepreneurs must fully understand the renewal process for a franchise. Sometimes the renewal is automatic, but in some cases it is up to the franchisor's discretion. The entrepreneur does not want to be taken by surprise as was one Second Cup franchisee in Toronto, who was shocked to learn that Second Cup would not be renewing his franchise. The result was a significant financial loss for the franchisee. Furthermore, the entrepreneur will want to consider any additional fees that must be paid on the renewal of the agreement. The entrepreneur will also want to clarify if the contract comes with a termination clause and what these terms entail.

8. WHAT CURRENT OWNERS SAY ABOUT THEIR FRANCHISE

When investigating a franchise, it is important to talk to other franchise owners to find out if they are happy with their decisions. Sometimes the franchisor will supply some contact information, but it is highly recommended that potential franchisees seek their own contacts, as it is unlikely that a franchisor would provide contacts who are unhappy with the system. (Unhappy franchisees are discussed in **Small Business in Action 5-7** below.) Some questions to consider asking a current or former franchisee include the following:

- Why did you choose this franchise?
- Are you happy with the choice?
- Did you have any problems with the franchisor? If so, how were they resolved?
- Are there any hidden costs or fees?
- Are you satisfied with the training and marketing assistance provided by the franchisor? Why or why not?
- Would you invest in this franchise again?

In general, most of the information should be provided in the disclosure statement or the prospectus. If the franchisor refuses to answer these questions, a potential franchisee should take a lot more time evaluating the franchisor.

Front-end procedure fees, royalty payments, expenses, and other information should be compared with that of franchises in the same field, as well as in different business areas. If a franchise looks good as an investment, the entrepreneur may request a full franchise package from the franchisor, which usually contains a draft franchise agreement or contract. The contract or franchise agreement is the final step in establishing a franchise arrangement. Here, a lawyer experienced in franchising should be used. The franchise agreement contains all the specific requirements and obligations of the franchisee. Things such as the exclusivity of territory coverage will protect against the franchisor's granting another franchise within a certain radius of the business. The renewable terms will indicate the length of the contract and the requirements. Financial requirements will stipulate the initial price for the franchise, the schedule of payments, and the royalties to be paid. Termination of franchise requirements should indicate what will happen if the franchisee develops a disability or dies and what provisions are made for the family. Terminating a franchise generally results in more lawsuits than any other issue in franchising. These terms should also allow the franchisee to obtain fair market value should the franchise be sold. Even though the agreement may be standard, the franchisee should try to negotiate important items to reduce the investment risk.

SMALL BUSINESS IN ACTION 5-7

UNHAPPYFRANCHISEE.COM

The name of the site says it all. UnhappyFranchisee.com is a website where unhappy franchise owners can vent their frustrations about their franchisor. In addition to allowing visitors to post both anonymous and signed complaints, the website maintains an active list of legal cases concerning franchisor-franchisee disputes and publishes research about franchising. The site also allows franchisors to dispute some of the posted information or to defend their franchising track record and practices. For example, UnhappyFranchise.com recently published a report noting the following information about A&W franchises:

A&W RESTAURANTS FRANCHISES 2008–2011

Franchises open January 2009	910
Franchises added 2009–2011	31
Franchises terminated/closed 2009–2011	167
Franchises terminated/closed (%)	18%

The information, which it took from A&W's disclosure documents, indicates a high termination/failure rate, something that would likely deter future franchisees. Kevin Bazner, president and CEO of A&W Restaurants, responded to this report on the website and cited several reasons to explain the store's poor performance, including co-branded stores (shared with another restaurant) and corporate restructuring issues.

Discussion Questions

1. Given that not all posts are signed, how much credibility would you give to the reviews on the site? Would you consider them at all? Why or why not?
2. Given that the information published about A&W was part of the company's internal records, would this affect your decision to purchase an A&W franchise? Why or why not?
3. Given that Bazner responded to the website, does he add credibility to the report and the website itself? Does Bazner's response offer enough to put potential franchisees at ease with their decision to purchase an A&W franchise?
4. Use the Internet to visit the site, look at Bazner's complete response. Does his response explain the high failure rate of A&W stores? Why or why not?

Unhappyfranchisee.com is attracting more attention as a source of information for potential franchisees. Some CEOs, like A&W's Kevin Bazner, monitor the site's information about their company.

© AWSeebaran/iStockPhoto

Because the signing of a franchise contract is a major step for the entrepreneur, the investigation should be thorough. **Appendix 5B** at the end of this chapter provides a comprehensive checklist for the prospective franchisee to use in this evaluation.

Table 5-6 lists the top franchises for 2019.

TABLE 5-6 **Top Franchises for 2019**

1. McDonald's	\$1.1M – \$2.2M
2. Symposium Cafe	\$665K – \$730K
3. Pizza Nova	\$450K – \$500K
4. Boston Pizza	\$1.7M – \$2.6M
5. UCMAS Mental Math	\$40K – \$60K
6. A&W	\$1.1M – \$1.7M
7. Tim Hortons	\$430K – \$480K
8. Triple Os	\$750K – \$1.5M
9. Oxford Learning Centre	\$109K – \$243K
10. Home Instead Senior Care	\$125K – \$145K

THE ENTREPRENEUR AS FRANCHISOR LO9

An increasingly popular method of entrepreneurship in franchising is not being a franchisee but, rather, selling franchises and becoming a franchisor. For example, John DeHart and Ken Sim, founders of Nurse Next Door, started the company with the goal of creating a large franchisor company. After establishing three stores on Canada's West Coast, the pair immediately went into hyper-expansion mode and quickly added 50 franchises in a short time. Before a prospective franchisor attempts to sell franchises, several requirements must be met. Is the type of business franchisable? What information is required? How much capital is needed? All these questions should be addressed in the process of becoming a franchisor.

WHAT BUSINESSES CAN BE FRANCHISED?

Franchises abound in many industries today. This phenomenon is reflected in the following statement by the U.S. Commerce Department: "Any business that can be taught to someone is being franchised."[47] The franchise business must have a sound concept. The franchise should be distinct, be practical, and fill a need. It must also be easy to teach and clearly communicated to others. It must be capable of being replicated and transferred to other geographic areas. The example in **Small Business Beginnings 5-2** reveals how this is so. Suzy Okun, a co-founder of the franchise Treats, which specialized in desserts, elaborated on this idea, saying at the time: "We sell a concept. We take what the palate already knows, and we make it electric! We take what the customer has already seen and do it differently."[48] Consumer research may be required to solidify the concept. Estimates based on sound research will be much more attractive to the prospective franchisee.

HOW DOES SOMEONE BECOME A FRANCHISOR?

Once prospective franchisors are satisfied that the business can be franchised, they must take several steps to develop the franchise. Some of the most important steps are discussed next.

1. Establish a Prototype.

The franchisor should set up and operate a prototype business long enough to iron out the bugs and get a clear picture of market demand. This business can also serve as a reference point for prospective franchisees to use in their evaluations. To be useful, the prototype should be earning a consistent profit.

2. Selling Franchises.

Entrepreneurs often get established in business by operating a single franchise. However, selling franchises after successfully managing their own has been the preferred route to follow for some. Such is the case with master franchisor Nicole Matta, who has obtained the rights to sell a U.S.-based line of high-tech, low-touch spa centres in Ontario for **Planet Beach Spray & Spa**. Planet Beach's services are fully automated. There are no massage therapists, but the company still provides body wraps, facials, full-body and deep-tissue massages, and UV therapy using high-tech equipment to deliver the treatments in private rooms. Growth for Planet Beach's Spas has been dramatic, and Matta is confident that this growth will be repeated in Ontario. She is planning to award eight to 10 franchises in the next year and to have about 40 locations in the next four to five years. With the company's help, Matta is able to provide marketing, financial, and operational assistance to prospective franchisees, which increases their chance of success.[49]

3. Prepare the Necessary Information.

Information prospective franchisees will require includes promotional literature regarding the franchise and detailed financial data not only for the company but also for a typical franchise. A prospective franchisee requires information on capital needed, potential income, cash flow projections, and future trends in the industry to make an informed decision. It is recommended that someone with accounting expertise be retained to assist in preparing this information.

4. Investigate the Legal Requirements.

The franchisor should investigate the legal requirements in setting up a franchising company. Some of these requirements include the following:

- Registration and disclosure with government agencies; as mentioned earlier, some provinces require detailed information before franchising can begin.
- The required business licences and incorporations.
- Other laws regulating the operations of franchises.

In addition, the franchise contract should be drawn up by someone with legal expertise to ensure that the rights of both parties are protected. The legal operations of the franchise and the responsibilities of both franchisor and franchisee are formalized in the franchise contract. The franchisor needs to decide which services and what assistance to provide, what restrictions to impose, and what to require from the franchisee in return.

5. Develop a Planned and Standardized Program of Operations.

Standardization of procedures is an essential part of a successful franchise and enables the franchisor to monitor operations more easily. The following quote about **Molly Maid**, a maid service franchise, illustrates the effective use of professionals in the development of the franchise system:

> *MacKenzie made full use of experts in setting up his company. He used two well-known accounting firms, one to develop an internal accounting system, and the second to construct a package for franchisees. A legal expert on franchising developed the franchise agreement, and a firm specializing in trademarks and patents set up the rules for use of the logo.*[50]

The operations manual is generally developed using the experience of the prototype business. As mentioned above, the methods or system used are typically the service that is franchised. The franchisor must ensure that the operations manual is understandable and easy to integrate into franchisee operations. The following quote about **College Pro Painters** shows the time and care taken in preparing the operations manual:

> *After graduation in 1974, he took a year off to travel around the world, and started to put together a manual for the operation of College Pro Painters. Drawing on the knowledge he had acquired at school, he developed a chronology for starting a business and systematically attached every topic from "Business Plan" to "Close Down" in what would become his corporate bible.*[51]

6. Establish a Support System.

After establishing standard operations, entrepreneurs will have to create a support system to assist franchisees in training and managing their company. Most successful franchisors have initial and ongoing training in place for franchisees and provide assistance in managing the ongoing operation of the business, including but not limited to staffing, marketing, and financial planning. As noted earlier, Boston Pizza one of Canada's most successful franchises, provides training for new franchisees in a corporate store and then sends a nine-person team to help train the staff before opening. Additionally, the franchisees can expect to be visited a minimum of four times a year for an assessment of operational performance and food quality. Boston Pizza also sends in secret shoppers throughout the year to help improve restaurant performance and maintains an advisory council to provide advice to store owners.[52] Nurse Next Door, as discussed, established a call centre and staffed it with trained operators to assist franchisees in managing their business. Boston Pizza and Nurse Next Door are not alone in this support, and other successful franchisors, such as Tim Hortons, Subway, and Harvey's, actively provide franchisees with a considerable amount of assistance in running their business.

7. Obtain Adequate Financing.

To franchise successfully, the franchisor will need capital to set up the prototype business, do the necessary market research, prepare the promotional literature and financial estimates, and develop the system of operations. A rapid expansion program may even require outside equity financing from a venture-capital company or other financial institution.

8. Find Franchisees.

After establishing standard operations, obtaining capital, and creating a support system, franchisors must find franchisees. A common method to do this is to advertise in trade publications and on the Internet or to rely on word of mouth. Franchisors should recognize that the selection of franchisees is very important to the long-term success of their firm. George Melville, co-owner of Boston Pizza, says, "You want somebody who is entrepreneurial and yet can work within a system. A lot of times you need some business acumen and some money, but you also need a personality."[53] Successful franchisors will spend significant resources finding and then selecting franchisees. Cora restaurant will spend two months evaluating franchise candidates and only one in 15 actually make the cut. Douglas Fisher, a Toronto restaurant consultant, says, "Franchisees are your partners and you need to pick them wisely. A heartbeat and money does not make a good franchisee."[54]

SMALL BUSINESS BEGINNINGS 5-2

SPRAY-NET COMING TO A HOME NEAR YOU

Carmelo Marsala, the owner and founder of Montreal-based **Spray-Net**, is an example of a small franchisor who can offer potential franchisees significant value if they choose to purchase his franchise system.

Spray-Net is a unique, mobile, home-painting business that specializes in applying a factory finish to non-wooden surfaces, such as aluminum and vinyl siding, brick, and stucco. While studying at Concordia University, Marsala earned extra money running a painting franchise. After his second year in business, he stopped taking on clients who wanted non-wooden homes, doors, or window frames painted as he wasn't happy with the end results. Traditional paint was resulting in a subpar finish and sometimes warped the siding. Marsala thought the lack of suitable products to repaint non-wooden surfaces represented a significant opportunity if he could create a paint that would work on various finishes. Marsala succeeded in creating a paint product that could be applied using a spray after investing in research and development, and working with a chemist. The end product offers consumers an industrial-strength factory finish, which Marsala guarantees for 15 years.

Given his lack of financial resources and his desire to quickly scale the business, Marsala opted to pursue the franchise model. He says franchising made sense as he could quickly scale the business, grow the brand and his team, and create economies of scale. Marsala initially offered franchisees an opportunity to buy a geographical territory, which included a mobile unit and access to his paint all for $80,000 plus a seven percent royalty. While initial franchise sales were slow, with only two

[continued]

[continued]

purchased at the outset, sales have progressed significantly, and Spray-Net now has franchises in 18 territories. Total revenue for the company in 2018 exceeded $8 million, and Marsala reports that most franchisee owners have reinvested by purchasing additional territories. The company is currently aggressively expanding both in Canada and the United States, and long-term plans are to take Spray-Net global. He notes that while franchising has allowed him to scale quickly, it did require more money to expand than he originally thought.

Discussion Questions

1. What are some advantages and disadvantages of franchising from the franchisor's perspective?
2. Spray-Net has not patented their paint or their technology. Would this concern you if you were a potential franchisee?
3. Use Internet resources to see what the current franchisee costs are for establishing a Spray-Net franchise. Based on information you can find online and information in this case, would you invest in a Spray-Net franchise? Why or why not?

FRANCHISING IN THE FUTURE

Franchising is expected to continue its rapid growth as new types of businesses incorporate franchising principles into their operations. Several trends are expected to surface in the future. The retail food industry, the largest sector of Canadian franchising, is expected to continue its growth but in more specialized areas, such as ethnic foods. This growth will provide numerous opportunities for entrepreneurs, but it also means greater competition for existing small businesses in certain industries. As mentioned previously, more and more service businesses are expected to become franchises. A high percentage of Canada's fastest-growing franchises are in the service industry.

Some franchises are experimenting with "piggybacking," in which two or more franchises operate in one outlet. This concept has been tried with gas stations/convenience stores and restaurants/video stores. The practice of converting existing chain outlets to franchises, or "branchising," is expected to continue as chains search for new sources of interest-free capital. Additional growth areas in franchising are "mini-franchises," which are small satellite versions of larger franchisees (such as a McDonald's in a Walmart) and mobile franchises that move from location to location on a seasonal basis.

LEARNING OBJECTIVES SUMMARY

LO1 **The potential advantages of buying a small business include the reduction of risk, time, set-up expense, and competition; capitalization of business strength; possible assistance from the previous owner; and easier planning. Potential disadvantages include problems with physical facilities, personnel, inventory, and accounts receivable; deterioration of the business' financial condition or market; and difficulty in negotiating a purchase price.**

LO2 **The common sources for locating a business for sale include classified ads, government departments, real estate brokers, word of mouth, and professionals such as lawyers, accountants, and bankers.**

LO3 **The key areas an entrepreneur should investigate in carrying out an industry analysis are sales and profit trends, degree of competition, state of the economy in the market area, legal restrictions, and social concerns that may adversely affect the industry in the future. To evaluate the internal aspects, the following should be addressed: previous owner's reputation, why the owner is selling the business, validity of the financial statements, condition of the assets, personnel, external relationships of the business, and existing records.**

LO4 There are three general approaches to valuing a business. The first method uses the asset value to determine the price. The second method uses the earnings of the business. The third method uses a combination of assets and earnings.

LO5 Franchising has enjoyed phenomenal growth in recent years. One reason franchising is popular is the increased incentives for franchisees. Franchising continues to allow many organizations with a proven concept or product to expand much more rapidly to meet demand.

LO6 The three types of franchises are (1) the manufacturer-directed franchise, in which the manufacturer of a product grants a dealer the right to sell the product; (2) the wholesaler-retailer–directed franchise, in which one member of the distribution channel, such as the wholesaler or retailer, initiates the organization of the franchise; and (3) the franchise company, in which a company sells a product, service, or system in exchange for an initial predetermined fee and an ongoing royalty.

LO7 Franchising offers the following advantages over the other two methods of starting a small business: a proven market and services, such as selection of location, purchase or construction of the site; financing; standardized methods of operating; advertising; volume purchasing; and training.
The potential disadvantages of franchising are lack of independence, cost of the franchise, unfulfilled promises, restrictions in the contract, saturation of the market, lack of security, cost of merchandise, and possible exaggeration of financial success.

LO8 Several key areas should be examined in evaluating a franchise. Information can be obtained from several sources, including the franchising company; the Canadian Franchise Association; professionals, such as lawyers and accountants; other franchisees; and government agencies.

LO9 Becoming a successful franchisor entails five steps. The first step is to develop a franchise prototype to iron out any difficulties. The second is to prepare the necessary information for the prospective franchisee. The third is to investigate the legal requirements in setting up a franchise company.
The fourth is to plan and standardize the program of operation to facilitate the monitoring of operations. The last step is to ensure that adequate financing is available to keep up with possible rapid expansion.

TIME TO TAKE ACTION

If you are interested in becoming an entrepreneur as a franchisee, learning more about franchising, or growing a business through acquisition, then this is the time to act. You may want to consider using some or all of the steps outlined below:

1. Start to study the industry in which you are interested in owning a business. Narrow the search to a few franchises or specific businesses. Conduct some research specific to the company, including identifying and assessing its marketing mix, value chain, and competition. Then look at the target market to identify the customers; talk to them to determine if they are satisfied, if they will continue to visit the location, and so forth.
2. Contact businesses or franchisors, and let them know you are interested in either buying a business or in becoming a franchisee. If you are looking to buy a business, then you should start to investigate the financials of the company and the personnel by using the methods discussed in this chapter. If it is a franchise, then you will ask to see additional information and to speak to franchisees.
3. Speak to people who have engaged in similar business decisions in the past. If you are buying a business, talk to people who have bought businesses about the pros and cons, how to structure a deal, and where to get financing. If you are interested in franchising, then speak to people who have owned and operated a franchise.

DISCUSSION QUESTIONS

1. Why are there so many different techniques for determining the worth of a firm? In any given situation, is there one right answer for a company's value? What effects do your answers to these questions have on the entrepreneur making an acquisition?
2. Being a franchisor seems to be a mechanism for growth, but what are the growth prospects for entrepreneurs that are franchisees? Isn't the entrepreneur limited in his or her ability to pursue all the different types of growth strategies?
3. Is being a franchisee simply substituting one type of employment for another type of employment?
4. What do you think is the best method of becoming an entrepreneur? Starting a business from scratch? Buying an existing business? Buying a franchise? Why?
5. Discuss in detail the steps you would follow in developing a housecleaning franchise system.
6. What possible benefits does a franchise realize in franchising its business instead of expanding through company-owned outlets? What method of expansion would you prefer? Why?

EXPERIENTIAL EXERCISES

1. Find a local business that is for sale, and investigate and evaluate the company. Determine whether the business is overvalued, fairly valued, or undervalued. If you had the capital, would you buy this business? Have other groups evaluate each business, and compare the results.
2. John Van Goegh wants to own his own business. His area of expertise is the sporting goods market. He has checked into opening his own store versus purchasing an existing store in the downtown area. The existing store is a seven-year-old proprietorship with sagging sales. There are four main sporting goods shops in the city (60,000 people). The existing business is in a prime location, and the market and product line are well established. The financial condition, however, includes a large number of accounts receivable. With this information, John turns to you as a consultant. What advice would you give John regarding whether to purchase the existing business or start his own? What additional factors should he consider? Justify your answer.
3. You are investigating the purchase of a fertilizer manufacturing plant. The results of your analysis of the firm are extremely positive, except for an unidentifiable annual payment of $100,000. On further digging, you learn that the $100,000 is being paid in fines for dumping toxic waste. The previous owner has determined that it costs less to pay the fines than it would to properly dispose of the waste by deep-well injection. In light of recent government actions, how would this situation affect your decision to purchase? Explain.
4. Sally's Bar and Grill is available for purchase. Sally's earnings for the past five years were as follows:

Last year, $50,000	Four years ago, $40,000
Two years ago, $60,000	Five years ago, $25,000
Three years ago, $30,000	

   Determine the value of the business, using the following methods (use current bank interest rates) and both general and weighted averaging methods:

   a. Capitalized earnings formula

   b. Times earnings method
5. Do an industry analysis for the existing grocery stores in your area. Complete your analysis by using all the areas mentioned in the text. Refer to the checklist in Appendix 5A.

6. Visit the website Entrepreneur.com and complete a search for the top franchises for the year, the fastest-growing franchises, and low-cost franchises. Then, complete the following activities:
   - Select one franchise from each category, and complete a profile of the company that can be submitted or presented to class.
   - Select one franchise, complete a full investigation, and conclude whether the franchise would be a good investment for the geographic region.
   - Compare the support, training, costs, and so forth associated with a low-cost franchise with one of the top or high-growth companies. Determine whether the added costs are justified.
7. Visit a local franchise in your city. Ask the manager what they think are the advantages and disadvantages of franchising.

COMPREHENSIVE CASE   DAN KIM: PART 2

Although the numbers Dan put together indicate that the Ladder Helper business might face several challenges, he decides to devote all his spare time to the venture. This is primarily because of the positive response that he has received from his co-workers and the local Home Hardware dealer, as well as numerous comments on the Internet, all agreeing that the product has potential. Dan is particularly excited about some of the positive comments on crowdsourcing sites, as they had come from all over the world, and he is convinced the product could have global appeal. Dan was so enamored by the response that he decided to put up a few units for sale using Kijiji and some Internet sites used by inventors. He quickly had to pull the ads down, as he sold 10 units within a few days, essentially running out of product. Feedback from customers has been positive, and this is encouraging Dan.

One of the decisions that Dan is concerned about is whether to keep manufacturing at home or rent a facility. Dan's wife, Suzie, has been pressuring Dan to consider manufacturing the product in China to reduce costs, but Dan insists that the product be made in Canada.

Regardless of how he establishes the manufacturing facility, one thing that Dan learned in his small business management class was that he should prepare a business plan. He therefore sets to work preparing the plan. The outline of Dan Kim's business plan for the Ladder Helper follows.

Introduction

My objective in starting this business is to become independent and develop a business that will provide an adequate living for my family and me. I anticipate that within three years, the product will experience high awareness and demand throughout Canada if not North America. At that time, I will look to expand globally. I have considerable expertise in construction and roofing, which has allowed me to be knowledgeable about the safety and convenience concerns associated with the use of ladders.

Marketing

The product is a light metal handrail that will attach to most aluminum extension ladders commonly used in the construction industry and many homeowners. It can be made inexpensively (estimated at $10 per unit) and has great profit potential (selling price estimated at $40 per unit or a 300 percent markup). I anticipate that anyone who owns a ladder would see the Ladder Helper's benefit and would be interested in purchasing it. I intend to promote the product on the Internet during the early days of the company, making use of social media sites, sites that allow for free advertisements such as Kijiji, and perhaps make use of some traditional promotion, such as newspapers and perhaps television advertising. I am also considering a crowdfunding campaign as a way to generate some initial sales and publicity. I am also hopeful that I will be able to generate some additional publicity for the product in newspapers and on the radio, because there is currently no other product like it on the market.

Physical Facilities

Although I now can manufacture the Ladder Helper in my garage, as sales increase, I will need to build, purchase or lease a small factory to meet the demand. I estimate that an adequate production facility, including the required equipment, will cost approximately $170,000. Since I have inherited land, I would ideally build my own plant on this property.

Financial

I currently have $20,000 of my own money to invest in the business and will need to raise the rest of the money. Ideally I would borrow the money from a bank. I am certain that the business will be able to generate the required income to make the interest payments on the loan plus provide a good living for my family.

Legal

I plan to operate the business as a private corporation to protect myself from any liability issues.

Personnel

The business will employ three people initially, including me. I will be in charge of the production process, assisted by two others. I will also handle the marketing and financial aspects of the Ladder Helper, with the help of my wife, Suzie.

Questions

1. Evaluate the business plan that Dan has prepared. Suggest improvements.
2. Where do you think Dan will be able to secure the funds required to start the business? Do you think the bank will lend him money? Why or why not?
3. How would you market the Ladder Helper? List some of your best ideas and share them with the class.

APPENDIX 5A

CHECKLIST OF CONSIDERATIONS IN PURCHASING A BUSINESS

THE INDUSTRY

1. What are the sales and profit trends in the industry?
2. What is the degree of competition? What competitive changes have taken place?
3. What is the nature of competitor strategies?
4. What is the state of the economy in the market? How is the business' performance affected by changes in the economy?
5. What existing or pending legal restrictions affect the operations of the business?
6. What social or cultural concerns affect the industry?
7. Are there any potential competitive or trading area changes that might affect the business?

THE PREVIOUS OWNER

1. Why is the owner selling the business?
2. Has the reputation of the previous owner contributed to the success of the business?
3. Will the previous owner help by providing assistance and advice after the sale?
4. Is the previous owner willing to finance all or part of the purchase?
5. Will the previous owner start a competitive business after the sale?

FINANCIAL CONDITION OF THE BUSINESS

1. Is the financial information provided accurate and indicative of the business' performance?
2. What is the history of profits going back at least five years?
3. Has the business gained or lost market share in the past five years?
4. How do the various financial ratios for the business compare with industry averages?
5. Does the business have a strong identity with customers or clients? Can this identity be maintained?
6. What prospects does the business have for increasing market share and profitability in the future?
7. If the business is currently unsuccessful, what are the chances of improving it with an infusion of capital or managerial expertise?
8. What value does the business place on goodwill?

CONDITION OF ASSETS

1. Are any special terms or conditions associated with the liquid assets?
2. Are the accounts receivable collectible?
3. Is the inventory old or obsolete?
4. Are the building and equipment up to date and paid for?
5. Are taxes and service costs paid on land?
6. Is the location good? Is it increasing or decreasing in value?
7. Is the lease good? What are the terms and conditions of the lease?
8. Have you verified the value of assets with a qualified chartered business evaluator?
9. Are the systems and processes efficient, timely, and compatible with your own?

QUALITY OF PERSONNEL

1. Do the employees of the business compare favourably with the industry in productivity and expertise?
2. Will the employees stay on with the business after the sale?
3. Has the business been progressive in meeting competitive demands regarding wage rates and employee benefits?

CONDITION OF EXTERNAL RELATIONSHIPS

1. Can favourable relations with suppliers be maintained?
2. Are financial sources appropriate and adequate? Can they be maintained?
3. Does the business have a strong support staff such as a lawyer, an accountant, and a consultant? Can these people be retained, if needed?

CONDITION OF RECORDS

1. Can the purchaser obtain key records, such as credit files, personnel files, customer lists, sales reports, and contracts?

APPENDIX 5B

A CHECKLIST FOR THE POTENTIAL FRANCHISEE: QUESTIONS TO ANSWER AFFIRMATIVELY BEFORE GOING INTO FRANCHISING

THE FRANCHISOR

1. Has the franchisor been in business long enough (five years or more) to have established a good reputation?
2. Have you checked better business bureaus, chambers of commerce, government agencies, the Canadian Franchise Association, industry associations, or bankers to find out about the franchisor's business reputation and credit rating?
3. Did the investigations reveal that the franchisor has a good reputation and credit rating?
4. Does the franchising firm appear to be financed adequately so that it can carry out its stated plan of financial assistance and expansion?
5. Have you found out how many franchisees are now operating?
6. Have you found out the "mortality" or failure rate among franchisees?
7. Is the failure rate low?

8. Have you checked with some franchisees and found that the franchisor has a reputation for honesty and fair dealings among current franchisees?
9. Has the franchisor shown you certified figures indicating exact net profits of one or more going operations that you have checked yourself?
10. Has the franchisor given you a specimen contract to study with the advice of your legal counsel?
11. Will the franchisor assist you with the following?
    a. A management training program
    b. An employee training program
    c. A public relations program
    d. Ways to obtain capital
    e. Good credit terms
    f. Merchandising ideas
    g. Design of store layout and displays
    h. Inventory control methods
    i. Analysis of financial statements
12. Does the franchisor provide continuing assistance for franchisees through supervisors who visit regularly?
13. Does the franchising firm have experienced and highly trained management?
14. Will the franchisor help you find a good location for your business?
15. Has the franchising company investigated you carefully enough to assure itself that you can successfully operate one of its franchises at a profit both to it and to you?
16. Have you determined exactly what the franchisor can do for you that you cannot do for yourself?

THE PRODUCT OR SERVICE

17. Has the product or service been on the market long enough to gain broad consumer acceptance?
18. Is it priced competitively?
19. Is it the type of item or service the same consumer customarily buys more than once?
20. Is it an all-year seller in contrast to a seasonal one?
21. Is it a staple item in contrast to a fad?
22. Does it sell well elsewhere?
23. Would you buy it on its own merits?
24. Will it be in greater demand five years from now?
25. If it is a product rather than a service:
    a. Is it packaged attractively?
    b. Does it stand up well to use?
    c. Is it easy and safe to use?
    d. Is it patented?
    e. Does it comply with all applicable laws?
    f. Is it manufactured under certain quality standards?
    g. Do these standards compare favourably with similar products on the market?
    h. If the product must be purchased exclusively from the franchisor or a designated supplier, are the prices for you, as the franchisee, competitive?

THE FRANCHISE CONTRACT

26. Does the franchisee fee seem reasonable?
27. Do continuing royalties or percentage of sales payments appear reasonable?
28. Is the total cash investment required and the items for financing the balance satisfactory?
29. Does the cash investment include payment for fixtures and equipment?
30. If you will be required to participate in company-sponsored promotion and publicity by contributing to an advertising fund, will you have the right to veto any increase in contributions to the fund?
31. If the parent company's product or service is protected by patent or liability insurance, is the same protection extended to you?
32. Are you free to buy the amount of merchandise you believe you need rather than required to purchase a certain amount?
33. Can you, as the franchisee, return merchandise for credit?
34. Can you engage in other business activities?
35. If there is an annual sales quota, can you retain your franchise if it is not met?
36. Does the contract give you an exclusive territory for the length of the franchise?
37. Is your territory protected?
38. Is the franchise agreement renewable?
39. Can you terminate your agreement if you are not happy?
40. Is the franchisor prohibited from selling the franchise out from under you?
41. Can you sell the business to whomever you please?
42. If you sell your franchise, will you be compensated for the goodwill you have built into the business?
43. Does the contract obligate the franchisor to give you continuing assistance after you are operating the business?
44. Are you permitted a choice in determining whether you will sell any new product or service introduced by the franchisor after you have opened your business?
45. Is there anything with respect to the franchise or its operations that would make you ineligible for special financial assistance or other benefits accorded to small business concerns by federal, provincial or territorial, or local governments?
46. Did your lawyer approve the franchise contract after studying it paragraph by paragraph?
47. Is the contract free and clear of requirements that would call on you to take any steps that your lawyer thinks are unwise or illegal in your province or territory, county, or city?
48. Does the contract cover all aspects of your agreement with the franchisor?
49. Does the contract benefit both you and the franchisor?

YOUR MARKET

50. Are the territorial boundaries of your market completely, accurately, and understandably defined?
51. Have you made any study to determine whether the product or service you propose to sell has a market in your territory at the prices you will have to charge?
52. Does the territory provide adequate sales potential?

53. Will the population in your territory increase over the next five years?
54. Will the average per capita income in your territory remain the same or increase over the next five years?
55. Is the existing competition in your territory for the product or service not too well-entrenched?
56. Are you prepared to give up some independence of action to secure the advantages offered by the franchise?
57. Are you capable of accepting supervision, even though you will presumably be your own boss?
58. Are you prepared to accept rules and regulations that you may not agree with?
59. Can you afford the period of training involved?
60. Are you ready to spend much or all of the remainder of your business life with this franchisor, offering this product or service to the public?

CHAPTER 6

FINANCING THE SMALL BUSINESS

LEARNING OBJECTIVES

By the end of this chapter, you should be able to:

LO1 Describe the financing problems experienced by small businesses.

LO2 Identify the types of start-up capital the entrepreneur may require.

LO3 Explain the stages of venture funding.

LO4 Illustrate a method for determining the amount of capital required.

LO5 Identify the sources of equity and debt funds available to start and operate a small business.

LO6 Explain the considerations in obtaining equity or debt financing.

LO7 Describe the elements to include when preparing a proposal to obtain financing for a small business.

SMALL BUSINESS PROFILE

RAZOR SULEMAN *Achievers*

Razor Suleman, 37, is the founder of Achievers, an employee-recognition company that was originally called I Love Rewards Inc. Suleman began his first business at 15, importing and selling hockey cards between Canada and the United States. The profit he generated from the first of his many ventures paid his tuition to Wilfrid Laurier University, where he studied business and economics.

Out of Suleman's Bricker Residence dorm room, he started his own campus-branded apparel company, Razor's Edge. After graduating from university, Suleman expanded his business to include supplying corporate-branded items for large businesses. Suleman soon discovered that nobody works harder for a coffee mug, and his clients needed more to give their employees an incentive for doing a job well. Branded apparel was not influencing behaviour or motivating employees to do a better job. Challenged by this obvious demand in the industry, Suleman created I Love Rewards in 2002.

I Love Rewards grew to become the leading web-based employee rewards and recognition solution provider. The company worked with top employers in North America to drive the behaviours and results most important to their organizations, and build a motivated and aligned workforce.

By mid-2005, I Love Rewards had 18 employees and $5 million in sales. This rapid growth created several internal management problems that led Suleman to reorganize and clearly set out his vision for the company. Much of the reorganization took the form of creative employee management practices, allowing Suleman to obtain financing to break into the U.S. market, which was integral to the company's growth. For the financial backing the company needed, he decided that venture capital was the best route to follow.

In 2008, I Love Rewards received $4 million during its Series A financing round, led by JLA Ventures with participation by Lawrence Capital. Success came rapidly after that, with sales nearly tripling in two years. In the summer of 2009, I Love Rewards accepted its Series B funding, led by Grand Banks Capital with participation from the Ontario Venture Capital Fund, Lawrence Capital, and JLA Ventures.

Photo by Peter Power/The Globe and Mail/The Canadian Press

Although this financing allowed I Love Rewards to achieve an increase in sales, it did cost Suleman his majority interest in the company he had founded. However, Suleman states, "You either have to give up control to get big, or you stay small."

In 2011, I Love Rewards opted to change its name to Achievers because Suleman felt the new name better described the company's goal of increasing employee engagement and driving performance. As he explains, "The new name highlights the values and philosophy that we use to help our customers to build great corporate cultures every day." Achievers shows no signs of slowing down, as the firm recently reported continued rapid growth including a 105 percent increase in year-over-year revenue, a 162 percent increase in employees, and an additional capital injection of $14 million from investors. According to Suleman, the company is not only growing but is also retaining customers: 84 percent of firms that work with Achievers return: "Our platform is sticky. Eighty-four percent of our entire user base comes back every quarter. Our churn is less than one percent."

Given Achievers' substantial growth, Suleman started to pursue an initial public offering for the company late in 2015, the process that would take Achievers public. As he was building a management team to prepare for the transformation from a private firm to a public one, Silicon Valley firm Black Hawk Network approached Suleman and bought the firm for $137 million. Suleman states, "They really made it compelling by keeping Achievers independent, keeping the team on board, keeping the brand."

Suleman is clearly not going to retire. Shortly after leaving Achievers, he joined **Alignvest Management Corporation** as a partner. The firm is committed to investing more than $200 million by purchasing and transforming businesses in the next three years. For an entrepreneur like Suleman, this may be the perfect fit. Suleman's one piece of advice to Canadian entrepreneurs is to think bigger. In a recent interview he refers to the famous line in the *Social Network* movie where Mark Zuckerberg's character realizes that while a million-dollar company is cool, what is *really* cool is a billion-dollar company. Suleman says Canadian entrepreneurs should think bigger and try to create businesses that make lasting changes to how things are done.

ACHIEVERS
achievers.com

SMALL BUSINESS FINANCING LO1

The inability to obtain adequate funding has often been cited as a major small business frustration, if not a primary cause of some small business failures. The entrepreneur may require financing not only to start the business but also to provide capital to fund ongoing operations.

One dilemma many entrepreneurs face is that funds are needed for expansion as the business grows. For example, Jessie Hambly—he and his brothers were featured in **Chapter 1**—started manufacturing Pressa Bottle, a specialized water bottle which allows the user to infuse fruits and vegetables juices into their water. As sales grew, the brothers needed money for inventory and sought out investors using crowdfunding.[1]

Although many small businesses experience difficulties because of their inability to obtain needed funds, statistics show that financing woes are often a symptom of other management problems.[2] Lack of managerial competence and experience can often result in the following specific financial problems:

- Underestimating financial requirements, leading to undercapitalization (shortage of cash) and, often, causing failure
- Lack of knowledge of sources of equity and debt capital, leading to either an inability to obtain funds or the failure to obtain them at the lowest cost
- Lack of skills in preparing and presenting a proposal for financing to a lender or an investor
- Failure to plan for future needs, resulting in last-minute financial crises
- Poor financial control of operations, leading to failure in payment of loan obligations

This chapter discusses each of these important areas to help entrepreneurs obtain financing to establish their business. Most of the information in this chapter is also applicable to the purchase of a business or the signing of a franchise contract. Although obtaining financing is not always easy, perseverance and hard work will usually pay off. For example, when Christopher Frey, Kisha Ferguson, and Matt Robinson began searching for the $300,000 they needed to fund their Toronto-based Canadian adventure travel magazine, ***Outpost,*** they had to be determined. In less than three months, the three owners telephoned over 200 potential investors. While the trio was initially unsuccessful in raising all the money needed, they did manage to come up with $50,000 in bridge financing. Two years later, after many failed attempts, the company negotiated a $1 million equity injection from BHVR Communications, a Montréal media and entertainment company.

THE IMPORTANCE OF CAPITAL AND PLANNING LO2

Entrepreneurs have probably heard the saying "cash is king," but until they are actively starting or managing an enterprise, they may not fully understand the statement. For a start-up venture, cash is needed to buy supplies and to purchase inventory and assets, while growing businesses need cash to pay employees, restock inventory, and conduct day-to-day operations. While profits are important, cash is the heart of the business; without it, a business will fail. For example, **Display Partners**, an Ontario company that specializes in moving trade-show booths, generated $573,000 in sales in its first year but could not finance the growth because the company was receivable rich and cash poor. The business eventually had to find a U.S. company that would purchase its receivables to provide needed cash. Entrepreneurs should be aware of the following issues when trying to raise capital:

- How much do you need? Entrepreneurs should determine the amount of funds needed. Investors will want to see a documented plan noting exactly what the money will be used for. If entrepreneurs are purchasing assets, investors will want to make sure they are providing exact costs and not rough estimates.
- When will the funds be used? Investors will want to know exactly when the money will be spent.
- How long will the money last? Entrepreneurs and investors have a vested interest in determining how long the requested money will last. For example, when Mitomicsinc, now **MDNA Life Sciences**, an Ontario biotechnology company, was searching for $3.3 million, it informed investors that the financing was to get its product from the science stage to the proof-of-concept stage, when more financing would be required.
- Where can the money be raised and what type of financing (debt versus equity) will be used? When first looking at the financial landscape, there appear to be many sources of financing, but as discussed below, the stage of the company will usually dictate the choice of funding available.
- Do you need funds immediately? If the company does not need money right away, it will be in a stronger bargaining position with both debt and equity investors. Entrepreneurs should pay attention to their burn rate, or how much money they are spending a month, and anticipate when they will be out of cash. By monitoring these factors, entrepreneurs will know the urgency associated with obtaining financing.
- Will I get anything else besides money? Often investors will contribute their knowledge and experience along with their money to a business venture. Equity investors in particular will often insist on overseeing if not contributing to the management of a company. For an entrepreneur, especially an entrepreneur with limited contacts or experience, these contributions are particularly useful.

DETERMINING THE AMOUNT OF FUNDS NEEDED

The first step in securing capital (funds) for the business is to determine the amount of money needed. Any lender or investor will want to see evidence of a systematic and thoroughly prepared statement of fund requirements. It is helpful to divide required funding into two categories: start-up costs and ongoing operating requirements. The entrepreneur's own funds available for the venture can then be subtracted from the projected required amounts to obtain the capital needed from outside sources, as shown in the following formula:

$$\text{Capital requirements} = \text{Start-up costs} + \text{Operating requirements} - \text{Owner assets available for investment}$$

START-UP COSTS LO3

Capital is required to finance land, buildings, equipment, and other items needed to start the business. **Table 6-1** is an example of a start-up schedule for a small retail store. Note the source provided for each number in the schedule. The owner should obtain and quotes from sellers of these assets and verify them with owners of businesses similar to their own. The owner should add a contingency factor for potential price increases during the planning and start-up phase.

TABLE 6-1 **Start-Up Cost Schedule**

ITEM	COST	SOURCE
Land and buildings	No cost—leased	If purchased, a similar business or quotes from suppliers
Equipment	$ 34,000	Other similar businesses or quotes from suppliers
Initial inventory	70,000	Other similar businesses or quotes from suppliers Use the formula Inventory = Projected sales/ Inventory turnover (300,000/4.3)
Wages (first two months)	6,000	Other similar businesses or current wage rates
Utilities and telephone		
First deposit	100	Quotes from provider
First two months	680	Quotes from provider
Rent (deposit)	500	Quotes from lessor
First two months	3,000	Quotes from lessor
Advertising agency/media	960	Quotes from advertising agency or media
Insurance (prepaid)	975	Quotes from insurer
Licences and permits	200	Quotes from municipal agency
Other prepaids	285	Other similar businesses
Contingency	3,300	
Total start-up requirements	**$120,000**	

Start-up capital is also required to finance some of the operating costs during this period. Usually a delay in sales revenues occurs for a start-up business, but many operating expenses are incurred before the business begins operating. The entrepreneur needs to estimate these types of expenses and include them in the capital requirements. The time until operations provide sufficient cash flow to finance expenses will vary, but it may be two to six months. Some of these types of expenses are the following:

The first step in financing is determining the start-up funds needed. A good way to estimate is adding up the capital costs and allowing for six months of working capital.

- Initial inventory
- First few months' payroll, including owner's salary
- First few months' utilities
- First few months' rent
- Initial advertising
- Prepaid items, such as utility deposits, rent deposits, and insurance
- Licences and permits
- Other operating costs to be paid before revenues are generated

Start-up costs may be difficult to project. Note the sources of information used to prepare this statement. Also note that operations of the business in the first two months should provide some cash to offset the initial start-up requirements, although this has not been included in this example.

ONGOING OPERATING COSTS

The entrepreneur should prepare a cash flow statement to calculate financial operating requirements after the start-up period. A cash flow statement, explained in more detail in **Chapter 9**, is simply a record of all projected cash inflows and outflows. An example of such a statement for the same business for which the start-up schedule appears is found in **Table 6-2**. In this monthly cash flow for a hypothetical business, it has been calculated that up to $34,000 may be needed to finance operations. This occurs in the first month.

TABLE 6-2 Sample Cash Flow Statement

	BEFORE START-UP	FEB.	MARCH	APRIL	MAY	JUNE	JULY	AUG.	SEPT.	OCT.	NOV.	DEC.	JAN.
Opening balance	$ 0	$(69,000)	$(65,285)	$(48,595)	$(31,905)	$(55,173)	$(34,871)	$(14,569)	$(36,839)	$(17,289)	$ 2,261	$(20,311)	$ 1,467
Bank loan	$ 35,000	0	0	0	0	0	0	0	0	0	0	0	0
Sales: Cash	0	12,000	12,000	12,000	13,750	13,750	13,750	13,750	13,750	13,750	13,750	14,250	14,250
Credit	0	0	12,000	12,000	12,000	13,750	13,750	13,750	13,750	13,750	13,750	14,250	14,250
Total receipts	$ 35,000	$(57,000)	$(41,285)	$(24,595)	$ (6,155)	$(27,673)	$ (7,371)	$ 12,931	$ (9,339)	$ 10,211	$ 29,761	$ 8,189	$ 29,967
Disbursements													
Furniture and fixtures	$ 34,000	$ 0	$ 0	$ 0	$ 0	$ 0	$ 0	$ 0	$ 0	$ 0	$ 0	$ 0	$ 0
Rent		1,500	1,500	1,500	1,500	1,500	1,500	1,500	1,500	1,500	1,500	1,500	1,500
Utilities		200	200	200	200	200	200	200	200	200	200	200	200
Promotion (2% of sales)		480	480	480	550	550	550	550	550	550	570	570	570
Telephone		140	140	140	140	140	140	140	140	140	140	140	140
Wages and salaries		3,000	3,000	3,000	3,000	3,000	3,000	3,000	3,000	3,000	3,000	3,000	3,000
Inventory	70,000	0	0	0	41,820	0	0	41,820	0	0	43,350	0	0
Maintenance and repairs		240	240	240	270	270	270	270	270	270	270	270	290
Professional fees		330	330v	330	330	330	330	330	330	330	330	330	330
Insurance		975	0	0	0	0	0	0	0	0	0	0	0
Interest and bank charges		1,420	1,420	1,420	1,208	1,208	1,208	1,960	1,960	1,960	712	712	712
Loan repayment													
Total disbursements	$104,000	$ 8,285	$ 7,310	$ 7,310	$ 49,018	$ 7,198	$ 7,198	$ 49,770	$ 7,950	$ 7,950	$ 50,072	$ 6,722	$ 41,742
Cash (+/–)	$ (69,000)	$(65,285)	$(48,595)	$(31,905)	$(55,173)	$(34,871)	$(14,569)	$(36,839)	$(17,289)	$ 2,261	$(20,311)	$ 1,467	$(11,775)

Note: 50 percent of monthly sales are cash and 50% are credit. The credit sales are collected in the next month.

If debt financing were used, the entrepreneur would most likely attempt to arrange a $35,000 line of credit (operating loan) with a lender to cover this amount when required. Such a method of financing would allow the business to withdraw and deposit funds on an ongoing basis as long as the total amount withdrawn at any point did not exceed $35,000.

THE OWNER'S NET WORTH

After estimating start-up and operating capital requirements, the owner should prepare a personal net worth and capability statement. Preparing this statement will not only help determine the amount of the owner's funds to invest in the business but will also probably be required by a lending institution if the owner needs to borrow the necessary capital. The essentials of the personal net worth statement are the same as those for a business' balance sheet. An example of a net worth statement appears in **Table 6-3**.

TABLE 6-3 **Suggested Format for a Personal Net Worth Statement**

Personal Net Worth Statement for ______________________

As of ______________, 20______

Assets		**Liabilities**	
Cash on hand and in banks	$______	Accounts payable	$______
Savings account in banks	______	Notes payable to banks	______
Canada savings bonds	______		
Accounts and notes receivable	______	Notes payable to others	______
Life insurance—cash surrender value only	______		______
Other stocks and bonds	______	Installment account (auto)	______
		Monthly payments $______	______
Real estate	______	Installment accounts (other)	
		Monthly payments $______	______
Automobile—present value	______	Loans on life insurance	______
Other personal property	______	Mortgages on real estate	______
Other assets	______	Unpaid taxes	______
		Other liabilities	______
		Total liabilities	______
		Net worth	______
Total	$______	Total	$______

DETERMINING TYPES OF FINANCING

Two general sources of funds can be used to finance a small business. The first is equity or ownership financing. The second is funds obtained from borrowing, usually referred to as debt financing (including trade credit). Many small businesses use both forms of financing to get established, although, as discussed below, the stage the business is in (start-up compared with high growth) will often affect the type and source of financing used.

BUSINESS STAGES AND FINANCING LO4

The type of financing entrepreneurs can access is usually dictated by the stage the business is in and the type of opportunities the company is pursuing. In Canada, start-up businesses are traditionally self-funded, with 84 percent of new ventures relying on personal savings, while ongoing businesses often use personal investment and retained earnings (49 percent). In addition, entrepreneurs who are just starting a business are more likely to be turned down for bank financing and usually have to sign a personal guarantee for debt.[3]

As illustrated in **Figure 6-1**, start-up companies are much more likely to rely on personal savings and personal lines of credit when compared with SMEs with a history.

FIGURE 6-1 Sources of Financing Used by Start-Up Firms in 2017*

Personal financing	84 percent
Credit from financial institutions	37.4 percent
Friends and/or family	16.9 percent
Trade credit from suppliers	16.4 percent
Retained earnings from other businesses	12 percent
Capital leasing	11.1 percent
Government loans, grants or subsidies	4 percent
Angel investors and/or venture capitalists	1.9 percent

Source: Statistics Canada, "Survey on Small and Medium Business Financing 2017," Revised March 21, 2019, https://www.ic.gc.ca/eic/site/061.nsf/vwapj/SFGSME-EFCPME_2017_eng_revised_March-21.pdf/$file/SFGSME-EFCPME_2017_eng_revised_March-21.pdf.

Figure 6-2 illustrates the types of financing used to maintain company activities in 2016.

FIGURE 6-2 Sources of Financing Used To Maintain Activities in 2016*

Owner equity, funds/assets	49 percent
Credit cards	30 percent
Personal loan/line of credit	19 percent
Leasing	14 percent
Friends and/or family	13 percent
Commercial mortgage	7 percent
Business Development Bank of Canada	6 percent
Angel investors and/or venture capitalists	3 percent

Source: Queenie Wong, "SME Financing Indicators," CFIB, October 2016, accessed August 20, 2019, https://www.cfib-fcei.ca/sites/default/files/article/documents/rr3412_0.pdf.

In addition to the stage a business is in, the type of opportunity that the company is pursuing is very likely to dictate the type of financing sought (**Table 6-4**). Entrepreneurs who are starting or managing a relatively small business that is pursuing a slow-growth strategy will often be limited to debt as their main source of capital, although they may use equity when dealing with small business angel investors, friends, relatives and crowdfunding. These smaller start-ups also pass through fewer stages as they travel from an idea to an ongoing business. Examples of these businesses include service companies, retail operations, and food and beverage businesses.

TABLE 6-4	Financing Small, Slow-Growth Businesses
EARLY STAGE	
• Seed capital	Relatively small amount to conduct market research and develop the business plan. Most likely sources are personal savings, personal lines of credit and/or credit cards, money from friends and relatives in the form of either equity or debt, crowdfunding, and government programs.
• Start-up	Funding to get the business running. The business is operating but it is unlikely that it is profitable. Financing is usually needed for working capital, inventory, and marketing. Most likely sources are personal savings, personal lines of credit and/or credit cards, loans from a chartered bank that are personally guaranteed, trade credit, money from friends and relatives either in the form of equity or debt, crowdfunding, government programs, and retained earnings.
EXPANSION/MAINTAINING OPERATIONS	
• First stage	Funding to maintain operations as the business is striving to become profitable. Financing is used primarily for working capital, marketing, and other day-to-day activities. Most likely sources are personal savings, retained earnings, trade credit, crowdfunding, personal or business lines of credit, and loans from chartered banks.
• Second stage	The business is profitable and may be starting a slow to medium-paced expansion. Financing is used for working capital and to fund expansion ideas. Most likely sources of financing are retained earnings, crowdfunding, commercial lines of credit, and trade credit.

Entrepreneurs who are pursuing a high-growth venture are much more likely to use equity and debt in financing their business. These businesses are usually in technology, health care, or knowledge-based industries, and they pass through numerous stages of financing and operations compared with low-growth SMEs. **Blume**, which is owned and operated by British Columbia sisters sisters Bunny and Taran Ghatrora, is an example of a company that has grown quickly and is attracting equity partners. Blume started out selling organic cotton tampons at farmers' markets, eventually moved to selling monthly subscription boxes, and is now a specialized online retailer and distributor of organic menstrual products. The company has seen sales soar. To further ignite growth, the sisters have accepted an investment of $3.3 million from investors.[4]

The three types of funding as the high-growth business develops are indicated in **Table 6-5**. The funding problems, as well as the cost of the funds, differ for each type. *Early-stage financing* is usually the most difficult and costly to obtain. Two types of financing are available during this stage: seed capital and start-up capital. Seed capital, the most difficult financing to obtain through outside funds, is usually a relatively small amount of funds needed to prove concepts and finance feasibility studies. Since venture capitalists usually have a minimum funding level of above $500,000, they are rarely involved in this type of funding, except in the case of high-technology ventures of entrepreneurs who have a successful track record and need a significant amount of capital. The second type of funding is start-up financing. As the name implies, start-up financing is involved in developing and selling some initial products to determine if commercial sales are feasible. These funds are also difficult to obtain. Angel investors are active in these two types of financing.

TABLE 6-5 Stages of Business Development Funding for High-Growth SMEs

Early-Stage Financing: Most likely sources of funding are personal investment by the entrepreneur, friends and family, crowdfunding, angel investors, and some venture-capital funding.	
• Seed capital	Relatively small amounts to prove concepts and finance feasibility studies
• Start-up	Product development and initial marketing but with no commercial sales yet; funding to get company operations started
Expansion or Development Financing: Most likely sources of funding are personal investment, crowdfunding, venture capital, and government programs.	
• Second stage	Working capital for initial growth phase but no clear profitability or cash flow yet
• Third stage	Major expansion for company with rapid sales growth at break-even or positive profit levels but still a private company
• Fourth stage offering	Bridge financing as the company prepares to go public
Acquisitions and Leveraged Buyout Financing: Most likely sources of funding are venture capital and bank financing.	
• Traditional acquisitions	Assuming ownership and control of another company
• Leveraged buyouts (LBOs)	Management of a company acquiring company control by buying out the present owners
• Going private	Some of the owners/managers of a company buying all the outstanding stock, making it a private company

Expansion or development financing (the second basic financing type) is easier to obtain than early-stage financing. Venture capitalists play an active role in providing funds here. As the firm develops in each stage, the funds for expansion are less costly. Generally, funds in the second stage are used as working capital to support initial growth. In the third stage, the company is at break-even or a positive profit level and uses the funds for major sales expansion. Funds in the fourth stage are usually used as bridge financing in the interim period as the company prepares to go public.

Acquisitions and leveraged buyout financing (the third type) is more specific in nature. It is issued for such activities as traditional acquisitions, leveraged buyouts (management buying out the present owners), and going private (a publicly held firm buying out existing stockholders, thereby becoming a private company).

There are three *risk-capital markets* that have been traditionally involved in financing a firm's growth: the *informal risk-capital market or angel investors,* the *venture-capital market,* and the *public-equity market.* As we will discuss, crowdfunding is starting to become an option for financing a firm's growth as well. Although all three risk-capital markets can be a source of funds for stage-one financing, the public-equity market is available only for high-potential ventures, particularly when sophisticated technology is involved. Recently, some clean technology and biotechnology companies raised their first-stage financing through the public-equity market, since investors were excited about the potential prospects and returns in this high-interest area. This also occurred in the areas of oceanography and fuel alternatives when there was a high level of interest. Although venture capital does provide some first-stage funding, the venture usually requires a minimum capital level of $500,000. A venture-capital company establishes this minimum level of investment because of the high cost of evaluating and monitoring a deal. By far, the best source of funds for first-stage financing is the informal risk-capital market.

EQUITY FINANCING LO5

Equity financing involves giving up ownership of the business in return for capital. The sources of equity financing are private investors, including personal funds, friends and family, informal investors better known as angel investors, corporate investors commonly called venture capitalists, and government.

Equity financing offers the following advantages:

1. There is no obligation to pay dividends or interest. This flexibility allows the firm to invest earnings back into the business in its early years, when these funds are usually needed most.
2. Often the original owner benefits from the expertise the investor brings to the business in addition to the financial assistance.
3. Equity capital expands the borrowing power of the business. Most lenders require a certain percentage of equity investment by the owners before they will provide debt financing. Thus, the more equity a business has, the greater is its ability to obtain debt financing.
4. Equity financing spreads the risk of failure of the business to others.

Disadvantages of equity financing include the following:

1. Equity financing dilutes the ownership interest of the original owner and leads to decreased independence. Because of this drawback, many owner-managers are hesitant to follow this route in obtaining capital.
2. With others sharing the ownership interest, the possibility of disagreement and lack of coordination in the operations of the business increases.
3. A legal cost may be associated with issuance of the ownership interest.

So which do Canadian entrepreneurs prefer? We reveal the answer in **Small Business in Action 6-1**.

SMALL BUSINESS IN ACTION 6-1

DO CANADIAN ENTREPRENEURS PREFER AN APPLE SEED TO A FULL TREE?

Would you rather own 100 percent of an apple seed or a smaller percentage of an apple tree? In other words, would you rather own a large share of a small business or a small to mid-size share of a large business? For many, the answer is pretty straightforward: it is almost always better to own a percentage of a larger business compared with full ownership in a much smaller one.

But not all Canadian entrepreneurs agree with that assessment. Canadian entrepreneurs have traditionally shunned equity sources of financing, because they do not want to exchange ownership for capital. Studies consistently indicate that small firms often refuse to share ownership in exchange for capital, and the majority of SMEs are dependent on debt for long-term financing. Many entrepreneurs view equity investors as individuals and companies that are looking for a quick return and care little about the actual business in which they are investing. As noted above, successful entrepreneur Vincent Fiore, owner of Partners in Credit, has avoided debt and equity in growing his firm and has instead relied on retained earnings. Other companies, such as **Original Joe's** restaurant, opted to issue debt and franchise their company to fund growth rather than sell equity in their firm.

Often entrepreneurs have to decide whether to give up equity in exchange for financing to grow their business. Would they rather own a piece of a large tree or keep 100 percent ownership of a small leaf?

Fer Gregory / Shutterstock.com

Yet entrepreneurs may be missing out: numerous studies in both Canada and the United States have revealed that equity-supported businesses are more successful, hire more employees, and are more likely to bring products to market. Razor Suleman, who is featured in the **Small Business Profile** in this chapter, recognized that equity financing was an important step in growing his business. Suleman notes that he had a choice: he could stay small and fund his business through retained

[continued]

[continued]

earnings, debt, and some small injections of equity financing, or he could take on large equity partners and grow his business into a much larger firm. Suleman eventually gave up majority ownership in his firm for the capital and assistance that helped him grow his business into the leading employee recognition company in North America.

Discussion Questions

1. If entrepreneurs knew all the facts, do you think they would be so quick to dismiss equity as a source of capital?
2. If you owned a growing business, would you make use of equity financing from investors? Why or why not?
3. Would you sell majority control of your business like Suleman did to access the capital to grow? Why or why not?

Personal Funds and Retained Earnings.

Few, if any, new ventures are started without the personal funds of the entrepreneur. As indicated at the beginning of this chapter, 84 percent of startups use personal savings, and three out of the four most common financing strategies involve personal guarantees. Entrepreneurs should realize that personal funds are not used only in small businesses—96 percent of the fastest-growing businesses in Canada as identified by *Canadian Business* magazine partly financed their business with a cash infusion from the owner. Not only are these the least expensive funds in terms of cost and control, but they are essential in attracting outside funding, particularly from banks, private investors, and venture capitalists. The typical sources of personal funds include savings, life insurance, or mortgage on a house or car. Pam Streeter, owner and operator of a small Halifax daycare and private school company, noted that she had to rely almost exclusively on personal savings when starting her business. In addition, growing firms use retained earnings to keep the business growing. For example, Vincent Fiore, owner of **Partners in Credit**, a Markham-based debt collection company says, "We've self-generated all our financing. It's all sexy to go out and want to get bigger, but I'm kind of old school. We use what we have to grow. Yes, it's a slower climb, but I don't have to worry about making payments to anyone at the end of the month." Fiore, much like many Canadian entrepreneurs, are re-investing profits back into their business. Kiane Eastmond, owner of **Sandbox Studios** went beyond personal savings during the early days of her now successful Toronto recording studio. Eastmond, whose business initially struggled, before a change in strategy, took on three extra jobs to help pay her bills and keep her entrepreneurial dreams alive. Eastmond successfully switched business strategies from discovering artists to working with popular musicians while simultaneously providing consulting services; which aided in expanding her business and acquiring a larger facility.[5]

Some entrepreneurs take this a step further and use personal credit cards to finance their start-up or to build their company. Kevin Fitzgerald, business consultant and founder of Aurora Microsystems in Sudbury, Ontario, originally applied to several banks for financing. After he was rejected by all of them, he used his credit cards to provide much-needed capital. He estimated in year one that he charged approximately $1 million to various credit cards.[6] As personal funds are often the easiest and cheapest type of financing available, entrepreneurs should monitor their own investment in the business. Some entrepreneurs end up relying more on personal funds than they originally planned and put their financial future at risk. They must be careful to balance the risks associated with pursuing their dream of owning a business and their financial

Like many successful entrepreneurs, Kiana Eastmond took on extra work during her company's early years to fund her entrepreneurial dreams. The investment has paid off as Eastmond's recording studio is expanding in the Toronto area.

Photo: Samuel Engelking

future. Gerry Schwartz, one of Canada's most successful entrepreneurs and current chairman and CEO of **Onex Corporation**, argues the opposite point, noting that entrepreneurs should be willing to put their finances at risk because it is often the only way they can follow their dreams. "Invest in yourself–don't be afraid to take virtually all of your assets, everything you can scrape together, and put it into your business."[7] For example, the co-founders of **Sweetpea**, Eryn Green and Tamar Wagman, an Ontario firm that produces and sells frozen organic baby food, both lament that they have put much more money into the business than originally planned. But the pair is hoping that their financial contributions will lead to a bigger payoff in the future. Thus they are willing to risk their money in hopes of fulfilling their dreams.

Outside providers of capital feel that the entrepreneur may not be sufficiently committed to the venture if they do not have money invested. Entrepreneur Michael Cerny states, "Be prepared to put your money where your mouth is. . . . The reality is that any reputable grade-A financial institution is going to expect you to put some kind of your own money up front to show your commitment and belief in your venture."[8] As one venture capitalist succinctly said, "I want the entrepreneurs so financially committed that when the going gets tough, they will work through the problems and not throw the keys to the company on my desk." A complete lack or very small commitment of personal funds invested in a project may hinder an entrepreneur's ability to gain financing.

Family and Friends.

After the entrepreneur, family and friends are a common source of capital for a new venture. They are most likely to invest because of their relationship with the entrepreneur. This helps overcome one portion of uncertainty felt by impersonal investors–knowledge of the entrepreneur. Young entrepreneurs often have to rely on family and friends as their main source of capital because they usually do not have any significant personal savings. For example, when Amanda Hunsley started her Calgary-based dance school, **Prestige Dance Academy Inc.**, she was only 21 years old and had difficulty raising money. Hunsley says that while lending agencies, such as banks, say they like young entrepreneurs, this is mostly lip-service and they do not want to lend young people money. Rather than giving up on her dream of running a dance studio, Hunsley brought her proposal to her parents, and they readily invested in their daughter.[9]

Although it is relatively easy to obtain money from family and friends, like all sources of capital, there are positive and negative aspects. The amount of money provided may be small, but if it is in the form of equity financing, the family members or friends then have an ownership position in the venture and all rights and privileges of that position. This may make them feel they have direct input into the operations of the venture, which may have a negative effect on employees, facilities, or sales and profits. Although this possibility must be guarded against as much as possible, frequently family and friends are not problem investors and, in fact, are more patient than other investors in desiring a return on their investment.

Many young entrepreneurs, such as the founder of Prestige Dance Academy Amanda Hunsley, have to rely on investments from family and friends to get capital to start their business.

Getty Images/Tetra images RF

To avoid problems in the future, the entrepreneur must present the positive and negative aspects and the nature of the risks of the investment opportunity to try to minimize the negative impact on the relationships with family and friends should problems occur. One thing that helps to minimize possible difficulties is to keep the business arrangements strictly business. Any loans or investments from family or friends should be treated in the same businesslike manner as if the financing were from an impersonal investor. Any loan should specify the rate of interest and the proposed repayment schedule of interest and principal. The timing of any future dividends must be disclosed. If the family or friend is treated the same as any investor, most conflicts can be avoided. It is also beneficial to the entrepreneur to settle everything up front and in writing. It is amazing how short memories become when money is involved. The details of the financing must be agreed on before the money is put into the venture, including such things as the amount of money, the terms of the money, the rights and responsibilities of the investor, and what happens if the business fails. A formal agreement with all these items helps avoid future problems. For example, when Eryn Green and Tamar Wagman, discussed above, went looking for investment dollars for their organic baby food business from their friends and family, they prepared and formally presented a full business plan outlining the opportunity. The pair wanted people to invest in their business because they believed in the concept and not just because of their relationship. By treating friends and family like formal investors, Green and Wagman managed to raise $150,000 for 10 percent equity in their company.[10]

Finally, the entrepreneur should carefully consider the impact of the investment on the family member or friend before accepting it. Particular concern should be paid to any hardships that might result should the business fail. Family members or friends should be investing in the venture because they think it is a good investment, not because they feel obligated.

Some entrepreneurs receive funding, consultation, and occasionally manual labour from their friends and family. When Craig Flinn was opening his award-winning restaurant, **Chives** in Halifax, his friends and family pitched in with more than just money. They helped him physically get his location ready, and many were his first customers. His grandmother pitched in as well, with a recipe for the restaurant's now famous biscuits.

Crowdfunding.

As discussed in previous chapters, an emerging trend in raising capital for business is crowdfunding. Crowdfunding occurs when entrepreneurs solicit small investments or donations from the public to fund the start-up or growth of their company. Originally, crowdfunding was used by social entrepreneurs and artists who solicited support from investors who donated funds over the Internet. Generally, investors or donors received little in the way of a return for their investment outside of a thank you and the knowledge that they had contributed to society's greater good. As crowdfunding websites, such as **Kickstarter** and **Indiegogo**, grew in popularity some entrepreneurs, such as Canadian Eric Migicovsky, made use of the sites to ask supporters or backers to contribute to the creation of a product and they would receive a reward, in most cases the product they were funding or a services in return for up-front money. Migicovsky raised over $10 million to produce the Pebble smartwatch and another $12.8 million to produce the Pebble 2. While being perhaps the most successful entrepreneur to use crowdfunding, Migicovsky is far from alone: contributions on Kickstarter topped $4.3 billion midway in 2019, up significantly from $320 million in 2012.[11] The total value of contributions on crowdfunding sites was expected to surpass $300 billion by the end of 2025.[12] Many Canadian entrepreneurs have successfully used crowdfunding to raise start-up money and to test market their products. For example, Alex Kennberg and Joshua Moore, two University of Waterloo students, recently raised more than $51,000 pre-selling their sleek Cobra wallet design on Kickstarter. Entrepreneurs are now starting to use crowdfunding to sell shares in their fledgling businesses or to borrow money, a practice sometimes referred to as *peer-to-peer lending,* which is discussed in more detail below.[13] The **National Crowdfunding Association of Canada** was formed as crowdfunding became more popular to develop and support the crowdfunding industry.

A major constraint for entrepreneurs who want to sell equity by using crowdfunding is navigating the different provincial and territorial laws in Canada. Currently, Canada does not have a national regulatory body like the Securities and Exchange Commission (SEC) in the United States, and crowdfunding laws are regulated by the provinces and territories. While Ontario has allowed entrepreneurs to use crowdfunding to raise capital since 2009, until 2014 the practice was technically illegal in other provinces and territories. A major breakthrough occurred for crowdfunding hopefuls in 2015 when British Columbia, Saskatchewan, Manitoba, Québec, New Brunswick, and Nova Scotia all agreed on harmonized rules on crowdfunding, which will allow entrepreneurs to raise upward of $500,000 a year for their firms. Along with allowing for crowdfunding, these provinces put into practice some protection for investors, such as limiting their investments in projects, ensuring transparency in contracts, and giving them the right to cancel an investment within a time limit.[14] Some equity websites, such as **Vested** and **FrontFundr**, have emerged as a direct result of the change in legislation. Entrepreneurs who live outside the provinces mentioned above will have to raise equity by using more traditional methods, although they may be able to circumvent the law by registering their company in one of the provinces that allows crowdfunding.

Even with the legal ambiguity, there is little question Canadian entrepreneurs are engaging in the practice of selling shares to the general public using crowdfunding. Some entrepreneurs are using social networking sites to avoid the rules mentioned above—in Canada, you can legally sell shares in a company to close friends. Given that social networking sites have allowed people to form relationships with hundreds if not thousands of people, these friends could become investors in a business. Other entrepreneurs are using international crowdfunding sites to sell shares in their company, or relying on peer lending. Some of the more commonly used sites include **SeedInvest**, **EquityNet**, and **Wefunder** in the United States. For example, serial entrepreneur Jay Giraud, founder of Vancouver-based Damon Motors Inc., a company that created technology to make motorcycle riding safer, is using SeedInvest with the goal of raising $3 million.[15]

Jay Giraud, founder of Damon Motors Inc., is planning on raising $3 million through equity crowdfunding to further develop his work on making a safer, smarter motorcycle.

Photo courtesy of Damon Motors Inc.

The major advantages of crowdfunding include the capital it can provide entrepreneurs, an increase in public profile, a way to test market a product or sometimes referred to as proof of concept, and an opportunity to get valuable feedback and advice from the public. The major disadvantages of crowdfunding include the lack of national laws in Canada allowing entrepreneurs to sell equity in their firm, the potential damage to entrepreneurs' reputations if they fail to meet their goals or build their products, and possible negative comments or publicity based on unmet promises or poorly produced products. **Small Business Beginnings 6-1** provides some insight in how to build a potentially successful crowdfunding campaign.

SMALL BUSINESS BEGINNINGS 6-1

CREATING A SUCCESSFUL CROWDFUNDING CAMPAIGN

As discussed through the text, the use of crowdfunding is growing in popularity for entrepreneurs as way to prove there is a market for their product/business and to raise capital. As a result, the number of crowdfunding campaigns have grown exponentially, and not all are successful. For every **Coolest Cooler** success story—the company raised in excess of $13 million on Kickstarter offering a free cooler as a reward to backers who supported their project—there are hundreds of thousands (280,077 and counting) of unsuccessful crowdfunding campaigns. Kickstarter statistics indicate that roughly 37 percent of projects are successfully funded and 12 percent of projects do not receive a single pledge. Creating a successful crowdfunding campaign is important to the entrepreneur given that success will prove their business model and could attract other potential investors to their business.

As such the entrepreneur may want to consider the following keys to crowdfunding success:

Understand your financials: As discussed below, sometimes, even fully funded campaigns do not provide enough money for the entrepreneur to successfully start their business or even meet their crowdfunding promises. Entrepreneurs should complete a full financial analysis of their capital requirements to start the business and to meet their crowdfunding obligations prior to commencing their campaign. It will be essential that entrepreneurs successfully select the appropriate price for products, offer rewards they can afford, and so forth. If entrepreneurs are using an equity site, it is even more important they understand their financial commitment to investors.

[continued]

[continued]

Study successful campaigns: Entrepreneurs should review as many successful campaigns as possible and compare and contrast them to unsuccessful campaigns. Entrepreneurs should pay attention to wording, videos, rewards, entrepreneur engagement, and so forth.

Select the appropriate site: There are differences between the major crowdfunding sites in terms of rules, fees, and benefits. For example, Kickstarter, which is the world's largest funding platform, screens all applications, can solely be used for creative projects, provides the entrepreneur with funds only if the project is fully funded, and charges fees in the range of eight percent. Indiegogo, on the other hand, will allow any type of project to be funded, has no application process, and will allow the entrepreneur to access the money even if the project does not reach its funding goals. Indiegogo only charges a four percent fee if the project is fully funded but charges a nine percent fee of the total money raised if the project does not meet its initial target. Indiegogo, while operating in more countries than Kickstarter has fewer users.

Plan your campaign: Entrepreneurs should realize that planning their campaign will take a significant amount of time. Michael Mayer, who surpassed his crowdfunding goal of $10,000 by raising $13,000 for his smartphone attachment, **Lookalu** says entrepreneurs should likely spend a minimum of three months planning their campaign. Mayer says you will need high-quality photos, video and, most importantly, a compelling story. Mayer recommends testing photos and concepts on social media as a way to solicit feedback. Business journalist Josh Kraus says that having a compelling or unique product is not enough to generate crowdfunding financial support and that a story and a hook are essential. A hook is something to get potential backers to complete the sale—and spend money. Kraus points to the successful **Bluffworks** Kickstarter campaign, which tagged the blazer they were selling as "the only blazer you'll ever need." Kraus says the catchphrase appealed to young consumers and hooked them into participating in the campaign.

Launching is not enough: Just placing your product or idea on a crowdfunding site is not enough. The entrepreneur has to bring attention to the campaign and quickly. Michael Mayer confirms the entrepreneur will have to hit between 30 and 40 percent of their funding goal in the first 36 to 48 hours in order to gain prominence on the crowdfunding site. Research indicates most successful campaigns rely heavily on family and friends during the initial launch to generate support. Entrepreneurs should be prepared to reach out to friends and family on social media, text, emails, and on the phone prior to, and during the initial launch of the campaign. Additionally, entrepreneurs should be prepared to contact influencers, journalists and even consider advertising their campaign online. For example, when the Hambly brothers were completing their crowdfunding campaign for Pressa Bottle, they did a series of local media interviews.

Be engaged and responsive: Once the crowdfunding campaign starts, the entrepreneur must continue to push friends and family to their site. Additionally, there will be opportunities to engage with initial backers. Do this often and in a positive manner. Entrepreneurs are sometimes surprised how much time they have to invest in managing their campaign once it's launched. Brother and sister Ronny Elfassy and Josie Elfassy-Isakow, who are mentioned in Small Business Beginnings 6-2, said they were surprised by how time consuming it was to manage their crowdfunding campaign.

Discussion Questions

1. Given what you have read in this and other chapters, is crowdfunding a worthwhile idea for an entrepreneur to pursue? Why or why not?
2. Imagine you have created a new revolutionary steak knife that will never have to be sharpened. Create a compelling message, or hook, for the product.
3. Crowdfunding can be time consuming. Why would an entrepreneur pursue this type of funding compared to other financing methods?
4. Use Internet resources to review the requirements for some of the equity crowdfunding sites and report on them to the class.

Interestingly, the three entrepreneurs discussed above, Eric Migicovsky (Pebble Watch), Alex Kennberg, and Joshua Moore (Cobra wallet), were all late in producing their products, leading to some negative publicity for their companies on crowdfunding and social networking sites. Although the entrepreneurs maintained open communication with their donors or investors explaining the delay, inevitably not everyone was happy, and some voiced their opinions online. Unfortunately, sometimes the entrepreneur even fails to deliver on their promised rewards. For example, Klever Freire founder of DreamQii Inc., wanted to build a drone but knew he needed funding. He set out to raise $100,000 on Indiegogo but significantly surpassed his goal, raising more than $2.2 million from 8,400 backers, many of whom thought they pre-paid $699 for a drone. As of 2019, he has failed to deliver any drones and many backers have unsuccessfully sought their money back. Freire says he is still trying to build the drone but was always clear with his backers, that they were investing in an idea, not a finished product.[16]

Supporters or backers of ideas on crowdfunding sites, as discussed in **Chapter 3**, are often offered rewards if the entrepreneur successfully commercializes a product. Consumers are not actually pre-purchasing a product when they support an entrepreneur, they are backing an entrepreneurial dream. In return, the entrepreneur is offering a reward if they successfully fulfill their goal. While crowdfunding sites attempt to make this clear, not all backers are aware how the process works, and some consumers think they are simply pre-purchasing a product.[17] Also, most if not all of the larger crowdfunding sites state they are acting as an intermediary by connecting creators or entrepreneurs to backers. As a result, none of the crowdfunding sites offer any type of guarantees or money back, nor do they offer any assessment of the validity of the entrepreneur or the idea. For example, Kickstarter states clearly the company makes no assessment of the validity of a project or the entrepreneur's ability to complete the project prior to posting the campaign on their site. Backers are free to make their own assessment of the different campaigns.[18] And what happens next? **Small Business Beginnings 6-2** provides a brief overview into what happens for the entrepreneur after completing a successful crowdfunding campaign.

SMALL BUSINESS BEGINNINGS 6-2

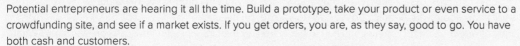

BEYOND CROWDFUNDING

Potential entrepreneurs are hearing it all the time. Build a prototype, take your product or even service to a crowdfunding site, and see if a market exists. If you get orders, you are, as they say, good to go. You have both cash and customers.

Yet that is not always the case. While there are many stories in the media of successful Canadian crowdfunding campaigns, these stories often don't always tell you is what comes next. While crowdfunding might provide the entrepreneur with proof of concept and some infusion of cash, the entrepreneur is then left to build the business. Often entrepreneurs need another injection of cash which can be difficult to obtain or only be obtainable at a high cost of capital. Entrepreneurs who may have been holding down a full-time job while using crowdfunding to test their idea suddenly have to balance work and entrepreneurship or make a choice between the two.

Double Fine Productions is an example of a company which ran what many would describe as an overly successful Kickstarter campaign to create a new adventure game called Broken Age. The campaign was so successful they raised in excess of $3.3 million U.S. roughly eight times their initial $400,000 goal. Yet the amount raised was not enough to fully fund the game's development. Double Fine had underestimated the transaction costs associated with accessing the funds, overspent on game production, and promised backers of their campaign rich pledges, including a documentary movie about the game's development, which they had to ship globally to 87,000 people. Double Fine opted to release half of the game and hold another crowdfunding campaign to fund the full game's development. Double Fine COO Justin Bailey offers that entrepreneurs who are hoping to rely only on crowdfunding to fund their business need to fully understand all the costs associated with crowdfunding, the actual full start-up costs of the business itself, and to be careful about promises to backers.

Similarly, brother and sister Ronny Elfassy and Josie Elfassy-Isakow of Toronto launched their MagneTreeBooks on Kickstarter. The books are made of magnetic pages and come with personalized magnets of friends and family that children can move around the pages when crafting a story. While their Kickstarter campaign did supply some capital, it was not enough to print a second run of the books, which they needed to grow sales. Since neither sibling could secure a bank loan, the pair started to drive for Uber and turned back towards crowdfunding to raise additional money for the business. Unfortunately, the siblings were not as successful in funding the business in the second round of crowdfunding and recently announced they are closing the firm.

Discussion Questions

1. Do you think a successful crowdfunding campaign is enough to serve as proof of concept? Why or why not?
2. Kickstarter charges roughly eight percent of funds raised for all successful campaigns. Do you think this is a fair percentage? Why or why not?
3. Based on what you have read in the text, would you be inclined to use crowdfunding for an idea for which you only have a prototype? Why or why not?

Informal Risk-Capital Market (Angels).

The informal risk-capital market is the most misunderstood type of risk capital. It consists of a virtually invisible group of wealthy investors, often called *business angels,* who are looking for equity-type investment opportunities in a wide variety of entrepreneurial ventures. Typically investing anywhere from $10,000 to $500,000, these angels provide the funds needed in all stages of financing, but particularly in start-up (first-stage) financing. In Canada, angel investors became prominent with the emergence of CBC's hit show *Dragons' Den.* The show features five well-known business angels called Dragons, who, as a group, listen to pitches from entrepreneurs who want the Dragons to invest both their money and their expertise into their business. While the show does have its share of detractors, it is one of the most popular shows on the network and regularly attracts over a million viewers to each episode. Similarly, angel investors are known in the United States through the popularity of *Shark Tank,* a show on ABC that is quite similar to *Dragons' Den.* In fact, two of the original Dragons, Kevin O'Leary and Robert Herjavec, now appear on *Shark Tank.* If you would consider pitching to the Dragons, read **Small Business Beginnings 6-3**.

SMALL BUSINESS BEGINNINGS 6-3

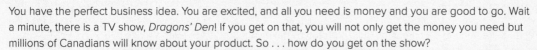

FIVE WAYS TO GET YOUR PITCH ON *DRAGONS' DEN*

You have the perfect business idea. You are excited, and all you need is money and you are good to go. Wait a minute, there is a TV show, *Dragons' Den*! If you get on that, you will not only get the money you need but millions of Canadians will know about your product. So . . . how do you get on the show?

Every year thousands of would-be entrepreneurs audition to get in front of the Dragons. But how can *you* stand out? What can you do to ensure you make the cut and appear on TV? *Profit* magazine author Deborah Aarts offers the following advice:

1. Go easy on gimmicks, such as models and children. Focus on the business idea.
2. Do your homework. Make sure you know who your competitors are and how you are different.
3. Have a good story. Be certain you and your idea are interesting to the audience.
4. Prove that you really need help. The show's executives state they are looking for companies that really need the money, not just entrepreneurs looking for publicity.
5. Keep your cool. Make sure you can answer questions and pitch under pressure.

In Canada, business angels are represented by the **National Angel Capital Organization** or NACO. The mission of NACO is to professionalize angel investing and to support early-stage companies in Canada.[19] While the organization says there is no way to tell exactly how many angels exist in Canada, although the number is estimated to between 20,000 and 50,000, NACO says they have 4000 plus members and from 2009 to 2018 its members have reported on 2,224 investments in 1,472 companies totalling $853.3 million.[20] Mary Ng, Minister of Small Business and Export Development says angel investments is vital for startups and early stage companies.[21] For example, when Mark Chaplin, founder, president, and CEO of Disc-Go-Tech, a manufacturer of DVD, CD, and video game repair kits based in Surrey, British Columbia, started his business, he found money by first draining his bank account and then asking family and friends for help. After exhausting his personal finances and raising as much money as he could from friends and family, Chaplin attempted to find capital from banks or venture capitalists with no success. He notes, "Neither myself nor my partners had any credit or assets, so the banks wouldn't look at us, and venture capitalists weren't interested unless we were looking at $1 million to $5 million." Chaplin then looked for angel financing to get the funds needed to start his company. He eventually succeeded and raised $300,000 for 20 percent of his company from a pair of angel investors.[22] Similarly, Shelby Taylor, founder of **Chickapea Pasta**, from Collingwood Ontario, developed an idea for a healthier chickpea lentil pasta. Taylor had purchased a health food store and notice that most people still ate lots of pasta but were not thrilled about the nutritional contents of the product. Taylor decided to create her own healthy pasta using chickpea and lentil flour, which resulted in a pasta that was high in protein, fibre, and iron. To raise the funds needed to bring her product to market, Taylor completed a Kickstarter campaign, and then successfully raised money through angel groups in Ontario. Taylor said she did this all pre-finished product and is grateful for the support of the angel financiers.[23]

Shelby Taylor, founder of Chickapea Pasta, successfully raised angel capital for her company prior to having a finished product.
Photo by Ellie Kistemaker

In addition to start-up financing, angels can bring a wealth of experience and knowledge to a venture. The majority of angels are entrepreneurs themselves and can offer advice on such important issues as strategic planning, management, and marketing. Hamilton entrepreneur Matthew Sheridan, founder of **Nix Sensor**, one of the fastest-growing companies in Canada, attracted ten angel investors after first achieving $70,000 in sales on Kickstarter. Sheridan attributes some of the angels' business knowledge in changing how he manages the company. Nix Sensor allows consumers to use a smart device to scan and match paint colours, but the company was outsourcing some of their technology development. Sheridan says some of his experienced investors urged him to complete the technology development in-house and that doing so enabled Nix Sensor to be more nimble and responsive to change, and to stay ahead of the competition.[24] Angel investor Robert Herjavec says, "The best deals for me are the ones where I can leverage my investment with my network, experience and facilities. That way I can increase their and my chances of making money."[25] In addition, since most angels are over the age of 50, they have usually accumulated a wide variety of contacts that the entrepreneur can use.[26] Firms funded from the informal risk-capital market frequently raise second- and third-round financing from professional venture-capital firms or the public-equity market.

To date, very little research has been done on the total amount of capital available to entrepreneurs through angel financing, but some research has indicated that the dollar amount may exceed the total venture-capital pool in the country. This notion has been supported by research in the United States that shows the amount of money available through angel financing surpasses the total amount available through venture capitalists.

The characteristics of these informal investors, or angels, are listed in **Table 6-6**. They tend to be well educated; many have graduate degrees. Although they will finance firms anywhere in Canada (and a few in other parts of the world), most of the firms that receive funding are within one day's travel. Business angels will make one to two deals each year, with individual investments ranging from $10,000 to $2 million with most ranging from $50,000 to $150,000. Angel investors are quite selective and fund only between 1 and 3 percent of the proposals that they screen. Angels traditionally prefer equity to debt financing, but sometimes they will offer a combination of the two, or just debt financing. Unlike venture capitalists, angel investors usually do not want to assume control of a venture and will structure their investment as a limited partnership or hold shares in a private corporation. Angels may or may not play an active role in the management of the firm, although they will often sit on a board of advisors or directors. In some cases, angels will join with other angels, usually from a common circle of friends, to finance larger deals.

TABLE 6-6 Characteristics of Individual Canadian Angel Investors

Demographic Patterns and Relationships

- Most are male.
- Most are at least 50 years old.
- Most are or were entrepreneurs.
- Most are well educated, with many having graduate degrees.
- Most have a net worth of at least $1 million and earn approximately $150,000 a year.
- Most are likely to invest in firms about which they have some background knowledge.
- Angels have the potential to bring much more than capital to a firm; they usually have a strong background in management and a variety of useful business contacts.
- Angels tend to invest in close proximity to where they reside.
- From those who responded in 2018, Central Canada has 72 percent of angels, 26 percent in Western Canada and only two percent are in Eastern Canada.
- Many belong to angel clubs.

Nature of Investment

- Most angel investments will either become limited partnerships or receive shares in a closely held corporation.
- Angels may or may not want to be actively involved in the management of the firm.
- Angels will usually sit on a firm's board of advisors or directors.

Investment Range

- Range of investment: $10,000 to $2,000,000, typically $50,000 to $150,000
- Average investment: $125,000
- One to two deals each year

Venture Preference

- They mostly finance start-ups.
- They are most interested in financing manufacturing, technology, and knowledge-based companies.

Approval Rate

- Most angels will reject anywhere from 97 to 99 percent of proposals they review.
- Of the 1 to 3 percent that are eventually approved, most have to go through an extensive due diligence process to ensure that they are reliable and the information presented in the business plan is accurate.

Risk/Reward Expectations

- Median five-year capital gains of 10 times for start-ups
- Median five-year capital gains of six times for firms less than one year old
- Median five-year capital gains of five times for firms one year to five years old
- Median five-year capital gains of three times for established firms over five years old

Reasons for Rejecting Proposals

- Risk/return ratio not adequate
- Inadequate management team
- Not interested in proposed business area
- Unable to agree on price
- Principals not sufficiently committed
- Unfamiliar with area of business

Is there a preference in the type of ventures in which they invest? While angels invest in every type of investment opportunity, from small retail stores to large oil exploration operations, some prefer manufacturing of industrial and consumer products, energy, service, and the retail/wholesale trade. In general, angels, such as venture capitalists, prefer ideas that are difficult to duplicate, offer some form of intellectual property protection, and are in a leading-edge sector, such as IT or clean energy. Additionally, angels prefer to invest in entrepreneurs with a proven track record. Angels want to see a history of success in running a business. The returns expected decrease as the number of years the firm has been in business increases, from a median five-year capital gain of 10 times for startups to three times for established firms over five years old. These investing angels are more patient in their investment horizons and do not have a problem waiting for 7 to 10 years before cashing out. This is in contrast to the more predominant five-year time horizon in the formal venture-capital industry. Investment opportunities are rejected when there is an inadequate risk/return ratio, a subpar management team, a lack of interest in the business area, or insufficient commitment to the venture from the principals.

Finding and Soliciting Angels.

As discussed above, it is estimated that there are between 20,000 and 50,000 Canadian angels who are willing to invest thousands of dollars in entrepreneurial start-ups. This number is set to grow as more and more senior executives retire and look to invest their savings. Jason Aparaga, president and CEO of Oakville-based **Spara Capital Partners Inc.**, says the number of retired people taking buyouts and the encouragement of other angels is fuelling the growth of angel investors across Canada. Even with the strong growth, most entrepreneurs claim the only thing more difficult than finding an angel is successfully negotiating a deal with one.[27] Thus entrepreneurs should consider the following when seeking out and negotiating with an angel investor:

- *Prepare well.* Make sure that you have a complete business plan before attempting to contact angels and that you have fully investigated the idea. While angel investors will invest in start-ups, they do not usually just hand over money based on a poorly researched idea. Before investing, most angels will insist on a due diligence process that is quite thorough, and entrepreneurs should assist them, whenever possible, by providing a complete business plan. Yasmine Kustec of the National Angel Capital Organization (NACO) recommends that entrepreneurs plan for capital well in advance and start to network with potential angel investors before they need money. Kustec notes that this will help establish a relationship with potential investors, build trust, and increase the likelihood of success when asking for money.[28]
- *Ask for referrals.* Angel investors, like most successful entrepreneurs, enjoy their privacy and it is often difficult to access their contact information. The best way to find an angel investor is through networking with existing contacts, such as bankers, accountants, lawyers, and financial planners. Since most angels rely on trusted friends and business partners to steer potential investments their way, they often let their associates know that they are looking to invest in start-up companies. In addition, many angels belong to angel clubs or groups, and by accessing the information for one angel, you may gain access to an entire group.
- *Screen potential angel investors.* Try to get as much background information as possible before contacting a potential angel investor. Since most angels limit investments to areas with which they are familiar, your chances of successfully receiving financing improve if you approach an angel who has either working or investment experience in the industry. If a potential angel lacks this knowledge, the entrepreneur may have a harder time accessing financing.
- *Prepare for the first contact.* When making initial contact with an angel, it is best to use the referral's name (after getting permission). Before making contact, entrepreneurs should prepare a short list of points that they want to cover in the conversation. The main goal of the conversation is to arrange a meeting where the entrepreneur can pitch their idea.
- *Pitch the idea.* Before meeting with an angel investor, they will most likely ask to see a brief business plan or an outline of the business model. The key to this is being as precise as possible while clearly outlining the potential of the business. When it comes time to pitch the idea face to face, entrepreneurs must focus on key points that emphasize their ability to succeed. Entrepreneurs should be able to explain, in a very short time and using everyday language, the size of the market and the problem that they are solving. Sean Wise, a

financing expert, provides this example of an ideal pitch for the pill Viagra: "People want to have sex longer than their bodies will allow. Our aspirin-sized, government-approved tablet is extremely effective at letting them do so." Kevin O'Leary says he puts a great deal of emphasis on the entrepreneur's pitch. "If you can't stand up in front of people and communicate what the deal is and how it works in four minutes, you're not going to be successful. All the rest—finance, marketing, system integration—is secondary, because you can always hire a systems person or an accountant. But someone has to be able to set the course and communicate the vision."

- *Prepare for a response.* Angels will usually respond to an idea pitch rather quickly. If the answer is no, entrepreneurs should ask why and react accordingly. Some common reasons for rejection and suggested responses are the following:

    1. *Incomplete proposal or lack of funds at this time:* Entrepreneurs can ask if they could pitch the concept again after completing the proposal or at a time when the angel thinks she or he may have more money to invest.
    2. *Weak management team:* insufficient return on investment: The entrepreneur could offer to re-pitch the idea after addressing these issues.
    3. *Not interested in that particular industry:* The entrepreneur could ask the angel to provide a reference to any potential investors who are familiar with that industry.
    4. *Not a good idea:* The entrepreneur should ask angels for their input—be polite and thank them for their time.

Jim Treliving, who is an avid angel investor outside of the television show *Dragons' Den,* notes that entrepreneurs should not hesitate to bring third-party validation for their product. Treliving says, "I don't know anything about software but if Bill Gates said [your software] was good, who would I be to argue?" Audry Larocque and Louis Brun, founders of Neuralitic Systems Inc., a Montréal-based IT company whose products and apps assist marketing managers in identifying customer needs, have successfully raised $20 million in money from investors and note that they used testimonials from early adopters to help investors see the potential of their idea.

Crowdfunding results can also offer validation or proof of concept for an entrepreneur. Angel investors will find it difficult to question if a market exists for a product when an entrepreneur comes in with either sales or pre-orders in hand. For example, Tyler Handley already had $300,000 in sales from Kickstarter when he approached angel investors with his authentic looking temporary tattoo business, **Inkbox**. Handley used his crowdfunding success to convince a group of angel investors to give him $1 million for 28 percent of his business. Handley says he needed the money to grow his company and sales have recently surpassed $5 million, up 928 percent in just two years.[29]

Entrepreneurs should be fully prepared to answer a variety of complex questions. They also have to display a willingness to accept advice during the pitch. As discussed above, most angels will want to contribute not only money but knowledge to the business. Bob Chaworth-Musters, founder of the **Angel Forum - Vancouver**, states, "A CEO's demonstrated ability to accept advice can make or break an application."[30]

If the angel investor agrees to invest, the entrepreneur should assist them in completing the due diligence of the business and of the entrepreneur. The entrepreneur should have the following ready:

- A list of 10 to 15 personal and business references including contact information
- Any letters from customers, suppliers, and creditors, including patent information, financial records, and so on
- Any other information that will allow the process to move forward

After the investigation of the concept is complete, the angel investor and the entrepreneur will draw up a legal agreement. Entrepreneurs should realize that while angel investors are willing to be flexible with their terms and invest in start-ups, they will still demand a much higher rate of return than a traditional lender. One angel investor who was participating in a research project on Canadian angel investors clearly stated, "A guy phoned the other day and asked me to consider a project. I said, 'I'll look at the venture, but I'll tell you right now, I'll want between 20 and 25 percent on my money.' The guy said, 'We can go to the bank and get better than that.' I said, 'What did you call me for then?'" These comments are reinforced by Kevin O'Leary, who states he is looking for returns of 10 to 20 and even 100 times his original investment. He says angels need these kinds of returns because only 20 percent of firms they invest in will actually become successful companies. Marie Chevrier, founder of **Sampler**, a direct-to-consumer sampling company, advises entrepreneurs to use a lawyer and make sure you understand every term you are agreeing to with an angel investor. Chevrier says negotiating fair terms with angels is one of the most valuable lessons she has learned.[31]

Research conducted by the National Angel Capital Organization (NACO) echoes these claims. The organization found that while angels can earn a healthy return on their investment, most of the return can usually be attributed to one or two successful companies that exceed expectations. NACO found that roughly 50 percent of angel investments fail to yield any return.

Angel Organizations.

A trend that has emerged in angel investing over the last decade is the formation of angel clubs or associations. Angels use these clubs to network with other angels, share investment opportunities, and pool money to invest in start-up ventures. The above-mentioned NACO, works co-operatively with angel groups to assist angels who are pursuing investment opportunities. Yasmine Kustec of NACO says that entrepreneurs who are looking for angels should contact NACO; it serves as a matchmaking service between companies in need of angels and angels in need of companies.[32] The general characteristics of angel organizations can be found in **Table 6-7**.

TABLE 6-7 Characteristics of Canadian Angel Investor Groups

- Almost all male, with women accounting for roughly 17 percent of angel groups.
- Most members are or were entrepreneurs.
- There are 6,918 members in angel organizations, with the average angel group having 256.22 members.
- Group size ranges with 33 percent of groups having between 51 and 100 members and 26 percent of groups having over 100 members.
- 57 percent of angel groups have been operating for more than five years and 28 percent more than 10 years.
- 67 percent of angel groups are not-for-profit and 27 percent for-profit.
- Two-thirds of groups charge a fee, with the fee ranging from $250 to $1000 a year.

Frequency & Nature of Investment

- Investment activity differs significantly among groups. Eight groups in Canada (27 percent) made more than 25 investments. While 24 percent of the groups made less than five investments.
- Ontario and Quebec have the most active groups of angel investors. Central Canadian angels accounted for 86 percent of total investments in 2018 compared to 11 percent in Western Canada and just 3 percent in Eastern Canada.
- 40 percent of 2018 investments were follow-on investments in firms the angels had already invested in.
- Angel groups often invest with other investors in a syndicate. The average syndicate investment in 2018 was $2.3 million.
- Angel groups frequently invest in small business with firms under 10 employees accounting for 74 percent of investments.
- Angels groups invest in business using a a variety of financial instruments including 37 percent using convertible debentures, 36 percent common shares, 23 percent preferred share, and debt accounting for 2 percent

Investment Range

- Range of investment: $10,000 to $2,000,000.
- Average investment: $282,167.
- $5,101,259 is the average 2018 investments made by angel groups.

[continued]

[continued]

Venture Preference

- Prefer to finance start-ups.
- Angels frequently invest in small business, with firms under 10 employees accounting for 74 percent of investments.
- Angels invest primarily in Communication and Technology Firms (45 percent), with Life Sciences representing 20 percent of investments.
- 53 percent of investments were valued between $2 and $4 million.

Approval Rate

- Angel groups received 6,541 requests for funding in 2018 and invited 17 percent to pitch while funding just 6.4 percent of applicants.
- Angel groups made 583 investments.

Risk/Reward Expectations

- Same as individual angels (See **Table 6-6**).

Reasons for Rejecting Proposals

- Same as individual angels (See **Table 6-6**)

Source: Mason, C (2019) 2018 Report of Angel Investing in Canada. National Angel Capital Organisation of Canada: Toronto: https://www.nacocanada.com/cpages/angel-activity-report

Angel clubs usually meet monthly to network and review one or two venture pitches from aspiring entrepreneurs. A recent survey of angel groups found they contributed at least $142.8 million in 2018 to 583 firms. Research conducted by NACO found that the size of the average investment is $282,167, and many angel groups are contributing follow-up or additional capital to existing entrepreneurs. Angels invest primarily in Communication and Technology Firms (45 percent) with Life Sciences representing 20 percent of investments. An example of a typical angel group is Ottawa's **Purple Angel**. The group is made up of former Bell executives who offer entrepreneurs one of two types of venture financing. They will invest approximately $150,000 in start-up companies that are having problems attracting venture capital, or they will invest upward of $1 million in companies that are successfully raising capital from other sources. Along with capital, the Purple Angel club will contribute ideas and contacts and assist in managing the venture. The founder of the group, Irving Ebert, describes the club as active angel investors who bring decades of experience to portfolio companies. To date, the Purple Angel club has provided funding to 29 companies, including as BTI Systems, a cloud-computing company that is now part of Juniper Networks, and **Renaissance Repair and Supply**, a company providing legacy and end-of-life network equipment alternatives, supply chain, sustaining engineering and repair services to extend the life of otherwise functional networks.

Generally, an idea pitched to an angel organization will follow this pattern:

1. Entrepreneurs hoping to pitch their idea to an angel group will submit an application. It helps to have at least one angel sponsor the entrepreneur to get on the meeting agenda. The sponsoring member usually meets with the entrepreneur before the meeting and completes an initial screening process. Entrepreneurs can still get on the agenda without a sponsor but it tends to be more difficult. Getting to the pitch stage is not easy. Angel investor and member of NACO Parm Gil states that most angel groups receive 100 business plans a year and on average only formally review one to five of them. Gil says there is value in entrepreneurs trying to get their business reviewed because they will receive valuable feedback that should help them manage their business.[33] Some clubs now ask the entrepreneur to pay a fee to present to the organization. The organizations that charge entrepreneurs will usually assist entrepreneurs in putting together their presentation and sometimes their business plan.
2. Before the meeting, the entrepreneur will provide investors with a summary of the company and key financial information.

3. Entrepreneurs will get 30 to 60 minutes to pitch their idea.
4. Angels will spend at least another 60 minutes asking questions.
5. If the group makes investing decisions together, then they will vote whether to invest in the idea. Voting members usually vote either for or against the idea, or for hearing further information. Some angel groups do not invest as a group, and after the entrepreneur's presentation individual angels will decide on their own whether to pursue the idea.
6. If the majority vote "yes" or "yes, but," then two to three angels will be assigned to the project to complete further due diligence and ensure that it meets the requirements of the group.

Refer to **Table 6-8** and **Table 6-9** for more information on Canadian angel investment groups.

TABLE 6-8 Regional Angel Groups

Central Canada	**Anges Quebec**
	Brightspark
	Capital Angels Network
	Maple Leaf Angels, Toronto, ON
	Northern Ontario Angels
	York Angels
Western Canada	**Angel Forum**™ - Vancouver
	Valhalla Angels
	Vantec Angel Network, British Columbia
Eastern Canada	**East Valley Ventures**
	Island Capital Partners

TABLE 6-9 Angel Group Investments

ANGEL GROUP	EXAMPLE OF INVESTMENTS
Maple Leaf Angels	**Wealthsimple**: Investment company, aimed at providing simple, low-fee investments.
	Bus.com: A charter bus company representing 2300-plus bus operators.
	Top Hat: Active-learning technology company.
Valhalla Angels	**Apartment Love**: One of the largest apartment finder websites in the world.
	Dealcloser: Website that allows lawyers and business clients to sign and complete contracts online.
	ChatterHigh: Helps students learn about career choices.
East Valley Ventures	**Hygge Power**: Smart power outlet that stores energy in case of a blackout and maximizes power use.
	Kognitive Spark: Augmented-reality software to assist in employee training and development.
	Squiggle Park: Online reading game to enhance children's reading comprehension.
Anges Quebec	**Bonlook**: Specialty eyewear retailer and manufacturer.
	GradeSlam: Chat-based tutoring for students..
	Trailblazer Games: Online and mobile games developer.

Corporate Investors.

Many companies are interested in investing in a small business in the hope that the value of their investment will increase over time. Often they then sell their ownership interest back to the original owners when the owners are in a better position to finance the business independently.

Companies whose major activity is investing in smaller and medium-sized businesses are called *venture-capital companies.* These companies use highly sophisticated evaluation techniques and accept only a small percentage of applications.[34] A venture-capital company typically looks for a business within a growth industry, with sound management and the potential for a return on investment of between 20 and 40 percent. For example, brothers David and Mark Ang, co-founders of **Second Closet**, recently received a $13.2 million investment in their growing firm from Whitecap Venture Partners. The venture capital firm was likely attracted by Second Closet's unique business model and potential for growth. Second Closet is a storage company that picks up items and stores them based in a warehouse charging clients on square footage basis which is cheaper than a traditional storage locker.[35]

Brothers David and Mark Ang, co-founders of Second Closet, initially worked with angel investors and, as the company grew, they brought in more formal investors from Whitecap Venture Partners.

Photo courtesy of Second Closet

Explore another VC success story in **Small Business in Action 6-2**.

SMALL BUSINESS IN ACTION 6-2

NEURALITIC OFFERS ENTREPRENEURS A ROADMAP TO VC SUCCESS

Montréal-based Neuralitic, an IT company that helps mobile operators understand customer behaviour to ensure long-term success, offers business owners and aspiring entrepreneurs a model to follow when looking for venture-capital investment. The company, which was co-founded by Audry Larocque and Louis Brun, managed to raise $20 million in just three years; more interestingly, they managed this between 2008 and 2011, when venture-capital money was not easy to come by. How did they do it? By building an innovative product, Seven Flow, and then targeting venture-capital investors who had a history of investing in the industry. When the co-founders met with venture capitalists, rather than focus on the product, they focused on how profitable the app could become. They secured $12 million in investments from five investors.

Drogatnev/Shutterstock.com

While sales were growing, the entrepreneurs soon needed additional capital and went back to the original investors along with other contacts. This time the pair faced some tough questions about why the original $12 million was not enough. The Neuralitic founders countered this by offering testimonials from early adopters and again focused their pitch on the potential financial success of the product and not the technology behind the app. The strategy worked because investors could see the long-term capital appreciation that could be made investing in the company. In 2013, the company was bought out by a larger U.S. firm, Guavus, which had raised $30 million to fuel its own growth just prior to the purchase. While the terms of the deal have remained confidential, reports indicate that the investors and founders of Neuralitic were happy with the sale of the firm.

Discussion Questions

1. Why do you think Neuralitic was successful in raising capital?
2. Do you think the sale of Neuralitic, a Canadian company, to a U.S. firm is a positive development? Why or why not?
3. If you were the owner of Neuralitic, would you have preferred to keep the company for yourself, or would you have jumped at the opportunity to sell your shares at a profit to a larger company? Why?

In 2018 the members of the Association of **Canadian Venture Capital Private Equity Association** invested some $3.7 billion in almost 534 businesses in Canada.[36] Of the investments, information and communication technologies (ICT) led the way with 66 percent of the money invested; 17 percent in the life sciences; and 7 percent was invested in clean technology. Regionally, Toronto has the majority of venture-capital (VC) activity in Canada, with $1.5 billion of invested capital, representing 41 percent of all disbursements; that city is followed by Montréal (24 percent) and Vancouver (11 percent).[37] Refer to **Table 6-10** for guidelines on dealing with venture capitalists.

TABLE 6-10 Guidelines for Dealing with Venture Capitalists

- Carefully evaluate which venture capitalist to approach for funding the particular type of deal. Screen and target the approach. Venture capitalists do not like deals that have been excessively shopped.
- Once a discussion is started with a venture capitalist, do not discuss the deal with other venture capitalists. Working several deals in parallel can create problems unless the venture capitalists are working together. Time and resource limitations may require a cautious, simultaneous approach to several funding sources.
- It is better to approach a venture capitalist through an intermediary who is respected and has an existing relationship with the venture capitalist. Limit and carefully define the role and compensation of the intermediary.
- The entrepreneur or manager, not an intermediary, should lead the discussions with the venture capitalist. Do not bring a lawyer, an accountant, or other advisors to the first meeting. Since there are no negotiations during this first meeting, it is a chance for the venture capitalist to get to know the entrepreneur without interference from others.
- Be very careful about what is projected or promised. The entrepreneur will probably be held accountable for these projections in the pricing, deal structure, or compensation.
- Disclose any significant problems or negative situations in this initial meeting. Trust is a fundamental part of the long-term relationship with the venture capitalist; subsequent discovery by the venture capitalist of an undisclosed problem will cause a loss of confidence and probably prevent a deal.
- Reach a flexible, reasonable understanding with the venture capitalist regarding the timing of a response to the proposal and the accomplishment of the various steps in the financing transaction. Patience is needed as the process is complex and time consuming. Too much pressure for a rapid decision can cause problems with the venture capitalist.
- Do not sell the project on the basis that other venture capitalists have committed themselves. Most venture capitalists are independent and take pride in making their own decisions.
- Be careful about glib statements, such as "There is no competition for this product" or "There is nothing like this technology available today." These statements can reveal a failure to do your homework or can indicate that a perfect product has been designed for a non-existent market.
- Do not indicate an inordinate concern for salary, benefits, or other forms of compensation. Dollars are precious in a new venture. The venture capitalist wants the entrepreneur committed to an equity appreciation similar to that of the venture capitalist.
- Eliminate to the extent possible any use of new dollars to take care of past problems, such as payment of past debts or deferred salaries of management. The new dollars of the venture capitalist are for growth, to move the business forward.

Government.

Government has traditionally hesitated to provide equity funding to small businesses. However, programs have been developed in recent years that permit government funding and incentives for venture-capital firms or allow for direct equity investment by government in the business. Some of these programs and agencies are described next.

Business Development Bank of Canada (BDC).

The **BDC** participates with other investors as a principal in the provision of investment capital in businesses it views as promising. Generally, the purpose of such financing is to provide an adequate equity base for the firm to receive funding from additional sources. The BDC is an important source of equity capital in Canada and offers roughly nine different capital programs, examples include an Industrial Innovation Fund, Women in Technology Venture Fund, and a IT Venture Fund. Chris Murumets, owner of **LOGiQ3**, a Toronto-based insurance company that has been consistently identified as one of the fastest-growing firms in Canada, says the BDC provides more than money to entrepreneurs. "We raised some money with the BDC. I like the BDC because it feels like they are on your side. That sounds fluffy but, as a business owner, it's nice to have these people guiding you through the process and helping you along the way." His comments are echoed by entrepreneurs Lee Van Iderstine of **Happier IT** and David Ciccarelli of **Voices.com**. Both owners of growing Canadian IT/Internet firms agree that the BDC is more open to financing and supporting entrepreneurs than are traditional banks. Iderstine, whose BC-based company provides IT solutions to small and medium businesses says, "We've used the BDC to fund product launches and sales efforts. A normal bank doesn't try to make it work, in our experience."

BOOTSTRAP FINANCING

One alternative to acquiring outside capital that should be considered is bootstrap financing. Bootstrap financing involves the entrepreneur relying on personal investment including retained earnings to fund the startup of a business.

The major advantages of bootstrap financing include:

1. If the firm succeeds, the value of the business is worth more to the entrepreneur as there is no debt or equity partners.
2. The entrepreneur has complete freedom to manage the business as they see fit.
3. Entrepreneurs who bootstrap tend to keep tight controls over costs and develop creative ways to conserve money.
4. If the business fails, and the entrepreneur has not personally borrowed any capital, there is no debt to pay off–and no disappointed equity partners.

The major disadvantages of bootstrapping include:

1. The entrepreneur takes on all the financial risk of starting or maintaining a business. Entrepreneurs who bootstrap will sometimes borrow money or use personal credit cards to fund their business. If the business fails, the entrepreneur is personally liable for borrowed funds.
2. The lack of capital can limit the entrepreneurs ability to grow the business.
3. Investors and sometimes lenders bring along mentorship and networking opportunities for the entrepreneur. By going it alone, the entrepreneur could lose out on opportunities.

Bootstrap financing also involves using any possible method for conserving cash. For example, some entrepreneurs will join business incubators such as Halifax-based **Volta**, which can offer entrepreneurs shared office space, access to mentors, and other business development services at a lower price than traditional suppliers.

Entrepreneurs can also take advantage of any supplier discounts available. Entrepreneurs with restricted cash flow need to take as long as possible to pay without incurring interest or late payment fees or being cut off from any future items from the supplier. The entrepreneur should always ask about discounts for volume, frequent customer discounts, promotional discounts for featuring the vendor's product, and even "obsolescence money," or allowing upgrade to an enhanced product at no additional cost. Savings can also be obtained by asking for bulk packaging instead of paying more for individually wrapped items as well as using co-op advertising with a channel member so that the cost of the advertisement is shared.

Some entrepreneurs have also encountered significant savings by working from home rather than leasing a space; locating their business in a smaller city; sharing space with another business; or by buying used equipment. **Recyc PHP Inc.** of Drummondville, Québec, used some of these strategies to save money. The business, which recycles disposable diapers, considered locations in both Montréal and Drummondville but after considering the costs, the management team decided to locate in the smaller city, saving the company a lot of money. The owners then purchased used production equipment at an estimated savings of $750,000 compared with purchasing new equipment.[38] Other examples include Toronto restaurant owner Zane Caplansky, who first started selling his deli sandwiches from the second-floor kitchen of an already-operating tavern.[39]

Consignment financing can also be used to help conserve cash. Some vendors allow entrepreneurs to place a standing order for the entire amount of goods to be used over time but take shipment and make payment only as needed, therefore securing the lower price of a larger order without having to carry the cost of the inventory.

Entrepreneurs have also managed to save money by offering equity to employees as payment or in addition to traditional compensation. For example, if a new business needs an IT person who may earn $75,000 a year, the entrepreneur may offer the job to someone for $25,000 a year plus a percentage of equity in the firm. If the business succeeds, the equity may end up being worth much more to the employee than the lost salary. Other times, an entrepreneur may be able to solicit free labour in return for equity. Lorax, a Nova Scotia–based oil and gas company, successfully persuaded some senior corporate managers who had recently retired to join the firm as employees for an equity-only compensation plan. Learn about one entrepreneur's reasons for bootstrapping his own company in **Small Business Beginnings 6-4**.

These are just some examples. The only possible limitation in bootstrap financing is the imagination of the entrepreneur. Another type of bootstrapping involves the entrepreneur being paid as quickly as possible from outstanding accounts as well as getting overdue accounts to pay.

Bootstrapping is particularly important at the start-up stage and in the early years of the venture when capital from debt financing (i.e., in terms of higher interest rates) or from equity financing (i.e., in terms of loss of ownership) is more expensive.

SMALL BUSINESS BEGINNINGS 6-4

FORMER VENTURE CAPITALIST OPTS FOR BOOTSTRAPPING OVER INVESTORS

When Qasim Mohammad left his corporate job as a venture capitalist to start **Repshift**, a Toronto-based customer advocacy company, he, surprisingly, shunned venture capital (VC). Repshift can be integrated into current customer management software to help sales people access customer references when completing sales acquisitions.

Mohammad says that three factors led to him opting to bootstrap his company. First, he wanted to put an emphasis on profits not growth. He notes he was inspired by other entrepreneurs who started software companies for less than $1000. Mohammad says he has managed to start his company for less than $20,000, all from personal savings, and has made use of such common bootstrapping techniques as accessing free office space and offering high payback to employees/contractors if Repshift does well long term in return for lower pay on the front end.

Mohammad says he also opted for bootstrapping as he wanted the independence to make mistakes and was unsure if the business could deliver the returns VC investors expect. Mohammad points out that VC investors normally have board representation with a company, and they can impact the founder's strategy and plans. By bootstrapping the company, Mohammad gave himself more freedom to make mistakes and the flexibility to pivot his business.

Discussion Questions

1. Based on the information in this case and the chapter, what do you think are some of the advantages and disadvantages of start-ups working with venture capitalists and angel investors?
2. Why would venture capitalists want to emphasize growth over profits? Why would this matter to a founding entrepreneur?
3. Does the information in the case and chapter make it more or less appealing to you to persuade venture capital and/or angel investors if you start a business? Why?

DEBT FINANCING LO6

Few small businesses are able to become established and continue operations without some sort of debt financing. About 30 percent of the money loaned to business in Canada is held by small businesses. A national survey found that 37.4 percent of small and medium-sized businesses used a bank for financial support, 11.7 percent have lines of credit, 10.3 percent have a credit card, 6.6 percent have a term loan and 4 percent have a non-residential mortgage.[40] Because of the high possibility that debt financing will be required, it is essential that entrepreneurs be aware of the advantages and dangers of using it. It is also important that they understand the sources of debt capital and the characteristics and requirements of various financial lenders.

Advantages and Disadvantages of Debt Financing.

Some of the positive benefits of using debt are as follows:

1. It is possible to obtain a higher return on investment by using leverage debt. If borrowed funds earn a higher return than the associated interest cost, it is possible to increase the overall return on investment for the business through debt financing. A $10,000 investment could be any productive asset or change in the business.
2. Interest costs in a business are tax-deductible expenses (assuming a profit is being made), whereas dividends paid as a result of equity ownership are not tax deductible.
3. Debt financing may allow greater flexibility in that there is no loss of ownership control.
4. Many small businesses have found it is often easier to obtain debt capital than equity capital. A study by Statistics Canada found that 86 percent of small business loan applications were approved.[41]

Some of the potential negative aspects of debt financing are as follows:

1. Interest must be paid on borrowed money. Interest costs can be high, and high interest expenses are a common problem in many failing businesses. Interest rates have been high in the past in Canada, and this caused serious hardship for many small businesses. The inability to pay interest costs resulted in the foreclosure or bankruptcy of many businesses. Although interest rates are currently low, the small business owner must monitor rate changes closely.
2. Debt financing creates additional paperwork requirements for the entrepreneur, and the lender may monitor the business.
3. When using debt financing, the total risk of the venture lies squarely on the owner's shoulders. There are no other partners or shareholders to assume some of this risk.

Sources of Debt Financing.

Several sources of debt financing are available to small businesses, including private lenders, corporate lenders, private lending institutions, and government agencies. Technology has opened up new sources of financing, as is discussed in **Small Business Beginnings 6-5**.

SMALL BUSINESS BEGINNINGS 6-5

OUT WITH THE OLD IN WITH FINTECH

FinTech is short for the relatively new term *financial technology*, which is used to describe new technology solutions for traditional banking and banking-related industries. FinTech used to describe how banks would use technology to better serve customers, but it has since taken on a much larger meaning.

Today, FinTech is more about startup companies that hope to replace traditional banking institutions by offering less-expensive but more-efficient services to under-served markets, such as entrepreneurs. In 2017, FinTech firms around the world attracted

$34 billion in investments and reached $33 billion in the first six months of 2018. In Canada in 2017, there were over 600 FinTech companies that attracted $520 million in investments, the majority of which are located in the Toronto region. Some of the better-known FinTech companies, all of which have been mentioned in this text, include Shopify, online website creator aimed at the sale of goods; Freshbooks, cloud-based accounting and invoicing system; and **Lightspeed**, small and medium business point of sale company.

Other lesser-known examples of FinTech firms whose focus is directly on helping entrepreneurs include:

Clearbanc: As discussed earlier in the book, Clearbanc provides money to entrepreneurs without asking them to pledge personal assets against loans. The company, co-founded by serial entrepreneur Michelle Romanow, charges six percent in interest with no extra fees. To be eligible, entrepreneurs provide Clearbanc with access to their bank accounts and must have a minimum of $10,000 a month in sales. Clearbanc is particularly interested in online entrepreneurs who can prove an infusion of cash will enable them to add increase marketing leading to a direct increase in sales. Michael McNaught of RV rental marketplace said it only took a few days for his company to access capital through Clearbanc.

Payfirma: a cloud-based payment processing company which enables firms to accept payments online or in person under one company account. Payfirma's fees are in the range of 1.99 percent compared to roughly 2.9 percent charged by traditional banks. Similiar companies include **Square** and Shopify's payment processor.

bitbuy: Allows consumers and businesses to buy, sell, and hold Bitcoin a cyrptocurrency. Other sites offering this include **Coinsquare** and **Kraken**.

For more detail about how a lending FinTech company works, read about Lending Loop in **Small Business In Action 6-3**.

Discussion Questions

1. What are some obstacles to entrepreneurs and Canadians using more FinTech services in their businesses and daily lives? How can FinTech companies overcome these obstacles?
2. Think about some financial services you use at banks and other traditional financial institutions. Select some of the financial services and create a FinTech company that can offer superior solutions. Ensure you can communicate the advantages of your new firm over traditional enterprises and pitch it to your class.
3. Use Internet resources to identify 5 to 10 new FinTech companies. Narrow your list down to the one or two you think will be the most successful in the long term. Communicate your results to your peers and/or instructor. Be sure to identify advantages for the new companies and barriers they will have to overcome.

Private Lenders.

One increasingly common source of debt capital for small business is the borrowing of funds from the owners of the business. These funds are called *shareholders' loans,* and they offer some unique advantages. It is estimated that approximately one-third of small business owners make a start-up loan to their own businesses.[42] Although the interest paid is a tax-deductible expense for the business, the repayment terms are flexible. In addition, lenders often view shareholders' loans as equity as long as the funds are left in the company. Some believe this method combines the advantages of equity and debt financing.

Another source of private debt is borrowing from other individuals, such as friends or relatives. As with shareholders' loans, it may be possible to structure flexible repayment terms. A new and growing trend in private lenders is online peer-to-peer lending, which is discussed below in the Lending Loop case (see **Small Business in Action 6-3**). Toronto-based Snakes & Lattes is an example of a company that found success using Lending Loop to expand their business. Founder Ben Castanie says he wanted to expand his company from a cafe to a full, on-site restaurant offering customers a complete menu. Aaron Zach, the COO, confirms that, in the past, the business relied on non-traditional lenders, who charged high interest rates, or government programs, which had a long approval process. Zach says Snakes & Lattes shared their financial information and company background with Lending Loop, who then assigned the company a credit rating and marketed the lending opportunity on their site. Within two-and-a-half hours, Snakes & Lattes had raised the required $100,000 at a fair interest rate.[43]

SMALL BUSINESS IN ACTION 6-3

LENDINGLOOP.CA: PEER-TO-PEER LENDING

Peer-to-peer lending has been catching on throughout the world as a way for businesses and entrepreneurs to acquire needed debt financing for their business. For example, **Lending Club** in the United States, which was originally founded to facilitate online personal loans, started allowing businesses to use the site to acquire capital in 2014. Until 2015, Canadian firms looking to borrow money from other Canadians had to follow strict rules, and lenders normally had to have met the requirements of being an accredited investor with a minimum of $250,000 in annual income.

This all changed when **Lending Loop** started their online lending platform. Lending Loop allows lenders with as little as $50 to lend the money to business owners who can use the funds for inventory, expansion, and other business operations. The process for both lenders and businesses is fairly simple. Lenders fill out an online application and after they are approved, they can view businesses that are looking for money. Lenders can access the company's bio, interest rates, and other terms and conditions. Lenders can receive up to 15 percent interest for the use of their funds. Lenders are attracted to peer-to-peer lenders as they can receive high returns on their capital, and some like the idea of supporting Canadian entrepreneurs. Peer-to-peer lending is not without risk, however. If the company to which lenders lend money goes out of business or fails to pay the loan, the lenders can lose all their money, and there is little to protect their investment.

Businesses that apply for a loan on Lending Loop fill in a simple one-page application. Lending Loop then verifies the creditworthiness of the company and lists the company for a loan. Lending Loop currently insists that firms must have been in business for at least two years and have annual revenue of at least $200,000 before approval.

Peer-to-peer lending is seen as advantageous to entrepreneurs because of its simplicity, the ability to access debt financing that they may not otherwise be able to get from banks or other lenders, and a fairly easy approval process. The major downside of peer-to-peer lending for entrepreneurs may be higher interest rates and other disadvantages associated with debt financing. Cato Pastoll, CEO of Lending Loop says, "We are confident that our platform will prove to be a compelling alternative to high-cost private lenders and overly conservative Canadian banks for small businesses that are looking for flexible financing at fair rates."

Discussion Questions

1. Peer-to-peer lending has grown into a billion dollar industry. Are you surprised how large the industry has become? What do you think are the reasons for the growth?
2. The returns offered to lenders are higher for business loans than personal loans. Why do you think this is the case?
3. Do you think it s ethical to charge people 15 percent to borrow money when the banks are charging much lower interest rates?
4. What type of companies do you think are most likely to be attracted to peer-to-peer lending?
5. Lending Loop is not allowing start-ups to access its service. Why do you think this is the case? Do you think start-ups should be given access to peer-to-peer lending?
6. The Canadian government has yet to regulate peer-to-peer lending for businesses. Should the government pass rules and regulations for the industry? Why or why not?

Corporate Lenders.

In some circumstances, other companies may lend funds to a small business. Often these are larger firms that have established some connection or working relationship with the small business. One example of such funding would be the granting of trade credit by a company to a small business that purchases merchandise from that company. Most small businesses use this source of financing wherever possible. Trade credit for inventory is normally financed for 30, 60, or 90 days, with discounts for prompt payment. Equipment is usually financed for up to five years, with a 20 to 30 percent down payment required.

Another type of lender associated with accounts receivable is a factor. Factor companies purchase accounts receivable from a business at a discount. The business obtains needed cash, and the factor collects the accounts receivable. An increasing number of businesses in Canada are enlisting factoring companies to obtain short-term financing.

The sale and leaseback is another form of financing involving other businesses. In this arrangement, the business sells an asset to another company, which, in turn, leases it back to the seller. The advantage of the sale and leaseback is that the seller not only has the use of the funds of the sale but also benefits from the tax deductibility of the lease payments.

Regular Private Lending Institutions.

This category includes companies whose major purpose is the lending of funds. The most common of these firms are the following:

- *Chartered banks.* A major source of small business financing is Canada's chartered banks. Banks have currently extended over $225 billion in credit to small and medium companies. At present, six major Canadian chartered banks and a multitude of foreign-controlled banks operating in Canada account for 72 percent of all small business debt financing.[44] While this is a sizeable amount of money, banks normally have stringent requirements for approving financing for new or small businesses. Banks normally require a business plan, a good to excellent credit rating, a personal guarantee, loan security, and a reasonable request. (For more details, see **Small Business in Action 6-4**.)
- *Trust companies.* Trust companies are geared primarily toward mortgages on long-term capital assets, such as land, buildings, and equipment.
- *Credit unions.* Credit unions are usually locally owned. They tend to be concerned primarily with personal loans and working with smaller companies. Since credit unions have a tendency to be more local in their approach, they tend to offer better financial service to small companies. In fact, the Canadian Federation of Independent Businesses recently concluded a study on access to capital in Canada and found that credit unions outperform the big five banks in financial service to small firms.[45] Matt Mould, founder of **Sport Systems Canada**, an Ottawa-based manufacturer of sports pads and floors, supports these findings. Mould says, "The credit unions listened to us in the beginning, when the chartered banks didn't . . . credit unions were instrumental in getting us started."
- *Finance companies.* These are high-risk lenders that charge a higher rate of interest than other agencies. As with credit unions, the majority of their loans are personal loans.

An additional source of small business financing that seems to be increasing is the entrepreneur's use of their credit cards to provide temporary assistance.

SMALL BUSINESS IN ACTION 6-4

DO CHARTERED BANKS LEND MONEY TO ENTREPRENEURS?

This is a rather simple question but the answer appears to be complex.

According to the Canadian Bankers Association, banks are major lenders to entrepreneurs, and as of 2017, banks had approved credit in excess of $225 billion to small and medium enterprises. The association points out that approval ratings are quite high at 87 percent, and the average loan is in excess of $300,000. The banks through their national association state they are important partners in small business financing in Canada.

So, based on these statements above, you may assume that banks are strong supporters of Canadian entrepreneurs.

Lane V. Erickson/Shutterstock.com

The Canadian Federation of Independent Businesses (CFIB) begs to differ. The non-profit agency completed a report titled *Battle of the Banks* in 2017. CFIB surveyed 11,400 small business owners and concluded access to financing was problematic for small businesses and particularly problematic for smaller firms. For example, on a scale of 1 to 10, micro-businesses, firms with fewer than five employees, ranked

[continued]

their access to bank financing as almost non-existent. In the survey, every bank scored under 4.6 out of 10 for access to financing with the three lowest ranking banks being HSBC (.9 /10), Royal Bank (3.5/10) and TD Canada Trust (3.6/10). CFIB's report did conclude that access to capital appears to increase with firm size and the age of the firm, but ultimately concluded that banks need to do more to assist small Canadian firms. CFIB CEO Dan Kelly says, access to banking services is important to small business success and the CFIB is challenging banks to better their small business offerings.

Evidence both statistical and anecdotal appears to back up Kelly's assertion that banks are not overly supportive of smaller businesses and startups. While the banks boast an 87 percent loan approval rate, the CFIB research indicates smaller firms have actual rejection rates as high as 22.3 percent. As discussed earlier in the chapter, banks supply approximately 30 percent of funds to startup companies and of this most, if not all, of the money is guaranteed by personal assets of the business or the entrepreneur. Additionally, the provincial and federal governments have all invested in various funding programs to assist startup enterprises that cannot access traditional capital through banking institutions. As stated by serial entrepreneur Chris Neville, banks really are not interested in lending money to startups or small companies. Raymond Luk, founder of **Hockeystick** a Toronto-based data management company says banks will not assist entrepreneurs unless their company is worth in excess of one million dollars.

Anecdotal evidence that banks do not lend money to aspiring entrepreneurs or small business is much stronger and perhaps best summed up by Michael Duck, CEO of **SureShot Solutions**, a growing Halifax company that manufactures restaurant equipment. Duck says, "Some people have this idea in their heads, they go into a bank with a business plan and good credit, the plan has strong projections and he will sell himself and his idea to the banker. Based on his business idea and credit, the bank will lend the entrepreneur the money. This is not how it works. Banks don't lend money based on business plans. They lend money based on assets, what the owner can pledge against the loan. If they cannot pledge anything, then they do not get any money. It's that simple." Co-CEOs Nik Grgic and Karl Gannon, owners of **FourQuest Energy Inc.**, an Alberta-based energy service company, echo Duck's comments. The pair, who have extensive experience in the oil industry, developed a clear business plan identifying a very large opportunity for their potential company. Yet when they started visiting banks, they couldn't find anyone willing to lend them money. In the end they settled for a $1 million loan from BDC, which was half of what they had hoped to raise. Even today as the company has grown to over $50 million in sales in a short time, they note they still struggle to find lenders. Kevin Carmichael, a business columnist for the *Financial Post*, writes that banks' traditional lending practices may harm the digital economy. He states that digital companies do not have traditional assets and, given their need for capital, many are being restrained by Canadian banks' aversion to risk.

Discussion Questions

1. Do you think banks should be willing to lend money based on a strong business plan and credit scores alone? Why or why not?
2. Since many angel investors make a healthy return on investing in start-ups, are banks missing out on an opportunity for profits by not investing in new or small companies? Why do you think banks are not doing this?
3. Since Canadian banks tend to be highly profitable and appear to benefit from some federal laws that limit competition, should they as a group be more willing to invest in small business given its importance to the Canadian economy. Do you think rather than invest in small business themselves that government should stipulate a percentage of bank loans be made to new businesses? Why or why not?

Government Lenders.

As discussed earlier, government agencies at both the federal and the provincial or territorial levels invest in Canadian small business. Not only is the BDC is the major source of federal money for aspiring and growing entrepreneurs, but the agency provides counselling assistance to small businesses as well. The federal government has created a one-stop website for entrepreneurs looking to grow their business and access capital on the **Innovation Canada** site. Entrepreneurs looking to access capital would be well served to use this site as a starting point. Two other significant government programs are the Canadian Small Business Finance Program and Futurpreneur, formerly the Canadian Youth Business Foundation, both of which we look at next.

Canada Small Business Financing Program (CSBF).

The **Canada Small Business Financing Program** is a loans program that aims to increase the availability of capital for existing small and medium-sized businesses that are looking to improve or expand their small business (startups can qualify for the program). The program allows business owners to apply for a maximum loan of $1 million at any of the participating lenders, including banks, credit unions, and caisses populaires, with the federal government acting as a guarantor for 85 percent of the lender's losses. The financial institutions make all lending decisions and are responsible for providing the funds and registering the loans. Both start-ups and existing businesses are eligible to apply for funding as long as they meet the program's requirements. Many entrepreneurs have successfully used this program to gain access to much needed funds and are happy with the interest terms of no more than 3 percent above prime for floating rates or 3 percent above residential mortgages for fixed rates. For example, Jim MacAulay used the CSBF program to open the **True North Diner**, a Halifax-based, 1950s-style diner. MacAulay says that traditional banks would never have lent him money without the CSBF program. MacAulay eventually sold his profitable business to an expanding restaurant chain.

Cozy Corner Saunas used a CSBF loan to gain access to much needed start-up capital. The business, based in Dartmouth, Nova Scotia, had a difficult time securing initial funds and relied on the CSBF program to get the business up and running. The firm's owner, Catherine Whittaker, confirmed that if it weren't for the loan from the program, she would not have been able to start her company. "Our business plan had just been approved, but the bank was uncomfortable lending us the entire amount requested," she says. "One of the bank officers offered to look into the Canadian Small Business Financing program for us. A few weeks later, we were accepted into the program and the deal went through! We had a perfect vision of what we wanted to do with our business and were determined to go forward. But as first-time business owners, we had very little capital or history to back us up," Whittaker explains. "The Canadian Small Business Financing program was really the deciding factor as to whether we were going to be able to move forward."[46]

Futurpreneur.

Futurpreneur, formerly the Canadian Youth Business Foundation, (CYBF) is a national non-profit organization funded by the federal government, which provides access to start-up and growth funds to young entrepreneurs who are 39 or younger. Futurpreneur provides entrepreneurs with access to up to $45,000 as well as professional mentorship. Futurpreneur is particularly attractive as a financing option to young entrepreneurs as it considers the applicant's character and the merits of the business plan, not collateral. In addition to capital, Futurpreneur ensures that all successful applicants work with a business mentor to assist them in running their business. To date, Futurpreneur has invested in more than 12,000 entrepreneurs, creating 10,000 businesses, whose businesses have created more than 50,000 new jobs, $300 million in tax revenue, and hundreds of millions of dollars in sales and export revenue.[47]

Provincial and Territorial Programs.

Provincial and territorial governments have provided tax and rebate incentives for the formation of small business investment companies, which function similarly to venture-capital companies.

The potential advantages of approaching a government agency are the following:

1. The agency may finance higher-risk or lower-equity ventures, which characterize many small businesses.
2. Government lenders may be more willing to rewrite loan terms and conditions if the business gets into trouble. They also tend to be less quick to foreclose on a failing business.
3. Government agencies may provide a lower interest rate than the chartered banks. Many provincial and territorial government lenders fall into this category. BDC rates, which are adjusted periodically, are usually similar to chartered bank rates.
4. Government lenders may provide some equity capital in the form of temporary ownership or grants, depending on the type of business and its location. (See the information provided in the Government Lenders section above.)
5. Government lenders may provide management counselling along with funding to assist the business.

Although the advantages may make borrowing from government agencies attractive, there are some potential disadvantages that the small business owner should be aware of:

1. A government agency usually requires more information to review a loan application than other lending institutions do.
2. The time required for approval of a loan tends to be longer than with private lending institutions.
3. Most government agencies exert more monitoring and control over the businesses to which they lend, and the agencies often require regular reports on operations.

In addition to the government agencies established to provide both debt and equity financing, several specific federal government programs also provide financial help for small businesses.

Most provinces and territories also have programs designed to provide financial assistance to the small business community.

DETERMINING THE TERM OF FINANCING

The small business owner should carefully evaluate the characteristics of the sources of financing we discussed and measure their suitability against the needs of the business.

The length of term and type of financing required may assist in making the decision among lenders, as **Table 6-11** shows. The table also illustrates the typical assets covered by the various terms of financing. The length of the term allowed by a lender is normally equivalent to the useful life of the asset, except in the case of land, which is often carried on a 20-year term.

TABLE 6-11 Matching Financing to Assets

TYPE OF LOAN	SOURCES	USE	SECURITY	LOAN CHARACTERISTICS
Short-term (demand) loans (3–6 months)	Banks, private sources, factoring houses, confirming houses	Receivables, line of credit, inventory (working capital items)	Assignment of receivables and inventory, personal guarantees, assignment of life insurance	Can be withdrawn on short notice; no fixed payment terms; interest, principal rates fluctuate
Medium-term (3–10 years) loans	Banks, term lenders, financial houses, leasing companies, foreign banks, private sources, and government programs	Equipment, furnishings, vehicles, leaseholds, and new business investments	Chattel mortgages, conditional sales contracts, or assignment of equipment insurance	Specific repayment terms; interest either fixed or floating with prime rate
Long-term (15–25 years) mortgages, bonds, debentures	Trust companies, foreign banks, private sources	Property, land and buildings, new business investments	Collateral mortgages, assignment of property insurance	Fixed repayment terms; fixed interest rates

An often costly mistake that some owner-managers make is to use funds obtained for long-term purposes to get them through short-term crises. Inevitably, this practice creates a more serious financial crisis a short while later. If capital requirements were underestimated, the owner should approach the lender again with this information and attempt to have the lender increase the funds provided.

PREPARING A PROPOSAL TO OBTAIN FINANCING LO7

When attempting to obtain financing, a small business owner should be aware of those areas about which the lender requires information. In addition to completing the loan application, the owner should include the financial projections. A detailed and well-prepared loan proposal goes a long way toward ensuring the approval of a loan application.

1. THE APPLICANT'S MANAGEMENT ABILITY

The lender will want to be sure the applicant has the skills, education, experience, and ability to make the business succeed. To evaluate the applicant's managerial ability, the lender will want to know the following:

How Much the Applicant Knows about the Business.

The lender will probably ask questions about the business or industry to ascertain the applicant's level of knowledge. The lender will also be interested in any previous experience the applicant has had that relates to the proposed business.

How Much Care Was Taken in Preparing the Proposal.

The lender will want to see a detailed plan of what the loan is for, as well as a listing of the other sources of financing for the project. The steps of a business plan outlined in **Chapter 4** should provide the basis for the financing proposal. Several statements will be required, and it is important that the applicant document the source of the information in those statements. The first statement is the lending proposal, which typically follows the format shown in **Table 6-12**.

TABLE 6-12 Loan Proposal Format

PROGRAM		FINANCING	
Land	$20,000	Bank loan	$60,000
Building	$50,000	Own funds	$20,000
Equipment	$10,000	Total	$80,000

In addition to the lending proposal, the lender will probably want to see a proposed income and cash flow statement for at least the first year of operations and probably longer. A balance sheet may also be required. These statements should be carefully prepared following the formats discussed in **Chapter 3** and **Chapter 9**. As mentioned above, each item on the statement should be well researched and well documented. The lender will want to know what provision has been made for the owner's salary and for contingencies. Often an entrepreneur is advised to enlist an accountant if the owner is weak in financial statement preparation.

2. THE PROPOSAL

The lender will assess the idea or proposal itself. Using the income statement and cash flow projections, the lender will assess the chances of repayment of the loan. The lender will evaluate not only the specific business but also industry trends, including the extent of competition and the experiences of similar businesses. The lender may also check with experts in the industry. Many chartered banks now have industry specialists on staff to assist in this type of evaluation. The pitfalls of a poor proposal are illustrated in **Small Business Beginnings 6-6**.

Some specific types of evaluation used in the lending industry follow:

- *Level of working capital*—the dollar difference between current assets and current liabilities. Working capital should be sufficient to meet current obligations as they become due and to finance delays in revenue caused by such items as accounts receivable.
- *Current ratio*—current assets compared with current liabilities. A healthy current ratio is 2:1.
- *Quick ratio*—current assets less inventories compared with liabilities. A healthy quick ratio is 1:1.
- *Debt-to-equity ratio*—percentage of owner's equity compared with debt. A minimum debt-to-equity ratio is 4:1 (25 percent equity). For smaller businesses, most lenders prefer to see 50 percent equity.

The lender will also want to see projections for the basic financial statements, such as the balance sheet and income statement. The fundamentals of these statements are also covered in **Chapter 9**.

Collateral.

Because of the security position on the loan, the lender will want to know whether another lender is also providing funding for the project and, if so, what collateral it has taken as security for the loan. The lender will want to ensure that the funds loaned will be secured by some form of saleable collateral. On capital assets, a lender generally allows no more than 80 to 90 percent of the value of the assets as security. The reason is that if the lender needs to realize on (repossess) the security, obsolescence, selling, and administration costs will reduce its value. The level of collateral may also vary by industry type, reflecting risk and type of asset.

SMALL BUSINESS BEGINNINGS 6-6

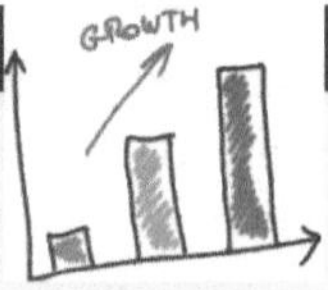

FINDING CAPITAL

Michael Dinn and Heidi Noble, co-owners in the restaurant industry for years, shared a dream of building a winery in the Okanagan Valley in British Columbia. Through their industry experience, they had built up some close connections with winemakers that they assumed would help them to get started. The only problem was that they did not have the finances. At first, they went to their families and got enough for a down payment on a two-hectare farm. However, it was not long before they were using their credit cards and had resumed their day jobs in Vancouver. On weekends, they began processing their first sample vintage on a limited basis with the help of a winemaker. Everyone agreed that the product was excellent. However, they needed substantial financing to construct the winery. They had difficulty obtaining the funding because of weaknesses in their proposal, including their lack of understanding of the business and the market, a failure to show a positive cash flow, the lack of equity, and a failure to create a sound business plan. Eventually, after finding a bank that was familiar with the industry, Dinn and Noble received the required funding and have now realized their dream of building a successful wine business.

At this point the entrepreneur may realize that they do not possess the required equity to secure adequate financing. In such cases, an investigation of the possibility of leasing instead of buying could be made. An increasing number of businesses are leasing assets to free up capital for other purposes. A recent study carried out by Trimark Seg Fund found that more than one-half (53.5 percent) of small business entrepreneurs have given personal guarantees to secure loans. Forty percent have used their homes, while 20 percent have used their savings.[48]

3. THE APPLICANT'S BACKGROUND AND CREDITWORTHINESS

In addition to the project itself and the applicant's managerial ability, the lender will require some additional information in judging the applicant's creditworthiness.

Personal Information.

In filling out a loan application, an applicant is usually required to file information typically included in a personal résumé–items such as age, marital status, education, and work experience. (Be careful to check the legal implications of certain questions.)

Present Debt and Past Lending History.

The lender will want a list of the current state of any loans outstanding and may require information about the applicant's past loan history as well. Most lenders are members of credit bureaus that can provide a complete credit history of the applicant. Lenders will generally use this source to verify the information provided by the applicant.

Amount of Equity the Applicant Has Invested.

All lenders want to know the amount of the applicant's personal funds going into the project. Usually, cash equity is required, but occasionally, capital assets or even sweat equity may be acceptable. The amount of equity funds required will vary depending on the risk associated with the project, but as mentioned, few lenders will provide financing if the applicant has less than 20 to 25 percent equity to invest in the business.

Will the Applicant Bank with the Lender?

Many lenders will request that the applicant's business accounts be transferred or opened with the lending bank. They may also require that a compensating balance be held in the account as collateral.

If the loan request is turned down, it is important that the entrepreneur find why and make adjustments to the proposal. Alternatively, several lenders should be visited to secure the necessary funding.

LENDER RELATIONS

Once financing has been obtained, it is important that the business provide up-to-date information to the lender regarding current operations and future plans. Regular financial statements and lease contracts can help establish trust between the banker and the owner-manager. Many businesses have found that maintaining a close working relationship with lenders helps ensure adequate levels of financing in the long run. A recent survey by the Canadian Bankers Association found that 78 percent of small businesses had positive relationships with their financial institutions.[49]

What do entrepreneurs do if they have investigated both equity and debt sources and are unable to obtain the needed capital? Probably the first thing to do is find out the reasons for refusal and possibly rework the proposal to bring it in line with the lender's requirements.

Changes may be necessary to make the proposed business more attractive to lenders or investors. As noted, one option that is increasingly being used to reduce the amount of funds required for capital purchases is to consider leasing or renting the asset. Leasing the asset generally does not require a down payment. The ability to obtain the lease is usually based more on the earning power of the asset and the business than on the background of the owner. Later, when the company is in a more stable condition, the owner may succeed in obtaining funds to make a purchase if they desire.

LEARNING OBJECTIVES SUMMARY

LO1 **Lack of managerial competence and experience can often result in such financing problems as underestimation of financial requirements, lack of knowledge of sources of capital, lack of skills in preparing and presenting a proposal for financing to a lender, failure to plan in advance for future needs, and poor financial control in payment of loan obligations.**

LO2 **Start-up capital includes initial inventory, deposits, and first few months' payments for payroll, utilities, rent, advertising, insurance, licences, and permits. Accounts receivable and any other operating costs that need to be paid before revenues are generated should also be planned for.**

LO3 **The type of financing entrepreneurs can access is usually dictated by the stage the business is in and the type of opportunities the company is pursuing. In Canada, start-up businesses are traditionally self-funded, while ongoing businesses often use personal investment and retained earnings. Entrepreneurs who are starting or managing a relatively small business that is pursuing a slow-growth strategy will often be limited to debt, while entrepreneurs who are pursuing a high-growth venture are much more likely to use equity and debt in financing their business.**

LO4 **An essential step in determining the amount of capital needed is to calculate the owner's net worth. This helps determine the amount of funds the owner has to invest in the company and will probably be required by a lending institution.**

LO5 **Three general sources of equity financing are private investors, corporate investors, and government programs. Sources of debt financing include owners of the business, corporate lenders, regular lending institutions, and government agencies.**

LO6 **The advantages of equity capital include the lack of an interest obligation, the expertise of the investors, expanded borrowing power, and the spreading of risk. The disadvantages of equity financing include a dilution of ownership, the increased potential for disagreements, and the cost incurred in the issuance of the ownership interest. The advantages of debt financing are the possible higher return on investment, the deductibility of interest, flexibility, and the ease of approval. The disadvantages include the interest expense, the additional paperwork, and the inability to spread risk among investors.**

LO7 **The criteria most lenders use in making the loan decision are the applicant's managerial ability, the proposal itself, and the applicant's background and creditworthiness.**

TIME TO TAKE ACTION

If you are interested in finding money to start a business or to grow an existing business, it is time to take action. Focus on doing the following from this chapter:

1. Determine your own net worth. Establish your cash position because it will affect how much money you need to raise.
2. If you have not done so already, determine how much money you need. Then decide on your optimal capital mix.
3. Start to discuss financial plans with potential sources of capital as early as possible, including bankers, potential investors among family and friends, and so forth.
4. Prepare your fundraising pitch, and start looking for capital. Remember—you will be successful if you work hard enough!

DISCUSSION QUESTIONS

1. What is the cheapest source of funds? When all other sources turn down your request for funding, what source is most likely to say yes? Why is this the case?
2. What are the advantages and disadvantages of debt and equity financing?
3. What do you think are the advantages and disadvantages of crowdfunding and angel investors?
4. Are investors on crowdfunding sites in need of some government protection, or do you agree that it is their money and they should be able to spend it as they see fit?
5. Should government provide loans for entrepreneurs starting new businesses? Should government guarantee loans for small businesses that are missing the necessary track record, assets, or other ingredients to obtain a commercial bank loan? What benefit do we, as a nation of taxpayers, receive from such loan guarantees?
6. An investor provides an entrepreneurial firm with the capital that it needs to grow. Beyond the capital, in what other ways can the investor add value to the firm? What are the possible downsides of having an angel or a venture capitalist as an investor in the business?

EXPERIENTIAL EXERCISES

1. Indicate whether each of the following is a start-up cost (S), an ongoing operating cost (O), or both (B).
   a. $1000 for first month's rent
   b. $25,000 for store fixtures
   c. $1000 for third month's rent
   d. Weekly cleaning fee of $250
   e. Purchase of $50,000 of inventory
   f. Payroll expense
   g. $50,000 for TV advertising
2. Imagine you are preparing a business plan for a small manufacturing firm in your province or territory. Using Internet resources, determine what government programs are available. How could each program help your client's business?
3. Search the Internet for services that provide access to business angels or informal investors. How do these sites work? If you were an entrepreneur looking for funding, how much would it cost to use this service? How many business angels are registered on the typical database? How many entrepreneurs are registered on the typical database? How effective do you believe these services are? (Use data, where possible, to support your answer.)
4. Interview an employee at one of the government agencies that offer equity or debt financing to small businesses. Determine the purpose, the merits, and the weaknesses of that program.
5. Interview a banker and someone at the Futurpreneur to determine what they look for in a loan application. Compare the differences.
6. Form an even number of groups in class, label half the groups as venture capitalists and the other half as entrepreneurs. Groups from each side will pair up, and their job is to negotiate a deal with each other based on the following information: the entrepreneur has a company that has revenue of $2 million; expected annual growth is 25 percent a year for five years and then 5 percent a year after that; the firm is looking for an investment of $5 million for 10 percent equity. Which venture-capital firm and entrepreneur groups negotiated the best deal?
7. Interview three small business owners about things they do (or have done) to bootstrap the financing of their business. How effective were these techniques? Be prepared to present this list to class and describe how the techniques work.
8. Go to a directory of venture capitalists and ascertain what percentage of funds for a typical venture-capital firm are invested in seed, start-up, expansion or development, and acquisitions or leveraged buyouts. What criteria do venture capitalists report using in their initial screening of business proposals?

COMPREHENSIVE CASE DAN KIM: PART 3

Dan is quite proud of his business plan and realizes that he has learned a lot in preparing it. He also realizes, however, that for the business to get off the ground, he needs to raise additional money. Suzie will only let Dan use $20,000 of their savings for the venture, but Dan is of the opinion that this will at least help them get started. Once the business is up and running, additional funds will be generated through sales of the Ladder Helper.

Dan has also decided that he would rather establish the manufacturing facility from scratch rather than lease or purchase an existing facility. This way he can arrange the building as it suits him, and he will not have to spend money to retrofit. In addition, Dan lives on an acreage which he inherited and he already owns enough property on which to construct the building. He estimates that constructing a small building of 2000 square feet will cost about $150,000. Although he can use some of the metal-cutting and bending equipment that he already has, another $50,000 is required to obtain the equipment needed to move to commercial production of the Ladder Helper. Dan also thinks that he will have to have a truck to haul inventory to the plant and perhaps to deliver the finished product to local purchasers. The estimated cost for a good used truck is $20,000. Initial inventory of aluminum is estimated at $20,000. The financing requirements total $240,000 (**Table 3-A**).

TABLE 3-A Ladder Helper Start-Up Costs

Building	$150,000
Equipment	50,000
Truck	20,000
Inventory	20,000

Armed with his business plan and his estimate of start-up costs, Dan goes to his local bank to obtain the required financing. He is surprised that his banker is less than enthusiastic about his proposal. His banker's response is clear: "First, I would never lend a brand-new corporation this money; you will need to mortgage your house and property. Second, you need more equity than this before I would consider a loan to you even with collateral. Third, you will need more detail on your costs. And finally I will need some indication that your business has the ability to make the loan payments." With his banker's words ringing in his ears, Dan is determined to show how this business could repay a loan. He goes home and starts to work up a proposed income statement, shown in **Table 3-B**.

TABLE 3-B Ladder Helper Year 1 Income Statement

Revenue: 5000 units at $40	$200,000
Cost of goods sold: 5000 units at $10	50,000
Wages	70,000
Utilities and phone	15,000
Net income	$ 65,000

When Dan takes this statement to the banker, he is told that more work needs to be done. Dan goes home to Suzie feeling pretty discouraged and is not sure what to do next.

Suzie and Dan decide to spend some time researching other potential sources of money online. Both are surprised to learn about the number of angel investors and angel groups in their region. Suzie thinks pursuing angel support for their business would be ideal because the couple will not be burdened with interest costs, which are associated with traditional bank financing. Furthermore, if the business fails, they will likely lose less of their own money. Dan is not as excited about angel investors as Suzie is. He argues with her that he wants to be his own boss; business angels would want to influence his decisions, and starting the company is something they can do on their own. Dan also thinks that if he sells equity in his business, he could be giving up millions in long-term profits if the company succeeds nationally and then globally.

Dan is becoming increasingly convinced that crowdfunding is the best way to solicit funds for the Ladder Helper. He has read numerous articles about entrepreneurs who have raised millions quickly on crowdfunding sites.

He is convinced that in a few days he could place some photos on Kickstarter with a product description and offer one Ladder Helper to every backer who donates $30 to his entrepreneurial dream as an incentive. He recognizes that this is less than his original selling price, but in his mind people would simply be pre-purchasing the Ladder Helper and early adopters should get a deal. Dan does some quick math and says if he pre-sold 3,000 Ladder Helpers at $30 a piece he would quickly have $90,000 in sales with costs of goods sold coming in at $30,000. This would represent a nice profit and he could then go to the bank with this evidence in hand. Although Suzie doesn't know much about crowdfunding, she thinks it might be more complex than Dan is imagining.

Questions

1. What items have been overlooked by Dan in both the start-up costs and the income statements for the Ladder Helperl?
2. What additional statements would the banker likely require?
3. Do you think Dan should consider other forms of capital like equity? Why or why not?
4. What advantages and disadvantages of angel financing is Dan missing out on in his assessment of this specific type of an investor? How might Suzie persuade him to change his mind?
5. Would crowdfunding be a good idea for Dan to pursue? What are some of the potential advantages and disadvantages of this strategy?
6. What information is Dan missing in calculating his potential crowdfunding campaign profits?
7. What advice would you offer Dan to help him improve his crowdfunding campaign?

CASES FOR PART 2

Clark's Sporting Goods
Jensen Roofing
Conrad's Photographer's Supplies
Kelly's Grill
Second Cup

CLARK'S SPORTING GOODS

Dave Clark plans to open a specialty sporting goods store in London, Ontario, as soon as he graduates from university there in the spring. Dave's concept is to go after X-game–type sports, offering both high-end and entry-level equipment and safety products that local residents would normally have to source online. He would also be quick to add trendy and unique products like the **Freebord**, which allows users to simulate snowboarding on pavement. Dave did a market demand analysis for such a store for one of his course projects and is confident the opportunity exists.

Dave's major problem is determining the amount of funds he will require. His father, will lend him $30,000 as a graduation gift to invest. He has located a store that rents for $3,000 per month (in advance) and has made an itemized list of the start-up costs as follows:

Merchandise (4 months)	$100,000
Shelves, racks, displays	5,000
Remodelling	4,000
Cash register (used)	800
Check-out counter	500
Office supplies (4 months' supply)	200
Telephone & Internet (annually)	1500
Utilities: $200/month	2400

Dave has made the following estimates:

- He can completely turn over his inventory every four months.
- In the first year, he plans a 60 percent markup on the cost of merchandise.
- He can get by on a salary of $2000 per month.
- He plans to hire one full-time employee at $2500 per month and one part-time employee at $1000.
- He plans to spend $2000 in opening promotion in the first month and $500 a month after the grand opening for advertising.

Questions

1. Estimate how much money Dave will need from outside sources to start his business.
2. Assuming Dave receives start-up financing from a local government program, the amount calculated in Question 1, will he require an operating line of credit during the first four months of operation? If so, how much?
3. Should Dave pursue debt or equity sources of funds to get started?
4. How could Dave quickly evaluate the likelihood of success of his business?
5. Should Dave open up this business? Why or why not?

JENSEN ROOFING

Robert Jensen has just completed a short entrepreneurial course at a local college as preparation for establishing his own roofing business. One of the main things that he learned in the course was the necessity of preparing a business plan for the enterprise. As a result, Robert went to work and within a few days put together the following business plan for Jensen Roofing.

Background

I, Robert Jensen, will be the sole owner of this proprietorship, which will install and repair roofs in the Lethbridge, Alberta, market area. I have completed an entrepreneurial course at the Lethbridge Community College and have had several years experience in the roofing business working for Charles Hill Roofing, the largest roofer in the Lethbridge area.

I want to start my own business to be independent and to obtain a higher financial compensation than I am currently receiving. I want everyone in Lethbridge and surrounding areas to know my company and the quality work we do.

Market Approach

The target market will be every person who owns a house, an apartment building, a warehouse, a condo, or an office building. The services we provide will cater to all people who own buildings that need roof repair or construction. We will provide all types of roofing materials and services. Eavestroughing will also be included in our business. Quality workmanship will be the building block of our business. We will have a one-year guarantee on all work.

Because the service Jensen Roofing will provide is of high quality, I will charge a slightly higher price on our product. I will try to maintain a 20 percent markup over costs to keep our prices fair to every customer. Jensen Roofing will use several forms of promotion. Brochures and pamphlets will be prepared and sent through direct mail to every homeowner in Lethbridge. I will us newspaper ads as well as ads for Kijiji. I will create a website and a Facebook page, and make use of Facebook Marketplace.

Physical Facilities

The business will be located in my home at first. This will save a considerable amount of money until the business gets established. Equipment, supplies, and opening inventory will be purchased from local suppliers. The following schedule provides a listing of the equipment and supplies that will be needed to get started.

Physical Requirements

1 work truck (used half ton)	$15,000
3-metric ton dump truck (used)	15,000
1 hoist	1,500
4 ladders (25 foot)	1,500
Computer system & website	3,000
Office equipment and supplies	1,000
Total	$37,000

Financial

To estimate potential revenue for Jensen Roofing for new houses, I have multiplied the average roofing job for new houses ($8000) by the number of new houses constructed in Lethbridge (400) in 2017 for a total of $3,200,000. For repair jobs I have taken the average dollar expenditure per household for the Lethbridge area (Urban Family Expenditure Data) of $100 and multiplied it by the number of homes (26,000) for a total of $2,600,000. Of this total of $5,800,000, I estimate that Jensen Roofing will obtain a 10 percent market share for a total revenue of $580,000. There are currently eight other roofers in the city, but because of my quality workmanship, I hope to increase the market share of Jensen Roofing to 20 percent within five years.

Projected income based on these estimates are given below:

JENSEN ROOFING PROJECTED INCOME—YEAR 1

Sales	$580,000
Cost of goods sold (45%)	261,000
Wages	100,000
Depreciation	2,000
Advertising	2,600
Insurance	1,200
Repairs and maintenance	5,000
Licences and permits	200
Professional fees	800
Interest (8% on $15,000)	1,200
Total	374,000
Net Income	$206,000

Jensen Roofing will obtain a loan from a local bank to finance $35,000 of the start-up requirement. I will be willing to pledge my home against the loan. The remaining $2,000 will be supplied by me, the owner. The financial records of the business will be prepared and maintained by an accountant.

Legal Requirements

The necessary business licences and permits will be obtained from the City of Lethbridge. Initially, the business will be operated as a proprietorship, and when the business becomes more established, I will consider forming a limited company.

Personnel

The personnel required to keep Jensen Roofing operating will vary from season to season. Because of the uncertainties of the weather, part-time employees will be used. Ads will be placed in the local newspaper to find workers for the business. I will also use the government employment agency of Canada Manpower. During the summer months, I may also look at hiring students. I estimate that on average I will have about five workers on the payroll. Training will take place on the job, which is appropriate for this type of work.

Question

1. Evaluate the Jensen Roofing business plan from both an investor's and a lender's point of view.

CONRAD'S PHOTOGRAPHER'S SUPPLIES

Richard and Karen Bingley are interested in going into a business related to their hobby—photography. For the last year, they have been good customers of Conrad's Photographer's Supplies, a sole proprietorship, owned by Shelley Conrad. Although the store is relatively new, they have become well acquainted with Shelley, who is a well-known photographer in the community. Shelley told the Bingleys that the store was doing well considering she opened it just over year ago. She noted that there has been a resurgence in print photography, especially among millennials, and this is helping her grow her business. More and more people have gotten involved in photography and with the resurgence of print photography, the industry was in a growth position. An increasing number of people seem to prefer an outlet where they can get advice about taking pictures as opposed to buying only for low prices.

However, one day Shelley confides in Karen that although she enjoys operating the business, it was taking much more time to run than she expected, and she is considering selling the business to devote more time to her professional photography. Shelley thinks Richard and Karen might be interested in purchasing the business, since they are such good customers and know a lot about photography.

Richard and Karen are quite excited about the idea and meet with Shelley to go over the entire business. They are impressed with the operation as all the equipment and fixtures are new, and they are especially impressed with the extensive and growing customer list. As they discuss the financial information (see below), Shelley indicates that she would sell the business for $80,000, slightly above the value of the assets of the company. Richard and Karen currently have $20,000 in equity and Shelley says that she is prepared to finance them over four years at 10 percent per annum. Because of her stature in the industry and her numerous connections in the community, Shelley has developed a good working relationship with her suppliers, which typically includes them granting 30-day credit on inventory. The store is located in an older urban neighbourhood, which has been growing as of late with an infusion of young people looking to live close to the city centre. She currently has a five-year lease on the building.

CONRAD'S PHOTOGRAPHER'S SUPPLIES INCOME STATEMENT

Sales	$511,000
Cost of Goods Sold	365,000
Gross Margin	146,000
Expenses	
Wages	60,000
Promotion	7,000
Rent	36,000
Utilities	6,000
Miscellaneous	2,000
Depreciation	5,000
Net profit	$ 30,000

CONRAD'S PHOTOGRAPHER'S SUPPLIES BALANCE SHEET

Assets	
Cash	5,000
Accounts Receivable (Film Processing)	1,000
Inventory	40,000
Fixtures	15,000
Goodwill	12,000
Total	73,000
Liabilities and Owner's Equity	
Accounts Payable	27,000
Debt	20,000
Equity	26,000
Total	$76,000

Questions

1. Suppose the Bingleys decided to start a photography store from scratch. Discuss how this decision would compare with the other two methods of getting into the business on (a) independence, (b) risk, and (c) information requirements.
2. In evaluating this business to purchase it, discuss concerns you would have about (a) the previous owner, (b) financial information, and (c) assets of the business.
3. Assuming the information in the financial statements is accurate, is Shelley Conrad's asking price a reasonable one? Use book value and capitalization of earnings methods to help you answer this question.
4. There is at least one adjustment to the balance sheet and two to the income statement that should be made to make these statements more accurate, which will affect the calculation of the price of the business. Make the adjustments and reevaluate the asking price.

KELLY'S GRILL

Kelly Orr works as assistant department manager in the ladies' wear department of a large department store in Kingston, Ontario. She enjoys her work but sees that chances of further advancement in her $45,000-a-year job are limited. For the past few years, Kelly has been thinking about starting her own business. As a teenager, she worked summers in a fast-food franchise and always wanted to own a restaurant. As she has two children, she resents having to work Thursday and Friday evenings and Saturdays, and she thinks that by owning her own business she can more easily take time off to be with her family. Her husband, a schoolteacher, has supported her working in the past but is a bit hesitant about Kelly risking her savings of $20,000 to go out on her own. They agree, however, that Kelly should investigate a few possibilities and obtain as much information as she can about the restaurant industry in Kingston.

For the past six months, Kelly has visited with several of her friends, looked at some prospective businesses, and checked with public officials to find out what information is available. She has obtained the following information:

Population of Kingston	95,000
Per-family away-from-home food expenditures	$190/month
Number of families in Kingston	28,000
Number of restaurants in Kingston	110
Average square footage per outlet	1,500
Cost of goods sold as percentage of gross sales	50%
Bank's lending rate	10%

Operating expenses, excluding rent, interest, and franchise advertising royalties, are estimated to be 35 percent of gross sales.

From several restaurant possibilities, Kelly has narrowed the decision down to three: a site in a shopping mall, a downtown restaurant that is for sale, and a fast-food franchise. All three involve a greater investment than Kelly was planning on. To get sufficient funds, the Orrs may have to remortgage their house.

Possibility A

The first potential site is a shopping centre that is currently under renovation. The centre is anchored at each end by two national department stores. Kelly is a bit concerned about the long-term viability of one of the stores given the poor financial results the company has been reporting for the past two years. The space Kelly is considering is 6,000 square feet and carries a rental of $20 per square foot, plus a royalty of 2 percent of gross sales. Although the rental costs would be high, Kelly is confident that the mall, once fully renovated, will generate considerable customer traffic, thus outweighing the rental costs. Also, the mall location is within a few minutes' drive from her home. However, the space is unfinished, and Kelly estimates she would need a minimum of $70,000 in equipment and $20,000 in leasehold improvements to get the restaurant started. As it stands now, the mall has a food court with nine operators and she would have the only sit-down restaurant.

Possibility B

The second potential site is a 2500-square-foot busy downtown lunchtime café that is for sale. The present owner is asking $150,000 for the restaurant and is willing to finance the sale at $50,000 down and $10,000 per year for 15 years. The space has been leased at $35,000 annually and is due to be renegotiated in three years. The location of this restaurant makes it attractive to lunchtime and late-afternoon customers. The restaurant has operated successfully for six years and is located close to several large office buildings.

Possibility C

The third possibility is to sign a franchise contract with a national fast-food chain that wants to expand into Kingston. The typical outlet size is 2000 square feet. The initial franchise fee is $20,000, plus an additional $150,000 to be financed through Kelly's bank with the franchise guarantee, which would lower the interest rate by 2 percent. Kelly would also pay 6 percent of gross sales as a royalty. They would train Kelly in one of its company-owned outlets at no charge and help with the start-up of her own outlet. She would, of course, be constantly monitored by the franchise—a point that makes her a bit uneasy.

Kelly needs to make a decision soon. All three prospects might be lost if she waits too long.

Questions

1. How well has Kelly thought out and prepared for her decision to start her own restaurant?
2. Based on the information provided, which of the choices open to Kelly would you advise her to make?
3. What additional information should she obtain before making this decision?

SECOND CUP

Ken and Mary Hatch are in the process of making a major career change. Ken has been caretaker for a local high school in Markham, Ontario, for 20 years, rising to the position of supervisor. Mary has worked in a coffee shop for eight years since their children entered school. They are considering opening their own coffee shop and are interested in a Second Cup franchise.

Second Cup is a successful, nationally known Canadian franchise that was established in 1975 in Toronto and has grown to more than 400 outlets across the country. Mary became aware from her employer that Second Cup was looking for franchisees in the Markham area, and she has collected the following information from the company. The franchise fee is $40,000, and there is a promotional royalty of 9.5 percent of gross sales. Second Cup estimates the total investment for an outlet in Markham to be an additional $400,000 for equipment and other start-up costs. Second Cup is also offering franchisees the opportunity to include Pinkberry frozen yogurt business to be housed within the coffee store. The additional fee for this is $5,000 plus $10,000 for equipment. This cost does not include the building, which Second Cup builds and then rents back to the franchiser.

Although the Hatchs do not have $400,000, they have saved $20,000 and have been assured by Second Cup that the bank will finance the remainder at 8 percent by being signed up with the franchising company. One of the Hatchs' concerns is that they have not managed a restaurant before, although Ken has supervised people in his caretaking job and Mary has worked in the coffee shop for eight years. The Hatchs are take some comfort in the fact that Second Cup offers a three-week course at their Coffee College to teach the fundamentals of the coffee and retail business.

The couple is also unsure of the value in pursuing the Pinkberry option. While its a relatively well-known brand in the U.S., the inclusion of Pinkberry as a store within a store concept is new in Canada and Second Cup can only provide anecdotal evidence of its popularity with Canadian consumers. To date Pinkberry is only in a few stores and sales have been in the range of $2000 a month on average per store with a gross margin of 55 percent.

They are both tired of taking orders from supervisors and see this opportunity as a way to be their own bosses with minimal risk. There are currently five other Second Cup outlets in Markham and three Starbucks coffee houses, which are their major competitors. There are also many other independent coffee shops and other fast-food outlets that sell coffee. However, with the city and coffee sales growing, the Hatchs are optimistic about their chances for success. They cite the fact that they will save considerably by purchasing all their supplies from the parent company and the fact that the well-organized operating and monitoring system will ensure that they operate at peak efficiency as reasons for optimism.

Second Cup has supplied the following sample financial statement to help the Hatchs in their planning (this includes Pinkberry revenue):

Opening cash balance	$ 20,000
Sales	900,000
Cost of goods sold	473,684
Total	$446,316
Expenses	
Advertising royalty	$ 18,000
Royalty on Gross Sales	67,500
Rent ($60 at 1000)	60,000
Insurance	5,000
Repairs and maintenance	5,000
Telephone, Internet and utilities	25,000
Wages	150,000
Miscellaneous	10,000
Total	$340,500
Net income	$105,816

The Hatchs are happy with the projections because the business would make $105,816. Ken estimates that 30 percent of the wages to employee will include money the couple would take as co-managers for running the business. Ken and Mary note that combining this with the profits from the business would almost double what they are earning in their current jobs.

This couple is about to make the final decision to leave their employment and sign this franchise contract.

Questions

1. What further analysis should they do before making this decision?
2. What specific questions about the financial information as presented by Second Cup should they ask?

APPENDIX 6A

PROVINCIAL EQUITY CAPITAL PROGRAMS

CANADA

Canada Business Network: Financing Your Business
canadabusiness.ca/eng/page/2852/

Canadian Venture Capital and Private Equity Association
cvca.ca

INDIGENOUS PROGRAMS

There are a substantial number of programs aimed at encouraging Indigenous entrepreneurs. The program links and descriptors can be found at:
canadabusiness.ca/starting/checklists-and-guides-for-starting-a-business/aboriginal/

ALBERTA

Alberta Government Capital and Financing Supports for Entrepreneurs
alberta.ca/capital-financing-supports-entrepreneurs.aspx

BRITISH COLUMBIA

Government of B.C. Investment Capital
https://www2.gov.bc.ca/gov/content/employment-business/investment-capital

MANITOBA

Government of Manitoba Innovation and Partnership Growth Programs
gov.mb.ca/jec/busdev/financial/

NEW BRUNSWICK

New Brunswick Innovation Foundation
nbif.ca/en

NEWFOUNDLAND AND LABRADOR

Pelorus Venture Capital Limited
pelorusventure.com

NOVA SCOTIA

Innovacorp Early Stage Venture Capital
innovacorp.ca
Nova Scotia Business Inc.
novascotiabusiness.com/

ONTARIO

Small Business Development Corporations Program
Investment in Ontario
investinontario.com
Mentorworks
mentorworks.ca

PRINCE EDWARD ISLAND

Prince Edward Island CBDC Association
cbdc.ca/en/prince-edward-island-association-of-cbdcs/programs
Prince Edward Island Small Business Development Grant
princeedwardisland.ca/en/service/small-business-investment-grant
Atlantic Canada Opportunities Agency
acoa.gc.ca/e/financial/venture.shtml

QUÉBEC

Québec Government Funding Program
canadastartups.org

SASKATCHEWAN

Community Bond/Social Bond Program
Labour Sponsored Venture Capital Program
Saskatchewan Immigrant Program

APPENDIX 6B

FEDERAL GOVERNMENT ASSISTANCE PROGRAMS FOR SMALL BUSINESS

PROGRAM	TYPE OF ASSISTANCE	LIMITS	PURPOSES	CONTACT OFFICES
Futurpreneur Canada **futurpreneur.ca/en/**	Financial assistance and mentoring	Up to $50,000 to candidates 18–39 years old unable to raise funding elsewhere and $30,000 for expansion funding	Help youth start businesses	Private
Program for Export Market Development **edc.ca/en**	Shares costs of specific export marketing efforts; encourages and assists export	Provides up to 50 percent of the costs incurred by a company in penetration of new markets; repayable if sales are made	Specific project bidding; market identification; participation in trade fairs abroad; bringing in foreign and domestic buyers; export consortia development;	Innovation, Science and Economic Development Canada regional offices

			sustained export market development; risk insurance	
Self-Employment Incentive Program	Provides temporary grants while entrepreneurs establish businesses	$200 per week	To assist with living expenses while an entrepreneur establishes a business	Employment and Social Development Canada
Atlantic Canada Opportunity Agency **acoa.ca**	Financial assistance for economic development and capital costs	Varies by type of project and industry	Improve the economic viability of businesses in Atlantic Canada and encourage entrepreneurship	ACOA offices in Atlantic Canada
Western Economic Diversification Canada **wd.gc.ca**	Financial assistance through grants	Maximum amount of assistance depends on which tier the applicant is in; level of support depends on nature of the project, need for support, value, and government economic objectives	Promote industrial and regional development in Western Canada	Innovation, Science and Economic Development Canada regional offices
National Research Council Canada: Industrial Research Assistance Program **nrc.canada.ca/en**	Financial assistance through grants and technical assistance	Varies according to which aspect of the program is applied for	Increase the calibre and scope of industrial research and development through the use of available technology	Industrial Research Assistance
Small Business Development Bond	Assistance through reduced interest rates on loans	Eligible small business corporations that use all their assets in an active business; one- to five-year loan; specific time restrictions on past loans to qualify.	Relieve the financial burden of interest rates on the small businessperson	All approved lenders
Technology Outreach Programs	Financial assistance	Small businesses can access information, receive grants and loans for implementing new technology	Promote innovation and use of new technology	Innovation, Science and Economic Development Canada

[continued]

[continued]

Business Development Bank **bdc.ca**	Loans and equity investment	Extend debt financing to small businesses; can also extend venture capital to small firms wanting to expand	Increase viability of small business	BDC offices
Patient Capital Program	Financial assistance	$230,000 for early-stage technology companies	Improve chances of success for new companies	Innovation, Science and Economic Development Canada
Canada Small Business Financing Program **ic.gc.ca/csbfp**	Loan guarantee of up to 85 percent of lender's losses on defaulted loans	$500,000 for equipment, property, improvements	Improve chances of success for small companies	Business and Industry Canada
National Indigenous Economic Development Board **naedb-cndea.com**	Financial assistance	Up to 40 percent (or $100,000) equity and 75 percent for marketing, innovation, and R&D for businesses own by Aboriginal people	Support and encourage formation and growth of businesses owned by Aboriginal people	Aboriginal Programs, Innovation, Science and Economic Development Canada
Co-Vision: Start-Up Financing Program	Financial assistance	Up to $100,000 and counselling	Help start-up entrepreneurs start a business for the first time	Business Development Bank of Canada
Xpansion Loan	Financial assistance	Up to $50,000	Develop new markets, attend trade shows, develop marketing plans, or purchase new inventory	Business Development Bank of Canada
Innovate **innovation.ised-isde.canada.ca/s/?language=en&lang=eng**	One-stop shop for all government financing programs			

PART 3

MANAGING THE SMALL BUSINESS

Part 2 of this text dealt with issues relating to the organization and establishment of a small business. Once the business has been established, the owner-manager should follow several management fundamentals to ensure that the business stays viable and competitive. Part 3 discusses five of these management areas. Chapter 7 looks at the marketing plan, with a focus on industry and competitor analysis and market segmentation. Chapter 8 discusses the marketing mix with an emphasis on managing promotion in the digital age. Chapter 9 covers the recording and controlling of the financial aspects of the business. Both marketing and finance are areas in which many entrepreneurs lack training and competence. Chapter 10 discusses some fundamental components of the internal operations or production aspects of the business. Chapter 11 reviews the principles of personnel management applicable to the small organization. Chapter 12 outlines the most relevant tax considerations for the small business and extends some of the legal discussion from earlier in the text.

CHAPTER 7

MARKETING MANAGEMENT

LEARNING OBJECTIVES

By the end of this chapter, you should be able to:

LO1 Describe the role of marketing planning in a business enterprise.

LO2 List the major steps in creating a marketing plan.

LO3 Explain why understanding the external environment of the organization is essential.

LO4 Recognize the importance of marketing research.

LO5 Describe effective customer relationship programs and why they are important.

LO6 Explain the reasons for identifying marketing goals and objectives.

LO7 Explain the importance of monitoring the marketing plan.

SMALL BUSINESS PROFILE

RONNEN HARARY, ANTON RABIE, AND BEN VARADI *Spin Master*

Ronnen Harary, Anton Rabie, and Ben Varadi are living what for many would be a childhood dream come true. The trio and close friends are owners of their own children's entertainment company in Toronto—Spin Master. Harary and Rabie serve as co-CEOs, while Varadi is in charge of product development with the title of chief creative officer.

The 40-something Canadians have taken the toy world by storm over the last two decades with such hot items as Paw Patrol; Bakugan Brawlers; Hatchimals; Liv Dolls; Air Hogs, a plane that flies on air power; Bukuna Mighty Beanz collectibles; and Bella Dancerella, a home ballet studio and instructional kit. In addition, they have signed partnership agreements with some of the biggest companies in North America, including Disney and McDonald's, to develop such toys as the SpongeBob SquarePants–inspired Bounce Rounds (inflatable, portable play gyms) and a McDonald's McFlurry Maker. The company reached over $1.6 billion in sales in 2018 and is the third-largest toy business in North America.

One of the most common questions people ask after hearing about the accomplishments of the three entrepreneurs is, "How did they break into a North American toy market that is characterized by large operators with equally large product development and marketing budgets?" A great deal of their success can be attributed to their initial marketing efforts and their focus on getting close to their customers to understand their wants and needs. In the company's infancy, it was clear the partners had a marketing plan: they would focus on customer knowledge, relationship management, and low-cost strategies.

The company's first product was Earth Buddy, a replica of a small doll head constructed of pantyhose and filled with grass seed and sawdust. The Earth Buddy would sprout grass when watered and placed near light. With only $10,000 for marketing, the three developed a marketing plan that was heavy on non-traditional marketing and PR, selling the product and their story to anyone who would listen. Their marketing plan was based on getting to know retailers who would purchase their products, and they created positive relationships with Zellers, Canadian Tire, and eventually Walmart. The product was a huge success, and they were on their way.

THE CANADIAN PRESS/Frank Gunn

They followed the product with Devil Sticks, a game for children, and they managed to sell 250,000 units in six months without using any traditional promotional campaigns. Their marketing plan once again relied on nontraditional marketing: they hired college and university students to demonstrate the game at playgrounds, local events, and malls, which created a huge demand for the product.

With Devil Sticks becoming a commercial success, the company received its biggest break when it was approached by two inventors with the idea of an air-powered airplane. The concept was simple enough: Children pump the plane full of air and then launch it, watching it soar upward of 15 metres. The result was a flying plane called Air Hogs. Rather than launch a massive retail and marketing campaign, Spin Master crafted a marketing plan where they focused on selling the product to specialty educational toy stores and through the Sears catalogue, using what they did well—PR and unconventional marketing methods. Knowing journalists, who in this case were their target market for PR, wanted stories on unconventional companies and products, they created a press kit based on a suitcase and filled it with an Air Hog, a plastic airline cup, a bag of peanuts, and a barf bag. They then sent it to numerous writers and editors. The campaign was very successful, and both *Time* and *Popular Science* magazines published stories on the airplane, with *Popular Science* calling it one of the best products of the year. Spin Master again hired students, this time sending them to air shows, demonstrating the product and creating a buzz among airplane enthusiasts. Sales were starting to soar. But the best was yet to come: the PR team at Spin Master managed to get

[continued]

[continued]

the product on NBC's *Today* show and Rosie O'Donnell's daytime talk show, creating major demand. The following year the company was ready to launch Air Hogs in traditional retailers, and it was a runaway hit.

A large part of Spin Master's success, as mentioned above, is an understanding of its customers and target markets. Iain Kennedy, former chief operating officer of Spin Master, says the firm is diligent about market research and compiles vast information on customers and the feedback they provide. According to Kennedy, this understanding of customers has enabled them to develop some of the hottest toys in the industry. Kennedy also notes the firm tracks the success of its marketing strategies in their marketing plan and uses the information to determine a return on investment for their initiatives.

The company, which pays close attention to trends in the toy industry, has re-positioned itself as a children's entertainment company. This change is the result of shifts in the business' environment, with children spending more time playing video games and using mobile applications. As a result Spin Master announced they would releasing several new apps in 2015, all based on their most popular products. "The company is transforming itself and setting itself up for its next phase," says Rabie. "We have been saying as a company for the last 10 years that we are not a toy company; we are a children's entertainment company focused on creating great content platforms for kids."

Spin Master is also growing up in a big way. When sales reached the billion-dollar level, the owners opted to take the company public. In 2015 they listed Spin Master on the Toronto Stock Exchange using the ticker symbol TOY. By going public, the company raised $220 million, which they are using for further expansion. But the founders structured the deal in such a way that they still control 98 percent of the voting rights or decision-making authority, which will allow them to continue to manage the firm as they see fit. With runaway hits such as Paw Patrol and Hatchimals, newer toys like Candylocks and Lollipets, and brand-new toys based on the successful movie *How to Train Your Dragon*—not to mention an ever-expanding list of digital offerings—the sky is the limit for the company.

SPIN MASTER LTD.
spinmaster.com

THE ROLE OF MARKETING MANAGEMENT IN THE SMALL BUSINESS

Marketing activities are often overlooked by owner-managers after the business has been established. Some possible reasons for this are that (1) owner-managers do not fully understand what marketing is; (2) owner-managers may not think it is necessary—that is, they may believe that if they have a good enough product, it will sell itself; or (3) owner-managers tend to be so busy with the day-to-day activities and problems of the business that they do not take the time to assess the market and develop a marketing plan. For example, Richard Carufel, in his recent column in *Agility* magazine, states that nearly 50 percent of small business do not have a marketing plan and the majority of businesses do not have any formal goals for 2019.[1]

Regardless of the reasons for failing to apply marketing principles in the small business, it is critical that the owner-manager understand and apply those principles. The business will likely be unable to hire a marketing specialist. Therefore, the owner-manager will have to do a considerable amount of marketing, not only to potential customers but also to suppliers, employees, bankers, and perhaps even government agencies. The **Small Business Profile** of Spin Master at the beginning of this chapter illustrates how important marketing is to the successful establishment of a company.

Many businesses do not have marketing plans, which can often lead to business failure.
Alistair Berg/Getty Images

The major purpose of this chapter, then, is to introduce the fundamentals of marketing that can help sustain the growth of the business. Some of the principles also apply to establishing a business and were mentioned earlier in the text. Other marketing principles form an important part of a business plan and were discussed in **Chapter 4**.

An owner-manager may become involved in the following marketing activities:

- Writing and maintaining the marketing plan for the business
- Defining the target customer (market niche), target customer characteristics, and information concerning that customer's product or service wants and needs
- Understanding those influences outside the business that will affect its operations
- Developing the product or service
- Developing the channel(s) of distribution
- Setting price levels for the product or service
- Providing information or promoting the product or service to those who are influential in its purchase

This chapter will discuss the relevant aspects of marketing plans, market segmentation, target marketing, customer profiles, the impact of the external environment on the company, and relationship marketing. **Chapter 8** will focus on the marketing mix, including a lengthy discussion on digital marketing and its impact on small and medium businesses. It is important to note, however, that these components need to be coordinated to prepare a marketing plan and managed together as a system to be most effective.

THE MARKETING PLAN LO1

The marketing plan is a significant element of the business plan for a new venture. It has a number of important functions or purposes. Primarily, the marketing plan establishes how the entrepreneur will effectively compete and operate in the marketplace and thus meet the business goals and objectives of the new venture. Once the strategies of how the business will operate have been established, the entrepreneur can assign costs to these strategies, which then links them to budgets and financial projections. The marketing plan, like any other type of plan, may be compared to a road map used to guide a traveller. It is designed to provide answers to three basic questions:

1. *Where have we been?* When used as a stand-alone document (operational plan), this would provide some background on the company, its strengths and weaknesses, some background on the competition, and a discussion of the opportunities and threats in the marketplace. When the marketing plan is integrated as part of the business plan, this segment would focus on some history of the marketplace, marketing strengths and weaknesses of the firm, and market opportunities and threats.
2. *Where do we want to go (in the short term)?* This question primarily addresses the marketing objectives and goals of the new venture in the next 12 months. In the initial business plan, the objectives and goals often go beyond the first year because of the need to project profits and cash needs for the first three to five years.
3. *How do we get there?* This question discusses the specific marketing strategy that will be implemented, when it will occur, and who will be responsible for the monitoring of activities. For example, **Tom's of Maine**, manufacturer of toiletries that only use natural ingredients, designed a marketing campaign focusing on using micro-influencers. The company had influencers ask their followers to write about the natural products, resulting in over 4 million potential customers learning about the product in three months.[2] Similarly, Winston Gust, owner of **Crossdock Group**, a Mississauga-based transportation company and one of the fastest-growing companies in Canada, uses social media, particularly LinkedIn, as a key component of its marketing strategy: "LinkedIn has become a very effective tool for us. Our theory now is: with all the social media at our fingertips, we should never have to make cold calls. There's always some way to connect with a person you want to talk to and get an introduction, so when you make the call, it won't be cold."[3]

Tom's of Maine used social media influencers to create awareness for their natural toiletries products.

Photo 97397056 © Mohamed Ahmed Soliman - Dreamstime.com

The answers to these questions are generally determined from the marketing research carried out before the planning process is begun. Budgets will also be determined and used in the income and cash flow projections.

Management should understand that the marketing plan is a guide for implementing marketing decision making and not a generalized, superficial document. The mere process of thinking about preparing a marketing plan can be helpful to the entrepreneur because to develop the plan, it is necessary to formally document and describe as many marketing details as possible that will be part of the decision process during the next year. This process will enable the entrepreneur not only to understand and recognize the critical issues but also to be prepared in the event that any change in the environment occurs.

Each year the entrepreneur should prepare an annual marketing plan before any decisions are made regarding production or manufacturing, personnel changes, or financial resources needed. This annual plan becomes the basis for planning other aspects of the business and for developing budgets for the year. **Tables 7-1**, **7-2**, and **7-3** provide suggested outlines for in-depth marketing plans. Variations of these outlines will depend on the market and nature of the product or service, as well as the general company mission. Lisa Shepherd, author of *Market Smart: How to Gain Customers and Increase Profits with B2B Marketing,* recently stated that an entrepreneur with no plan could start by using four sheets of paper, conducting some research, and on each piece of paper answering one of four basic questions:[4]

1. Who is your target market?
2. What is your value proposition?
3. What is the message?
4. What tools will you use to connect to your target market?

TABLE 7-1 **Marketing Plan for a Consumer Products Company**

I. ANALYZE AND DEFINE THE BUSINESS SITUATION—past, present, and future

An analysis of where we are, perhaps how we got there. Data and trend lines should go back three to five years. Suggested items to cover:

A. The scope of the market (class of trade)
B. Sales history by products, by class of trade, by regions
C. Market potential, major trends anticipated
D. Distribution channels:
   1. Identification of principal channels (dealer or class of trade), sales history through each type
   2. Buying habits and attitudes of these channels
   3. Our selling policies and practices
E. The customer or end user:
   1. Identification of customers making the buying decision, classified by age, income level, occupation, geographic location, etc.
   2. Customer attitudes on product or services, quality, price, etc. Purchase or use habits that contribute to attitudes
   3. Advertising history: expenditures, media and copy strategy, measurements of effectiveness
   4. Publicity and other educational influences
F. The product or services:
   1. Story of the product line, quality development, delivery, and service
   2. Comparison with other approaches to serve the customers' needs
   3. Product research; product improvements planned

II. IDENTIFY PROBLEMS AND OPPORTUNITIES

A. In view of the facts cited in (I) above, what are the major problems that are restricting or impeding our growth?
B. What opportunities do we have for:
   - Overcoming the above problems?
   - Modifying or improving the product line or adding new products?
   - Serving the needs of more customers in our market or developing new markets?
   - Improving the efficiency of our operation?

III. DEFINE SPECIFIC AND REALISTIC BUSINESS OBJECTIVES

A. Assumptions regarding future conditions:
   - Level of economic activity
   - Level of industry activity
   - Changes in customer needs
   - Changes in distribution channels
   - Changes beyond our control, increased costs, etc.
B. Primary marketing objectives (the establishment of aim points and goals). Consider where you are going and how you will get there. Objectives are the necessary base of any plan, since a plan must have precise direction.
C. Overall strategy for achievement of primary objectives. The division's overall strategy to accomplish its primary objective—sample: shifting of sales emphasis, products, or classes of trade; changes for improvement of sales coverage; etc.

[continued]

[continued]

D. Functional (departmental) objectives. In this section "explode" your primary objectives into sub-objectives, or goals, for each department. Show the interrelation vertically, by marketing project. Show time schedule on objectives below:
   1. Advertising and promotion objectives
   2. Customer service objectives
   3. Product modification objectives
   4. New product objectives
   5. Expense control objectives
   6. Workforce objectives
   7. Personnel training objectives
   8. Market research objectives

IV. DEFINE MARKETING STRATEGY AND ACTION PROGRAMS—to accomplish the objectives

A. Here, *detail the action steps,* priorities, and schedules relating to each of the functional objectives above. If, for example, one of your estimates was "an increase in sales of product X from 10,000 to 20,000 units," now is the time to pinpoint specific customers. In order to explain who must do what, and when, you can show the interaction of the departments listed above (III-D) and how their objectives serve to meet this increased demand.

B. If one of your objectives was to introduce a new product by "x" date, now show the details and deadlines, production schedule, market introduction plans, advertising and merchandising support, sales and service training needed, etc. Define responsibility and dates for each step.

C. Alternatives—In the event of a delay in a project or program, what alternative plans are available?

V. CONTROL AND REVIEW PROCEDURES

How will the execution of the plan be monitored?

A. What kinds of "feedback" information will be needed?

B. When and how will reviews be scheduled (departments, regions, etc.)?

C. Date for full-scale review of progress vs. plan.

Source: David S. Hopkins, *The Marketing Plan,* The Conference Board, 1981. Reprinted with permission of The Conference Board of Canada.

TABLE 7-2 Marketing Plan for a Business-to-Business Company

Marketing Plan Outline

For each major product/product category: Time Period—One, Three, and Five Plus Years

I. MANAGEMENT SUMMARY

What is our marketing plan for this product in brief?

This is a one-page summary of the basic factors involving the marketing of the product in the plan period, along with the results expected from implementing the plan. It is intended as a brief guide for management.

II. ECONOMIC OUTLOOK

What factors in the overall economy and industry will affect the marketing of the product in the plan period, and how?

This section will contain a summary of the specific economic and industry factors that will affect the marketing of this product during the plan period.

III. THE MARKET—qualitative

Who or what kinds of market segments constitute the major prospects for this product?

This section will define the qualitative nature of our market segments. It will include definitive descriptions and profiles of major distributors, specifiers, users, and/or consumers of the product.

IV. THE MARKET—quantitative

What is the potential market for this product?

This section will apply specific quantitative measures to this product. Here we want to include numbers of potential customers, dollar volume of business, our current share of the market—any specific measures that will outline our total target for the product and where we stand competitively now.

V. TREND ANALYSIS

Based on the history of this product, where do we appear to be headed?

This section is a review of the past history of this product. Ideally, we should include annual figures for the last five years showing dollar volume, accounts opened, accounts closed, share of market, and all other applicable historical data.

VI. COMPETITION

Who are our competitors for this product, and how do we stand competitively?

This section should define our current competition. It should be a thoughtful analysis outlining who our competitors are, how successful they are, and what actions they might be expected to take regarding this product during the coming year.

VII. PROBLEMS AND OPPORTUNITIES

Internally and externally, are there problems inhibiting the marketing of this product, or are there opportunities we have not taken advantage of?

This section will include a frank commentary on both inhibiting problems and unrealized opportunities. It should include a discussion of the internal and external problems we can control, for example, by changes in policies or operational programs. It should also point to areas of opportunity regarding this product that we are not now exploring.

VIII. OBJECTIVES AND GOALS

Where do we want to go with this product?

This section will outline the immediate short- and long-range objectives for this product. Short-range goals should be specific and will apply to next year. Intermediate to long-range goals will necessarily be less specific and should project for the next three to five years and beyond. Objectives should be stated in two forms.

(1) Qualitative—reasoning behind the offering of this product and what modification or other changes we expect to make.

(2) Quantitative—number of accounts, dollar volume, share of market, and profit goals.

IX. ACTION PROGRAMS

Given past history, the economy, the market, competition, etc., what must we do to reach the goals we have set for this product or service?

This section will be a description of the specific actions we plan to take during the coming plan period to ensure reaching the objectives we have set for the product in VIII. These would include the full range of factors composing our marketing mix. The discussion should cover what is to be done, schedules for completion, methods of evaluation, and assignment of accountability for executing the program and measuring results.

Source: David S. Hopkins, *The Marketing Plan,* The Conference Board, 1981. Reprinted with permission of The Conference Board of Canada.

TABLE 7-3 Marketing Plan for a Service Company

Marketing Plan Outline

For each major bank service:

I. MANAGEMENT SUMMARY

What is our marketing plan for this service in brief?

This is a one-page summary of the basic factors involving the marketing of the service next year, along with the results expected from implementing the plan. It is intended as a brief guide for management.

II. ECONOMIC PROJECTIONS

What factors in the overall economy will affect the marketing of this service next year, and how?

This section will include a summary of the specific economic factors that will affect the marketing of this service during the coming year. These might include employment, personal income, business expectations, inflationary (or deflationary) pressures, etc.

III. THE MARKET—qualitative

Who or what kinds of organization could conceivably be considered prospects for this service?

This section will define the qualitative nature of our market. It will include demographic information, industrial profiles, business profiles, and so on, for all people or organizations that could be customers for this service.

[continued]

[continued]

IV. THE MARKET—quantitative

What is the potential market for this service?

This section will apply specific quantitative measures to this bank service. Here we want to include numbers of potential customers, dollar volume of business, our current share of the market—any specific measures that will outline our total target for the service and where we stand competitively now.

V. TREND ANALYSIS

Based on the history of this service, where do we appear to be headed?

This section is a review of the past history of this service. Ideally, we should include quarterly figures for the last five years showing dollar volume, accounts opened, accounts closed, share of market, and all other applicable historical data.

VI. COMPETITION

Who are our competitors for this service, and how do we stand competitively?

This section should define our current competition, both bank and nonbank. It should be a thoughtful analysis outlining who our competitors are, how successful they are, why they have (or have not) been successful, and what actions they might be expected to take regarding this service during the coming year.

VII. PROBLEMS AND OPPORTUNITIES

Internally and externally, are there problems inhibiting the marketing of this service, or are there opportunities we have not taken advantage of?

This section will contain a frank commentary on both inhibiting problems and unrealized opportunities. It should include a discussion of the internal and external problems we can control, for example, changes in policies or operational procedures. It should also point to areas of opportunity regarding this service that we are not now exploiting.

VIII. OBJECTIVES AND GOALS

Where do we want to go with this service?

This section will outline the immediate short- and long-range objectives for this service. Short-range goals should be specific and will apply to next year. Long-range goals will necessarily be less specific and should project for the next five years. Objectives should be stated in two forms:

(1) Qualitative—reasoning behind the offering of this service and what modifications or other changes we expect to make.

(2) Quantitative—number of accounts, dollar volume, share of market, profit goals.

IX. ACTION PROGRAMS

Given past history, the economy, the market, competition, and so on, what must we do to reach the goals we have set for this service?

This section will be a description of the specific actions we plan to take during the coming year to ensure reaching the objectives we have set for the service in VIII. These would include advertising and promotion, direct mail, and brochure development. It would also include programs to be designed and implemented by line officers. The discussion should cover what is to be done, schedules for completion, methods of evaluation, and officers in charge of executing the program and measuring results.

Source: David S. Hopkins, *The Marketing Plan,* The Conference Board, 1981. Reprinted with permission of The Conference Board of Canada.

While Shepherd obviously does not think this is an ideal marketing plan, given that many firms have no plan at all, this could be a good starting point.[5]

Entrepreneurs should recognize that the marketing plan is only as good as the information on which it is based. As such, most successful marketing plans are built on market research including secondary and primary data. A thorough discussion of market research can be found in **Chapters 2** and **3** in the text. Business owners who want to create a successful marketing plan should normally engage in market research before drafting the plan, monitor customer feedback, and amend the plan accordingly. As illustrated in the opening **Small Business Profile**, Spin Master Toys has invested time engaging in market research and evaluating their marketing efforts.

CHARACTERISTICS OF A MARKETING PLAN LO2

The marketing plan should be designed to meet certain criteria. Some important characteristics that must be incorporated in an effective marketing plan are as follows:

- It should provide a strategy for accomplishing the company mission or goal.
- It should be based on facts and valid assumptions (**Table 7-4**).
- An appropriate method must be described to implement the marketing plan.
- It should provide for continuity so that each annual marketing plan can build on it, successfully meeting longer-term goals and objectives.
- It should be simple and short. A voluminous plan will be placed in a desk drawer and likely never used. However, the plan should not be so short that details on how goals will be accomplished are excluded.
- The success of the plan may depend on its flexibility. Changes, if necessary, should be incorporated by including "what if" scenarios and appropriate responding strategies. For example, Indigenous artist and entrepreneur Nigel Fox notes that his marketing evolved as he was running his business. He changed his focus from selling paintings direct to consumers to selling prints of his works online. This led to an increase in sales.[6]
- It should specify performance criteria that will be monitored and controlled. For example, the entrepreneur may establish an annual performance criterion of 10 percent of market share in a designated geographic area. To attain this goal, certain expectations should be set at given time periods (e.g., at the end of three months we should have a 5 percent share of market). If not attained, then new strategy or performance standards may need to be established.

TABLE 7-4 **Facts Needed for Market Planning**

- Who are the users, where are they located, how much do they buy, from whom do they buy, and why?
- How have promotion and advertising been employed, and which approach has been most effective?
- What are the pricing changes in the market, who has initiated these changes, and why?
- What are the market's attitudes concerning competitive products?
- What channels of distribution supply consumers, and how do they function?
- Who are the competitors, where are they located, and what advantages and disadvantages do they have?
- What marketing techniques are used by the most successful competitors? By the least successful?
- What are the overall objectives of the company for the next year and next five years?
- What are the company's strengths? Weaknesses?
- What are the company's production capabilities by product?

Clearly, the market plan is not intended to be written and then put aside. It is intended to be a valuable document, frequently referred to, and a guideline for the entrepreneur during the next time period.

THE MARKETING SYSTEM: INFLUENCES ON THE SMALL BUSINESS LO3

Since the term *marketing plan* denotes the significance of marketing, it is important to understand the marketing system. The marketing system identifies the major interacting components, both internal and external to the firm, that enable the firm to successfully provide products or services to the marketplace. In the marketing system, the external environment and the internal environment affect the entrepreneur or business owner, which, in turn, affects marketing decisions and the development of marketing strategies through the marketing mix, which then affects consumers. The customers, through their actions, provide feedback to the entrepreneur. The system can be seen in **Figure 7-1**.

FIGURE 7-1 **The Marketing System**

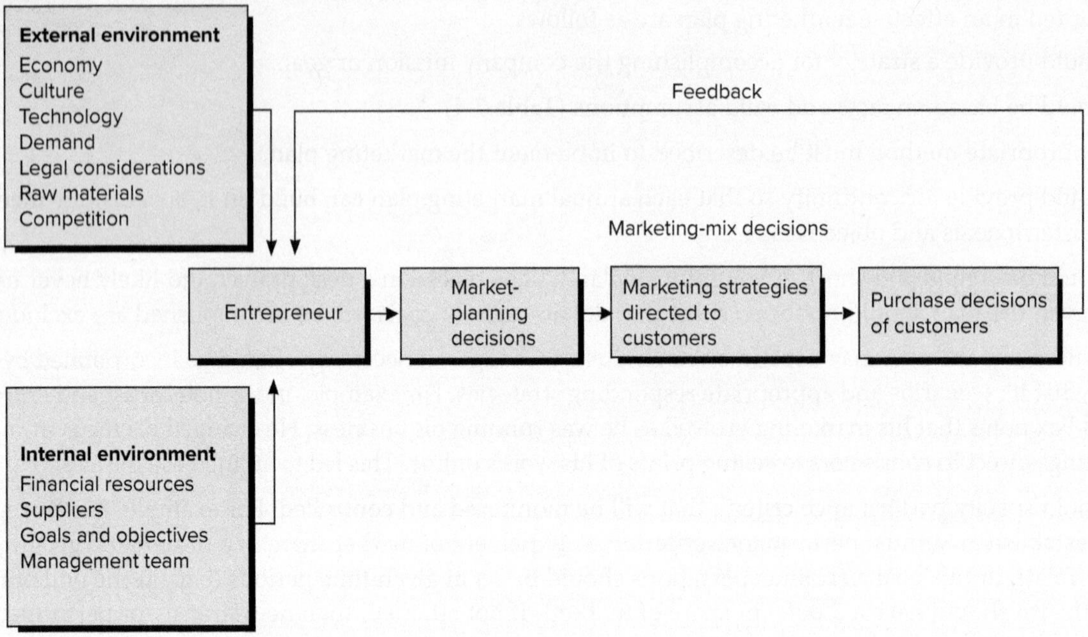

As evident above, the environment (external and internal) plays a very important role in developing the marketing plan. These factors should be identified and discussed in the industry analysis section of the business plan. Note that although some of these factors are typically uncontrollable, the owner-manager can do some things to effectively respond to some of these external influences:

- Identify which external conditions affect the business.
- Set up a system to continually monitor the relevant external influences. For the owner-manager, this might mean regularly obtaining reports, newsletters, and studies that contain up-to-date information on these conditions.
- Adjust internal operations to respond to changes in these external influences most effectively.
- Some of the most common external influences that can affect the small business and thus affect the information to be collected are the economy, the competition, legal restrictions, the social and cultural environment, and technology.

The Economy.

The state of the economy in the market area is a critical external condition. For many products and services, market demand is directly related to upturns and downturns in the economy. Small businesses often are able to react more quickly than large businesses to changes in the economy.

The Competition.

As mentioned in **Chapter 1**, a small business usually finds itself competing against larger firms over which it has no control. New technology used by competitors is another factor in assessing competition, especially in many growth industries. In some cases, the small business may gain competitive advantages because of its size. By accurately identifying prospective competitors and their strengths as well as weaknesses, the entrepreneur can develop a more effective strategy. Attempts should be made to clearly identify the competitive advantage for the business. Many entrepreneurs have found their competitors' websites are helpful resources when analyzing their strategy and future plans.

Legal Restrictions.

This potential influence includes the laws and regulations with which the business is required to comply. The owner-manager should keep up-to-date with any legislation that might affect business operations. Some entrepreneurs obviously have to pay more attention to changes in laws and regulations than other business owners. For example, firms such as those focusing on family law and mediation must ensure they stay abreast of any and all changes in the legal system.

Social and Cultural Environment.

This factor encompasses trends in the culture in which the business operates that may affect demand. The culture may dictate norms that the population is generally hesitant to violate or suggest new growth industries that can be attractive opportunities. For example, Dr. Wendy McLelland and Greg Habstritt founded Vets To Go, a Calgary-based home veterinary service which was recently named one of the fastest-growing firms in Canada. McLelland and Habstritt identified the trend of pet owners treating pets like family and saw the growing demand for vet services that were less stressful for pets. As traditional veterinarians have been slow to adopt to changing customer demands, Vets To Go has been able to establish a successful and thriving business.[7]

Greg Habstritt and Dr. Wendy McClelland run Vets To Go, one of the fastest-growing businesses in Canada. The pair noticed that pet owners were looking for in-home vet care that would reduce the stress on animals.

didesign021 © 123RF.com

Technology.

New technology can be a significant factor in the success of a small business. Failure to recognize and adopt technology can spell disaster for the entrepreneur. Likewise, developing and using it can be an important competitive edge.

Table 7-5 illustrates how the owner of a small business can work with all these uncontrollable conditions.

TABLE 7-5 Management of the External Influences

EXTERNAL INFLUENCE	POSSIBLE CHARACTERISTIC	SYSTEM TO MONITOR	POSSIBLE INTERNAL ADJUSTMENT
Economy	Inflation rate Unemployment level	Relevant government and industry reports	Lower prices Increase advertising
Competition	Competitor strengths and weaknesses Competitor's use of new technology	Competitors' new products Competitors' reactions to your strategies	Alter product or service Select specific target market
Legal	Laws affecting your business Pending changes in laws	Legislative changes from government documents and industry reports	Alter product or service Make promotional changes
Social and cultural	Lifestyle trends Demographic studies Purchase patterns	Industry and government reports recording social statistics and purchases	Provide new products or services Change distribution channel Change promotional themes and levels
Technology	Trends	New product reports Fast-growing company literature	Alter product

In addition to the external environmental factors are internal environmental factors, which are more controllable by the entrepreneur but can also affect the preparation of the marketing plan and implementation of an effective marketing strategy. Some of the major internal variables are discussed next.

Financial Resources.

The financial plan, discussed later in the text, should outline the financial needs for the new venture. Any marketing plan or strategy should consider the availability of financial resources and the amount of funds needed to meet the goals and objectives stated in the plan.

Employee Capabilities/Management Team.

It is extremely important in any organization to make appropriate assignments of responsibility for the implementation of the marketing plan. In some smaller organizations, the owner-manager may be solely responsible for implementing the marketing plan. Yet if they lack the skills or capabilities, the owner may want to make use of experts, enlist volunteers, and so forth. It does not make sense for a micro-enterprise to plan for an ambitious online marketing campaign to be implemented by the owner who lacks such skills. If the small business is larger, the entrepreneur must be sure to build a management team that possesses the skills to manage the marketing plan.

Suppliers.

The suppliers used are generally based on a number of factors, such as price, delivery time, quality, and management assistance. In some cases, where raw materials are scarce or there are only a few suppliers of a particular raw material or part, the entrepreneur has little control over the decision. Since the price of supplies, delivery time, and so on, are likely to affect many marketing decisions, it is important to incorporate these factors into the marketing plan.

Company Mission.

As indicated in **Chapter 4**, every new venture should have a mission statement. This statement, which helps to define the company's mission, basically describes the nature of the business and what the entrepreneur hopes to accomplish with that business. This mission statement or business definition will guide the firm through long-term decision making. For example, Dr. Julia Levy, executive chair and former CEO of the Canadian biopharmaceutical company QLT, states, "Companies must define their collective values in a mission statement; the statement will define where the company goes in the next number of years and how it will get there."[8]

Kasey Kaplan, founder of KWK Studio, co-founder of Urban FT, and a contributor to *Forbes* magazine, echoes Levy's comments. He notes that a mission and value are ultimately what a company is built around. He explains that, initially, an entrepreneur starts a new business that is usually run by a small group of people who understand why the company was created. But as the business grows, and more employees are added, the mission statement becomes more important as it will ensure the business stays focused on its value.[9]

THE MARKETING MIX

The environmental variables will provide important information in deciding what will be the most effective marketing strategy to be outlined in the marketing plan. The actual short-term marketing decisions in the marketing plan will consist of four important marketing variables: product or service, pricing, distribution or place, and promotion. These four factors are referred to as the *marketing mix*. Each variable will be described in detail in the strategy or action plan section of the marketing plan discussed in the next chapter. Although flexibility may be an important consideration, the entrepreneur needs a strong base to provide direction for the day-to-day marketing decisions. Some of the critical decisions in each area are described in **Table 7-6**.

TABLE 7-6 Critical Decisions for Marketing Mix

MARKETING MIX VARIABLE	CRITICAL DECISIONS
Product	Quality of components or materials, style, features, options, brand name, packaging, sizes, service availability, and warranties
Price	Quality image, list price, quantity, discounts, allowances for quick payment, credit terms, and payment period
Distribution/Place	Use of wholesalers and/or retailers, type of wholesalers or retailers, how many, length of channel, geographic coverage, inventory, and transportation
Promotion	Media alternatives, message, media budget, role of personal selling, sales promotion (displays, coupons, etc.), and media interest in publicity

STEPS IN PREPARING THE MARKETING PLAN

The major steps in preparing the marketing plan are as follows:

1. Examine the product/service and market situation.
2. Review company goals and restraints.
3. Set marketing objectives that are specific and measurable.
4. Determine the marketing strategies and prepare action programs.
5. Re-evaluate programs against objectives.
6. Draft the marketing plan, with steps to monitor progress of programs.
7. Match feasibility of programs against resources.
8. Finalize the marketing plan,

Following each of these steps will allow the owner-manager to create a formal marketing plan. The main steps are outlined and discussed by using examples to help you fully understand the necessary information and procedure for preparing the marketing plan. It is important for entrepreneurs to realize that the marketing plan must be updated frequently. Business owners must constantly ask themselves: Have my target customers changed? How has it changed? Do I need to reshape my marketing mix to reflect these changes? For example, Canadian retailer Harry Rosen had to redesign its marketing mix when it realized that the average age of its customer had increased from 38 to 43. Dennis Campbell of **Atlantic Tours & Travel** had to change the long-term objectives of his tour company to increase usage by families. While the tour company is seeing the number of seniors who travel increase, it has also realized that as people age they will eventually travel less. Thus the company must expand its reach into younger demographics if it wants to be successful.

DEFINING THE BUSINESS SITUATION

The *situation analysis* is a review of where we have been. It responds to the first of the three questions mentioned earlier in this chapter. It also considers many of the factors that were defined in both the environmental analysis section of the business plan (see **Chapter 4**) and the industry analysis discussed earlier in this chapter. Investors will also want to see your market potential and market share calculations for your business as well.

To fully respond to this question, the entrepreneur should provide a review of past performance of the product and the company. If this is a new venture, the background will be more personal, describing how the product or service was developed and why it was developed (e.g., to satisfy consumer needs). If the plan is being written after the new venture has started, it would contain information on present market conditions and performance of the company's goods and services. Any future opportunities or prospects should also be included in this section of the plan.

The industry and competitive environment have already been discussed in an earlier section of the business plan. Thus, the entrepreneur should simply review some of the key elements of that section to provide a context for the marketing segmentation and actions stated in that section of the business plan.

MARKET SEGMENTATION AND TARGET MARKETING: BEYOND THE BASICS LO4

Most entrepreneurs will have heard of the concepts of target marketing and market segmentation before investigating their business idea. *Market segmentation* is simply defined as breaking down a marketplace into categories of buyers who share similar characteristics. *Target marketing* is the process of looking at what segment your company can most profitably serve, and then modifying your product, price, placement, and promotion to deliver to them more value than your competition can.

Entrepreneurs should recognize that they cannot target everyone, especially with a new or smaller business. In fact, many small business experts will tell aspiring entrepreneurs to target a niche market for the greatest likelihood of success. For example, Tyson Leavitt, founder of Alberta-based **Charmed Playhouses**, builds luxury playhouses for children with a base price of $3500 and the most expensive model costing $200,0000. While Leavitt would love to sell these playhouses to everyone, he knows the reality is that most families are not spending tens of thousands of dollars on a child's backyard toy. As such, Leavitt first breaks the market into potential playhouse buyers then segments by income and other characteristics.[10]

When textbooks describe the segmentation process, much attention is given to demographic information, such as age or income, and to geographic segmentation. Very little attention is paid to psychographic segmentation and the need to segment by buyer behaviour. As a result, these texts often contain examples such as "Jeannie's high-end clothing store is going to target middle-aged women who have a university degree and earn an above-average income." At first this might sound fine, but there are significant problems with that type of target, including the following:

- Not all women like to shop at the same location. Some may prefer a downtown district; others may prefer a shopping mall.
- Not all women are willing to pay the same amount for clothing regardless of income or education.
- Of the women who prefer extra advice and service with their clothing purchases, some are willing to pay a small premium for this, while others are willing to pay a large premium.

Now imagine that Jeannie's store is located in the downtown core, is relatively small (about 1000 square feet), offers modern business dress and a high level of service, and charges a moderate premium. Do you think the original segment of middle-aged, university-educated, above-average income earners is a good target market? The obvious answer is no. Such a broad segment could have Jeannie wasting thousands of dollars promoting her products to people who are as likely to shop at a discount store, such as Winners, as they are in her store.

What Jeannie has to do is take her market segmentation to the next level. This is sometimes referred to as *true target marketing* or *need-based segmentation.* Lawrence Stevenson refers to this as "need segmentation" in his book *Power Retail,* where he notes five characteristics that segmentation must have to be useful:

1. *Meaningful:* Segments must be different from one another to the point that two segments would be unlikely to be attracted to the same marketing strategy.
2. *Mutually exclusive:* Each segment must be mutually exclusive and collectively exclusive, meaning that each customer group belongs to only one segment.
3. *Measurable:* Each segment must be measurable in both market share and market potential to the business.
4. *Substantial:* Each segment must be large enough to represent a group of potential customers. If a large enough group of customers does not fit into the segment, then it may not be a segment at all.
5. *Actionable:* The entrepreneur should be able to promote the product offering to the segment. Look back at Jeannie's original target market, is it truly actionable?

Michelle Strum, owner of Halifax Backpackers Hostel, has said that listening to feedback from her customers has been key to her success.
Photo courtesy of Michelle Strum, Halifax Backpackers Hostel

How does an entrepreneur develop segments that meet all the qualities discussed above? Through market research. Entrepreneurs must know the buying habits of their customers, their pre- and post-purchase behaviours, their motivation for buying, and so on. Simple demographic information is never enough. Barry Cohen and Michael Rybarski in their book *Start-up Smarts: The Thinking Entrepreneur's Guide to Starting and Growing Your Business,* state that business owners should treat marketing as a science.[11] The pair recommends that entrepreneurs take the time and effort to fully understand their customers, what makes them buy certain products, and how they want to receive information. For example, Joanna Griffiths, founder of Toronto-based **Knix**, a manufacturer of stylish leak-proof underwear for new mothers, attributes her success to getting to know potential customers using online forums and social media. Griffiths says she spent considerable time talking to potential clients and conducted surveys to understand what consumers were looking for in product selection. After listening to consumers, she created a body-positive underwear and bra company which has reached in excess of $5 million in sales.[12] Similarly, Michelle Strum, owner of **Halifax Backpackers**, takes time to learn what her clients want and tailors her hostel to meet their needs. Her hostel has been open for over 10 years now, and she recently expanded to include a coffee shop and a separate beach house.[13]

Joanna Griffiths, founder of Knix, invests considerable time listening to her customers. She values feedback for every part of the business, from the design stage all the way to the women featured in Knix marketing material. Griffiths is reinventing the intimates category, creating products that make women more comfortable in their own skin, all designed, modelled, and worn by real women.
Photo courtesy of Knix

Let us look at Jeannie's clothing store again. Jeannie should initially segment her market using demographic information, but then she should complete the segmentation process by conducting market research using observations, focus groups, and survey work. From this information, she would determine that four market segments meet the standards outlined by Stevenson above:

1. Price-conscious women who shop on the weekend in the suburbs
2. Bargain hunters
3. Price-insensitive women who seek advice and shop frequently
4. Price-insensitive women who seek advice and shop seasonally

By looking at the four categories, Jeannie can see that she cannot profitably appeal to the first group, as they likely have a family and will shop at malls and box stores. The second group will most likely frequent Winners, Walmart, and similar stores. But both the third and fourth groups are potentially profitable, large, mutually exclusive, measurable, and actionable. Jeannie can now fine-tune her marketing mix to appeal to these segments.

While this type of segmentation appears daunting to an entrepreneur, it is worth the time and investment. Proof can be found in the results of some of the largest companies in Canada. Shoppers Drug Mart owes much of its success to the strategy of appealing to price-insensitive convenience shoppers and health-focused advice shoppers. The same is true for Canadian Tire, one of the few mass merchants that has thrived in the presence of Walmart and Costco. Canadian Tire reviewed its extensive database of credit card holders to identify advice-seeking handymen and convenience shoppers as targets that they could profitably serve.

The key steps in moving your segmentation beyond the basics include the following:

1. Decide what general market or industry you want to pursue.
2. Divide the market into smaller groups based on the characteristics of the customer and buying situation. These may include the following:
   - Demographic
   - Geographic
   - Psychographic (e.g., personality and lifestyle)
   - Motivation (e.g., rational, emotional)
   - Influencers (e.g., anyone else influencing a decision, importance of opinion leaders)
   - Price sensitivity
   - Desired benefit (e.g., product features)
   - Usage (e.g., rate of use)
   - Buying conditions (e.g., frequency, time of year)
   - Awareness of buying intentions (e.g., familiarity with product and willingness to buy)
3. Make sure the segments are meaningful, mutually exclusive, measurable, substantial, and actionable.
4. Select a segment or segments to target.
5. Develop a marketing plan that integrates product, price, placement, and promotion.

A note of caution should be used in segmentation. Entrepreneurs often incorrectly assume the segment that produces the most revenue is the one that is the most profitable. This is incorrect and dangerous. Entrepreneurs must analyze the costs of each transaction, the time involved, the method of communication, and the cost of goods sold order to truly determine which segment offers the most profit potential. For example, Anwar, an investment salesman, has determined that teachers in his area offer his business the most potential sales and thus the most potential profit. Anwar, however, is ignoring that teachers take a great deal of time in deciding whether to purchase investments, and he will have to spend an average 12 to 15 hours per year acquiring each account and then another 10 to 15 hours per year speaking to each teacher about questions and concerns. Dentists, on the other hand, are fewer in number, and, while they offer less potential revenue, most dentists will require only an hour or two per year deciding whether or not to invest and then only two to three hours per year dealing with questions and concerns. Based on this information, dentists should be the target market as they offer the most profit potential.

Let us assume that an entrepreneur has developed a unique liquid cleaner that could clean a restaurant grill at operating temperatures; remove grease from household appliances; clean whitewall tires, bumpers, upholstery, and engines; and clean boats. At least four markets could be identified from its uses: restaurants, households, automobiles, and boats. Each market is then segmented based on the variables discussed above. The entrepreneur finds that in the restaurant market there is little competition, the product's advantages are most evident, and massive marketing resources are not necessary for entry. On this basis, the entrepreneur chooses the restaurant market. This market is then segmented by province and territory, type of restaurant (e.g., fast-food, family), and whether the restaurant is part of a hospital, school, company, and so forth. Each of these segments is evaluated, and the entrepreneur chooses to initially target independent family restaurants in a specific region, such as within a single province.

This market offers the greatest opportunity because no other product exists that can perform grill cleaning at operating temperatures and without damage to the grill. The threats in this market include ease of entry and potential imitation by major competitors: in fact, a number of large firms, such as Colgate-Palmolive and Procter & Gamble, may be interested in the market. However, regardless of the threats, the greatest opportunity is presented in the restaurant grill-cleaning segment. This becomes the target market. **Table 7-7** gives a general example of purchase characteristics of various age groups. **Small Business in Action 7-1** provides a real-world example of an entrepreneur who understood his target market.

TABLE 7-7 Purchase Characteristics for Various Ages

In Their Teens

This group has an increasing amount of money to spend on clothing, cosmetics, and entertainment products. They also have a major influence with family purchases.

In Their 20s

This group is not yet financially secure. They demand instant gratification, lasting value, and tangible benefits. Purchase decisions are often based on subjective factors.

In Their 30s and 40s

These people have high incomes and high debt. They are individualistic, striving for self-fulfillment, and concerned about social and environmental issues. They look for information before buying.

In Their 40s and 50s

Prosperous and facing retirement, they purchase for sentimentality, brand loyalty, and convenience.

In Their 60s and 70s

They tend to have lots of leisure time. They seek financial security, quality, and value. They rely on knowledge and experience.

In Their 80s and older

This group spends heavily on health care, travel, and security products.

SMALL BUSINESS IN ACTION 7-1

FIGHTING, EXTREME SPORTS, AND FANTASY FOOTBALL—LEONARD ASPER'S TAKE ON TARGET MARKETING

Leonard Asper, former CEO of Canwest Global Communications, is back in the media business, this time with **Anthem Sports and Entertainment**, a business that is clearly aimed at a specific target: males between the ages of 25 and 45. Asper says he learned a lesson in his final days of running Canwest in 2010, when advertising revenue was declining for almost every media product he had, except for a few specialty networks, like **HGTV**. Asper says, "You need targeted destinations for communities that are passionate about the subject."

[continued]

[continued]

When Asper decided to start a new media company, he took this lesson to heart and listened to perhaps his most important potential clients: advertisers. Advertisers were telling Asper, and others, that reaching males both on television and online was increasingly difficult. Asper decided to venture back into the media world, this time with a targeted approach focusing on offering media to male audiences. Asper's first move was to acquire the **Fight Network** and the **Pursuit Channel**, a hunting and outdoor network.

Leonard Asper, founder of Anthem Sports and Entertainment, is trying to create a portfolio of media businesses aimed specifically at male audiences. Asper's latest project, the Fantasy Sports Network, is aimed at the 35 million predominantly male fantasy sports players.

Photo by Kevin Van Paassen/The Canadian Press

Asper wasn't finished. He made perhaps his biggest gamble in 2014 when he launched the **FNTSY Sports Network**. The cable and online media provider focuses on providing content for fantasy sports players, which is a $4 billion industry with 35 million participants in North America alone. Asper says, "The one thing that convinced me to do this is watching my staff and never being sure if they are working when they have their computers on or if they are checking fantasy sites, because they are all doing it." Asper's latest network won't need to spend on acquiring expensive sports content; rather, it can provide the information and sports analysis that fantasy players are looking for, in a user-friendly format. Yet some critics maintain that audiences—even fantasy sports players—are not interested in a 24-hour fantasy network and contend that viewers won't turn in often enough to generate substantial advertising revenue. Asper counters with his belief that specialty channels are the way of the future. "People thought 'How can there be an entire channel devoted to golf?' but now The Golf Channel is in 82 million homes. It's an obvious trend and we're trying to capture it. . . . That's where sports channels are going. The whole world is going to a channel for every sport."

Discussion Questions

1. Do you think Asper's strategy of targeting a male audience will be successful? Why or why not?
2. Given women are increasingly interested in fantasy and extreme sports, should Asper consider changing his message to advertisers that his company is aimed predominantly at men between the ages of 25 and 45? Why or why not?
3. Asper is the former CEO of Canwest Global, a large company founded by his father that eventually went bankrupt. What do you think are some of the potential advantages and disadvantages of Asper's background?
4. Some business experts state that media, especially television media, is a poor investment because of the high costs of content, declines in user rates, and the increased time people are spending online. After reading this Small Business in Action box, do you think Asper will be successful, or is traditional media, such as television and mainstream radio, fading away?

CUSTOMER PROFILE

After selecting target markets, entrepreneurs should develop a comprehensive customer profile based on their needs and buying behaviour. The entrepreneur must be sure to include all the information from the segmentation process and expand on it to deal with such factors as the following:

- Demographic questions
- Customer attitudes on price and quality
- Where customer currently buys product
- Where customer wants to buy product
- Influence of advertising
- Quantities and frequency of purchase
- Why customer buys product

Based on this information, Jeannie's clothing store from the example earlier in this chapter would use a customer profile similar to the following:

- *Demographic information:* Women ages 40 to 55, income $85,000-plus, university degree, highly computer-literate
- *Frequency:* Shop frequently in the downtown core, often weekly or biweekly
- *Products:* Willing to pay a premium for quality products upward of 20 percent compared with shopping district stores
- *Service:* Associate service with quality and are willing to pay a premium for personal service
- *Motivation:* Can be motivated by both rational and emotional influences
- *Lifestyle/personality:* Read frequently, travels, share a desire to be perceived as fashionable and upper-class by society, want to be trendy and hip, influenced by friends and fashion magazines
- *Advertising:* Most susceptible to online and one-to-one marketing or one-to-small-group marketing
- *Buying decision:* This group will buy from me because I have connections in Paris that will allow me to bring the latest fashion trends to the region. In addition, I have built a database that will allow me to know each customer on a personal level and engage in one-to-one marketing, and I have hired experienced salespeople to provide meaningful advice to customers.

Study this information further in the hypothetical case in **Small Business in Action 7-2**.

SMALL BUSINESS IN ACTION 7-2

TARGET MARKET FOR A HYPOTHETICAL SMALL RESTAURANT

Diane and Sam have always dreamed of opening a restaurant. They have recently acquired a small commercial property in a busy urban location, ideal for a restaurant. The following is their proposed target market.

Demographics

Age: 30–49

Income: higher than average ($40,000–$80,000)

Occupation: professionals, managers

Education: university graduates

Lifestyle (Psychographics)

Activities: exercise and participation in sports, high social interaction; low TV usage and high reading; husband and wife both work, enjoy the outdoors, attend cultural events

Interests: appearance, health, fashion

Opinions: conservative economically, liberal on social issues

Personality: achievement-oriented, outgoing, independent

Purchase Characteristics

What: high-quality and high-priced menu items

Where: high-class restaurant, international cuisine

When: evenings and weekends

How much: frequently eat away from home, 50 percent higher than national average

Majesticca/Shutterstock.com

[continued]

[continued]

Purchase Motivations

Benefits sought: superior quality of food, service, atmosphere, variety of menu

Influencers

Reference groups and social class the main influencers in choice of restaurant, through word of mouth

Discussion Questions

1. Review the target market, discuss areas where it is strong, and identify weaknesses.
2. What information could be added to enhance the target market?
3. Develop a target market and a customer profile for a well-known Canadian chain, such as Lululemon or Sport Chek. Compare your customer profile with those of your classmates to identify areas for improvement.
4. Do you think small business should spend significant time and resources on creating customer profiles? Why or why not?

CONSIDERING STRENGTHS AND WEAKNESSES

It is important for the entrepreneur to consider strengths and weaknesses in the target market. For example, referring to the liquid grill cleaner, the primary strength in its market is clearly its unique application: It can be used on a hot operating grill with no discernible odour. Other strengths might relate to the fact that the company has experience in the restaurant business and understands the customer.

Weaknesses could relate to the production capacity limited by space and equipment. In addition, the company lacks a strong distribution system for the product and would have to depend on manufacturers' representatives. Lack of cash to support a heavy promotional effort could also be identified as a weakness.

We discuss various aspects of the marketing mix of a real social enterprise in **Small Business in Action 7-3**.

SMALL BUSINESS IN ACTION 7-3

STORYTELLING AND SOCIAL ENTERPRISE

Mark Marsolais-Nahwegahbow, Ojibwe and Band Member of the Whitefish River First Nation in Birch Island, Ontario, has created a social enterprise: **Birch Bark Coffee Company** which has a goal of bringing clean water to First Nations communities throughout Canada. Marsolais-Nahwegahbow says he founded his company when he learned about the Third World–like conditions of the drinking water in many Indigenous communities and he wanted to do something to help. With this goal in mind, Birch Bark Coffee Company was born.

Mark Marsolais-Nahwegahbow founded Birch Bark Coffee Company, a social enterprise that is cause-driven to help First Nation communities access clean drinking water.

Photo courtesy of Birch Bark Coffee Co.

Birch Bark is an organic, fair trade, and SPP-certified coffee company that donates two dollars from every bag of coffee sold from the Birch Bark Coffee Company website and one dollar from retailers carrying the coffee in their stores to purchase the certified water-purification systems for Indigenous homes across our nation.

Marsolais-Nahwegahbow collaborates with a water company who has been in business for 40 years and is responsible for building the "All Canadian-Made" water purifiers that are both washable and have a cartridge that is biodegradable. The supplier has offered to sell him the purifiers at a discount, enabling him to donate one water purification machine for every 50 bags of coffee sold from his website and 100 bags sold from a retail store.

Marsolais-Nahwegahbow says that Indigenous people are storytellers, and he shares his story to educate and bring awareness to people about the lack of clean water in First Nation communities. Marsolais-Nahwegahbow created what he refers to as an "Indigenous Inclusion Continuum," which demonstrates encompassing everyone who is involved with his coffee: from whom he sources his coffee beans, the customers, the retailers, and the communities he helps. He specifically highlights the Latin American farmers, also of Indigenous descent, from whom he sources his beans; Latin America is well-known for some of the best coffee in the world. Marsolais-Nahwegahbow also mentions Just Us Roasters, a co-op that only roasts organic coffee beans, has been helping Birch Bark Coffee Company reach their goals.

He notes that his coffee and company's story touched many hearts and beans are now being roasted four days a week because retailers cannot keep his organic product on the shelf. Birch Bark started selling only in Ontario in 2018; but by 2019, the company has already started to see purchases internationally and in the U.S.

Discussion Questions

1. Birch Bark's founder, Mark Marsolais-Nahwegahbow has been very successful in generating media and using storytelling to sell his products. As the company grows, what will be some of the challenges in relying on this form of promotion?
2. Companies are always trying to create a distinct marketing mix to appeal to their target markets. Create one or two potential target markets for Birch Bark Coffee and match the company's marketing mix to the potential targets.
3. There are a number of social enterprises that donate a percentage of revenue to social causes but which have not reached the same level of success as Birch Bark. Why do you think Birch Bark has been so successful? Do you think the success is sustainable? Why or why not?
4. Do you think Birch Bark should have expanded so quickly into other countries? Why or why not?

CUSTOMER RELATIONSHIP MARKETING LO5

Investors often want to see some information in the marketing plan that focuses on how the company plans to build a relationship with its most profitable customers. Even if investors are not looking for this, most entrepreneurs should be trying to establish long-term relationships with customers. The key to proper relationship marketing is the realization that 70 to 80 percent of a business' profits can actually come from a very small percentage of customers, as illustrated in **Small Business Beginnings 7-1**. Confirming this information, American Express has determined that retained customers buy more often and spend more money than new customers.[14] It is with these customers that the entrepreneur is going to want to build a relationship.

Much has been written about building relationships with all customers—and in some businesses this is possible—but for many businesses it is not feasible, and the entrepreneur can waste time and money trying to build relationships with people who do not offer much in return. For example, if a local car dealership tried to build a relationship with all its customers, it might end up allocating the same amount of marketing and research dollars to someone who buys a new car every two years and someone who buys a new car every 10 years. Entrepreneurs should focus on building relationships with their most profitable customers and customers that show the most potential to offer profits in the future. Therefore the car dealership should focus its energy on building a relationship with the person who buys a car every two years and attempt to convert the person who buys a car every 10 years into a more frequent purchaser.

One of the best tools in customer relationship marketing (CRM) is the use of a database to track customer buying habits, personal information, and anything else that is relevant. By analyzing this information, the entrepreneur can select appropriate customers with whom to build relationships. Ken McLean, a financial planner with Investors Group, realizes the simple principle that he must build a relationship with his most profitable customers to be successful. McLean has identified that 70 percent of his profits come from only 20 percent of his clients, and so he spends extra time servicing the needs of this key group. McLean offers accounting services at tax time, takes clients golfing, and hosts annual Christmas and summer events. Furthermore, McLean has built an extensive database of these clients, learning birthdays, career aspirations, retirement goals, and anything else that may be relevant so that he can tailor his products to his target market. **Harry Rosen**, one of Canada's most successful retailers, has adopted the same principle as McLean and serves as a great example of how relationship marketing can work for larger businesses. The retailer makes use of an extensive customer database that goes beyond just recording basic demographic information. The database will typically include information on vacation destinations, sizes, time of year the person shops, personal relationships, and so forth. Rosen then builds its sales and marketing strategy around this information and two simple premises: (1) clients always come first, and (2) keep clients for life.

SMALL BUSINESS BEGINNINGS 7-1

KNOW THY CUSTOMER

When founder Dennis Goll got **West Wind Aviation** off the ground over 35 years ago, it was a one-aircraft operation fuelled by high ambition. Today, the president and CEO has transformed this humble business into Western Canada's largest general aviation services company, employing more than 250 people. It has recently been recognized as one of Canada's 50 Best Managed Companies. Goll attributes the success of the company primarily to understanding the consumer: "We've identified underserved markets quickly and homed in on those opportunities. We have also embedded customer service into our corporate culture. It's not just idle talk here. I've often told employees to not worry about numbers and think about customers' needs first." As a result the company is committed to customer service training for everybody in the company, from maintenance staff to accountants.

The keys to establishing an effective relationship marketing program are the following:

- Start with proper segmentation and target marketing.
- Identify the most profitable customer groups.
- Identify groups that show potential to become more profitable.
- Solicit further information on customers.
- Develop products and services that are mutually beneficial.
- Allocate your marketing budget so that you spend the majority of money appealing to your most important customers.

The Database Information System.

A critical part of most effective CRM is the development of a database information system focused on the consumer. The emergence of database marketing is based on the premise that past behaviour is the best indicator of future purchase patterns. The increase in computer power and storage capabilities, coupled with decreasing costs, now enables organizations to deal directly with customers on an individual level.

Database Marketing for the Small Business.

A customer database is an organized collection of comprehensive data about individual customers or prospects, including geographic, demographic, psychographic, and behavioural data. The database can be used to locate good potential customers, tailor products and services to the special needs of targeted consumers, and maintain long-term customer relationships. Database marketing is the process of building, maintaining, and using customer databases and other databases (products, suppliers, resellers) to contact and transact with customers.

A small business can use databases for both business-to-business as well as business-to-consumer marketing. In business-to-business marketing, the salesperson's customer profile may contain such information as the products and services the customer has bought, past volumes and prices, key contacts, competitive suppliers, status of current contracts, estimated customer expenditures for the next few years, and assessments of competitive strengths and weaknesses in selling and serving the account. In consumer marketing, the customer database may contain a customer's demographics, buying behaviour, and other relevant information. Several simple and inexpensive database software programs are now available to assist small businesses in being more responsive to their customers.

Developing a database information system requires five steps:

1. Begin with the customer information that the organization already has. Such information might include sales records, requests for information, credit files, and other customer data.

2. The next step is to obtain more information. This might be received through warranty cards, surveys, mail-in coupons, rebates, and contests. A relatively new method of obtaining information is to use the Internet. Not only can companies manually track some online activity but a variety of companies and software applications enable a business to learn more about its customers by monitoring web habits, as illustrated in **Small Business in Action 7-4**. Care should be taken in obtaining information and permission should be sought for this information to be shared with other organizations.
3. Organizations may be able to supplement these data by accessing information available from a variety of public and private sources. Government and private market studies may profile different types of consumers and their purchase behaviours. Other databases might be obtained from credit card companies and banks.
4. The organization must then process the information. The acquisition of a database software system will be required. There are now a number of inexpensive systems available, or the business may need to have a customized model developed to suit its purposes. Such a system should allow the business to see the relationship between the data and the behaviour of the customer.
5. The last step in the development of a database system is to use the data to develop a highly specific profile of the company's customers.

SMALL BUSINESS IN ACTION 7-4

SOMEONE IS ALMOST ALWAYS WATCHING YOU

The title may sound scary but it's true, at least for people's online and mobile activity. Some of the largest organizations in the world, such as Facebook and Google, are tracking not only your activity on their sites but also your other online browsing activity. These firms then use this information to sell to firms who want to target you with advertising based on your Internet usage. Other software tools, such as **KISSmetrics**, have been developed to help businesses identify the behaviour of web users. Users of KISSmetrics can not only identify who is visiting their site but track their actions as well. This information can be used to tailor offerings and improve sales. Since the company's inception, it has tracked the web use of 4.5 billion people and their 36 billion interactions.

Many consumers are quite surprised to find out their online activity and locations are being tracked by companies.

Gajus/Shutterstock.com

Companies watching you may not be limited to the online world either. More businesses both large and small are now making use of GPS data to track consumers' whereabouts. Using services such as **Thumb Vista**, firms can send coupons, advertising information or texts about their business to people in physical proximity to their firms. When they combine this information with knowledge gleaned from your Internet usage, businesses may know more about you than you do.

Some companies have become even more creative when tracking their users and likely have breached privacy laws in Canada and the United States. Aaron's, a rent-to-own store, has recently gotten into hot water for installing software in laptops, which enabled the company to use the computer's web cam to see what its customers were doing. The software, called PC Rental Agent, has been the subject of a number of consumer complaints because of its use to capture pictures and video of people in very intimate moments. While Aaron's appears to have crossed the line with their software, the use of other tools, such as Google Alerts, HootSuite, and KISSmetrics, are considered to be perfectly legal and acceptable business practices.

Discussion Questions

1. Do you think organizations should be able to track who visits their websites and monitor their online behaviour?
2. Do you think it is a worthwhile investment for businesses to monitor and respond to social media discussions about their companies? Why or why not?

[continued]

[continued]

3. Did Aaron's cross the line with its monitoring tools?
4. If you started a business would you make use of online tools to track people's Internet activity? Why or why not?
5. Do you think it is a good business practice to monitor smartphones and push out coupons and ads to potential customers? Why or why not? Do you think the practice is ethical? Why or why not?

CRM Databases and Retention.

As discussed, one of the most critical keys to the success of the small business is retaining its customers. An increasing number of organizations are realizing that the cost is much higher to attract a new customer than to retain an existing one. As a result, expenditures for customer retention activities have now surpassed expenditures on customer attraction in North America.[15] By getting to know customers and creating a database, entrepreneurs are more likely to be able to target clients and offer products and services they are interested in. This is llustrated in **Small Business in Action 7-5**, but another example is **Olivier Soapery**, which has created a unique family approach to business from the beginning. The New Brunswick–based company manufactures eco-skincare products, and its founder and president, Isabel Gagné, believes that the secret of a successful business lies in creating long-lasting relationships with customers. Her family approach to selling is what makes her business different from others: "Whenever you call, you get a real live person and never a machine. And that's fundamental to my company," Gagné says. The firm sells quality products through retail stores, a company website, a comprehensive distribution network, and loyal clients. Olivier now markets 140 products and has started franchising the business.[16]

SMALL BUSINESS IN ACTION 7-5

THE LOYALTY PUZZLE

Sunterra Market, an Alberta-based independent grocery operation, knows about customer relations. The company first introduced its loyalty program, Fresh Rewards, in 2000 and has seen steady growth, with five stores in Calgary and two in Edmonton.

What differentiates Sunterra's loyalty program from others is that it is not discount based—it is pure rewards. The program is simple and easy: the customer gets one point for every dollar spent in any store; Sunterra pays them back at about three cents on the dollar. So, if you have 3330 points, you get a $100 gift certificate for Sunterra. There are two modes of redemption for Sunterra's reward program: high level and low level. In high level, you fill in a form and send it in or place your redemption online. Low level is done in the stores for items such as a $10 gift card or something even as small as a cookie.

While some larger Canadian firms are abandoning loyalty programs, Sunterra markets is expanding theirs to better connect with customers.

Sunterra is expanding and always looking for more ways to connect with its customers. They have a birthday mail-out that allows any customer who signs up for the rewards program to receive a card in their birth month with a coupon for a free piece of cake or cup of coffee.

Discussion Questions

1. Do you think reward programs, such as the one described above, make a difference to the company's bottom line? Why or why not?
2. In recent years, some larger Canadian companies, such as Second Cup, have abandoned their rewards programs. What are some of the advantages and disadvantages of using rewards as a way to retain customers and generate sales?
3. If you were starting a small retail business, would you implement a rewards program? Why or why not?

The small business should have a natural advantage over large businesses in customer service and retention because of the ability to develop a more personal relationship with the customer. Many large businesses, in their attempts to increase volume of sales, simply cannot provide the level of service that a small business can. This is because service tends to be individualized and time-consuming to provide. The small business needs to remember that in most situations, the offering of excellent service is what will set it apart from large business and provide an important competitive advantage.

To provide effective customer service and retention, the small business should do the following:

- *Identify the types of service to offer:* These service activities, of course, should be tailored to the needs of the target market of the business. As discussed, the effective use of customer databases and customer profiles will assist the entrepreneur in achieving this goal.
- *Budget adequate funds for this activity:* Employee training, guarantees, and other service activities will require a financial investment.
- *Handle customer concerns and complaints effectively:* Research has shown that if a business handles a complaint quickly and satisfactorily, 70 to 95 percent of customers will continue to patronize the business.
- *Do better than expected:* Although the business may need to advertise the service, many have found that the best policy is to provide better service than their customers expect. Christine Magee, founder of Sleep Country Canada, maintains this point of view: "When a customer comes in the door, we want to exceed their expectations."[17]
- *Do not disappoint the consumer:* The chances of retaining a customer primarily depend on the level of satisfaction received through the experience with the business. Specific activities that can be used to increase the chances of satisfaction are quality products and services, rebates and rewards, follow up contacts and thank-yous, requests for suggestions, and guarantees.
- *Regularly evaluate customer service and retention programs:* Ensure that your programs are effective and meet the needs of your customers.

ESTABLISHING GOALS AND OBJECTIVES LO6

Before any marketing strategy decisions can be outlined, the entrepreneur must establish realistic and specific goals and objectives. These *marketing goals and objectives* respond to the question "Where do we want to go?" and should specify such things as market share, profits, sales (by territory and region), market penetration, number of distributors, awareness level, new product launching, pricing policy, sales promotion, and advertising support.

For example, the entrepreneur of a new frozen diet product may determine the following objectives for the first year: 10 percent market penetration, 60 percent of market sampled, distribution in 75 percent of the market. These goals must be considered reasonable and feasible given the business situation.

All the goals discussed are quantifiable and could be measured for control purposes. However, not all goals and objectives must be quantified. It is possible for a firm to establish some other types of goals or objectives: research customer attitudes toward a product, set up a sales training program, improve packaging, change the name of a product, or find a new distributor. It is a good idea to limit the number of goals or objectives to between six and eight. Too many goals make control and monitoring difficult. Obviously, these goals should represent key areas to ensure marketing success.

DEFINING MARKETING STRATEGY AND ACTION PROGRAMS

Once the marketing goals and objectives are established, the entrepreneur can begin to develop the marketing strategy and action plan to achieve them. These strategy and action decisions respond to the question "How do we get there?" As indicated earlier, these decisions reflect on the marketing mix variables that will be discussed in-depth in **Chapter 8**.

BUDGETING THE MARKETING STRATEGY

Effective planning must also consider the costs involved in the implementation of these decisions. If the entrepreneur has followed the procedure of detailing the strategy and action programs to meet the desired goals and objectives, costs should be reasonably clear. If assumptions are necessary, they should be clearly stated so that anyone else who reviews the written marketing plan (e.g., a venture-capital firm) will understand these implications.

This budgeting of marketing action and strategy decisions will also be useful in preparing the financial plan. Details of how to develop a financial plan are discussed in **Chapter 9**.

MONITORING PROGRESS OF MARKETING ACTIONS LO7

Generally, monitoring of the plan involves tracking specific results of the marketing effort. Sales data by product, territory, sales rep, and outlet are a few of the specific results that should be monitored. What is monitored depends on the specific goals and objectives outlined earlier in the marketing plan. Any weak signals from the monitoring process will give the entrepreneur the opportunity to redirect or modify the marketing effort to allow the firm to achieve its goals and objectives. Remember, all marketing efforts need monitoring. Swiss Media Inc., a natural health products producer and frequent user of guerrilla marketing (free samples), measures the impact of its sampling program by monitoring regional sales and its website traffic, comparing the data before and after its sampling program. Other measures can be simpler. Brian Scudamore, owner of 1-800-Got-Junk?, a Canadian-based international junk-hauling franchise, established a customer relations program that focused on wowing customers, starting with their call centre and the customer's first contact with the company. To measure this program, he employs a great deal of formal metrics, but he is also known to simply call his own call centre to see how workers are treating potential customers.

CONTINGENCY PLANNING

Generally, the entrepreneur does not have the time to consider many alternative plans of action should the initial plan fail. However, as stated earlier, it is important for the entrepreneur to be flexible and prepared to make adjustments where necessary. It is unlikely that any marketing plan will succeed exactly as expected.

WHY SOME PLANS FAIL

Marketing plans are ineffective or fail in meeting marketing goals for different reasons. In fact, failure may also be considered a matter of degree, since some goals may be met and others missed completely. The overall failure of the plan will be judged by management and may depend on the mere solvency of the organization. Some of the reasons for failure can be avoided if the entrepreneur is careful in preparing the marketing plan. Some of the more common reasons for failure that can be controlled are as follows:

- *Lack of a real plan.* The marketing plan is superficial and lacks detail and substance, especially regarding goals and objectives.
- *Lack of an adequate situation analysis.* It is invaluable to know where you are and where you have been, before deciding where you want to go. Careful analysis of the environment can result in reasonable goals and objectives.
- *Unrealistic goals.* This generally results because of a lack of understanding of the situation.
- *Unanticipated competitive moves, product deficiencies, and acts of nature or catastrophe.* With a good situation analysis, as well as an effective monitoring process, competitive decisions can be assessed and predicted with some degree of accuracy. Deficiencies in the product often result from rushing the product to the market. For an act of nature or a catastrophe–such as an oil spill, flood, hurricane, or war–the entrepreneur has no control.

LEARNING OBJECTIVES SUMMARY

LO1 **The marketing plan designates the response to three questions: Where have we been? Where are we going? How do we get there? A marketing plan is a key part of business planning, and much like a business plan, it must be monitored and updated frequently.**

LO2 **The marketing plan entails a number of major steps, including defining market segments, selecting target markets, and developing customer profiles.**

LO3 **Some of the most common external influences affecting the small business are the economy, the competition, legal restrictions, the social and cultural environment, and technology. In dealing with external influences, the owner-manager must identify which external conditions affect the business and then set up a system to monitor and effectively respond to changes in those influences.**

LO4 **To be able to respond effectively, it is generally necessary for the entrepreneur to conduct some marketing research. This research may involve secondary sources or a primary data collection process. Information from the research will be very important in determining the marketing mix factors or the marketing strategy to be implemented in the marketing plan.**

LO5 **Customer relationship management is important to the long-term success of business. One important tool in customer relations management is the use of databases.**

LO6 **Goals and objectives must be established. These goals and objectives must be realistic and detailed (quantified, if possible).**

LO7 **The marketing plan should be monitored to discern the success of the programs. Any weak signals will give the entrepreneur the opportunity to modify the plan or develop a contingency plan. Even with careful scrutiny of the marketing plan, many plans will fail.**

TIME TO TAKE ACTION

1. Conduct additional research on your industry, competitors, and customers. Start to build a profile of your main competitors, including such things as their target market(s) and their marketing mix. Expand this profile to identify your competitors' strengths and weaknesses.
2. Review the major factors in the external environment that can influence your business. Identify any potential changes in the environment that can affect your business.
3. Determine who your target customers will be. Develop a complete profile by answering the questions from this chapter. Interview or survey your potential customers to learn their opinion about your business and strategies.
4. Use the Internet to review some of the common social media monitoring tools. Which ones would you consider using? Why? Create a table outlining the name, use, price, strengths, and weaknesses of each tool.

DISCUSSION QUESTIONS

1. What are the advantages of developing a very detailed marketing plan compared with a short plan that could be drafted on a few pages? Do you think it is valuable for businesses to invest a considerable amount of time developing a detailed marketing plan? Why or why not?
2. As noted in the chapter, many businesses do not have a marketing plan. How does this affect your opinion of the usefulness of the document?

3. One argument in favour of market segmentation and target marketing for small companies is they often lack the resources to market to large groups of people. Is this still true with the technology available today?
4. What is the difference between traditional target marketing and the more enhanced target marketing discussed in this chapter?
5. Is market segmentation just a nice way of using stereotypes to sell your products? Can people really be classified so easily into groups that share common needs, wants, and demands?
6. Segmentation is the process of breaking a population down into smaller groups. Is it possible for a small business to oversegment? How might that be detrimental to the success of the business?
7. Many businesses both large and small are using online tools, specifically social media, to track the Internet use of customers and potential customers. Do you think this is ethical? Why or why not?
8. Why is customer retention so important? What are some of the things businesses can do to improve retention?
9. What are some of the key steps in establishing marketing goals for a business? Do you think goals have to be quantifiable? Why or why not?

EXPERIENTIAL EXERCISES

1. Define the target market(s) for your university or college. What are the target market demographics, lifestyle characteristics, purchase characteristics, and purchase motivations? Create a customer profile for one of the target markets.
2. Identify the major competitors for your local college or university. What are their strengths and weaknesses? Where do you see an opportunity in the market to create value and grow enrolments for your school?
3. Review the external environment for your university or college. What changes are you anticipating that could affect business? What can your school do to benefit from these changes?
4. Develop an idea for a new business that will operate in the local economy. Define the target market(s), create a customer profile, and examine in detail the factors in the external environment that will affect the business.
5. Develop a marketing mix (i.e., product, promotion, price, distribution) for a high-end restaurant that you would like to open.
6. Interview a local small business owner and find out what his or her marketing strategy is. Determine the promotional strategy. Are these strategies similar to those discussed in the chapter?

CHAPTER 8

MANAGING THE MARKETING MIX

LEARNING OBJECTIVES

By the end of this chapter, you should be able to:

LO1 Recognize the importance of the marketing mix.

LO2 Explain how products and services are created.

LO3 Explain the differences in marketing to consumers and marketing to businesses.

LO4 Discuss three methods of price setting.

LO5 Identify the major steps in a promotion campaign.

LO6 Compare and contrast different promotional tools.

SMALL BUSINESS PROFILE

CHRISTIAN LUNNY AND AARON WOJNOWSKI, Musi

martin-dm/Getty Images

Christian Lunny and Aaron Wojnowski from Winnipeg, Manitoba, appear to be typical young men in their early 20s. Aaron recently graduated from the University of Manitoba and Christian is managing his own business, Dash Agency, a digital marketing firm. Yet there are a few things that set them apart from many people their age. Aaron taught himself to code in grade nine and Christian developed an interest in digital media and computer interfaces at a young age. When the two met in high school, it was natural to think they might start a business together someday. What perhaps set the pair apart is that day occurred shortly after meeting.

Lunny and Wojnowski recall the story, saying they were with their friends and trying to listen to free music on YouTube, and while there is a lot of free video content, there isn't an easy way to stream YouTube songs onto your phone or organize songs and artists. With this problem in mind Lunny and Wojnowski set out to create an ISO, or Apple app, which would allow users to easily play songs from YouTube and other free content providers. A short time later Musi was born. Musi is an app, which takes free songs from YouTube and SoundCloud and allows the user to play them on their smartphones. The benefits of Musi include access to free music, easy playlist organization, the ability to immediately queue videos to play up next or on demand, multi-band equalizer for in depth adjustment of audio levels and easy ways to build and share music video playlists with friends.

The business partners put the app in App store and started to promote their it locally through social media with their friends and some initial public relations. Given their lack of money, Lunny and Wojnowski, started to think more about App Store optimization and what potential users would be searching for when online. The partners noted that the keywords they were using in describing the app were "YouTube organizer" and no one was searching for this term. But when they changed the key words to include, "free" and "music download" the popularity of the app took off. Almost overnight their downloads went from very few to 15,000 a day—and then to 30,0000 a day.

The next question to come along is how they would monetize or make money off the app. Wojnowski recalls he was initially set against having ads on Musi, that he thought it would take away from the user's experience. But they eventually ran some banner ads with the condition that they would not overwhelm the app. Wojnowski says they key was using banner ads that didn't take away from the operability of the app or ruin the site. Apps that are around a long time are more profitable than apps that are focused on short-term revenue. For example, an app which gets some initial users and quickly adds a lot of advertising tends to lose users swiftly until they are forced to cease operations; they make very little money. While an app that is around a long time tends to make much more money if they gradually increase advertising without taking away from the app's functionality. Following this long-term strategy, Musi was soon earning a few hundred dollars a day, which eventually grew to thousands per day. A turning point came when Musi started to work with companies such as MoPub, which specializes in helping entrepreneurs maximize revenue from their apps. Shortly afterward connecting with MoPub, daily revenue tripled.

Lunny further states what has set them apart is their focus on their core values: they want to create the best app that allows users to stream music from YouTube and other free providers. The results are clear: Musi has many positive reviews on the app store, the app has been downloaded 12 million times in over 150 countries. Musi is a private company and the owners report annual revenue in the millions.

THE ROLE OF THE MARKETING MIX IN SMALL BUSINESS LO1

As mentioned in the previous chapter, marketing activities are sometimes overlooked by entrepreneurs. A key element in the marketing plan is establishing the correct marketing mix. A good marketing mix will create value and long-term relationships with target customers, and distinguish a business from its competitors. For example, Shopify, which allows businesses to easily create online stores, has created value for its target customers—businesses that want to sell products online—by creating an easy-to-use product, pricing it competitively by charging a royalty on a percentage of sales, and marketing the business using a number of nontraditional promotions that appeal to their target audience. The remainder of this chapter will discuss elements of the marketing mix and provide entrepreneurs with a variety of strategies to appeal to targeted customers.

DEVELOPING THE PRODUCT OR SERVICE LO2

As mentioned in the previous chapter, the product or service to be offered should be designed to meet target market demand. To ensure responsiveness to consumer demand, the owner-manager should think of the product or service in terms of the ways and extent to which it satisfies consumer need. A prototype of the product should be prepared and tested with a representative sample of the market. This type of information should be collected before finalizing the production decision.

Some major decision areas about which the small business owner should be knowledgeable when developing a product strategy are discussed next.

DEVELOP PRODUCT OR SERVICE POLICIES

Product policies should cover such items as quality level, product or service depth and width, packaging, branding, level of service, and warranties.

DECIDE HOW THE PRODUCT WILL BE MANUFACTURED

For many small businesses, contracting with another firm to manufacture the product is advantageous. This may be an especially viable alternative during the early stages of a business, when the risk is usually higher. After the product has achieved market acceptance and the volume of production has increased, it may be more cost effective to acquire the manufacturing capability.

UNDERSTAND THE PRODUCT LIFE CYCLE

All products and services have a life cycle, as **Figure 8-1** shows. As the product moves from the introduction to the decline stage in its life cycle, the marketing strategy for the product and even for the business may also change. This means changes may be required in pricing, in distribution, in promotion, and even in the product or service. Knowing that the product or service has a life cycle helps the owner-manager plan for any necessary adjustments to the marketing strategy when the maturity stage is reached. Such modifications can help prolong the life cycle of the product or service. Strategies include the following:

- Appeal to a new target market.
- Adjust the product or service to meet changes in customer needs.
- Increase promotion to enhance frequency of purchases.
- Emphasize different uses or characteristics of the product or service.
- Offer a new product or service.

FIGURE 8-1 **Product Life Cycle**

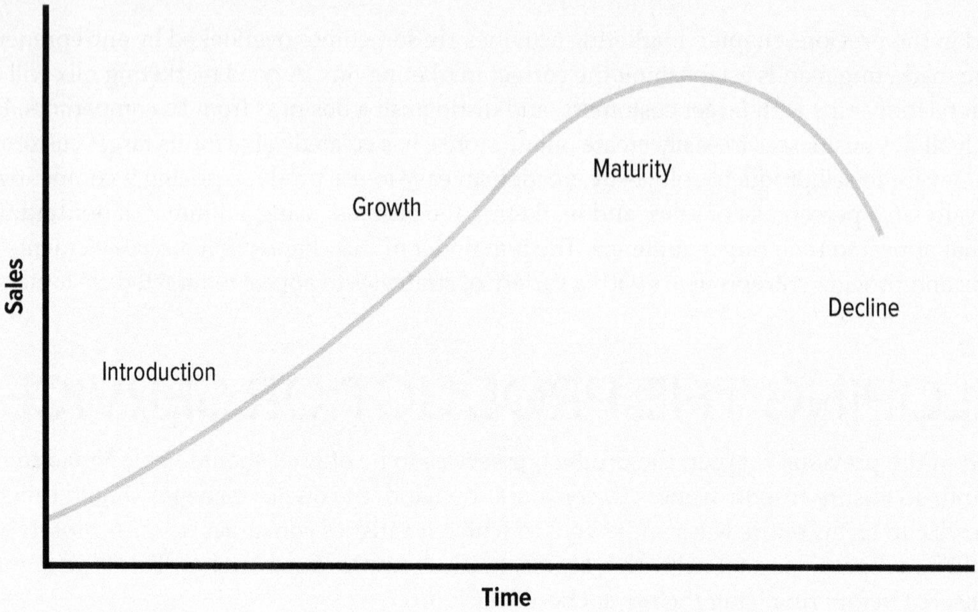

- Introduction expenses high
- Sales slowly increase
- Negative or little profit
- Highest profit
- Sales increasing
- Competition starting to appear
- Sales stagnating
- Heavy competition
- Profits beginning to level off
- Decreasing sales
- Declining or no profits

Product life cycles in many industries, notably the high-technology areas, are getting shorter. This has an impact on the long-term planning for the business.

DETERMINE FACTORS THAT MAY ACCELERATE PRODUCT OR SERVICE ADOPTION

Research shows that consumers generally adopt new products or services at different rates. Those who purchase first are the innovators or early adopters. In Canada, roughly seven percent of the population can be classified as innovators who like to try brand new products. Another 27 percent of the population are open to adopting innovative solutions and 44 percent of the population would be considered cautious adopters. Based on this information, it is clear Canadians are open to trying new products and services.[1] This willingness to adopt innovative solutions is something young Vancouver entrepreneurs Amir Ahani and Alex Mazinani are counting on as they market their new company, **TechPOS.** TechPOS has developed a POS system with an accompanying scale designed specifically for cannabis distributors. TechPOS scales weigh cannabis to one-tenth of a gram—more accurate than most current POS scales and, the business partners note, their cloud-based POS operating system is easier to use and has more features then their competition does. Although the company is new, Ahani and Mazinani have plans to carve out a large share of the cannabis industry.[2]

While the innovators and early adopters typically make up between seven and 34 percent of the Canadian market, they have a far greater influence because the rest of the market usually looks to this group before purchasing. After the small business owner has identified the innovators and early adopters within the target market, every attempt should be made to test market the product or service to that group first. In Canada, early adopters are heavy Internet users, visit crowdfunding sites, and 23 percent more likely to use public transportation. If the early adopters accept the product or service, they may even do much of the initial promotion on social networking sites, such as Facebook, Twitter, Pinterest, Instagram, Tumblr, and so forth. Early adopters also have higher income levels ($90,000 in Canada), are better educated, are more socially active, are more willing to take risks, and have greater exposure to printed media.[3] Firms that are interested in appealing to these groups will often use social networking sites and print ads in subways and buses. For example, **Snakes and Lattes**, a Toronto-based board game and coffee shop, used social media to attract early adopters to its business. According to Snakes and Lattes owner, 27-year-old Ben Castanie, social media sites, such as Facebook and Twitter, have been essential in attracting clients to his business.[4]

In addition to understanding the characteristics of innovators and early adopters, the small business owner should be aware of the factors that can speed up product adoption and attempt to capitalize on them. Some of the more important factors are discussed below.

Relative Advantage.

If the product or service appears to have a significant advantage over existing ones, and if this advantage can be communicated effectively, it is more likely to have a faster adoption. This is the case for Shopify: not only was the company's online store building platform easy to use, but it was also richer in features when compared with competitors.

Complexity.

If the product or service is difficult to understand, the adoption rate is typically longer. In such a case, promotion should have informational or educational content. For example, Halifax-based **Lorax Systems Inc.** has developed an oil and diesel filtration system that will eliminate fuel leaks and spills at residential and commercial properties. Given that the product is new, and the system somewhat complex, a great deal of Lorax's marketing initiatives include personal selling in which representatives explain how the product works. John Zafris, one of the company's shareholders who has worked in sales, says the adoption process has been slow as people have to first learn about the product and understand its benefits.[5]

Divisibility.

A product or service that can be purchased in small amounts with a minimum of social or financial risk usually has a quicker adoption rate. For example, the **Pet Peppy**, a nylon carrying case for pets that can be used on airplanes, has resulted in sales in excess of $2 million in only three years for Oakville, Ontario, entrepreneurs Bilal Chaudhry and Suhaib Sajjad. Consumers like both the simplicity of the carrying case and the low cost of the product.[6] Other examples of companies offering low-risk items include the **RimRoller**, a small tool that enables users to roll up the rim on Tim Hortons' cups. That company amassed large sales after appearing on CBC's *Dragons' Den.*[7]

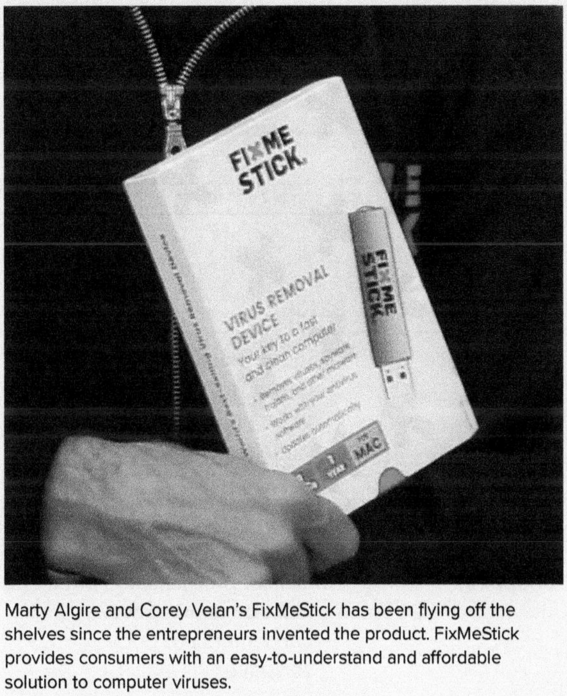

Marty Algire and Corey Velan's FixMeStick has been flying off the shelves since the entrepreneurs invented the product. FixMeStick provides consumers with an easy-to-understand and affordable solution to computer viruses.

Photo courtesy of FixMeStick Technologies Inc.

Communicability of Results.

If the results of using the product or service are quickly evident and easily communicated to others, its adoption will be more rapid. For example, Marty Algire and Corey Velan of Montreal, creators of FixMeStick which was discussed in **Chapter 3**, had a simple, easily communicable solution to the problem of computer viruses. Consumers can take a USB stick and plug it into their computer. The USB would detect and fix any potential hazards to their machine, and the stick sells for less than $30, which makes the product even more attractive.[8]

In summary, the less risk associated with the purchase decision, the more rapid the adoption rate. Therefore, the owner-manager should do as much as possible to reduce risk for the consumer when introducing a new product or service. Providing information and offering a guarantee or warranty as part of the purchase are commonly used methods for reducing risk.

UNDERSTAND HOW THE CONSUMER CLASSIFIES THE PRODUCT OR SERVICE LO3

Marketers use a standard classification system in categorizing consumer products. This system can be valuable in developing the marketing strategy for the small business:

- *Convenience products.* Products that are purchased with minimal effort. They may be necessities, unplanned purchases, or emergency goods.
- *Shopping products.* Products that are purchased only after comparison with similar products. Comparisons may be made on the basis of price if competing products are viewed as similar or in terms of quality or style if competing products differ.
- *Specialty products.* Products that inspire substantial brand or product loyalty in consumers. As a result, they are willing to spend considerable effort to locate and purchase the brands and products they desire. Patrice Mousseau's product falls into this category, as is illustrated in **Small Business in Action 8-1**.
- *Unsought products.* Products that consumers are unaware of, such as new innovations, like the Shockbox helmets discussed in **Small Business in Action 4-3** in Chapter 4, or life insurance. Given that the products are unsought, they are the toughest to sell and often involve a great deal of promotion or personal selling.

Table 8-1 illustrates strategy implications for each of these classifications. The focus of the marketing strategy is determined by how the target consumer classifies the product or service.

TABLE 8-1 Strategy Implications for Product Classifications

TYPE OF PRODUCT	PRICE	DISTRIBUTION	PROMOTION
Convenience	Although usually lower-priced goods, the markups tend to be high. Within a certain range, price is not important to the consumer.	Products should be located close to consumers, either in relation to where they live or within the store. Availability is important to the customer.	Promote availability. Use point-of-purchase displays for impulse goods.
Shopping	For similar products, the price must be competitive, as consumers are price sensitive.	Products should be located close to competing products to aid comparison.	Promote price advantage for similar products or quality/style advantage for dissimilar products.

	For dissimilar products that are still competitive, price is not as important to the consumer.		
Specialty	Within a certain range, price is not important to the customer.	Location is not important to the customer.	Promote the outlet that carries the product or brand.
Unsought	Consumers may be very price sensitive for products which they may not want to buy, like insurance. Early adopters of new products maybe less concerned about price than late adopters for innovative products	Location depends on the product	Given that the product is new or one consumers do not want to buy, promotions need to focus on education. Consumers need to learn why they need the product.

SMALL BUSINESS IN ACTION 8-1

HEALTHY BABY, HEALTHY BUSINESS

Patrice Mousseau is an Ojibway from Fort William First Nation's Community who says she didn't set out to be an entrepreneur. She was just looking for a solution to a problem when she created **Satya**, an eczema treatment cream. Yet a few years after starting her business, Mousseau's eczema cream is carried in over 700 stores, she has plans to introduce six new products, and she wants to expand globally.

Mousseau notes she created her organic, fragrance-free, filler-free eczema cream shortly after her new baby was born. Her daughter's skin had developed red welts and Mousseau recalls going to the doctor and being given the diagnosis of eczema. She was told of the traditional treatment: steroid creams. But Mousseau, who was previously a broadcast journalist, was concerned about the impact of steroid creams on her baby and opted to research alternative treatments, including traditional Indigenous medicine. After a few days, Mousseau cooked up what she thought would be an eczema cure in her crock-pot and applied it to her daughter's skin. A short time after applying the treatment her daughter's eczema was cleared.

Mousseau's story could have ended with the successful treatment of her daughter. But she attended an entrepreneurship conference and was inspired to start a business selling her organic cream. She first started selling at farmers' markets, selling $110 on the first day. Mousseau soon expanded her sales to craft fairs and local retailers. When she reached 70 retailers, Satya caught the attention of Purity Life Health Products, a national distributor. Once they started selling her cream nationally, her product was quickly placed in 700 stores.

In addition to helping people with eczema, Mousseau wants to assist working mothers. She now employs six mothers, all of whom work flexible schedules based on their children's needs. On top of flexible scheduling, Mousseau is paying her employees a Vancouver living wage of $22 an hour. Her long-term plans include building her own manufacturing centre on Aboriginal land to create additional jobs in First Nation's Communities.

Discussion Questions

1. How would you describe Satya's rate of adoption? Slow or fast? What factors discussed above impacted product adoption? Please use specific terms from the text and expand on your answer?
2. How would you classify Mousseau's product? Why?
3. Do you consider Mousseau to be a social entrepreneur? Why or why not?
4. Read the next section, **Developing the Distribution System**. Based on what you learned, what are some of the strengths and weaknesses of Satya's distribution strategy?

UNDERSTAND HOW BUSINESSES CLASSIFY THE PRODUCT OR SERVICE

Business products or services are used specially by businesses in their operations. Businesses classify their products or services based on their use and the classification of business purchases falls into seven categories: raw materials, major equipment, accessory equipment, component parts, processed materials, supplies, and industrial services. Often, entrepreneurs looking to sell to other firms classify business purchases as capital or supply purchases for marketing decisions. Capital purchases may be considered large for the purchaser and often involve more contact and personal selling from the supplier. Supply purchases are relatively routine and inexpensive and require less contact from the manufacturer or supplier.

Given that 80 percent of the fastest-growing firms in Canada sell to other businesses, it is important that aspiring entrepreneurs recognize the importance of business-to-business sales. Karl Gannon, co-founder of Albertan-based **Four Quest Energy Inc.**, provides a good example to use when comparing the difference between selling to consumers and to other businesses. While consumer sales can have relatively short periods of contact and not be overly complex, business to business sales normally involve more contact time and complexity. Gannon, whose business is one of the fastest-growing firms in Canada, meets with clients numerous times a year, almost always face to face so that he can understand their needs and build a relationship. Gannon says, "Our philosophy is that it's better to meet one person seven times a year than seven people one time each. If we go see a client seven times in a year, we'll know who they are, how their business is doing and how we can help them. And if we can help their business, they can help ours."[9]

DEVELOPING THE DISTRIBUTION SYSTEM

Many entrepreneurs develop an excellent product but lack the knowledge about the best way to get it to the end users or customer. An effective distribution system should provide the product or service to the right customer, at the right place, at the right time, and in the right quantity. For example, when Eryn Green and Tamar Wagman founded a frozen organic baby food company called Sweetpea, they struggled with getting their product into stores. At first, they started slowly selling their products at baby groups, yoga classes, and trade shows, and by using some small store demonstrations. However, they knew that to make this product a commercial success, they would need distribution in large retail stores. In Ontario, they sold directly to some of the supermarkets, but in Western Canada, they realized they would have to enlist the services of a distributor with a wide distribution network that could also represent their specialty product adequately to compete with other natural baby foods. They were successful in signing with **SunOpta**, which achieved distribution in over 100 stores in the west.[10] This, coupled with their growing Ontario distribution, now means Sweetpea products are in over 350 stores nationwide.[11]

The distribution channel is the path the product or service follows from the producer to the customer. It includes the different organizations or individuals who will assist in this movement toward consumption.

The small business owner needs to address three main distribution decision areas: the type of channel to use, the length of the channel, and the number of distributors authorized to sell the product.

CHANNEL OPTIONS

A small business can follow essentially two channel paths, although various combinations of these types of channels are possible.

Manufacturer to Customer (Short-Direct Channel).

This type of channel involves distributing the product or service directly to the customer or consumer. The transportation and selling functions are carried out by the owner-manager or the sales staff. While many small businesses often lack the financial capacity or expertise to hire and train their own sales forces, the Internet has enabled many small firms to pursue this strategy at low costs. In fact, online sales have resulted in firms achieving much higher margins on their products as they have effectively cut out middlemen such as wholesalers, distributors, and/or retailers. For example, **Indochino**, the world's leader in made-to-measure suits, was founded by 22-year-old Kyle Vucko and 26-year-old Heikal Gani while they were studying at the University of Victoria in British Columbia. Selling menswear direct to consumers, the pair grew Indochino to millions in sales with a valuation in excess of $50 million.[12]

Manufacturer to Wholesaler/Retailer to Customer (Long-Indirect Channel).

In this type of distribution channel, the wholesaler or retailer purchases the product and resells it to another channel member or to the consumer. The manufacturer assumes less risk with this method but generally has a lower profit margin and less control over the distribution. The small business may use this type of distribution channel by going to a retailer or wholesaler directly or visiting a trade show attended by these intermediaries. Many products receive their initial start from successful trade show experiences. For example, Jamie Draves, of Georgetown, Ontario, owner of **Katan Kitchens** and **Quinta Local Superfoods Inc.**, has successfully used trade shows to sell his Ontario-grown superfood, quinoa, to retailers.[13]

CHANNEL LENGTH

The decision regarding channel length will depend on the concerns of the manufacturer, as mentioned above. It also involves examining the product and market characteristics listed in **Table 8-2**.

TABLE 8-2 Deciding on Channel Length

DIRECT-SHORT CHANNEL (MANUFACTURER TO CUSTOMER)	INDIRECT-LONG CHANNEL (MANUFACTURER TO WHOLESALER/ RETAILER TO CUSTOMER)
Implications for Manufacturer	
More expensive to set up	Cheaper to set up
Greater potential return	Less return
More risk	Less risk
More expertise needed	Less expertise needed
Product Characteristics	
Perishable	Standardized
Technical	Inexpensive
Large, bulky	Proven demand
Expensive	
Market Characteristics	
Geographically concentrated	Geographically dispersed
Low product awareness	High product awareness
Sales effort required	Less sales effort required

CHANNEL INTENSITY

Another channel decision is how many distributors or dealers will be allowed to sell the product. Generally, products that require greater selling effort, seller knowledge, and sales expertise are best distributed through a more-exclusive arrangement. For example, when Spin Master Toys (see the **Small Business Profile** in Chapter 7) started selling Air Hogs, an air powered toy plane, the company initially focused distribution efforts on hobby shops and specialty toy stores, where merchants would be more likely to take the time to explain the product. Standardized or convenience-type products usually call for a more intensive channel system. Because product availability is important in such a system, many dealers are allowed to carry the product.[14]

SOCIAL SELLING/MULTI-LEVEL MARKETING

An increasingly popular form of distribution channel used by small and large organizations is social selling often referred to as multi-level marketing. In a typical social selling system, individuals associate with a parent company as an independent contractor or franchise and are compensated based on their sales of products or services, as well as sales achieved by the people they bring into the business. This type of selling is typically through personal contacts or at group social gatherings. For example, both Steeped Tea and Poppy & Peonies (handbags), which are discussed in **Chapter 2**, are highly successful social selling companies that have grown to millions of dollars in revenue by having individual associates sell their products primarily at fun parties for women.[15]

Social selling organizations typically provide the entrepreneur with well-prepared training manuals and motivational meetings. The attractions of this type of marketing to the individual entrepreneur include flexibility, the ability to work from home, and the promise of high income. More and more products and services have been added to social selling in recent years, and expansion onto the Internet has vastly increased the market average for organizations and entrepreneurs. As of 2019, there are 1.3 million Canadians generating $2.58 billion in revenue acting as independent sales consultants for over 75 direct sales companies.[16] Readers who are interested in social selling should visit the Direct Sellers Association of Canada at **dsa.ca** to see industry statistics and member organizations.

SMALL BUSINESS BEGINNINGS 8-1

AMAZON AND SMALL BUSINESS AN "INTERESTING RELATIONSHIP"

Is Amazon good or bad for small business owners? The answer might depend on who you ask. Amazon offers free shipping and low prices, and sells virtually everything. Why would a consumer want to drive to a small business, find parking, go into a store, wait in line, and then drive home. Alternatively, in a few seconds, a shopper can purchase an item online and have it delivered to their home, often within 24 hours. Clearly Amazon is bad, very bad for small business.

But wait a second, many small businesses, five million in total, sell through Amazon. By using Amazon, small businesses can reach millions of global consumers something they would never be able to do on their own. In fact third-party retailers sold more goods through Amazon than Amazon itself. Third-party retailers sold an astonishing $116 billion in 2018 alone! Many small businesses are entirely dependent on Amazon for most if not all of their sales. As an example, Pet Peppy, discussed earlier in this chapter, earned over $2 million in revenue in three years just selling their expandable nylon pet carriers on Amazon's American site. Also, Instant Pot, a new kitchen gadget, started selling on Amazon and soon the site accounted for 90 percent of the firm's sales.

Still, critics of Amazon are not so sure. They argue Amazon can destroy a small business' brand and that the site charges high fees to its sellers. Critics also point to the many independent businesses that have closed their brick-and-mortar locations in recent years with the owners citing online competition as the main reason for shutting down.

If you are a small business owner and you want to use Amazon to reach a global marketplace, then consider the following steps. First, educate yourself. Take advantage of Amazon's seller's forum online or attend a seller's conference and/or a class in person. Next, set up an Amazon seller's account. This can be either an individual account, which charges a per-unit amount, or a business account, which charges a flat subscription fee. You can then choose to ship the products yourself or have Amazon warehouse and ship products for you. The entrepreneur's next step is creating a product listing, including a description and, of course, a photo of the item. Experts advise that product descriptions should highlight the problem-solving capabilities of the product and include a call to buy. Entrepreneurs may consider offering incentives to current customers to shop on Amazon, ask happy customers to complete product reviews, and/or use some of Amazon's product promotions to boost sales. And remember, the higher your initial sales, the more likely your product will be displayed when customers use Amazon's search.

Discussion Questions

1. How would use describe the channel length and path for businesses selling primarily on Amazon?
2. What are some of the advantages and disadvantages for small businesses selling on Amazon?
3. Do you think Amazon is good or bad for small business? Why?
4. Use Internet resources and read about how small businesses can grow their sales on Amazon. Report your findings back to the class.

SETTING THE PRICE FOR THE GOOD OR SERVICE

LO4

Another marketing strategy variable within the control of the owner-manager is the setting of price for the product or service. Pricing is a critical part of the marketing strategy; the small business cannot afford to make a pricing mistake in a competitive industry. Unfortunately, many small business owners struggle with this element of the marketing mix, and a common criticism is that many small entrepreneurs are mispricing their products. Additionally, small and medium enterprises are facing competitors using a variety of pricing tools to gain a competitive advantage, as well as consumers who have easy access to pricing information on the Internet. For example, Walmart and Target use psychological pricing strategies to help them maximize profits, and online retailer Amazon uses "dynamic pricing," which uses algorithms to track past shopping habits and adjust the price of items based on the personal habits of individual shoppers.[17]

To approach price-setting effectively, entrepreneurs must understand the factors that affect prices. These factors can be classified as either external or internal. External influences, as discussed in the previous chapter, include the state of the economy in the market area, the extent of competition, possible legal restrictions, cultural or societal attitudes toward certain price levels, and target market demand. Typical internal influences on pricing policy are internal costs, the firm's long-run objectives, and pricing policies as set by the owner-manager.

In setting price levels for the product or service, the entrepreneur may find that some of these factors are more influential than others. As a result, businesses use three general bases for price setting that take these influences into account: cost, demand, and competition.

COST-BASED PRICING

In cost-based pricing, the major influence is the cost of producing the product for the manufacturer, of purchasing and selling the product for the retailer, and of providing the service for the service firm (internal influence). **Table 8-3** illustrates the use of cost-based pricing in each of these types of business.

TABLE 8-3 Cost-Based Pricing Methods

Manufacturing Firm	
Direct material cost per unit	$ 18.00
Direct labour cost per unit	21.00
Variable overhead (manufacturing)	10.00
Fixed overhead (factory)	30.00
Total manufacturing cost per unit	79.00
Selling cost per unit	3.00
General overhead (allocated per unit)	5.00
Total cost per unit	87.00
Desired profit	13.00
Selling price	$100.00
Retail Firm	
Cost of merchandise	$ 50.00
Selling and storage (estimated)	20.00
Estimated markdowns	5.00
Desired profit	25.00
Selling price	$100.00

[continued]

[continued]

In retailing, the difference between the price and the cost of inventory is known as *markup*. In this example, it is $50 and is usually expressed as a percentage in the following manner:

$$\text{Percentage} = \frac{100 - 50}{100} = 50\%$$

Service Firm

Estimated cost of providing service per customer	$ 60.00
Estimated overhead costs per customer	20.00
Desired profit per customer	20.00
Selling price	$100.00

After the costs have been determined, a percentage markup is added to reflect the firm's profit objective. The owner-manager should realize, however, that the initial markup is seldom achieved. Markdowns and inventory shrinkage should be estimated (see **Table 8-3**) and built into the markup calculation.

DEMAND-BASED PRICING

Demand-based pricing uses consumer sensitivity to price as the major factor in arriving at the final price level (external influences). Usually research in the form of surveying potential customers and observing what competitors are charging will be required to assess acceptable prices for products. **Figure 8-2** illustrates the results of such a survey incorporated into a demand curve. Each point on the line shows the quantity demanded at the related price. For example, at a price of $30, demand would be 10 units; at $20, demand increases to 16 units. In this example, the total revenue at the $30 price is $300 (30 × 10),

FIGURE 8-2 **Consumer Price Sensitivity: Demand Pricing**

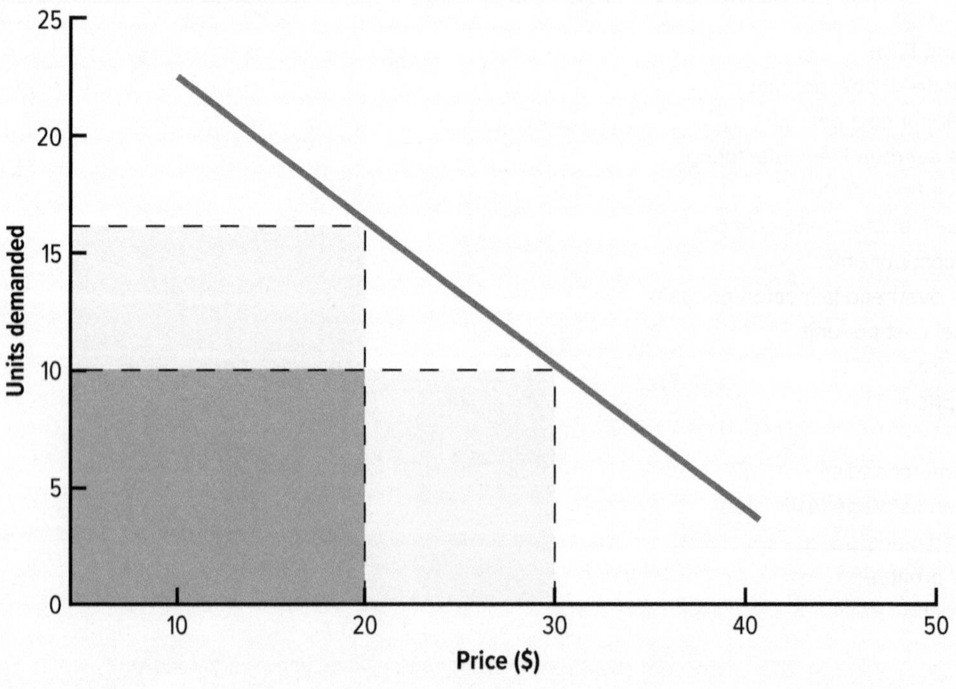

whereas at $20 the total revenue is $320 (20 × 16). This situation can be described as *price elastic*. In price-elastic situations, price increases have a negative effect on demand. For some types of products (convenience and specialty) and some industries (those with little direct competition), price may be less important to the purchaser, and thus a change in price may not significantly affect demand. If this condition exists, it means the business has much more freedom and flexibility in setting prices than it would in a more competitive and price-sensitive situation. For example, Canada Goose has established that consumers are not very price sensitive when purchasing its branded products, especially its winter jackets. As such, the company has established a policy where retailers are not allowed to discount its products.

For products and services already on the market, existing price levels and industry experts may provide valuable information to assist in setting demand-based prices.[18]

COMPETITION-BASED PRICING

Firms in a growing number of industries are using competitive pricing in which the major considerations in setting prices are the price levels and policies of competitors (external influences). Many firms conduct ongoing price checks on the competition to guide their own pricing. The small firm may want to set prices at a fixed percentage above, equal to, or below competitors' prices. Most markets today tend to be very price sensitive. As a result, entrepreneurs may have to resort to discounting prices to attract customer attention and patronage. However, in doing so, the entrepreneur should be aware of the final markups and be careful that discounting price does not conflict with the product or business image.

VALUE-BASED PRICING

Some business experts are starting to argue that small business owners should not rely too heavily on only one of the above methods of pricing as each is problematic. Andreas Hinterhuber, an Austrian pricing consultant, says that most SMEs tend to set their prices based on their costs or what the competition charges. By slavishly matching rivals' prices, he says, "you completely abdicate pricing [control] and let someone else dictate your destiny. . . . In general, pricing is undermanaged, in both small and large companies."[19] Hinterhuber is one of many who argue that small firms should embrace value-based pricing, which is becoming more popular with businesses. With value-based pricing, the entrepreneur makes sure that a clear association with the product or service and its benefits takes place. Such value components might be service, quality, or environmental factors. If this is done effectively, the seller has an easier time attracting and selling to target customers because they can more readily see the benefits. In addition, this strategy facilitates reaching customers who care more about value than cost alone.

PROMOTION LO5

Gone are the days of the philosophy "Build a better mousetrap, and the world will beat a path to your door." Today, most businesses must actively provide information to the purchaser. For the entrepreneur, finding low-cost but effective ways to promote the business or product is a challenge. Knowledge of the options and the use of creativity can help stretch the promotional dollar. When drawing up promotional plans, entrepreneurs may choose from a number of different media to convey their message, including TV, radio, newspapers, and magazines. While all offer some advantages and disadvantages, they share one common characteristic: they all cost money. Rather than spend a great deal of time discussing traditional promotional methods, which are sometimes not feasible for start-ups and small enterprises, we will briefly discuss them, then focus on tools that offer entrepreneurs significant potential at low costs. They include guerrilla marketing, public relations (PR), content marketing, and Internet or digital marketing, which includes the use of social media.

STEPS IN A PROMOTIONAL CAMPAIGN

How does the owner-manager prepare the promotional program for the product, service, or business? The following steps are essential in carrying out a promotional program that can be used as a guide for the small business.

1. Set Promotional Objectives.

Specific objectives should be set before the promotion. Typical examples are the desired percentage increase in sales, the amount of traffic to be generated, and the percentage of awareness increase desired.

2. Determine the Target of the Promotion.

Although, in many cases, the target will be the ultimate consumer, often it will be an intermediary in the distribution channel or another group that has considerable influence over the purchase.

3. Understand the Target's Needs and Perceptions of the Product or Service.

Once the target of the promotion has been determined, it is essential that information be gathered about members of that group with regard to their needs, media habits, and perceptions of the product category or specific product or service.

4. Develop the Relevant Theme.

The next step is to develop a theme for the promotion that will reflect responsiveness to target needs and perceptions and help achieve the promotional objective. It is important that only one theme be used, since too many themes or too much information can confuse the consumer and lead to unsatisfactory results.

5. Determine the Method or Media to Use.

The decision about which promotional type to use often depends on the relative importance of creating awareness or closing the sale. **Table 8-4** lists the strengths of each previously mentioned type of promotion with respect to these purposes. As the figure illustrates, advertising, public relations, and some sales promotions tend to be more effective in creating awareness, whereas personal selling tends to work better for achieving or closing the sale.

TABLE 8-4 **Effectiveness of Promotion Types**

	PERSONAL SELLING	SALES PROMOTIONS	PUBLIC RELATIONS	ADVERTISING
Create awareness of product or business	Weak	Weak	Strong	Strong
Develop interest in product	Weak	Medium	Weak	Strong
Increase desire to purchase product	Medium	Medium	Weak	Medium
Achieve product purchase	Strong	Medium	Weak	Weak

6. Develop a Specific Promotional Message.

Once the theme and medium have been determined, it is possible to develop the specific type of message to be used. As **Table 8-4** points out, some types of information are not appropriate for certain types of media. Care should be taken to ensure that the benefits of the product are clearly communicated.

7. Set the Promotional Budget.

Once the method of promotion is determined, it is possible to estimate the cost of the promotion. Several methods are used to determine amounts to spend on promotion. The most common approach is the percent of sales method. Standard percentages for various businesses can serve as a guide in using this method. The percent of sales method is theoretically weak but simple to apply, which explains its high rate of use by small businesses. A business owner should remain flexible in using these percentages, however, as market and product conditions may necessitate a deviation from the averages.

8. Implement the Promotional Program.

An essential feature of implementing the program is proper timing. Certain times of the year, the week, and even the day may be inappropriate for promoting the product or service to the target market.

9. Evaluate the Effectiveness of the Promotion.

The owner-manager should attempt to evaluate the promotional effectiveness to aid in future promotions. Evaluating effectiveness is much easier if specific objectives, such as those mentioned earlier, are set. Observations of results and surveys may be used in this evaluation. The mechanics of using primary research methods were discussed earlier in the text.

As this chapter illustrates, many aspects are involved in the marketing plan of a small business. The way all these aspects are integrated so that they compose a clear and coordinated strategy often spells the difference between a successful and an unsuccessful business.

TYPES OF PROMOTION LO6

A small business can use a variety of methods to provide information about its product or service: advertising, sales promotions, personal selling, traditional promotions, nontraditional promotions (including guerrilla marketing and public relations), and Internet or digital marketing.

Advertising.

Advertising is a non-personal form of promotion. It is directed at a mass audience through various forms of media, such as television, radio, newspapers, magazines, billboards, the Internet, and direct mail. A small business owner should be aware of the strengths and weaknesses of each of these types of media and exactly when each is appropriate. This information is presented in **Table 8-5** and discussed in further detail below. One of the most rapidly growing vehicles for small business advertising is through the Internet. The Internet is not only an effective means of advertising but also an excellent tool for securing customer feedback. More will be discussed about small business and the Internet later in this chapter.

TABLE 8-5 Advertising for Small Business

MEDIA TYPE	ADVANTAGES	DISADVANTAGES	PARTICULAR SUITABILITY	TYPICAL COSTS
Newspapers	Flexible Timely Local market Credible source	May be expensive Short life Little "pass along" Non-selective audience	All local retailers or for definable areas similar to circulation	One-page ad: large market ($2000–$4000); small market ($500–$800) (prices depend on length of contract)
Television	Sight, sound, and motion Wide reach	Cost Clutter Short exposure Less selective	Definable market area surrounding the station's location for certain products	30 seconds of prime time: large local market ($750–$1000); small local market ($200–$300)

[continued]

[continued]

Direct mail	Selected audience Personalization Flexible	Relatively expensive per contact High "throw-out" rate	New and expanding businesses; those using coupon returns or catalogues	Approximately $1 per contact
Radio	Wide reach Segmented audience Inexpensive	Audio only Weak attention Short exposure	Business catering to identifiable groups: teens, commuters, homemakers	30 seconds of prime time: large local market ($175–$250); small local market ($35–$60)
Magazines, including trade publications and catalogues	Very segmented audience Credible source Good reproduction Long life Good "pass along"	Inflexible Long lead times Costly	Restaurants Entertainment Identifiable target markets Mail order Chains	Approximately $30,000 for one-page four-colour ad in *Chatelaine* (French and English)
Outdoor	Flexible Repeat exposure Inexpensive	Mass market Very short exposure	Amusements Tourist businesses Brand-name retailers	One month of prime location billboard, large market ($2500–$3000)
Telephone directories	Users in market for goods or services Continuous ads Costs relatively low	Limited to active shoppers Limited visibility Not dynamic	Services Retailers of brand-name items Highly specialized retailers	Inexpensive— depends on size of ad
Internet	Inexpensive Requires computer hardware and expertise	Difficult to measure results Cannot see and try Lack of privacy Viruses	Information products	"Sign on" fee varies by type of ad
Trade shows	Many buyers High exposure Time saving	Cost	Product sold in chain stores	Varies

Because the small business typically does not have a lot of money to spend on advertising, it is important that the entrepreneur find effective ways to promote the business economically. Co-op and shared advertising are two ways of doing this.

With co-op advertising, the manufacturing company shares the cost of advertising with the small retailer if the retailer features the manufacturer's products in those ads. Both the manufacturer and the retailer get more advertising per dollar by sharing expenses. Co-op advertising is used most frequently by small retailers, but unfortunately, many small retailers do not take advantage of this type of assistance.

In shared advertising, a group of similar businesses forms a syndicate to produce generic ads that allow the individual businesses to dub in local information. This technique is especially suitable for small businesses that sell relatively standardized products or services. The result of this form of advertising is higher quality ads and significantly lower production costs.

Sales Promotions.

Sales promotions are also non-personal forms of promotion, but they are directed at a much more restricted audience than is advertising. Examples of sales promotions are point-of-purchase displays, coupons and discounts, trade shows and exhibitions, and contests. Sean O'Reilly, owner of Barrie-based Shorex Roofing

Corp., says that his firm has successfully used coupons from day one. When he first started his business, he had staff visit people door to door, and hand them a brochure with a coupon for 25 percent off. O'Reilly notes that customers who were thinking about hiring a roofing company had a choice, they could go to the phone book and start making calls or they could talk to the salesperson at the door who was handing them a paper worth 25 percent off the cost of a job.[20] More recently, online coupons have become increasingly popular, and small through large businesses are using such promotions to increase sales. Business journalist Jagoda Hryszko offers the following suggestions to small companies who are trying to create a successful coupon strategy:

- The design should catch people's attention.
- There should be an expiration date to keep the offer attractive.
- Have a clear and concise message.
- Have a clear call to action for consumers.[21]

In recent years "deal of the day" coupons have become an emerging trend in business as they offer consumers deep discounts, and entrepreneurs a new method of promoting their product (see **Small Business in Action 8-2** for additional information).

SMALL BUSINESS IN ACTION 8-2

GROUPON—A DIFFERENT KIND OF COUPON

Traditionally, coupons offered customers a small savings off the price of a product. For example, you may receive 10 to 25 percent of your money back after purchasing a brand of laundry detergent at a grocery store; or perhaps local restaurants will offer a two-for-one coupon in the daily newspaper. But that all changed in 2008 when **Groupon** was founded. The company, which can be described as an online social-buying website, promotes coupons that offer consumers deep discounts of anywhere from 50 to 90 percent.

Some companies use Groupon to get rid of inventory or to establish relationships with customers. The deep discounts don't usually leave the merchant with much profit after also paying Groupon's fee.

Annette Shaff/Shutterstock.com

Groupon, was originally founded as a "deal-of-the-day" site where interested consumers agree to purchase a coupon but no sales occur until a minimum number of buyers are reached. Once a targeted number of buyers have been reached, the deal becomes unlocked, the consumer's credit card is charged, and they can print the coupon. Today, Groupon offers both deal of the day and other coupons but no minimum purchases are required.

When Groupon first emerged, many companies liked the concept because they saw it as a low-cost way to acquire customers. Firms that used these online promotions paid no upfront money and had their name and logo emailed out to thousands, and in some larger urban centres, millions of people. But reviews from participating businesses have not all been favourable: many have cited the high cost of participating in the program as a deterrent. For example, at a minimum the coupons usually offer consumers a savings of 50 percent off the cost of a purchase. So a participating restaurant would offer $100 worth of food for $50. This closely resembles traditional coupons discussed above where consumers could buy one meal and get another for free. But Groupon needs to make money as well, and they normally charge 50 percent of the sale price of the coupon, or in this example, $25. So a participating restaurant would be selling $100 worth of food for only $25. Given that most restaurants only net a small percentage of gross sales, they would incur a substantial loss to participate in the program. Another complaint is that this type of coupons creates a negative image about the business. And some businesses have complained that Groupon can be slow to pay the participating business its share of the money, resulting in businesses

[continued]

[continued]

incurring hefty expenses to deliver the product or service without seeing the money come into their business for weeks, if not months.

Proponents of Groupon argue that these coupons can work for some businesses. For example, some products and services have a high enough markup that businesses can afford to offer them at a deep discount. Furthermore, some companies, especially those in the service industry, are more prone to acquiring repeat customers after a successful purchase. Coupon sites are also useful for businesses that are trying to generate sales during slow periods, that want to get rid of unwanted inventory, or that have high fixed costs, such as hotels, cruise ships, or even small tour operators. For example, Cirque du Soleil in Toronto has used Groupon to sell tickets to its show Alegria. Given that most of their costs are fixed, selling tickets at a deep discount is likely better than having the seats sit empty. Utpal Dholakia, from Rice University, completed a study of companies using Groupon and recommended companies use the site to establish long-term relationships with consumers. He says the best strategy is to use Groupon to encourage multiple visits to a firm by creating coupons that require more than one visit to realize the full value of the discount.

Discussion Questions

1. What are some of the potential advantages and disadvantages to firms that offer Groupon coupons?
2. The case above cites some examples where Groupon coupons may make sense. Develop some additional alternatives where participating in "Groupon-type" programs would be beneficial to firms.
3. Do you think Cirque du Soleil is making a good business decision selling tickets at 50 percent off using Groupon? What are the benefits of this? What are the disadvantages?
4. If you ran a business would you offer consumers Groupon deals? Why or why not?

Trade shows are also a cost-effective method of promotion for the small business. Research indicates that more than 80 percent of visitors at trade shows are decision makers, and more than 60 percent plan to make a purchase. For example, Leif Quraeshi of **QHouse Kids**, a Montreal-based distributor of specialty children's toys, says attending trade shows such as the Toronto Gift Show has been key for the company acquiring new clients, testing products, and getting customer feedback. He believes that for his company—and many others—long-term business growth comes from personal relationships and face-to-face contacts, which trade shows provide.[22] Entrepreneurs who are using or are considering using trades shows to boost revenue should consider the following tips to ensure success:

- Create a plan that includes objectives and a budget. Entrepreneurs should pre-determine what they want to accomplish. For example, is the plan to create awareness for your company or generate sales and/or leads?
- Plan for the trade show in advance. Entrepreneurs should research to find an appropriate event for their product, advertise the event, and plan on how they and their employees will interact with participants.
- At the event, entrepreneurs will want to generate interest for their display using eye-catching booths, video, or perhaps some interactions.
- Entrepreneurs will want to focus on creating relationships with attendees and follow up on leads as soon as possible.
- A final assessment should be completed to determine if attending the show was a success.

Personal Selling.

The conditions conducive to a short distribution channel or an emphasis on personal selling were discussed earlier in this chapter. Most businesses will require some personal selling as part of their marketing strategy and in some cases personal selling is essential to success. For example, Dwight Gerling, managing director of Toronto-based **DG Global Inc.**, visits Japan and other Asian countries three to six times a year to build relationships with customers. Gerling says, "The Asian culture is all about relationships . . . they appreciate me coming over, as they see me more as a friend than just as a business partner."[23] Owner-managers will undoubtedly be required to promote themselves, their businesses, and their products to customers, bankers, suppliers, and government agencies through personal selling. For example, Alberta Metis entrepreneur, Jordan Jolicoeur, owner of **Carvel Electric**, says his first large contract with KMC's pipeline was as a result of the relationship he established with the company. [24] Calum McGuigan, the 27-year-old owner of **Fervent Events**, still recalls making cold calls when he first started his business. McGuigan's marketing company, which is one of the fastest-growing businesses in Canada, started with him running the business in his spare time, cold-calling potential clients after working all day at a call centre.[25]

If salespeople are employed, they will need to be trained not only about product or service knowledge but also in selling skills. Other aspects of training, supervision, and motivation of a sales force are discussed in detail later in the text.

Traditional Promotional Methods.

Traditional promotional tools use a variety of media for the delivery of a company's message. As mentioned, these tools include direct mail, telephone directories, newspapers and magazines, TV, radio, and trade shows. While these methods can be effective, they generally have higher costs than other forms of promotions, sometimes have limited exposure time, and are rarely interactive.

Direct Mail.

Direct mail is one of the most effective methods for SMEs to promote their business. Firms can tailor direct mail packages to certain segments of the population, and it is relatively easy to produce materials that produce measurable results. In general, direct mail packages will include a letter that is written to grab a reader's attention and then a sales/promotional package. Generally, a good direct mail campaign will produce five customers (responses) for each 100 sent, although there have been campaigns that have produced much higher results. When costing your campaign, keep this 5 percent in mind—determine the costs of your package and the potential results based on a 5 percent response rate, and determine if it makes financial sense.[26] Tom St. Louis, who specializes in SME marketing, advises companies to spend their marketing money on direct mail to current customers first. Then—and only if there is money left over—should SMEs spend money on lead-generating marketing. Another advantage of direct mail is the ability to test different messages. SMEs can easily compare one direct mail package with another one to see if the response rate varies and then select the more effective package.[27]

Canada Post's **Business Matters** portion of their website provides a great deal of direct mail research, helpful hints, videos, webinars, and even the opportunity to speak to someone online.

Telephone Directories.

This is a common form of advertising for small businesses. Essentially, firms take out an advertisement or a listing in the local directory. The ads are considered credible and have a longer shelf life compared with those in newspapers and magazines. They are, however, costly, and more and more consumers are shunning large, printed directories in favour of Internet solutions.

Newspapers/Magazines.

Entrepreneurs will generally advertise in newspapers/magazines using display ads or classifieds. The ads allow for some targeting of consumers, can be run at different times of the year, and are considered a credible source of information. The downsides are the short life for many publications and the costs. Classified ads are usually less effective than display ads, but they cost substantially less. While some firms only use display ads, there have been some remarkable stories of businesses getting strong results by using classified advertising. A small Montréal retail spa business runs a weekly classified ad advertising a hot tub for sale. The ad reads like an individual is selling a new hot tub that is still in the box—but the business is the one selling the tub. The firm keeps running the ad because it has been highly effective. Much like many forms of traditional advertising, newspaper and magazine advertising is being affected by the Internet. As more people use tablets and mobile devices to read newspapers and magazines, some businesses are questioning the value of print ads.

Radio.

Radio commercials are usually less costly than TV ads, but they offer the ability to tailor a message to a specific audience and are easy to produce. Radio advertising has declined in recent years as advertisers are spending their money on other forms of promotion.[28] The disadvantages of radio advertising are the presentation (audio only) and the short exposure.

Television.

SMEs usually advertise on TV by purchasing time to run commercials. Larger firms are now engaging in product placements, but the costs associated with these are often beyond new entrepreneurs. The advantage of commercials is they include sight and sound and can be aimed at a specific audience. The biggest downsides are the high costs and their short exposure. Former restaurant owner Jim MacAulay believes differently. MacAulay argues that too many small firms overestimate the cost of advertising on TV and underestimate the value. He notes that he spent less than $10,000 to advertise his restaurant, The True North Diner, throughout Atlantic Canada on TV. He saw a 30 percent increase in sales over the two months that the ads ran. MacAulay says the ads also resulted in strong sales after they stopped running. For his business, TV was much more effective than other forms of media.

Nontraditional Promotional Methods.

Nontraditional promotional methods can be defined as pursuing traditional business goals of sales and profits through non-conventional means. Nontraditional methods are usually low in cost, generate both exposure and sales, but may or may not be interactive with consumers. The two major types of nontraditional promotions are guerrilla marketing and public relations (PR).

Guerrilla Marketing.

Guerrilla marketing consists of entrepreneurs developing creative, catchy, and—most importantly—low-cost methods to attract attention to their business and to sell their products. For example, some companies have hired college students to stand in airports with signs sporting a company's web address to lure online visitors. Other companies stage contests, hire mascots, or arrange for special events, all of which draws attention to their business at very little cost. Shopify, discussed throughout this text, generates a great deal of business and buzz for itself by running Build-A-Business competitions. On a smaller scale, Indigenous entrepreneur Shara Wilson of **Finawear** ran a contest in the Spring of 2019 asking her customers—new and long-term—to take selfies wearing her clothing which feature authentic aboriginal art.[29] Consumers had to tag her for a chance to win prizes. Guerrilla marketer Calum McGuigan, the owner of Fervent Event mentioned earlier, says, "Guerrilla marketing is about being innovative and creative."[30] His firm has staged flash mobs, put on fake public weddings, handed out free samples, created sidewalk art, used murals, opened popup shops, and held parties to promote products and services. McGuigan says that guerrilla marketing shocks people out of their normal routine and leaves a lasting impression: "One day you walk to work and you see something peculiar like a tug-of-war, a flash mob, chalk art, a free sample, a Guinness world record attempt. etc. . . . you take a second and then perhaps a third look. You're intrigued, and hopefully it's left a positive emotional experience with you. Guerrilla marketing reaches smaller more concentrated groups than traditional methods, but leaves more memorable impressions."[31]

Social media has made guerrilla marketing even more effective. Social media offers businesses more opportunity to engage in online guerrilla marketing activities using a variety of options, ranging from user-generated content, online games, online contests, and so forth. Additionally, social media can be combined with more traditional guerrilla marketing campaigns to create a wider reach. After all, when people see an interesting flash mob, or a fake wedding, the first thing many onlookers do is to share pictures and posts with their social media contacts allowing businesses to reach a wider audience.

Two mistakes entrepreneurs often make with guerrilla marketing are to wrongly associate it with smaller enterprises or to question its effectiveness. This is simply not the case, as demonstrated by **lululemon**, one of the largest sports retailers in North America. To promote its high-end and high-cost yoga pants, the retailer has used a variety of brand promotions, including offering their brand ambassadors products to try, discounts to customers who shop in the nude (online), in-store yoga classes, and writing inspirational sayings on chalkboards to promote products.[32] Lululemon also relies heavily on the Internet and buzz from social media to promote its products.[33] Vancouver's Vega, a supplement manufacturer, clearly dispels any rumours that guerrilla marketing is ineffective. Vega sets up pop-up stores or booths in retail locations that carry their products and gives away free smoothie samples—the catch being that customers have to mix the smoothie themselves using a bicycle powered blender. The first time Vega tried the promotion, sales soared 700 percent in 10 days at the retail location.[34] Vega has done so well that its founder, Charlie Chang, recently sold the company for $550 million.[35]

Other examples of guerrilla marketing efforts include the following:

- Contests or raffles
- Artists hanging paintings or photographs in doctors' offices
- Sticky notes posted where people can see them
- Free samples
- Public demonstrations
- People wearing or using a company's product

Guerrilla marketing events, such as flash mobs, can shock people into taking a second look and leave a lasting impression.

wjarek/Shutterstock.com

Note that guerrilla marketing is different from stealth marketing (see **Small Business in Action 8-3** box). When companies engage in guerrilla marketing, consumers are generally aware of the company's intentions. Stealth marketing attempts to fool or mislead consumers into buying products. For example, in guerrilla marketing, a company may post something online or in a chat group and let users know the post came from a business or an individual representing a business. If the company was engaged in stealth marketing, it would post information online and pretend to be a regular consumer. The stealth marketer is hoping to mislead consumers into thinking a peer is recommending a product or service.

SMALL BUSINESS IN ACTION 8-3

STEALTH MARKETING VERSUS NONTRADITIONAL MARKETING—CAN YOU TELL THE DIFFERENCE?

In stealth marketing, companies undertake promotions to advertise to consumers without them being aware they are the object of a marketing plan. Stealth marketing often uses deception to convince consumers to buy products or to create awareness for a company. It is different from unconventional marketing (such as PR or guerrilla marketing) because the objectives of the company are often concealed from consumers. For example, CBC recently ran an exposé on the use of stealth marketing in Canada and discovered a marketing firm that hired people to set up fake social networking accounts on sites such as Facebook. The people would befriend others and then make products and service recommendations on behalf of clients. Given that people, especially young people, put a higher value on peer recommendations, the business was successful in promoting products and events throughout the country. Another common form of stealth marketing is

Some businesses have hired people to establish social networking accounts under false names to promote products or services. This is referred to as "stealth marketing" and, while not illegal, it is unethical.

Frui / Dreamstime.com

[continued]

[continued]

to post fake reviews on such sites as Yelp or TripAdvisor. Some business owners and/or managers will create false accounts, pose as customers, and draft favourable reviews about a product or service. Given that research has found that a slight increase in ratings can positively affect sales, the motives for entrepreneurs and managers are quite clear.

Yet the lines between stealth marketing and nontraditional marketing are becoming blurred. Using product placements and celebrity endorsements as examples, these activities are considered acceptable to some yet seen as unethical by others. People are increasingly unsure whether to classify marketing activities as nontraditional or stealth. For example, some alcohol and smartphone companies have hired attractive or popular people to use their products in public; businesses have urged online friends to support their company or products in online contests; and some videos on YouTube, while appearing to be shot by amateurs, are really professionally concealed product placements or endorsements.

So far, the Canadian government has not adopted any laws to regulate or eliminate stealth marketing. While some consumer groups are advocating for rules to protect consumers, others are stating that the lines between stealth marketing and nontraditional marketing have become so close that rules or laws would not work. Furthermore, companies that engage in stealth campaigns risk consumer backlash, which serves as its own deterrent.

Discussion Questions

1. Do you think stealth marketing is ethical? Should it be illegal?
2. Should government create laws to protect consumers from fake or misleading recommendations on Facebook, Yelp, and TripAdvisor? Would it be possible to enforce such a law?
3. From the examples above, do you think smart phone and alcohol companies that hire attractive or popular people to use their products are engaging in unethical behaviour? Why or why not?
4. Are companies such as Apple, which spend millions on product placements, engaging in stealth marketing? Do you think product placements are an acceptable form of advertising? Why or why not?
5. Would you use stealth marketing to help you sell a product or service? Why or why not?
6. How would you differentiate between stealth marketing and guerrilla marketing? Could you argue they are one and the same? Why or why not?

Public Relations (PR).

Public relations is defined as generating positive awareness of your company. PR is a highly effective form of promotion that has been used by large and small firms. Spin Master Toys, the third-largest North American toy company, shunned traditional advertising for years and instead concentrated on PR. PR offers the benefits of being free and is often viewed more favourably by consumers. Business author Pamela Bartlett argues that PR should be incorporated into every business plan because it increases credibility and sales. Bartlett says, "When a third party, such as the media, endorses a product or service, the company gains credibility. Consumers are much more likely to make a purchase based on third-party endorsement than an advertisement."[36] Unfortunately, many new and smaller firms do not engage in PR because they believe it costs a lot of money or is nothing more than having a newspaper story written about their grand opening. PR consultant Susan MacDonald disagrees that PR is only for large firms, noting that PR is a democratic process that rewards those who learn how the media works. She says firms that work hard and commit to the process can expect good results through PR.

Aspiring entrepreneurs should make PR a key component of their marketing and communication strategy. As cited above PR is free, provides credibility, and allows firms to engage with the public. Business owners should recognize that effective press releases follow a formula, much like the one presented by Mia Wedgbury, president of High Road Communications, a Toronto-based public relations agency, in an article in *The Globe and Mail*. Wedgbury states that there are four sacred rules to writing press releases:

- *Lead with your strength.* What do you want the press to read first? Remember this is not a promotional piece; you are alerting the media to something that their readers will find interesting. Do not waste time with fluff; rather, get to the point, and sell the story.

- *Answer the question "So what?"* Demonstrate to the media why there is a demand for your company, product, or service, and why their readers will be interested.
- *Let others do the talking.* Offer expert opinion, testimonials from customers, and so forth. This adds credibility.
- *Send it off with a pitch.* Use email to send it to reporters. Ensure that the message entices them to read the release.[37]

Examples of good public relations activities include the following:

- Develop a press kit. Many entrepreneurs wonder how their competitor always manages to be in the local paper and on TV. Chances are they have developed a press kit that consists of company information, pre-written stories, and pictures, which they have sent to reporters, editors, and so on.
- Write articles for a newspaper, newsletter, or community guide.
- Write letters to the editor.
- Participate in discussions either online or through traditional mediums.
- Host events.
- Offer services as a guest speaker.

Digital or Internet Marketing.

The Internet or the use of digital marketing offers small and new businesses a cost-efficient method of reaching customers anywhere in the world. Much has been made in the press about using the Internet as a central point of all marketing activities because it allows entrepreneurs to present consumers with a significant amount of information at lower cost than traditional methods. Additionally, and perhaps more importantly, digital marketing, enables companies to reach out to consumers and engage in interactive conversations with them using a variety of tools, including websites, social networks, and mobile applications. Various digital and social media options are presented below. An entrepreneur can use as few or as many that will work to build relationships with customers. Discover how to organize your online marketing in **Small Business Beginnings 8-2** later in this chapter.

Company Web Pages.

As previously noted, websites enable companies to post a great deal of information on the Internet for pennies, enable interactive communication between firms and consumers, allow for direct sales of products to customers, assist in procuring supplies, and so forth. Excellent websites are fast, facilitate communication with visitors, contain all essential information that customers are looking for, are easy to navigate, and have a domain name that is easy to remember. Unfortunately, having a website is not enough; for a website to assist your business, it has to get visitors—one way to do this is to register with search engines and build a search-friendly site.

In developing a website, an entrepreneur needs to remember that a website is a communication vehicle and should address the following questions: Who is the audience? What are the objectives for the site? What do you want consumers to do on visiting the site? Is the website an integral part of the venture's total communication program? In addressing these questions, the entrepreneur needs to structure the website and organize the information to effectively engage the target market. This requires that the material be fresh, with new material added on a regular basis. The material should be interactive to engage the individual. And, of course, the website needs to be known and as visible as possible. As such, business and owners and managers will also want to ensure that their website works well with mobile devices. Mobile devices are quickly becoming the preferred device for consumers to access the Internet. *Globe and Mail* business columnist Marie Chevrier writes, "We're collectively addicted to mobile and its something that marketers should recognize and prioritize." Chevrier points out that U.S. consumers spend more time on their mobile phones than on PCs.[38]

Any business with a website must ensure it works well on mobile devices. Consumers are now using mobile devices more than PCs to access the Internet.

scyther5/Shutterstock.com

SMALL BUSINESS IN ACTION 8-4

DRAGONS' DEN EFFECT

One of the best forms of PR is to get your product or service on TV. Whether it is being on the nightly news, serving as an expert on a televised panel, or just having your company in the background of a story, these can often cause sales and public awareness of your company to rise. In the U.S. the gold standard for companies was to get on the *Oprah Winfrey* show. Entrepreneurs knew having their business featured on *Oprah* would increase sales and customer awareness. Some entrepreneurs like Brian Scudamore, founder of 1-800-GotJunk?, actually made appearing on *Oprah* a key goal for his company, a measure if he was successful, and something to springboard expansion plans. Scudamore did eventually land a spot on *Oprah,* and shortly after the episode aired, the firm received 3000 calls from customers—up 300 percent from the usual—and 500 franchise inquiries.

In Canada, the equivalent of the Oprah show is CBC's hit series *Dragons' Den.* As discussed in several chapters in this book, *Dragons' Den* has entrepreneurs pitch their business to a group of angel investors called Dragons. Successful bidders can leave with an investment in their business, while unsuccessful entrepreneurs leave empty-handed and occasionally have their business skills degraded by the investment panel. Occasionally, entrepreneurs are criticized so much that viewers may wonder why people would want to appear on the show, as it is not unusual for some Dragons to refer to entrepreneurs as crazy or insane.

Yet the entrepreneurs who get on the show are far from crazy. While many pitchers are no doubt interested in the investment money from the Dragons, the PR benefits even from a rejected pitch can be significant. In fact, the positive boost in sales and awareness companies experience after being on the show has been given an official reference by CBC—"The *Dragons' Den* Effect." For example, when **Saxx Underwear** founder Trent Kitsch appeared on *Dragons' Den,* he didn't leave with a deal; but the next day his company's online sales soared from the usual $1000 to roughly $35,000. Kitsch says every entrepreneur should aspire to be on the show not only for the potential investment but also for the publicity; an opportunity for your business to be seen by millions. Another entrepreneur, Zane Caplansky appeared on the show looking to get money to franchise his food truck concept, **Caplansky's Delicatessen**, which featured what he claimed were the best smoked-meat sandwiches in Toronto. While the Dragons enjoyed his product, they did not think his business was worth an investment, and one Dragon in particular, Kevin O'Leary, started calling Caplansky "Insane Zane." The result of his rejection on air was a 50 percent rise in sales a month after the show aired. Other failed pitches report strong results as well, including the **Stilt Guys**, performers . . . on stilts. While the company was unsuccessful in raising any money, the owners note that even their brief appearance on the show led to other PR opportunities that helped them expand the business: "Despite being on air for only a minute, we were able to make a big impression. Local media has loved talking to us and finding out what the experience was like. Considering most TV ads are only 30 seconds, having a full minute on one of Canada's most watched national TV shows is like winning a huge advertising grand prize!"

Emily Rudow recently drafted an article describing the impact of her *Dragons' Den* experience. Rudow pitched **Oneiric Hockey**, specialized hockey underpants that enable children to dress quickly, notes that pitching on the Den had significant impact on the business. She say web traffic surged the year of the pitch and was up 927 percent year over year. Furthermore, 38 percent of the traffic occurred the week the pitch aired and through the subsequent two weeks. Revenue also increased, with 71 percent of online orders coming from the time of the pitch on November 16 through December 31. She says being on the Den also increased the company's credibility with consumers and dealers as the pitch was watched two million times. Tournament and direct sales have gone up 50 percent since the show aired.

The most successful example of the "*Dragons' Den* Effect" goes to Holy Crap cereal. After appearing on the show, company co-founder Brian Mullins was hoping to see annual sales increase to $600,000 a year. Instead sales skyrocketed to over $5 million.

What accounts for such strong results? The show is number one in Canada and two in five Canadians watched an episode this past year. Faythe Pal, chair of the Canadian Institute of Marketing and CEO of **Hands of Time, Inc.**, a Toronto-based management corporation, says it is a coup to appear on the show: "All of that exposure, all of the commercial lead-ups, all of the promotional marketing. Even if you don't win, to get that full engagement where your products can then be sold on [the CBC] website, and your story can continue being told. It's amazing."

Discussion Questions

1. What are the advantages and disadvantages of appearing on *Dragons' Den*?
2. Many entrepreneurs appear to be quite upset by some of the Dragons' comments about their businesses and ideas. Do you think the potential of being called insane on national TV is worth the PR for a company?
3. If you had a business, would you try to get on *Dragons' Den*? Why or why not?
4. Many of the so-called successful bidders do not end up receiving any financing support from the Dragons after the show has aired. Given this information, are you more or less likely to recommend the show to an aspiring entrepreneur? If the Dragons agree to invest in a concept on the air, should they not have to honour their statements? Why or why not?

Search Engine Optimization (SEO).

When consumers use Google, Bing, or Yahoo! to search for a company, a product, or a service, businesses want to ensure their firm not only comes up in the search results but is featured prominently on the list. Evidence indicates that firms that appear frequently and higher up in search lists have more visitors to their web pages. SEO attempts to create websites that result in more frequent and higher ratings. While this is not an exact science, entrepreneurs will want to build a site that has clear title tags, has content pages that use words that relate to the purpose of the site, has clear document links, and has many pages. They also need to update the site frequently.

Additionally, SEO experts recommend business owners consider the following recommendations to achieve better search results:

- Use words customers actually use to describe their service.
- Avoid changing a website's address, as Google search has a tendency to favour older sites.
- Increase the number of external links, as these strongly influence Google algorithms.

Embrace social networking by providing clear links to the business' social media sites. In general search engines favour websites that are shared, liked, or discussed more frequently.

Pay-Per-Click Advertising (PPC).

Pay-per-click (PPC) advertising allows firms to bid on key words or phrases relevant to their target market. When a consumer enters the phrase or word in the search engine, the company will appear under the results section, and their ads will appear on the side of the viewer's screen. Common PPC advertisers are Google AdWords, Yahoo! Search Marketing, and Microsoft adCenter. **Prollenium Medical Technologies**, a manufacturer of cosmetics based in Aurora, Ontario, serves as a successful example of PPC advertising. The company purchased specific search terms through Google AdWorks and Yahoo! for $2000 per month, which have resulted in an increase from 1000 to 50,000 monthly visitors. The company now attributes 90 percent of company sales to PPC advertising. The other popular form of PPC advertising is having companies place ads on websites that they pay for only when their ad is clicked.[39]

Online Newsletter.

Online newsletters can be created as standalone websites or be sent to customers via email. Since the newsletters are almost always permission based, containing material your customers are interested in, they can build and strengthen relationships with customers and drive traffic to your website at a very low fee.

Direct Email to Customers.

Email marketing is just direct marketing to customers via the Internet. Since the Internet is used to communicate with customers, businesses can send a great deal more information compared with traditional direct mail at a substantially reduced cost. Email has an almost unlimited number of uses and can be used to welcome customers, to encourage people to visit your website or make a purchase, to provide additional information, or to send videos, blogs, newsletters, and podcasts. Emails can also be used to supplement other forms of marketing, and research indicates that including email as part of a direct mail campaign increases response rates by 40 percent; when used in conjunction with telemarketing the response rate jumps by 76 percent. Note that email marketing is not spam, a practice in which companies send out emails to random lists of people; rather it is permission-based marketing. For example, Milk Handmade, a women's clothing shop which specializes in ethically produced goods from independent designers, recently engaged in a successful email campaign. The campaign targeted current customers with the title Secret Sale, whereas customers could come to the store and take an additional 50 percent off anything on the sales rack. The campaign resulted in a 43 percent open rate, a ten percent click through rate and $1000 in sales in only three days.[40]

Banner Advertisements.

Banner ads were one of the first forms of Internet marketing. Banner ads are placed on websites (for a fee) in an attempt to attract visitors to a website, purchase a product, or solicit further information. Banner ads can be advantageous because they allow entrepreneurs to target customers, but they may or may not be cost effective, depending on their placement. The key to using banner ads is to place them on sites that are appropriate to your target audience, have attractive ads that are visually appealing, and offer consumers some benefit by clicking on the advertisement.

Affiliate Programs.

Affiliate programs are online partnerships where one company posts links to your website if you do the same in turn. Affiliate programs are attractive to entrepreneurs because of their low cost and ability to target a specific audience.

Online Classified Advertising Sites.

Kijiji, Facebook Marketplace, and Craigslist all allow users, including businesses, to post online classified ads. Kijiji, the most popular of the three in Canada, is the country's 13th most visited site.[41] Kijiji allows companies to post individual classified advertisements and banner ads that appear at the top of a user's computer screen. Facebook Marketplace has only recently started to allow businesses to post classified ads on their site. The Marketplace allows users to interact with people and firms selling products and services as they visit the social media site. While relatively new, Facebook Marketplace already has over 800,000 users and a number of small business owners are successful using the site to sell products and services.[42] For example, Chris Neville, who owns a landscaping and real estate business in Nova Scotia, states, "Facebook Marketplace is quickly starting to rival Kijiji got my most effective form of advertising. Both sites are excellent and superior to other forms of marketing in costs and quality of the business they generate. While I still use other forms of marketing such as Facebook posts and other forms of social media, most calls for our services and/or apartments come from Marketplace and Kijiji."[43]

Online Auction Sites.

A number of online auction sites allow businesses and consumers to sell items in an auction format. Generally, individuals or companies post items for sale and take bids on their products or services. eBay is the best known of all these sites and one of the most commonly visited sites in the world. eBay allows users to sell items in online auctions or operate online eBay stores. Many small businesses are attracted to the site for its global reach, ease of use, and custom features. For example, Quebec couple Yossef Vidal and his wife Shoshana have been selling watches, handbags, and jewellery on eBay since 2013. They recently celebrated surpassing $10 million in total sales and have three full-time employees working for their eBay store **WatchVendor**.[44] Similarly, immigrant Virendra Rajawat, who moved from India to Toronto, is running a thriving eBay business, **Sonatona**. Rajawat imports gemstones from India and sells them on eBay, generating annual sales in the $250,000 US range. He says being honest and taking professional photos are some of his secrets to success. Rajawat, who sells to customers in America, Germany, United Kingdom, and France, says eBay has enabled him to pay for his children to go to university and for him to earn a living.[45] Every year eBay celebrates the achievements of successful Canadian entrepreneurs with eBay awards. The 2017 winner, Vasilios Sakellaropoulos, operates an online office supply store, **universaldatasupplies**, through eBay; he specializes in laser toner, which brings annual sales in excess of $1 million.[46]

Gamification.

Gamification is applying the concepts and application of game thinking to affect behaviour. Simple gamification concepts include having consumers collect points, badges, or other incentives. Common examples of gamification on websites and mobile applications include providing rewards for people or players who accomplish certain tasks, establishing levels of participation and enabling consumers to track their progress through various levels, providing virtual currency or coupons, adding elements of competition to a website, and so forth. For example, Cheryl Ng's company FouFou Brands, a Canadian retailer of high-end pet products, used numerous gamification features on her website when she first started her business in 2005. FouFou Brand web visitors could play games on the site, including trying to move a dog through a maze, and collect various rewards.[47] This fun offering helped build her following and she has successfully rebuilt her website. Other examples include consumer feedback sites that rank the users' level of participation; users are urged to provide additional feedback or participate more to unlock the next level. Sometimes, unlocking levels comes with awards, and in other cases, the achievement itself is the award.

Online Games.

In addition to adding gamification elements to websites and apps, many companies are delivering promotional messages during game play or sponsoring games as a way to communicate with consumers. These can take the form of virtual product placements, online scavenger hunts, and so forth.

Podcasts.

Podcasts are audio or video clips that can be downloaded on a mobile, such as a smartphone or a tablet. The keys to creating a good podcast include getting to your point quickly, creating something entertaining, and using conversational language. Podcasts are not just for reaching young consumers either; in fact, research indicates that podcasts influence business-to-business purchase decisions as well. As one buyer noted, "It's nice sometimes just to listen to the information." Podcasts can result in increased web traffic, better relationships with listeners, and in increase in sales. Research indicates that 63 percent of podcast listeners will purchase products featured in podcasts.[48]

Webinars.

Webinars have been described by entrepreneurs as the best sales tool to come along since the advent of the Internet. Webinars are web-based seminars where you can engage in a full sales pitch with customers regardless of their location. One Nova Scotia entrepreneur stated that it is like a conference call on steroids. Sales staff can use the full interactivity of the web to sell clients on the wonders of their products but at a low cost.

Social Networking.

In addition to the Internet marketing methods mentioned above, businesses are increasingly using social networking to promote their businesses with consumers. Social networking sites are online communities where people can meet new people, talk to current friends, and build their networks. Businesses are using social networking sites to talk to customers, create online communities, promote and sell products and services, and learn more about consumers and competitors. Popular social networking sites include Facebook, LinkedIn, Twitter, Snapchat, Pinterest, Instagram, Youtube, and Tinder.

Facebook.

Facebook is the third-most–visited site in Canada and globally has over 2.23 billion active users, more than 66 percent of whom visit the site daily.[49] Facebook allows companies to create targeted ads, profiles, distribute information, such as product details or coupons, share pictures and videos, and encourage people to engage in online discussions. Most small and large businesses use Facebook to share information, pictures, and sales with consumers.[50] For example, the **Stratford Festival** successfully used Facebook to post a one-day coupon aimed at increasing ticket sales from new and lapsed patrons. The end result of the campaign was an increase of three times the tickets sold. Aaron George, the company's social media coordinator, had this to say about the use of Facebook: "Using Facebook as a media tool has definitely been beneficial for us. It's given us the reach of television with the targeting capabilities of a direct mail campaign. It allows us to target lapsed patrons or reach those who came to a performance a few years ago, and gave us a great return on ad spend. Facebook Ads have helped us strengthen our digital brand presence, increase ticket sales and cultivate new audiences."[51]

Terre Bleu Lavender Farm used Facebook to double its visitors and triple its annual sales.

Ingram Publishing/SuperStock

Facebook's targeted advertising is highly effective as it creates groups of people who have similar interests and buying behaviour based on their social conversations and web browsing history. Companies can purchase this information from Facebook and use it to create targeted advertising. For example, **Terre Bleu Lavender Farm**, located in Milton, Ontario, doubled its number of visitors and tripled sales year over year using Facebook-page-like ads, along with an increase in posts to its Facebook page.

Facebook is also engaged in a significant effort to expand its abilities to help companies connect with consumers. The company is investing heavily in its search function, Facebook Search, which allows users to find information that was posted on the social network. So consumers who are looking for a bakery in their neighbourhood may search Facebook instead of using Google. Facebook says that its search is a semantic search engine—meaning it will give you results related to the context of your search terms.

In addition, Facebook has launched Instant Articles, an online product that allows companies to create graphically pleasing and content-rich articles and videos in a short time. Companies can then distribute the articles using a variety of social media channels.

The use of Facebook, along with other social media sites, is really limited only by the creativity of the entrepreneur. For example, Marie Chevrier of Toronto founded **Sampler**, an online company that assists businesses in using Facebook to distribute product samples. Chevrier states that the old way of providing samples by handing them out at public events is ineffective as firms may not reach their target market and they could have difficulty tracking results.[52] Her solution was to create an app that can be installed on Facebook fan pages and that allows people to request samples or share samples with their friends. The result is that samples are aimed more directly at people in the target market and its easier to track results.[53]

LinkedIn.

LinkedIn has been described as Facebook for professionals. The social networking site currently has 120 million members, whose profiles appear online very much like a résumé. Members can network with one another, join specific groups, and communicate. Businesses have been using LinkedIn to recruit employees, to find out information about potential clients, to share information about their business, and to strengthen relationships through communication.[54] For example, ClubRunner, a sports-management software business based in Oakville and one of the fastest-growing companies in Canada, used LinkedIn to target potential customers. The company provided interesting content on software management to readers on their LinkedIn page and asked readers to review the company's brand online. The result of the campaign was a 40 percent increase in sales leads.[55]

Twitter/Online Blogs.

Blogs are websites where people can express their opinion on any issue they want to. Twitter and Tumblr are two of the most popular sites in Canada, but others exist as well. Twitter limits people to messages or tweets of 140 characters and is frequently in the top 10 monthly visited websites by Canadians. Tumblr, like Twitter, allows people to express opinions but does not limit what people can say. Many small businesses are using Twitter and Tumblr to post information about their business including sales promotions, to answer questions from consumers, and to attract people to their firm's websites and network.[56] For example, Alan Smithson co-founder of SmithsonMartin Inc., a company that made software and hardware for professional DJs, stated that he used Twitter to start conversations with potential clients and to create online friendships with customers.[57] Social media consultant Ross Simmonds urges business owners to start conversations with key customers and stakeholders on Twitter. He states that people with Twitter accounts are more likely to read posts about them and directly answer their Twitter messages.

Some businesses are also blogging but doing so from their company webpage or using blogging software. These blogs have a tendency to be longer and offer more information than on Twitter and Tumblr. Jim Estill, former CEO of SYYNEX Canada and current CEO of **Danby**, both located in Ontario, says **blogging** allows him to stay in touch with key stakeholders.[58] Michael Jagger, president of Vancouver-based **Provident Security and Event Management Corp.**, dedicates a set number of hours a week to his blog and notes that it is part of the company's overall marketing strategy. Jagger thinks blogging leads to closer ties with current customers and generates new sales.[59] The advantages of blogging include the low costs, the ability to reach wide audiences, and the chance to reach customers on a personal level.

Snapchat.

Snapchat is a relatively new form of social networking where participants chat in real time on their mobile devices. Snapchat, which has 188 million active users, allows people to share pictures and other content, comment on others' posts, and so on. While Snapchat is only the seventh-most–popular social media site in Canada, 90 percent of users are between the ages of 13 and 24 and almost all users are under the age of 34. Business owners can use Snapchat ads to promote their business, post pictures of products, offer incentives, as well as create online contests and storyboards. Snapchat is also an ideal way for businesses to communicate with the public. Given the demographics of Snapchat users, the social network is ideal for businesses who want to reach young, mobile consumers.[60]

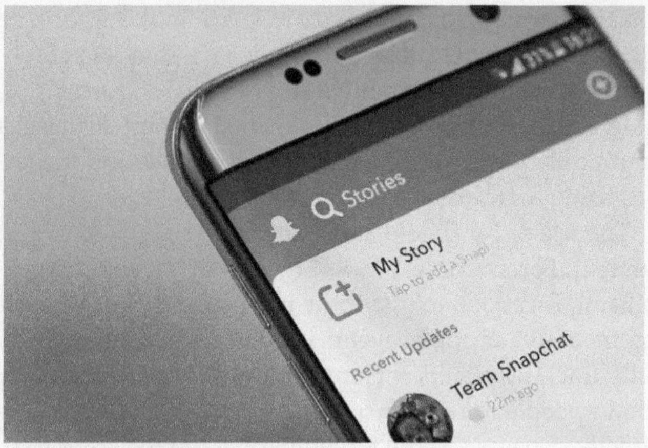

Snapchat is a relatively new marketing tool for businesses. Experts anticipate its use will spread, especially among companies who wish to target young, on-the-go consumers.

Photo 94992879 © Dimarik16 - Dreamstime.com

Photo-Sharing Sites (Instagram, Pinterest).

A number of photo-sharing sites allow users to post and share photos with their friends online. The most popular is Instagram with over 1.1 billion monthly users, of which 500 million log on daily. Instagram users tend to be younger, with 71 percent of users under the age of 35; these consumers are willing to following brands (60 percent) and purchase products or services they discovered on the site (30 percent).[61] Instagram is also home to influencers who, as discussed below can have significant impact on your business. Small business owners who want to use Instagram should create a business profile in order to access the free analytics, which will help them understand who is visiting their site. When posting content on Instagram business owners can post pictures and videos, create stories, generate advertisements, make use of hashtags, run contests, and work with influencers.

Pinterest is the fifth-most–visited social media site in Canada. Users can save pictures and videos called *pins* to their personal bulletin boards called *pinboards.* Pinterest is especially popular among women aged 25 to 54 who Pinterest refers to as "Deciders" because they control roughly 80 percent of household spending. Pinterest users also tend to come from households with higher income and higher education, and most users will use Pinterest to aid in making purchase decisions. Pinterest is particularly important to women as they plan for moments in their lives like weddings, vacations, parties, and meals.[62] Small business owners can use Pinterest to promote products and services, engage with users, run contests and offer incentives.[63]

Video-Sharing Sites (YouTube).

YouTube enables companies to share videos with millions of daily visitors. The site, which is the second most visited site in Canada, allows participants to load video clips onto the sites and display them for the public to see.[64] Business and individuals can also create their own YouTube channel to build a loyal following. The videos can act as mini-commercials for products or services, be infomercials, attract prospective employees, or serve as a means to generate PR for a company. Entrepreneurs who want to use YouTube should ensure that their movies appeal to their target markets, are unique, run no longer than five minutes, and have a trailer with the video that provides a link to the company's website. For example, the worldwide Free Hugs campaign has relied on YouTube to promote its initiative throughout Canadian cities. Jim McElgunn, a small business writer, offers entrepreneurs the following advice when creating video material: "Videos should be short, get to the important material in the first 15 seconds, encourage return visits by offering a variety of videos, engage and communicate with viewers."[65]

YouTube also provides advertising, including TrueView ads (better known as skippable ads), non-skippable ads, and bumper ads. The benefits of TrueView ads are they are relatively inexpensive to purchase and rarely watched by uninterested viewers given they can be skipped after five seconds. Businesses only pay for ads that play for 30 seconds or longer and when the consumer has engaged in a follow-up like a click on a link. Non-skippable ads run at the start of videos or during video play. Non-skippable ads work best when the content appeals to the viewer of the video. Bumper ads only last six seconds and appear at the end of the video the viewer is watching. Bumper ads are relatively inexpensive, as the business placing the ad will only pay when the viewer clicks through to the provided web link and the ads have a wide reach.[66]

Dating Apps and Mobile Marketing.

Tinderand other dating apps represent a new type of social media. Tinder allows for location-drive interaction among users who can first acknowledge one another and subsequently chat online. Companies are just starting to use dating apps as part of their promotional strategy. But given the young user base and the location-centric theme of the interactions, as well as the ability to engage in targeted advertising and communicate with consumers, entrepreneurs can expect to see the use of Tinder accounts and Tinder advertising to grow. To date, business has used Tinder for advertising, to offer promotional pricing including coupons, for contests, and to engage with users.

SMALL BUSINESS BEGINNINGS 8-2

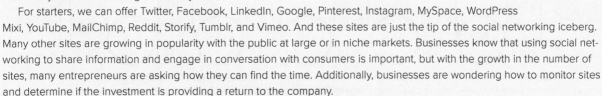

SOCIAL MEDIA DASHBOARDS

How many social networking sites can you name?

For starters, we can offer Twitter, Facebook, LinkedIn, Google, Pinterest, Instagram, MySpace, WordPress Mixi, YouTube, MailChimp, Reddit, Storify, Tumblr, and Vimeo. And these sites are just the tip of the social networking iceberg. Many other sites are growing in popularity with the public at large or in niche markets. Businesses know that using social networking to share information and engage in conversation with consumers is important, but with the growth in the number of sites, many entrepreneurs are asking how they can find the time. Additionally, businesses are wondering how to monitor sites and determine if the investment is providing a return to the company.

Ryan Holmes of Vancouver, B.C., founded **HootSuite.com** in 2008 with the idea that marketers and/or entrepreneurs should be able to manage multiple social media campaigns from one central website. HootSuite.com allows companies to send messages to a variety of social media sites, including all those mentioned above, and to an additional 24 social networking sites, all from one online dashboard. Using HootSuite, small and large companies can type information into one central location and have it distributed throughout their social networks. HootSuite can also provide businesses with analytics about who is viewing their message and reactions to their information from consumers and help companies understand the value of their investment in social networking. Holmes, whose company was recently valued at $750 million, has more than 16 million business users, including 800 of the Fortune 1000 (America's largest companies), the White House, and the Prime Minister's Office.

Mobile marketing is the use of mobile devices to communicate marketing messages. Smart entrepreneurs should recognize that mobile devices, such as smartphones, tablets, watches, and other wearables, are rapidly replacing traditional computers as access points for Internet uses such as email, online searches, web browsing, social media, video, and so forth (**Figure 8-3**). Consider these facts: 73 percent of people always have their mobile device with them; people pick up their mobile device 150 to 200 times a day; and customers, particularly young customers, are spending more than two hours a day on mobile devices.[67] Business owners must create web pages with the mobile user in mind to ensure effective marketing and communication with customers.

- *Apps or applications:* Companies are now creating apps, or applications, for use on smartphones. Research indicates that consumers spent more time using apps in 2018 then they did watching traditional TV, and Google has recently made changes to its search product to allow for the searching of apps.[68] Entrepreneurs can use apps to build businesses, engage consumers, and provide services and content, as illustrated in **Small Business in Action 8-5**. Sometimes the apps can simply be used to distribute meaningful content, such as the Tim Hortons app, which helps users find the nearest Tim Hortons location and engages consumers with the products or services. Entrepreneurs can also use apps as the sole basis for their business. For example, Checkout 51, a Canadian coupon app founded by Noah Godfrey, Pema Hegan and Andrew McGrath, provided consumers with a list of deals or coupons for products that changes frequently. Consumers can purchase these products at any retailer that they want and simply take a picture of the receipt. Consumers then use the app to submit a picture of the receipt and maintain an online bank account of savings. When the amount reaches $20, they are sent a cheque.[69]

FIGURE 8-3 **Mobile Device Use Is Skyrocketing**

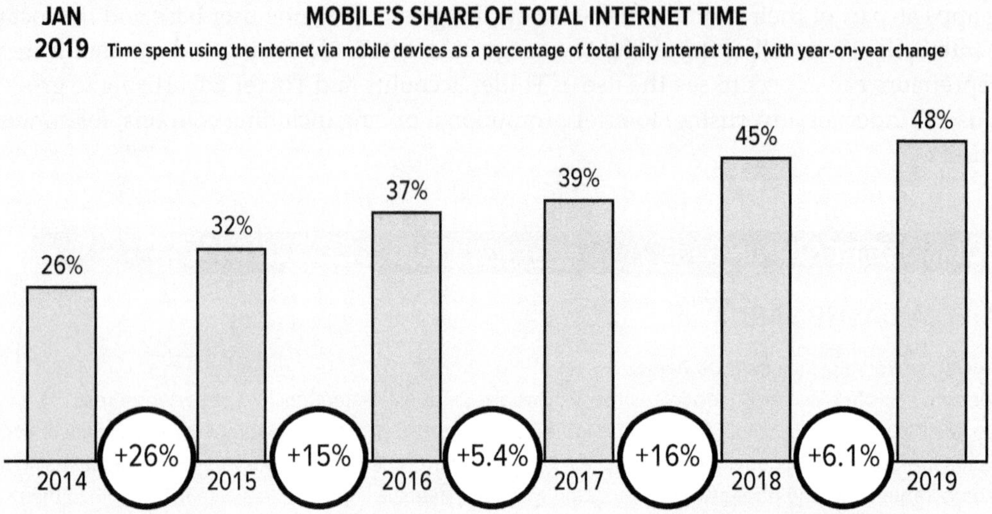

Source: Figure: Jan 2019 – Mobile's Share of Total Internet Time, from: Hootsuite & We Are Social (2019), "Digital 2019 Global Digital Overview," retrieved from **https://datareportal.com/reports/digital-2019-global-digital-overview**. Used by permission of DataReportal

- *Text/SMS messages & MMS:* Many companies use short message services and smartphones to send quick text messages to potential customers. For example, at the 2011 World Beach Volleyball Championship in Halifax, several sponsors used text messages to alert people about drink specials and opportunities to win prizes. As text messages are normally read within four minutes of receipt, customers are likely to receive them and respond. Many companies are going beyond words and using multimedia marketing services (MMS) to also send consumers images, video, and audio. Businesses can use SMS or MMS to send coupons, to engage in discussions with customers, to provide customers with incentives or just valuable information to further build their brand. Firms will often first provide customers with an incentive to opt into receiving texts and then send them follow-up information. In a World Beach Volleyball Championship example, people where urged to send a message to Volleyball to receive updated scores and one drink coupon. Sponsors then used text to market other products, promote their companies websites, and build their brands.
- *QR codes:* These are block bar codes that link print and other forms of media advertising to websites using a mobile device, which scans and reads the code. Some retail store owners have been posting QR codes near the entrance of their store to attract people in by offering coupons, information on popular products, and pictures or videos.
- *Proximity/location-based marketing:* Software can now allow companies to send out real-time advertising and communication to potential customers when they are in close proximity to a business. For example, a restaurant located on Sainte-Catherine Street in Montréal can send out ads, menus, and/or coupons to potential customers walking in the area, via their mobile device. Twitter has recently announced that it will be able to support location-based advertisements or tweets. **Kiehls**, a retail skin care company operating in North America, recently engaged in a very successful proximity based mobile marketing campaign. The retailer first encouraged consumers to opt into receiving SMS and MMS messages containing information on sales and products from the firm and then sent them up to three messages a month based on their proximity to the stores. Kiehls reported that 73 percent of customers who signed up to receive messages made a purchase as a result of the campaign.[70]

- *Voice search:* While paid search dominates digital advertising for firms, the rapid growth of mobile devices may lead to a decline in industry. Unlike video and social media use, which is similar on mobile devices and traditional computers, some elements of search do not work as well on mobile devices. As a result, voice search using Apple's Siri or Microsoft's Cortana are becoming increasingly common. Entrepreneurs will want to tailor their websites with this in mind. For example, it is recommended that websites now directly answer key questions such as who, what, where, and why about firms so they work better with voice.

Content Marketing.

Content marketing is the use of marketing to create valuable and relevant content such as blogs, newsletters, videos, and so forth, to acquire or retain customers. Companies that engage in content marketing are hoping to enhance their brand with consumers and ultimately become a valuable resource. The end result is their sales will improve as consumers view the company as a source of helpful, relevant, or entertaining information. Strong content marketing campaigns have been used to improve brand awareness, increase traffic to a website, increase the number of registered users for a website, and create sales. **Mint**, an online retailer of financial planning products, is an example of a firm that enjoyed great success with content marketing. The company started not by selling products but by offering readers content on money management, budgeting, and so forth. Given the target audience was young professionals, articles such as "Cheap Dates" and "How-To Guide: Paying for College" were attractive to the demographic. After building a following, the online company was then able to introduce products to their already loyal visitors. The strategy was so successful that Intuit eventually bought Mint for $170 million.[71] **Corinna vanGerwen**'s gift wrapping company also uses content marketing for her independently owned and operated firm, which specializes in creating a lasting impression with gift wrap. She notes that she has spent no money on marketing; rather, she is on Pinterest, Twitter, and LinkedIn, and publishes a newsletter in which she offers consumers valuable information on gift wrapping.[72]

For 2019, the latest trends in content marketing include a focus on quality versus quantity—businesses both large and small are recognizing that quality content is better than nonstop content. To attract visitors to company web pages and social media feeds, the key is to have quality material that is valuable. The emergence of separate, content-only pages means that more and more companies are creating separate content-only sites that offer visitors a rich information resource. Although the sites support the brand, they will not ask for direct sales. Finally, an increased emphasis on engagement and communication will see content marketers not only looking to provide information but also to communicate and engage visitors. Marketers will view and respond to reader reactions, comments, ratings, and so forth.

Social Media Influencer Marketing.

Influencer marketing is the use of social media influencers to sell a product or service. Influencers are people who have the ability impact the purchasing decisions of their followers because the influencer is perceived to be knowledgeable and/or important. Originally influencers were limited to celebrities—local, national or global—and, prior to social media, the extent of influencer involvement tended to be capturing them using a product in public. However, with the increased use of social media, the impact of online influencers has become instrumental to the marketing of many companies both large and small.[73]

Online influencers often appeal to a specific niche, have significant impact on their followers, and can be effective in marketing a business. **Intrepid Travel** offers one such example. When Intrepid began offering vegan tours, they worked with vegan influencers to promote their new products. Influencers posted pictures to Instagram, tweeted, and generally shared information about the tours to their followers, who often purchased tours and/or shared information about the tours with their like-minded social networks. Alyssa Kerbel, CEO of the Toronto-based organic made in Canada children's clothing store **Mini Mioche**, says when influential photographer Jeff Mindell posted a picture of his son wearing one of her company's hats, the item quickly sold out of stock.[74]

While small business owners likely cannot hire Kylie Jenner, who makes $1 million per sponsored Instagram post, there are 500,000 known active influencers from whom they can choose.[75] Many business advisors note that smaller influencers, who tend to be less expensive, are often ideal to work with as they tend to actively engage and form stronger relationships with their followers leading to greater influence. For example, **AnthroDesk**, a small standing desk business in Etobicoke, uses micro-influencers (between 1,000 and 50,000 followers) to write blog posts about their desks. Rather than pay the influencers, the company provides them with free desks as a reward for working with their followers.[76] Kamaj Silva, used influencers to grow his Mississauga-based monthly sneaker club company, **Sneakertub**. Silva didn't pay influencers. Instead, he gave them free sneakers, which led to some of the influencers sharing information about his company with their followers.[77] Entrepreneurs looking to work with micro-influencers can use such sites as **Tinysponsor**, who help firms source, create, and price influencer marketing campaigns. For those who are unsure about the impact of influencer marketing, a recent Neilson study found that influencer marketing generates 11 times greater return on investment (ROI) then traditional marketing, and 70 percent of millennials make purchases based on recommendations from peers.[78]

SMALL BUSINESS IN ACTION 8-5

SOCIAL MEDIA GUERRILLA MARKETING: TURNING SUCCESSFUL EXAMPLES INTO SMALL BUSINESS SOLUTIONS

As discussed in the text, both large and small businesses are using guerrilla marketing to boost sales and create awareness for businesses. Some of the most compelling examples in recent years include Jagermeister's undercover party campaign. The company used its Snapchat account to send out clues to the company's subscribers to an event it was holding and the campaign went viral. People were checking their phones, chatting about the possible location of the party, and who could potentially be attending. Jagermeister, an early adopter of Snapchat, says the app appeals to the company as its users tend to be young, and they often access the app while out at a bar.

Companies are combining social media and guerrilla marketing to produce innovative marketing campaigns.

Photo 151779327 © Motortion - Dreamstime.com

Candy bar maker, Modelez, also created a popular Snapchat contest where you had to take a picture of a candy bar and then draw on it using Snapchat draw. The company then created a micro website to highlight the best artwork, bringing more attention to the campaign.

Another guerrilla marketing example comes from the marketing team for the film Ex Machina. The marketers opted to use Tinder to market their film at a local music festival. The marketers inserted a picture of an attractive woman and, when people swiped right, they were asked a series of questions eventually leading to a video promoting the film. Domino's is a frequent Tinder user, especially around Valentine's Day when the company featured a photo of an attractive pizza. If people swiped right, they received a coupon code.

Discussion Questions

1. Think about the current university or college you are attending. What would be some of the potential advantages and disadvantages of the institution using a guerrilla marketing campaign?
2. Create a list of potential social media guerrilla marketing ideas for your university or college. Select what you think would be the best idea and describe it fully. Who will be your target market for your marketing campaign? What app will you use? Why? What will the promotion look like? How can you track results?
3. Small businesses can often look to see what is working for large firms and copy some of their concepts/ideas. Thinking about a small bar, a new summer hockey camp, and an independent clothing store, list five to seven potential social media guerrilla marketing ideas for each. Select one of the three businesses and what you think would be the best idea, then describe it fully. Who will be your target market for your campaign? What app will you use? Why? What will the promotion look like? How can you track results?

LEARNING OBJECTIVES SUMMARY

LO1 A key element in the marketing plan is establishing the correct marketing mix. A good marketing mix will create value and long-term relationships with target customers and distinguish a business from its competitors.

LO2 Product development involves idea generation, product testing, and ultimately, if successful, commercialization.

LO3 Consumer marketing involves less detail and a shorter buying cycle compared with business marketing.

LO4 The three methods of setting price are cost-based, demand-based, and competition-based pricing.

LO5 Within a marketing plan, businesses usually have a promotional plan that includes objectives, information about target markets and an understanding of their needs, a theme, strategies and tools, messages, budgets, the timing of implementation, and a method of evaluation.

LO6 There are a variety of ways to provide information about a product or service: advertising, sales promotion, personal selling, public relations, Internet marketing, and so forth. Businesses are becoming increasingly reliant on the Internet and social networking sites to promote their businesses. Today, businesses typically use a mix of traditional media, public relations, and Internet marketing, including social networks, to sell their products or services. The major points of difference among promotional tools are cost, impact, and level of consumer engagement.

TIME TO TAKE ACTION

If you are drafting a business plan for a course or starting an actual business, it is likely time you started to seriously think about your marketing mix.

1. If you are selling products or services, list the attributes that consumers will find appealing. How does the product or service compare with those of competitors? Determine an asking price, and be prepared to justify the price to classmates and investors.
2. Develop a promotional campaign for your business, following the guidelines in the text in this chapter. Make sure you use some of the effective, low-cost promotions such as guerrilla marketing, PR, and social networking. Decide specifically which social networking sites you will use and why. Present your promotional campaign to the class, and ask for feedback and suggestions.
3. Visit with some local businesses that use social networking sites to promote their products and services. Ask them what strategies and promotions have worked for them. What strategies and promotions have not worked well? Consider revising your promotional campaign based on their responses.

DISCUSSION QUESTIONS

1. What elements make up the marketing mix? What is the purpose of the marketing mix in a marketing plan?
2. Where is Kellogg's Corn Flakes in the product life cycle? What has Kellogg done to prolong the life cycle of this product?
3. Why is appealing to early adopters important to a firm?
4. What methods of pricing do small firms normally use? What are some of the problems with pricing products using these methods?
5. Do you think there is a difference between guerrilla marketing and public relations? Why or why not?
6. What are the advantages of using the Internet and social networking sites as a company's major form of advertising?

EXPERIENTIAL EXERCISES

1. Develop a marketing mix (i.e., product, promotion, price, distribution) for a bakery.
2. Form small groups and develop public relations and guerrilla marketing activities for your college or university. Select the best five ideas, and present them to the class.
3. Which pricing system would you use for the following products? Why?
   a. Campbell's soup
   b. Toronto Blue Jays season tickets
   c. Patio furniture
   d. Automobiles
4. If the cost of merchandise is $100 and it is sold for $150, what is the markup on cost? On selling price?
5. You have been approached to develop an advertising campaign for a new local discount golf franchise. The owners realize they need to develop awareness among consumers but have only a small amount of funds available for advertising. Which media type would you use for the advertising campaign? Justify your decision to use or not use each media type.
6. Interview a local small business owner, and find out what their marketing strategy is. Determine the promotional strategy. Are these strategies similar to those discussed in the chapter?

CHAPTER 9

FINANCIAL MANAGEMENT

LEARNING OBJECTIVES

By the end of this chapter, you should be able to:

LO1 Identify the fundamentals of small business accounting.

LO2 List the various types of accounting systems a small business can use.

LO3 Describe how technology can help the small business manage its finances.

LO4 Illustrate how to evaluate the financial operations of the small business.

LO5 Explain the important aspects of credit management for the small business.

SMALL BUSINESS PROFILE

CHRIS NEVILLE *Entrepreneur Finds Accounting and Controlling Costs Are Keys to Success*

Chris Neville of Sydney, Nova Scotia, was always interested in entrepreneurship and owning his own business. Neville states his dream was to be an entrepreneur, to be able to set his own destiny, and to have unlimited earning potential. So it was no surprise to his friends when Neville started his first business, a hockey identification camp for aspiring players, when he was only 20 years old. The camp was highly successful, and Neville quickly jumped into another business: manufacturing and selling calendars to university students. With two successful ventures under his belt, and still a student at the University of New Brunswick, where he eventually earned his Master's degree in Business Administration, Neville began looking for larger ideas. He soon discovered online gaming and successfully started lifeofsports.com, an online gaming site specializing in poker tournaments aimed at university students, which he grew to over 100 employees in six different countries. Neville sold the company to Gr88.com in 2010, when he felt the timing was optimal to maximize his value in the business.

Photo courtesy of Chris Neville

Now with some time on his hands, Neville decided to venture into real estate and started KayJim Developments in 2010, a company he named after his parents. The company flourished, and he quickly acquired 139 units, mostly in his home town of Sydney, Nova Scotia. Neville confirms he was always fascinated with real estate and felt it was a great way to grow his investments. But as his company quickly grew, Neville realized he was not completely prepared for the financial management involved with being a landlord to a large number of units. As he says, "We went from a few buildings to over 100 rather quickly, and managing rental units is different than other businesses in so many ways. For one, people want to pay using a variety of methods, and in some buildings we bought, rent was collected in cash, late collections were the norm, and the bookkeeping systems were often scribblers or loose paper."

Undaunted, Neville very developed formal rules for collecting rent, standardized the accounting systems from previous building owners, and started working with a professional accountant. Neville also notes that with so many rental units, controlling costs was vital to maximizing revenue. He says saving money on home heating oil, snow removal, and garbage collection are often overlooked by other growing property developers, and by spending time with his accountant and by negotiating hard with vendors, he managed to save thousands.

Neville soon expanded into other businesses, including Vision Landscaping and Vision Snow Removal, and he recently purchased two spas. Neville notes the key to his long-term success is his belief in strong financial management practices and working closely with his accountants to control costs: "As I expand into other areas, I always look to my costs and setting up strong financial management practices. By working with my accountants, I can ensure systems are in place and my businesses all run well."

THE NEED FOR FINANCIAL RECORDS

Financial management skills are important for a small business, as **Small Business in Action 9-1** shows. But business owners frequently lack these skills. One survey found that 24 to 45 percent of Canadian small business owners did not understand basic financial measurement ratios used in evaluating their businesses.[1] In fact, entrepreneur and contributing writer to **Small Business Trends**, Adam Sonnhalter says that some business owners will almost cry when they are asked to explain their financial statements.[2] Rob MacDonald, co-founder and President of **Envirobate**, an environmentally friendly construction company based in Halifax, says that understanding a company's finances is essential to long term success. MacDonald who has grown the business from a micro enterprise to a growing firm with 110 employees says, "Without understanding where your revenue is coming from, your expenses, and your ratios, it's hard to become a sustainable success. Every business owner should take the time to learn about their company's finances, as this knowledge will enable them to make better decisions and to grow their business."[3] The partner-owners of reMixed Snacks illustrate this in Small Business Beginnings 9-1.

SMALL BUSINESS IN ACTION 9-1

MANAGING CASH FLOW

Pieter Spinder is president of Calgary-based **Carmen Creek Gourmet Meats**. This company processes bison meat throughout Canada and the United States. A large part of the success of the business—Carmen Creek was ranked the second-fastest-growing company in Canada by *Profit* magazine in 2009—is Pieter's thorough and detailed working with the financial numbers. He updates his Excel workbook several times a day and sends cash-flow updates to staff every two or three days. He also distributes weekly margin reports so that the firm can quickly trim spending if rising costs eat into margins. Being on top of the numbers provides Carmen Creek with the flexibility to make cost-saving changes and move quickly to take advantage of new market opportunities. It has also improved relations with the company's banker. Because Spinder is such a meticulous bookkeeper, the bank was convinced to increase the company's line of credit to cover extra expenses that arise occasionally.

Discussion Questions

1. Do you think most entrepreneurs are as thorough with their financial management as Spinder? Why or why not?
2. Is Spinder's attention to detail too thorough, given that most business' expenses ebb and flow a bit? Would you like to work in an environment like this? Why or why not?

Failure to understand and manage the financial aspects of a business can be disastrous for the small business owner. The need for competence in this area is continually growing as new technology and greater competition in many markets require closer monitoring of operations and quicker decision making. Keeping proper records can warn the owner-manager in advance of future financial difficulties and help plan the growth of the business.

Another reason for proper record keeping is to satisfy government requirements. The fact that the Canada Revenue Agency (CRA) requires accurate record keeping to calculate a business' tax liability may actually benefit the small business.

Record keeping is also necessary if a business must borrow money. Lenders will require that proper record keeping be followed to ensure that debt obligations are met. The availability of accurate and current records of the operations of the business is also essential for the evaluation and control of business operations. **Figure 9-1** illustrates the various uses of accounting information.

FIGURE 9-1 **Uses of Accounting Information**

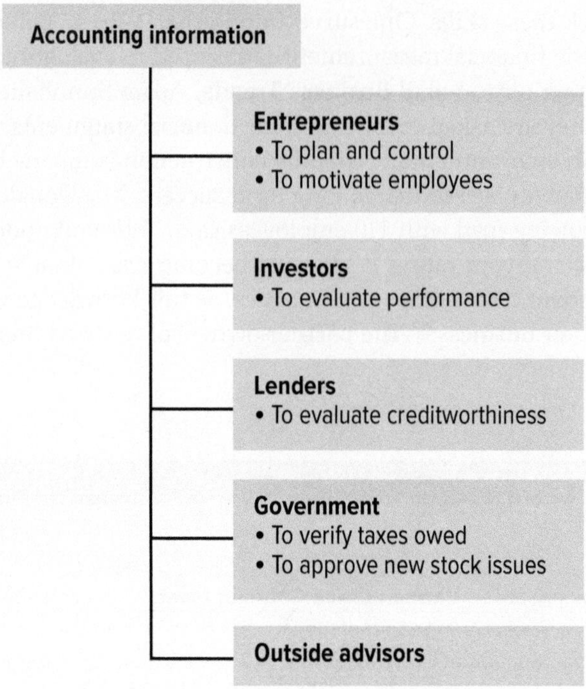

Small business owners may be tempted to neglect the financial aspects of the business in favour of the day-to-day operational aspects, such as production, personnel management, and marketing. Often this is because they have an incomplete understanding of how to manage the record-keeping system effectively. Understanding the managerial aspects of record keeping requires reviewing some basic accounting fundamentals.

Isabelle Lam and Jamie Lee, co-founders of reMIXED, have been able to create attractive branding and grow their snack food business to over 30 retail locations, all with a personal investment of only one thousand dollars each.

Photo courtesy of reMIXed

SMALL BUSINESS BEGINNINGS 9-1

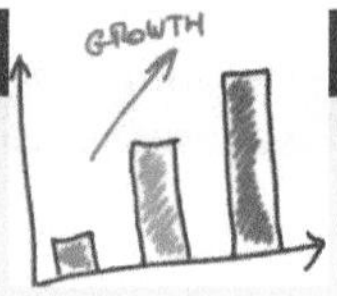

BOOTSTRAPPING TOWARDS FINANCIAL SUCCESS

Isabelle Lam and Jamie Lee, co-founders of **reMIXED**, launched the business as students enrolled in McGill's Dietetics and Nutrition program. The friends started selling cookie-jar mixes at local craft fairs and became excited with the opportunity of starting a larger business. The business partners realized there was a lack of healthy snack food alternatives, and their mixture of dehydrated apples and beans combined with chocolate not only tastes good but also provides consumers with 10 grams of protein. Lam and Lee explain that people need protein throughout the day not just during mealtime, and their snack food, called Bean Bark, meets that need.

Since their company's launch, the business partners have managed to secure 30 retailers to carry the product, and created labels and packaging, all with a initial investment of only $2,000 into their business. The partners didn't have a lot of money as students, so they bootstrapped the business, meaning they cut costs wherever possible, re-used personal items in their business, and kept a close eye on expenses. Future plans for the budding entrepreneurs include an expansion of the business' product lines and the addition of new retailers.

Discussion Questions

1. Do you think it's easier to keep track of expenses at the start of the business? Why or why not?
2. As reMIXED grows, what financial and accounting systems should the company put in place? Why?

THE ACCOUNTING CYCLE LO1

Table 9-1 illustrates the basic process by which transactions of the business are translated into financial statements.

TABLE 9-1 The Accounting Cycle

Recording of transactions (journal)	→	Classification of transaction totals (ledger)	→	Summarizing of data (financial statements)

RECORDING TRANSACTIONS

Transactions are recorded chronologically (as they occur) in a record called a *journal.* Many types of journals are used. In a business in which few transactions occur, these entries may be made manually. In many retail businesses, the daily cash register tape total may be used to record the revenue journal entries. The cheque register can be used to record payments or disbursements. In businesses with a large number of transactions, the journal may be kept mechanically by a bookkeeping machine or by a computer.

Accounting uses double-entry recording. This means the amounts of each transaction are recorded twice. This procedure accurately reflects the fact that each transaction affects two parts (accounts) of the business. Often a decrease in one means an increase in another. For example, if a desk costing $400 is purchased and paid for in cash, the amount of cash in the business decreases by $400 and the value of the office furniture in the business increases by $400. The use of double-entry accounting also allows for double-checking of the accuracy of the entries.

Table 9-2 illustrates how some typical recording entries might appear in a small business journal. In each of these transactions, for every increase in one account, a corresponding decrease occurs in another account. At the end of the period, the totals of increases and decreases at the bottom of the page for a number of transactions should be equal.

TABLE 9-2 Typical Journal Entries

		DR.	CR.
Jan. 1, 2020	Cash	2,000	
	Accounts receivable		2,000
	Received from Bill Smith on account.		
Jan. 5, 2020	Equipment	4,500	
	Cash		4,500
	Purchased equipment for cash.		
Jan. 20, 2020	Inventory	2,000	
	Accounts payable		2,000
	Inventory is purchased on account.		
Jan. 31, 2020	Accounts payable	500	
	Cash		500
	Liabilities of $500 are paid with cash.		
Jan. 31, 2020	Cash	8,000	
	Sales revenue		8,000
	Sales of $8,000 are made during the month.		

CLASSIFYING TRANSACTION TOTALS

Once the transactions have been accurately and properly recorded, the next step is to group or classify similar transactions. These groupings or classifications are called *accounts* and are entered into a book called a *ledger.* The ledger keeps a running balance of the dollar amounts in each account so that the net totals are known at the end of each period. As with journal entries, a ledger may be kept manually or by computer. **Table 9-3** shows some accounts of a typical ledger for service, retail, and manufacturing firms. The recording and classifying steps of the accounting cycle are usually referred to as *bookkeeping.* Many small businesses have found it valuable to hire an accountant to set up the bookkeeping system most appropriate for their businesses.

TABLE 9-3 Typical Ledger Account Titles Used for Some Types of Businesses

SERVICE FIRM	FOR A RETAIL FIRM ADD THESE ACCOUNTS	FOR A MANUFACTURING FIRM ADD THESE ACCOUNTS
Sales	Sales returns and allowances	Machinery
Cash	Sales discounts	Accumulated depreciation: Machinery
Accounts receivable	Furniture and fixtures	
Accounts payable		
Land	Accumulated depreciation: Furniture and fixtures	Cost of goods sold: Raw materials Direct labour Factory overhead
Building		
Accumulated depreciation: Building	Merchandise inventory	

SERVICE FIRM	FOR A RETAIL FIRM ADD THESE ACCOUNTS	FOR A MANUFACTURING FIRM ADD THESE ACCOUNTS
Accumulated depreciation:	Cost of goods sold:	
Office equipment	Purchases	
Office supplies inventory	Purchase returns	
Retained earnings	Purchase discounts	
Salaries expense	Transportation in	
Telephone expense		
Advertising expense		
Office supplies expense		
Depreciation expense: Building		
Depreciation expense: Equipment		
Miscellaneous expense		
Salaries payable		
Utilities expense		
Licences and taxes expense		
Insurance expense		
Accounting and legal expense		

SUMMARIZING DATA

The third step in the accounting cycle (which is usually carried out by an accountant) involves taking the account totals from the ledger and putting them together to form the financial statements. These statements indicate the past success and current position of the business. It is important that the small business owner understand what financial statements mean and how to use them. For example, Sonnhalter, who was discussed earlier in the chapter, notes that entrepreneurs need to understand their financial records so they can understand how to achieve their financial goals. He points out that owners usually know how much profit they want to take home, but without understanding where they are spending money, they cannot determine how much revenue is required for them to achieve those after-expense goals.[4]

Essentially three financial statements are important to the small business owner: the balance sheet, the income statement, and the cash flow statement.

Many small businesses employ professional accountants to put together their financial statements.

Source: © Rob Daly / age fotostock

Balance Sheet (Statement of Financial Position).

The balance sheet presents, in summary form, a snapshot of what the business owns and owes at any point in time. Those items the business owns are termed assets, and those owed are either liabilities (owed to sources outside the business) or equity (owed to owners). **Table 9-4** illustrates a balance sheet for a hypothetical small business. Assets and liabilities are generally listed in order of liquidity, with the most liquid being first. Usually, assets and liabilities are divided into current (to be consumed in one year) and non-current (in more than one year).

TABLE 9-4 Balance Sheet

SMALL BUSINESS CORPORATION BALANCE SHEET AS OF DECEMBER 31, 2020		
Assets		
Current assets:		
Cash	$ 3,449	
Accounts receivable	5,944	
Inventories	12,869	
Prepaid expenses	$ 389	
Total current assets		$22,651
Fixed assets:		
Land, buildings, and equipment cost	26,926	
Less accumulated depreciation	$13,534	
Total fixed assets		$13,392
Other assets:		
Investments	$ 1,000	
Total other assets		$ 1,000
Total assets		$37,043
Liabilities and Shareholders' Equity		
Current liabilities:		
Accounts payable	$ 6,602	
Other current liabilities	$ 825	
Total current liabilities		$ 7,427
Other liabilities:		
Mortgage payable	3,000	
Total liabilities		10,427
Shareholders' equity:		
Common stock	15,000	
Retained earnings	11,616	
Total shareholders' equity		26,616
Total liabilities and shareholders' equity		$37,043

Income Statement (Statement of Profit and Loss).

The income statement shows the results of the operations of the business for a given period. This statement, introduced in **Chapter 3**, is an integral part of the feasibility analysis and the business plan. The profit or income is determined by taking revenue from operations and subtracting expenses incurred in earning that revenue. **Table 9-5** illustrates an income statement for a hypothetical small business.

Cash Flow Statement or Statement of Changes in Financial Position.

The importance and format of the cash flow statement was discussed in **Chapter 6**. This statement is similar to the income statement except that only cash inflows and outflows are shown. Managing cash can be vital to a business, especially a new one. Business expert Rosemary Peavler confirms that cash is king in businesses, especially startups and, while profits are nice, cash flow is essential.[5] Michael Whittaker, owner of Dieppe, New Brunswick–based deli meat manufacturers **Bonté Foods**, says strong cash flow management helped him manage his business when when he lost a major client. He asserts that by understanding where his cash was going, he was able to make some changes to the management of his business quickly, which helped him cut costs and eventually grow sales.[6]

TABLE 9-5 Income Statement

SMALL BUSINESS CORPORATION INCOME STATEMENT FOR THE YEAR ENDED DECEMBER 31, 2020

Net sales	$197,000
Cost of goods sold	123,000
Gross margin on sales	74,000
Operating expenses	
Selling expenses	
Advertising expense	1,200
Sales salaries expense	18,300
Depreciation expense—store equipment	2,000
Total selling expenses	21,500
General expenses	
Depreciation expense—building	3,000
Insurance expense	675
Miscellaneous general expenses	425
General salaries expense	7,200
Total general expenses	11,300
Total operating expenses	32,800
Net operating margin	41,200
Other expenses	
Interest expense	2,750
Net income before income taxes	38,450
Income taxes	14,350
Net income	$ 24,100

In recent years, it has been common to examine not only the cash flow position of a firm but also all the asset and liability accounts over time. This practice has led to the popularity of a statement called "the statement of changes in financial position." As the name implies, this statement presents balance sheet account changes from one period to the next. It can help explain why a business has a positive net income but a decrease in cash for the same period of operation, a situation that mystifies some small business owners. The examination of the statement of changes in financial position can be complex. An example of a cash flow statement for a hypothetical small business appears in **Table 9-6**.

TABLE 9-6 Cash Flow Statement

SMALL BUSINESS CORPORATION CASH FLOW FORECAST JANUARY TO JUNE, 2020

	JAN.	FEB.	MAR.	APR.	MAY	JUNE
Cash receipts:						
Sales in 2020	—	$25,000	$ 7,500	$10,000	$10,000	$10,000
Accounts receivable for 2019	$19,000	13,000	6,000			
Other:						
Equity funding		10,000				
Total cash receipts	$19,000	$28,000	$13,500	$10,000	$10,000	$10,000

[continued]

[continued]

Cash disbursements:						
Cost of sales						
Labour	$ 5,000	$ 5,000	$ 5,000	$ 7,000	$ 7,000	$ 7,000
Materials	400	800	800	1,000	1,100	1,100
Transport	300	400	400	500	400	400
Accounts payable from 2019	12,000	10,000	10,000	6,000		
Selling expense	400	800	800	800	800	800
Administration	250	550	550	550	550	550
Fixed-asset investment						
Long-term repayment			2,500			2,500
Income tax instalment			3,000			3,000
Interest on debt			680			640
Long-term debt						
Bank loan (other cash source)	$ 400	$ 350	$ 270	$ 370	$ 430	$ 440
Total cash disbursements	$18,750	$17,900	$ 24,000	$16,220	$10,280	$16,430
Monthly cash surplus (deficit)	$ 250	$10,100	$–10,500	$–6,220	$ 280	$–6,430
Accumulated cash surplus (deficit) for first six months of 2020	250	10,350	–150	–6,370	–6,650	–13,080

ACCOUNTING SYSTEMS FOR THE SMALL BUSINESS

LO2

Small businesses use several types of accounting systems. Variations occur because of differences in company size, type of business (retail, service, manufacturing), industry, number of transactions, and expertise of the owner. The following is a brief description of some of the more common general systems used.

MANUAL SYSTEMS

Although few businesses use manual accounting systems today, some very small enterprises may find them useful, particularly at start-up. A survey found that nearly one million Canadian small businesses still do their accounting manually.[7] Examples of such systems are the one-book, one-write, and multi-journal systems. The basic accounting steps of journal and ledger entries are made in these systems. An example of a simple one-book system is shown in **Table 9-7**.

TABLE 9-7 Illustration of a One-Book Accounting System

1	2	3	4	5	6	7	8	9	10
			BANK		REVENUE SALES/ MISCELLANEOUS		EXPENSES WAGES/ ADVERTISING/ OTHER		
DATE	DESCRIPTION	CHEQUE NUMBER	IN	OUT					
Sept. 1/20	Wages paid for August	25		5,000		5,000			
Sept. 8/20	Sales for week 1		8,000		8,000				
Sept. 12/20	Paid utility bill	26		800					800
Sept. 15/20	Sales for week 2		6,500		6,500				
Sept. 19/20	Paid advertising bill	27		400			400		

OUTSOURCING FINANCIAL ACTIVITIES

A business can outsource financial activities such as cash receipts and disbursements, payroll, accounts payable, bank reconciliations, general ledger maintenance, budgeting, preparation of interim financial statements, and information technology activities. Some small businesses have found that this option can be quicker, easier, and less costly, and it does not require financial expertise. Small business experts such as Alika Cooper, a Business Development Manager, say hiring an account can be quite helpful; and entrepreneurs have the option to outsource their accounting in the early years of their business and than hire an in-house accountant as the business grows.[8]

SMALL BUSINESS COMPUTER SYSTEMS LO3

A valuable use of technology is in the management of the financial aspects of the business. Many software programs have been developed specifically for small businesses. This software may maintain bookkeeping and accounting of transactions, maintain a database of inventories, assist in making capital investments, and allow financial performance evaluation.

These applications allow for increased speed and accuracy of maintaining records, improved service to customers, improved and more timely information to managers, and reduced operating costs. Note that the selection of software is the most important aspect of the computer decision. Software that will carry out the operations the small business requires should be selected first, followed by the hardware on which the software will run. This ensures that the hardware is powerful enough to handle the demands the software places on the computer. Some of the more popular accounting programs for small businesses according to *PC Magazine* Reviews are Quickbooks, FreshBooks, ZoHo Books, Billy, GoDaddy Bookkeeping, Zero, Wave, and Working Point.[9] A new trend in accounting systems is Internet-housed software solutions, such as Canadian market leader FreshBooks, discussed in more detail in **Small Business in Action 9-2**. Businesses, especially service businesses, find FreshBooks appealing as they can access key information regardless of where they are located.

SMALL BUSINESS IN ACTION 9-2

FRESHBOOKS

FreshBooks is the Toronto-based world leader in cloud-based accounting systems. The company, which was founded by Mike McDerment in 2003, has transformed itself to offer accounting and billing solutions for small companies via the cloud. The "cloud" essentially means firms can access information from anywhere and everywhere they want to. By being in the cloud, FreshBooks also had an easier time expanding globally, as they did not have to fight for shelf space or look for distributors.

While FreshBooks was originally aimed at small IT firms, it now specializes in service-based firms where, McDerment says, there is a lack of accounting solutions. McDerment states, "We are particularly focused on service-based businesses, where people—including butlers, bakers, and dog walkers—are paid for their time and expertise, and whose needs are not particularly well met by generalized accounting software." FreshBooks allows people to maintain easy and accurate billing records, accept various forms of payment, and create financial statements.

FreshBooks continues to grow, with more than 24 million users in 160 countries and $8 billion in annual invoices.

Discussion Questions

1. What are some advantages of FreshBooks?
2. FreshBook's niche is service firms, which often bill for their services in very small increments. What are some of the advantages and disadvantages of such small incremental billing?
3. Do you think some entrepreneurs would be hesitant to use FreshBooks because the software is stored in the cloud? Why or why not?

SMALL BUSINESS IN ACTION 9-3

INBOX MARKETER'S SIX-MILLION-DOLLAR DISEASE

Gts/Shutterstock.com

Randall Litchfield, co-founder of Toronto-based **Inbox Marketer**, said that in 2011 his firm became infected with a disease he calls $3 million-itis. No sooner did he think his firm was cured than $6 million-itis occurred. The cause of Inbox's disease? Quickly growing sales to $3 million and then to $6 million. That's when Litchfield realized that his company's accounting and financial processes were not equipped to deal with sales of this size. Litchfield noted that while the sales numbers may differ from firm to firm and industry to industry, eventually all growing companies have to take control of their financial and accounting systems to ensure their growth is well managed. He says Inbox Marketer's lack of systems and procedures negatively affected administrative staffing, budgeting, and calculating of ratios and cash flow, and made his firm more vulnerable to fraud.

Rather than let his firm stay sick from an accounting and financial perspective, Litchfield dealt with the problem. He had an accountant audit his financial systems and make recommendations. Following the accountant's suggestions, Inbox Marketer moved to an accrual-based accounting system that allowed for quarterly comparisons. The system enabled the company to prepare budgets and forecasts and work on a strategic plans that included financials for the following three to five years. Litchfield says the changes gave management a much better sense of control of the company's finances and future.

Discussion Questions

1. Why is it important to have an accrual-based system?
2. Litchfield had been using a cash-based accounting system. What are some of the advantages and disadvantages of a cash-based system?
3. What are the advantages and disadvantages of more formal accounting systems?
4. Given that Litchfield has grew his business to $6 million in sales without spending much time on financial and accounting systems, do you think the company's corporate culture would adapt to more formal controls and planning? Why or why not?

MANAGEMENT OF FINANCIAL INFORMATION FOR PLANNING

The first part of this chapter dealt with the fundamental aspects of collecting and maintaining the financial information within the business. This information is of minimal value, however, unless it is used to monitor, evaluate, and control current operations, as well as to plan for the future.

SHORT-TERM FINANCIAL PLANNING

Short-term financial planning consists of preparing an estimated future financial result of operations of the business. Such pro forma (projected) financial statements serve as a blueprint for planning operations. The projected income statement is generally referred to as a budget and was described in **Chapter 3** in the preparation of the feasibility analysis. Although budgets can provide many benefits to an organization, a recent study found that only 47 percent of small business owners maintain a budget.[10] A budget, however, can be a very valuable financial tool for the following reasons.

Clarification of Objectives.

A budget forces an organization to anticipate future operations and set goals and procedures to accomplish them.

Coordination.

The budgeting process draws employees and departments together and brings them into the planning process to input into the budget information relevant to their responsibilities.

Evaluation and Control.

A budget allows the owner-manager to quickly determine discrepancies that may require investigation. Such an investigation is often called *variance analysis.* It also allows comparison of planned (budgeted) amounts with actual results, which can improve effectiveness in the long term. **Table 9-8** shows how to establish and use a budget. After the comparison of budgeted (planned) and actual results, attempts can be made to explain the reasons for any differences. Consequently, changes might be made to correct the differences or refine the budgeting process.

TABLE 9-8 Use of a Budget

SMALL BUSINESS CORPORATION INCOME STATEMENT FOR THE YEAR ENDED DECEMBER 31, 2020

	BUDGETED	ACTUAL	DIFFERENCE	EXPLANATION
Net sales	$197,000	$180,000	$17,000	Sales targets not reached
Cost of goods sold	123,000	120,000	3,000	Material costs increase
Gross margin on sales	74,000	60,000	14,000	
Operating expenses				
Selling expenses				
Advertising expense	1,200	1,200	0	
Sales salaries expense	18,300	18,300	0	
Total selling expense	19,500	19,500	0	
General expenses				
Depreciation expense—store equipment	2,000	4,000	2,000	Additional equipment purchased
Depreciation expense—building	3,000	3,000	0	
Insurance expense	675	1,200	525	Premium increase
General salaries expense	7,200	7,200	0	
Miscellaneous general expenses	425	600	175	
Total general expenses	13,300	16,000	2,700	
Total operating expenses	32,800	35,500	2,700	
Net operating margin	41,200	24,500	16,700	
Other expenses				
Interest expense	2,750	3,200	450	Rate increase
Net income before income taxes	38,450	21,300	17,150	
Income taxes	14,450	7,455	6,995	Marginal rate decrease
Net income	$ 24,000	$ 13,845	$10,155	

LONG-TERM FINANCIAL PLANNING

Three types of long-term financial planning decisions can affect the small business–decisions regarding capital investment, capacity, and expansion.

The Capital Investment Decision.

Most long-term planning includes the question of future capital purchases. This may involve the acquisition of land, buildings, equipment, or even another business. Although sometimes running lean is a better choice, as is illustrated in **Small Business in Action 9-4**. The small business owner needs to have a simple but accurate way to determine whether the decision will be financially sound. Some of the more commonly used methods of estimating future return for capital investments are discussed next.

SMALL BUSINESS IN ACTION 9-4

LEAN MANAGEMENT YIELDS SUCCESS

Anne Larcade, president and CEO of **Sequel Lifestyle Hotels and Resorts**, has found that running a lean company by paying attention to financial information has allowed the company to offer lower prices and be successful in a very competitive industry. One key aspect of this policy is to have no office space by having all managers and back-office staff work from home. That yields savings of close to $100,000 per year. It also increases employee creativity and productivity. Sequel has also embraced technology to run leaner. Larcade has found that understanding the financial aspects of business has been a key to profitable operations as well. Sequel teaches all 250 staff to read financial statements so they better grasp cost management.

Call centres are not used, unlike competitors, and this also results in significant savings. Lean overheads allow Sequel to charge 30 percent lower property-management fees than its competitors. This advantage helps the firm increase revenues and profits each year at a rate much higher than the industry average.

Discussion Questions

1. What are some of the advantages and disadvantages of allowing staff to work from home?
2. Some business experts question the trade-off of efficiency versus cost savings in Sequel Lifestyle Hotels and Resorts' model. They note that, while office costs are reduced, people in traditional offices are more efficient because of supervision, and they have greater opportunities to collaborate, which leads to improvements in operations. Do you think people in traditional offices are better employees? Why or why not?

Rate-of-Return Method.

This method estimates the annual rate of return of the new investment. After this value has been determined, it can be compared with alternative investments. **Table 9-9** shows how a rate of return for a capital asset is determined.

TABLE 9-9 Rate-of-Return Method

STEPS	EXAMPLE
1. Calculate total cost of investment.	$50,000
2. Estimate depreciable life of investment.	5 years
3. Calculate average value of investment over life. Beginning value ($50,000) plus end value (0) divided by 2 equals average value.	$\frac{\$50,000}{2} = \$25,000$
4. Estimate average annual profit over depreciable life (net of depreciation)	$10,000
5. Average profit divided by average investment.	$\frac{\$10,000}{\$25,000} = 40\%$

Note: A reasonable rate of return on a capital investment is between two and three times the prime rate of interest. Using this criterion, the 40 percent rate of return in this example represents an attractive investment.

Present Value Method.

This method employs the time value of money in looking at future cash inflows and outflows. Future inflows and outflows of cash are discounted because cash held today is worth more than cash received or paid in the future. Present value rates are collected from present value tables, which most accounting and finance texts provide. The rate required to equalize discounted outflows (for the purchase of the assets) and discounted inflows (income from the assets) represents the discounted rate of return of the asset.

Payback Method.

This method, which is similar to the rate-of-return method, estimates the number of years required for the capital investment to pay for itself. **Table 9-10** illustrates how the payback method is used.

TABLE 9-10 Payback Method

STEPS	EXAMPLE
1. Calculate total cost of investment.	$50,000
2. Estimate depreciable life of investment.	5 years
3. Calculate annual depreciation charge.	$ 10,000
4. Estimate average annual profit over depreciable life.	$ 10,000
5. Cost of investment divided by cash inflow (profit + depreciation)	$\frac{\$50{,}000}{\$10{,}000 + \$10{,}000} = 2.5$ years

Note: The payback period for the capital investment would be 2.5 years. As this is considerably less than the depreciable life of the asset, it appears to be an attractive investment.

The Capacity Decision.

Another important financial planning decision for the small business, especially the small manufacturer, is the size and extent of operations. Financial management techniques related to capacity help answer such questions as how many units should be produced and how large the plant should be. A useful technique for answering these questions is break-even analysis.

The *break-even point* is the point at which the level of output (in units or dollars) is equal to fixed and variable costs. By applying break-even analysis, the small business owner can determine the minimum level of operations required to financially break even. The use of break-even analysis could form an important part of the feasibility analysis discussed in **Chapter 3**. The formula for break-even analysis is shown below:

$$\text{BEP} = \frac{\text{Fixed costs}}{\text{Profit per unit}} = \text{BEP in units}$$

or

$$\text{BEP} = \frac{\text{Fixed costs}}{\text{Profit as percent of sales}} = \text{BEP in dollars}$$

where

Fixed costs = Costs that will not vary as production increases

(e.g., costs of plant, equipment, and some overhead expenses)

Profit per unit = Selling price – Variable costs

The resulting graph (**Figure 9-2**) illustrates at what price and output the break-even point occurs given fixed and variable costs.

FIGURE 9-2 Break-Even Analysis

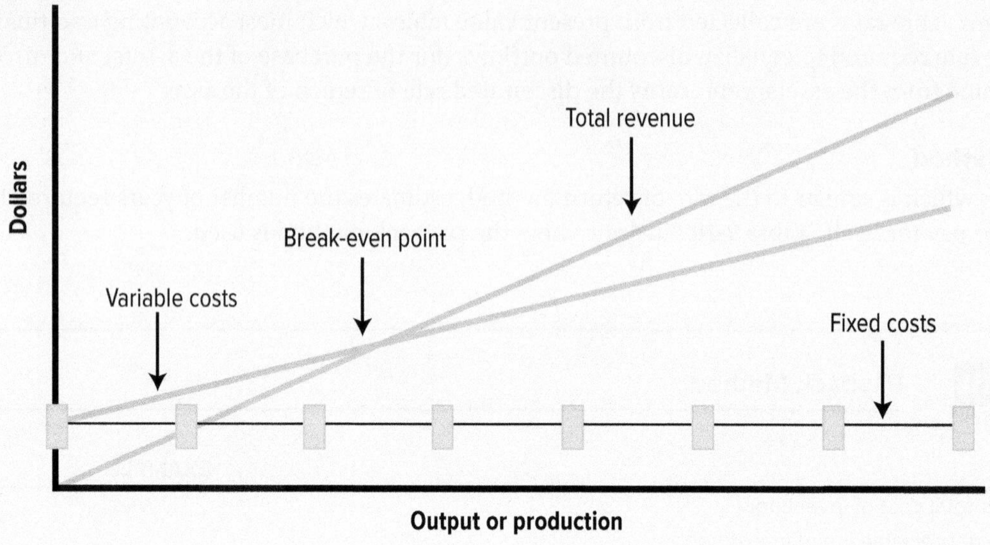

The Expansion Decision.

Break-even analysis can also be used to help the owner-manager decide whether to expand the scope of operations. The same formulas can be used but only on an incremental basis, as follows.

The Effect of Fixed-Cost Adjustments.

$$\text{BEP} = \frac{\text{Additional fixed costs}}{\text{Profit per unit}} = \begin{array}{c}\text{Additional unit volume needed to}\\ \text{cover additional fixed costs}\end{array}$$

$$\text{BEP} = \frac{\text{Additional fixed costs}}{\text{Profit as percent of sales}} = \begin{array}{c}\text{Additional sales volume needed}\\ \text{to cover additional fixed costs}\end{array}$$

The Effect of Variable-Cost Adjustments.

Another use of incremental break-even analysis is to measure the effects of changes in the components of the formula such as variable costs. The following example illustrates this calculation:

$$\text{BEP} = \frac{\text{Fixed costs}}{\text{New profit/unit}} - \frac{\text{Fixed costs}}{\text{Old profit/unit}}$$

$$= \text{Additional unit volume needed to cover additional variable cost}$$

$$\text{BEP} = \frac{\text{Fixed costs}}{\begin{array}{c}\text{New profit as}\\ \text{percent of sales}\end{array}} - \frac{\text{Fixed costs}}{\begin{array}{c}\text{Old profit as}\\ \text{percent of sales}\end{array}}$$

$$= \text{Additional sales volume (in dollars) needed to cover additional variable costs}$$

EVALUATION OF FINANCIAL PERFORMANCE LO4

Quantitative evaluation of the performance of the business is an essential management task. Many small business owners rely on their accountants to look after the financial end of the business because they lack the financial knowledge themselves. An accountant may be essential for preparing year-end financial statements, but few small businesses can afford ongoing financial management advice from this source. The small business owner is well advised to acquire a basic working knowledge of some key financial evaluation components of the business. This can enable the owner to monitor and control operations throughout the year, not just at year-end. Richard Abbass, co-founder of Deep Down Cleaning, a commercial cleaning business in Halifax that he has grown to 110 employees, is a good example of this. Abbass says he constantly monitors revenue and one major expense: labour. He notes, "We have grown every year since inception, not huge growth, but we have always grown. I pay close attention to this to make sure the trend is still there. The other area I monitor is our cost of labour. We are a labour-intensive business and it's important to review the figure on an on-going bases."[11]

Several measures can be used to evaluate the results found in the financial statements. Some of the more common techniques are described next.

MANAGEMENT OF CURRENT FINANCIAL POSITION

One critical problem many small businesses face is a shortage of cash to finance operations. Some small business owners find it hard to understand that as their businesses become successful and grow, this tends to create a strain on operating funds, as illustrated in **Small Business in Action 9-5**. Equally hard for many to understand is the situation in which the income statement shows a profit but the cash position of the business has deteriorated.

SMALL BUSINESS IN ACTION 9-5

THE LEGENDARY STORY OF TED ROGERS, FOUNDER OF ROGERS COMMUNICATION, AND CASH FLOW MANAGEMENT

The story goes something like this: During Ted Rogers' early years of business, his company often lacked the cash to pay creditors. Rather than pick and choose who would be paid, he would put all of their invoices into a hat and draw them out one at a time until the money was gone. The following week he would repeat the process. When one supplier heard about this selection method, he called hollering and yelling, urging the company's owner to pay him and abandon the "invoice hat." Ted Rogers's reply was straight, to the point, and quieted down his angry creditor, "If you keep yelling at me, I won't put your company's invoices in the hat next week." While the story may be an urban myth, it does give you some insight into how even the most successful entrepreneurs had to stretch out accounts payable during the early and lean days of doing business. Of course, this was very early in Rogers' career, as he eventually started Rogers Communications, one of Canada's most-successful companies, and one he remained involved with until he died in 2008.

Ted Rogers, founder of Rogers Communications, used a variety of methods to pay his accounts payable, especially early in his career.
Toronto Star / Getty Images

Discussion Questions

1. Do you think Rogers' method of bill paying was ethical? Why or why not?
2. Do you think Rogers' strategy would work today? Why or why not?
3. What other solutions could Rogers have sought out to pay his creditors on time? Why do you think he didn't try any of these solutions?

The reason these situations occur is that most small businesses do not operate on a cash basis of accounting. (Some service businesses, farmers, and fishermen do use cash basis accounting methods, however.) The system used is called an *accrual-based accounting system*. With an accrual system, a transaction need not involve a cash transfer to be recorded. For example, a sale of merchandise is recorded as revenue for income statement purposes whether it is paid for in cash or purchased on credit. Likewise, many non-cash transactions may affect the income statement, whereas some cash transactions may not.

The above discussion illustrates the need to closely monitor the cash position of the business. As indicated, this is difficult to do by examining only the income statement. The balance sheet and cash flow statements are essential components of monitoring cash position. To understand this better, see **Small Business in Action 9-6**.

SMALL BUSINESS IN ACTION 9-6

GLOW PROMOTIONS: GROWING WITH A FOCUS ON THE BOTTOM LINE

Dave O'Connor, founder of **Glow** recalls how he became an entrepreneur, "I was looking for business ideas, something new and different, and I came across a town where there were mobile signs everywhere, and I thought, 'well there is a business that doesn't exist on a large scale in Halifax'." A short time later Glow Signs was created. O'Connor, who is a natural salesperson, started to expand the business and quickly added new clients and innovative ideas. He notes, "We were the first to use fluorescent letters on our signs in the area, and we really worked to have our signs stand out."

Dave O'Connor has grown a small mobile sign business into an Atlantic Canada brand. It is so well known that if you mention Glow, people know you're talking about the leading event company in Atlantic Canada.

Photo courtesy of Dave O'Connor

Always looking to expand, O'Connor says he started to almost immediately think about what else he could sell to his clients. He remembered his prior experience working at a bank where they were always trying to cross-sell customers: you have an account with us, now a mortgage, an RRSP, insurance, and so forth. The banks understood that, once you have happy customers and you get to know them and their needs, it's easy to assist them. O'Connor says the traditional expansion trajectory for a mobile sign business is graduating into a full-service sign company. However, when he looked around the Halifax region, he noticed that there were several existing businesses and they were already doing a very good job. He says, "I want to go into businesses where I can be either number one or number two in the area. When I looked at becoming a full-service sign business, it would have been hard to reach those goals." He continues: "It was very competitive business, there were several companies, all doing a very good job, all of who had invested significant money into their business."

O'Connor says what excited him was the promotional aspect of the business. He was buying a few extra promotional pieces, such as banners and sky signs, and saw potential there. He recalls a pivotal moment that came early in his business: while showing a potential client all the promotional signage and equipment O'Connor had available, the client expressed disappointment. "He told me he expected more. I then realized I had to really invest into the business to grow." O'Connor says he attended trade shows and started to search the Internet for new ideas. Although, this was around 1996 and the Internet was relatively new, he did find some innovative concepts and started to grow his promotional business.

O'Connor says his searching paid off but it wasn't on the promotional side. As he was searching for innovative ideas, he came across a business that was renting bouncers—commercial, air-filled play structures—and noticed how much the children loved playing on them. He met with the business owner, learned as much as he could, and bought three used bouncers. And so Glow Inflatables was born. O'Connor says, "The inflatable business excited me as I thought we could become a leader. Unlike signs or even promotions there was a real opportunity. I also knew I had to invest in the business, as I learned that lesson in promotions and put money into the business." O'Connor says inflatables really worked for him as corporate events, schools, and universities loved having something fun for children to enjoy.

O'Connor continued to expand using his cross-selling skills learned at the bank; soon Glow Rides and Games was added, then Glow Party, Concessions and Catering, and eventually a party store including themes and events. It was at this time O'Connor says he learned another valuable lesson about financial management. Although he was really focused on growing his sales, when he received his year-end statements, they were not as strong as he thought they should be. While he believes that growing revenue should be the Number One concern for an entrepreneur, financial management should be Number One-A.

The financial report results forced O'Connor to closely monitor expenses, access monthly financial statements, and take an active role in financial management. He also started to rein in expenses by taking actions such as adding personal time sheets and putting GPS on company vehicles. O'Conner says, "I could really grow sales, but I learned if you don't take care of your costs, then you can easily find yourself in a position where you are not making *any* money. We put in more accountability and the business improved as a result." O'Connor adds that he invests heavily into his business every year, and that managing cash flow in a business that has a strong seasonal component and variability in service is important. "We have 40 full-time staff, but that grows upwards of 150 from the Spring to end of December to accommodate the extra business. So managing expenses and having accountability is important. Plus every event, every rental can be different. So establishing financial accountability helps us become more efficient."

Today, O'Connor continues to expand. He recently placed all his business units under the umbrella of Glow the Event Store, where he has added Glow Event Rentals, Glow Furniture, Glow Tents, Glow Lighting and Special Effects, Glow Christmas—a huge corporate party centre he created with a family theme—and more. O'Connor says the company has become the one-stop event store in the region, and in each category they are number one or number two. O'Conner has also added two large seasonal Halloween pop-up stores and has franchised his company to Sydney, Nova Scotia. O'Connor says future plans include continuing to grow revenue by making sure he is active in the financial management of the firm, and continuing to invest in his business. Due to his active community involvement and entrepreneurial leadership, O'Connor was recently honoured as the "Entrepreneur Leader of the Year" by the Halifax Chamber of Commerce.

Discussion Questions

1. O'Connor places a heavy emphasis on growing revenue and cross-selling. What are some of the advantages and disadvantages of his strategy?
2. O'Connor notes that he only wants to enter into businesses where he can be Number One or Number Two in the region. Do you think this is good strategy? Why or why not?
3. Why would managing cash flow be more challenging for O'Connor based on his business activity?
4. What advice would you give to O'Connor for managing his company's financials?

If the cash position of the business needs to be improved, an effective way to do so is to reduce the length of time from payment for inventory to receipt of payment for the inventory once it is sold. This cycle has three essential components:

1. Time taken to pay accounts payable
2. Time taken to sell inventory
3. Time taken to receive payment for inventory

Table 9-11 illustrates how to use these components in reducing this cycle for a hypothetical business. Additional information about estimating cash requirements for an increase in sales is provided later in the text.

TABLE 9-11 Financial Management

SMALL BUSINESS CO. LTD. BALANCE SHEET AT DEC. 31, 2020

ASSETS		LIABILITIES	
Accounts receivable	$100,000	Accounts payable	$ 40,000
Inventory	50,000	Bank loans	100,000
Fixed assets	$140,000	Shareholders' equity	$150,000
Total assets	$290,000	Total liabilities and shareholders' equity	$290,000

SMALL BUSINESS CO. LTD. INCOME STATEMENT FOR YEAR ENDED DEC. 31, 2020

Sales	$750,000
Cost of goods sold	500,000
Gross profit	250,000
Expenses	200,000
Net profit	$ 50,000

[continued]

1. Time taken to pay accounts

$$= \frac{\text{Accounts payable}}{\text{Cost of goods sold}} \times 365 \text{ days}$$

$$= \frac{\$40,000}{\$500,000} \times 365 \text{ days}$$

$$= 29.2 \text{ days}$$

This means that, on average, it takes 29.2 days to pay for inventory purchased.

2. Time to sell inventory

$$= \frac{\text{Inventory}}{\text{Cost of goods sold}} \times 365 \text{ days}$$

$$= \frac{\$50,000}{500,000} \times 365 \text{ days}$$

$$= 36.5 \text{ days}$$

This means that, on average, it takes 36.5 days to sell the inventory.

3. Time to receive payment

$$= \frac{\text{Accounts receivable}}{\text{Sales}} \times 365 \text{ days}$$

$$= \frac{\$100,000}{\$750,000} \times 365 \text{ days}$$

$$= 48.67 \text{ days}$$

This means that, on average, it takes 48.67 days to receive payment for inventory sold. The business cycle for this company is:

$$36.5 \text{ days} + 48.7 - 29.2 = 56 \text{ days}$$

To increase the cash position, suppose the business was able to increase the accounts payable and decrease the turnover and receivable day totals for each component by five days. The result of these actions is shown in the list below.

1. *Time taken to pay accounts:* A five-day increase substituted in the formula would increase accounts payable from $40,000 to $46,849, with a resulting increase in cash of $6849 ($46,849 – $40,000) by using the above formula. This five-day increase might be accomplished by obtaining extensions from suppliers or simply not paying accounts payable until absolutely required.
2. *Time to sell inventory:* A five-day decrease substituted in the formula would decrease inventory from $50,000 to $43,150, with a resulting increase in cash of $6850 ($50,000 – $43,150). Such a decrease might be a result of increased advertising, more careful purchasing, or greater incentive to salespeople.
3. *Time taken to receive payment:* A five-day decrease substituted in the formula would decrease accounts receivable from $100,000 to $89,733, with a resulting increase in cash of $10,267 ($100,000 – $89,733). Such a decrease might be accomplished by increasing the intensity of collection procedures or submitting charge card receipts more often.

The total effect of these measures on the cash position of the company would be $6849 + $6850 + $10,267 = $23,966 increase. The owner-manager, of course, would have to balance this increase in cash against the costs of accomplishing the five-day increases or decreases.

EVALUATION OF FINANCIAL STATEMENTS

Once the financial statements have been prepared, several relationships between various account totals can assist in evaluating the operations of the business. This evaluation of relationships is called *ratio analysis*. It can be used to compare the financial performance of the business with those of other similar businesses or with previous results for the same business.

Reports of financial ratios for other businesses are prepared by industry associations and Statistics Canada and can be found on the Statistics Canada, Strategis, and GDSourcing websites. These reports are collected from many businesses across the country; thus, when using them, it is important to use comparable businesses from the same industry.

Financial ratios can also help in isolating and analyzing weaknesses within the business. Four categories of ratios are commonly used in evaluating a small business. Each is discussed next with a general statement regarding whether the ratio is acceptable. The ratios of certain industries, however, may deviate from these averages. Illustrations of these ratios for a small business appear in **Appendix 9A**.

Liquidity Ratios.

Liquidity ratios assess the business' ability to meet financial obligations in the current period. Two liquidity ratios are commonly used: the current ratio and the acid test or quick ratio. The calculations for these ratios are as follows:

$$\text{Current ratio} = \text{Current assets: Current liabilities}$$

This figure, expressed as a ratio, should be higher than 1:1 and usually between 1:1 and 2:1.

$$\text{Acid test or quick ratio} = \text{Current assets} - \text{Inventories: Current liabilities}$$

The quick ratio is more suitable for businesses that have a high level of inventory. A ratio of 1:1 is considered healthy. If the liquidity ratios are lower than they should be, the business may have difficulty meeting obligations within the year and will have a hard time raising further debt capital. Actions that could improve the liquidity ratios are increasing current assets without a corresponding increase in current liabilities, such as through equity financing or increased long-term debt.

Productivity Ratios.

Productivity ratios measure the efficiency of internal management operations. They include the inventory turnover ratio and the collection period ratio.

The calculation of the inventory turnover ratio is as follows:

$$\text{Inventory turnover} = \frac{\text{Cost of goods sold}}{\text{Average inventory at cost}}$$

or

$$\text{Inventory turnover} = \frac{\text{Sales}}{\text{Average inventory at retail price}}$$

Inventory turnover reveals the number of times the inventory is turned over (sold) in a year. Average turnover rates vary considerably by industry but usually should not be lower than two to three times. An inventory turnover that is too low may reflect poor inventory buying in terms of either being overstocked or buying low-demand inventory.

The collection period is calculated as follows:

$$\text{Collection period} = \frac{\text{Accounts receivable}}{\text{Daily credit sales}}$$

This ratio reflects the average number of days taken for purchasers to pay their accounts to the business. Normal collection periods are 20 to 40 days. If the collection period is too long, it may mean the credit-granting policy is too loose, the administration of billing is too slow, or the collection of accounts is too lax. Solutions to poor productivity ratios include better buying and more emphasis on selling and collections.

Profitability Ratios.

Profitability ratios measure the effectiveness of operations in generating a profit. There are four ratios in this category.

The first ratio is gross margin:

$$\text{Gross margin} = \text{Sales} - \text{Cost of goods sold}$$

This figure, usually expressed as a percentage of gross sales, can be used for comparisons. Gross margin for an individual product is calculated by subtracting cost from selling price and is commonly called *markup*. Average gross margins usually range from 20 to 50 percent. If gross margins are lower than they should be, the cause may be poor buying, failure to emphasize high-margin items, theft or spoilage, or price levels that are not current.

The profit-on-sales ratio measures profit as a percentage of gross sales:

$$\text{Profit on sales} = \frac{\text{Net profit (before tax)}}{\text{Sales}}$$

Typically, the average falls within 1 to 5 percent. A lower than average profit-to-sales percentage can reflect a problem with either pricing or expenses. Pretax profits are normally used, since the tax rates may vary by jurisdiction and industry. In addition, reporting agencies that publish industry standards may use pretax profits as a comparison.

The third profitability ratio is the expense ratio:

$$\text{Expense ratio} = \frac{\text{Expense item}}{\text{Sales}}$$

Many specific expenses on the income statement may be expressed as a percentage of gross sales. These figures can then be compared with those for similar businesses.

The return-on-investment ratio reflects the profitability of the owner's investment:

$$\text{Return on investment} = \frac{\text{Net profit (before tax)}}{\text{Owner"s equity}}$$

This ratio may be compared not only with those for other similar businesses but also with alternative investments. If compared with the bank rate of interest, it is important to remember the risk associated with the business. Thus, the return on investment should be higher than the bank rate to compensate for this.

Debt Ratio.

The debt-to-equity ratio measures the solvency of the business, or the firm's ability to meet long-term debt payments:

$$\text{Total debt to equity} = \text{Total debt: Owner's equity}$$

Acceptable debt ratios vary, but generally, it should not be greater than 4:1. A lender normally will not provide further financing to a firm with a higher ratio. To improve the debt ratio, the small business may need to increase the equity investment or reduce debt through operations.

CREDIT AND THE SMALL BUSINESS LO5

A major concern for many small businesses in their attempt to reduce the length of the business cycle is control of credit. The owner-manager should understand the fundamentals of credit granting and management to effectively control receivables. Before deciding to extend credit, the owner-manager should be aware of the costs and potential difficulties involved in granting credit, as well as the advantages of its use. The attractiveness of such a program is less today, since the majority of consumers can use bank credit or debit cards for their purchases. However, many small businesses have found success by offering gift cards and loyalty rewards programs as a form of credit.

ADVANTAGES OF CREDIT USE

The advantages of offering credit include the following:

- A credit program will undoubtedly increase sales and will probably be necessary to remain competitive.
- Credit customers are more likely to be loyal to the store or business.

- Credit customers tend to be more concerned with quality of service than with price than are cash customers.
- The business can maintain information about and a record of credit customers and their purchases that can help in business planning.

DISADVANTAGES OF CREDIT USE

A credit program can also create certain difficulties:

- There will generally be some bad debts when using a credit program. The number of bad debts depends largely on how strict the credit-granting policy is and how closely accounts are monitored.
- Slow payers cost the business in lost interest and capital that could be used for more productive investments. It is estimated that in many businesses, losses resulting from slow payers are greater than losses from bad debts.
- A credit program increases bookkeeping, mailing, and collection expenses. Purchase records need to be kept, statements mailed, and accounts monitored and collected. As a result, many small businesses decide against offering their own credit programs.

MANAGEMENT OF A CREDIT PROGRAM

If the small business owner decides to use a credit program, some essential steps should be followed to ensure maximum effectiveness.

Determine Administrative Policies.

This includes such items as choosing application forms, setting credit limits for customers, choosing procedures to follow on overdue accounts, determining which records to keep, and deciding when to send statements.

Set Criteria for Granting Credit.

A small business owner-manager may want to assess many of the same areas a lender would evaluate in considering a small business loan, although perhaps not in the same detail. Some essentials would be past credit history, other accounts held, monthly income, references, and bank used. A small business is well advised to use the services of a credit bureau located in most cities or a commercial agency, such as Dun and Bradstreet, to evaluate customers' creditworthiness.

Set Up a System to Monitor Accounts.

Proper management of accounts receivable involves classifying accounts by the length of time they have been outstanding. This process is called *aging of accounts receivable.* Common categories used are under 30 days, 30 to 60 days, 60 to 90 days, and over 90 days. Experience shows that the longer an account is outstanding, the smaller is the chance of collecting it. Therefore, special attention should be paid to overdue accounts.

Establish a Procedure for Collection.

A uniform procedure should be set up regarding the use of overdue notices, phone calls, credit supervision, legal action, and a collection agency. Lax supervision of accounts has led to many small business failures, so this is an area of credit management that cannot be ignored. An example of such a collection policy appears in **Table 9-12**.

One form of collection sometimes used by small businesses is a factoring company, which, as discussed in **Chapter 6**, can also be a source of small business financing. This type of company purchases accounts receivable for cash (at a discount) and attempts to collect them. In some cases, a factoring company handles the overall credit program for the business and even provides debt financing.

TABLE 9-12 An Example of a Collection Policy

	30 DAYS	45 DAYS	60 DAYS	75 DAYS	90 DAYS
Communication	Letter, telephone; copy of statement	Letter, telephone; copy of statement	Letter, telephone	Letter, telephone	Registered letter or lawyer's letter
Message	Overdue account, please remit	Pay in 15 days, or deliveries will be stopped	Deliveries stopped; pay immediately	Pay in 15 days, or account will be turned over for collection	Action is being taken
Action	None	None	Stop deliveries	None	Use collection agency or small claims court

Source: *Small Business Review*, pamphlet (Toronto: Thorne Riddell Chartered Accountants).

USE OF BANK DEBIT AND CREDIT CARDS

Because of the high costs and risks involved in operating their own credit programs, many small businesses find the most effective way to offer credit is to use bank debit and credit cards, such as Visa and MasterCard. The use of credit cards and electronic banking by consumers has now surpassed that of cash and cheques in Canada. The credit card companies assume the risk of bad debts and cover much of the administration costs of bookkeeping and issuing statements in return for a fee—usually from 1.5 to 6 percent of sales, depending on volume. Because of the high ownership of these cards by consumers, most retail and service firms find their use essential to enhancing sales. In Canada, small business owners are becoming more vocal about what they see are ever-increasing transaction fees for some credit cards, notably reward and premium cards (see **Small Business in Action 9-7**). Visa Canada's 2013, "So, you think you want to *smallenfreuden*?" viral marketing campaign urging consumers to charge everyday items, such as coffee and bread, to their credit cards was particularly bothersome to the Canadian Federation of Independent Businesses (CFIB). The CFIB argued that the campaign increased the costs of doing business for smaller firms, the ones who can least afford it, and were vocal about wanting Visa to end its marketing efforts.[12]

Most businesses allow the use of debit cards, such as Interac. Much like the bank credit card, the debit card automatically transfers the sale amount from the customer's account at the bank to the business' account. The obvious advantages of debit cards are the quick repayment and reduction of accounts receivable. For a monthly fee, the business can be assured of on-the-spot transfers to its bank for a transaction. The costs of offering this service are approximately $50 per terminal per month or a percent of sales.

SMALL BUSINESS IN ACTION 9-7

REWARDS CARDS—WE BENEFIT BUT WHO PAYS?

Aeroplan, TD Rewards, and RBC Travel Card are just some of the growing number of premium reward cards in Canada. People love taking out their rewards card and charging anything from small convenience items, like coffee, to large purchases, such as entertainment centres. After all, who does not love getting something for nothing? Provided you pay off the balance every month, you can enjoy rewards, such as travel, gift cards, coupons, and more, none of which will cost you a dime.

But someone has to pay for these free items, and who that someone is may surprise you. It is not **Visa** or **MasterCard**, the card issuers, or even the banks that supply them. Rather, it is the merchants who pay in the form of fees. Last year, merchants in Canada paid $5 billion in total credit card fees, and a growing percent of the fees are from premium or reward-type cards. Unlike regular credit cards, debit cards, or cash, where transaction and bank fees are relatively low, premium cards come with much higher fees, sometimes more than double that of a regular transaction fee. These transaction fees can amount to 3 percent or more for every sale. Many small business owners are saying the extra fees premium cards charge are hurting their business' bottom line.

Visa counters that argument, stating the cost of accepting credit cards really amounts to the cost of doing business. Visa states, "Retailers also receive many benefits, including guaranteed payment, faster checkout times, enhanced security and fraud protection, reduced cash handling costs, and access to hundreds of millions of cardholders from around the world." Furthermore, Visa points out, the average credit card transaction fee in Canada is 1.6 percent and the fee has been stable for 10 years.

The Canadian Federation of Independent Businesses (CFIB) has brought the matter of higher transaction fees for premium cards to the Competition Bureau Canada. In its arguments, CFIB points out that average transaction fees are higher in Canada than in Australia, Denmark, the United Kingdom, and New Zealand, and is asking that changes be made to the current system. The CFIB wants merchants to be allowed to refuse to accept certain premium credit cards and be able to add a surcharge to consumers who want to use them. Under the current system, Visa and MasterCard can stipulate that a merchant must accept all their cards, not just the ones they want to accept. Furthermore, merchants are not currently allowed to charge a surcharge to credit card purchases in Canada.

Consumers in Canada love earning rewards, such as free travel, when they use their credit cards. But many Canadians don't realize that these trips and other rewards are usually paid for by merchants in the form of higher fees.

Chris Ryan/Getty Images

Discussion Questions

1. Do you think Visa and MasterCard are acting ethically in passing the cost of paying for consumer rewards cards to merchants in the form of higher fees? Why or why not?
2. Do you think Visa is correct in stating that the transaction fees ranging from 1.5 to 3 percent are worth the advantages of being able to accept credit cards?
3. As a consumer, how would you feel if merchants could refuse to accept certain credit cards you use? Would you accept paying an extra fee for the right to use a rewards card? Why or why not?
4. Do you support CFIB's position as outlined in the case above?

LEARNING OBJECTIVES SUMMARY

LO1 **The fundamentals of small business accounting include the three-step process of the accounting cycle: (1) recording the transactions (journal); (2) classifying the transaction totals (ledger); and (3) summarizing the data (financial statements). The three financial statements important to the owner-manager of a small business are the balance sheet, the income statement, and the cash flow statement.**

LO2 **The common types of bookkeeping systems used by small businesses today are manual systems (the one-book system, the one-write system, the manual multi-journal system), the outsourcing of certain functions, and small business computers.**

LO3 **Computers today can perform many functions to help the small business manage its finances. Some of the more common are recording bookkeeping and accounting transactions, creating and maintaining databases, assisting in capital investment decisions, and evaluating financial performance. Using technology can improve speed and accuracy in record keeping and reduce operating costs. Several accounting programs and cloud-based services are now available to small businesses.**

LO4 **Ratio analysis enables the small business owner to compare the financial performance of the company with that of other firms in the industry and with the company's own past performance. Common financial ratios include liquidity ratios, productivity ratios, profitability ratios, and debt ratios.**

LO5 **The advantages of offering credit are a likely increase in sales, increased store loyalty, and improved information about purchases. The disadvantages are bad debts, slow payers, and administration costs. Essential aspects of administering a credit program are defining administrative policies, establishing credit-granting criteria, setting up a system to monitor accounts, and establishing a procedure for collection.**

TIME TO TAKE ACTION

Now is the time to start to think about managing your business and personal expenses.

1. If you are writing a business plan for this course, develop a list of start-up and ongoing expenses if you have not done so already. Next, bring the list to some entrepreneurs in similar companies or business consultants, and ask them to point out inaccuracies or areas in which you can save money. Assess their recommendations and comments. If you believe they are reasonable, incorporate them into your business plan.
2. In addition to business expenses, reviewing your personal expenses can be a meaningful exercise. Create a financial plan and a monthly budget. Bring the budget to your peers and perhaps a financial planner, and consider their feedback. What, if any, changes could you make?

DISCUSSION QUESTIONS

1. Is it more important for an entrepreneur to track cash or profits? Does it depend on the type of business and/or industry? What troubles will an entrepreneur face if he or she tracks only profits and ignores cash? What troubles will an entrepreneur face if he or she tracks only cash and ignores profits?
2. How useful is a financial plan when it is based on assumptions of the future and we are confident that these assumptions are not going to be 100 percent correct?

EXPERIENTIAL EXERCISES

1. Create a personal financial snapshot for yourself. Where do you want to be financially in one, three, five, and ten years? How will you get there?
2. If you are writing a business plan, prepare a financial snapshot for your business. Where do you want your company to be in one, three, five, and ten years?
3. Create a list of start-up expenses for your business plan or for a business you may want to open. Wherever possible, verify these expenses with sources. Estimate only when you have to. Where do you think you could save money on start-up expenses? If time permits, bring your list to others who have started companies, and ask them if the list is complete and if it is possible to save money in certain areas.
4. Prepare cash flow and income statements for a potential business you may want to open. If time permits, bring these to other entrepreneurs and people in your network. Solicit their advice to determine if the numbers are realistic.
5. Research the software packages available to help entrepreneurs with the financials for a business plan. Which do you believe is the best? Why?
6. Companies planning to make an initial public offering (IPO) must submit a financial plan as part of their prospectus. From the Internet, collect prospectuses from three companies, and analyze their financial plans. What are the

major assumptions made in constructing these financial plans? Compare and contrast these financial plans with what you would expect of a financial plan as part of a business plan.

7. Draw up pro forma statements for your venture idea. (Note that the students must source these.) Then break into small groups to review your expenses and try to find ways to generate savings. Try to reduce expenditures by at least 20 percent per business plan.
8. For the following transactions, indicate which accounts are changed and by how much:
   a. Feb. 14, 2020—Received $1000 from Frank Johnson on account.
   b. Feb. 14, 2020—Purchased equipment for $1500 (paid cash).
   c. Feb. 15, 2020—Paid owner Bill Cartwright $2000 for January's salary.
   d. Feb. 18, 2020—Paid telephone bill of $90.87.
   e. Feb. 19, 2020—Bought ice cream on account, $395.00.
9. Calculate the rate of return for the following investment. The total cost of the investment is $250,000, the depreciable life of the investment is 10 years, and the annual profit (net of depreciation) is $30,000. What considerations other than financial ones exist?
10. Assume the annual depreciation charge for the investment in Problem 9 is $25,000. Determine the payback period of the investment.
11. Determine the break-even point, in dollars, for an investment with fixed costs of $100,000 and an estimated contribution of 60 percent. How much revenue would it need to produce before you would invest?
12. a. From the balance sheet and income statement of Sam's Paint and Drywall, determine the following ratios:
      (1) Current
      (2) Inventory turnover
      (3) Profit to sales
      (4) Return on investment
      (5) Total debt to equity
    b. From Dun and Bradstreet's key business ratios on industry norms, evaluate each of the above ratios.

SAM'S PAINT AND DRYWALL FOR YEAR ENDED DECEMBER 31, 2020
(in thousands of dollars)

ASSETS		**LIABILITIES AND NET WORTH**	
Cash	$ 12	Accounts payable	$ 15
Inventory	41	Notes payable—bank	4
Accounts receivable	18	Other	20
Total current assets	71	Total current liabilities	39
Fixed assets:		Long-term liabilities	41
Vehicles	10		
Equipment	15		
Building	22		
Land	23	Total net worth (owner's equity)	61
Total fixed assets	70		
Total assets	$141	Total liabilities and net worth	$141

Income Statement December 31, 2020 (in thousands of dollars)

Sales	$280
Less: Cost of goods sold	186
Gross margin on sales	94
Less: Operating expenses	81
Net profit	$ 13

13. Dick's Draperies has gross sales of $15,000 per month, half of which are on credit (paid within 30 days). Monthly expenses are as follows: wages, $3000; utilities and rent, $2000; advertising, $300; and miscellaneous, $500. Inventory is purchased every three months and totals $30,000 for each order. Yearly expenses paid for in advance are insurance of $1000 and a rent deposit of $700. Prepare a six-month cash flow statement for Dick's Draperies. What advice would you give this business based on the cash flow statement?

COMPREHENSIVE CASE DAN KIM: PART 4

Dan still needs to raise money to fund his business and is sure crowdfunding will work. He has listened to Suzie and has invested a fair bit of time learning about the process of establishing a successful crowdfunding campaign. Dan has invested in a promotional video, written a great introduction and explanation for Ladder Helper, and increased his social media contacts. Dan has also decided to offer one Ladder Helper per $30 donation as a reward to all backers for supporting his business venture. Dan and Suzie are now both excited about the possibilities of crowdfunding, and they decide to launch on March 15th, just prior to Spring when many people will be looking to complete renovations and contractors see a rise in their business. While the pair are optimistic, Dan has also lowered his expectations about the number of backers he anticipates and creates a campaign where he will meet his goal if 500 people support his idea. Dan understands that this will only result in $15,000, but it would be enough money to prove his concept and allow him to consider other forms of financing.

On the day Ladder Helper's crowdfunding campaign launches, Dan reaches out to all his social media contacts and asks them to share the crowdfunding link and talk about the idea. Suzie also reaches out to her friends and family through social media and as luck would have it, one of them writes for a national newspaper. Her cousin, who writes for the *National Times* and has a loyal Twitter following, loves the idea of the Ladder Helper and quickly shares the information on social media before following up with an article in the business section of the paper. Between Dan and Suzie's well-designed crowdfunding campaign, use of social media, and the free public relations, their crowdfunding campaign exceeds expectations and in 30 days Dan has achieved donations from 2500 backers.

With $75,000 in what amounts to pre-sales Dan is convinced he must build his factory. After much discussion Suzie and he agree to mortgage their home and borrow money to build a facility. While it delays Dan's ability to complete his Ladder Helper rewards, Dan manages to quickly get a factory built, hire some help, and start to build Ladder Helpers for his crowdfunding backers.

Dan realizes that while the $75,000 he raised through crowdfunding is a good start, the business is far from sustainable. He is unsure how to promote the business though and doesn't want to spend any money on marketing as he is starting to worry, he may not make any money off of his crowdfunding campaign. With labour, manufacturing and now mortgage costs, Dan is becoming increasingly concerned about his ability to manufacture the Ladder Helper at a reasonable cost.

Given his financial concerns, Dan raises the price of the Ladder Helper to $40 and invests time in promoting the Ladder Helper on social media and email. While he doesn't bother creating a marketing plan, he does work tirelessly at night talking about his product on Facebook, emailing information to construction companies, hardware stores and sending Tweets. Dan's hard work pays off and he is rewarded with an additional 1750 orders at $40 a Ladder Helper.

Although Dan underestimated many of his expenses and start-up costs, he provided much of the labour and expertise himself to defray part of this shortfall. As the year progresses, orders for the Ladder Helper continue to increase as a result of Dan's marketing efforts, and Dan begins to think that the business could really work.

Suzie has kept track of the receipts and disbursements and at the end of the first year of operations takes all the financial information to their accountant. A couple of weeks later, the accountant calls them in. They are very disappointed in the results (see **Table 9-A**). While reviewing the statements with their accountant, she provides some industry averages to help them in planning for the next year (see **Table 9-B**). They are quite nervous about taking the statements to their banker. Dan and Suzie are hopeful their investor will see that sales are increasing and will be satisfied with this.

TABLE 9-A

The Ladder Helper Income Statement: Year 1

Sales	2500 @ $30	$ 75,000	
	1750 @ $40	70,000	$145,000
Cost of Goods Sold	4750 @ $12	57,000	
Wages		80,000	
Employee Benefits		6,000	
Utilities		17,000	
Repairs & Maintenance		4,500	
Insurance		1,000	
Amortization		17,000	
Interest and bank charges		10,400	$192,900
Net Income			($47,900)

The Ladder Helper Income Statement: End of Year 1

Assets	
Cash	$ 2,250
Accounts Receivable	3,800
Inventory	10,250
Building & Equipment	153,000
Land	50,000
Total Assets	$219,300
Liabilities & Owner's Equity	
Accounts Payable	$ 36,800
Bank Loan—Current Payable	23,400
Bank Loan—Long Term	117,000
Owner's Equity	42,100
Total Liabilities & Owner's Equity	$219,300

TABLE 9-B

SELECTED RATIOS FOR METAL FABRICATING COMPANIES

Current Ratio	1.52:1
Gross Margin	23.2%
Profit on Sales	6.1%
Profit on Net Worth	21.13%
Collection Period	59 days
Inventory Turnover	4.2
Debt to Equity	1.1:1

Before Dan saw the statements, he had contemplated expanding his small factory by building an addition and adding some new equipment at a cost of $80,000 with a life of 10 years. He had estimated that this expansion would bring in an additional income of $10,000 per year. With the first year's performance, however, Dan is not sure whether he should make this investment.

Questions

1. What were some of the methods Dan and Suzie used to create a successful crowdfunding campaign? What other strategies could they use?
2. Dan is marketing his Ladder Helper through Facebook, Twitter, and email. Why do you think he opted for these methods? Should he expand his social media presence? Why or why not?
3. What do you think about Dan's strategy of investing no money in marketing? Do you agree with him? Why or why not? What other non-paid forms of marketing would you recommend to Dan.
4. Evaluate Dan and Suzie's financial management practices.
5. Using the ratios provided by the accountant, evaluate Dan's business and make suggestions for improvement.
6. Using the financial information provided, calculate a break-even point and rate of return for the new expansion. What additional information would Dan need to do a payback analysis of the proposed expansion?

APPENDIX 9A

USE OF FINANCIAL RATIOS FOR A SMALL BUSINESS (AUTOMOTIVE DEALER)

RATIO	METHOD OF COMPUTATION	LAST YEAR	MOTOR VEHICLE DEALER PREVIOUS YEAR	INDUSTRY AVERAGE	EXPLANATION
1. Liquidity a. Current	Current assets: Current ratio	1.09 times liabilities	1.05 times	1.1 times	Satisfactory: This dealer has the same ability as is common in this industry.
b. Quick ratio	Current assets – inventories: Current liabilities	0.33 times	0.45 times	Not available	
2. Productivity a. Inventory turnover	Cost of goods sold/Average inventory (at cost) or Sales/Average inventory (at retail)	7.41 times	7.41 times	6.0 times	Good: This dealer has a higher turnover rate than the average dealer. This may indicate a higher sales level or lower inventory levels.

[continued]

[continued]

b. Collection	Average inventory at retail/Daily credit sales	13.56 days	16.01 days	12 days	Fair: The collection period is longer than average, which may indicate the need to tighten the credit policy; however, it seems that some action has already been taken.
3. Profitability a. Gross margins	Gross sales – Cost of goods sold as a percent of sales	10.71%	12.28%	16.70%	Poor: The inventory may be obsolete, or company prices may be too low.
b. Profit on sales	Net profit (before tax)/ Gross sales	0.85%	– (0.6%)	0.6%	Good: Expenses are being kept in line.
c. Expense ratio	Expense item/ Gross sales	11.69%	13.59%	Not available	Good: The company is making an effort to cut expenses.
d. Return on investment	Net profit (before tax)/ Owner's equity	10.49%	– 1.74%	9.0%	Good: This company is more profitable than most in the industry. It is clear that action is being taken to improve profitability of this firm.
4. Debt a. Total debt to equity	Total debt/ Owner'sequity	325.89%	376.09%	398.20%	Good: This dealer depends less on debt financing than is common in this industry. An intentional move has been taken in this direction.

Note: The symbol / denotes division.

CHAPTER 10

OPERATIONS MANAGEMENT

LEARNING OBJECTIVES

By the end of this chapter, you should be able to:

LO1 Explain the production process.

LO2 Describe the management of the components of the physical facilities of a small business.

LO3 List the types of layouts used in small manufacturing firms.

LO4 List the factors to consider in planning the layout of a retail store.

LO5 Explain the methods of purchasing and controlling inventories in a small business.

SMALL BUSINESS PROFILE

COSTA ELLES, *Ela! Greek Taverna*

Hero Images/Getty Images

Costa Elles came to Canada with his parents in the 1970s after fleeing Greece as a political refugee. Elles' father, who was a priest, stressed two important requirements for being successful in life: education and work ethic. Elles recalls that he grew up playing and loving soccer. While his father was pleased to hear that he was working hard on the field, most of his father's focus was on school and education. With his love of soccer and a strong belief in education, Elles eventually moved to Halifax, where he attended St. Mary's University and was a student athlete. After graduating with a commerce degree, Elles ventured back to Greece, where he embarked on a professional soccer career for a short while before returning to Halifax. During Elles' early career, he coached soccer and worked as a sales representative for Moosehead Brewery. During his time as a sales rep, Elles noticed there were no authentic Greek restaurants in Halifax, and the idea of creating a great Greek restaurant became his passion. A short time later, Elles and his partner, Chris Tzaneteas, opened Opa in the Halifax downtown core. From the start, Elles envisioned that Opa would provide guests with an authentic Greek experience, and the partners put processes in place to ensure this would happen. Sourcing products was essential to the company, and they established the practice of using only the freshest and the highest-quality ingredients. In addition, controls were established to ensure that the dishes were cooked and served properly and that authentic, high-quality food was served consistently. Elles states that they wanted Opa to be a top-notch Greek restaurant, and that could only occur with the finest products and attention to detail.

Opa soon became a hit in the Halifax community, and Elles and Tzaneteas expanded their company, Eat It Two Entertainment, to include various restaurants and bars, including Seven (a high-end restaurant), Argyle Bar and Grill, Mosaic, and eventually two other Opa locations. The pair attributed much of their success to attention to detail and a core belief in being committed to using the best ingredients. It was during this time that Elles thought there could be a franchising opportunity for Opa and renamed the chain Ela! Greek Taverna, which was a name they could trademark. Elles notes that a key to establishing a successful franchise is finding the right people and putting in systems that they can follow. Every franchisee has to be able to produce the same authentic meal, and rules and controls have to be in place to ensure consistency. Furthermore, as Elles states, controlling costs is very important in the restaurant business, and a franchisor wants to know that in addition to great food, they are buying into a great business model that includes cost and portion controls. Now, after a number of years in business and an amicable split from his business partner, Elles thinks he has the right systems in place to ensure a positive Greek experience and is looking to grow his restaurant chain using the franchise model.

ELA GREEK TAVERNA
elagreektaverna.ca

MANAGEMENT OF INTERNAL OPERATIONS LO1

The management of internal operations is part of the physical facilities section of the business plan (see **Chapter 4**). Operations management is one area in which many small business owners have their greatest strength. They know how to produce a quality product or provide a quality service, and their primary interest often lies with this aspect of the business. **Small Business in Action 10-1** illustrates the potential problems of inefficient management and production. Although they may have production expertise, many entrepreneurs lack the management skills to maintain quality and control. Typical areas needing attention are cash flow, production costs and product quality, inventory management, and physical facilities issues. As mentioned in earlier chapters, the entrepreneur is often weaker in the areas of marketing and financial management than in managing the production process. As a result, many entrepreneurs find it advantageous to outsource some of these services. A study by PricewaterhouseCoopers found that 73 percent of Canadian businesses outsource one or more business processes.[1] Some of the typical services are financial management, human resource management, income tax preparation, marketing, call centre and customer care, and mail-room operations.

SMALL BUSINESS IN ACTION 10-1

MIND YOUR METRICS

Chris Bolivar, former president of Optamedia Inc., said during the first few months after establishing Optamedia, he noticed that although sales were good, the net income was off by as much as 10 percent. Optamedia was an Edmonton-based advertising agency that successfully merged with a rival marketing company, McRobbie in 2009 to form McRobbie Optamedia and eventually evolved into Free. So how did he accomplish this growth?

"I'd look at projects and wonder why they were taking so long," he says. He then realized that neither he nor his staff was keeping track of time spent on client work, which meant the firm was regularly underestimating how long it took to complete projects. Bolivar corrected the problem by introducing a time-accounting program that employees must fill out to get paid. Each month, he ran reports on accounts, tracking hours worked in relation to project milestones and overall budget. As a result, net income doubled, productivity was up, and estimating of new jobs was more accurate. This, along with other improvements, resulted in Optamedia being named as one of *Profit* magazine's Hot 50 start-up companies and directly affected the bottom line for the company. Bolivar notes that as a result of the successful merger and management changes, income is up over 40 percent, and company assets are up 100 percent.

Discussion Questions

1. Given that Optamedia was a start-up when Bolivar instituted the operations procedures, do you think this made the implementation easier or more difficult?
2. Do you think employees would be responsive to this rigour in reporting work? Why or why not? Would you want to work in a company with this much rigour in reporting? Why or why not?
3. What are some of the pros and cons of rigorous employee reporting?

THE PRODUCTION PROCESS

The production process involves the conversion of inputs, such as money, people, machines, and inventories, into outputs—the products or services provided. **Table 10-1** illustrates this application for manufacturing, wholesaling, retailing, and service businesses. The owner-manager's task is to organize the production process of the business so that the outputs (products) can be produced efficiently.

The priority evaluation and review technique (PERT) and other flowchart systems have been developed to help organize the production process. A simple example of such a system is shown in **Figure 10-1** for a manufacturing firm. By visually plotting the tasks and required time, the owner-manager can minimize down time and ensure the most efficient production. Continual efforts should be made throughout the process to ensure quality control.

TABLE 10-1 Examples of Production Systems

TYPE OF BUSINESS	INPUTS	PROCESS	OUTPUTS
Apparel manufacturer	Cloth, thread, buttons	Store—Cut—Sew—Press—Ship	Dresses
Wholesaler	Large volume per order of each product	Store—Sort—Package—Ship	Smaller volume of a product in each order
Retailer	A volume of each of many products to the ultimate customer	Store—Customer display—Package	Low volume of a few products to each customer
Laundry (service firm)	Dirty clothes	Sort—Wash—Press—Store	Clean clothes

FIGURE 10-1 Priority Evaluation and Review Techniques (PERT)

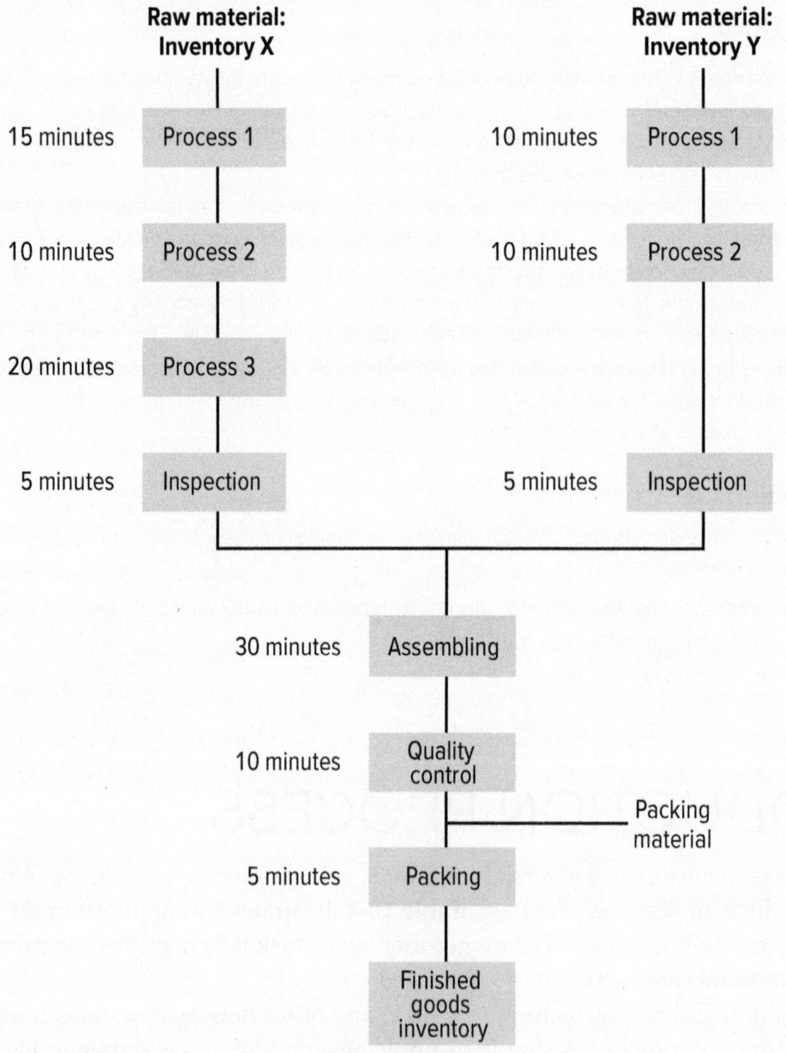

Total work time = 120 minutes   Critical path time = 95 minutes

TOTAL QUALITY MANAGEMENT

Many small businesses have been able to develop a competitive advantage by ensuring superior quality in their products and services, as evidenced in **Small Business in Action 10-2**. This is referred to as *total quality management.* Total quality management (TQM) is a philosophy of management focusing on problem solving and control. An organization that focuses on TQM uses factors such as consumer-driven product quality, efficient distribution, quick response, continuous improvement, elimination of waste, and top management leadership and commitment as measurement tools. These systems are often developed in conjunction with other business and engineering disciplines by using a cross-functional approach.

To achieve this type of standard, the business owner must meet several requirements:

- Realize that the business is going to exist in the long run so that it is more concerned with long-term performance than short-term profits.
- Involve employees in decision making so that they also see the need to ensure overall superior quality.
- Invest time and effort in training employees adequately.
- Develop standards by which quality performance can be measured.
- Continually measure internal performance through internal systems and externally by surveying customers and other key parties.

Some small businesses, particularly those interested in exporting their products, have found it advantageous to get their products quality certified through the International Standards Organization (ISO 9000). Although costly for the small business, the certification process can lead to more efficient business processes, positively impact quality, improve supplier relationships, and provide an effective marketing hook.[2] ISO 9000 is an international reference for quality requirements in business-to-business dealings. Quality management standards (QMS) are used by leading businesses worldwide to implement a management system that guarantees conformity and the quality of the processes followed to output products and services.[3]

SMALL BUSINESS IN ACTION 10-2

GODIN GUITARS STRIKES THE RIGHT CHORD

Robert Godin recalls he wanted to be a professional musician, specifically a guitar player. Yet, he admits he was more passionate than talented and, rather than chase an unrealistic dream, he decided to see if could turn his love of music into a more traditional occupation.

Godin recalls the pivotal music era of the late-1960s and early '70s when the guitar began to emerge as the lead instrument for rock bands. He noticed that guitar strings were not easy to manipulate and started to customize guitars using banjo strings and other additions. Based on his early success, he decided to try making guitars from scratch and fell in love with the process.

Godin started to manufacture acoustic guitars in Quebec, and today he produces stringed instruments under six different brand names including Godin, Norman, Seagull, Simon & Patrick, La Patrie, and Art & Lutherie. While **Godin Guitars** has become the largest North American seller of guitars, the company, which is based out of Montreal, still manufacturers primarily in Quebec with five factories in the province and one more in New Hampshire.

Godin Guitars, founded by Robert Godin and now run in co-operation with his two sons Simon and Patrick, continues to manufacture guitars in North America.

Left: Simon Godin Center: Robert Godin Right: Patrick Godin, Photo courtesy of Godin Guitars.

[continued]

[continued]

Godin and his sons, Simon and Patrick, who now run the business for him, state that while most of their competitors are now building products for significantly less money overseas, they continue to manufacture in North America in order to maintain quality assurance. Simon Godin says manufacturing in-province allows them to follow production from start to finish because, he points out, making quality instruments is difficult to rush. He explains that it can take upwards of two years to just dry the wood and six to ten weeks to make an instrument in North America. If instruments were made overseas, the production time could be as short as two weeks, but they would lose their ability to monitor the process.

Godin has also invested heavily in their North American production facilities and their employees. The company's factories specialize in certain instruments, they make use of robot technology to ensure precision, limit errors, and maximize efficiencies. The firm has also designed and built their own manufacturing tools allowing them to consistently produce superior products. Finally, Godin actively encourages employee engagement in the manufacturing process and rewards employees with a generous profit-sharing plan.

Godin Guitars has also invested in a unique sales process that enables them to offset some of the higher costs associated with manufacturing in North America. Godin sells direct to most retailers, including their international customers, and their distribution centre can normally place products in a retailers hand in less than three days after an order is placed. The result of "Godin Direct" is that retailers, especially smaller shops, do not have to purchase products from distributors who add in their own margins or mark-up. Given that some small retailers were sourcing guitars from a regional distributor who were buying from a national distributor, this process removes several layers of mark-up from the products.

Godin customers rave about the quality of the products, the fact that they are manufactured in Canada, and that they are priced competitively. Given their continued investment in manufacturing and the "Godin Direct" distribution system, perhaps the company can buck the trend of moving manufacturing facilities offshore.

Discussion Questions

1. Based on the material in this chapter, do you think Godin Guitars is following Total Quality Management Standards (TQM)? Why or why not?
2. Given that even the largest guitar producers are manufacturing outside of North America do you think Godin's insistence of only making products in North America is sustainable in the long term? Why or why not?
3. Based on the management's insistence of manufacturing in North America and the creation of "Godin Direct," which helps many small independent retailers, would you consider Godin Guitars to be a social enterprise? Why or why not?
4. What are some of the advantages and disadvantages associated with Godin's North American manufacturing and "Godin Direct"?

PHYSICAL FACILITIES LO2

Planning the physical facilities was discussed briefly in **Chapter 3** as part of the preparation of the feasibility analysis. Selection of the location for the business was introduced in **Chapter 4** as one of the steps in organizing a business.

Although it is not necessary to review that information again, it is critical for the owner-manager to recognize that the physical facilities must be closely monitored and maintained to ensure they are efficient and up-to-date. Locations are never static—populations, businesses, and traffic patterns shift continually. This trend has caused many excellent locations to deteriorate over the years.

Some aspects of the physical facilities that should constantly be evaluated are illustrated in **Table 10-2**. The table ranks the importance of each physical facility characteristic based on the type of small business.

LAYOUTS

Effective management of the interior layout of the business can greatly enhance productivity. Small businesses use several types of layouts. The layout selected varies by industry and by scope of operations. In determining layout, it is advisable to draw up a floor plan to better use available space.

TABLE 10-2 Business Building and Site-Rating Table

FACTORS	RETAILING	SERVICE	MANUFACTURING	WHOLESALING
Building feature:				
Age	1	4	3	4
Space	1	3	1	4
Configuration	1	4	4	3
Appearance	1	3	3	4
Frontage	1	4	4	4
Access	1	2	1	1
Interior use:				
Floor space	2	3	1	1
Room dimensions	1	3	1	4
Ceiling heights	2	2	2	4
Stairways, elevators	3	3	1	1
Window space	1	3	4	4
Utility services	3	1	1	3
Improvement potential:				
Building exterior	1	3	4	4
Building interior	1	3	2	2
Site	1	2	3	4
Surrounding	2	2	3	4
Streets and walks	2	3	3	3
Access	1	3	2	1
Expansion	2	1	1	1
Site and environment:				
Street and service areas	1	2	2	3
Setback and frontage	1	3	4	4
Parking	1	2	2	3
Surrounding businesses	2	3	4	4
Area environment	2	3	4	4

Key to ratings: 1 = critical; 2 = very important; 3 = not ordinarily important; 4 = minimum importance

LAYOUTS FOR MANUFACTURING FIRMS LO3

Here are some key areas to consider in planning the interior of a manufacturing plant:

- Location of utility outlets for machines.
- Location of receiving and shipping areas for raw materials and finished goods.
- Safety aspects.
- Adequate lighting capability throughout.
- Provision for easy plant maintenance and cleaning.

Small manufacturing firms use essentially three types of layouts: product layout, process layout, and fixed-position layout, each of which is discussed next. **Small Business in Action 10-3** provides another view to setting up a layout for the small business.

Product Layout.

The product layout is suitable for the business that manufactures just one or only a few products. It closely resembles the production line of a large factory. **Figure 10-2** illustrates the floor plan of a typical product layout.

FIGURE 10-2 **Product Layout**

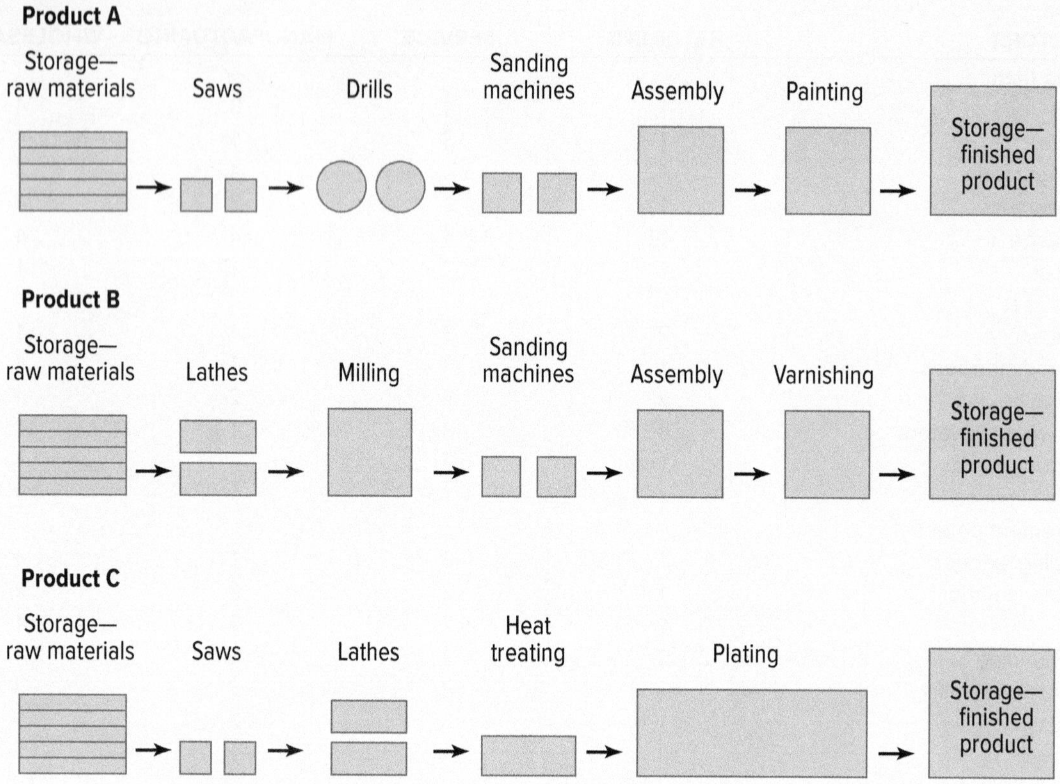

The product layout closely resembles one in a production line.

John A. Rizzo/Getty Images

The product layout generally allows for economy in both cost of and time required for production, as each part of the manufacturing process is carried out in sequence.

Process Layout.

The process layout is designed for factories that manufacture many different or custom-made products. In this layout, similar processes are grouped together and the product moves back and forth among those areas until completed. The process layout is often more expensive and requires more management time to ensure efficiency. **Figure 10-3** illustrates a process layout for a small factory.

FIGURE 10-3 **Process Layout**

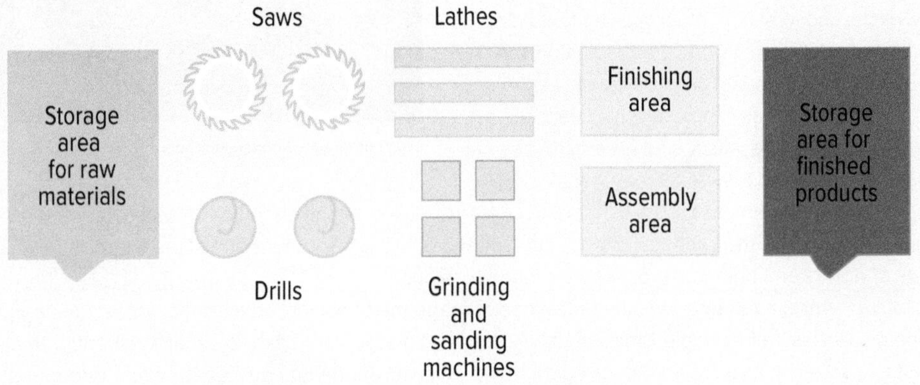

Fixed-Position Layout.

In the fixed-position layout, the product remains in a fixed position throughout its manufacture. The production processes move to the product. As one might expect, this type of layout is used for very large and cumbersome products and is used infrequently by small businesses. **Figure 10-4** illustrates the fixed-position layout.

FIGURE 10-4 **Fixed-Position Layout**

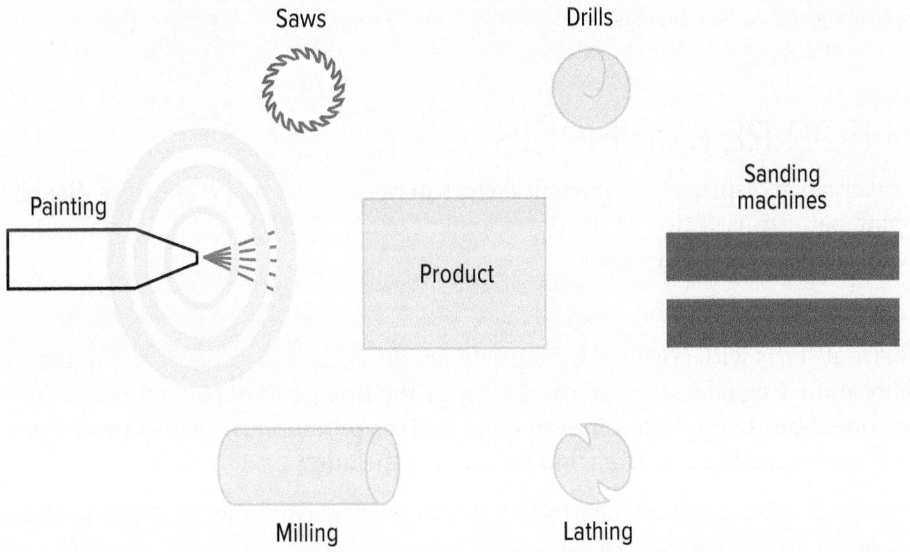

SMALL BUSINESS IN ACTION 10-3

PRODUCTION IMPROVEMENT

pisaphotography/Shutterstock.com

When the auto industry was in crisis from 2008 through 2012, Chris Wood, president of **Marwood Metal Fabrication Ltd.**, located in Tillsonburg, Ontario, was concerned. His business provided automobile parts to the major automakers. But Wood used his concerns to make a change: he turned to a lean management philosophy known as *kaizen*—Japanese for "continuous improvement." He thought it would usher in a more efficient way to produce the components. The *kaizen* system allows groups of workers from throughout the company to brainstorm intensively about the way they do their work, to identify waste, and to cut out processes that add cost but not value. After completing that work, the production line at Marwood began tightening up and productivity increased.

Wood notes that he was initially apprehensive in adopting *kaizen* management because he was fearful his employees would resist changes to the traditional way they were doing business: "I thought we were going to have a lot more trouble with buy-in on the shop floor—I was worried there'd be resistance to change." Instead, Wood says, the changes in production methods brought in as a result of the exercise have saved the company millions of dollars and helped it prosper after the recession.

Business consultant Anselm Almeida, who helped Wood manage the transition, advises that *kaizen* management is not only for manufacturing processes. For example, firms can apply the principles to their cash flow management or their information management systems. By reducing process and focusing on being efficient, improvements can be made throughout an organization. Scott Shpak, a business journalist, cautions that the system of lean management is not perfect. Although most firms that employ lean management practices do see some initial improvement, the constant drive for increased efficiency can negatively affect employee morale and can lead to less efficient workers.

Wood remains committed to the management process because, as he states, it has resulted in a much more efficient and profitable firm. His advice to small manufacturers is that they cannot afford to do things as they have always done them, especially when the economy and consumers are rapidly changing.

Discussion Questions

1. Do you think implementing changes, like the ones discussed above, is easier or more difficult in times of financial crisis?
2. Do you think there is a danger in the *kaizen* system of making change for the sake of change? How can companies ensure this does not happen?
3. List and discuss the potential pros and cons for adopting a *kaizen* system.

LAYOUTS FOR RETAIL FIRMS LO4

Interior layout and creative display are important factors in the success of a retail store. Sensitivity to consumer needs and shopping patterns is critical to the development of an effective layout. In planning the layout, the retailer will need to analyze several key areas.

Window Displays

Successful retail layout starts with creating appropriate window displays—a key factor in determining if consumers enter a retail location. Consider the window display as the first point of contact with customers. Window displays can also communicate important information, such as promotions, type of products sold, quality of items, and price. Keys to creating effective window displays include[4]:

1. *Layering:* Start with information on the window, then place items midway between the window tall backdrops.
2. *Storytelling:* Window displays should communicate a theme or an idea. Some common themes include changing seasons and holiday shopping.

3. *Simplicity:* Window displays do not have to be overly complex: they should inspire shoppers to walk into the store to see more items.
4. *Boldness and innovation:* Capturing people's attention continues to be difficult. Catch their interest using props, colours, and imagery.
5. *Display variety:* Displays should be changed to create renewed interest. Change can range from simply replacing a few items in the window to a completely re-doing the entire display. The latter usually signals the start of a new retail season.

Allocation of Selling versus Non-selling Space.

Experience in retailing shows that some areas of a retail store are more productive and draw more traffic than others. This phenomenon is illustrated in **Figure 10-5**. Generally, the space at the front and to the right is more productive space. Obviously, selling space should be planned for the most productive areas of the store. The space at the front of the store is referred to a the *threshold* or *decompression zone.* For smaller retailers, this is the first few feet inside the retail space. At this point, people are transitioning from being pedestrians to customers in your store. Here, they will make quick judgments about the layout, prices, and quality and attractiveness of the facility. It's important to note that 90 percent of shoppers in North America will turn right upon entering a store. Entrepreneurs will want to ensure the displays in these areas are attractive and offer high-demand and high profit-margin items. Most successful retail layouts have customers walk a path throughout the store, creating stopping points along the path. Successful stopping points grab the consumers attention and can include retails racks of interesting items, placement of promotional products, and/or a change in how items are being displayed. Finally checkouts or point of sales should be on the left as customer complete their journey through the store.[5]

FIGURE 10-5 **Rankings of Space Importance in a Typical Retail Store**

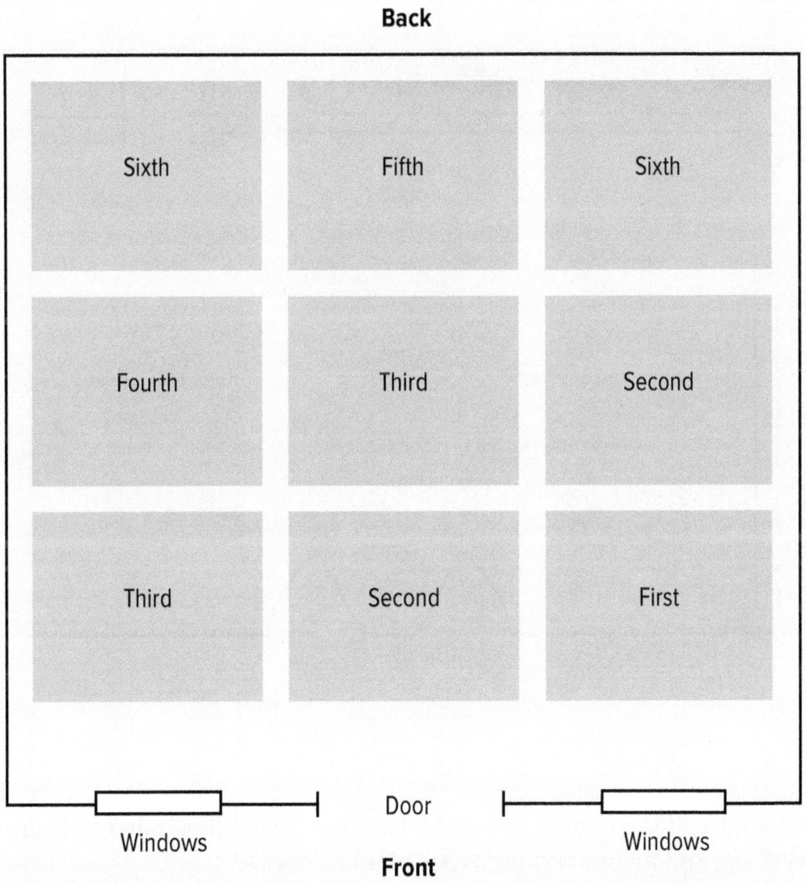

Allocation of Space among Departments and Products.

The same principle discussed above should be applied in allocating space among departments and products, with the most profitable being placed in the high-traffic areas, if possible.

Classification of Merchandise.

Previous chapters discussed the classification of consumer goods—convenience, shopping, and specialty goods. Each merchandise classification may require a slightly different placement in the retail store based on the purchase motives associated with that class of goods. For example, convenience items are often found close to heavier customer traffic flow. Shopping goods might be placed by competing brands, and specialty or demand items at more inaccessible parts of the store.

Location of Displays and Products on the Shelf.

The small retailer should acquire expertise in a number of display techniques. Placement of merchandise on a shelf or counter can lead to increased sales, as certain areas are more productive than others. Merchandise placed at eye level and at the ends of aisles generally sells better. Two types of layouts are used by retail stores: the grid layout and the free-flow layout.

Grid Layout.

The grid layout is organized with customer convenience and retailer efficiency in mind. Grid layouts have traditionally been used in stores such as supermarkets and hardware stores. **Figure 10-6** illustrates a grid layout.

FIGURE 10-6 **Grid Layout**

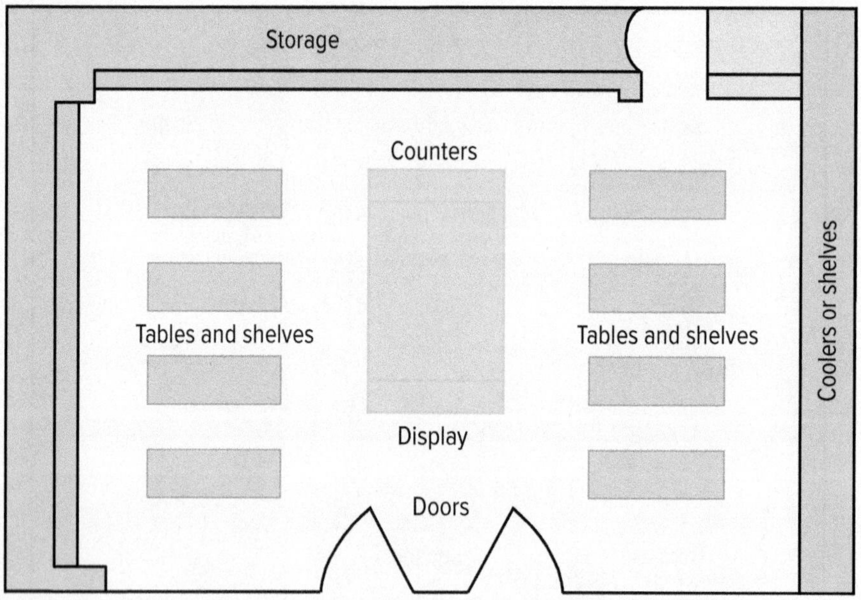

Free-Flow Layout.

Some types of merchandise are purchased in a more relaxed atmosphere that allows customers more time to browse. For such merchandise, it is common to use the free-flow layout illustrated in **Figure 10-7**. This type of layout is suitable for clothing and many specialty types of merchandise.

FIGURE 10-7 **Free-Flow Layout**

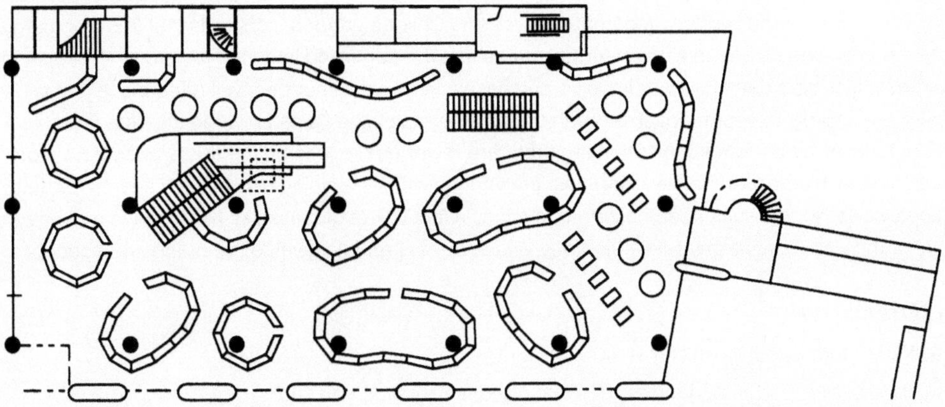

Many larger retail stores use combinations of the grid and free-flow layouts. Most small retailers, however, generally use one or the other type. **Small Business in Action 10-4** describes the innovative layout of a well-known retailer.

SMALL BUSINESS IN ACTION 10-4

NAVIGATING IKEA

Although it may seem odd to talk about a store solely in terms of its layout, if anyone deserves the honour, it's **IKEA**. Most people who have visited the store, whether or not they enjoyed the experience, can say that if there is anything that makes IKEA different, the store layout is high on the list. And most will admit that IKEA has some awesome information architecture going on.

In the main lobby, you'll find an array of sensible and well-marked services. There are restrooms and pay-phones, and even phone numbers for local buses and taxis. You can also find a huge diagram of the store in the lobby.

On the first level, IKEA has everything laid out for people who know what they are looking for. As well, you can browse bins of "take-me-home-now" items. Here you will also find self-serve furniture aisles and a bistro. But of course, IKEA would prefer you to move up the stairs, to the second level, where things really get interesting.

IKEA has managed to stand out in the industry by maintaining an attractive store layout.

nomadFra/Shutterstock.com

The second level is devoted to those people who aren't exactly sure what they want. All of IKEA's merchandise is laid out in context or, as some have called it, in room displays. This is perfect for anyone who isn't a decorator because IKEA provides the vision. As well, on this level you are guided to move in one direction. And in case you get confused, just look down! There are arrows on the floors and even signs at critical junctures that explain that you're moving through the store in a planned, straightforward manner. All of this, of course, has been purposely created. And while you can certainly move around in IKEA in your own way, chances are you'll feel odd doing so. But that's all part of IKEA's plan, proving that, if any store has an edge when it comes to retail layout, it's IKEA.

Critics of IKEA's business practices, while admitting the stores are successful, question the ethics of the store layout and staffing decisions. They contend the stores are designed in a way to encourage, if not ensure, people spend more time

[continued]

[continued]

shopping, resulting in consumers spending more time than they originally planned. For example, it has been found that shoppers spend on average two hours in IKEA, which is more than double the time they spend shopping for groceries. Alan Penn, director of the Virtual Reality Centre for the Built Environment at University College London, contends that IKEA's strategy is to keep customers in the store as long as possible. Penn further states that the confusing layout of the store, where shoppers follow arrows, encourages consumers to make more impulse purchases. Penn says shoppers will often place items in their shopping cart, knowing they are unlikely to venture back through the store and pick the items up when they are ready to leave. The result is more impulse purchases by customers. Additionally, there are fewer employees on the floors of an IKEA store compared with similar merchants. The result is consumers walking past the various impulse display bins as they search for help, which usually results in additional sales. Yet consumers do not seem to mind. In fact IKEA's global sales have grown every year since 2001, an accomplishment that would make any retailer jealous, and shoppers remain loyal to the brand and concept.

Discussion Questions

1. Do you think IKEA's store layout is ethical? Why or why not?
2. What are the advantages of IKEA's store design? What disadvantages do you see?
3. Why do you think shoppers are willing to spend so much time visiting an IKEA store?
4. Could a small start-up retailer mimic IKEA's layout? Why or why not?
5. Why wouldn't other larger retailers establish store layouts like IKEA? Would such a layout work for a grocery chain or a retailer, such as Walmart? Why or why not?

LAYOUTS FOR SERVICE FIRMS

Because the operations of service firms are so diverse, it is difficult to provide standard information on layouts. Some service firms, such as restaurants, more closely approximate the layouts of retail stores. Many of the principles discussed earlier for retailing apply here. For those service firms that are more similar to manufacturing firms, such as repair shops, the principles of manufacturing layouts may be more appropriate.

Small retail clothing stores tend to use a free-flow store layout to encourage customers to stop and browse.

fiphoto © 123RF.com

PURCHASING AND CONTROLLING INVENTORIES LO5

The cost of purchasing and holding inventories can be substantial and have significant impact on the viability of a business. A recent study concluded that businesses could save anywhere from two to six percent of their annual spending if they made some small but significant changes to how they bought supplies. While two to six percent may seem like a small number, it would take a 15 percent increase in sales to replicate its impact on the bottom line. The small changes that would result in such a significant savings include cutting out unnecessary expenses as well as price-checking or comparison shopping. Entrepreneurs should recognize that consistently making these changes do not require much effort and the savings can be substantial over time.[6]

Because a small business generally has limited economic resources, it is critical that it give inventory management a high priority. The following sections discuss areas about which the small business owner should be knowledgeable in purchasing and controlling inventories.

SOURCES OF SUPPLY

The chapters on marketing and business planning discussed various aspects of the distribution channel from the seller's point of view. The same principles apply in this section, but from the buyer's position. The owner-manager should know which suppliers are available. Purchases can usually be made directly from the manufacturer, from an agent of the manufacturer, from a wholesaler, or from a retailer. Although sources vary considerably among industries, most small business owners purchase their inventories from wholesalers.

By comparison shopping and buying only necessary items, entrepreneurs can save between two and six percent annually on all purchases. The savings are the same as a 15 percent increase in sales on a company's net income.

Image Source/Kevin Kozicki

One question most small businesses must answer is whether to purchase from one supplier or from many. In purchasing from only one supplier, the buyer is assured of consistent quality; and the supplier may offer favourable treatment, such as discounts and guaranteed supply in case of shortages, although orders may be too small to divide. But consider that other suppliers may periodically offer lower prices. Opting for purchasing from many suppliers may also spread the risk for the entrepreneur. The small business owner must weigh these pros and cons in making this decision.

Source for Sports is one of the better-known buying groups in Canada. Roughly 150 independent sports stores have combined together to buy large quantities of sporting goods items at discounts.

Photo courtesy of Source for Sports

Many small business owners find it advantageous and cost effective to pool purchases with other companies. This may be done on an informal basis, but this choice usually involves the business joining a purchasing group or franchise system. For example, Sports Distributors of Canada, better known as Source for Sports, is a buying group consisting of independent sports store owners across the country. Purchasing as a group enables local sports store owners to take advantages of large-volume discounts.[7] This type of arrangement may also be used to purchase group insurance and benefit plans for employees.

Other methods of achieving potential savings on purchasing include buying in large quantities, seasonal buying, consignment buying, and receiving price discounts for paying in cash.

EVALUATING SUPPLIERS

Small business owners generally use the following criteria, among others, to evaluate suppliers.

Dependability.

The owner-manager should evaluate how dependable the prospective supplier will likely be. Dependability will undoubtedly be more important for some companies and even for some types of products than for others.

Cost.

Obviously the cost of inventories will play a major role in supplier selection for the small firm.

Services Offered.

Typical services offered by suppliers are delivery, discounts, credit, promotion, promotional support materials, return policies, guarantees, and technical assistance. Willingness and ability to provide these services at all hours may be an important factor in the selection of a supplier.

DETERMINING ORDER QUANTITIES

Estimating the quantities of inventories to order requires several essential items of information.

Order Lead Time.

Estimate the time taken to process the order at both shipping and destination points and to transport the item(s). This is called *order lead time* and is illustrated by the distance between points B and C in **Figure 10-8**. An increasing number of businesses have instituted a just-in-time (JIT) inventory policy. In this approach, the order is placed so that the inventory arrives "just in time" to be used in the production process. This system is appropriate for manufacturers that have computer capabilities, are confident in the dependability of suppliers, and require large amounts of inventory.

FIGURE 10-8 **Order Points**

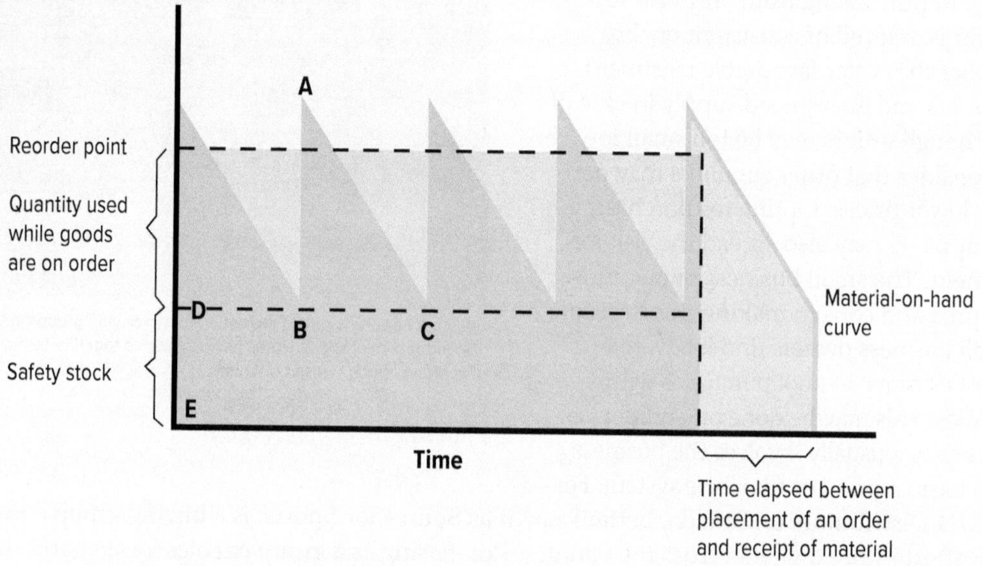

The basic idea of JIT is to reduce order sizes and time them to arrive as close to when they are needed as possible. The intent is to minimize a business' dependence on inventory and cut the costs of moving and storing goods. JIT is used more often by producers than by retailers. There are notable differences between a JIT approach and a more traditional approach. **Table 10-3** illustrates these differences.

Sales or Production Estimate.

The owner-manager will need to make a realistic projection of inventories to be sold or consumed in the manufacture of the finished product for the period. Methods of obtaining this type of information were discussed in **Chapter 3**. This rate of sale throughout the period is shown by the diagonal line A–C in **Figure 10-8**.

TABLE 10-3 JIT and Traditional Inventory Comparison

JIT INVENTORY	TRADITIONAL INVENTORY
Small orders and frequent deliveries	Large orders and infrequent deliveries
Single-source supplier for a given part with long-term contract	Multiple sources of suppliers for same part with partial or short-term contracts
Suppliers expected to deliver product quality, delivery performance, and price; no rejects acceptable	Suppliers expected to deliver acceptable level of product quality, delivery performance, and price
Less emphasis on paperwork	Requires more time and formal paperwork
Delivery time and quantity can be changed with direct communication	Changes in delivery time and quantity require new purchase orders

Minimum Inventory Levels Required.

No business wants to run out of inventory, especially if the inventory consists of important items. It is therefore common to carry a minimum basic inventory for many items. This inventory is often called *safety stock* and is shown as the distance between D and E in **Figure 10-8**. The size of safety stock usually depends on such factors as the importance of the inventory, volatility of demand, and dependability of sources of supply.

Inventory Currently on Hand.

The owner-manager should have an accurate estimate of inventories on hand. To monitor current inventory levels on a continual basis, a perpetual inventory system can be used. Details of this type of system will be discussed later in this chapter. For many businesses, a perpetual system requires a computerized inventory system, which an increasing number of small businesses can now afford. Once current inventory levels have been determined, the owner-manager can incorporate those amounts into various methods to determine order quantities.

Methods for Determining Order Quantities.

Some of the more common methods used to determine order quantities follow.

Minimum-Turnover Method.

This method uses the inventory turnover formula for the business in determining amounts of inventory required. For example, if inventory turnover for the business is 4 (four times per year) and projected sales for the period are $200,000, the required inventory is calculated as follows:

$$\frac{\text{Sales}}{\text{Inventory}} = \text{Inventory turnover}$$

$$\frac{\$200{,}000}{\text{Inventory}} = 4$$

$$\text{Inventory} = \frac{\$200{,}000}{4} = \$50{,}000$$

Hence, the minimum required inventory at retail value for the period is $50,000.

Maximum-and-Minimum Method.

Some small businesses set acceptable maximum and minimum limits on inventory levels. Whether inventory is measured in dollar amounts or number of units, reaching these limits indicates it is time to order and specifies the amount to order. This method is frequently used by small businesses for merchandise of lower unit values.

Open-to-Buy Method.

This method of calculating order quantities, used extensively in retailing, uses the following formula (the components were discussed earlier):

Open to buy = Maximum inventory – Merchandise on order – Merchandise on hand

where

Open to buy = Inventories that can be purchased
Maximum inventory = Expected sales + Safety stock required

A-B-C Analysis.

This method of inventory management recognizes that some items of merchandise are more important to the business than others. The level of importance is influenced by such factors as higher sales, high unit value levels, higher profitability, or more importance in the manufacture of the finished product.

With A-B-C analysis, the most important inventory (A items) is watched more closely to ensure it is managed efficiently. The B and C items, being less important, may require less detailed monitoring and control. **Table 10-4** gives an example of A-B-C analysis.

TABLE 10-4 A-B-C Analysis

	A ITEMS	B ITEMS	C ITEMS
Percentage of total inventory value	65%	25%	10%
Percentage of total list of different stock items	20%	20%	60%
Inventory method used	Minimum turnover EOQ Maximum turnover	Minimum turnover	Eyeballing
Time allocation	Time-consuming and precision needed	Less time-consuming estimates	Rough estimates only

Administration of the Buying Process.

The owner-manager should be familiar with the mechanics of purchasing. Knowledge of the different kinds of discounts and purchase terms and conditions is essential, as are efficient receiving, checking, and marking of merchandise to minimize inventory costs and reduce shrinkage.

INVENTORY CONTROL

As discussed earlier, efficient purchasing requires proper monitoring and control practices. Three essential aspects of inventory control are determining the unit of control, the method of valuing inventories, and the method of monitoring inventory levels.

Unit of Control.

Most firms keep track of their inventories by dollar amounts. This approach is called *dollar inventory control.* Dollar inventory control is suitable for firms with large amounts of inventory at a relatively low per-unit value.

Some businesses that have relatively small amounts of inventory keep track of inventories in numbers of units. This method is called *unit control.*

Valuation.

Generally accepted accounting principles allow inventories to be valued at the lower of cost or market value. It is very important that an accurate valuation of inventory levels be calculated, because, as **Table 10-5** shows, inventory levels directly affect the net income of the business at the end of the period.

TABLE 10-5 Valuation of Inventories

Sales − Cost of goods sold − Other expenses = Net income

where

Cost of goods sold = Beginning inventory + Purchases − Ending inventory

Using the relationships in these formulas, you can see that if ending inventory is overstated, cost of goods sold will be understated by the same amount and net income overstated by that same amount. Therefore, a valuation error of $100 will translate into either an overstatement or an understatement of net income by $100.

Monitoring.

There are essentially two methods of monitoring inventories. The first, periodic inventory, involves physically counting and recording the merchandise to determine inventory levels. Periodic inventory calculation is required at least once each year for income tax purposes. It is costly and time-consuming to carry out, however, so most businesses use this method no more frequently than required.

Employee theft is more likely to occur at smaller firms. Given that the financial impact of theft can be greater for small business compared to large companies, entrepreneurs must ensure they have proper systems in place to deter such activity.

Photo 126282351 © Andrey Popov - Dreamstime.com

The second type of inventory monitoring, perpetual inventory, involves continuous recording of inventory increases and decreases as transactions occur. Historically, this system was feasible only for a small businesses with low levels of high-unit-value inventory. Database management programs have made the perpetual inventory system a reality for many small businesses. These systems use bar codes that identify inventory purchases and sales. By using this system, sales can be tracked, inventory levels can be monitored, and orders can be made. Examples of inventory software programs that small businesses can use are Ordor, Cin7, Fishbowl, Veeq, Unleashed, and QuickBooks Pro.[8] These programs are relatively inexpensive and are regularly updated. Some small businesses find that developing a customized program, even though more costly, better suits their needs to manage inventory effectively. Inventory control is also enhanced by performing various evaluation analyses, such as calculating turnover, comparing budgeted amounts with actual inventories, and analyzing inventory disappearance (shrinkage).

Security of Inventory.

Preventing loss of inventory (shrinkage) is a major challenge for most small businesses. In fact a recent study concluded that most cases of employee theft occur at smaller firms.[9] The business should develop a detailed procedure for ordering, receiving, marking, handling, and monitoring all inventories. The system selected will vary, depending on the type of business. Additionally, some small businesses are investing greater attention and more money in better securing inventory throughout the supply chain. Such devices as radio frequency identification (RFID) are increasingly being used to track inventory as it moves through the distribution channel.

THE SMALL BUSINESS—SUPPLIER RELATIONSHIP

One key to the success of operations management is the relationship that the business maintains with its suppliers. Because of the size of the business and relatively small volumes of purchases, the small business tends to be at a disadvantage compared with large businesses in receiving favourable treatment from suppliers. It is therefore important that the owner-manager implement policies and procedures that can ensure a successful relationship with the supplier. Examples of such policies and procedures are as follows:[10]

1. Define clear, identifiable, and measurable objectives for your supplier management strategy.
2. Be prepared to work with the supplier to identify and define the roles that each will perform. Consider your relationship a partnership to achieve the objectives stated above.
3. Attempt to employ technology to share data relating to forecasting, product movement, and financial evaluation.
4. Evaluate suppliers regularly with an objective, standardized framework that is both quantitative and qualitative.

SUPPLY CHAIN MANAGEMENT

Many successful small businesses recognize the value in developing a network of interconnected businesses to provide products and services to the end customer. Supply chain management includes the movement and storage of raw material, work-in-process inventory, and finished goods from point of origin to point of consumption. This means that the small business places high priority on coordination and collaboration with channel partners, such as suppliers, intermediaries, third-party service providers, and customers.

LEARNING OBJECTIVES SUMMARY

LO1 **The production process involves the conversion of inputs—money, people, machines, and inventories—into outputs—the products or services provided.**

LO2 **The physical facilities must be continually monitored because the conditions that contribute to their effectiveness will not remain static.**

LO3 **The three types of layouts used by small manufacturing firms are the product layout, process layout, and fixed-position layout. The product layout is used when the business manufactures large numbers of just one product or a few products. The process layout is designed for factories that manufacture smaller numbers of many different or custom-made products. The fixed-position layout is used for very large or cumbersome products.**

LO4 **In planning the interior layout of a retail store, the retailer needs to analyze the allocation of selling versus non-selling space; the allocation of space among departments and products; classification of the merchandise; and the location of displays and products on the shelf. The two types of layouts used by a retail store are the grid layout and the free-flow layout. The grid layout, typically used in a supermarket, is organized with customer convenience and retail efficiency in mind. The free-flow layout has a more relaxed atmosphere that is conducive to browsing. This type of layout is suitable for clothing and many specialty types of merchandise.**

LO5 **The essential considerations required to estimate quantities to order are: order lead time; sales or production estimate; minimum inventory levels required; and the inventory currently on hand. Some methods used to determine order quantities include the minimum-turnover method, which uses inventory turnover calculations; the maximum-and-minimum method, which indicates the time to reorder and amounts to order; the open-to-buy method, used in retailing; and A-B-C analysis, which prioritizes types of inventory.**

TIME TO TAKE ACTION

1. Depending on your business or business plan, start to create standard operating procedures. Be sure to address such questions as how you will maintain quality control, standards, and so forth. You may find it helpful to contact entrepreneurs or managers with similar companies and ask for their advice.
2. If your business is a retail location, then visit other retailers. Take pictures and notes about their store layout. Create a document, using your computer, on how your store will be laid out. Ask experienced entrepreneurs to comment on the layout of your store.

DISCUSSION QUESTIONS

1. What kind of layout should be used for the following manufacturing firms?
   a. Golf club manufacturer
   b. Independent bottler
   c. Bob's Machine Shop
2. What kind of layout should be used for the following retail firms?
   a. Clothing store
   b. Motorcycle shop
   c. Small grocery store
3. Answer the following questions regarding the location of food items in a grocery store:
   a. Where are bread and milk located? Why?
   b. Where are chocolate bars and other candies located? Why?
   c. Where on the shelf are the top name-brand items located? Why?
   d. Where are the high-margin items positioned in the store and on the shelves? Why?

EXPERIENTIAL EXERCISES

1. Visit a small retail store or manufacturing plant and evaluate the layout.
2. Frank Newhart is opening a new DVD electronics store but has not determined which DVD supplier to use. Frank has narrowed the choice to two sources. Supplier 1 is newly established and sells the units for $60 apiece. Supplier 2 is a well-established firm and sells the units for $75 each, with a 7 percent discount on orders over 50 units. Evaluate each supplier from the information given. With this information, develop different scenarios in which Frank would choose supplier 1 or supplier 2.
3. Interview three business owners to determine which inventory ordering system they use and why.
4. Interview a small business owner to learn why he or she selected a particular supplier. Find out what criteria were important to the owner in making the choice.
5. How could a small business improve the quality of a product or service that it offers? Discuss the information provided in this chapter.

COMPREHENSIVE CASE DAN KIM: PART 5

Dan worked long and hard to improve the financial condition of the business as a result of the statements received at the end of the first year of operations. He has been able to make some adjustments in operations, move some short-term debt to long term, and obtain additional equity that allowed the business to receive adequate financing for the second year. His banker was also influenced positively by the upward sales trends for the Ladder Helper. In addition to allowing the existing operation to receive stable financing, the bank also agreed to finance the addition to the building that Dan had been contemplating. The banker agreed that this building would be needed to meet the growing demand for Dan's product.

With the new addition underway, Dan is now considering revising the interior space of the plant. Until now, he has employed an assembly-line type of production process, as he makes only one product. However, Dan is starting to get orders for different-sized ladders (which require a variation in the size and type of Ladder Helper), as well as for other accessories, such as safety braces to prevent ladders from moving sideways when placed against a building or roof. Given the possibilities for increasing his line of products in the future, Dan wonders whether his current manufacturing layout is still effective.

Dan is also concerned about inventory levels. He started out using the industry average for manufacturing plants to order initial inventory, but he soon realized that the industry average did not apply to a small plant like his. He then tried to order high volumes of inventory to get a better price, but he found that if the metal was sitting too long in inventory, costing him in interest expenses. Conversely, Dan does not want to run out of metal and cause a stoppage in the production process.

Dan is currently purchasing the metal used in fabricating the Ladder Helper from a local plant in Hamilton. He is, however, continually receiving calls from salespeople from outside the area offering better prices. This is also a concern for Dan. All these dilemmas are weighing heavily on him and taking him away from making the Ladder Helper units. He often thinks how nice it would be to just be involved in the manufacturing part and not have to worry about such things as buying metal and selling Ladder Helpers.

Questions

1. Discuss the layout options for Dan's company, considering the increased space and changes in product line.
2. What advice could you give Dan regarding his inventory ordering and management practices?
3. Discuss the criteria that Dan could use to evaluate suppliers for metal.

CHAPTER 11

HUMAN RESOURCES MANAGEMENT

LEARNING OBJECTIVES

By the end of this chapter, you should be able to:

LO1 Explain the importance of human resources management to the small business.

LO2 Illustrate the methods of planning for hiring and training employees.

LO3 Identify the principles of effective human resources management for the small business.

LO4 Describe the skill areas an owner-manager can strengthen to improve personal leadership and people skills within the organization.

LO5 Identify the legal requirements relating to personnel of the small business.

LO6 Explain the procedures for administering a small business payroll.

SMALL BUSINESS PROFILE

JASON TAFLER, UNYTE HEALTH

Photo courtesy of Jason Tafler

Jason Tafler recalls his past corporate experiences. He was a workaholic, frequently spending in excess of 80 hours a week at various corporate jobs including an investment banker (twice), building and selling a media company, and working at Rogers as a top 15 executive. He says he frequently ignored signs from his body that all was not well as he attended meetings, met deadlines and answered emails. Tafler admits he was addicted to work and the thrill of achievement.

Then suddenly, Tafler says, he almost lost it all. During a morning meeting at the office, he started to bleed internally and over the course of a day and a half he would lose almost half his blood volume. He recalls lying in bed thinking he may die. At this moment, Tafler reveals, all he could think about was his wife, young son and that he would have to change the way he was living if he survived.

After a short time Tafler's health improved, and he made the decision to leave Rogers to pursue entrepreneurship. Tafler founded Unyte, a company with a mission to create and acquire a suite of effective neural or mind-body solutions to help guide as many people as possible to happier, healthier, and more meaningful lives.

Unyte's first product, called Interactive Meditation, is a relaxation and stress management training tool that helps people learn awareness, self-regulation and resilience through real-time biofeedback, interactive breathing exercises, and mindfulness programs. Unyte recently added to its product suite by acquiring Integrated Listening Systems, a Denver-based neurotechnology company founded in 2007 that integrates auditory, movement, and cognitive exercises to improve brain function. Together, Unyte Interactive Meditation and Integrated Listening Systems have built a community of over 10,000 healthcare professionals in 40 countries, helping hundreds of thousands of children and adults achieve clinically significant improvements in learning, attention, behaviour, and performance.

Unyte originally raised $300,000 from Kickstarter and Indiegogo, and more recently the company raised capital from the Canadian Business Growth Fund, a Canadian private equity firm that helps domestic businesses grow into global leaders.

Tafler also wants to create an organization and corporate culture where there is a focus on compassionate leadership and an emphasis on long-term results. Tafler says it is important for employees to take the time to take care of themselves and put their health first, as an emphasis on self-care will lead to improved performance and creativity, and increased productivity and focus. With this in mind, Unyte offers employees such benefits as daily meditation sessions, weekly yoga classes, complimentary snacks and drinks, and flexible work hours.

UNYTE HEALTH
unyte.com

HUMAN RESOURCES MANAGEMENT AND THE SMALL BUSINESS LO1

Management in an organization has often been defined as getting things done through other people. Small business owners are personnel managers, even if their main strength or interest lies in the production, financial, or marketing aspects of the business.

Often small business owners are reluctant to learn human resources management (HR) fundamentals because they believe these principles apply only to larger organizations. But in any size of business, not focusing on HR often results in problems: frequent turnover of staff, lack of motivation and initiative, lack of harmony among employees, high absenteeism, frequent grievances, and high overall employee costs. The incidence of these problems appears to be high in small business. A study by Industry Canada (now Innovation, Science and Economic Development Canada) found that successful entrepreneurs believe that owner-managers' biggest challenge and most time-consuming activity is personnel.[1] A second study, conducted by the the BDC, titled *Labour Shortage: Here to Stay,* found that close to 40 percent of small and medium-sized businesses are experiencing difficulty in hiring and that there is a direct link between a shortage of workers and a firm's ability to grow.[2] These findings are echoed by the Canadian Federation of Independent Business (CFIB), which recently found that roughly 50 percent of small businesses had difficulty finding qualified labour; this translates to over 430,000 vacant positions across Canada. And 47 percent of business owners said the shortage of skilled labour is limiting their potential growth. For example, Nicholas and Jean-Francis Drouin, co-founders of Quebec-based Produits Matra, a growing manufacturer of pine windows and doors, say the shortage of skilled workers is so bad that they have to turn away sales as the company doesn't have the staff to do all the work. With Baby Boomers retiring and low unemployment, the firm is constantly recruiting new staff. Fortunately, Produits Matra has been able to fill positions recently by hiring recent immigrants and offering enhanced incentives to retain workers.[3]

Jordi Morgan of the CFIB says that small business owners often end up doing more work when there are staffing challenges, thus limiting growth.[4] Despite these predictions and trends, CFIB has also found that employees in small companies are significantly more likely to rate their workplace as "good" than are those in large firms. The reasons for this apparent high level of satisfaction are the increased flexibility in the workplace and a closer relationship with the owner.[5] Small businesses have a natural advantage over large businesses in these areas. It is critical that the entrepreneur use the techniques described in this chapter to maintain that advantage.

As the business grows, the owner-manager's workload generally expands. Because there is a limit to what one person can do, the business may suffer if the owner fails to hire new employees and delegate responsibilities to them. In most cases, when this occurs, the entrepreneur will have difficulty making the transition from a startup to a growing, well-managed business that maintains its success over a long period of time. If a company is successful, eventually an entrepreneur will have to share the management of the firm or create a *management team.*

The reputation of a business in the community can be affected by employees' satisfaction with their jobs. The level of employee satisfaction can be enhanced or lowered by the owner-manager's use of personnel management principles. This is especially true in the retail and service industries. Motivated and competent personnel are one characteristic of a business that the competition may find difficult to duplicate.

As small and medium-sized business owners recognize the importance of investing in their employees, they are increasingly focused on employee training. In the CFIB report, *Small Business, Big Investment: Improving Training for Tomorrow's Workforce,* the authors found that 91 percent of business owners believe training is important to grow their business; and 53 percent of firms provide formal training, with 37 percent offering informal training for a combined investment in excess of $14 billion annually. Given the shortage of skilled labour in Canada, entrepreneurs are more than willing to invest internally to grow their workforce.[6]

Given all these factors, it is essential that the owner-manager have some knowledge of personnel administration principles to sustain the success of the business. This chapter covers planning for personnel, hiring, and ongoing personnel management in the small business.

PLANNING FOR HUMAN RESOURCES LO2

There is an old saying in business: "If I hire someone who fails to perform, then I have made a mistake." What this essentially means is that an owner is responsible for the people they hire; if they fail to live up to expectations or—worse—steal, lie, or harm the company's reputation, then the person who hired them is ultimately responsible. If the saying does not convince you of the need for a detailed human resources plan, then simple math might. The cost of a poor hiring decision to a company's bottom line is a net loss of two to four times that person's annual salary. This calculation includes the costs associated with the original staffing process, training the person, the realization that person is ineffective, removing the employee from the organization, and then hiring a replacement; all of this costs a company thousands of dollars. In addition, unlike larger firms, in a small business one bad hire can destroy a company's culture. C. Lee Smith founder and CEO of **SalesFuel**, an online sales enabler, recalls he mistakenly hired the wrong person several years ago and the company is still recovering from the mistake.[7]

To avoid poor hiring decisions and to ensure productive and engaged people are working for a small business, a human resources plan should be developed. Questions to consider in a human resources plan include how many employees the company will require currently and in the next one to three years; what training programs will be provided; where candidates will come from; what job requirements will need to be met; how and how much employees will be compensated; and what employee policies should be in place. While this sounds like a substantial amount of work, investors will want to know your answers to these questions. Furthermore, this information will assist you when it comes time to hire and administer people in your organization. The best way to ensure that all these questions are addressed is by completing the following tasks:

1. Determine the requirements.
2. Establish an organizational structure (for every planned hire, draw a new chart).
3. Prepare job descriptions, including job titles, qualifications, duties, reporting lines, compensation, training necessary, and potential career paths.
4. Develop human resources policies, such as sick leave, bereavement leave, a tardiness policy, and so on.
5. Develop a hiring plan.

Determine Personnel Requirements.

The first step in planning for personnel is to determine the number of jobs or tasks to be done; the shift schedules, if applicable; the level of expertise required; and the number of people needed to perform those tasks. This process may already have been carried out as part of the feasibility analysis discussed in **Chapter 3** or in business planning in **Chapter 4**.

The person who makes the hiring decision is responsible for the success or failure of the people hired.

© Blend Images/Alamy

Set the Organizational Structure.

The second step in personnel planning is to integrate tasks and employees so that the owner can visualize how the different parts of the plan will work together. This formalized plan is commonly called an *organizational chart.* In the very small (two- or three-person) business, the organizational chart may simply be a division of responsibilities, as in Figure 11-1. In a larger business, the organizational chart shows the lines of responsibility for each member of the organization. An organizational chart for a small retail store appears in Figure 11-2. Each business possesses unique characteristics that dictate how to set up the organizational chart. Some of the more

FIGURE 11-1 **Division of Responsibilities for a Very Small Business**

Partner A	Partner B	Partner C
↓	↓	↓
Marketing	Production	Finance

FIGURE 11-2 **Organizational Chart for a Retail Furniture Store**

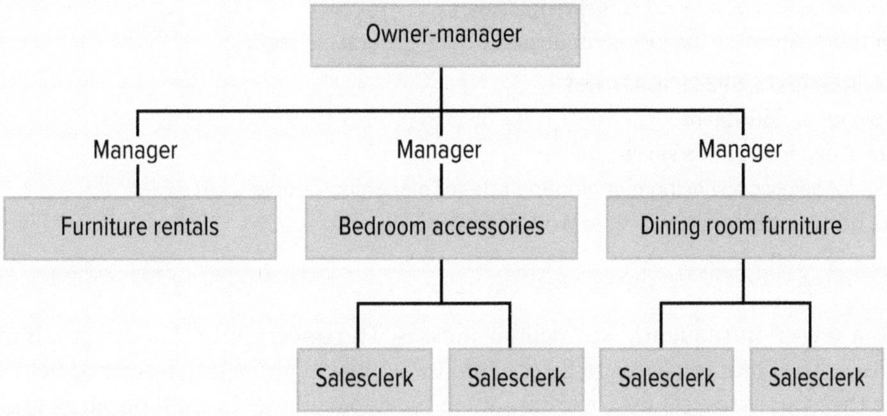

common approaches are to organize by (1) function performed, such as sales, purchasing, or promotion; (2) type of merchandise or department, as in Figure 11-2; or (3) geographic territory.

In setting up the organizational structure, it is good to follow these general rules, which have been found to contribute to a successful operation:

- Each employee should report to only one supervisor. This arrangement is called *unity of control or command.*
- Similar functions should be grouped together, if possible.
- There is a limit to an individual's span of control. Span of control is the number of people who can be directly supervised by one person. The proper span of control varies according to the combined characteristics of the manager, the subordinates, and the job.

Prepare Job Descriptions.

The third step in personnel planning is to prepare job descriptions and specifications. Before hiring employees, a detailed listing of the job or task duties (job descriptions) must be made. The job description briefly explains what is to be done, how it is to be done, and why it is done. This information goes into the job specification—a statement of the skills, abilities, physical characteristics, and education required to perform the job. As mentioned earlier, part of the job description may be included in the policy manual. Table 11-1 illustrates a job description and specifications for an employee of a small business.

Develop Personnel Policies.

The fourth step in personnel planning is to formally develop personnel policies. Including these policies in an employee policy manual can help prevent many personnel problems. For the very small business, this may simply be a list of some do's and don'ts; a larger business may provide a booklet to each new employee.

TABLE 11-1 Job Descriptions and Specifications for a Sales Manager, Hardware Store

JOB DUTIES DESCRIPTION	
	Reports to the general manager
	Is directly responsible for floor salespeople
	Suggests markdowns on slow items
	Controls inventory
	Authorizes merchandise returns
	Occasionally meets with suppliers to learn about new products
	Maintains good customer relations at all times
	Takes care of written correspondence concerning sales
	Does any other task relevant to the job as requested by the general manager
PERSONAL REQUIREMENTS SPECIFICATIONS	
	High school diploma or equivalent
	At least two years' experience in a similar job
	Initiative; instinct for sales; convincing manner; aptitude for managing people
	Self-disciplined; good appearance; willing to work overtime

Policy manuals are used infrequently in small businesses. The uncertainty that can result may create serious employee difficulties. The common areas to be covered in a policy manual are described below. Minimum standards for many of these areas are set by government labour departments in each province and territory.

- Job descriptions clearly outline the duties, responsibilities, and reporting lines for employees, as mentioned previously.
- Working conditions include such things as hours of work, coffee breaks, and other expectations of management.
- Holidays and leaves outline statutory holidays, paid vacations, and procedures for taking a leave of absence.
- Remuneration and pay consist of a listing of details of the payroll, such as date of payment, time periods included, and reviews of pay levels.
- Employee benefits provided by the firm, such as bonuses, profit sharing, extended health and dental insurance plans, and employee discounts, should be clearly stated.
- The grievance procedure consists of a description of the procedure employees are to follow if they have a concern or grievance within the organization.

THE HIRING PROCESS

After the personnel plan has been developed, the next step is to review various sources for potential employees and make the selection.

SOURCES OF EMPLOYEES

A study by the Canadian Federation of Independent Business indicated that the most common methods of recruitment for small businesses were referrals from friends and employees (used by 69 percent of companies), media ads (used by 41 percent), unsolicited applications (used by 37 percent), and government agencies (used by 17 percent).[8] The following are some other potential sources of employees for small businesses.

Recruitment from Within.

For most organizations, recruiting from within the firm is the most common course if current employees have the qualifications. Hiring an outsider to perform a supervisory job instead of someone within the organization usually has a negative and disruptive effect on the business. Firms like, **HRDownloads** use recruitment from within as a key part of employee retention. CEO Anthony Boyle states that they always look to current employees first because it helps the firm keep key people. "We always post internally first and try to promote from within," says Boyle. "And we set lofty goals and offer huge incentives. We give away more stuff here than the Price is Right did in the 80s: big-screen TVs, trips and more, even for groups that don't generate revenue." Boyle's strategy is working as his firm has experienced five-year revenue growth of over 3000 percent.[9]

Other Businesses.

To reduce training costs, employees from competing firms or similar industries can be hired. Such employees generally will have some background in the industry or business that can be easily transferred. The recruiter, however, will have to use this approach carefully to avoid a negative reaction from the competition, particularly in smaller markets.

Employee Referrals.

Current employees may be asked to recommend acquaintances to fill available jobs. This method has the advantage of providing some prior knowledge of the individual's background. Some firms, such as Toronto-based Achievers, provide employees with incentives for making successful referrals. A downside of this method is it may have a negative effect, however, if the new employee proves unsatisfactory.[10] Still even with the downside, some employers swear by the benefits of employee referrals. For example, Mandy Rennehan, founder of the Oakville-based retail construction and service firm **Freshco**, has over 300 employees, all of whom were hired using employee referrals. Rennehan confirms that her happy employees are her best recruiters for new hires because they promote the company culture to others in the industry.[11] Read about some other business incentives for hiring and keeping the right people in **Small Business in Action 11-1**.

SMALL BUSINESS IN ACTION 11-1

AVENUEHQ: USING FLEXIBLE BUSINESS PRACTICES TO ATTRACT AND RETAIN EMPLOYEES

When Chris and Rebecca Troelstra launched their company Realty Butler in 2013, they could not have envisioned a future change of the company name to **AvenueHQ** or openly talking about their aspirations to create a billion-dollar business. The married couple founded Realty Butler, a Vancouver-based company, to act as the real estate agents' agent. The firm provides a technical platform for real estate agents along with services such as creating websites and social media management, all of which are assist the real estate agent in building their brand. The couple note that their company allows real estate agents to focus on creating stronger relationships with clients by removing the concerns about website development, posting to social media, and other web-related activities.

While the firm was doing well and had hired 12 employees by 2017, the founders opted to re-brand themselves in 2018. Rebecca reveals there was a bit of a disconnect between the name and the services they offered—after all they were not butlers. But another part of the impetus for the re-brand was the desire to expand into the U.S. market. AvenueHQ now has customers in California, Oregon, Washington, Minnesota and Connecticut, as well as all the major markets in Canada.

With the rapid growth, came a need for additional staff and, by the end of 2018, the firm had grown to 90 employees. CEO Chris Troelstra says the firm has been successful in recruiting talent due to their flexible work schedule. He says employees can come and go as they please as long as the work is getting done, noting the company is also flexible on employee vacations, working from home, and personal hours. In addition, AvenueHQ provides its employee with benefits such as stock options, standing desks, spending cards for gym or ski memberships, and more. Rebecca, who is the company's chief operating officer, says the company wants to stand out not only in recruitment of talent but in retention by creating a strong work environment. Right from the start, the partners wanted to build a company where people can be themselves and reach their potential.

[continued]

[continued]

Chris and Rebecca Troelstra, founders of AvenueHQ, offer flexible working conditions and other perks to attract and retain employees.

Photos courtesy of AvenueHQ

Discussion Questions

1. What are the advantages of AvenueHQ's business model? Why is this model scalable?
2. AvenueHQ allows for very flexible working hours. What are the advantages and disadvantages of this strategy for a growing company?
3. As outlined above, AvenueHQ not only provides employees with flexible working hours but offers other perks as well. Would the company be in a better position for employee recruitment and retention if they became a bit more rigid in their working hours, reduced the perks, and put all of the money they would save back into employees' hands by increasing their salaries? Why or why not?

Advertising and Using Social Media.

Small businesses frequently advertise for employees in local newspapers or using online ads on sites, such as **Eluta**, **Talent Egg**, **Glassdoor**, **Workopolis** or **Monster**. With the cost of newspaper advertising rising and readership declining, more firms are finding online advertising optimal, as they can often post more details about the job online for less money. In addition, the Internet has replaced newspapers as the traditional source of information for job hunters.

Many companies are posting jobs and searching for leads on LinkedIn, Facebook, Twitter, Youtube, and other social media.

Cifotart/Dreamstime.com

Small and large companies alike are also using social media to post jobs and to find qualified leads. Many companies are posting jobs and searching for leads on LinkedIn, Facebook, Twitter, and YouTube among other platforms. Business author Shannon Bowen-Smed says social media allows firms to go beyond traditional job postings and should be a key component of recruitment strategies (see **Small Business in Action 11-2**). Bowen-Smed says social media can be used to reach passive job searchers by creating conversations on social networking sites, such as

LinkedIn, and firms can highlight their positive corporate culture on Twitter and Facebook, making their company more appealing to job seekers.[12] For example, Toronto-based Razor Suleman recently distributed job postings for 17 positions to his employees, who then placed them on their Facebook status updates, tweeted them to friends who re-tweeted them, and shared them through LinkedIn networks. Suleman explains that the average cost of a newspaper ad is $5000, while an online job board costs $700. Another comparison would be with recruitment firms that charge a percentage of a new hire's salary; the price tag of using one to fill these 17 positions would be $260,000. Instead, Suleman is paying a total of $1800 for wine and cheese at the open house that applicants are invited to. Companies such as Best Body Bootcamp and many others are using similar means to find new employees. Experts say that for reach, speed, and recruitment branding, social media sites are here to stay.[13]

SMALL BUSINESS IN ACTION 11-2

LINKEDIN'S IMPACT ON EMPLOYEE RECRUITMENT

While LinkedIn was originally founded as a social networking site for professionals, it has transformed itself into a site where people expand their networks, look for work, or are found by potential employers who often browse the site for qualified leads. In addition to job postings, LinkedIn now offers companies the following tools to assist them in recruiting candidates:

1. LinkedIn Recruiter allows companies to browse the profile of all LinkedIn users so they can contact people who may be interested in working for their firm.
2. LinkedIn Employment Branding services allow companies to build a career website on LinkedIn to network and attract employees.
3. LinkedIn allows companies to advertise their job offerings.
4. LinkedIn Talent allows firms to manage incoming applications and recruitment marketing.

Denys Prykhodov/Shutterstock.com

Spark Internet Marketing Corp., a Toronto-based firm, recently used LinkedIn to fill a position with a unique technical skill set—SEO management. Rather than advertise the job, Spark's executives posted information about the job in some of LinkedIn's groups and quickly filled the position.

The major advantage of using social media recruitment is the low cost, as sites such as LinkedIn and Facebook do not charge. Additionally, firms can access passive job seekers—people who would consider applying for a job they see but are not actively looking for work. The other major advantage is reach; not only will postings easily reach all followers, but people are also inclined to share information they see on social media that they think others will be interested in.

Discussion Questions

1. What do you think are the advantages and disadvantages of using social media sites to recruit employees?
2. What types of companies do you think are best suited to using LinkedIn and other social media sites for recruitment? Which types of companies do you think are poorly suited to using LinkedIn? Why?

Employment Agencies.

Employment agencies sponsored by provincial governments are one source of new hires. **Employment and Social Development Canada** offices also have lists of peoples looking for work. This can be a potentially valuable source of employees, particularly for positions that do not require highly technical expertise. Private employment agencies typically are not used by small businesses to recruit employees, but they may be helpful in recruiting highly skilled employees.

Educational Institutions.

Small businesses also use universities or colleges as sources for employees. The entrepreneur may appeal directly to students or work with career offices at the institutions. These sources can be helpful as they provide access to new and well-educated workers. While the workers are sometimes lacking in experience, most small business owners report they are now hiring younger workers. In fact, 54 percent of firms with 20 to 99 employees say they are recruiting more younger workers to offset the labour shortage.[14] Businesses also hire students who are in co-operative educational programs to fill vacancies. For example, Kinduct Technologies, a small Halifax-based data and analytical company, say they hire co-op students to attract potential full-time employees to the company. They confirm that the students bring new ideas, are innovative, and help the company identify new opportunities.[15]

Immigrant Agencies

With the shortage of workers across Canada, recruiting employees from underused segments of the labour market is becoming more appealing to small and medium-sized business owners. Because employment rates for new Canadians fall below employment rates for the overall population, they are an attractive labour pool filled with potential for business owners. For example, Calgary coffee shop owner Rahim Merali says he hired Syrian refugees not only to help them get started in their new home country, but also because he needed to find hard-working employees.[16]

Many small business owners such as Assam Hadhad and Rahim Merali, who are discussed in this chapter, are hiring newcomers to Canada to address the labour shortage.

Photo by George Rose/Getty Images

To date, business owners are less inclined to recruit newcomers as a strategy to combat the shortage of labour. Entrepreneurs interested in recruiting immigrants can work with the national Immigration, Refugees and Citizenship Canada Office or a host of provincial departments, agencies, and not-for-profit groups.[17] As discussed earlier in the book, some immigrant entrepreneurs are hiring newcomers to the country to address the current skilled-labour shortage. Nova Scotia–based Peace by Chocolate, founded by Syrian refugee Assam Hadhad, has already hired four refugees and is planning on hiring upwards of 45 more over the next few years.[18]

THE SCREENING PROCESS LO3

Once potential employees have been identified from one or more of the above sources, the owner-manager faces the task of selection. Several screening devices can be used to help select employees. Most successful companies use several screening methods to ensure the candidate is the right one for them. For example, Mandy Rennehan, who was discussed above, makes use of numerous screening techniques as she believes her company's culture and people are essential for success. Rennehan starts with a basic interview with a focus on personality and fit. "The first interview is just, 'Do we like this person?'" she says. "If we feel that your personality is not going to gel in this culture, you don't get a second one–it doesn't even matter about your skill set." If the candidate gets past the first interview, they then undergo a series of tests, including an aptitude test, a tools test, a handheld device test, and a simulated talking test. Only then would the candidate be hired.[19] Learn more about how Mandy Rennehan built her successful company in **Small Business in Action 11-3**.

SMALL BUSINESS IN ACTION 11-3

MANDY RENNEHAN: BLUE COLLAR CEO

Mandy Rennehan recalls her entrepreneurial journey started at age 10 when she discovered that fisherman needed bait for their traps. Rennehan says she would sneak out of her house in the middle of the night and find bait at low tide. The next morning, she says, she would sell the bait to the fisherman for 10 percent less than her competitors. Thus began a thriving business. Along the way, she became interested in construction and started to buy tools, eventually learning to build log cabins while still in high school.

When she finished high school, Rennehan decided to leave Yarmouth, packing up her belongings in a hockey bag to work on farms. Rennehan didn't have time for a formal trade school education; instead, she called skilled tradespeople and offered to work for free. By the age of 22, she had learned most of the major trades and word of her excellent construction skills spread, which encouraged her to move to Toronto to pursue additional opportunities. While in Toronto, she started specializing in retail store interiors and furthered her reputation so that by the age of 24, she was contacted by a major retailer based out of San Francisco to bid on a significant retail renovation contract. Rennehan fondly remembers showing up for the meeting and being called "Canada" by the person who greeted her and then being told she had seven minutes to speak to the people at the boardroom table. Rennehan left an hour later with a $4 million contract and an invitation to the CEO's house for dinner to meet his wife and family.

Fast forward to 2019 and Rennehan's company **Freshco** has established a North American reputation for quality in the retail construction industry. Freshco's niche is not the outside of retail stores, but rather, handling everything for the interiors, including maintenance, handling installations, and completing interior refreshes, which generally occur every three to five years. Freshco's customers include Nike, Apple, Banana Republic, and Sephora, and the firm boasts a five-year growth rate of 224 percent.

Rennehan says that like most labour-intensive businesses, Freshco is struggling to find enough employees. She indicates part of the challenge is that many trade schools have empty classrooms as more people are opting for university education over learning a skilled trade. She also notes that women are not encouraged to pursue trades, and this further limits the potential number of employees.

Rennehan says that even with significant demand for employees, she has opted to hire less, favouring quality over quantity. She adds that she likes loyal and audacious people and structures her interview process in a way to discover if a candidate has these characteristics. She will also ask people what projects they would make for money, for love, and who would they work alongside with in their dreams.

Given Rennehan's emphasis on quality over quantity, she wants to ensure that anyone she hires will remain at the company. To do that, she ensures Freshco is a fun place to work by providing such perks as standing desks, office ping-pong tables, and mentors. The company also encourages its employees to participate in projects that give back to the community. As a result of this investment in her employees, Rennehan's bottom line is less than the industry standard by 10 to 12 percent, a difference she is happy to live with because she considers the money an investment in retention and morale.

Rennehan has also adopted the title of Blue Collar CEO and uses it to encourages others, especially women, to pursue skilled trades. She says she adopted the title so people not only understand her background but also just how much success can be found working in the trades.

Discussion Questions

1. What are some of the advantages of Freshco's business model?
2. Rennehan bases a lot of her hiring decisions on intuition. Do you think this is a sustainable long-term strategy? Why or why not?
3. What suggestions would you make to Rennehan to improve her hiring process?
4. Why do you think people, and parents, are encouraging people to go to university rather than trade schools? What, if anything, should be done to promote the trades?

Application Form or Résumé.

Many small businesses will have a potential applicant submit a résumé or an application form. These documents can be a valuable screening tool and a time saver for the owner because they provide the candidate's education, work experience, and skills. Applicants who do not have the required background or skills do not have to be interviewed or hired. An application form need not be lengthy to be useful, as Figure 11-3 illustrates.

FIGURE 11-3 **Application for Employment for a Small Business**

First Name ______________________ Last Name ______________________

Address (Home) ______________________ Tel. ______________________

Address (Work) ______________________ Tel. ______________________

Languages: Spoken ______________________ Written ______________________

Secondary Education

Years School City Diploma

Postsecondary Education

Years School City Degree/Diploma

Work Experience

(begin with most recent)

From ________ To ______________ Employer ______________________

Title ______________________ Nature of Duties ______________________

Salary ____

Reason for Leaving ____

____

____

Work Experience

From ________ To ______________ Employer ______________________

Title ______________________ Nature of Duties ______________________

Salary ____

Reason for Leaving ____

____

____

Other Information

References	Name	Address	Title
1.			
2.			
3.			

Signature Date

The Employment Interview.

Although the application form or the submission of a résumé may screen out several potential employees, an interview is normally required to make the final decision. The employment interview is particularly important for jobs requiring interpersonal contact, because it allows the interviewer to judge appearance, poise, and communication ability. A helpful tool in interviewing is an interview guide, which focuses the discussion and provides a consistent base of information from which to compare applicants. Interviews normally start with an introduction, then questions are asked about the résumé, open-ended questions may also be asked, and PAR (problem–action–result) questions may round out the interview. (We will return to PAR questions at the end of this section.) At the end, it is common for the potential employee to make additional comments and ask questions. Jerry Fitch, president of Toronto-based **Marberg Staffing**, says preparation is the key to a successful interview. Fitch advises employers to start by formulating a job description and basing the questions on the corresponding skills. Research on interviews indicates that while PAR questions are very common, no magic questions will help employers find the best person.[20] For example, Rowan O'Grady, president of Hays Recruitment Canada says he likes going through candidates' job history one position at a time to find out what they enjoyed about the company and what they found frustrating. O'Grady says it helps him pick out inconsistencies.[21]

Checking References.

The third screening device is the checking of references. Most application forms require the applicant to list both personal and business references. As might be expected, business references are more valuable because they provide information regarding the individual's past work record.

Checks made by telephone or in person with business references are preferred to written responses. The writer of a letter of reference may have little or no idea of the requirements of the job. Also, past employers are sometimes reluctant to write uncomplimentary letters of reference. Specific questions should be asked about the candidate's performance and about whether employers would consider rehiring the person. More companies are also using social media sites to screen candidates or to learn more about applicants. The issue is discussed in more detail in **Small Business in Action 11-4**.

SMALL BUSINESS IN ACTION 11-4

USING SOCIAL MEDIA TO REFERENCE CHECK

Business owners and human resources professionals are increasingly screening applications by visiting the applicants' social media sites. *Forbes* magazine recently reported 37 percent of employers use social networks to screen potential job candidates. These companies are scanning social media sites to see if a person presents a professional image, to decide whether the person will fit into the company's corporate culture, and to learn more about a person's credentials and experiences. Not only are companies attempting to learn more about potential employees by scanning social media sites, but roughly 33 percent of businesses that engage in the practice have also opted not to hire someone based on what they have discovered on social media.

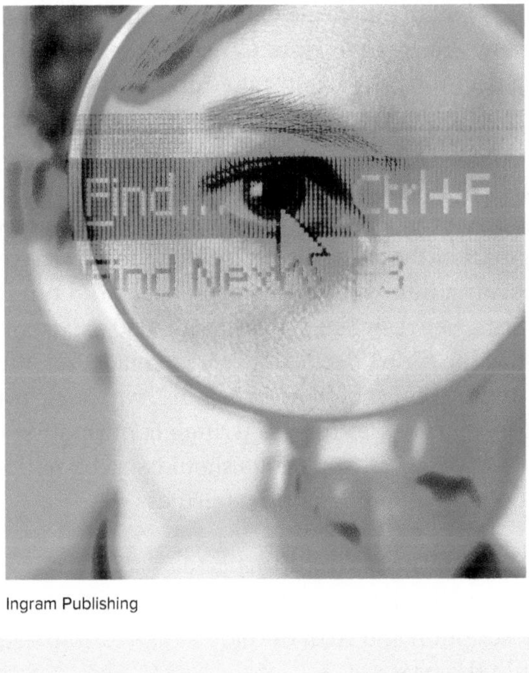

Ingram Publishing

Some social media users, particularly younger users, may find this use of social media reference checking disconcerting, as they think social media sites are private and employers should recognize this when screening applicants. Many business owners and human resources professionals counter with the fact that the information is publicly available and should be considered. A recent study by Dr. Amy Thurlow, a professor at Halifax-based Mount Saint Vincent University, on the acceptable use of online information may shed some light on the opposing viewpoints. Dr. Thurlow discovered that older people thought all information in the public domain, including information on social media sites, was public content, and it was fair to use such information in any way that they saw fit. Others, in particular younger people, indicated that it was not the poster's responsibility to control what they put on their social media site; rather, the visitor of the site should be expected to know what is private and what is intended for public viewing.

[continued]

[continued]

Discussion Questions

1. Do you think potential employers should look at people's social media pages as part of the hiring process? Is this practice ethical or unethical? Why?
2. Once employees are hired, do you think employers should monitor their social media usage? Why or why not?
3. Who is responsible for privacy on social media sites—the person who posts the information or the person who visits the site?
4. If you managed or owned a business, would you visit a candidate's social media sites as part of the hiring process? Why or why not?

Tests.

Many small and large businesses use various types of intellectual, ethical, and physical tests as part of the screening process. Some specific tests being used increasingly in small businesses are proficiency and skill tests (to perform a particular trade, craft, or skill), vocational interest tests (to assess long-term interest in the job or company), aptitude tests (to determine how a person might perform on a given job), and polygraph tests (to measure level of honesty).

CANDIDATE SELECTION AND NOTIFICATION OF THE HIRING SELECTION

After engaging in a screening process, the owner or manager selects the most appropriate employee(s) for the position. Normally, selection is based on ranking how potential candidates did on their interview, tests, and other screening methods; making comparisons; and picking the candidate viewed as superlative. One often overlooked selection measure, which employers should not leave out, is the question of *fit.* Fit generally refers to how a potential employee will work within the organization's culture based on personality and habits. Rowan O'Grady, President of **Hays Canada**, notes that far too many employers give a low priority to fit when making hiring decisions. As a result they do not always select the right candidate for their firm. O'Grady says, "People tend to prioritize tangible things–skills, experience, references–over fit. The problem is, these things don't always signal whether an employee is right for a job."[22] O'Grady's solution is to get to know candidates by mixing in both traditional screening techniques and social interaction. O'Grady thinks including social interaction in the screening process will result in a better assessment of whether the candidate will integrate well and enjoy being part of the business. In fact, in a recent survey of employers by Hays Canada, roughly 50 percent of employers admitted to hiring people who did not fit into their organizational culture–mistakes that ultimately cost firms between $10,000 and $100,000 each.[23]

Once the hiring decision has been made, an offer of employment should be made to the successful applicant. This notification should be in writing, with a clear indication of the terms and conditions associated with the job. Most businesses require written confirmation of acceptance of the offer by the applicant.

All unsuccessful applicants should also be notified. Failure to provide this courtesy can have a detrimental effect on the reputation of the business.

Do's and Don'ts of Hiring

Poor hiring can be as much of a problem as not controlling cash flow. Entrepreneurs should always start with a job description and then develop a plan to staff each position. The following is a list of do's and don'ts that will assist in the process:

Do:

1. Write a detailed job description. You will be lost without one.
2. Prepare interview questions in advance, and ask everyone the same questions. You could be subject to a human rights complaint if you do not follow this procedure.

3. When interviewing, screen the résumé to verify that the facts are true. Then move on to PAR-type questions.
4. Provide candidates with a reasonable description of the job and a timeline of the hiring process.
5. Take notes throughout the interviewing process. It is impossible to remember everything.
6. Try to limit the number of candidates that you interview.
7. Make sure that you check references thoroughly. Prepare questions in advance, and make sure that the reference can provide an accurate assessment of the candidate's work record.
8. Test the candidates. For example, if you want them to speak in public, design a simulation where they have to speak to a room of people; if they need to speak another language, give them a language test.
9. Make use of external testing tools, such as ethics, honesty, or aptitude tests. Even small companies can make use of online testing tools that range in price from as little as $10 to about $250. Thomas Savundra uses psychometric tests to ensure that new employees share his web-hosting company's values.

Don't:

1. Don't rely only on the interview process as a selection method. The interview has proven to be a poor tool in selecting candidates.
2. Don't become stuck on one qualification. If you originally wanted an MBA and someone applied for the position without one but with 10 years of job experience, do not dismiss them from the process.
3. Don't rely on non-work-related references. Many résumés are filled with references from volunteer commitments, politicians, or religious leaders, and they will rarely speak poorly about people who volunteer their time or vote for them.
4. Don't ever assume the candidate is telling the truth. In fact, one prominent HR group notes that 25 percent of job applications contain a major falsehood.

When interviewing candidates for the job, it is best to rely on the PAR method of questioning to be sure that you have a true idea about the candidate's skills in certain areas. The PAR method is based on a simple premise that the best predictor of future behaviour is past behaviour. The PAR process is as follows:

- **P:** Present the candidate with a problem that they would have had to overcome in a past job that is related to the position for which you are hiring. If you are hiring for a sales position, ask questions such as, "Can you give me a time when you had to close a particularly tough sales call?" or "Can you tell me about a time that you had to deal with angry customers?"
- **A:** Ask the candidate what action they took to resolve the problem.
- **R:** Ask if the result was positive or negative. Note that the entrepreneur should pay close attention to the result segment of the answer. Some candidates may come up with innovative solutions to problems, but if the results are not positive, this is a strong indicator that they probably did not take the right course of action.[24]

PERSONNEL MANAGEMENT LO4

Once employees have been hired, the owner-manager's responsibility is to see that they are properly trained, satisfied with the working conditions to continue working there, and—probably most important—motivated to work hard and show initiative. Most small businesses are not in a position to hire a professional personnel manager to ensure that these desirable conditions exist. However, the owner-manager can foster these conditions by using the concepts of personnel management discussed in this section and by crafting HR polices. The BDC found that small and medium-sized firms with strong HR policies were more likely to retain people, attract new employees, and grow their business.[25]

THE INTRODUCTION PERIOD

The first few months on the job are crucial to the employee's overall satisfaction and length of stay with the business.

The First Week.

One of the most frequently mentioned characteristics of good working conditions is the whether the owner-manager makes the employees feel like part of the organization.[26] Much can be done in the first week to communicate to employees that they are valued members of the business. New employees should be introduced to co-workers, shown the locations of employee facilities, informed of any company regulations, and encouraged to ask for additional information as needed. Employees should be talked to frequently during the introductory period, not simply left alone to read the company policy manual as larger companies sometimes do.

Many employers find it helpful to set some short-term goals toward which new employees can work within the first week or two. These goals can be discussed at the conclusion of the agreed-upon time. This communicates not only that the employer is interested in the employee but also that the business is results- and goal-oriented. Mandy Rennehan of Freshco, which was discussed earlier in this chapter, assigns new employees personalized caricatures, nicknames, and a mentor to ensure they are welcome and can learn about their jobs.[27]

THE PROBATIONARY PERIOD

Most employers find it advantageous to use a probationary period of three to six months for new employees. The probationary period allows the employer to further assess the new employee's suitability for the job. At the conclusion of a satisfactory probation period, the employee becomes permanent and may be entitled to a pay increase and other benefits of a permanent employee.

TRAINING

The purpose of the training program is to increase productivity and to provide enrichment opportunities. In addition, successful training programs can reduce employee turnover, allow for less supervision, and increase employee morale. Properly trained employees acquire a sense of worth, dignity, and well-being, as well as increased skill levels. As discussed at the beginning of this chapter, 91 percent of business owners believe training is important to grow their business, and small businesses make use of both formal and informal training by investing in excess of $14 billion annually in employee development. Nikolai Bratkovski, co-founder of Toronto-based Opencare, says that his company has created innovative training practices to retain staff. Opencare employees are provided with career coaches to help them establish individual goals, encourage a shared company culture, and help settle internal disputes. Bratkovski says the money he spends on coaching is worth the investment, and his firm's growth from 12 to 50 employees in a few short years proves his investment is working.[28] Read more about Bratkovski's success with Opencare in **Small Business in Action 11-5**. Serial entrepreneur Mike Kappel, founder and current CEO of Patriot Software, says successful small business training should start with a plan, occur at regular intervals, engage employees and impact performance reviews.[29] Businesses use many forms of employee training. Two of the more common are discussed next.

SMALL BUSINESS IN ACTION 11-5

NIKOLAI BRATKOVSKI: TALENT IS THE KEY TO SUCCESS

Serial entrepreneur Nikolai Bratkovski is co-founder and CEO of **Opencare**, a Toronto-based healthcare-recommendation service that has grown from 13 employees in 2016 to 40 in 2019. Founded in 2012, the company matches new patients with dentists, has raised in excess of $30 million, and has seen sales soar. But he considers the key to startup success to be the business' employees or, using his sports analogy, the team.

Noting that entrepreneurs often do not understand the key to startup success, Bratkovski argues that it is not a great business idea, nor the amount of money an entrepreneur can raise; instead, the people the entrepreneur surrounds themselves with is the vital component. Bratkovski says the three things entrepreneurs should do to be successful are: (1) define your organization's culture; (2) be cutthroat in recruiting; and (3) develop your employees.

Bratkovski says he finds it frustrating hearing people say they have a great culture because there is a beer fridge at the office. Instead, he argues, culture is a set of values that helps direct how employees see the world and provides a framework for them to make decisions. He says entrepreneurs should hire people who fit within the culture. Otherwise, hiring someone who doesn't fit will undermine or destroy the company's most valuable asset: its culture. Bratkovski adds that entrepreneurs should emphasize hiring top performers. While that focus may require entrepreneurs to be cutthroat in recruiting, he reminds all entrepreneurs that there is a war for talent and their success depends on employees.

Finally, Bratkovski says firms have to invest in their people. Developing employees will build a successful company, although, he notes, in Toronto (and this applies to the rest of Canada as well), there are so few entrepreneurs who have scaled their companies to millions of customers. So how does developing employees in this environment work? Bratkovski says his firm finds mentors for employees from all over the world. For example, if someone in his company wants to know about customer acquisition through Facebook advertising, he aligns them with the top people at Facebook, Uber, Thumbtack, or one of many other top-performing, high-growth companies. His goal as CEO is to connect his employees with people who have the technical abilities and experience in scaling a business.

Bratkovski has successfully followed his own suggestions and in September 2019, LinkedIn included Opencare on their list of the 25 hottest Canadian companies to work for.

Discussion Questions

1. Do you agree with Bratkovski's assessment that the entrepreneur's business idea and money they raise are not as important as the employees they surround themselves with? Why or why not?
2. Bratkovski has had great success in matching his employees with global experts. Do you think this practice will be sustainable in the long term? Why or why not?
3. Why would patients and dentists use Bratkovski's patient-matching service?

On-the-Job Training.

On-the-job training is the most frequently used method by small businesses. It is perhaps the best method of training for routine and repetitive types of work. The business may assign another worker to work closely with the new employee in a mentor system or apprenticeship. Formal apprenticeship programs are offered by many educational institutions and are growing rapidly, with approximately 300,000 apprentices currently registered in Canada.[30]

Just-in-Time (JIT) Training.

One of the more common types of employee training that is particularly suitable for small business is short-term or project training. Because of rapid advances in technology, many jobs are changed or displaced every three to five years.[31] It is predicted that in the future, an organization's core workforce will need to be continually training as new skills are required. This just-in-time (JIT) training may be provided by professional training agencies or simply downloaded onto employee computers.

Formal Classroom Training.

Businesses use many varieties of formal classroom training, but only a few have been used by small businesses. One such system is a co-operative type of program with an educational institution. This allows the employee to attend classroom instruction and training part-time. In Canada, the government provides financial assistance for employee training programs. These programs are discussed later in this chapter.

Some businesses hold periodic seminars in which they bring experts from various fields to the business.

THE OWNER-MANAGER AS LEADER AND PERSONNEL MANAGER

Entrepreneurs are often the primary managers in their business, and their ability to lead and their leadership style is quite important to the success of the firm.

Leadership Style.

While some people are natural leaders, for those not in that category, leadership skills can be developed and learned. Business author and researcher Jim Collins notes (see **Small Business Beginnings 11-1**) that successful leaders put the company first, surround themselves with highly qualified people, and then provide them with the decision-making tools and resources to do their job.[32] Leadership experts Jim Kouzes and Barry Posner, co-authors of *The Leadership Challenge*, state that leadership can be learned and that great leaders follow several basic principles, which they refer to as the practices of exemplary leadership.[33] They have found that such strategies work with large and small companies alike. The practices are as follows:

- *Find your personal voice by clarifying your personal values:* Essentially successful leaders establish expectations for themselves and then must reinforce these values daily in their actions.
- *Model the way:* Great leaders act as exemplary role models to employees.
- *Inspire a shared vision:* Create a vision of where you want your company to be. Then enlist others who share the same dream.
- *Challenge the process:* Do not accept any process or problem as unchangeable. Leaders should continually search for new opportunities to grow their company.
- *Enable others to act:* Collaborate–it improves performance. Create a climate of trust, and strengthen others by providing confidence and fostering accountability.
- *Encourage the heart:* Recognize contributions, pay attention to what is occurring, expect the best, recognize those who perform well, celebrate victories, and create a spirit of community.[34]

Another step in this process is self-evaluation to understand your own leadership or management style. Sometimes, owners are so preoccupied with running the technical or market side of the business that they give little thought to the kind of leadership example they set for employees.

SMALL BUSINESS BEGINNINGS 11-1

BUILDING A GREAT COMPANY

Jim Collins's book *Good to Great* is widely considered one of the best management books ever written, with over two million copies sold. Inside the book are tips and lessons on how to lead and build a great company. Entrepreneurs will want to pay close attention to Collins's thoughts on leadership, management, and culture:

Great companies have great leaders. Great leaders put the company first, are less about ego and more about results, give credit to employees, and are tireless workers.

Great companies have great employees. Leaders must recognize what characteristics are needed in their management team at different stages in their company's growth and make the appropriate hires and/or changes.

The right employees are a company's best assets.

If you hire the right people, they will already be motivated. Focus on hiring right, and don't waste time on motivation. Great leaders spend little time on motivation.

A great culture is one of both freedom and accountability. A leader must allow his managers the freedom to make decisions but they must be held accountable.

TABLE 11-2 Leadership Styles in Canadian Small Business

SOLO	OSMOSIS	MANAGERIAL	SYSTEMS	FIGUREHEAD
Does everything	High level of control over business but does spend time developing managers	Sets objectives and lines of authority	Develops systems and direction	Owns business but has little to do with it
Little delegation		Controls results but delegates more on procedures	Allows employees to set some objectives and determine how they are met	Complete delegation
Very small firms	High level of contact with employees	Less employee contact		

For entrepreneurs, several styles appear to be successful. A study of Canadian entrepreneurs found five different types of leadership. Table 11-2 describes each type.[35]

The effectiveness of the owner-manager's leadership style may vary, depending on the characteristics of the business and its employees. However, certain styles generally are more successful in the long run. Whatever the owner-manager's style, concern for both the people within the organization and the production process is important.

Time Management.

A second critical aspect of successful people management is efficiently managing your own time. Time management is often difficult to apply in small businesses. So many operating crises and interruptions take place in the normal course of a day that the owner-manager may feel that much of the advice in time management literature is impossible to employ. However, some basic time management concepts can be used successfully in a small business. Some of the more important concepts are discussed next.

Recognize the Importance of Time.

Much time wasting results from a failure to recognize the importance of our time. The first step in improved time management, therefore, is to have a sincere desire to use time more efficiently.

Re-examine and Clarify Priorities.

Priority planning may be long or short term. Long-term planning involves setting objectives that the owner and business are projected to meet over a period of months or years. Long-term objectives, which are a part of the business plan, as discussed in **Chapter 4** as part of the establishment plan of the business, provide direction for the firm. This strategic plan serves as the guideline for all operations of the business. Short-term priority planning deals with the use of time on a daily or weekly basis. It involves prioritizing tasks and working on those that are most important.

Analyze Current Time-Consuming Activities.

This step requires keeping a diary of the daily activities of the owner-manager. Most people find the results of this step surprising. Often they find they spend time on less important items at the expense of more important ones. One small business owner spent several hours arguing over a $25 increase in building rental instead of using that time to evaluate the suitability of the overall location.

Implement Time-Management Principles.

The owner-manager may be able to eliminate common time-wasting traps and use time more efficiently by implementing the following practices:

- Avoid procrastinating on difficult but important decisions in favour of easier but less important ones.
- Use the most productive time of the day for the more important decisions or analyses. For some people, this may be early in the day, and for others it may be later. Many have found it beneficial to schedule routine or enjoyable tasks during their least productive time.
- Read only relevant information. Stop reading, and start searching. Use travel, waiting, or otherwise unproductive times for reading.
- Use e-mail less and the telephone more. If possible, handle e-mails only once in a given time.
- Operate with a minimum of meetings. Make sure meetings are results oriented and have definite starting and ending times.
- Delegate as much work as possible, recognizing that the owner-manager is still ultimately responsible for the decision or action. A more detailed discussion of delegation in small businesses appears in **Chapter 13**.

ORGANIZATION CULTURE

In addition to managing employees and setting the vision for the company, the actions of the founding entrepreneur will also define the organizational culture. Organizational culture is the blend of values, attitudes, behaviours, dress, and communication styles that make one business different from another. Business owners should recognize that their decisions will affect the way their employees interact with one another and with customers. For example, Costa Elles, owner of **Ela!**, a Halifax-based Greek restaurant, is in the process of creating a customer-first culture. He recently had a staff meeting where he wrote the word "yes" on a board. He then gave a speech in which the central theme was "just say yes" to what customers want. If customers want to substitute food—say yes; if customers want to order off the lunch menu at dinner—say yes; and so forth. Later in the week, Elles observed an exchange in which a chef was questioning a server's order as she allowed for uncommon substitutions in the three-course meal. Elles said the server listened to the chef saying that the substitution would be difficult and then reminded him that their motto is "say yes." The chef then agreed with the server and made the food. The end result, according to Elles, was a happy customer, and happy customers come back. Elles has since bought pins and other signs for the employees displaying the word "yes" to get the message across.[36]

When creating a corporate culture, the owner must ensure it is aligned with the strategy in the business plan. For example, Fran Bigelow, founder of **Fran's Chocolates** in Seattle, has been able to get her employees, including her management team, to consider themselves artisans, focus on detail, and strive for perfection. Bigelow feels that this strategy is effective for her venture because of her premium product line but might result in disaster for someone marketing a high-volume, low-cost manufactured product. Owners must then ensure their actions confirm the chosen culture. For example, Elles has taken to waiting tables in his restaurants and always goes above and beyond to ensure customer satisfaction. Other employees see this and follow his lead.

After establishing the culture, entrepreneurs must ensure they hire people who have the personality to fit within the culture. For example, if the business owner wants people with a positive attitude, then they should create a hiring process that weeds out people who are pessimistic. Sophie Bond, publisher of ***The Upper Canadian Antiques Showcase***, a Grimsby-based magazine, wants a positive corporate culture and places an emphasis on personality when hiring. Bond recently posted a job with the following line: "Complainers need not apply." Finally, the reward system must encourage people to act in a way that reinforces the corporate culture. For example, if a firm wants people to be innovative, even those who try innovations and fail must be rewarded.[37]

MOTIVATION, ENGAGEMENT, AND LOYALTY

Successful managers are able to generate employee engagement and strong loyalty from their employees. Engaged employees are motivated employees working toward company goals. Engaged employees work hard and are creative and productive. Entrepreneurs and managers in engaged workplaces have open communication lines and creative benefits that provide a comfortable work environment. Employee engagement expert Mark Royal of Hay Group says the key to an engaged workforce is having leadership that lays out a clear plan for the company so people know they are working in a winning organization. The second aspect is one of reciprocity where people want to know when they perform they will get something in return. Royal states, "Employees have to know that when they do go above and beyond, they'll be noticed and recognized for it."[38]

It is no accident, however, that these conditions exist in some companies and not in others. In a recent Angus Reid survey, reasons for employees' dislike of their jobs were examined.[39] The results are shown in Figure 11-4. Some owner-managers understand and are able to apply these critical principles in human relations management. Two important principles concern working conditions and employee needs.

FIGURE 11-4 **Reasons Employees Dislike Their Jobs**

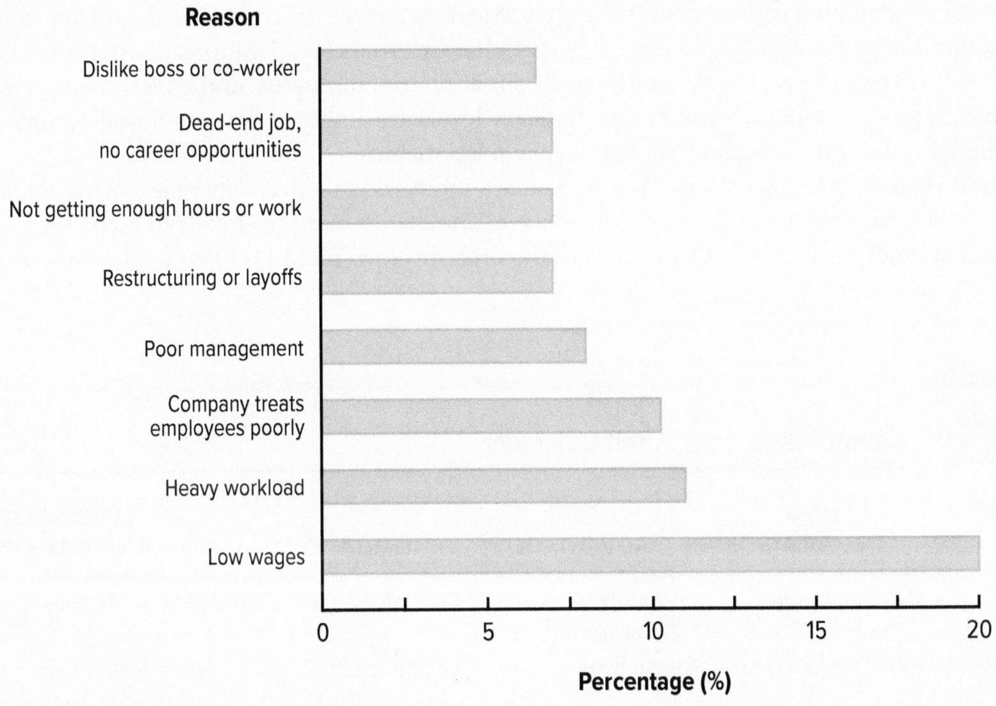

Working Conditions.

Employee satisfaction with general working conditions has been shown to reduce employee turnover. Although these factors may have minimal motivational impact, they are important in developing loyalty to the organization.[40] Some working conditions that may have this effect are the physical characteristics of the workplace, the level of supervision, relationships with co-workers, and company policies.

Employee Needs.

Understanding employee needs and providing the means for them to fulfill unmet needs can be a powerful motivational tool for the owner-manager. Employees' needs include adequate pay, feedback from management, the feeling of being a valued part of the organization, the possibility for advancement, extra responsibility or authority, recognition and praise by management, esteem of peers, a sense of achievement, and the challenge of the job. Studies have indicated that employees who are engaged and fulfilled at work are more likely to be productive and to stay with their employer.

PAYING EMPLOYEES

Small business owners face stiff competition from large companies and even government in paying employee wages. Many think they cannot afford to meet this competition. However, the value of a key employee cannot be overstated for many small businesses. As a result, many owner-managers have recognized that they must be competitive in paying key employees.

Employees are concerned about both absolute and relative wage levels. This means employees are usually aware of and concerned about their level of pay relative to those of their co-workers. Employee pay levels are very difficult to keep confidential in a small business. Often, a wage increase for one employee will be seen by other employees not as a reward for that employee but as a decrease in pay for themselves. This, of course, can cause unrest within the organization.

Wage levels are generally set using external and internal factors as a guide. Externally, the owner-manager may want to assess wage levels in similar or competing industries. Many provincial and territorial governments publish wage survey data that can assist in this regard. Most owner-managers can find out what the wage levels are in their communities through an informal survey. Other external considerations in arriving at wage levels might be cost-of-living increases, the demand/supply situation for employees, and government regulations. Internally, considerations employers use in setting salary levels are ability to pay, employee performance levels and requirements, and, as just mentioned, relative pay relationships.

Remuneration can offer employees security and have a motivational effect. There are many methods of paying employees, each with advantages and disadvantages. The owner-manager needs to tailor the pay plan to meet the needs of employees as well as the goals of the organization. Table 11-3 lists some of the more common

TABLE 11-3 Salary Plans for a Small Business

TYPE OF PLAN	HOW CALCULATED	ADVANTAGE	LIMITATION	BUSINESSES USING THE PLAN
Salary	Per hour or per month	Security Simplicity	Lack of incentive	Many businesses—routine tasks
Commission	Percentage of sales	Incentive	Lack of control Lack of security Lack of simplicity	Automobile sales Housing industry Some retail products requiring extra selling effort
Cash bonus on individual performance	Bonus on reaching objectives or quota	Security Incentive	Can be complicated	Retailing Manufacturing
Profit sharing on company performance	Percentage of profits distributed	Incentive Cooperation in organization	Can be complicated Amounts too small to motivate	Manufacturing Retailing Knowledge-based/service
Stock bonus	Predetermined percentage to employees based on objectives	Long-term interest in organization Incentive	Some employees want only cash	Manufacturing Knowledge-based/service

SMALL BUSINESS IN ACTION 11-6

PAY FOR PROFIT

Trevor Wasney, owner of **Arctic Spas** Oakville Group Inc., has seen the benefit of switching to profit-based compensation, which pays sellers for generating margin rather than revenue. Before the switch, Wasney paid his employees on a revenue-based commission tied to listed product prices and began running into trouble when poor performing salespeople began slashing prices and throwing in free merchandise just to secure a sale. On the advice of a fellow hot-tub retailer, Wasney decided to make the switch, and almost immediately his sales reps cut down on both price-chopping and throwing in free products. Since implementing the system, Arctic Spas has held its profit margins during slow years and increased them during good ones. Wasney has also seen how the system has helped motivate and retain his best employees.

Arctic Spa switched from a revenue- to a profit-based compensation program to ensure profit margins remain consistent.

Ariel Bravy/Shutterstock.com

Discussion Questions

1. Most firms base employee commission on revenue not sales. Why do you think this is the case?
2. What are some of the potential problems when changing an employee compensation system? How can these be avoided?
3. In profit-compensation systems, salespeople will normally want to sell the merchandise which produces the highest profit. How can this negatively affect consumers? What measures can be put in place to protect consumers?
4. Develop an alternative compensation plan for Wasney. Then, develop arguments to explain why he should switch to your plan.

methods of paying employees in small businesses and describes their advantages and limitations (see also **Small Business in Action 11-6**). Many organizations use combinations of these plans. A recent survey of top employees who left large organizations to work for smaller companies revealed that the main reason was the possibility of owning equity in the firm.[41]

FRINGE BENEFITS

Increasingly, small businesses need to provide fringe benefits to attract and retain employees. A survey of the 100 fastest-growing small businesses in Canada indicated that only 65 to 75 percent of employee compensation should be salary. The rest can be made up of bonus, profit sharing, stock options, and commissions.[42] Profit sharing has become increasingly common as entrepreneurs have found that linking employee compensation to the success of their business helps motivate employees. For example, the president of **QuickContractors.com**, Trevor Bouchard, says profit sharing helps keep employees focused and more concerned about keeping expenses low to maximize profits.[43] Other common benefits include bonuses, employee discounts, pension plans, disability and life insurance, and extended health and dental insurance.

If the small business has enough employees, it may be able to qualify for group insurance plans that reduce the cost of providing this benefit. Frequently, these plans are available through industry associations. Total costs of providing employee benefits are rising, and the owner-manager should monitor such costs closely. The Employee Benefit News Canada Organization reports that employee benefit programs typically cost from 2.5 to 9.1 percent of total payroll, depending on which benefits are offered.[44] Businesses may benefit by comparing the costs and services of several benefit providers to ensure they have the most cost-effective plan.

There are other work-related fringe benefits the business might offer to increase employee satisfaction and motivation are discussed next, but see **Small Business in Action 11-7** for a growing trend in smaller businesses.

SMALL BUSINESS IN ACTION 11-7

IS FIDO THE KEY TO EMPLOYEE HAPPINESS?

A growing trend in business is the practice of employees bringing pets, especially dogs, to the workplace. In fact, June 21 is designated International Take Your Dog to Work Day, although some companies, such as **HootSuite.com**, allow employees to bring their pet to work every day. HootSuite's CEO Ryan Holmes brings his own dog into work daily and says allowing pets in the office is an inexpensive way to improve employees' physical and mental health. His comments are echoed by Liz Palika, author of the book *Dogs at Work*, who states, "Employees are generally happier with a dog in the workplace."

In a recent article in *USA Today*, Small business owner Rhonda Abrams highlighted some additional advantages of bringing pets into the workplace. She notes that allowing pets at work actually helps with recruitment, and all of her job ads note her office is dog-friendly. Abrams also points out that allowing employees to bring their dogs to work positively impacts employee retention and, echoing previous statements, improves office morale.

Not everyone agrees that dogs in the workplace are acceptable, and some opponents raise issues of productivity, safety, and allergic reactions. A small survey conducted by *Canadian Business* magazine found that the key to successfully integrating dogs into the workplace was to create dog-free zones and policies around appropriate care and handling of the animals.

Many firms are starting to allow pets, especially dogs, to come to work with employees. Managers think this practice creates employees who are more engaged and loyal.

Monkeybusinessimages/Dreamstime.com

Discussion Questions

1. What do you think are some of the advantages and disadvantages of allowing pets, specifically dogs, in a workplace?
2. Given that the research on the impact of animals in the workplace is rather limited, would you allow employees to bring pets to work if you were in charge? Why or why not?
3. Conduct some research on the Internet about pets in the workforce. What is the current position of the literature on employee morale and productivity?

Job Rotation.

With job rotation, employees are periodically allowed to exchange jobs with other employees. Used in factories, this program can not only increase employee interest and motivation but also assist in training workers.

Job Sharing.

Some firms have found success in allowing employees to share their jobs. The possibility of two part-time workers may satisfy the job requirements and increase the satisfaction of those who may not want to work full time. It is estimated that over 170,000 Canadians job-share, according to Statistics Canada.[45]

Working from Home.

An increasing number of businesses are allowing employees to complete some or all of their work at home. Although this option may not be available for all types of small businesses, if it is an option if may be viewed as a valuable benefit to some employees. In a recent survey, 65 percent of employers said employees are more productive when they work remotely and cite other advantages such as saving money on office space. Working remotely does come with some some challenges for both employees and owner-managers as it can reduce access to leadership, reduce the likelihood of collaboration, and possibly impact organizational culture negatively.[46]

Flexible Hours.

Some firms have experienced increases in productivity by allowing employees a work schedule other than the nine-to-five schedule common in many industries. As discussed earlier in the chapter, real estate company AvenueHQ allows employees to essentially come and go as they wish; this works because the firm's co-owners focus on employees' results not on hours worked or where the work takes place. A recent survey by the Conference Board of Canada found that 85 percent of Canadian firms offer employees some type of flexible hours. The survey also found that employees would take pay cuts and reduce their vacation time if they could incorporate more flexibility in their day. Given the increased difficulty in attracting and retaining employees, small business owners may want to adopt some of these practices.[47]

Employee Suggestion Systems.

Many companies have some form of employee suggestion system. Recently, some companies have taken this idea a step further by offering employees money and/or time to implement their suggestions. For example, **Arrow Group**, one of the fastest-growing companies in Canada, provides employees with Arrow time. This is time to work on individual projects from home or the office. Arrow's president, Sam Ibrahim, says, "Some of our best innovations have come from people thinking on their independent time." The National Association of Suggestion Systems, reports that some 3000 formal suggestion systems operate in the United States, generating more than 300,000 ideas and saving companies more than $800 million annually.[48]

Table 11-4 provides a description of five fast-growing employee benefit programs. Additional assistance benefit programs may be available through a number of private companies that specialize in this area, such as Benefits Interface Inc. See **Small Business in Action 11-8** to understand how one company pulls together everything discussed in this section to create a deliciously successful retail business.

TABLE 11-4 Five Hottest Employee Benefits

1. Spending Accounts	Many firms that cannot afford flexible benefit plans are turning to spending accounts funded by company or employee contributions. They can be used to cover a range of health or dental expenses. When employees contribute a portion of their salaries (say 2 percent) to these funds, that income is not taxed.
2. Health Promotion	More employers offer non-medical benefits aimed at "wellness." Staff is allowed certain sums for such items as gym memberships, health-risk assessments, psychological counselling, and personal training.
3. Increased Choice	There is more choice in structuring benefit plans. Staff choices depend on how much they wish to spend, or on other variables such as their state of health or access to other benefits.
4. Flexible Work Hours	To help families juggle increasingly complex schedules, more firms let workers set their own hours. It could be 9 to 5, 7:30 to 3:30, or four 10-hour days.
5. Employee Input	More employees are being asked for their input on operational matters, but at a cost. Staff who suggest benefits changes, for instance, are held responsible for the program's success. If costs exceed the plan, they must make up the balance.

SMALL BUSINESS IN ACTION 11-8

PURDY'S CHOCOLATES BUILDS EMPLOYEE LOYALTY

Karen Flavelle, president of Vancouver-based **Purdy's Chocolates**, has acknowledged that her loyal employees are the main reason the company has been so successful. Her company uses profit sharing, internal promotions, training, and team building to build a motivated and loyal workforce. As a result of these programs, Purdy's employees work on average for nine years at the company, which is significant when we consider that over 50 percent of her workers are classified as front-line retail employees, a group that is known for its transient nature. This lack of turnover has allowed Purdy's to reduce training and re-staffing costs. Flavelle offers three tips to building a successful workforce:

Photo 37245151 © Yelena Rodriguez - Dreamstime.com

- *Hiring right:* Managers often go through four or five interviews while retail workers are interviewed at least twice.
- *Training:* Employees need to understand the business, and by providing quality training, the company can promote from within.
- *Praising and paying well:* Purdy's pays 20 percent higher than other retailers, and profit sharing is provided to all employees.

Discussion Questions

1. Do you think Flavelle's approach can work for other retailers? Why or why not?
2. What do you think are some of the advantages and disadvantages of providing front-line workers with so many benefits?
3. Do you think organizations are morally obligated to pay and treat front-line workers better? Are they ethically obligated?

CONTROLLING AND EVALUATING EMPLOYEE PERFORMANCE

Many of the practices previously mentioned may contribute to a more motivated and loyal workforce. It is essential, however, that this motivation be directed toward achieving the firm's objectives. The owner-manager needs to effectively evaluate progress toward goals and objectives and inform employees of their progress. This can be done through a regular performance appraisal.

Another method for accomplishing this is the management by objectives approach (MBO), which is used in many organizations. A simplified version of MBO that is suitable for the small business is described in *Putting the One Minute Manager to Work.*[49] The five steps in this method (called the *PRICE system*) are as follows:

- *Pinpoint:* Define the performance area to be evaluated (e.g., sales for a retail clerk).
- *Record:* Set up a system to monitor and record performance in that area (e.g., the cash register tape).
- *Involve:* Manager and employee jointly set goals and a strategy for reaching those goals in that performance area (e.g., dollar sales per month).
- *Coach:* The manager observes performance periodically, perhaps making suggestions but allowing the employee considerable freedom to work toward the agreed-on goals.
- *Evaluate:* At the end of the agreed-on period, assess performance, reward positive results, and set future goals.

The value of the PRICE system is the clear line of communication between employer and employee in directing the employee toward goals and evaluating the employee's progress.

HANDLING GRIEVANCES

Employee grievances, or concerns, arise in most organizations. They can have a negative effect on the morale of the organization, but they can also be positive and helpful if handled properly. The following are some principles for effective grievance management:

1. Implement a precise method whereby employees can express grievances. It is important that the organizational lines of authority be followed in this case. If at all possible, the grievance should be expressed to the immediate supervisor. This procedure should be laid out in the policy manual.
2. Employees need assurance that expressing their concerns will not jeopardize or prejudice their relationship with the employer. A wise employer will recognize that many grievances are legitimate and, if acted on, can help the organization.
3. There should be minimal red tape in processing complaints. Employees need to feel that someone is really listening to their concerns.
4. Owner-managers need to understand that some employees may be hesitant to raise a concern directly. In these situations, the suggestion box is effective.

TERMINATING THE EMPLOYEE

If the owner-manager makes a decision to terminate an employee, it is important to follow due care in regard to legislation and regulations concerning this matter. While legislation varies by province and territory, the following should be adhered to: justifiable reasons for the termination provided, adequate notice provided, appropriate severance and vacation pay provided (if applicable), necessary documentation completed (such as the record of employment), and if warranted, letters of explanation or reference for the employee provided.

UNIONIZATION AND THE SMALL BUSINESS

Most small businesses do not have unions operating within the organization. As the firm grows, however, and as employees become farther removed from the owner, the possibility of union-related activity increases. The owner-manager should recognize that unions are formed when a majority of employees believe that a union would better serve their employment needs than the existing system. For example, **Just Us Coffee**, a Nova Scotia-based coffee roaster, had one of its retail locations unionize in 2013, as workers at the Halifax store expressed concern about working hours and the distribution of tips. The owners of the firm, a co-operative, expressed surprise at the union movement and dismissed the union's organizers. After the dismissed employees filed complaints with the labour board, they were hired back, and Just Us accepted a union in the Halifax location. Union organizer Shay Enxuga says, "One of the biggest reasons we wanted the union was to put a system in place to negotiate things within our collective agreement. We don't want to just count on the benevolence of our bosses. But also because unless we have a union, there's a power dynamic going on between us and our bosses where we're not protected. One of the reasons we want to have a union is to have a grievance process, where we could be legally protected in case of mistreatment, like being dismissed."[50]

Effective human relations policies can go a long way toward discouraging union establishment in the firm. Some small businesses in certain industries may be required to hire unionized employees.

In these situations, the requirements for both the employer and the union are set out in the Labour Relations Act in each province and territory. Some of the more common aspects of collective bargaining that may affect the small business owner are the following:

- The contents of an agreement must deal with wages, benefits, and working conditions.
- Both parties must meet and bargain in good faith. However, an employer need not reveal company data that they prefer to keep confidential.

- The owner cannot discriminate against an employee for union involvement.
- Both employers and unions are bound by the terms and conditions of the collective agreement.
- Disputes concerning interpretation of the agreement must be resolved by an arbitrator.

GOVERNMENT REQUIREMENTS AND ASSISTANCE LO5

The owner-manager should be aware of relevant government labour laws and programs that affect the management of personnel. A brief discussion of such laws and programs for all levels of government follows.

FEDERAL GOVERNMENT

The federal and provincial governments provide training and employment programs to hundreds of thousands of Canadians each year. Some specific programs include the following:

- *Job entry programs* provide training for unemployed or undertrained people for up to one year.
- *Skill shortage and skill investment programs* provide financial assistance and training for up to three years for skill upgrading as a result of technological change within the company.
- *Job development programs* provide training and financial assistance for the unemployed, disadvantaged persons, women, persons with disabilities, older workers, and members of visible minorities.
- *Innovation programs* provide funds to test new solutions to labour-market-related problems.
- *The Community Futures Program* helps finance local committees for development training and employment initiatives in areas experiencing economic hardship.

For more information on each of the above programs, contact the local Canada Employment Centres or provincial departments of economic development and/or labour.

The federal government also has some legislation in the areas of employment standards, employment and pay equity, and hiring practices. Because of some overlaps in jurisdiction with the provinces and territories, details are discussed in the next section.

PROVINCIAL AND TERRITORIAL GOVERNMENTS

Each province and territory in Canada, through its human resources or labour department, has set labour standards with which every owner-manager should be familiar.

Job Discrimination.

Each provincial and territorial government has passed legislation concerning human rights in the workplace. Entitled *Bills or Codes of Human Rights*, they are administered by provincial and territorial human rights commissions; this legislation has jurisdiction over businesses not federally owned or regulated. Like their federal counterparts, these regulations are designed to prevent discrimination in the workplace.

Pay and Employment Equity.

Recently, some provinces and territories have enacted legislation to ensure equality of pay and employment opportunity regardless of gender, race, religious affiliation, or ethnic origin.

Working Conditions and Compensation.

Numerous legal requirements govern the conditions under which retail employees work. Of importance to the small business owner are wage and hour requirements, restrictions on the use of child labour, provisions regarding equal pay, workers' compensation, employment insurance, and the Canada Pension Plan.

Employment Standards.

Both the federal and provincial or territorial governments administer a considerable amount of legislation related to employment standards and labour relations. At both levels of government, ministries of labour have primary responsibility in this field of regulation. In addition, both levels have legislation that allows for the establishment of unions and collective bargaining agents in the form of provincial or territorial labour relations acts and the federal Canada Labour Code (**laws-lois.justice.gc.ca/eng/acts/l-2/**). The Canada Labour Code also deals with many aspects of fair labour standards, labour relations, dismissal procedures, severance allowances, and working conditions. Similarly, each province and territory enforces statutes covering minimum wage rates, hours of work, overtime, holidays and leaves, termination notices, employment of young people, and information requirements on the statement of earnings and deductions.

Employment Safety and Health.

Employment safety and health programs are designed to reduce absenteeism and labour turnover. Most provinces and territories have passed industrial safety acts to protect the health and safety of workers. These laws govern such areas as sanitation, ventilation, and dangerous machinery. In addition to legislation, provincial and territorial governments, as well as employers, provide programs and training designed to accomplish similar purposes.

Workers' Compensation.

Workers' compensation is an employee accident and disability insurance program required under provincial and territorial law. It covers employees who are accidentally injured while working or who are unable to work as a result of a disease associated with a particular occupation. Although these programs vary, they generally provide for medical expenses and basic subsistence during the period of disability. Employers help pay for the program through assessments from the Workers' Compensation Board or Workplace Safety and Insurance Board. The assessment rates represent a substantial operating expense; thus, they must be planned for and managed with considerable care.

Wage Subsidy Programs.

These programs provide financial assistance that encourage businesses to hire additional employees. Interested entrepreneurs should contact either their provincial economic development and/or labour departments or use the federal government websites to access information.

Provincial and Territorial Training Programs.

These programs provide job training and skill development incentives to upgrade the labour force. Often such programs include a wage subsidy to small businesses that hire new employees. Contact a local labour department for details on these programs.

MUNICIPAL GOVERNMENTS

Local or municipal government regulations related to industry generally are confined to such areas as licensing, zoning, hours of operation, property taxes, and building codes.

Municipal authorities also exercise an especially strong influence over food establishments. For instance, a municipal licensing system for restaurants and other food services establishments may be in effect. Health inspectors may make periodic and sometimes unannounced inspections. Any store that sells wine, beer, or liquor may require a licence from provincial or territorial liquor-licensing authorities.

RECORD KEEPING FOR EMPLOYERS LO6

Every employer should maintain an employee file that includes such information as the employee's original application form, work record, salary level, evaluation reports, and any other pertinent information. One of the most important employee record-keeping tasks for the owner-manager is completing the payroll. There are several essential steps in managing a payroll system for employees.

EMPLOYEE REMITTANCE NUMBER

As an employer, the owner-manager collects employee income tax on behalf of the government as a deduction from the employee's wage. Before remitting this amount to the Receiver General, the employer must obtain a remittance number, available by contacting the nearest office of the Canada Revenue Agency.

PAYROLL BOOK

The employer should use accounting/scheduling software or a payroll book to record employee time worked and the required deductions. The most popular payroll software included **Gusto**, **QuickBooks Pro**, and **Simple Pay Canada**. Paper payroll books can be ordered online or can be obtained from most business supply or stationery stores.

Monthly Remittance.

As mentioned above, each payday the employer is required to make the appropriate deductions and remit them, as well as the employer's share of Canada Pension Plan (CPP) and employment insurance (EI), to the Canada Revenue Agency. This remittance is made on a prescribed form similar to that in Figure 11-5. This form contains the remittance number, the current payment amount, and a cumulative record of payments to date.

Year-End Statements.

At the end of the calendar year, the employer is required to total and reconcile the year's remittances with the Canada Revenue Agency's totals. This is done on a T4-A summary form provided by the Canada Revenue Agency.

It is also the employer's responsibility to fill out for each employee a record of earnings and deductions for the year on a T4 slip. The T4 slip (Figure 11-6) is completed by reviewing totals from the payroll book and is required to be sent to the employee by the end of February of the following year.

An increasing number of small businesses have found it to be cost effective to hire another firm to handle the payroll function. This is called *outsourcing* and has extended into other areas as well because of the increasing complexity of some of these functions.

CONTRACT EMPLOYEES

A growing number of small business owners use a contract employee to meet part or all of the business' labour requirements. These workers are considered independent contractors and as such are not employees of the company. The contractor or the contracting company simply invoices the small business for services rendered. Contract employees may be hired for a particular project and can be long term. They may also be hired for temporary purposes and paid a fee to provide a short-term service. Although the owner-manager still manages these people, the calculation of CPP, EI, or other benefits is not required. This typically results in a reduction in costs to the small business of about 10 to 15 percent. However, some companies have experienced increased costs. It must also be remembered that some positions and tasks may not be suitable for the contract employee,

FIGURE 11-5 **Remittance Form**

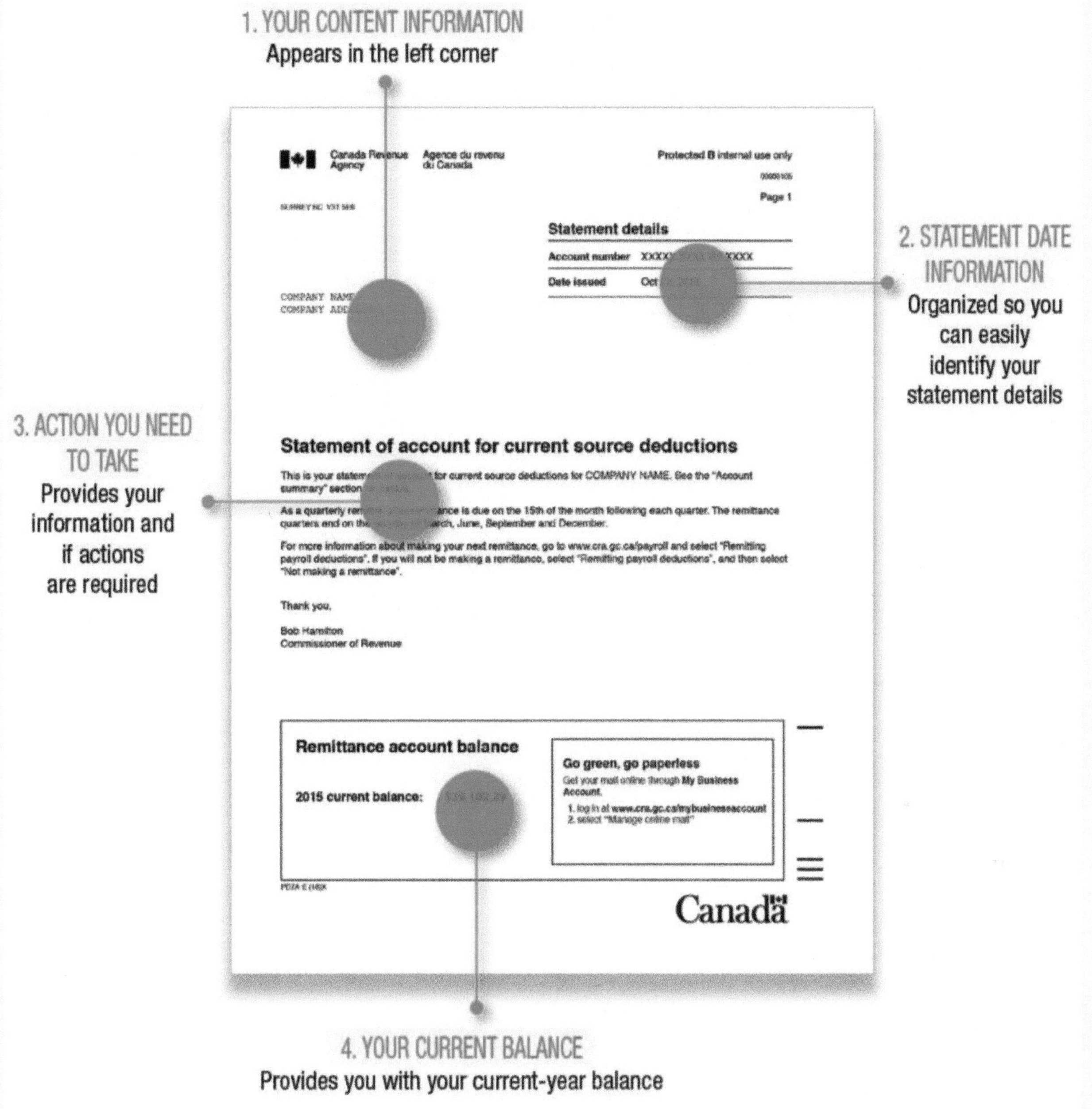

Canada Revenue Agency, Remittance Form – PD7A – Statement of account for current source deductions, from: https://www.canada.ca/en/revenue-agency/services/about-canada-revenue-agency-cra/understanding-noticesletters/pd7a-statement-account-current-source-deductions.html. Reproduced with permission of the Minister of National Revenue, 2019.

and issues of motivation and loyalty may be a problem for contract workers. Therefore, a contract employee may be more appropriate for temporary or project-type jobs. Other difficult issues relating to contract employees involve new privacy legislation, labour standards, performance appraisal, and terminations. The owner-manager should be aware of the legal differences in managing contract and traditional employees.

FIGURE 11-6 **T4 Slip**

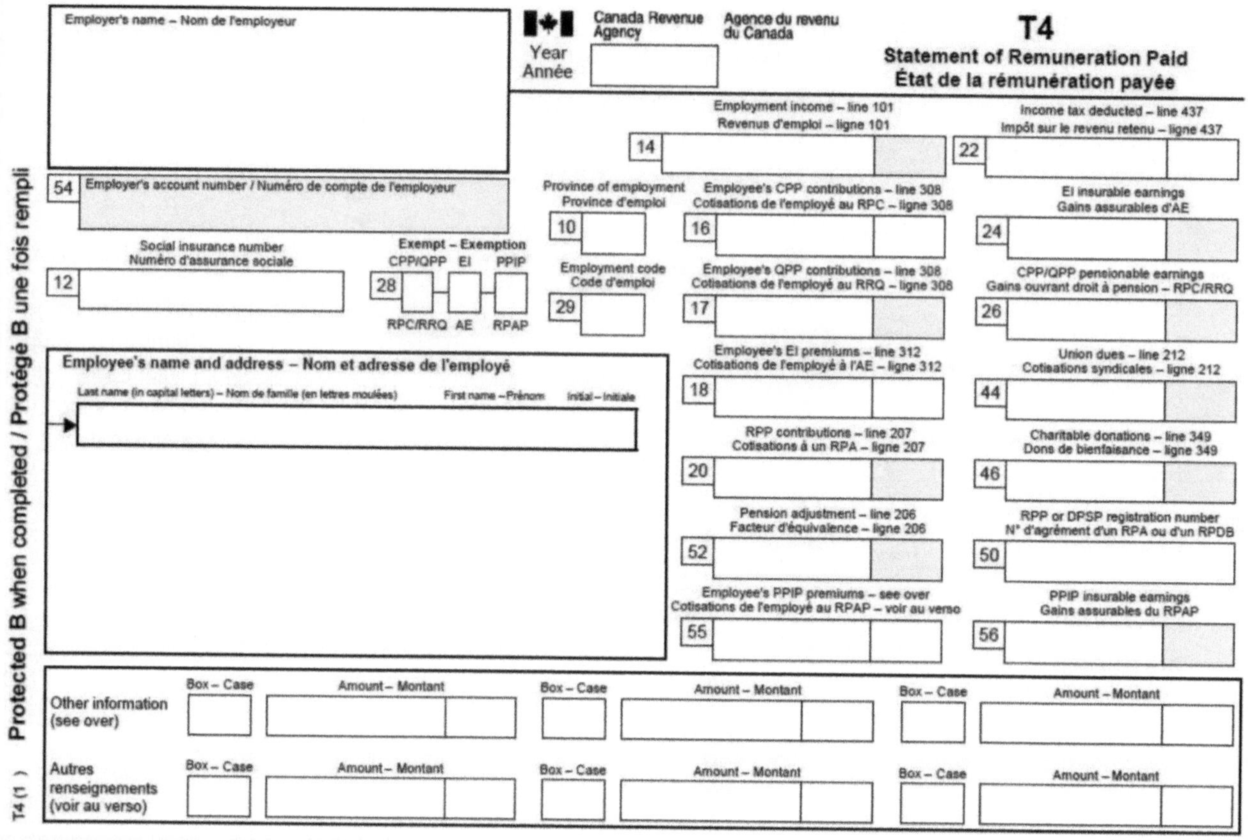
Employer's name – Nom de l'employeur

Canada Revenue Agency / Agence du revenu du Canada

Year / Année

T4

Statement of Remuneration Paid
État de la rémunération payée

54 Employer's account number / Numéro de compte de l'employeur

Social insurance number / Numéro d'assurance sociale — 12

Exempt – Exemption — 28 CPP/QPP, EI, PPIP / RPC/RRQ, AE, RPAP

Province of employment / Province d'emploi — 10

Employment code / Code d'emploi — 29

14 Employment income – line 101 / Revenus d'emploi – ligne 101

22 Income tax deducted – line 437 / Impôt sur le revenu retenu – ligne 437

16 Employee's CPP contributions – line 308 / Cotisations de l'employé au RPC – ligne 308

24 EI insurable earnings / Gains assurables d'AE

17 Employee's QPP contributions – line 308 / Cotisations de l'employé au RRQ – ligne 308

26 CPP/QPP pensionable earnings / Gains ouvrant droit à pension – RPC/RRQ

18 Employee's EI premiums – line 312 / Cotisations de l'employé à l'AE – ligne 312

44 Union dues – line 212 / Cotisations syndicales – ligne 212

20 RPP contributions – line 207 / Cotisations à un RPA – ligne 207

46 Charitable donations – line 349 / Dons de bienfaisance – ligne 349

52 Pension adjustment – line 206 / Facteur d'équivalence – ligne 206

50 RPP or DPSP registration number / N° d'agrément d'un RPA ou d'un RPDB

55 Employee's PPIP premiums – see over / Cotisations de l'employé au RPAP – voir au verso

56 PPIP insurable earnings / Gains assurables du RPAP

Employee's name and address – Nom et adresse de l'employé

Last name (in capital letters) – Nom de famille (en lettres moulées) / First name – Prénom / Initial – Initiale

Other information (see over) / Autres renseignements (voir au verso) — Box – Case / Amount – Montant

Protected B when completed / Protégé B une fois rempli

T4 (1)

Canada Revenue Agency, T4 Slip, from: https://www.canada.ca/en/revenue-agency/services/tax/individuals/topics/about-your-taxreturn/tax-return/completing-a-tax-return/tax-slips/understand-your-tax-slips/t4-slips/t4-statementremuneration-paid.html. Reproduced with permission of the Minister of National Revenue, 2019.

LEARNING OBJECTIVES SUMMARY

LO1 **Sound personnel management is a key to the success of a small business because motivated and competent personnel are one aspect of a business that may be unique and difficult to duplicate.**

LO2 **The organizational chart integrates tasks and employees so that the owner can visualize how the different aspects of the plan will work together. An effective way to prevent many personnel problems is to have a policy manual covering such areas as job description, working conditions, holidays and leaves, remuneration, and employee benefits.**

LO3 **The principles of human resource management start with the development of a proper hiring process that is applied consistently to every candidate, as well as organizational policies that guide the hiring process. Human resources must have a plan that includes job descriptions, recruitment plans, training plans, and policies to ensure employees know the organizational rules and how they will be evaluated.**

LO4 **The owner-manager should apply the following concepts of personnel management: assess their leadership style, work on time management by avoiding procrastination on important decisions or tasks, assess priorities, and use the most productive time of the day for the important decisions.**

LO5 **Legal requirements for the personnel aspects of small business are applicable from federal, provincial or territorial, and municipal governments.**

LO6 **The following are the steps in administering a payroll system: obtain an employee remittance number, obtain a payroll book, make the appropriate deductions and remit them with the employer's share to the Canada Revenue Agency, total and reconcile the year's remittance at the end of every calendar year, and send out T4s.**

TIME TO TAKE ACTION

By this stage in the entrepreneurial process, readers should be working on their business plan or even perhaps running their business. Entrepreneurs should consider the following action steps:

1. Complete a personal SWOT analysis. In what areas of management will you need help?
2. Complete an organizational chart and staffing plan for your business.

DISCUSSION QUESTIONS

1. Discuss the relative advantages and disadvantages of the various compensation plans used in small businesses.
2. What industries can you think of in which profit sharing would be less successful? Why?
3. Discuss the relative advantages and disadvantages of the different types of fringe benefits for a small manufacturing company. If possible, interview employees of such a business to find out which of these benefits are the most attractive.
4. Recently, a small business increased the wages of its employees, but its productivity is still inadequate. What are some possible reasons for this low level of productivity?
5. After reading this chapter, what do you believe will be the most critical small business personnel problem in the future?

EXPERIENTIAL EXERCISES

1. Interview two small business owners to find out their personnel policies and how they communicate those policies to their employees.
2. Ask three employees of small businesses what they like and dislike about their jobs. What personnel policies could be used to remedy the dislikes?
3. Determine how three employees of various small businesses were recruited for their present positions. What seems to be the most popular source from which to recruit employees for small businesses? Why?
4. Study some online job boards or LinkedIn job advertisements, and choose three examples of good job advertisements and three examples of poor job advertisements. Be prepared to explain your choices.

COMPREHENSIVE CASE DAN KIM: PART 6

Dan resolved the inventory and layout concerns with the help of a consultant whom his banker had suggested. With the expansion of the plant, Dan was able to meet demand for orders of the Ladder Helper and some additional products. Sales were increasing, and the problems with finances that had caused concern earlier seemed to be less troublesome.

However, partway through year two an additional problem began to surface. It involved his personnel. With increased demand and plant expansion, Dan had hired four additional employees. Three were put to work in the metal fabricating part of the business, and the other was hired to work full time with marketing and distribution. The two employees who had started with Dan had both left for higher-paying jobs, so Dan had hired six new employees in a short time. The first couple of hires were found through ads on Kijiji, but lately Dan had simply gone down to the local Canada Manpower office and found the required workers.

Dan is becoming increasingly discouraged with the time and hassle involved in managing employees. On many occasions, he would have liked to have fired an employee, but the hiring and training processes seem to take so long that Dan feels that he cannot afford a slowdown of the production process with demand being what it is. He realizes that the type of employee he is hiring possesses little education, but as a small business owner, he simply cannot afford—nor does the job require—better trained employees. He currently pays employees $1 above minimum wage, which is well below union rates, but he increases the wage as the employee finishes the on-the-job training. He also intends to give all employees a raise each year based on seniority. Because the business is losing money, however, Dan does not feel that he can afford raises to employee wages at this time.

Some of the employee problems that particularly bother him are employees wanting more money and better benefits; workers threatening to leave for higher wages if he does not increase their wages; work slowdowns when he is not physically present at the plant; poor quality work and too much wasted metal as a result of fabricating errors; and the appearance and conduct of some of the younger workers. This last problem especially annoys Suzie, who is frequently in the plant working on the finances.

In addition, on some occasions, Suzie has been in the plant and has given some direction to the workers when Dan is away. The employees simply ignore her because she is not the boss.

Questions

1. Evaluate Dan's personnel procedures.
2. How could Dan motivate his employees?
3. What should be done differently for the marketing person? Why?
4. What outside assistance might be available to help Dan with his personnel problems?

CHAPTER 12

MANAGEMENT HELP: MENTORS, BOARDS OF ADVISORS OR DIRECTORS, AND TAX ASSISTANCE

LEARNING OBJECTIVES

By the end of this chapter, you should be able to:

LO1 Illustrate how mentors, boards of directors, or boards of advisors can be used.

LO2 Explain the importance of understanding the nature of the Canadian tax system.

LO3 List 10 fundamental tax management principles the owner-manager should know.

LO4 Describe specific tax-related programs that apply to small business.

SMALL BUSINESS PROFILE

DEVON BROOKS, Sphere

Devon Brooks may be young, but her talent, ability to triumph through great challenges, and clarity on value-based leadership have already earned her extraordinary recognition.

In 2012, *PROFIT* magazine acknowledged Brooks when they named her "1 of the 30 most fabulous entrepreneurs in Canada," alongside such heavy hitters as Joe "Fresh" Mimran, Guy Laliberte, and Steve Nash.

Thus far, her entrepreneurial journey or "adventure," as she has put it, "resembles a path and no path at all"—and, for the wisdom it has allowed her, she would not have it any other way. Brooks had sailed around the world by age 16. At 21, she actualized her second-year school project, at the London College of Fashion, founding a category-defining franchise, Blo Blow Dry Bar, along with her co-founders and loved ones, Judy Brooks and Val Litwin.

"The Blo concept is a simple one," explains Brooks, "choose off a 'hair menu' and get your hair washed and styled in a short period of time for less than you would pay in a salon format. It is what my founders and I called 'fast, affordable, catwalk quality hair'," she says. Brooks and her mother and co-founder, Judy Brooks, came up with the idea when reminiscing about how frazzled attendees looked at a previous "top 100 women in business" event. "It was a gender equality issue as far as we were concerned. The time and cost of services at that point were forcing women to sacrifice self-care in their very busy schedules. . . . It's difficult to factor in the time for aesthetics you'd like, the modern woman has much to do." The Blo concept made that luxury affordable and fast. Six months after Brooks submitted the business plan as a school project, the founding team of three launched their first location. They innovated strong franchise systems and were quickly recognized for their edgy brand, with taglines such as "cause you can't blo yourself" and "you're not cheating on your hairdresser." "Hair cadets" (the "Blocabulary" name for its clients) were rolling in and so were franchise requests. They were onto something big, and it was not just the hair.

The Canadian-born business has been credited for igniting what has become a global market category.

izusek/E+/Getty Images

Today, the business is managed by the Toronto-based operating team the founders merged with in 2010. Blo has 65 locations around the world and continues to grow.

Working with that volume ignited something for Brooks and completely altered her lens on leadership. She notes, "It can't just be effective, it has to be meaningful and connected to the roots of the lives of its people. . . . If you don't know what people are dealing with, you can't know what they need," she explains. The lack of authenticity in the sharing of business stories compelled her. "We all have a perception issue, when we look at what we think is the success of others. Almost nothing is what it seems." She began speaking publicly about the abuse and violence she had endured at 18, when she was raped, and again at 21, just after launching Blo, when an assailant forced his way into her home, attacked her, and held her against her will until she was able to free herself. She never looked back. Brooks advocates personal evolution, from mental wellness to sex and relationships, with raw conversation: speaking to thousands, on many stages, including TEDx and Pecha Kucha; joining the board of directors and spearheading the marketing committee of a feminist anti-violence organization (**wavaw.ca**) to make her hometown of Vancouver a safer place for women; and supporting, mentoring, and advising businesses and aspiring entrepreneurs who want to make a cause-based impact in their communities. At 24, she became the youngest-ever mentor of the Canadian Youth Business Foundation, now known as Futurepreneur, and went on to represent Canada at two G20 Young Entrepreneur Summits. Brooks has a hunger for greatness and is skilled in awakening greatness in others. Her mentees noted, "as our business grows, our mentoring grows as well. Each session is more helpful than the last. We are extremely grateful for what Devon has brought to us, and we hope to continue to grow with her."

While serving as a mentor, Brooks started to formally engage in business coaching. She says coaching can be both powerful and transformational as it can help people reach their potential, achieve their goals, take leaps, and spark change. Given the positive impact of coaching, Brooks says she wanted to help coaches and seekers connect. That's how she came up with the idea of Sphere, an app that connects people and coaches, and has just launched in a beta test. What differentiates Sphere, Brooks says, is the quality of the coaches. Brooks has already signed fifty coaches who have agreed to pay a monthly membership fee as well as a percentage of sales to Brooks' company. Investors certainly see value in Brooks' new project as she has raised $800,000 in initial financing. According to Brooks, coaching needs to be innovated, and she believes Sphere will do that by becoming the go-to app for Millennials seeking a coach.

SPHERE
sphereishere.com/

ADVISORS AND SMALL BUSINESS LO1

When entrepreneurs are planning and starting their business, they will often seek out assistance from more experienced entrepreneurs or mentors. Many successful entrepreneurs, such as Brian Scudamore, founder of **1-800-Got-Junk?**, state that seeking the advice of experienced leaders helped them grow their company. In addition to mentors, many entrepreneurs will form boards of advisors or directors to assist them in growing their company. Entrepreneurs should also be willing to engage in discussions with lawyers, accountants, and business counsellors as they move their business from just an idea to startup to a growing enterprise. As noted, by *Globe and Mail* business author Jennifer Warawa, entrepreneurs should be willing to hire and consult with outside experts, such as accountants, as it enables them to focus on why they started the business, provides work-life balance, and can help increase their business.[1]

This chapter will first introduce the concept of mentoring and advisors and then proceed to discuss tax management, a very important topic in small business.

USE OF ADVISORS

Entrepreneurs will usually use outside advisors, such as accountants, bankers, lawyers, advertising agencies, and market researchers, as needed. These advisors, who are separate from the more formal board of advisors discussed below, can also become an important part of the organization and thus will need to be managed just like any other permanent part of the new venture.

The relationship of the entrepreneur and outside advisors can be enhanced by seeking out the best advisors and involving them thoroughly and at an early stage. Advisors should be assessed or interviewed just as if they were being hired for a permanent position. References should be checked and questions asked to ascertain the quality of service and the compatibility with the entrepreneur or the management team.

Hiring and managing outside experts can be effectively accomplished by considering these advisors as advice suppliers. No manager would buy raw materials or supplies without knowledge of their cost and quality, and the same approval process should apply to advisors. Entrepreneurs should ask these advisors about fees, credentials, references, and so on, before hiring them.

Businesses often rely on outside advisors, such as CPAs and lawyers, to ensure they are making appropriate decisions.

© Rob Daly/age fotostock

There are many good sources of advisors, such as other small business owners, chambers of commerce, universities, friends, and relatives. However, once advisors have been hired, the entrepreneur should question their advice. Why is the advice being given? Does following the advice make sense for the business? Make sure you understand the decision and all its potential implications.

Mentors.

Often the first stage in formal advice is the use of a mentor. Mentors can be used on an ad hoc basis or formally assist the entrepreneur in running the company on an ongoing basis. Mentoring often takes the form of a new business owner forming a relationship with an experienced mentor. The experienced entrepreneur offers advice and guidance to an entrepreneur who is in the early stages of running a business. For example, the founders of Canadian toy giant **Spin Master** relied on several business mentors in the toy industry as they were building their company. But mentorship does not have to be just at the start-up stage of a business—many experienced entrepreneurs make use of mentors. Larry Wasser, a mentor for the Rotman School of Management says, "Getting a mentor at any stage can always help because there's always something that an external advisor, an unbiased party who hasn't worked within the business' walls, can bring."[2] Brian Scudamore of the above-mentioned 1-800-Got-Junk? still uses mentors even though his company has surpassed $100 million in sales.[3]

Two major benefits of mentoring is that it offers one-on-one communication and it will enhance your skill set. Managers of the Futurpreneur program, which primarily supports startups, believe so strongly in the mentoring process that they insist all loan applicants who receive funding from the organization establish a formal mentor relationship. Research strongly supports Futurpreneurs' mandated mentoring as 70 percent of mentored businesses last longer than five years compared with 30 percent of new businesses that will not survive the first 24 months, and 50 percent that won't last five years.[4] Entrepreneurs also attest to the importance of mentors as 92 percent of mentored entrepreneurs confirm their mentors have had a direct impact on their businesses' growth and ability to survive.[5] As discussed in **Chapter 6**, Matthew Sheridan, founder of Nix Sensor, attributes some of his success to his angel investors who also acted as mentors. Sheridan says their advice has impacted his company's strategy and helped his business stay ahead of his competitors.[6] Giovanna Minenna founder of three Winnipeg businesses, including **BrowsbyG**, says if she could give entrepreneurs one piece of advice it would be to find a mentor as their guidance is the best path for an entrepreneur's success. She says her mentors helped her by providing tough feedback, assistance with contracts, improvements to her website, and her marketing plan.[7]

Given the value of mentoring, surprisingly few small businesses make use of the practice. A recent survey indicates that only 22 percent of entrepreneurs had a mentor in place when they started their business. That same survey indicates that 80 percent of entrepreneurs wished they had a mentor.[8] Jay Dingwall, CEO of Famous Folks, the Toronto marketing agency discussed in **Chapter 1**, says the he constantly spoke to people when he started his business asking for advice. He confirms the use of both formal and informal mentors is essential to startups, especially businesses managed by young entrepreneurs.[9] Sue Underhill, owner of **Maximum Physiotherapy** in Collingwood, Ontario, echoes Dingwall's comments, saying mentors are valuable because they touch on things entrepreneurs may not even think about, often preventing new entrepreneurs from making costly mistakes.[10]

Giovanna Minenna says mentoring has helped her in a number of ways with her business, Brows by G Inc. She says mentors can provide advice and also ask difficult questions. Minenna advises anyone who wants to be an entrepreneur to find a mentor.

Photo courtesy of Giovanna Minenna

Todd O'Keefe's story is typical of many Futurpreneur successes. While O'Keefe was enrolled in his PR degree course, he was soon sure about two things: one, he enjoyed PR and marketing, and, two, he wanted to run his own consulting firm rather than work for someone else. O'Keefe states, "Running my own company is a dream and I had to make it happen." Rather than wait till he graduated, O'Keefe started writing his business plan and soliciting clients in the fourth and final year of his degree. O'Keefe decided to focus on small and micro-sized businesses as a way to build his portfolio and work with clients that normally would not be able to afford the services of larger firms. O'Keefe says, "Small firms need PR work, too; they may not need it all the time, but no one is trying to specifically serve this market, as most firms would rather deal with larger clients who have bigger budgets." O'Keefe quickly found a couple of clients and successfully earned a Futurpreneur loan that comes with a mandatory mentorship program to further finance his enterprise. O'Keefe notes, "Getting the financing was wonderful, but equally valuable was their insistence that I work with a mentor. My mentor has assisted me every step of the way in starting my firm, and I will continue to rely on them in the future."[11] O'Keefe's advice to other PR and marketing grads who dream of working for themselves is to find mentors who can assist them and go for it.

Finding and Selecting Mentors.

Entrepreneurs should seek out mentors in almost the same way they should look for employees. Entrepreneurs should start by listing their own personal strengths and weaknesses, noting where they lack knowledge and require assistance. They should then prioritize areas for development. Although they may need assistance and advice in numerous areas, entrepreneurs should identify key areas of their business where advice would have the most meaningful impact. From here, they should craft a job description for their potential mentor, the description should include such things as the education and experience they will be looking for in a mentor.[12]

Mentoring is an investment in time, and both the entrepreneur and the mentor will want to ensure the relationship is a productive one. For example, an entrepreneur who is starting an online fantasy sport business and lacks fundraising knowledge should likely look for a mentor who has successfully raised money for an online company. A common mistake for entrepreneurs is to work with whatever mentor is easy to find, not necessarily the right mentor. Entrepreneurs should of course be willing to ask for advice and assistance from a variety of people, even establishing short, informal mentor relationships. But a more formal mentor relationship, one with an ongoing commitment of time, should result in significant help for the entrepreneur. Rick Spence, a business author, says, "The ideal mentor is an entrepreneur who's in a similar business, but one that is non-competitive to yours. He or she will usually have a few more years' experience than you have, and should have overcome many of the same challenges you're facing now."[13] Entrepreneurs can seek out mentors from their networks or by contacting such organization as the **Young Presidents Organization of Canada**.

Greig Clark, founder of College Pro Painters, says using a board of advisors assisted him in growing his business.

Hannamariah/Dreamstime.com

Managing the Mentor Relationship.

Mentor relationships are like most relationships: they have a beginning, a middle, and an eventual end. At the start of the mentor relationship, entrepreneurs should be honest about their expectations. Entrepreneurs should come overly prepared for the first meeting with a list of questions, expectations on meeting times, and what they hope to gain from the relationship. Similarly, well-established mentors will likely come with questions for the entrepreneur. If after the first meeting, the entrepreneur and mentor agree to a relationship, a formal meeting and communication structure should be established. While it is common for business owners to email or phone mentors with quick questions, established monthly or biweekly formal meetings allow for a more meaningful exchange of ideas and lead to a more productive long-term relationship. Entrepreneurs should also recognize that mentors, like employees, may come and go. An entrepreneur who is managing a start-up may need a very different mentor as they prepare for international expansion. Much like when doing employee evaluations, entrepreneurs should consider the value their mentor is bringing to their relationship, and if their needs have changed, they should be willing to change their mentor.

Board of Advisors or Directors.

Some entrepreneurs will form a board of advisors to assist them in managing their business. When a business is either a public corporation or going public, it will be legally required to form a *board of directors*, which was discussed in the section Components of the Plan in **Chapter 4**. Brian Scudamore notes that having a board for 1-800-Got-Junk? has greatly assisted him in running his business. Scudamore notes, "If you [entrepreneurs] don't have a mentor board of advisors, get one soon–it offers the best education money can't buy." Greig Clark, founder of College Pro Painters, confirmed that forming a formal advisory board of seasoned business leaders helped him in running his company. Clark points out that 28 percent of private firms, among the fastest-growing firms in Canada, use a board of advisors. Rob Bracey, president of a Toronto-based IT firm, started a board of advisors after attending a Microsoft partners' conference where the speakers pointed out that firms with a board are on average much more profitable than those without one.[14] In fact, a study by Pierre Cléroux, VP research and chief economist at BMO, found significant support for establishing an advisory board: "We did a study with Statistics Canada where we compared the performance of companies for three years before they created an advisory board, and three years afterward. On average, their sales increased by 66 percent. The results are really telling. Having an advisory board gives you a better vision of where you want to go, and will make your business perform better."[15]

The board of advisors may serve a number of functions:

- Reviewing operating and capital budgets, providing accountability and discipline
- Developing longer-term strategic plans for growth and expansion
- Supporting day-to-day activities
- Resolving conflicts among owners, partners, or shareholders
- Ensuring the proper use of assets
- Developing a network of information sources for the entrepreneur

Boards can provide an important reality check for the entrepreneur or owner of any non-corporate type of business. Robin Chase, the founder of **Zipcar**, a self-service car rental business, regularly calls on a group of advisors to help her hash out ideas, provide recommendations for advancing her company, or just get a mental check. Chase finds that the flexibility of a board of advisors in size, background requirements, number of meetings, and compensation makes these boards a very desirable alternative to the more formal boards of directors.[16]

Yet, even with compelling information in support of using advisors, only six percent of Canadian entrepreneurs have an advisory board (see **Small Business in Action 12-1**). Of those entrepreneurs with a board, 86 percent say it has had a major impact on their business. That impact can be strategic, as discussed above, but, as other entrepreneurs point out, advisors can provide significant assistance on day-to-day matters. Jean-Yves Sarazin of Montreal-based Groupe Delom recalls that at his very first advisory board meeting he was referred to a new financial institution, saving him thousands of dollars in interest charges.[17]

SMALL BUSINESS IN ACTION 12-1

THE ABCs OF BOARDS

Many entrepreneurs cringe when they think of forming a board of directors or advisors. They are concerned with giving up control of the company or losing their ability to make quick decisions. What is important to remember is that any company about to go public legally requires a board. An effective board, whether it is a board of directors or advisors, is often cited as the main reason that businesses have thrived rather than just survived. A strong board should provide entrepreneurs with the following:

- *Access:* A board will link entrepreneurs to people and capital that they may not have normally met on their own.
- *Credibility:* Board members are usually experienced entrepreneurs. Investors will be more willing to invest when they know that entrepreneurs can draw on the advice of knowledgeable advisors.
- *Strategic thinking:* Board members will be able to draw on their experience and provide advice to entrepreneurs.

A study by BMO concluded that firms' sales went up 66 percent after forming a board of advisors.

©Jose Luis Pelaez Inc/Blend Images LLC

[continued]

[continued]

- *Education:* Entrepreneurs should think of board members as a mentoring club. Most board members are usually willing to mentor individuals and companies.

Planning

1. Start with an assessment of the strengths and weaknesses of the company's owner or management team. Look for board members who can provide missing strengths and shore up weak areas. David Bookspan, founder of customer-focused companies **Monetate** and **Dreamit**, says it's relatively easy to find people to fill in knowledge gaps.
2. Determine how many board members you want in advance. The optimal number for a small to medium-sized company is five to seven members, although new and smaller companies can use fewer.
3. Establish a list of firm objectives for the board. The board should focus more on strategy and not on daily administrative tasks.
4. Determine how you will compensate board members. If you expect to have them meet and conduct real work, you should expect to compensate them with either money or a small amount of equity. Founders usually pay advisors anywhere between one quarter of one percent up to one percent in compensation.

Recruiting

1. Avoid family and friends. They have no objectivity.
2. Start with your own network of accountants, lawyers, and other business associates and build referrals.
3. Try to recruit people with experience who have managed similar companies in the past or at least worked in the industry. As baby boomers start to retire, the number of potential board members increases substantially.
4. Do not over-recruit. Sometimes entrepreneurs ask anyone and everyone to be on their board—remember that you are trying to address gaps in the management team and make the company more attractive to investors.
5. Do not immediately use the first three people who agree. Rather, take your time, and find the right people.

Managing the Board

1. Growing companies should schedule monthly meetings. At the very minimum, an effective board should meet bimonthly. Remember that technology today allows for members to be in different locations for meetings.
2. At board meetings, entrepreneurs should consider themselves to be team leaders or as leaders among equals. Entrepreneurs must be willing to give up some control if the board is to be effective.
3. Ensure that every meeting has an agenda that allocates the majority of meeting time to strategic issues. Reviewing reports and daily administrative matters should be kept to a minimum.
4. Do not be afraid to assign homework. If board members are willing, and they will be if they are getting paid, assign some work for them to do outside the meeting.
5. As your company evolves, so should the board of directors. New board members should be added and other members replaced as the company grows.

Discussion Questions

1. What do you see as some of the advantages and disadvantages to using an advisory board?
2. Do you think brand new companies should spend money and pay members of an advisory board? Why or why not?
3. Would smaller businesses be better off using mentors and paid outside advisors or should all firms form an advisory board? Why?

The purpose of the board of advisors is to provide important leadership and direction for the new venture, and participants should be carefully chosen. Entrepreneurs should do the following when selecting board members:

- Select individuals who can work with a diverse group and will commit to the venture's mission.
- Select candidates who understand the market environment or can contribute important skills to the new venture's achievement and planning goals.
- Select candidates who will show good judgment in business decision making.
- Identify candidates by using referrals from business associates or from any of the external advisors, such as banks, investors, lawyers, accountants, or consultants.

TAXATION AND SMALL BUSINESS LO2

Chapter 4 presented a brief outline of small business tax requirements. It was noted that various types of business and property taxes are levied by federal, provincial or territorial, and municipal governments. The calculation of and liability for most of those taxes are relatively straightforward and are not discussed again in this chapter. Income taxes, however, can be more complicated and more subject to interpretation, and can have a greater impact on the planning and cash flow of the business. Therefore, this chapter focuses primarily on this area.

The Canadian Federation of Independent Business (CFIB) reports that the total tax burden is the top concern of small and medium-sized enterprises (SME), as shown in **Figure 12-1**. Individuals who reside and corporations that operate in Canada are liable for federal and provincial income taxes. These taxes are applied on income that is received or receivable during the taxation year from all sources minus certain deductions. Federal and provincial or territorial tax agreements govern the procedures by which the federal government is empowered to collect taxes and remit portions to the provinces and territories. Some provinces and territories, including Quebec and Alberta, now collect their own corporate income taxes.

FIGURE 12-1 **Total Tax Burden Remains Top SME Concern**

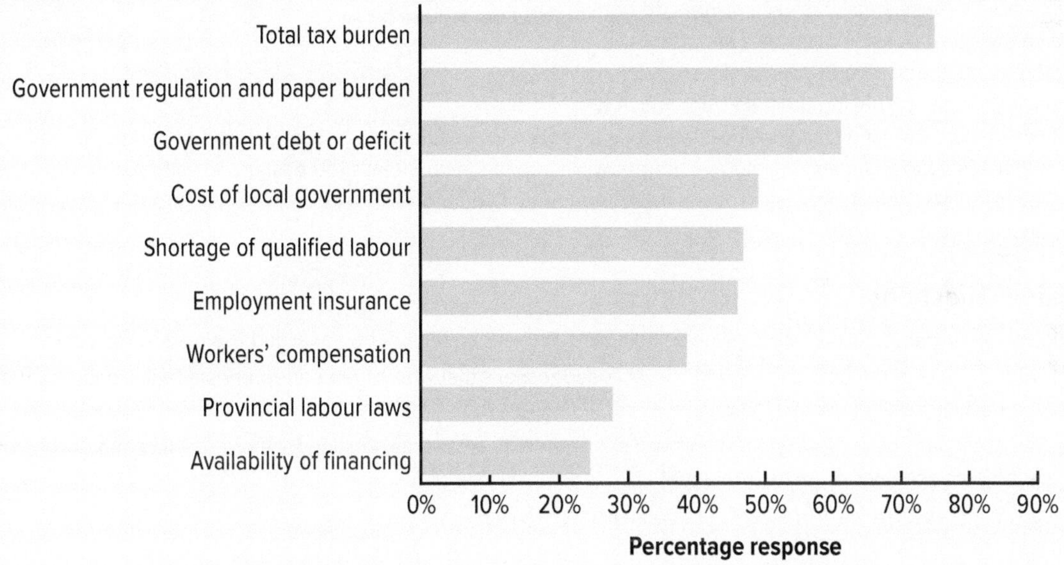

Because of the complexity of tax principles, the frequency of legislative changes concerning taxes, and the provincial and territorial differences in application, a detailed treatment of tax management for small business is beyond the scope of this book. This chapter briefly discusses some general tax management principles and programs. Although it is essential for owner-managers to have some knowledge of these principles in managing and planning their businesses, they are strongly advised to seek professional advice in preparing tax returns and investigating methods of minimizing tax liability (see **Small Business in Action 12-2** to understand why). An accountant or a bookkeeper who is up-to-date on tax changes and is experienced in working with small businesses can help the entrepreneur avoid many difficulties. This person may also assist with personal income taxes for the entrepreneur because often business and personal tax considerations are closely interrelated.

SMALL BUSINESS IN ACTION 12-2

THE LITTLE SHOEBOX OF HORRORS

Kellis/Shutterstock.com

Karen Yull, a tax specialist at Grant Thornton LLP and author of *Smart Tax Tips,* describes as the "little shoebox of horrors" the experience where a client arrives with a box or bag full of receipts. It is then the accountant's job to make sense of the business expenses while keeping the tax payable and the accountant's fees to a minimum. Yull knows the frustration that can accompany this task and suggests that a small organization can go a long way in managing personal and business expenses for tax purposes. Small business owners are usually the ones who pay for things with cash and often have all their personal and business expenses coming out of the same account. A lot of time and money can be saved by simply keeping business affairs separate from personal banking and by keeping track of all expenses. Although it may sound like a simple solution, time and again Yull has seen small business owners mixing professional and personal expenses, leaving the difficult task of sorting expenses to the accountant.

Yull offers a few suggestions to business owners to help at tax time. Because small business owners do not usually have their own pension plans, it is important to plan for retirement. If members of your family are working in your business, consider paying them a salary, which will help the tax situation. By using small business credit cards solely for business purposes, you can separate personal and business expenses. Also, maintaining your own ledger will make the accountant's job easier and will save money in accounting fees. The last piece of advice is perhaps the most important: if you are unsure about what you are doing, seek help from a professional.

Discussion Questions

1. Why do you think many small business owners find it difficult to separate their personal and business expenses?
2. In small groups or as individuals, come up with a list of suggestions that would help entrepreneurs better organize their finances, particularly as they pertain to taxes.
3. The government has been cracking down on small entrepreneurs at tax time, looking for more receipts and documentation. What are the pros and cons of such a strategy?

The government requires the small business owner to report the profits the business makes as *income* (for tax purposes). This should not be confused with the income the owner makes from the business, which may or may not be taxable, depending on the legal form of the organization. This chapter deals primarily with the income tax considerations of the organization.

Some owner-managers may not be overly concerned with income taxes and thus may do little tax planning. This lack of concern may be due to one of two factors. First, the business may currently have no tax liability; in other words, it is losing money. This situation, of course, will be only temporary because the business will eventually become profitable or cease to exist. Second, the owner-manager may not understand the impact of taxes on the cash flow of the business. As **Table 12-1** illustrates, an increase in the tax rate of only 10 percent translates into a tax liability that would require an additional $100,000 in sales to offset. When owner-managers understand the full effects of a lower or higher tax liability, they will want a working knowledge of tax principles and programs.

TABLE 12-1	Impact of Tax Rate on a Business
Taxable income	$50,000
Increase in tax rate from 20% to 30%	20% of 50,000 = $10,000
	30% of 50,000 = $15,000
Increased tax liability	15,000 − 10,000 = $5000
Profit as a percentage of sales	5%
Sales required to offset tax	5000/5% = $100,000

Note: The extra $100,000 in sales would also incur an additional $1500 tax liability.

GENERAL TAX MANAGEMENT PRINCIPLES LO3

Small business owner-managers should be aware of 10 fundamental areas of tax management.

CONTINUAL TAX PLANNING

One of the most disturbing aspects of tax statement preparation for owner-managers is learning that they have incurred an unnecessary tax liability. This situation usually arises because the accountant received and prepared the return too late to take advantage of favourable programs and deductions.

It is critical, therefore, that owner-managers be aware of the tax consequences of business operations throughout the year, not just at or after the year-end (see **Small Business Beginnings 12-1**). Up-to-date income statements can assist in forecasting income trends, allowing some advance tax planning. Many simple software programs are now available that can help entrepreneurs in the information and tax management function.

The Canada Revenue Agency (CRA) requires that income tax be paid in instalments throughout the year. Individuals operating proprietorships and partnerships are required to remit quarterly instalments for the amount of taxes they incur. Corporations must submit monthly instalments based on their prior year's tax liability. Again, planning will be required to comply with this regulation.

SMALL BUSINESS BEGINNINGS 12-1

VICTORIA SOPIK AND JENNIFER NASHMI: KIDS & COMPANY

Victoria Sopik was running nonprofit day-care centres in Toronto in 2001 when she recognized a need in the child-care market that was not being met by existing services. "I also realized that the non-profit service I was running was limited because it was in schools, the space was limited, and it catered to children age two and older," said Sopik, herself a mother of eight.

As a result, she set up Kids & Company with Jennifer Nashmi, a chartered accountant who had worked with Sopik in her previous business. Together they targeted the lucrative corporate market. They spent a year preparing a business plan and doing market research by interviewing potential corporate clients. They discovered that there was a significant need for child care for company employees, but these companies did not want to provide it themselves. The pair set up centres in downtown locations close to

Christopher Futcher/Getty Images

[continued]

[continued]

company offices and outfitted them with webcams so parents could view their children occasionally from work. Sopik and Nashmi also offered emergency backup services that parents could use when they had no access to regular child care.

Although they felt that they had a winning concept, the startup was not without its difficulties. Obtaining the necessary funding when each centre took almost $500,000 to open up was a problem. Although banks were interested in using their service, they would not lend Sopik and Nashmi the money to get started. Finally, the two entrepreneurs were successful in obtaining start-up financing from an angel investor friend. Once adequate financing was in place, signing up clients happened quickly.

Sopik and Nashmi's success has been due to more than identifying a niche in the market. Their backgrounds and experience have also been a major factor. Sopik had a long and distinguished career in the child-care industry. She also has a business degree from the University of Western Ontario, which has been helpful in the management aspects of the business. Nashmi's accounting and financial experience included over 10 years with various high-tech and service organizations. Her expertise in the financial aspects of the business has allowed Kids & Company to successfully manage and minimize the tax consequences of the company's growth and success. Nashmi indicates that a rapidly growing company in a difficult economy and continually changing tax environment needs considerable expertise to navigate such volatile times.

The results of Sopik and Nashmi's efforts have been outstanding. Although reaching their goal to become a $50-million business has been slower than they desired, Kids & Company's growth has still been phenomenal. It has been recognized as the number one growth company in Canada by *Profit* magazine. The number of employees has risen and the company has opened up centres in the United States. Key client companies include Royal Bank, CIBC, Rogers, Coca Cola, Procter and Gamble, Deloitte, and Manulife Financial. The company was recognized as one of the top employers in Canada from 2013 to 2017.

Discussion Questions

1. What are some of the factors that enabled the company to be successful?
2. Do you think their company will be able to reach its lofty growth targets? Why or why not?
3. Given that anyone can start this type of business, are you surprised more competition has yet to emerge? Why?
4. What type of advisors should someone look for if they wanted to start a firm similar to the one above?

TAX DEFERRAL

One unwritten rule of tax management concerns tax deferral. This means that owner-managers should attempt to put off paying taxes as long as legally possible for at least two good reasons. First, they have the use of the tax money for the period of the deferral. This money can be put to productive use in the business or other investments. Second, tax laws may change, resulting in a decreased liability in the future.

Several specific programs facilitate deferral of tax liability. Some of these programs are discussed later.

INCOME SPLITTING

The tax system for individuals in Canada is a progressive system whereby a higher taxable income results in a higher percentage tax liability. Because of the progressive nature of taxes, splitting incomes between spouses and other family members or among partners will result in a reduced overall tax liability, as **Table 12-2** shows. If done within a family, the spouse and children will likely be taxed at lower rates, which would further reduce this tax liability. Note that the federal government has recently announced they will be changing the tax rules in order to limit income splitting in businesses. However, family members won't be impacted if they can prove they are active in the business and spend more than 20 hours a week working for the firm throughout the year.[18]

MARGINAL TAX RATES

The marginal tax rate is the tax rate applied by CRA to the next dollar of income earned. Knowledge of an individual's marginal rate can be helpful in planning income and expenses. For example, if an owner-manager has a marginal tax rate of 30 percent, each dollar of income earned will incur a tax liability of 30 cents, whereas each dollar of expense incurred will save 30 cents in tax liability. Thus, awareness of the current marginal rate allows the owner-manager to calculate the after-tax effects of extra income and expenses.

TABLE 12-2 Impact of Tax Rate on a Business

Business income = $60,000

	A.		B.
	If one person declared the income:		If two people split the income:
	Income = $60,000		Income = $60,000
	Tax rate = $6108.90 + 22% of $19,274		Partner A = $30,000
	Tax liability = $10,349.18		Partner B = $30,000
			Tax rate for each = 15% of $30,000
			Tax liability A = $4500
			Tax liability B = $4500
			Tax liability for A + B = $9000

Tax savings by splitting income = $10,349.18 − $9000 = $1349.18

Another benefit of knowing the marginal rate is the possibility of moving that rate to a lower bracket by incurring some additional expenses before year-end–provided, of course, that the expenses are necessary. Like income splitting, this principle has the most value for the proprietorship and partnership.

DEDUCTIBLES

The small business owner should be familiar with those expenses that are deductible in the calculation of taxable income. The onus is on the taxpayer to keep proper records, since the burden of proof for these expenses lies with him or her. This means the owner-manager must keep receipts of business expenses. An often neglected aspect of this practice is the failure to obtain or keep receipts of expenses for which the owner-manager paid personally on behalf of the business. These expenses may seem too small to justify keeping track of. However, if the tax rate is 25 percent, a mere $4 of unrecorded expense can result in an increased tax liability of $1. According to generally accepted accounting principles, an expense is defined as a payment or a liability created to earn income. To determine whether certain expenses are deductible, the owner-manager should consult an accountant, CRA, or such publications as the *Master Tax Guide* published by Commerce Clearing House. Some of the more common small business expenses that may require explanation follow.

Accounting and Legal Expenses.

Only those expenses incurred to earn income are deductible. Expenses incurred to incorporate the business or prepare a personal tax return are not deductible.

Advertising.

Advertising expenses are deductible only if used in Canadian media and targeted at Canadian consumers.

Business Entertaining.

Business entertaining expenses incurred in one's home are not deductible. Neither is the purchase of club memberships or yachts. Other types of legitimate business entertaining, however, are deductible.

Automobile Expenses.

For personal vehicles, the portion of expenses used for business purposes is deductible, but records must be kept to verify those amounts. Usually, the business portion is the number of kilometres expended on business travel prorated to the total kilometres travelled. In addition, automobile lease costs and interest costs on vehicle loans are also deductible business expenses.

Interest Expense.

Interest expense is deductible for business loans but not for personal loans. Some experts counsel that to maximize this deductible, personal savings should be used to finance personal expenses, if possible, rather than business expenses.

For a corporation, another interest-related matter is a loan to the business by a shareholder. This is a fairly common form for financing a business because it offers some significant advantages. The interest is a deductible expense to the business, but the repayment terms may remain flexible, depending on the ability of the business to pay and the wishes of the owner-lender. In a sense, the shareholder's loan combines the advantages of both debt and equity financing. Note that interest paid to shareholders must be included in their income.

Repairs and Improvements.

Repairs are deductible expenses, but improvements should be depreciated at the specified CCA (capital cost allowance) rates. CCA rates are percentages that can be subtracted from a capital asset cost and allocated as a business expense. It is often unclear what portion of the expenditure is a repair and what portion is an improvement. An accountant should be consulted in making this allocation.

Office Expenses.

Office expenses are deductible and can be an important area for the owner-manager whose office is in the home. In such a case, a portion of household expenses, such as utilities, mortgage interest, insurance, repairs, and taxes, can be listed as business expenses. The portion to deduct depends on the size of the office relative to the size of the house. Care should be taken in including depreciation as an office expense, since it could be deemed to be recaptured and added to taxable income and result in the loss of the principal residence capital gains exemption. Small business owners should consult with an accountant to verify the level of home expenses that qualify as a deduction.

An increasingly popular way of taking advantage of these expenses is contracting out. Many employees have left employment with an organization and have contracted out their services to that company. Although this may allow them to take advantage of some of the above deductions, care must be taken to be sure that it is not an employment arrangement. Discussion with a tax accountant should be held if such a plan is being contemplated. Also, consult the CRA guide for the distinction between an employee and a subcontractor.

GOVERNMENT TAX-RELATED PROGRAMS LO4

Numerous government programs and policies in Canada affect the tax management practices for the small business. It is important that the entrepreneur be aware of these programs to take advantage of their benefits. The following is a summary of some of the more important items for the owner-manager.

Special Tax Rate Deductions.

Small Business Deduction (SBD).

The small business deduction is 11 percent of active business income for an incorporated, Canadian-controlled, private business. This special rate applies to the first $500,000 of income.[19] The Canadian government announced that this rate will decrease to 9 percent in 2019.[20] For income above this limit, the federal tax rate is 19.5 percent (28 minus 8.5 percent). **Table 12-3** illustrates the significance of this program for a small business. In addition, provincial tax rates for small businesses range from 3 percent (Alberta) to 8 percent (Québec). These lower rates allow small businesses to retain more of their earnings in the business for reinvestment.

Investment Tax Credits.

In some provinces, residents are eligible for investment tax credits on purchases of qualified property. All taxpayers are eligible for tax credits on qualified scientific research expenditures (SRTCs). Canadian-controlled private corporations may apply for a 35 percent SRTC, while all other taxpayers may apply for a 20 percent SRTC.

TABLE 12-3 **Effect of the Small Business Deduction**

Business income = $50,000	
No small business deduction:	Small business deduction:
Tax rate = 28%	SBD = 28% − 17% = 11%
Tax liability = $14,000	Tax liability = $5500
Difference in tax liability = $8500	

Other tax credit programs that may be of interest to small businesses are the Apprenticeship Job Creation and Investment Credits for creating child care spaces.

Deferral Programs.

Some programs that allow tax deferrals are very popular with owner-managers of small businesses:

1. *Deferred profit sharing.* DPS allows for a deferral of part of the business profits that have been registered for payment in the future to employees. The payment amount is taxable to employees only when received but is a deductible expense in the year in which it is set aside or registered. The entrepreneur should see an accountant regarding this deferral program.
2. *Registered retirement savings plan.* RRSPs allow the owner-manager to put money into a registered plan that will be taxed only when received at a future date, presumably when the taxpayer is in a lower tax bracket. Budget changes have increased the contribution limits of RRSPs.
3. *Bonus deferral.* This program permits the business to deduct an accrued bonus or wage as an expense but allows a certain time period (180 days) to pay the amount. This amount is not taxable until received. The bonus deferral thus may effectively allow the business an expense in one year but defer tax liability in the hands of the recipient to the following year.
4. *Tax-free savings account.* Similar to the RRSP, this relatively new program allows the small business owner to avoid paying tax on interest earned on savings. Up to $5000 can be added to the TFSA each year (without a specific level of earned income as required with RRSP contributions).

Accelerated Capital Cost Allowance.

This program allows an increased depreciation rate (capital cost allowance) to be applied as non-cash expenses to certain classes of assets in calculating taxable income. Capital cost allowance rates can be obtained from an accountant or the tax department or by consulting the *Master Tax Guide.*

Small Business Financing Programs.

These programs allow the incorporated business to borrow money from a chartered bank at a reduced interest rate. This is made possible because of special tax treatment these banks receive from the CRA. Only businesses unable to obtain ordinary debt financing are eligible for this program.

THE INCORPORATION QUESTION

One decision regarding the establishment or growth of the business that owner-managers face is incorporation. **Chapter 4** discussed the relative merits and weaknesses of the proprietorship, the partnership, and the incorporated company. Some significant differences in tax treatment also exist among these different forms of business.

As mentioned above, with the small business deduction, the federal tax rate for an incorporated business is about 11 percent. If the business is a partnership or a proprietorship, the business income is brought into the owner-manager's personal tax return. This return includes various other personal deductions and exemptions.

The individual's personal rate may be higher or lower than the rate for an incorporated business. If the minimization of tax liability is the major concern, the owner-manager would pursue incorporating when the tax rate for the business was lower than the personal rate. The incorporation question is influenced by more than just the tax liability for the different legal forms of business; many government programs are available only to incorporated businesses. Examples of the tax consequences of the different legal forms of business are shown in **Table 12-4**.

TABLE 12-4 Income Tax for Different Legal Forms of a Business

	BOB JOHNSON LTD. CORPORATION	BOB JOHNSON PROPRIETORSHIP	BOB AND SUE JOHNSON PARTNERSHIP
Revenue	$100,000	100,000	100,000
Expenses	80,000	80,000	80,000
Net Income	20,000	20,000	20,000
Tax Consequences	Taxed at the corporate rate. (Bob's salary is a business expense.)	Income brought into and taxed at personal rate. (Bob's salary is not a business expense.)	One-half of income partner's income and rates. (Salary to Bob and Sue are not business expenses.)

THE REMUNERATION QUESTION

Another difficult decision owner-managers must make is how to be paid by the business. In the proprietorship and the partnership, payment to the owner is treated as a drawing from the business and is not a deductible expense (or taxable income). In the corporation, an owner can be paid with a salary or with dividends. These methods of payment receive significantly different tax treatment and vary by province and territory. The owner-manager should consult with an accountant before making a decision in this area, because federal budgets have changed the difference in tax treatment of salary and dividends. Currently, surtaxes imposed by the federal and some provincial governments result in a slightly higher income tax paid when remuneration is taken in dividends if the owner's taxable income exceeds $55,000.

TRANSFERRING THE BUSINESS: CAPITAL GAINS

Many small business owners wanting to transfer their businesses to others have encountered considerable difficulty. Some tax considerations significantly affect how the business is transferred. Tax changes involving capital gains exemptions have made it much easier to transfer the business to family members or others. Currently, CRA allows an $800,000 lifetime capital gains exemption on the shares of a small business corporation.[21]

GOODS AND SERVICES TAX (GST) OR PROVINCIAL SALES TAXES (PST) AND HST

Although the GST and PST are value-added taxes that are not levied on the income or profits of the small business, they are taxes on sales revenues achieved by the small business and require a significant effort on the part of the small business. The federal GST is currently set at 5 percent of the sale price, whereas the PST rates vary by province or territory. The amount of both taxes (Harmonized Sales Tax or HST) is added to the retail price of the product. Accurate record keeping is required to collect, record, and remit GST or HST amounts to the government. **Figure 12-2** illustrates the type of information required for submission to CRA by the small business. If the small business has sales of less than $30,000 per annum, no GST or HST collection and remittance is required. The small business owner should consult the CRA or the provincial or territorial revenue department for information about how the GST and PST or HST apply to their business.

FIGURE 12-2 Goods and Services Tax Return

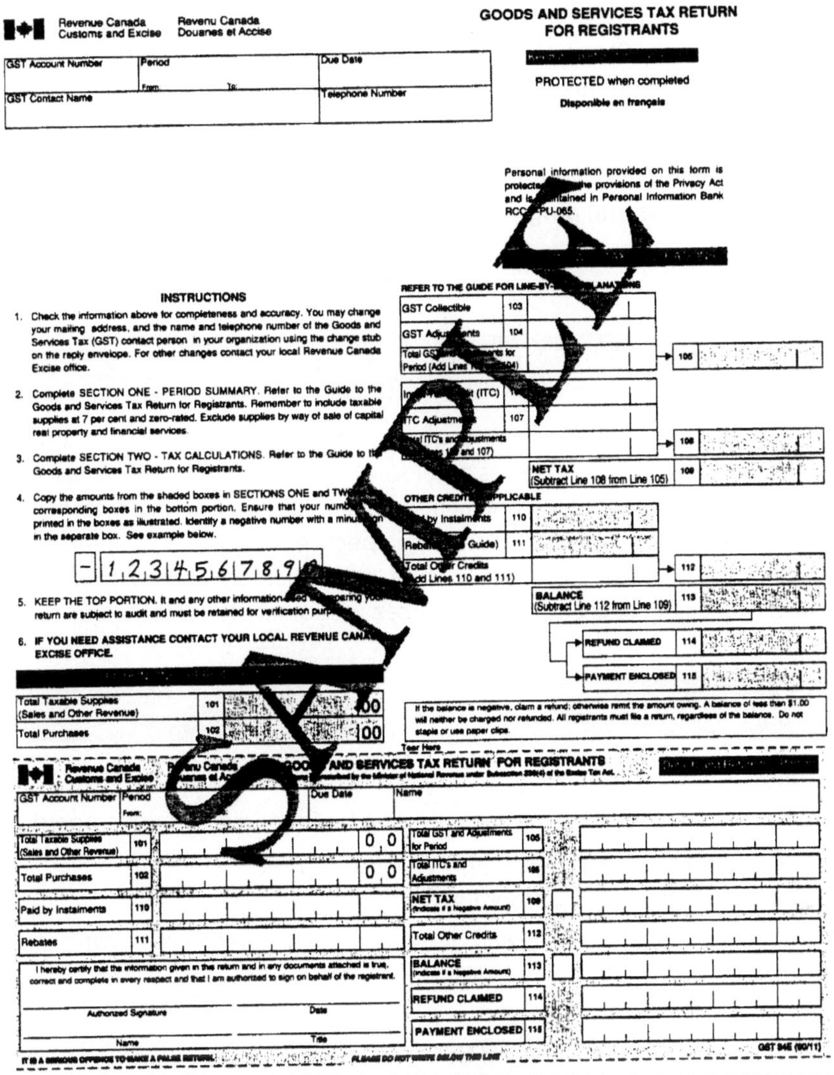
Revenue Canada Customs and Excise — Revenu Canada Douanes et Accise

GOODS AND SERVICES TAX RETURN FOR REGISTRANTS

[redacted]

PROTECTED when completed

Disponible en français

GST Account Number	Period From: To:	Due Date
GST Contact Name		Telephone Number

Personal information provided on this form is protected under the provisions of the Privacy Act and is maintained in Personal Information Bank RCC/P-PU-065.

INSTRUCTIONS

1. Check the information above for completeness and accuracy. You may change your mailing address, and the name and telephone number of the Goods and Services Tax (GST) contact person in your organization using the change stub on the reply envelope. For other changes contact your local Revenue Canada Excise office.
2. Complete SECTION ONE - PERIOD SUMMARY. Refer to the Guide to the Goods and Services Tax Return for Registrants. Remember to include taxable supplies at 7 per cent and zero-rated. Exclude supplies by way of sale of capital real property and financial services.
3. Complete SECTION TWO - TAX CALCULATIONS. Refer to the Guide to the Goods and Services Tax Return for Registrants.
4. Copy the amounts from the shaded boxes in SECTIONS ONE and TWO to the corresponding boxes in the bottom portion. Ensure that your numbers are printed in the boxes as illustrated. Identify a negative number with a minus sign in the separate box. See example below.

   - 1,2,3 4,5,6 7,8,9

5. KEEP THE TOP PORTION. It and any other information used in preparing your return are subject to audit and must be retained for verification purposes.
6. IF YOU NEED ASSISTANCE CONTACT YOUR LOCAL REVENUE CANADA EXCISE OFFICE.

REFER TO THE GUIDE FOR LINE-BY-LINE EXPLANATIONS

Line		No.
GST Collectible		103
GST Adjustments		104
Total GST and Adjustments for Period (Add Lines 103 and 104)		105
Input Tax Credit (ITC)		106
ITC Adjustments		107
Total ITC's and Adjustments (Add Lines 106 and 107)		108
NET TAX (Subtract Line 108 from Line 105)		109
OTHER CREDITS IF APPLICABLE		
Paid by Instalments		110
Rebates (See Guide)		111
Total Other Credits (Add Lines 110 and 111)		112
BALANCE (Subtract Line 112 from Line 109)		113
REFUND CLAIMED		114
PAYMENT ENCLOSED		115

	No.	
Total Taxable Supplies (Sales and Other Revenue)	101	00
Total Purchases	102	00

If the balance is negative, claim a refund; otherwise remit the amount owing. A balance of less than $1.00 will neither be charged nor refunded. All registrants must file a return, regardless of the balance. Do not staple or use paper clips.

Tear Here

Revenue Canada Customs and Excise — Revenu Canada Douanes et Accise — GOODS AND SERVICES TAX RETURN FOR REGISTRANTS

GST Account Number	Period From:	Due Date	Name

	No.			No.	
Total Taxable Supplies (Sales and Other Revenue)	101	0 0	Total GST and Adjustments for Period	105	
Total Purchases	102	0 0	Total ITC's and Adjustments	108	
Paid by Instalments	110		NET TAX (Indicate if a Negative Amount)	109	
Rebates	111		Total Other Credits	112	
			BALANCE (Indicate if a Negative Amount)	113	
			REFUND CLAIMED	114	
			PAYMENT ENCLOSED	115	

I hereby certify that the information given in this return and in any documents attached is true, correct and complete in every respect and that I am authorized to sign on behalf of the registrant.

Authorized Signature — Date

Name — Title

IT IS A SERIOUS OFFENCE TO MAKE A FALSE RETURN. — PLEASE DO NOT WRITE BELOW THIS LINE — GST 34E (90/11)

SAMPLE

Canada Revenue Agency, GST34-2, Goods and Services Tax/Harmonized Sales Tax Return for Registrants. Reproduced with permission of the Minister of National Revenue, 2019.

LEARNING OBJECTIVES SUMMARY

LO1 **Advisors will often be necessary in a new venture. Outside advisors should be evaluated as if they were being hired as permanent members of the organization. Information on their fees and referrals can help determine the best choices. A board of directors or board of advisors can provide important management support for the entrepreneurs in starting and managing the new venture. The board of advisors is a good alternative to a board of directors when the stock is held privately or in a family business.**

LO2 Basic tax knowledge allows the small business owner to save money that would otherwise be paid in taxes. Continual tax planning ensures that the owner-manager is aware of the tax consequences of business decisions throughout the year rather than just at year-end.

LO3 The 10 fundamental areas of tax management of which the owner-manager should be aware are (1) continual tax planning, (2) tax deferral, (3) income splitting, (4) marginal tax rates, (5) deductibles, (6) knowledge of government tax-related programs, (7) the incorporation question, (8) the remuneration question, (9) capital gains, and (10) GST or PST and HST.

LO4 Some of the more important government tax-related programs are the small business deduction, investment tax credits, deferral programs, accelerated capital cost allowances, and small business financing programs.

TIME TO TAKE ACTION

The chapter spends significant time discussing managerial help and mentors. Now is time for you to take action. Using Question 1 in the Experiential Exercises as a guide, develop a list of potential mentors for either your entrepreneurial or work aspirations. Start to contact the mentors using email or social media. Meet with mentors and outline your goals, either from a business startup perspective or a career perspective, and ask them about their willingness to mentor you. Follow the steps outlined in the chapter to establish a mentor relationship. It would be a worthwhile exercise to share your experiences with other students in your class.

DISCUSSION QUESTIONS

1. What are the advantages of using a mentor compared with a board of advisors?
2. Does the old saying "You get what you pay for" apply to a board of directors or a board of advisors?
3. Explain why the year-end date is significant in tax planning.
4. Which variables affect the decision to incorporate?
5. Discuss with an accountant the advantages and disadvantages of the different owner compensation methods in a corporation.

EXPERIENTIAL EXERCISES

1. Complete a personal SWOT analysis. What areas of management will you need help with if you start a business? Create a job description for a potential mentor. Where would you find your mentor?
2. Interview entrepreneurs about their use of mentors or a board of advisors. Ask who mentored them or was on their board, how they selected the advisors, and whether the relationship was worth their investment in time.
3. The year-end for Wave Waterbeds is soon approaching. The proprietor, Tom Newcombe, estimates that the company currently has taxable income of $5500. He would like to purchase a new cash register worth $2000. Determine the tax liability if Newcombe purchases the cash register before or after year-end; cash registers are depreciated at 20 percent. When would you advise Newcombe to purchase the cash register? Why?
4. The owner-manager of L.A. Construction has just incurred expenses listed below. Which expenses are tax deductible?
   a. Incorporation expenses
   b. Advertising expense in Canada and in the United States
   c. Truck repairs of $2000
   d. Costs of maintaining a residential phone used for business purposes

5. What is the tax liability for the following proprietorship's taxable incomes?
   a. $5496
   b. $10,942
   c. $34,999
   d. $63,000
6. Determine the federal tax liability for the following companies:
   a. A Canadian-controlled incorporated company with $25,000 taxable income
   b. A Canadian-controlled incorporated company with $25,000 taxable income that qualifies for a small business deduction
   c. Same as part (b), but the business qualifies for the 5 percent manufacturing credit
   d. A proprietorship with taxable income of $25,000
7. Ask a consultant or an accountant when a business should incorporate. What are the important considerations?
8. Start the process of creating an ideal board of advisors for your potential business. Create a list of roles with the requisite skills and knowledge you will be seeking. If you want to take this question further, create procedures for managing the board as outlined in the chapter.

CASES FOR PART 3

Derocher's Market
Home Smart Hardware Store
Martha's Designs
Sadie's Country n' Western Store
Dale's Sport Pursuit
Susie's Fashions
Taylor Construction Company
The Barrow Bracket
Threadz
Garner Men's Wear
Boomerang Bouncers Entertainment

DEROCHER'S MARKET

Derocher's Market opened a new store in Québec City in January 2019. Although the firm has been in business for three generations, the neighbourhood in which the original store stood had become shabby, and many of its loyal clientele had moved to the suburbs. The present owner, Claude Derocher, decided to follow the population move. The new store is located next to a several other small independent businesses near more than 70 four-storey apartment buildings that house more than 400 families. Many more apartment buildings are under construction, as well as three- and four-bedroom single-family homes in several nearby housing developments. The nearest competition is located approximately three kilometres northeast of the present shopping centre.

In preparation for the grand opening, Claude Derocher purchased many varieties of canned juices, fruits, and vegetables. In addition, he carries a number of varieties and lines of cheeses, frozen foods, other dairy products, fruits, vegetables, and meats. To display and sell all the stock, it is necessary to use valuable aisle space as islands for various bulk cheeses, canned fruits, and dry groceries, such as potato chips, pretzels, and the like. The store size is 17 by 27 metres. The store layout, shown in **Figure 1**, is as follows:

- A: display area for crackers, breads, and cookies
- B: refrigerated area for frozen foods, frozen desserts, and packaged cheeses
- C: display area for olives, pickles, other condiments, canned fruit, and fruit juices
- D: display area for canned vegetables, canned fish, breakfast cereals, and dried fruits

- 1: island display for bulk cheeses
- 2, 3: island display for soft drinks
- 4: area for shopping carts

FIGURE 1 **Present Store Layout—Derocher's Market**

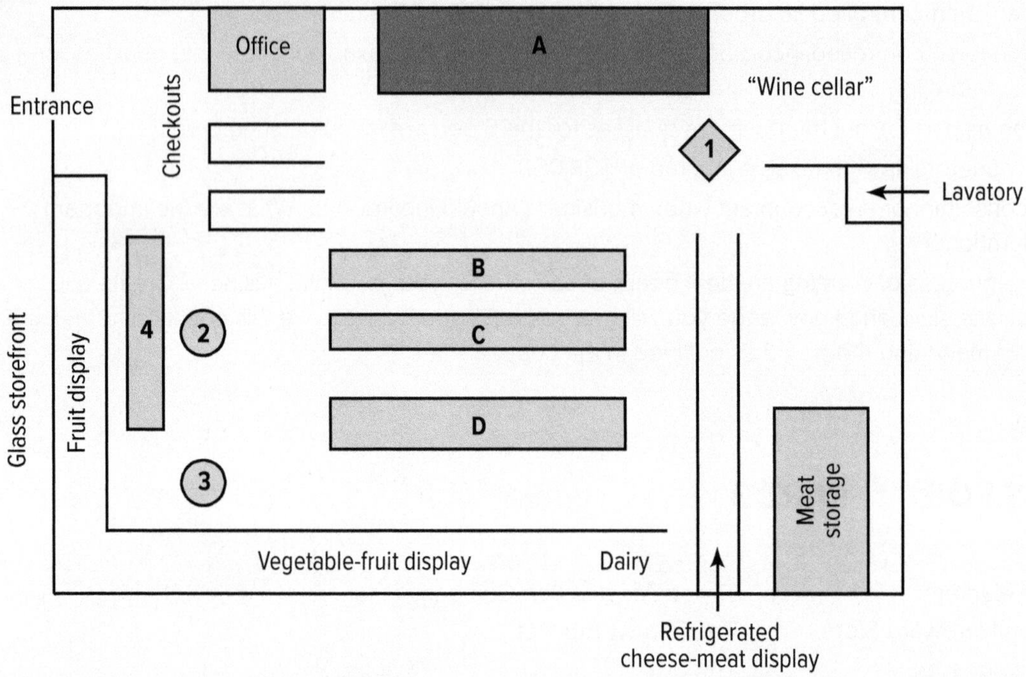

The store employs eight full-time people. These consist of six clerks and two assistant managers—one manager for meat and dairy and the other for grocery, produce, and frozen foods.

During the first four weeks of operation, several things were determined:

1. There are far too many employees for the type of work needed.
2. There is far too much congestion of shoppers at certain in-store locations.
3. There is a build-up of customers at the check-out stations.
4. Many customers have inquired as to where to find various food items.
5. Several of Derocher's employees have indicated that some changes need to be made to the interior layout of the store.

After receiving this input, Derocher is not sure what to do. The present layout seems unsatisfactory, but he does not want to spend a lot of money making changes.

Questions

1. Based on **Figure 1** and the observations of the first four weeks, what are the weaknesses of the present store layout?
2. Develop a layout that might solve these problems.

HOME SMART HARDWARE STORE

Home Smart is a small hardware store located in Meyburn, Saskatchewan, an agricultural community with a population of about 9000. Merchandise stocked includes automotive and farm supplies, furniture and appliances, sporting goods, plumbing and electrical supplies, and giftware.

The owner is Peter Lovely, a prominent businessman in the community who also owns another business that occupies a large portion of his time. Because of this, Lovely has delegated considerable authority to the manager of the store, John Ferns. In July 2018, Lovely and Ferns decided to hire a new employee to be trained as an assistant manager. They first discussed the possibility of promoting one of the store's existing employees, but Lovely thought none of them would be suitable as assistant managers because they were either too old or did not want the extra responsibility. Doug Ferns, John's uncle, was already 63 years old and, though working full time, had indicated he wanted to work fewer hours and begin to ease into retirement. Sue Mikita, 52, had been with the company for 12 years but had concentrated on the giftware side of the department. Ferns did not think she had an adequate knowledge of the farm supply side of the business, which produced the most revenue in the store. Ruth Huddy, 61, had worked for the company for only six years, mostly part time, and although she was very competent and knowledgeable, Ferns felt she was also too old to fill the position. The only other employees were part-time students who worked Saturdays and summers.

Lovely and Ferns decided to advertise for an assistant manager on some local job websites and on Kijiji. This resulted in a few enquiries, but no applicants who met the two criteria Ferns and Lovely considered most important: familiarity with the people in the community and knowledge of agriculture. Lovely and Ferns met again in August to discuss the lack of prospects. Lovely suggested that he might contact Noel Branlen, an acquaintance who lived in Meyburn, about coming to work for the company. Branlen currently worked in a town some 40 km away, and perhaps he could be attracted back to his home town. Branlen was young—only 25—and knew the people in the community. Lovely approached him and found out he was interested in working for him but required a salary higher than Lovely and Ferns had planned for this position. If they agreed to pay the salary he requested, Branlen would be paid a higher wage than the other hardware department employees except Ferns himself. Although Lovely and Ferns were worried about this, they decided to hire Branlen and requested that his salary be kept confidential. Branlen would be in a training position for approximately six months and would then assume the position of assistant manager of the store.

Things went smoothly at first, but after a few months, it is evident to Lovely that some problems are surfacing. Lovely notices antagonism between Branlen and the other three regular employees, and so do the store's customers. In discussing Branlen's progress with Ferns, Lovely learns that Branlen is frequently late for work, his appearance is unsatisfactory, he is very slow in gaining essential product knowledge, and Ferns has had several complaints from customers about him. In addition, Branlen himself has contacted Lovely directly and expressed his disillusionment with the job and with his supervisor, John Ferns. He indicates that Ferns is not providing adequate training for the products or the authority to order inventory, set prices, and so on. Also, when Ferns has his day off, several sales are lost because none of the employees knows the information customers required. Branlen also mentions that as assistant manager he should not have to sweep the floors as he has been required to do on several occasions. He further requests that he be granted time off two afternoons a week to take a management course at a local college to help him prepare for the managerial aspects of his job.

Lovely discusses the problem again with Ferns, who says that as soon as Branlen proves himself, he will be given the requested authority. He is very opposed to letting Branlen take time off for a management course, so this request is turned down.

Toward the end of November, Branlen contacts Lovely to see if he can take some of his vacation just before Christmas. When Lovely mentions this request to Ferns, Ferns is very opposed to it because this is the busiest time of the year for the store; furthermore, in the past employees had worked for a year before they took their holidays. However, Lovely allows Branlen to take the vacation.

The store gets through the Christmas rush and inventory taking without serious incident, but things get progressively worse thereafter. Nine months after his hiring, Branlen hands in his resignation, saying he is going back to university. Lovely is relieved that this problem employee is leaving and hopes that the same problems will not recur next time.

Questions

1. Comment on the possible reasons why Noel Branlen's employment was unsuccessful.
2. How could Home Smart successfully compete against the threat of competition from Walmart or Home Depot?

MARTHA'S DESIGNS

Martha Millwork needs to make some important decisions regarding her clothing manufacturing business. Started as a hobby in the mid-2010s, the business has grown to the point where she has opportunities to expand the scale of operations so that it can become a full-time commercial enterprise. She is unsure of which markets to pursue, which marketing channels to use, and the extent of product line that would be the most effective.

Martha lives in Grenfel, Saskatchewan, and she had started sewing clothing for herself and her children in 2009. Her skill and talents were first shown publicly during the summer Agribition celebration in Regina in 2018, at a fashion show she organized. As a result of this initial show, she received orders from interested buyers, and the hobby soon became a part-time business that she operated out of her home in Grenfel. Company sales have grown steadily since that time and reached close to $30,000 in the latest fiscal year. Although this only brought a profit of $5000, Martha has fine-tuned the business so that an increase in sales also means a larger profit percentage.

Martha's Designs specializes in high-quality, fashionable women's and men's coats made from canvas, denim, and Hudson's Bay and Pendleton wool blankets. The coats are designed to be comfortable, sophisticated, and original. They also feature fur and leather trims. Several coat designs are available, and Martha modifies existing designs and creates new ones on an ongoing basis. The coats are well-made, with high-quality materials, and are priced from $300 to $600. The clothes are fashionable and modern. This blend of fashion, function, and tradition make a unique finished product that she has successfully sold to buyers from across North America and Europe.

As the owner-manager, Martha designs the coats and cuts the fabric. She usually orders materials only after receiving an order for a particular coat. The cut pieces, trim, and notions are sent to one of two part-time local seamstresses who do the sewing in their own homes. Martha carefully inspects each garment on completion. The purchasing of materials is an important aspect of the production process, since the cost of materials is such a large part of the cost of goods. Fabric is purchased at the lowest possible price, but Martha is aware that better prices are available if she increases the size of her orders. The unique trims used on the coats are purchased primarily from local suppliers.

Recently, Martha was approached by the town of Wolseley (estimated population 1000), which is about 15 kilometres from Grenfel, to be a part of a sewing plant that the village is planning to establish. The village intends to purchase sewing machines and other equipment and contract out the sewing services of the workers to interested firms, such as Martha's Designs. Martha realizes that to make such a change in operations worthwhile, Martha's Designs will have to increase its production volume dramatically. This proposal is attractive because of its low financial risk, the opportunity for increased production efficiencies, and the flexibility to produce a greater volume of coats.

Martha's marketing efforts to date consist primarily of fashion shows, displays at events, a basic website, newspaper advertising, a small amount of social media activity, and a brochure. Each year she organizes several fashion shows in Alberta, Montana, North Dakota, and Saskatchewan. In the past, some of these were in conjunction with other events, such as the agricultural exhibitions, rodeos, and athletic events. Each show is the result of coordinating the individual efforts of models, commentators, hairdressers, make-up artists, sound specialists, musicians, and publicity staff. Displays are set up at various trade shows and even at events such as Canada Day celebrations. In addition, a small amount of advertising has been done in newspapers, such as the *Regina Leader Post* and other local papers. Martha uses advertising to promote general awareness and to promote good community relations.

With a potential increase in production capacity, Martha has to plan the company's future marketing strategy. She is confident that demand for her company's unique clothing exists and that volume could be increased enough to result in significant material purchase savings, which would lower production costs. A major decision is which marketing channel to use. Until now, sales have been made directly to purchasers of the clothing. Martha thinks she might achieve an increase in volume by selling through retail stores or clothing wholesalers, but she is unsure which type of retail store would most effectively reach her target customer. An alternative is to continue selling directly to customers but to expand her online presence. Her current website amounts to a few pictures and her contact information. She would have to invest roughly $10,000 to have a fully functional website, and she has done very little to promote her business on social media. She is wondering if creating a website and using social media wouldn't lead to a significant increase in sales. Martha is also unsure if people would buy her unique products without seeing them in person.

Martha is also thinking about increasing the sales of men's and children's coats. Although this strategy would add to her product line and create additional design work, it could also make the line more marketable by broadening its appeal.

A final decision to be made is how to support the sales efforts. Should she use more advertising, or should she concentrate on setting up sales booths at trade shows? There are many trade shows, and deciding which to attend would be difficult.

As Martha considers the alternatives available to her, she is beginning to realize that her company is at an important crossroads—to continue its growth, it would have to enter new markets and expand production capacity. Martha's Designs is a cottage industry on the verge of becoming a small manufacturer.

Questions

1. Discuss the implications of Martha Millwork's potential expansion.
2. Evaluate the distribution channel options and promotional implications associated with them if Martha's business expanded.

SADIE'S COUNTRY N' WESTERN STORE

Sadie Rogers is the owner of a western-wear clothing and gift store located in Champion, Alberta. Champion is a small town of 500 located about 150 kilometres south of Calgary and 100 kilometres north of Lethbridge, Alberta. Several other smaller communities are within a 100-kilometre radius of Champion, as well as numerous rural farmers. Champion is located on one of two major highways from Lethbridge (and the United States) to Calgary. Other amenities located in the small town include a school, bank, post office, restaurant, hotel, grocery store, hardware store, farm machinery dealership, and services, such as insurance, a beauty salon, and a small library.

Sadie established her store two years ago after a successful five-year experience owning the town's grocery store. With this first venture, she was pleasantly surprised that such a small community could support a grocery store, and she was especially pleased that she was able to draw residents from some of the other communities to her store. The margins in the grocery industry were not very high, however, and she contemplated using her experience, expertise, and knowledge of the community with a clothing and gift store. She reasoned that if she could have the same success in drawing customers with higher-margin merchandise, the business could really be profitable. She therefore sold the grocery store and started her current business. She named it Sadie's Country n' Western Store.

Sadie's Country n' Western is located on the main street and is part of a mini-mall with a beauty salon, grocery store, and bank. Sadie's features a huge selection of clothing for men, women, and children (including jeans, shirts, jackets, footwear, hats, and accessories), gifts, collectibles, toys, furniture, jewellery, cards, and gift wrap. She has maintained a close working relationship with Wrangler, which has become her most profitable brand. The store also carries a line of rancher supplies, such as saddles, bridles, and other cowboy accessories. She imports many of these products from the United States, which allows her to carry products that are exclusive in southern Alberta.

Sadie defines her target market as customers within a 90-minute drive of her store. Interestingly, the majority of her market comes from outside Champion. There are a few direct competitors to her store in the towns within a 100-kilometre radius. However, Sadie feels that the main reason she is able to draw customers from outside her community is because of her marketing efforts and low prices.

Because of her low overhead, Sadie makes sure that her prices are lower than her competitors'. She regularly visits these stores in other communities and does price checks. Sadie's promotional activities include direct emails, which she sends to customers throughout the region, some mail flyers, distributed throughout southern Alberta, and her Facebook and Instagram postings, which often highlight low prices on standard products and some of her unique products. Sadie's also offers discounts to 4H and rodeo club members, guest appearances by well-known rodeo professionals, and various contests and giveaways.

Sadie has been very pleased with sales as she nears the end of her second year of operations. Results have been remarkable considering the small size of the community in which she is located. Although sales have exceeded expectations, she has some concerns about the profitability of the business and is anxiously awaiting the year-end results.

Questions

1. How do you account for the ability of Sadie's Country n' Western Store to attract customers from outside the local community?
2. Evaluate Sadie's marketing strategy. What additional things might she do to enhance sales?
3. Evaluate Sadie's pricing strategy. Relate your evaluation to the classification of consumer goods.

DALE'S SPORT PURSUIT

Dale Jorgensen has developed a new online game for sports enthusiasts similar to Trivial Pursuit, except that all the questions are about sports. The game involves asking questions about players, teams, statistics, and records in all of the major North American professional and amateur sports. As the participants answer the questions correctly, they move around the online board, which is patterned after a racetrack. The first participant to cross the finish line is the winner. One of the great features of the game is that participants do not have to be in the same region to play. Friends can compete against one another regardless of their geographic location. Dale is also considering adding a feature where people can simply log in and play against any other people online. Eventually, he would like to develop an online chat component to his game.

Dale has worked with his friend Amanda, an app developer, and they have made a prototype of the game and he is now in the process of developing the marketing plan. Dale currently works for a national sporting goods chain in Toronto as a retail sales associate. Dale is now 38, and he would like to turn this idea into the type of business that would allow him to leave retailing and be his own boss. Dale has an extensive background in athletics, having played junior hockey for three seasons and participated in amateur baseball until he was 16. He enjoys attending professional sporting events, and most of his good friends meet often to discuss sports. He has tested the prototype of his game with these friends, and they have indicated to him that he has the makings of a million-dollar product if he can market it effectively.

Assume that Dale has come to you for guidance in developing the marketing plan for his product. As Dale has little experience in marketing or managing a business, he wants you to help him develop a marketing strategy for Sport Pursuit.

Questions

1. Discuss how the concept of product classification would give Dale direction regarding price, distribution, and promotion strategy.
2. What additions should Dale make to the game to make it more user friendly?

3. How should Dale market the game? What strategies should he employ?
4. Give two to three examples of how public relations and guerrilla marketing could work with this product. Mention an advantage and a disadvantage of using this promotion.

SUSIE'S FASHIONS

As part of his MBA course requirements at Simon Fraser University in British Columbia, Darren Richards has received a student consulting assignment with a small clothing manufacturer in Vancouver. The firm has been in operation a little over a year and has received funding from the government agency funding small businesses. However, it is experiencing cash flow problems. There is a concern that the business, Susie's Fashions, will have to either close or obtain additional funds. Darren spends considerable time wading through the financial data and finally comes up with the approximate statements shown in **Figure 1**.

FIGURE 1 Financial Statements for Susie's Fashions

SUSIE'S FASHIONS BALANCE SHEET AS AT JANUARY 31, 2019

ASSETS		**LIABILITIES AND OWNER'S EQUITY**	
Current assets:		Current liabilities:	
Cash	$ 2500	Accounts payable	$ 8,450
Accounts receivable	815	Current portion of debt	1,000
Inventory	9,765	Total current liabilities	9,450
Prepaid expenses	275	Long-term liabilities	
Total current assets	13,355	Debt	14,000
Fixed assets:		Total liabilities	23,450
Equipment	3,500	Owner's equity	(6,595)
Total assets	$16,855		

INCOME STATEMENT FOR YEAR ENDED JANUARY 31, 2019

Sales:		
352 dresses	$35,200	
298 robes	26,820	
Other miscellaneous	15,200	
Total sales		$ 77,220
Cost of goods sold:		
Dresses	6,336	
Robes	7,152	
Other miscellaneous	2,500	
Total cost of goods sold		15,988
Expenses:		
Wages (including Susie's)	42,000	
Rent	24,000	
Utilities and phone	3,200	
Interest	1,000	
Repairs and maintenance	3,000	
Total expenses		73,200
Total cost of goods sold and expenses		89,188
Net profit (loss)		**$ (11,968)**

Susie Mikado had emigrated to Canada from Hong Kong about five years earlier. Being a hard worker and having worked in a clothing factory in Hong Kong, she got a job immediately at a dress-manufacturing factory. After three and a half years, she had accumulated some funds and decided to start her own small business making selected clothing primarily for the large Asian population in the Vancouver area. Susie has an obvious talent for selecting fabrics and designing garments and, through her family and friends, has developed a reputation as a skilled seamstress.

Susie located her business in the Chinatown district of Vancouver in a leased space of about 1200 square feet. The location is far from ideal as she is on the third floor of a hair salon and she constantly hears that people do not know her business exists. To make renovations, buy equipment, and pay other initial expenses, she borrowed $15,000 and put $5000 of her own funds into the venture. She hired two part-time employees, paying them $16 per hour to assist in sewing the clothing items. The production process is simple: each employee and Susie make a garment from beginning to end.

Darren Richards visits Susie's Fashions to assess the situation and determine what can be done to solve the cash flow problem. He is impressed with the product line, which exhibits quality work. Susie's produces primarily two garments. The first is a Chinese-style dress retailing at $100, and the second is a kimono-like robe retailing at $90. Sales are based almost entirely on word-of-mouth, as Susie spends no money advertising. In examining the production process, Darren notices numerous interruptions occur as family and friends of the workers frequently come by to visit. He estimates, however, that on average the dresses take four hours to make and the robes take three hours. The average dress takes about three yards of material, and the robes average four yards. The fabric for both items cost Susie about $6 per yard.

Darren is concerned about the management of the firm. Although Susie hired two employees, she often hires family or friends to help for a few days at a time when they, as she puts it, "need some money." He is most concerned, however, with the financial procedures Susie is following. Because there is no record-keeping system, he has difficulty determining paid and unpaid bills from the assortment of receipts, scraps of paper, invoices, and notes Susie keeps. Deposits and withdrawals from the bank account have been made but not recorded. Susie's salary is not recorded, but Darren learns that she withdraws $500 per week.

Questions

1. Briefly evaluate Susie Mikado's approach to running her own business.
2. Examine the pricing system for Susie's clothes.
3. Assuming miscellaneous clothing and robe sales stay the same, how many dresses would Susie's have to sell to break even?
4. Evaluate the financial statements prepared by Darren Richards in both form and content.
5. What kind of financial record-keeping system would you advise for Susie's Fashions?

TAYLOR CONSTRUCTION COMPANY

In September 2019, George Taylor realized a lifelong dream by starting his own construction company. He had worked for several construction firms in Québec over the years and had been a foreman on several large projects before he started his own firm. He is a hard worker and has developed a reputation as a capable and sought-after foreman by many companies. Since starting Taylor Construction Company, George has succeeded in obtaining several profitable contracts, which keep him very busy. One day he was visiting with a friend, Rob Dumont, over lunch. The following conversation reveals that things are not so great at Taylor Construction.

Rob: How is your business doing, George? You've sure been busy lately.

George: Yes, we've got lots of work, but you can't imagine the problems I've had with employees. I never dreamt it would be such a hassle.

Rob: What kinds of problems are you talking about?

George: Take your pick! When we started up and got our first contract, I needed six labourers, so I ran an ad on Kijjii and I got 19 applicants. I was surprised that most hadn't worked anywhere consistently and some didn't even finish high school. Even the ones I hired were lazy and undependable. I spent half my time replacing those who quit or whom I fired. Since then things haven't really improved much.

Rob: Maybe you should spend more time training them.

George: More time? As it stands now, I have to be with them almost constantly on a job and tell them what to do every step of the way. If I leave one of them in charge when I have to be away, the others resent it. It seems like they're always bickering with each other.

Rob: I wonder if you should train a foreman to supervise the workers.

George: I tried that. The work that he supervised was poorly done, and on top of that he padded his hours. I even noticed a few tools missing. When I confronted him with it, he quit.

Rob: Can't you spend a little more money and find some better-qualified and motivated employees?

George: My labour costs are too high already! Even though I don't hire union workers, I have to pay pretty close to those rates, and they are high. Once in a while a hard worker comes along, but before long peer pressure from the others seems to drag him or her down to their level.

Rob: It sounds pretty hopeless.

George: The worst part is that just last month I gave all my employees a bonus. I distributed it based on how long they had worked for me and thought I had explained it to them. However, after I gave it out, several of them were upset, and I even had two quit on the spot. Can you believe that? I'm seriously considering shutting down the business and going back to working for my old firm.

Questions

1. Why do you think George has gotten into this situation?
2. What recommendations would you make to George?

THE BARROW BRACKET

Gary Anderson operates an accounting firm in Fredericton, New Brunswick. Although his accounting business is successful and he enjoys it, Gary has always wanted to invent a product and take it to market. In his spare time, Gary recently developed a metal bracket that, when attached to a wall, allows you to hang a wheelbarrow on the wall of a garage or shed. Gary feels that this simple metal product could provide wheelbarrow owners with a major saving of space. Named the Barrow Bracket, the product has received positive comments from several friends and some retail hardware store managers. Gary has obtained a patent on the product and has made a number of them in his garage. He believes that the Barrow Bracket would be an ideal product for most homeowners who own wheelbarrows, and it may even be of interest to some businesses and retail stores.

With his steel press located in his garage, Gary can make 100 Barrow Brackets per day with the material costing him $5. He is hoping that he can sell the product for $10 and that eventually sales will increase to the point that he can build his own manufacturing facility and retire from his accounting practice. Given his personal savings and retirement funds, he will not need the Barrow Bracket to provide enough money to replace his income when he retires from his accounting practice, but he would like to supplement his savings.

The major decision Gary faces now is determining the most effective way to market the Barrow Bracket. He has identified three distribution channel options, which all seem viable. The first is to sell to a national retail hardware chain, such as Canadian Tire or Home Depot. This method would guarantee substantial sales, but Gary is unsure of the profit margin he could make on each bracket. The second option is to hire manufacturer representatives to sell the Barrow Bracket. Manufacturer representatives are independent salespeople who sell to retail stores and receive a commission on these sales. These salespeople typically represent several manufacturers as they travel around to various retail stores. The third option is to sell the product online and perhaps consider a crowdfunding campaign to generate some initial interest.

Since Gary does not have a lot of expertise in marketing, the decision of the appropriate marketing channel is especially troublesome to him. In addition, Gary does not want to spend a lot more money on the venture because he has already invested most of his spare cash to develop the product and obtain the patent.

Questions

1. Evaluate the three distribution options for Gary using the information provided in the textbook regarding long and short channels.
2. Discuss the implications for setting the price of the Barrow Bracket for each of the three distribution options mentioned.
3. What other marketing costs may Gary have overlooked?
4. What would you recommend to Gary and why?

THREADZ

Threadz is a small, independent retail women's clothing store located in London, Ontario. London is a city of 336,000 in southwest Ontario and has a large young adult population because of the university and colleges located in the area. The owner-manager of the store is Jennifer Byers. Jennifer established Threadz eight years ago after graduating from university with a bachelor's degree in business management. During her high school and university days, she worked in various retail clothing stores and gained valuable experience for this kind of business. Her father, a successful entrepreneur, provided start-up capital and other assistance for the venture.

Although sales have increased steadily each year, Jennifer has been concerned recently that this success is starting to fade and will be short lived unless something is done soon. Last year, sales were virtually the same as the previous year, and the rate of growth in sales has declined in each of the last three years. Because Threadz is an independent retailer, Jennifer is concerned that stiff competition from the well-known chains is luring away her customers with their lower prices, greater choice, and large advertising budgets. In addition, online sales of clothes continue to grow, and companies that rent clothes to women are starting to emerge.

The Threadz outlet contains 500 square metres of selling space and targets the 20- to 35-year-old aspiring professional woman. Jennifer's competition comes from such stores as Banana Republic, Club Monaco, and RW and Co. There are many other clothing retailers that are somewhat competitive, but Jennifer is of the opinion that they are not focused on exactly the same customer that Threadz targets. Jennifer describes her target market as the upper-middle-class woman who is "on the go" and requires clothes that are easy to "mix and match" and are "for any occasion." Threadz's target market comprises a decreasing circle of women who enjoy the shopping experience. Because of career obligations, women in this market tend to shop during lunch breaks, in the evenings, on weekends, as well as online. Threadz is located in downtown London and is accessible to a large work population and the residential market. The downtown has many eating places and night clubs, which also contribute to pedestrian traffic at midday and in the evenings.

Jennifer has operated the store in the past with her as manager, an assistant manager, and two sales clerks. Recently, she hired a new assistant manager, Sarah Hetherington, who graduated from a retail management diploma course at a local college. As Jennifer is discussing Threadz's current sales dilemma with her, Sarah asks her if she has thought of establishing a database program in an attempt to retain the customers she suspects she is losing. Sarah indicates that such a system would help in better customer relationship management (CRM), and would assist her in her social media promotions. Although she is aware of CRM, Jennifer thinks that such systems are far too expensive for a small, independent retailer like Threadz. She is not sure that she can afford another marketing cost as she is already spending 4 percent of sales on promotion, above the industry average.

Threadz's promotion budget comprises social media, her website, special events, newspaper advertising, and participation in various local retailer promotions. Much of her marketing continues to be to a large group, and to her Instagram and Twitter followers. Sarah explains that technology costs have come down and that a database system might help Threadz provide better service to its existing customers. Such a system could profile these customers and monitor their purchasing behaviour to tailor special offers to them. As the system is developed further, Sarah explains, it could also be used to target new customers.

Another use would be to exchange this information with other organizations, such as restaurants, jewellery stores, and shoe stores, that have the same target market as Threadz. A main benefit, according to Sarah, would be that this system could provide in-store sales personnel with immediate information about its customers so that the store could provide more personal treatment. Jennifer sees some of the advantages of the system that Sarah is suggesting but is unsure whether it is worth the financial investment.

Questions

1. Evaluate the advantages of the system that Sarah Hetherington is suggesting.
2. What concerns should be explored with this system?
3. What steps should be followed in setting up a CRM system for Threadz?
4. What other promotional suggestions might improve Threadz's performance?

GARNER MEN'S WEAR

Garner Men's Wear is a relatively small, independent men's wear retailer located in Oshawa, Ontario, that has been operating for more than 30 years. The owner, Adam Garner, previously worked for 10 years at Tip Top Tailor, a national chain of men's formal clothing, before starting his own store. Although the first few years were difficult as the business was getting established, Adam was eventually able to develop the business and provide superior service while offering high-quality men's clothing at competitive prices. His target market is made up of middle-aged executives and professionals, most of whom he knows on a first-name basis. Adam has always felt that if he takes care of his best customers, the financial part of the business will take care of itself. He is comfortable with this philosophy because he really does not enjoy all the bookwork that is part of running a business.

Recently, however, he has become concerned about the performance of the business. One of his concerns includes the financial aspects of the business. He seems to always have lots of customers, but when he gets his financial statements from his accountant about two months after the year-end, he is surprised and disappointed to find that the net income of the business has dropped to $10,000 and there is no cash in the business bank account. Assume that you have been called in to evaluate Adam's business. He provides you with the following financial statements for the last two years:

Garner Men's Wear Ltd. Balance Sheet

ASSETS	**2019**	**2020**
Cash	$ 10,000	$ 0
Accounts Receivable	90,000	120,000
Inventory	50,000	80,000
Fixed Assets	140,000	130,000
TOTAL	$290,000	$330,000
LIABILITIES		
Accounts Payable	40,000	50,000
Long-Term Debt	100,000	120,000
Owner's Equity	150,000	160,000
TOTAL	$290,000	$330,000

[continued]

[continued]

Garner Men's Wear Ltd. Income Statement

	2019	2020
Sales	$750,000	$720,000
Cost of Goods Sold	500,000	490,000
Gross Profit	250,000	230,000
Expenses	200,000	220,000
Net Profit	$ 50,000	$ 10,000

Questions

1. Comment on the financial management practices of Adam Garner in managing Garner Men's Wear.
2. Calculate and discuss the significance of each of the following for Garner Men's Wear:
   a. Current ratio
   b. Inventory turnover
   c. Debt ratio
   d. Return on investment
   e. Return on sales
3. How many days are there in this company's business cycle? (That is, how long is it taking to convert cash spent back to cash available?)
4. Where did the $10,000 cash from the 2019 statement go in 2020, even though the business made $10,000 income during 2020?

BOOMERANG BOUNCERS ENTERTAINMENT

As Cam Bean sits at his desk on March 1, he feels he needs to make some decisions about his strategy for using online tools to take his business to the next level. Cam has decided that April 1 will be his last day as a tax trust lawyer for a firm that employs 175 other lawyers just like him. He is not enjoying this profession, but it pays the bills. After three years of running a small part-time business, Cam and his wife/business partner feel the time is right to focus solely on his own business and have Cam devote his energies into making the business a full-time endeavour.

Cam Bean is 32 years old. His wife, Janet, is also his business partner. They have four young children. Cam has a joint law/MBA degree, and Janet has an education degree. Cam grew up in a family with a small-business and entrepreneur background. Janet's parents worked for very large aerospace firms. Three years ago, Cam decided to make some extra income on weekends by renting out air bouncers to people for recreational activities. Bouncers are large, inflatable, tent-like structures, sometimes known as moonwalks, spacewalks, jumps, inflatables, and by several other names. Often they are shaped in well-known themes, such as Spiderman or Cinderella. Cam got the idea for the air bouncers from a college friend who had a thriving business in bouncers in Kansas City, Kansas. Cam lives in Calgary and thought this might be a nice way to bring in extra income on the weekends.

Cam and Janet called their small part-time venture Boomerang Bouncers Entertainment. The bouncers are usually rented for five hours at a time at a cost on average of $600. Boomerang Bouncers Entertainment delivers and sets up the jumps. They make sure everything is safe, clean, and dependable. At the end of the rental time, Boomerang then picks up the bouncer and takes it back to inventory to be rented out again. The market for these jumps includes day cares, schools, family parties, church and club socials, and corporate parties. Weekends are usually the busiest time. The business is seasonal and things slow down from November to February each year.

In their first year, Cam and Janet invested in two bouncers at a cost of $7500 each. With these two bouncers, they generated sales of $32,400 on 54 unit bookings. The next year, Cam thought they would expand this business with two more bouncers and another $16,000 investment. In year two, they generated sales of $102,000 on 170 bookings. In year three, they went to a total of six bouncers and sales went to $150,000 on 250 bookings. They almost always have multiple requests for bouncer rentals on weekends that they cannot fulfill because all the bouncers are already booked. Cam has found that he really enjoys the business and can hardly wait for his work day as a tax lawyer to end so he can take time for Boomerang Bouncers Entertainment. He decides to quit his tax job and operate Boomerang Bouncers full-time, with a total of 20 bouncers.

This decision to go full-time with 20 bouncers means Cam has to make a number of other decisions. He has to hire more drivers for delivery and increase his marketing efforts to keep all the bouncers rented as much as possible.

Cam uses his website and social media to generate a lot of his sales. He also advertises in local community papers read by parents of school-age kids, uses word-of-mouth, and makes some person-to-person sales for commercial accounts. Commercial clients are relatively new for Boomerang as Cam's business has primarily focused on children and family parties. Commercial clients tend to rent multiple bouncers out for corporate events and social functions and, unlike birthday party clients, commercial clients seem less concerned about price and often want the bouncers for less time. While these accounts are less price sensitive, Cam finds they require more upfront work on the sales side and tend to be more demanding in terms of executing on bouncer set up and take down. They also want Cam to provide staff to operate the bouncers for them.

As Cam is leaving his job to run Boomerang full time he is concerned about what type of client he should target. His current target market consists of weekend birthday parties where he drops the bouncers off and picks them up. He always aims to drop them off early to give the family some time with the bouncer, and no one seems to mind if he picks them up a little later than expected. As it stands, he can get by with minimal staff this way. However, Cam is becoming quite intrigued by the potential for commercial clients. He feels he could actually raise his bouncer rental fees to $900 on average, with some bouncers fetching upwards of $1200. Yet these clients will want at least two operators with each bouncer rental—operators Cam will have to compensate at $15 each per hour—and the bouncer delivery and pickup times will have to be precise. This will require additional staff and force Cam to become very efficient in operating the business.

The selection of his target market will also influence his marketing. Cam will need to generate at least $225,000 in bouncer rentals this coming year to justify leaving his job. His plan is to grow that number to $300,000 the following year and then reach $500,000 in annual sales shortly after that. Birthday and party rental clients appear to respond to social media and website material that highlight children having fun, with an emphasis on the bouncers being left for extended periods of time and being run by the party host. While Cam hasn't changed his website or social media to appeal to corporate clients, it appears they would be interested in renting bouncers if he could provide trained operators to manage the bouncers, have strict rules in place to ensure children had fun but were always safe, and guarantee the scheduled for drop-off and pick-up times of the bouncers.

Questions

As a consultant to Cam, answer the following questions:

1. What are the advantages and disadvantages of family party versus commercial clients?
2. Do you think Cam could target both markets? Why or why not?
3. What client group would you ultimately recommend to Cam to target? Based on your recommendations, what changes if any will he have to make to his business?
4. What other services or products could Cam offer to clients to increase his sales?

5. Cam has not spent much time promoting his business. What are some non-traditional methods Cam could use to increase public awareness of Boomerang Bouncers? Why did you choose these methods?
6. What social media sites do you think Boomerang should use to market his business for birthday party clients? What sites should Cam use for corporate/commercial clients?
7. Select one target customer and develop a list of ideas that Cam could use to market his business using social media.

PART 4

LOOKING TO THE FUTURE

Part 4 focuses on management of the small business for the long term. If a business is being managed effectively and increasing sales and profitability have resulted, the owner-manager will face the question of expansion. If growth of the business is desired, some changes will be required within the organization. Chapter 13 discusses the preparations needed.

Chapter 14 discusses the methods of transferring ownership of the business to someone else. Many key considerations in this regard have legal and tax implications with far-reaching consequences for the owner-manager. An option other than transferring ownership to another person is involving family members in the business. The majority of small businesses are, in fact, family-owned and family-operated. Chapter 14 also examines the special characteristics of such businesses.

CHAPTER

13

MANAGING GROWTH

LEARNING OBJECTIVES

By the end of this chapter, you should be able to:

LO1 Describe the problems that success and growth can bring to the small business.

LO2 Examine the characteristics of the stages in the business life cycle.

LO3 Explain how to sustain the business despite the difficulties created by growth.

LO4 Illustrate the importance of planning for growth.

SMALL BUSINESS PROFILE

CHRIS WEBB & VICTORIA FOULGER, PAVIA Gallery - Espresso Bar & cafe

Businesses grow for many reasons, sometimes an entrepreneur envisions an opportunity, or in other cases consumers fuel growth with demand for a product or service. In the case of Victoria Foulger and Chris Webb, co-founders of PAVIA Gallery–Espresso Bar & Cafe, the pair grew their business because one location was not enough to create the type of lifestyle and ethically responsible company they aspired to operate.

Webb and Foulger, partners in life and in business, first started PAVIA in 2011 on Herring Cove Road, a rural part of Halifax Regional Municipality on the outskirts of the blue-collar neighbourhood Spryfield. Webb says that while the location was perhaps unusual, the partners thought they could make it work if the difference in products and service they offered customers was worth driving the extra distance. Foulger and Webb state that they wanted to create an authentic Italian-style café with an emphasis on fair-trade products and ethical business practices. Foulger says that they had an idea to create a café and gallery just as the building on Herring Cove came up for sale. They thought if the business did not work, they would at least have an asset in the building. Foulger looks back at the decision saying that people thought they were crazy, remortgaging their homes, and quitting their jobs to open a coffee shop in Herring Cove. She says on one occasion a person came into the business and let them know that when the coffee shop failed, they would take the building off their hands.

Photos courtesy of @threesixfive.media

When Foulger and Webb opened PAVIA in 2011, the café quickly became known for home-baked products and excellent fair-trade organic coffee. Webb notes that the business' first break came with a positive review in the provincial newspaper, *The Chronicle-Herald*. Webb says he was surprised by the amount of business the positive review brought the company and how much customers appreciated the baked-from-scratch goods and organic products. Webb noted people loved to discover the café, which captured a truly authentic Italian experience.

Foulger and Webb recall that by 2013, even though PAVIA had attracted a loyal following among locals and tourists alike, the business was not generating enough profits for both to work within the business full time. In addition, while they envisioned creating a completely organic, fair-trade business, the costs of doing so were prohibitive given their one, somewhat remote location. Foulger and Webb state that the business partners were faced with a choice: they could expand and grow the business, or one of them would have to re-direct their efforts elsewhere. At that time, Halifax was in the process of creating a new downtown library and were soliciting bids from interested companies to operate a coffee shop on the premise. Webb and Foulger decided to pursue the opportunity, and worked on their application package for many late nights over the 2013 holiday season. Their hard work paid off when, in 2014, Webb and Foulger were awarded the tender for not one but two locations in the new and heavily visited Central library.

But, as Webb notes, this unexpectedly good news meant they had to quickly manage rapid expansion. PAVIA needed staff, and Webb and Foulger needed to organize their resources—and fast. Given both Webb, who is also an artist, and Foulger, who previously worked in health care, are naturally creative and results-orientated people, they developed some

[continued]

[continued]

unique ideas to quickly staff their two new locations. First, the pair hosted a couple of unique hiring nights, meeting and informally interviewing people, and making staffing decisions in a relatively short period. Next, the couple immersed themselves in their work by investing long hours planning their expansion. The two new locations opened in the library in late December 2014.

In 2016, PAVIA expanded once again, this time into the Art Gallery of Nova Scotia where they signed a ten-year agreement to run a licensed café on the main floor of the building. With this agreement, PAVIA also become the exclusive caterer for on-site events. Webb says that the result of the exclusive contract led to an increase in the catering side of the business, allowing PAVIA to expand in this direction as well. Webb says that PAVIA has distinguished itself from other catering companies by focusing on farm-fresh, high-quality, organic foods and their willingness to pay more for ingredients. Webb points out that while organic, free-trade ingredients, such as chocolate and sugar, cost more, using them results in superior product offerings for their customers.

When asked about the benefits of expansion, Foulger and Webb offer interesting responses. First, the pair agree their expansion efforts allow them to continue working within PAVIA, the business they created. But more importantly, note the co-founders, that growth and success has enabled them to build and operate the environmentally friendly, sustainable business they aspired to start back in 2011. Webb and Foulger each said that success has allowed them to source more locally, to bring in more fair-trade products, and to be committed to the environment. Webb states that he wants PAVIA to be a conduit for people in downtown Halifax to invest in rural farms, and both he and Foulger aspire to create a zero-waste food business. The pair also prioritize supporting local charities and have successfully raised money for the YWCA and the IWK Children's Hospital.

PAVIA
paviagallery.com

SMALL BUSINESS AND GROWTH LO1

As illustrated below, short-term success and subsequent growth do not always lead to a trouble-free business operation. Often, success and growth compound the complexities and difficulties of managing the business.

But even with the challenges discussed in this chapter, there are many advantages to growing a business. Many entrepreneurs work the same number of hours whether the business is pursuing a growth strategy or simply providing an income for its founder. One of the differences between a business pursuing a growth strategy and a business opting to stay small is that the earning potential of the growth business is much more significant. Former CEO of Lakeport Brewing Income Fund Teressa Casciola says, "One of the only differences between a small and large business is the size and volume of transaction. But the higher volume and larger transaction enables larger businesses to pay their owner much more money, which translates into nicer homes, cars and vacations."[1] Rebecca MacDonald, Executive Chair and founder of Toronto-based **Just Energy** states that larger companies are also better prepared to handle downturns in the economy, saying, "Unless your business is growing, it's stagnating. Keeping the business small, you don't have a diversification portfolio, so you are counting on all the eggs in one basket. You cannot sustain the bad times as much as big business can. You can get in trouble way quicker."[2] Victoria Sopik, president and CEO of Thornhill, Ontario–based **Kids & Company**, a child-care company that specializes in 24-hour care catering to corporate clients and emergency care, says she has been growing her business as quickly as possible to gain market share and put the company in a position to fend off any potential competition. Other advantages of growing a business include raising capital more easily; attracting and retaining quality employees compared with small, stagnant companies; and building an asset out of the business that can be sold for more money than small firms with low-growth stories.

To avoid the pitfalls of growth and changes in the market, owner-managers should try to ensure long-term viability early in the life of the business. First, owner-managers need to understand the life cycle of the business to effectively plan for the future. Second, they should be aware of some of the more common growth problems a business is likely to face. Finally, owner-managers should take specific steps in planning for the growth of the business.

THE BUSINESS CYCLE LO2

The business cycle of the small enterprise is similar to the product life cycle discussed in **Chapter 8**. For many small businesses that have only one or two products, the business cycle and the product life cycle may be the same.

Figure 13-1 illustrates the changes required by a small business as it moves through its life cycle. The vertical axis represents the growth index, usually measured by gross sales, market share, or profitability. The horizontal axis measures the time taken to pass through the stages of the cycle. The time a business stays in one stage depends on several variables. Many small businesses take several years to move through the life cycle, while others pass through all four stages within a couple of years. This shorter life cycle is common in high-technology industries. The characteristics of the stages of the business cycle are discussed next.

FIGURE 13-1 **The Life Cycle of a Business Concept**

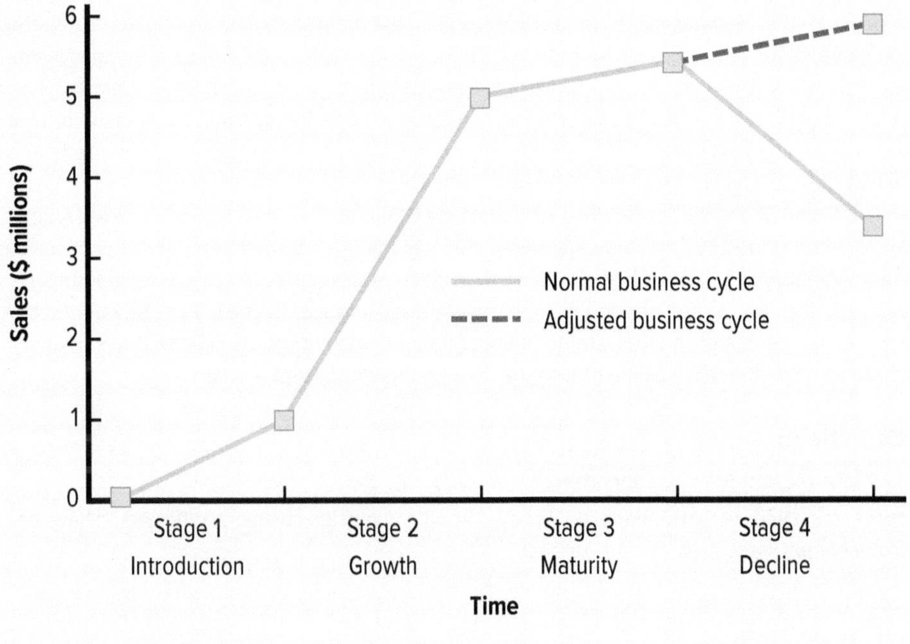

INTRODUCTION

Stage 1 is the start-up stage of the small business. It is characterized by expenditures made for both product development and introductory promotion and by low profits, particularly in the early days of the business. Stage 1 also usually includes a narrow market, a very limited product line, and involvement in most aspects of the business by the owner-manager. The owner's role tends to be more technical and entrepreneurial in this stage. As discussed In **Small Business Beginnings 13-1**, the founders of Mabel's Labels invested a significant amount of time in just gaining visibility for the company, and, during the early stages of their business, they were involved in all aspects of running the company.

SMALL BUSINESS BEGINNINGS 13-1

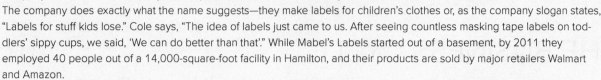

LABELS LEAD TO MILLIONS

Mabel's Labels does not sound like a high-growth company. But you may not want to tell that to the four company founders, Julie Cole, Cynthia Esp, Julie Ellis, and Tricia Mumby, who reside in southern Ontario. The company does exactly what the name suggests—they make labels for children's clothes or, as the company slogan states, "Labels for stuff kids lose." Cole says, "The idea of labels just came to us. After seeing countless masking tape labels on toddlers' sippy cups, we said, 'We can do better than that'." While Mabel's Labels started out of a basement, by 2011 they employed 40 people out of a 14,000-square-foot facility in Hamilton, and their products are sold by major retailers Walmart and Amazon.

The partners, who wanted to grow their firm beyond local parents, have successfully used social media and online sales to sell over 50 million labels in 97 countries. Their initial social media objectives were to first get visibility for their firm and then engage followers. The company initially targeted highly influential mommy bloggers, who are always looking for new content. The partners sent free labels to bloggers they targeted and held contests with them to gain visibility. Mabel's Labels also created volunteer "Buzzmamas," women who would post positive news about the company on their social media pages. After using bloggers and Buzzmamas to gain visibility, the company used their own social media pages and website to develop a community of followers. "Moms talk about products they love and hate like it's their job," says Cole. To keep their community engaged, they hold online events and discussions about things mothers are interested in. For example, the company hosted an online discussion about whether parents should send their children to camp. The discussion had a camp counsellor as a guest, and he answered questions from many of the followers. Cole says their online business, which has become a true community of followers and supporters, has been recognized by Inc.com as one of the top 20 Awesome Facebook Fan Pages and Hubspot's The 15 Best Facebook Pages You've Ever Seen.

As Mabel's Labels grew, the founders also made several business decisions aimed at supporting growth. The partners realized they had to let go of minor aspects of the company to focus on the big picture. They brought in consultants to assist with their human resource development and to fill the gaps in other areas, they hired a PR firm to grow sales in the United States, and perhaps most importantly, they hired a retail consultant, Gerald Harris, to help them pitch to Walmart. Harris along with the partners visited Walmart armed with a new product—blank non-custom labels that can survive both the dishwasher and the washing machine—along with market research supporting the concept. The meeting was a success, and the company landed a contract with Walmart Canada and subsequently Walmart in America.

With rapid growth, Mabel's Labels was approached in 2016 by CCL Industries with a takeover offer. Although initially the company was uninterested in the offer, the founders recognized that the business needed deeper pockets to continue to fuel growth. So, after a short negotiation period Mabel's Labels was acquired by CCL for $12 million. Co-founder Julie Cole said that the business was over a decade old and needed an injection of capital to get to the next level. She added that CCL can provide this investment for the company and that three of the four co-founders are staying on with the firm. Cole notes that she wants Mabel's Labels to grow and that was the reason the co-founders negotiated this deal.

Discussion Questions

1. What are some of the reasons Mabel's Labels became so successful?
2. Rather than agree to a takeover, the founders could have brought in outside investors. What would have been the advantages and disadvantages associated with this strategy?

GROWTH

Stage 2 of the business cycle, growth, is usually characterized by the establishment of a market share, or acceptance, and expansion of the product line or markets. It may also take the form of internal or external expansion, such as a merger or franchising. During this period, sales grow at an increasing rate. For example, a number of small businesses that sell products to help people grow cannabis at home have reported significant increases in sales. **Grow Daddy Canada**, a Prince Edward Island e-commerce store, has noted sales have increased 60 percent from October 2018 through the Spring of 2019; and **Indoor Growing Canada** has doubled the size of its operations since it was founded two years ago.[3]

At the end of the growth stage, however, competitive pressures begin to take their toll, necessitating changes in business strategy. Promoting the business to customers, investors, and employees is important at this stage of the business life cycle. Most small businesses find that this stage requires increased capital to finance the expansion. The business may have orders to purchase but receives payment when the product or service is delivered. Therefore, financing to cover inventories, equipment, and employees is required before sales occur. Both Grow Daddy Canada and Indoor Growing would need capital to hire additional staff and to purchase inventory to sell to their expanding client base.

As mentioned above, most high-growth firms indicate that this is the stage at which the most severe cash flow problems occur in. As **Small Business in Action 13-1** illustrates, even when Montréal e-retailer **Beyond the Rack Inc.**, grew its sales from $4 million to $80 million, it continued to need outside capital to cover the costs of growth; even after raising $78.6 million from 2009 to 2016, they filed for bankruptcy protection from creditors.[4]

Companies such as Grow Daddy Canada, which sells kits and supplies to people who want to grow cannabis at home, have seen sales surge after the federal legalization of cannabis for personal use. While such companies are happy with the surge in sales, growth comes with requirements for additional capital and employees.

Photo 134483937 © Dmitry Tishchenko - Dreamstime.com

MATURITY

Stage 3 is characterized by a levelling of sales because of increased competition or a decrease in demand. During this stage, the owner-manager must make some important strategic decisions to avoid moving into stage 4, decline. Out of necessity the strategy of the business is to become more competitive. Such a strategy may involve adding new products, expanding to new markets, or adjusting or improving existing products in some way. The goal of such actions is to lengthen the life cycle, as illustrated by the increase in sales during the decline stage of the adjusted life cycle in **Figure 13-1**. The owner's responsibility becomes much more managerial during this stage. For example, Richard Abbas, founder and president of Deep Down Cleaning, a commercial cleaning business based in Halifax, says that growth during the early stage of his company was rapid. But eventually it started to slow.[5] To maintain growth and diversify income, Abbas started to rent out high-end cleaning equipment and expanded into industrial clean-ups.

SMALL BUSINESS IN ACTION 13-1

BEYOND THE RACK INC.

Beyond the Rack Inc. was a Montréal-based, online, flash retailer that sold name-brand fashion and household items to its members for as much as 80 percent off the cost in traditional stores. Flash retail is a form of retail in which a company posts pictures of items it is selling for a limited time. Flash retailers, including Beyond the Rack, do not take possession of merchandise before selling it; rather, they wait for orders to come in and then place demand orders with their suppliers. This type of flash retail allowed Beyond the Rack to avoid the extra cost of taking possession of unsold merchandise and storing items in warehouses. The firm passed the savings onto consumers. While this process does add some extra time in getting products into the hands of consumers, shoppers appeared to be willing to wait because of the deep discounts on the site. Beyond the Rack founder and former CEO Yona Shtern said, ". . .we [Beyond the Rack] do not stock the majority of the merchandise we sell; we place demand orders with our vendors after taking customer orders on our site. This model allows us to offer exceptional pricing at some cost to delivery time. Our loyal customers are happy to pay less in exchange for slightly longer delivery times."

[continued]

[continued]

Beyond the Rack was recognized as one of the fastest-growing e-retailer in the United States by *Internet Retailer* magazine as the company's sales grew from under $4 million in 2009 to over $150 million in 2014. But, for several reasons, the company was not profitable. First, the firm spent over $30 million on marketing in 2015 and 2016 attempting to expand rapidly into the competitive U. S. market. They also increased the number of employees from 75 in 2010 to to 333 by 2015. Even with the increased number of employees, Beyond the Rack suffered from slow customer service, and the losses mounted. One company employee noted that the business was not scalable because expenses rose as the business grew. Industry analysts stated that Beyond the Rack mistakenly changed its business model when is added non-branded, low-cost Chinese products to its flash sale website.

With losses mounting, the business went into bankruptcy protection in 2016 stating it lost $17.1 million dollars with $44 billion owed to creditors. While the business may have seemed like a failure, experts were not surprised when a buyer emerged. Even with all of its problems, Beyond the Rack had in excess of 14 million subscribers and 450,000 active buyers. Shortly after entering into creditor protection, Beyond the Rack was purchased and is operating today using the flash sale model to sell such luxury brands as Prada, Burberry, Gucci, and Coach.

Montréal-based Beyond the Rack was the largest flash retailer in Canada, with sales in excess of $150 million. Flash retail allowed the company to sell items before taking possession of them. This enabled Beyond the Rack to sell name-brand fashion at 80 percent of retail prices.

Discussion Questions

1. What are the advantages and disadvantages of Beyond the Rack's sales method?
2. Beyond the Rack spent a significant amount of money on public relations and marketing in an attempt to grow and grab market share. As a result, the firm was not always profitable. What are the advantages and disadvantages of this strategy?
3. Imagine you are a potential investor. Would you invest in a company like Beyond the Rack? Why or why not?
4. Why would selling non-branded Chinese products be problematic for Beyond the Rack?
5. Were you surprised a buyer emerged for the company? Why or why not?
6. Some retail analysts say the flash sale model is dead. They ask why consumers would continue to check flash sales sites when they know they can buy discounted items daily on Amazon. Do you agree with this sentiment? Why or why not?
7. What would you suggest Beyond the Rack's new management does to ensure long-term sustainability?

DECLINE

As you saw in **Figure 13-1**, stage 4 involves a decrease in both sales and profits. Unless action is taken to reverse this trend, the business will fail.

Table 13-1 shows an example of the growth of a business and subsequent operational and strategy changes that should take place. The actual dollar level of sales relating to the stages of the life cycle will vary depending on the growth of the market, the type of industry, and the owner's objectives. However, **Table 13-1** also points out the need to deal quickly with the changes that growth in sales can create.

TABLE 13-1 Stages of Growth

APPROXIMATE SALES LEVEL	MARKET	PRODUCT	OWNER-MANAGER
\$0–\$1,500,000	One market	One or limited line	Involved in day-to-day aspects of the business, such as buying, selling, and financial management
\$1,500,000–\$4,000,000	Expanding into new markets	Adding new products in same category	Some organizational change allowing supervisor to oversee greater part of day-to-day operations
			Greater need for financial evaluation
			Greater need to obtain capital to finance growth
			Some delegation required
			Development of managers
\$4,000,000+	Established markets: continued expansion to new markets	Adding new products in different categories	Managers run day-to-day operations and report to owner
			Communication and information important
			Training for management development
			Establishment of proper controls

PROBLEMS CREATED BY GROWTH LO3

To anticipate growth difficulties and make plans to minimize them, the owner-manager should be aware of some of the problems that can be expected to accompany growth.

OWNER-MANAGER FATIGUE AND STRESS

Stress levels rise when the scope of the business and the magnitude of its problems increase. For example, John DeHart and Ken Sim, co-founders of Nurse Next Door Home Healthcare Services Inc., had successfully grown to 1000 employees and \$20 million in revenue in four short years. Yet one day at work, the pair realized that they no longer liked their business, nor did many of their managers actually like them. The founders of Nurse Next Door were so focused on growth that it had negatively affected the work environment.[6] Rather than sell their firm, which they discussed, the pair opted to create a new vision, remove employees who they identified as problematic, and revamp some of their human resources practices, including their hiring process. To ensure an engaged workplace, the co-founders then invested more money in training managers. The result was an increase in growth and a happier work environment for the entrepreneurs and the employees.

LACK OF COMMUNICATION

As the scope of operations grows, the former closeness between owner and business dissipates. Many owner-managers resent this loss of closeness and even curb their growth objectives as a result. As a firm grows, owners often struggle with letting go of managing every part of their company. For example, Rebecca MacDonald says that when she first started the business, she was involved in every detail of managing the firm. But as the business grew, she had to let her managers do their jobs, which was something she struggled with. "At one point I was involved in everything, from sales to marketing to gas procurement," notes MacDonald. "It was almost like letting a child leave home. It was hard for me. But I wanted to allow my talented people to do what they were hired to do."

HUMAN RESOURCES PROBLEMS

One of the biggest challenges facing growth companies is human resources related. Many companies are facing staffing challenges because they cannot find enough skilled workers, while other companies are adding employees so quickly that they failed to develop enough formal structures to manage their employees, often leading to low morale and high turnover. A lack of both qualified staff and formal human resources practices can negatively affect growth. For example, Halifax-based, make-your-own-wine company, **Noble Grape** grew from one store to eight in Halifax over a short time. As the company grew, co-founders and brothers Stephen and Mark Haynes focused on sales and didn't create any formal human resources structures.[7] Eventually employees started to complain that there was no consistency in how the firm was being managed. This eventually led Stephen to develop a formal human resources guide, including rules on sick leave, vacation days, and so on to ensure formal practices were used in all locations. Employees were happy with the consistency and that many of their benefits were now in writing.

LACK OF COORDINATION

Various aspects of the business may become specialized and less integrated with the overall operation as a business grows. This often results in increased conflicts among departments and individuals within the organization. Employees who in the early stages of the company life cycle performed many duties are often reluctant to give up some of those responsibilities to specialists. Such resentment can lead to conflicts within the organization.

SHORTAGE OF CASH

Growth and expansion typically require financing that the business has not yet generated. Merchandise may have been sold or services rendered but cash not yet received, even though cash is still needed to acquire new inventories or to fuel growth. *Canadian Business* magazine produces a list of the fastest-growing companies in Canada and many of them, including 40 percent of the top 15, have yet to make any money. As noted above, Beyond the Rack achieved sales in excess of $150 million but still needed to raise $36 million in capital to fuel growth.[8] Another example of a firm that had to overcome a shortage of cash was **Aecometric Corp.** Its president, Jill Anderson, discovered the importance of managing cash-flow during a recent downturn in her business. Her firm, which makes custom burners and other heavy industrial equipment, narrowly missed going out of business because of the economic slump. Large-scale construction projects were brought to a halt and clients started taking longer to pay, which caused the firm to miss payroll three consecutive times. To keep the firm afloat, Anderson cut her workforce from 22 to 6 and remortgaged the family farm. Although sales are up, Anderson has become a very careful manager of cash flow. It is important that the owner-manager estimate the cash requirements of an increase in sales.[9] See **Table 13-2** for an illustration of how to do this.

TABLE 13-2 **How to Estimate the Cash Requirements for an Increase in Sales**

To make the calculation, a business needs the following information:

- The increase in sales planned ($)
- The time frame for adding new sales (days)
- The company's gross profit margin, gross profit ÷ net sales (percent)
- The estimated additional expenses required to generate additional sales ($) (extra overhead)
- The company's average collection period (days)

To calculate the amount of additional cash needed, use the following formula:

Extra cash required = [(New sales – Gross profit + extra overhead) × (Average collection period × 1.20*)] ÷ (Time frame in days for adding new sales)

*The extra 20 percent is added as a cushion.

Consider the following example:

The owner of Ardent Company wants to increase sales by $75,000 over the next year. The company's gross profit margin is 30 percent of sales (so its gross profit on these additional sales would be $75,000 × 30 percent = $22,500), its average collection period is 47 days, and managers estimate that generating the additional sales will require an increase in expenses of $21,300. The additional cash that Ardent will need to support this higher level of sales is

Extra cash required = [($75,000 – $22,500 + 21,300) × (47 × 1.2)] ÷ 365 = $11,404

Ardent will need $11,404 in extra cash to support the additional sales of $75,000 it plans to bring in over the next year.

LOW PROFITABILITY

Low profitability is common in rapidly growing businesses. As discussed above, approximately 40 percent of the 15 fastest-growing companies in Canada according to *Profit* magazine are not making any money. Considerable expenses are incurred in research and development of markets during the growth period.[10]

BREAKDOWNS IN PRODUCTION EFFICIENCY

Declining production efficiency, as evidenced by unmet schedules, increases in quality assurance problems, and consumer complaints, are common in rapidly growing companies. Robert Sher, founder of **CEO to CEO Inc.**, a business consultancy firm which specializes in helping firms grow, states that many founders are strong salespeople but as sales increase they often lack the operations efficiencies to manage growth. Sher notes that a strong human resource team, including people with experience in operations management is essential to ensure growth is managed correctly. Sher says, "What's absolutely important is that you have an executive that loves operations. Many CEOs don't—they're sales types, they're creative, they're engineers. You need executives that really pride themselves on seeing that the trains run on time."[11]

LACK OF INFORMATION

Lack of information with which to evaluate the business' performance often accompanies rapid growth. As the owner-manager becomes increasingly removed from day-to-day operations and the scope of the business outgrows manual information retrieval, a more automated system is often needed to generate the required data.

OWNER LIFESTYLE

An often overlooked contributor to business failure caused by growth relates to personal lifestyle decisions of the owner as the business begins to be successful. A larger house, bigger car, or exotic vacations based on the expectation of continued growth often leave the owner unable to meet personal obligations.

EVALUATING THE GROWTH QUESTION

Owner-managers should answer four important questions before proceeding to expand the business.

IS THE BUSINESS ONE THAT CAN GROW?

A preliminary step in dealing with the question of growth is to evaluate whether the product or business is one that can grow. Restricted markets or products that have volume production restrictions are difficult to expand. Many service businesses that rely on the special expertise of their owners also fit into this category. Rapidly changing industries, such as those found in high technology, suggest concerns of rapid obsolescence. This is particularly critical if the capital investment of growth is large. However, one successful technology company illustrates how working with the right partners can offer avenues for growth. Read more in **Small Business in Action 13-2**.

SMALL BUSINESS IN ACTION 13-2

SECUREKEY TECHNOLOGIES INC.

Brian A Jackson/Shutterstock.com

Have you ever ordered something online? If you are like most people, you likely have. The process has become very simple: the consumer clicks on an item, enters a credit card number, and waits for their package to arrive. If the item can be downloaded, the consumer can access their order using a computer or mobile device in seconds.

But as online sales have grown, so has online theft and fraud. In the transaction described above, all that is needed is a computer, a tablet, or an online device to place the order and credit card numbers. The actual credit card is not required. Thieves can use a variety of tricks to get your credit card number, including skimmers and mobile cameras. They can then spend thousands of dollars online without ever stealing your card. Greg Wolfond, founder and CEO of **SecureKey Technologies Inc.**, knew how to change this. His Toronto-based company worked with Intel in 2011 to allow computers and mobile devices to recognize credit and bank cards. Online transactions became more secure as people were required to have the physical card to make a purchase, using the "tap" feature on their cards when making a purchase, increasing the security of the system.

In addition to online credit card recognition, SecureKey Technologies created a strategy to allow one set of online credentials to deal with multiple online sites or access points by creating the product SecureKey Concierge. Customers using SecureKey Concierge no longer have to memorize various usernames and passwords but can access multiple sites using one secure sign-in system. Consumers benefit from easier access to sites, some of which they may not visit frequently, while businesses can ensure clients and employees that they are who they say they are.

In 2012, SecureKey announced the launch of their innovative service that allows people to use their online banking sites for accessing online services from the Government of Canada. Thus consumers can benefit from the security of their online banking system to access government documents and information.

Discussion Questions

1. What are some of the advantages and disadvantages of SecureKey's systems as described above?
2. Would you be more comfortable tapping your credit card against your iPhone or iPad compared with typing in your credit card information? Why or why not?
3. Do you think people would be comfortable accessing all the websites they visit using one sign-in system? Why or why not?

IS THE BUSINESS OWNER PREPARED TO MAKE THE EFFORT?

Expanding a business will require additional time and effort on the part of owner-managers. The decision owner-managers must make is whether they are ready to increase effort and prepare for the stress or be content with a smaller but less demanding business. Many successful small businesses have chosen not to grow for precisely this reason. This decision not to grow is one which has been applauded by American business consultant Ed Hess. Hess states that some firms with owners who are not prepared to change and are run by people who do not want to grow are better off staying small.

DOES THE OWNER-MANAGER HAVE THE CAPABILITIES TO GROW?

The owner-manager should assess whether the needed capital, labour, and expertise can be obtained to deal effectively with growth. This was the case with Abdulfatah Sabouni, a Syrian immigrant who came to Calgary in 2016. Sabouni, who manufactured soap in Syria, lost everything in the recent war, and was uninterested in making soap in Canada. But after vending at a Calgary festival and quickly selling out the soap that he had manufactured in the Middle East, he changed his mind. Sabouni created Aleppo Savon, a soap made with laurel oil, and now has a Canadian factory and one retail location. He is planning to open more stores throughout Canada while expanding his wholesale business. Sabouni appears to be in a good position to succeed as he has all the qualities listed above: the skills and expertise of soap-making and running a business, capital from retained earnings to fuel his expansion plans, and a large labour pool in his new home city.[12]

HOW SHOULD THE OWNER-MANAGER PURSUE GROWTH?

If growth is desired, several approaches may be taken in pursuing it. The most common strategies (some of which were already mentioned) are as follows:

- Pursue new markets for the product or service. This may involve different geographic (domestic or foreign) or demographic markets. Since Canada is relatively small on a global scale, many companies pursue exporting or international expansion as their main strategy. For example, **Kicking Horse Coffee** has successfully expanded into the American market. Company founder Elana Rosenfeld says the company's initial expansion lacked structure and so wasn't successful. Rather than give up, Kicking Horse changed their approach and targeted one region at a time. Rosenfeld says the U.S. is so large that a business has to look at it as many countries rather than just one. Her approach of expanding region by region has worked, and Kicking Horse can now be found across America.[13] Of the fastest-growing companies in Canada identified by *Canadian Business* magazine, 58 percent of them are pursuing international expansion. For example, **Flow**, which sells Alkaline Spring water from Aurora, Ontario, has expanded into the China. Sales have been strong as Chinese consumers perceive Canadian water as safer and of higher quality.[14]
- Increase sales of existing products or services by increasing the frequency of use. This can be done through increased promotion or, sometimes, it happens organically through industry growth. For example, Toronto's **Downtown Camera** is experiencing a surge in sales as more young people are picking up analog cameras rather than using digital.[15]

- Add new products or services or modify existing ones to increase sales. For example, **Three Farmers**, a Saskatoon-based business founded by sisters Natasha and Elysia Vandenhurk, originally started by selling camelina oil at farmers' markets and have grown the business by 476 percent in five years and adding 11 employees. After their initial product offering of camelina oil, they added chickpea snacks to diversify revenue.[16] Similarly, some of the small and large green house operators throughout Canada have switched from growing vegetables to cannabis as the margins on cannabis are much higher than vegetables.[17]
- Find new uses for the product or service and promote these uses to the market.
- Acquire other small companies or merge with another organization. For example, GoodLife has become the largest health club company in Canada following an expansion and acquisition strategy. Over the last decade GoodLife has purchased the Nubody gyms in Atlantic Canada, Toronto-based Extreme Fitness, and several Gold's gyms locations in Western Canada. After also building over 100 new locations, the company owns in excess of 300 fitness centres.

GoodLife has expanded throughout Canada by opening up new facilities and acquiring smaller gyms.

Photo 118010528 © Roberto Machado Noa - Dreamstime.com

PLANNING FOR GROWTH LO4

Once the decision to expand has been made and the method of expansion has been determined, a plan for growth should be developed. A growth or strategic plan is a blueprint of future actions. Planning is an essential but often overlooked part of management. The importance is illustrated by London, Ontario–based company Diagnostics Biochem Canada. Before expanding into new markets with its diagnostic kits, the company spent significant time gathering information, and studying competitors and the business environment. As CEO Manon Hogue described it, this planning allowed the company to gain first-mover advantage in growing economies.[18] Dan Shimmerman, former president and CEO of Varicent Software Inc., notes that planning was essential in expanding his company. Shimmerman, eventually grew his company to the point that IBM purchased the firm.[19]

Some small business owners want to expand but don't create a full plan or completely understand the market, learning as they go instead. For example, Toronto-based, **Eatable Food Inc.**, which sells alcohol-infused popcorn, expanded to the American market less than a year after they started their business. Company founders Charlene and Vince Li soon discovered that cross-border shipping is expensive and comes with challenges. They also found out that American and Canadian tastes are not the same. While Canadians prefer Scotch-whisky–infused caramel popcorn, Americans opted for peanut butter-and-jelly–flavoured and merlot-flavoured popcorn. Undaunted by these challenges, the company founders have established preferential shipping rates, increased the order amount that qualifies for free shipping, and created plans to expand into brick-and-mortar retailers.[20]

Planning can be a challenge when most small business owners feel snowed under by the daily operations and often think planning is a nuisance. However, small business owner-managers who are able to periodically step back from the organization and objectively assess its overall direction are generally better able to cope with the environmental changes that will affect the business. It may be advisable for owner-managers to employ professional management in the business if the management problems of rapid growth are due to their own limited capabilities. Many entrepreneurs have found that following this course of action has allowed them to focus on the areas that they have greater expertise and interest in.

Finally, conditions change so rapidly in many industries that plans have to be altered frequently. The need for constant adjustment discourages many small business owners.

THE EXPANSION PLAN

Chapter 4 discussed the essential elements of the start-up business plan. Many similarities exist between the start-up plan and the expansion plan. The business plan as introduced in **Chapter 4** includes projecting for growth and expansion as well. The steps in the expansion plan are discussed here.

When JJ Bean Café expanded from Vancouver to Toronto, the company set a goal of establishing 40 retail locations in the region, all supported by a coffee-roasting facility in North York.

Photo 131336502 © Standret - Dreamstime.com

Set Objectives.

The first step in the planning process is to set the objectives the business is to accomplish. As mentioned previously, it is important to set specific objectives so that the outcomes can be measured. Objectives may include dollar sales, market share percentage, or dollar profits. For example, when Vancouver coffee company **JJ Bean Café** expanded into the Toronto market, founder John Neate opened up a coffee roaster in North York, which he believes will support the 40 cafes he plans on opening.[21]

Determine Alternatives.

The second step includes identifying possible strategies to achieve the objectives. It also involves forecasting the possible outcomes of different alternatives.

Select the Best Alternatives.

Alternatives should be selected with a view toward long-term success. The components of this success are the company's capability and the potential growth of the area.[22] As mentioned previously, growth could occur geographically, by reaching new markets, or by adding new products.

UNDERSTANDING THE REQUIREMENTS OF GROWTH

Rapid growth will necessitate some fundamental changes within the organization. Some of the requirements of growth are discussed next.

Greater Management Depth.

Owner-managers must realize that an expansion of management depth must accompany the expansion of the business. This will require more skills or harder work on behalf of owner-managers. Because they may already be stretched to the limit, such expansion usually consists of training subordinates to handle some of the managerial responsibilities. This involves training and delegation, two personnel practices owner-managers are often hesitant to incorporate into their management styles. But as the business grows, owners must spend more time thinking and less time doing. This also means they must move from task delegation to functional delegation, allowing key people to manage various functional areas of the business. Greater management depth can also be achieved through the use of functional specialists outside the company such as accountants, lawyers, directors, or mentors.

Staffing.

As firms grow, they will also require additional staff and or managers. Given the aging workplace in Canada many firms struggle to hire skilled employees. Any expansion plan should contain human resources recruitment strategies. Some firms, such as Winnipeg-based Broadview Networks Inc., have adopted programs to enhance the skills of its employees so they can meet the ever-changing needs of the firm. According to Broadview's president, Michael Orloff, the company has adopted a training program for every one of the firm's employees to grow the skills of the company.[23]

Intelligent Expansion.

A common problem among small business owners is that in their effort to succeed, they start too many diverse projects. They often do so without evaluating whether they have the productive or marketing expertise, or the resources to accomplish the expansion. They may also ignore the potential effects of unplanned expansion on their existing products. The decision to expand should incorporate continuity, experience, and intelligence. For example, Meal-kit company **Fresh Prep** has been in a slow, well-planned expansion mode in the rapidly expanding meal kit business. The Vancouver company, founded by young entrepreneurs Husein Rahemtulla, Dhruv Sood, and Becky Switzer, signed up 200 customers in their local area then spent time determining how they could be sustainable compared with their competitors. Rahemtulla says if they expanded too quickly there was a chance they would lose focus on operations. After spending time learning the business and planning their expansion, the business partners plan to expand to Victoria, Calgary, and Edmonton initially, then move into the Toronto and Montreal markets.[24]

Additional Capital.

Any expansion in the business will require additional money to finance added productive capacity, inventory, and/or personnel. Entrepreneurs may either have to reinvest profits, borrow funds, or solicit investors. As discussed in **Chapter 6**, there are advantages and disadvantages associated with raising capital through any of these methods. Such actions can take time, increase the entrepreneur's risk of failure, and can potentially dilute the entrepreneur's ownership in the business. Fresh Prep, which was discussed above, has recently raised $3.3 million from investors to fuel expansion.[25]

One way to achieve high growth even with limited capital may be to franchise the business or the idea. Although becoming a franchisor requires a certain amount of capital, franchising may allow a firm to expand rapidly without needing large amounts of funds. Michael Gerber, author of the bestselling entrepreneurship book *The E-Myth Revisited: Why Most Small Businesses Don't Work and What to Do About It*, has studied a number of the world's best brands and concluded that franchising their system is what enabled them to grow quickly but at a controlled pace. Brian Scudamore, CEO of 1-800-Got-Junk?, a Canadian franchisor of a junk removal business, notes that franchising has enabled him to grow his company with partners (franchisees) into the world's largest junk removal business.[26] Learn about another successful franchise in **Small Business in Action 13-3**.

SMALL BUSINESS IN ACTION 13-3

ENVIRO PAVING CORP.

Enviro Paving Corp. is using the franchise model to successfully grow its business throughout North America. The company, which uses recycled tires to pave driveways, is enjoying significant growth as people are looking for more environmentally friendly products. Unlike traditional asphalt driveways, Enviro-recycled driveways do not leak toxins into the ground and come with a five-year guarantee. Current franchise owner Ron Bristow tried the product at his home in Innisfail, Alberta, and liked it so much he bought the franchise rights for two territories, including Central Alberta. Bristol says, "We can put it over asphalt, concrete, paving stone, sidewalk blocks," adding that there's a recycled plastic product that can be used to create the necessary base for the rubber coat elsewhere—such as on bare ground. "It'll support over 100,000 pounds per square foot."

Enviro Paving Corp., a company that paves driveways with recycled tires, is using the franchise model to grow its business in Canada.

Marekusz/Dreamstime.com

As noted in previous chapters, one advantage of franchising for the franchisors is that they can grow their company quickly, often using other people's money; and franchise owners tend to be very interested and committed managers. The downside is franchisors give up a large portion of their potential net income to the franchisee, often settling for an initial franchise fee and a percentage of sales, better known as a royalty. While royalties are in the range of 5 to 15 percent of annual sales, they still fall well short of 100 percent profits.

Discussion Questions

1. What do you think are some of the challenges a small company like Enviro Paving Corp. may face in trying to grow using the franchisor-franchisee method?
2. What other methods of growth could Enviro Paving Corp. pursue as an alternative to franchising?
3. Enviro Paving Corp. is a relatively new company, with a new concept. Many prospective franchisees would assume it's a more proven concept because they are pursuing growth via franchising. Is Enviro Paving Corp. under a moral obligation to explain this to potential franchisees or is it strictly buyer beware?
4. Would you invest in an Enviro Paving Corp. franchise? Why or why not? What are some strong arguments for investing in the company.

Financial Information.

Often, increased sales obscure the fact that the profitability of the business is declining or even negative. As the business grows, it is increasingly difficult—but more important—for owner-managers to obtain accurate information about the profitability and productivity of the business. The use of accounting software by many small businesses has greatly helped in this area. As the business grows, there is a greater need to use information technology. Owner-managers should regularly project future financial requirements so that cash shortages do not occur.

Organizational Change.

As owner-managers realize they can no longer be involved in every aspect of the business, the organizational structure will require alteration. This is necessary to establish a clear understanding of reporting and responsibility centres in the business. The aim is to reduce the owner's span of control, allow managers the space to make decisions, and let owners focus on planning and long-term strategy development of the business. It can also allow the owner more time to foster coordination within the firm. As the firm grows, the owner can make greater use of advisory boards and professionals, as discussed in **Chapter 12**.[27] At the same time, owner-managers must resist the temptation to overdo the bureaucracy of the organization. An entrepreneurial culture (which likely contributed to the business' success in the first place) must be retained if growth is to continue.

Implementing Managerial Controls.

As a business grows, it becomes more difficult to control. Through the use of informational and organizational methods, a system of goals, performance levels, and evaluations must be put into place. As discussed earlier in the text, the integration of new software into small business operations has greatly enhanced owner-managers' ability to control all aspects of the business. Such measures as ratio analysis, bench marking, inventory turnover, margins, and cost controls are examples.

Monitoring the External Environment.

The final growth requirement is that owner-managers should focus greater attention on the external environment of the business. These external forces serve as a guide to the long-term strategic planning in which owner-managers now must engage. Important external forces are technological change, competition, consumer demand, social and cultural norms, legislation, and the state of the economy.

To keep their companies strong and encourage growth, managers need to do the following:

- Invent new applications for products and services.
- Find new sales and distribution channels.
- Rethink internal processes.
- Enhance technological content.
- Provide employees with upgradeable, saleable skill sets.
- Disseminate internal information effectively.[28]

LEARNING OBJECTIVES SUMMARY

LO1 **Problems to anticipate as a result of growth are the owner-manager's increased fatigue and stress, lack of communication, human resources problems, lack of coordination, shortage of cash, low profitability, breakdown in production efficiency, lack of information, and possible decreases in employee morale.**

LO2 **The four stages of the business cycle are (1) introduction, which is characterized by the owner investing in start-up expenses and marketing; followed by (2) growth, in which the business attracts customers; (3) maturity, when sales level off; and finally (4) decline, when sales fall off and the business may eventually cease to exist.**

LO3 **To acquire the knowledge to deal with growth problems, the owner-manager should address three areas. First, review the business life cycle. Second, be aware of the common growth problems that arise. Third, know the steps to take to plan effectively for growth.**

LO4 **Growth planning is often overlooked because of the failure to understand the planning process, lack of time, and the constant changes occurring in the industry. The three steps in developing an expansion plan for a small business are (1) setting objectives, (2) identifying all the possible strategies or alternatives for achieving the objectives, and (3) choosing the best and most viable alternative.**

TIME TO TAKE ACTION

If you are following the steps in this book, you are well on your way to your entrepreneurial dreams or hopefully at the very least a great grade in your course. The focus of this chapter is on growth strategies and dealing with the implications of growth. Whether you are running a growing business or hope to be, it is never too early to plan for growth. After reading this chapter, you should complete some or all of the following activities:

1. Determine what your business goals are. Look at your business idea or operating business. Is the business large enough to meet your goals? Generate some ideas that will grow your business. If necessary, review **Chapter 2**'s discussion on creativity.
2. Check out the Internet or your local book store, and read material on people who have grown a small business into a large one. Try to determine what strategies they used. Comment on any changes in the management structure of the company. If possible, interview some entrepreneurs who have grown their business. Identify their strategies, and discuss with them what, if any, changes occurred in how they manage their company.
3. If you have not already done so, complete a personal SWOT analysis, writing down your personal strengths and weaknesses. Now review where you want your company to grow to in the next three, five, and ten years. Then note areas where you have to develop if you want to maintain your position as owner-manager.

DISCUSSION QUESTIONS

1. What are some of the advantages of growing a business?
2. What problems should the owners be aware of when expanding? How might these problems be dealt with?
3. What are the requirements for growth?

EXPERIENTIAL EXERCISES

1. The owner-managers of a small, successful hair-cutting company want to expand their business. Their growth objective is to have 35 percent of the local hair-cutting market in two years' time.
   a. What steps could they take to determine the feasibility of their expansion?
   b. Outline a brief expansion plan.

2. Interview the owner-manager of a successful small business and evaluate the potential for further growth. Would you recommend expansion for this firm? Why or why not?
3. Visit three small businesses that you suspect have varying sales levels. Determine the market, product, and degree of owner-manager involvement in each business. Are your results significantly similar to those in **Table 13-1**? Explain.
4. Identify three of the fastest-growing companies in your region. What opportunities have they pursued to achieve this level of growth? What growth mechanism have they used (internal, joint venture, acquisitions, franchising, etc.)?
5. Use research to come up with three examples of founding entrepreneurs who stepped aside once the firm had grown to a certain size and brought in a professional manager. What relationship did the entrepreneur continue to have with the firm after the transition? Provide an example of a founding entrepreneur being forced out of the position of CEO to be replaced by a professional manager.
6. Form groups and assume the roles of top management at your university or college. Develop expansion strategies and objectives to grow the business. Present your findings.

COMPREHENSIVE CASE DAN KIM: PART 7

Despite the personnel problems, Dan is able to persevere and keep the plant running. Toward the end of the second year of operations, Dan's business seems to be really taking off. Sales have reached $700,000 by October, mainly because of distribution of the Ladder Helper and accessories across Canada, as well as a growing number of sales from the United States. He has added some accessory products and their sales are also contributing to the positive company performance. This expansion necessitated renting additional manufacturing space nearby and doubling production. Dan secured patent protection for the Ladder Helper and its accessories, and now has several ideas for new but related products.

However, the major concern that Dan has is that the business has grown to the point that he is putting in 18-hour days. It seems that every day new crises arise and he is the only one who has either the expertise or the interest to deal with these problems.

Despite the sales success, the business continually experiences cash flow problems. Dan has to pay for the metal COD, but the retail hardware chain that has exclusive rights for his products only pays him once per month. This results in a continual operating deficit until this payment is received.

The plant personnel problems continue to cause a lot of stress, and with the additional plant, this has compounded. Dan finds that he is going from one plant to the other to try to ensure quality production. Times when he has been on the road, the quality has slipped and a number of customer complaints have been received. Although his marketing person is a hard worker and capable, Dan has to oversee marketing and review the financial condition of the business. Finally, he has to ensure that the loan payments to the bank are made.

His family life has essentially disappeared. The dream of owning his own business and having the freedom to do what he wants is turning into a nightmare. All the problems of trying to run the business were compounded when Suzie announced that something had to be done, she wanted to see her spouse and spend time with him. Dan realized that he misses Suzie and wants to spend more time with his family. As a result, he is contemplating selling the business or altering the organization somewhat to allow for more time for his personal life.

Question

1. Identify the problems that growth has caused with Dan's business and discuss possible solutions.

CHAPTER 14

MANAGING THE TRANSFER OF THE BUSINESS

LEARNING OBJECTIVES

By the end of this chapter, you should be able to:

LO1 Explain the importance of planning for the long-term and the possible transfer of ownership of the small business.

LO2 Review the unique characteristics and problems of owning a family business and passing it on to family members.

LO3 Explain the critical considerations in selling the business to employees or to outsiders.

LO4 Review information pertaining to the closing down of the business.

SMALL BUSINESS PROFILE

DANA REISS, Canada Goose

In 1957 Sam Tick, an immigrant to Canada, founded Metro Sportswear Ltd. in Toronto, a company that specialized in woolen vests, raincoats and snowmobile suits. In the 1970s David Reiss, Sam's son-in-law, joined the company and invented a volume-based, down filling machine, and the company began selling Snow Goose parkas, mostly for public sector workers, such as police and park rangers. David Reiss' son, Dani Reiss, joined the family company in 1997 in order to earn enough money to travel. Soon after joining the company, the younger Reiss realized that customers felt a connection with the "Made in Canada" label. The youngest Reiss noted that many customers associated the product with their ideal image of the Canadian wilderness: "I realized people had an emotional connection to 'Made in Canada.' The experience of owning one of these jackets was like trying on a piece of Canada." As a result, Reiss convinced his father to change the name of the business to Canada Goose. Within the year, Reiss' father asked him to take over as CEO of the business.

Once he assumed control of the company, Reiss faced a major decision—should he follow his competitors and outsource production, or should he continue to manufacture jackets in Canada? Reiss says he struggled with the decision because many experts advised him to manufacture in China where he could save substantially on costs. He opted to follow his instinct and continue to produce the coats in Canada. "We took that opportunity to stay in Canada, and by doing that we became successful. The strategy of sticking around [helped] the perception that we are the champions for 'Made in Canada,' and people appreciate that. You can't be a luxury brand without the history and the heritage."

Reiss then opted to change the way the company was marketing its products by focusing on telling a story about the company and its coats. The stories were based on feedback from customers and featured the tagline "Ask anyone who knows," which is a reference to any customer telling you how great the product is. "We tell the stories of the people who actually use our products. . . . People who live and work in the coldest places on earth, like Antarctica and Northern Canada, our original market."

Rick Madonik / Getty Images

The company's savvy marketing, combined with some luck, resulted in the company's coats being used in the hit movie *The Day After Tomorrow.* In addition, a number of celebrities were photographed wearing the coats, including Kate Upton on the cover of the *Sports Illustrated* swimsuit edition, former Boston Red Sox star David Ortiz, actor Matt Damon, and Lil Uzi Vert, a platinum-selling rap artist who released a song titled *Canada Goose.* As sales grew, Reiss' next decision was how to maintain momentum. Business experts wondered if the company would revisit the question of producing products in other countries or diversify by licensing the brand. Rather than diversify or license out, the younger Reiss is opting to stay the course as a niche brand manufactured in Canada. Reiss says, "I believe a lot of brands have lost an element of their soul by outsourcing to Asia. If you look at some of the world's greatest brands, like Louis Vuitton—it is all made at 27 factories in France . . . we are not a mass brand. The strongest brands in the world are true to what they say."

Reiss' plans for the company accelerated from 2013 to 2017 and included a shift away from wholesale to focusing on direct-to-consumer sales both online and in stores. Canada Goose also opened a number of flagship stores in major global cities to throughout the world including Toronto, New York, and London.

As the firm continued to grow, Reiss was looking to inject capital in the business and to profit from the firm's success. In 2013 he sold majority interest in the

[continued]

[continued]

company to Bain Capital, an American private investment firm. Under the terms of the deal, Reiss has stayed on as CEO and is a large minority shareholder. The sale of the majority interest allowed Reiss and his family to maximize value and successfully transfer ownership of the business while still maintaining some control. Reiss notes that Bain has invested a considerable amount of money into Canada Goose, which will enable the company to continue to build and grow the brand with manufacturing remaining in Canada.

In 2017, Bain Capital and Reiss moved to maximize their return on investment by taking Canada Goose public on the Toronto and New York Stock Exchanges. Bain and Reiss, who agreed to a $250 million dollar-value for Canada Goose in 2013, saw the value of the firm soar to $2.29 billion only four years later. Reiss, who sold $70 million worth of shares with the Initial Public Offering (IPO), kept 24 percent of the outstanding shares which were worth $500 million dollars at the time of the IPO.

The Canada Goose story continues after two ownership transfers and with the founding family still at the helm of the company, even after successfully harvesting their equity in the business.

CANADA GOOSE
canada-goose.com

LONG-RANGE PLANNING LO1

As mentioned in **Chapter 13**, relatively few owner-managers engage in formal long-range planning. One reason is the unpredictability of the future because of changes in the economy, technology, consumer demand, and legislation. However, one outcome that is predictable for small business is that the owner-manager will not be able to manage the business forever. Someday the business will be transferred to others or be closed down. Because of the time, effort, money, and commitment owner-managers have put into their ventures, they generally want the business to continue to grow and prosper and hope to realize a financial gain, sometimes referred to as *harvesting,* for their efforts in starting and building the organization.

To ensure this continuity for the business, owner-managers need to plan early for the time when they will no longer be in charge. Many small business owners are uncomfortable about this prospect. As a result they procrastinate, avoiding the issue until shortly before the transfer of ownership becomes a necessity. Most succession experts advise that planning should be done five to ten years in advance.[1] Given today's legislation and tax laws, such a lack of planning can be extremely costly and damaging to both the owner-manager and the new owners of the business.

In addition, succession rates, which are already rising, are predicted to increase further as many baby boomers look to exit their businesses. According to a 2017 study by BDC, roughly 60 percent of small and medium-sized business owners are over age 50, and close to 50 percent of these entrepreneurs plan on leaving their businesses in the next three years.[2] Similar succession statistics were reported as early as 2012 in the the National Entrepreneurship survey conducted by *Canadian Business* magazine. That survey found roughly 50 percent of small and medium enterprise (SMEs) owners plan to sell their business within five to ten years, with 16 percent looking to sell soon. If business owners stick to their timelines discussed in that 2012 survey, roughly 60 percent of Canadian SMEs will have changed hands by the time you are reading this text. Research conducted by the Canadian Federation of Independent Business (CFIB) supports the findings, with 71 percent of entrepreneurs reporting that they plan to sell their business within 10 years.[3] Pierre Somers, in his *The Globe and Mail* article titled "The Succession Planning Crisis: How to Transfer Your Legacy to Millennials," notes that the majority of Canada's 2.3 million firms are still owned by baby boomers, and for every two retiring business owners there is only one suitable replacement.[4] Benjamin Tal, deputy chief economist with CIBC world market, says that 310,000 Canadian SME owners plan to transfer control of their business in the next five years.[5] Some experts involved in the buying and selling of businesses, such as Brent Boyd, think the number of firms hitting the marketplace at the same time could be devastating to entrepreneurs looking to cash in on the sale of their firm. Boyd is forecasting that 80 to 90 percent of firms will not actually find a buyer.[6] Jordan Gould, a Toronto-based specialist in succession planning, echoes Boyd's comments, saying that many firms, especially those with less than $8 million a year in annual revenue, may have no one to sell to.[7]

Some experts are predicting that there will be so many businesses for sale in the coming decade that 80 to 90 percent of them will not find a buyer.
Andy Dean Photography/Shutterstock.com

The key to successfully transferring ownership of a business is planning for succession. Yet the majority of entrepreneurs do not appear to have any formal plans. In a 2016 survey by BMO Wealth Management, they found that roughly 70 percent of business owners had no formal succession plan and only eight percent of owners had an up-to-date written plan. In the National Entrepreneurship survey mentioned above, only 18 percent of respondents indicated they had a formal written plan, and 44 percent admitted to no plan at all. According to small business expert Mark Groulx, it can take years to prepare for the sale of a business.[8] Succession expert Jordan Gould suggests that many small business owners have their heads in the sand when it comes to proper succession planning. Gould notes that succession planning is at minimum a five- to 10-year process, and entrepreneurs who do not like planning for the long term lack the capacity to think about this.[9]

Given the number of businesses that could be sold in the coming decade, entrepreneurs should be familiar with the possible outcomes for the business, the relative merits of those outcomes, and some key implications of each.

ALTERNATIVES FOR THE BUSINESS

The owner-manager can anticipate four possible outcomes for the business: transferring ownership to family members, selling the business to an employee, selling the business to outsiders, and closing down the business or declaring bankruptcy. We'll discuss each option here. Regardless of which option the entrepreneur choose, before transferring ownership of a business, they should do everything possible to get the business in a condition to maximize the value of the firm. As noted earlier, this maximization of the value of the firm is sometimes referred to as *harvesting*.

SUCCESSION PLANNING

Succession planning, much like traditional business and expansion planning, involves the entrepreneur first developing alternatives and then selecting the best strategy for the firm. In the case of succession planning, most entrepreneurs want to remove themselves from their business and maximize profits. In some cases, especially in family businesses, entrepreneurs are motivated to leave control of their firm to certain individuals and may accept less money to do so. Still, the process of removing oneself from the business can be difficult for the entrepreneur and something they may have to think hard about. For example, Daniel Hershcovis, a Calgary-based CPA, states that one of his clients described the succession planning as the equivalent of being diagnosed with a terminal illness. The client revealed that he felt he was selling his identity after a lifetime of building his firm.[10]

The key steps in a strong succession plan are discussed below.

1. Plan Early and Plan for the Unexpected.

Most experts agree the sooner entrepreneurs start to plan for their exit, the better. For example, Ron Foxcroft, founder of Fox International Inc., recognized at age 55 that he needed a plan to eventually exit his business. Part of the plan should include the method or choice of exiting the business. Foxcroft, after learning neither of his sons wanted to manage the company, developed a plan where the chief operating officer would eventually take over the management of the firm.[11] The other aspect of the plan should include tax planning. In Canada, the owner and those in their family who own shares in the firm could be eligible for capital gains tax exemptions in the amount of $835,716. Doug Robbins, founder and president of Robbinex Inc., a brokerage specializing in selling businesses, says that most firms are saleable, but some need time to get their financial and management practices into a condition where they are attractive to buyers. Robbins further adds that if you are in a hurry to sell your business, the price you receive might be much less than it is worth.[12]

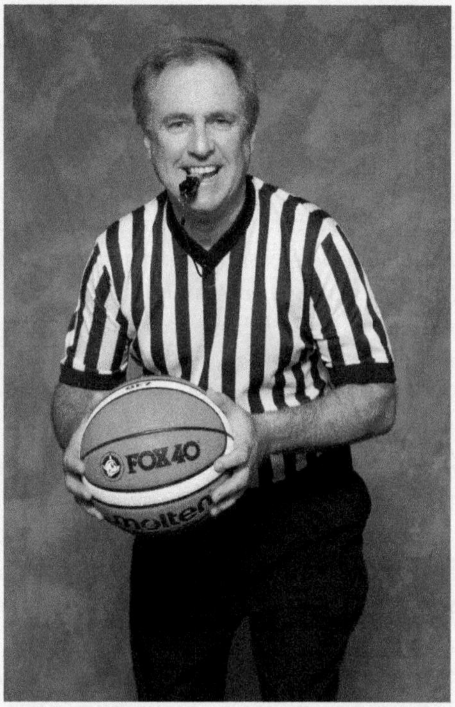

Ron Foxcroft is among the minority of entrepreneurs who start succession planning early. When neither of his sons expressed interest in taking over his business, he looked internally for a successor and found one in his Chief Operating Officer.

Photo courtesy of Fox 40

Succession plans should also plan for the unexpected. While most owners envision a smooth transition in which they gradually leave the firm, owners should have plans to manage sudden illness or even death. For example, when Jack Simpson, then–owner-operator of **CANA Construction Ltd.** died unexpectedly, he didn't have a clear successor in place. While his son, John, did ultimately take control of the business, the younger Simpson did engage in a dispute with his sister over the management of the firm. As a result of his experience, John has established a clear contingency plan for his company, taking into consideration untimely illnesses or death. He updates his emergency succession plan each year, taking into consideration his senior management team and the skills and ambitions of his children.[13]

2. Start to Gradually Remove Yourself from the Business.

Many entrepreneurs, especially those in smaller businesses, are so involved that their company could not run without them. If entrepreneurs want to sell their firm, then they must start to build a management team or train employees to make decisions without them. Owners want to ensure the business can be run efficiently and effectively when they are gone. For example, Tom Duffey owns and operates **Tom Duffey Hockey Schools** throughout Atlantic Canada. The name alone and the fact that he manages all on-ice sessions will make it difficult for him to sell his firm. As one business consultant said, what value does Tom Duffey Hockey Schools have without Tom Duffey? Entrepreneurs should also start to create a business plan or operations guide outlining how they manage their firm. This can be included in a sales package. Buyers will want to know about key suppliers, employees, customers, and internal plans and practices.

3. Start to Prepare Financial Statements.

Potential purchasers of a business are normally interested in the cash flow a company can provide. Thus, purchasers pay particular attention to EBITDA, or earnings before interest, taxes, depreciation, and amortization. As discussed in **Chapter 5** on buying a business, purchasers will often look at net income or EBITA and multiply the amount 2 to 10 times to determine a rough value of the firm. Often when entrepreneurs are preparing financial statements, especially income tax returns, they overstate expenses by running personal items through the company, engaging in travel to conferences or professional development events, or employing family members who do not play an active role in the firm. Entrepreneurs who are looking to maximize the value of their firm should try to increase their EBITDA as much as possible by growing sales and eliminating unessential expenses. Richard Niedermayer, a partner in Stewart McKelvey notes, business owners should keep a clean balance sheet, grow revenue, manage costs and put reputable managers in place if they are looking to make their company look like a good target.

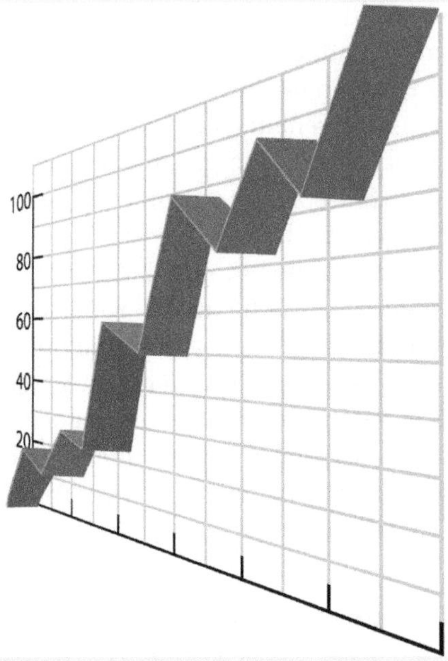

Prospective purchasers of a company want to see steady, reliable sales.

Michaeldb/Dreamstime.com

4. Continue to Invest in the Firm

Prospective purchasers will want to see that the business is being maintained and the owner is investing in the company. Very few prospective buyers want to purchase a business with decaying assets or one which has failed to pursue opportunities. Commercial real estate agent Kenzie MacDonald notes, "Many entrepreneurs who are looking to sell their business are trying to keep as much money as possible by limiting investment in the firm as they start to consider selling the company. At the same time, they want to maximize the sales price. What they don't realize is the two are counterproductive. If you limit investment, you will usually end up with a lower sale price for your company." MacDonald advises that the bigger payout is in the sale of the business and entrepreneurs should continue to invest in their firm as they plan for their departure. This is exactly what Sydney, Nova Scotia, entrepreneur Chris Neville did with his spa business. Although Neville's main focus was on real estate, he acquired two spas as a way to diversify his holdings. After realizing the spa business wasn't for him, he continued to invest in the buildings and create promotions to build a loyal clientele. His continued investment enabled Neville to sell the spa businesses at a premium a few years later.[14]

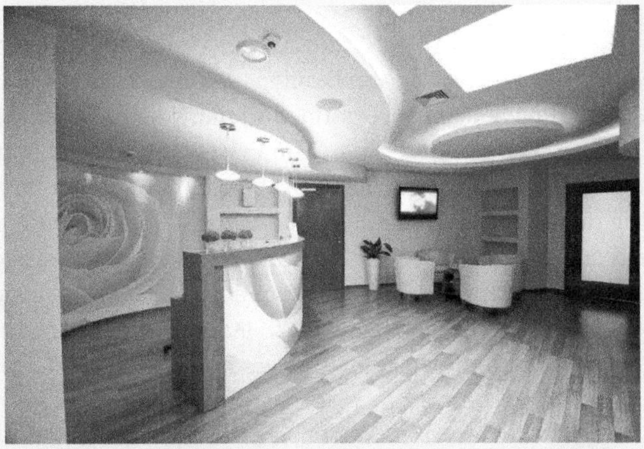

Entrepreneur Chris Neville realized he didn't want to be in the spa business after acquiring two firms in Sydney, Nova Scotia. Rather than sell them quickly, Neville continued to invest in the businesses, which made them more attractive to purchasers.

Photo 22319735 © Sebastian Czapnik - Dreamstime.com

5. Grow Stable Revenue.

As stated briefly above, part of any succession plan should include maximizing incoming revenue. Of particular importance is regular revenue or income that occurs time after time. Prospective buyers like to know there is consistent revenue.

6. Get an Evaluation of the Firm.

One of the biggest shocks to entrepreneurs is discovering what their business is actually worth. Some entrepreneurs describe getting the first offer as a "slap-in-the-face moment" and as a result some business owners decide not to proceed with investigating the sale of their company. Business consultant Mark Groulx says for many entrepreneurs the value of their firm puts their pride on the line. "It's the ultimate measure of what [entrepreneurs] did with their company." Michael Lamm, a merger and acquisition consultant states, "[Entrepreneurs] think their company is terrific, has all these bells and whistles, and is worth an enormous amount of money. When we tell them, 'Here's the reality,' some owners are able to accept that. But others say, 'I'm not going to sell my company, ever!' They'll take it to the grave."[15] By getting an evaluation done in advance, entrepreneurs can get a true sense of what their firm is worth and, in some cases, the time to recover from the shock of the valuation.

Consultant Michael Lamm reveals that when some entrepreneurs hear what their business is worth, they are so upset they consider it a slap in the face.

© esolla/iStockPhoto

7. Consider Hiring Professionals.

Often buyers, especially buyers of larger companies, will have lawyers and accountants evaluating a potential purchase decision. Entrepreneurs may want to bring in consultants to assist them in not only getting their firm in a position to be sold but also helping negotiate the process. Business brokers, lawyers, and many accountants specialize in this area.

TRANSFERRING OWNERSHIP TO FAMILY MEMBERS LO2

Keeping the business in the family is a common method of transferring the business. Many Canadian family businesses have been successful, and many small business owners want to pass the business they have inherited or built to their children. In a 2016 **Pricewaterhouse-Coopers (PwC)** survey, 38 percent of business owners planned to pass the ownership of the company to family members. Interestingly, and perhaps reflective of the aging demographic of family-run businesses and the increased seriousness of their succession plans, this number is significantly lower than the 55 percent who planned on passing their business to family members in 2012. Another interesting statistic is the rising number of family-business owners who plan on bringing in professional management as they work to leave ownership of the business in the hands of the family. In 2014 only 11 percent of family business owners noted they would bring in professional managers and this number has increased to 27 percent in 2016.[16]

Still, few owners of family businesses are planning for succession. In the above-mentioned PwC survey, only 18 percent of business owners have a formal succession plan. This evidence mirrors a recent survey by the Canadian Association of Family Enterprise (CAFE), which discovered 80 percent of family businesses had no formal succession plans. These findings are echoed in another recent survey conducted by *Canadian Business* and Deloitte, which showed that only 17 percent of family-owned businesses in Canada have succession plans.[17] In some cases, this transfer occurs with considerable tension—as evident in the McCain dispute discussed in **Small Business in Action 14-1**.[18] Because a family-owned business has many unique characteristics, it is important to review the problems and potential solutions in managing this type of organization.

Estimates of the extent of ownership within a single family indicate that approximately 90 percent of all businesses in Canada are family owned and family operated, and employ close to 60 percent of the Canadian workforce.[19] Although a majority of these firms are small businesses (see **Small Business in Action 14-2**), a significant number of family-owned large companies exist. Almost 35 percent of the Fortune 500 companies are owned or controlled by a single family.[20] In Canada, family involvement in business is also significant as approximately 40 percent of the largest 100 companies on the Toronto Stock Exchange (TSX) have handed control to a second or even later generation.[21] One survey of the 500 fastest-growing private corporations in

SMALL BUSINESS IN ACTION 14-1

McCAIN FOODS DISPUTE

One of the most interesting and legendary succession planning disputes in Canada occurred at McCain Foods when the two founding brothers, Harrison and Wallace McCain, battled over who would replace them as CEO.

Keith Homan/Shutterstock.com

Harrison and Wallace McCain, former owners of **McCain Foods**, a billion-dollar frozen-food empire, provide an example of how difficult succession planning can be. For years, McCain Foods' two founding brothers co-managed the company. The brothers often appeared to be a perfect management match, with Harrison, the extrovert, assuming the role of spokesman for the company, focusing on sales and expansion, and managing the overseas operation, while Wallace, three years Harrison's junior and an introvert, spent his time running the North American operations and looking after the details of company business. The two brothers were co-CEOs, with each possessing a veto over final decisions; between them they controlled 66 percent of the company's shares, with the remaining 33 percent divided among their two late brothers' children.

The company successfully ran this way for over 30 years, reaching sales of approximately $3.5 billion in 1993 with operations in 11 countries. Together the brothers were a perfect management match and best friends. Unfortunately, this all unravelled when the touchy subject of succession came to the forefront. Both men had sons who worked within the company at one time or another, but only Wallace's son, Michael, had managed to climb the corporate ladder and gain enough experience to take over as CEO. Wallace was becoming adamant behind closed doors that if the pair was to name a successor, Michael should receive the job. Harrison disagreed; he thought Michael was still too inexperienced and lacked people skills. He felt that their late brother's son, Allison, would be a better choice but admitted Allison needed more experience before he would be ready to lead the company. As an alternative, Harrison pushed to bring in an outsider (not a family member) to take over the reins of the company until Michael matured or Allison was ready to assume the leadership role.

The situation came to a head when Wallace flew to the company's head office in the United States to appoint Michael as CEO of McCain Food's U.S. operations. To outsiders, the move made sense because Michael had held a number of high-level management positions within the company and was currently serving as president of McCain's U.S. frozen juice company where he engineered a turnaround, reversing years of losses and turning the company into a money maker. But few people knew that Harrison was dead set against the promotion and asked Wallace not to proceed with the announcement: "I never claimed Michael was stupid or that he was lazy. I just felt that he wasn't ready and that his appointment made us look bad to the professional managers we employed around the world. I told Wallace his son's promotion wasn't justified and was far too nepotistic." Wallace proceeded with the announcement and, for the first time, ignored the long-time mutual veto that either brother could use at his discretion.

After this, it was only a matter of time before significant changes were made to the company's management team. The board of directors had the power to terminate one of the brothers, and Harrison gathered support from the other family members to successfully oust Wallace from his position as co-CEO. Wallace countered with a lawsuit, and the two brothers agreed to have Judge Ronald Stevenson adjudicate the matter with the binding authority of a court but behind closed doors. After hearing the case, the judge ruled that the board did have the legal right to oust Wallace but offered some recommendations with his ruling that might be an acceptable compromise to both sides. He suggested that both brothers resign as co-CEOs as soon as an outsider could be found to fill the role, the brothers should stay on as consultants, family members with ambition should be patient, outside directors should be brought in to sit on the board, and the family should consider going public. Harrison refused the compromise that Wallace was now willing to accept, and he fired his brother.

Rather than stay in New Brunswick, Wallace moved to Toronto and tried to find an alternative exit from the family business. He tried to sell his shares but could not find any takers outside the family who were willing to become a minority shareholder in a family enterprise. He considered selling his shares to Harrison, but they could never agree on a price. Finally, he used the

[continued]

[continued]

leverage of his shares and his strong business connections to acquire the financing to purchase Maple Leaf Foods, a competitor of McCain Foods'. His son, Michael, soon joined him under the Maple Leaf banner, taking over the role of president and CEO. Harrison and Wallace continued their feud almost up to the time of Harrison's death. Wallace died a short time later. Michael McCain is still the CEO of Maple Leaf, and Allison McCain, Harrison's choice of successor, has taken over as chairman of McCain's board of directors, although the day-to-day operations are managed by an outside CEO.

Discussion Questions

1. Are you surprised by any elements in the case above? Which elements did you find surprising, and why?
2. What type of compromise would have been possible to avoid such a lengthy dispute?
3. Do you think non-family members working in the company would have been surprised or objected to Michael McCain assuming the role of CEO? Why or why not?
4. Were you surprised to learn that the brothers continued their feud almost up to the time of Harrison's death?

the United States undertaken by *Inc.* and *USA Today* found that 33 percent of spouses and 28 percent of children are involved in family business operations.[22] Listed below are some facts: consider that Canadian family businesses

- Account for 80 to 90 percent of firms
- Generate more than 60 percent of GDP
- Employ, directly and indirectly, around 6 million people
- Create 50 percent of all new jobs
- Represent roughly 40 percent of the largest 100 public companies started as family businesses (many still are)
- Outperform non-family businesses
- Stay in existence longer than non-family firms
- Generate approximately $1.3 trillion in revenue every year

SMALL BUSINESS IN ACTION 14-2

SUCCESSFUL FAMILY BUSINESS

Before George Thomson, founder of **Paradise Island Foods**, passed the family business on to his two sons, Len and Kevin, he insisted that they first prove they were assets to the business. Len, now president of the company which is based in Nanaimo, British Columbia, says that his father wanted them to first gain hands-on experience in the food industry, as well as learn to work for other people. The Thomson sons first learned the ropes in grocery retailing in other companies and then moved up the ladder at Paradise Island Foods, before finally taking over their father's enterprise.

baibaz/Shutterstock.com

The company worked closely with a chartered accountant and lawyer to structure a succession plan to help them through the business ownership transition. The transition was made over three years so that the sons could reach their comfort level and make adjustments. They had experts work on tax planning, one of the more complex matters in the business. (As stated elsewhere in this text, businesses can benefit from a third-party point of view, and BDC Consulting offers entrepreneurs expertise regarding transition planning.)

Communicating effectively to customers, suppliers, and employees in advance is a key factor in the success of the ownership transition. To prepare key people for the transition, and ensure there wouldn't be any surprises, Thomson shared his plans with the senior management team six months in advance. Communicating to customers and suppliers was crucial in the process because of the strong rapport Thomson had built with them.

Today, the Thomsons have proven themselves to be capable owners by bringing different strengths to the business. Kevin, vice-president of operations, is a natural for sales development, while Len is more focused on the production side of the business. The business is achieving steady growth, and the Thomsons have seen highly positive results since taking over.

Discussion Questions

1. What are some of the benefits to planning for succession as outlined in the case above?
2. Did the family miss any steps in their planning process? If so, what steps were missed?
3. If you worked in a management capacity in the family business, knowing the intent to leave the company in the hands of family members, would you continue working for the firm? Why or why not?

Despite the predominance of family businesses in Canadian society, relatively few survive into the second and third generations. The *Canadian Business* and Deloitte survey found only 25 percent of businesses make it to the second generation and 11 percent reach the third.[23] This succession problem also appears to be occurring more frequently today because many entrepreneurs who launched in an economic boom 30 years ago are now nearing retirement.[24] What are the reasons for this apparent lack of continuity? One of the major problems occurs in family businesses when the firm reaches the second and third generations, and shares of the firm continue to be diluted among family members. For example, the Irving Group of New Brunswick, which was founded by legendary business icon KC Irving, originally had a simple succession plan. KC noted that his three sons would equally split the shares in the firm, and the oldest would be in charge.[25] While this plan initially worked, as his children's children had families, shares in the firm became more and more divided. Recent news stories have discussed the internal succession problems as the growing family struggles to create a clear succession strategy. In 2017, Erin Anderssen published a particularly insightful story about the stress succession planning has had on the family as Kenneth Irving discussed the impact on his mental health with the journalist. The story cites both the difficulties and pressure involved in passing on a successful company from generation to generation.[26] Observation also shows that if some unique considerations in operating the family business are not recognized and planned for, they can cause considerable difficulties for the enterprise. Family involvement in a business may have a detrimental effect not only on the business but also on family relationships. Additionally, unique challenges result when spouses own and operate a business together. Statistics Canada estimates that 31 percent of all self-employed persons have their spouses as partners.[27]

Planning for Succession in the Family.

The owner-manager has both a difficult task and an excellent opportunity in preparing children to become involved in the business. Some difficulties include providing proper training, adequate motivation, and a supportive atmosphere so that the child is able and willing to come into the business. Research shows that fewer than 50 percent of children who worked in family businesses expect to return after receiving their college or university education, and only 20 percent plan to return to the business within five years of their graduation.[28] For example, Dani Reiss, the current CEO of Canada Goose Jackets and the feature of the **Small Business Profile** at the beginning of this chapter, noted that he had no intention to work for the family business once he graduated from university. Dani started to work there as a summer job, but once he became involved with the firm, he fell in love with the stories associated with the jackets.[29] Other studies indicate that 70 percent of family businesses are either liquidated or sold after the founder retires.[30] It is apparently difficult for the parent to instill in the child the personal interest in the business the parent has. One school of thought is that parents may take too passive a role in attempting to interest their children in the business. They assume the children will find a profession more interesting and rewarding for them.[31]

Another common scenario is that of the parent-owner who is unwilling to give up control or allow the child a say in the business. For example, Shannon Bowen-Smed had to threaten her mother with her resignation from the family company if she continued to dismiss her input in the business. Bowen-Smed had joined Calgary-based **Bowen Workforce Solutions Inc.** in the early 1980s and had worked in more progressive jobs but she wanted to expand and diversify the company. She eventually took control of operations and has grown annual sales from $1 million to $33 million. Conversely, it is also common for the inexperienced child to want to make changes the parent believes will be detrimental to the business.

Running a family business also offers a great opportunity to provide on-the-job training and background for the child that is not otherwise possible. The parent-owner can also assess the child's progress and level of preparation over a longer period than would be possible if hiring an outsider to manage the business. In addition, the owner-manager's business philosophy and style may be taught to the child who is apprenticing for management and ownership of the business.[32]

Figure 14-1 provides questions that should be asked before transferring the business to an heir.

FIGURE 14-1 **Mom and Pop Quiz: How Succession-Ready Is Your Company?**

Consider this a final exam that your family business should take before it advances from one generation to the next. Developed by Scott E. Freidman, an attorney, author, and consultant specializing in family-business issues, the Family Business Scorecard is a comprehensive, 100-question survey designed to identify problem areas, especially those that can directly affect a planned succession. "Three types of people should take this quiz," Friedman explains. "Adult family members who work in the business, adult family members who don't work in the business but are stakeholders, and key non-family employees and advisors, such as the firm's lawyer, accountant, and financial planner. How much of a consensus there is among the participants can be as revealing as the answers themselves." We have adapted 10 yes-or-no questions from the quiz to help give readers a quick take on how they are doing.

1. Our family has customized its decision-making process to require various levels of consent (by different family members or outside advisors) for issues of varying significance.
2. Our key non-family employees are satisfied with the manner in which family members are brought into and employed by our business.
3. All family members, regardless of sex or birth order, will be considered as possible successors for the business.
4. Our succession criteria include formal education, job experience outside our business, and job experience inside our business with increasing responsibility.
5. A written agreement establishes rules for buying, selling, and transferring ownership interest in our business.
6. If our business leader suffered a catastrophe, our family would be prepared to react.
7. Spouses of family members have a meaningful forum in which to air their views on subjects affecting the business.
8. Adult family members have begun working on their estate plan.
9. Senior family members approaching retirement age look forward to pursuing interests outside our business.
10. Our family has considered the merits of adopting an alternative dispute-resolution mechanism in the event of family conflict.

If you answered no to five or more of these questions, or if the people in your company who took the test gave different answers to the same questions more than four times, your business would benefit from a more complete analysis by an advisor.

Tax and Legal Implications of Transferring the Business to Family Members.

Increasingly complex considerations in transferring a business to heirs are the legal and tax implications. One specific tax consequence of transfers of business ownership within a family concerns capital gains. In Canada, one-half of the capital gain (defined as the increase in value of the asset since acquisition of the business or since 1972, whichever is shorter) on the sale is added to the income of the person disposing of the asset (the business). This rule applies a "deemed disposition" rule (to family) in that the business is deemed to have been sold at market price whether or not the market price was actually paid.

SMALL BUSINESS IN ACTION 14-3

FAMILY SUCCESSION—WHEN FAIR IS NOT EQUAL

Estate planning for parents is often simple. If they have two children, their estate is divided equally, 50 percent to one child and 50 percent to the other. The same formula can be applied when there are three children, four children, and so forth. Essentially, in the minds of both the parents and the children, fair and equal are a one-in-the-same concept. What is equal is fair, and what is fair is equal.

This principle does not always hold true when there is a family business as part of the estate. Often the parent's desire is to see the business stay in the family and suddenly what is fair may in fact not be equal. Consider the Oswald family dairy farming business in Steinbach, Manitoba, which is currently being run by third-generation farmer Brent Oswald. Brent, who has two other brothers, was the only family member interested in working in the business. After he was married, his parents began the succession process, which included evaluating all the farm's assets. Once this was completed, the asset value was frozen, and new shares in the farm were issued. Brent noted that this was done to ensure he could pay for the assets over time and the business could be flexible. The distribution though was not equal, which Brent's father, Edwood, explained to his other children and their spouses. Edwood gave the other brothers lump sum cheques and stated that Brent was financially tied to the family farm going forward and if the farm fails then he would lose everything while the brothers received a cash payment which was not hinged on the success or failure of the farming business. Edwood states that this unequal distribution of his estate was not initially appreciated by his other children.

The Oswald succession, described above, is similar to the unfolding story of Don Sundgaard's succession planning with his third-generation poultry farm. Sundgaard, who has two daughters and a son, Trent, says only his son was interested in pursuing farming for a career. Sundgaard encouraged his son to come back to the farm but only after he met two conditions: first he had to attend post-secondary school to further his education, and second, he had to work for someone else for a period of time. Trent followed his father's guidance, earning a renewable resource degree followed by several years working for various farms, including an aquaculture farm and large poultry operation in the Bahamas. When Trent returned to the farm, the succession planning process started, and while not completed, Don notes that there will not be an equal distribution of assets. He says that the value of his land and farming quota has gone up significantly since he took over the farm and that it would be nearly impossible for Trent to pay market value for the assets and to continue the farm.

Discussion Questions

1. Why is the continuation of the family business often more important than the equal distribution of assets to the owner of the business?
2. Given that most family businesses fail, would it not be more prudent to harvest the business at the highest valuation possible and equally divide the money among the children?
3. Do you think it is ethical and fair to value the continuation of the family business over an equal distribution of the estate? Why or why not?
4. Imagine you are one of the children in a family business. Your parents wish to keep the business running, so they are dividing the estate in the following way: 50 percent is going to one of your siblings while you are your other sibling each receive 25 percent. Would you be happy with this distribution? Why or why not?

In the past, the federal government allowed a tax-free rollover or capital gains deferral to a spouse and children up to a maximum capital gain of $200,000. This applied to Canadian-controlled private corporations. If the heir sold the shares (or business) to someone outside the family, the capital gain would be realized and a resulting tax liability incurred. Canadian tax law also allows for a $813,600 lifetime capital gains exemption. This provision allows for the transfer of ownership of the business with little capital gains consequence, whether or not the business is an incorporated company.

Obviously, these changes have affected the tax consequences of transferring the business to heirs. Although most of these changes have been positive from the point of view of the small business, they are complex and may differ by province and territory. Therefore, counsel should be sought from a legal or tax expert before making a decision in this area.

Another important task when considering transferring or selling the business is determining its value. Assistance should be sought from an accountant or a member of the Canadian Institute of Chartered Business Valuators.

Methods of Transferring the Business to Family Members.

In deciding which method to use in transferring all or part of the business to the heirs, owner-managers first need to clarify their own objectives in making the transfer. Some common transfer-related objectives are the following:

- Owner-managers want to keep a reasonable amount of control over the business until the heirs are of an age and competence level to assume their responsibilities.
- Although owner-managers want to maintain control of the business, they also want the heirs to maintain their interest in and commitment to the business.
- Owner-managers want to distribute the business assets (ownership) so that the heirs (if more than one) will recognize this distribution as fair.
- Owner-managers want sufficient access to income or assets from the transfer of the business to maintain an adequate standard of living.
- Owner-managers want to achieve an orderly transfer of the business to minimize the tax consequences for both parties.

Some of the most common methods of transferring ownership to the heir(s) are discussed next.

Through a Will.

When the transfer is made through a will, ownership of the business does not pass to the heir until the owner dies. This method may satisfy the owner's objective of maintaining control of the business, but it fails to address any of the other objectives mentioned. For example, serious tax consequences may arise if the business is unincorporated. In such a situation, the previous owner's income is calculated at the date of death. If the business has an irregular business cycle and a death occurs at the wrong time of the year, a large income (and higher tax liability) may result. The heirs would then have to deal with this tax liability.

Purchase and Sale of the Business.

This method may not satisfy the owner's objectives unless it takes place gradually over a number of years. Such an agreement can remain flexible within the family to accomplish the objectives of both the owner and the heirs. A "deemed disposition" is viewed to have taken place at market value whether or not that amount was actually paid. Purchasing the business gradually may provide an incentive for the heir and also allow the parent to maintain the desired control for the required time.

Gifting Program.

In the absence of gift taxes, part or all of the business may be gifted to the heirs. The most common method of doing this is gradually, over several years. This option is likely feasible only if the owner is not dependent on proceeds of the sale for their income.

Life Estate.

A life estate is used primarily when the significant assets are real property. This method transfers the ownership or title of land or buildings to the heir, with the condition that the previous owner has a position of control until they die. The extent of control can diminish as the heir becomes more involved in the business. Immediately on the parent's death, the title automatically passes to the heir. This method accomplishes many of the aforementioned objectives.

Joint Ownership of the Business.

In this method of succession, the parent can transfer shares of the business to the child (if the business is incorporated) or transfer an ownership interest to the child in the form of a partnership (if it is not incorporated). In both situations, the parent can retain control over the business by providing the child with a different form of ownership, such as a different class of share (corporation) and a limited partnership interest (not incorporated).

In a corporation, this type of arrangement may also provide the beneficial tax advantage of freezing the value of the shares. In both methods, the voting or controlling interest may be transferred gradually as the interests, abilities, and conditions warrant.

Potential Problems in a Family Business.

Several problems may surface in the family-owned business. Recognition of these potential difficulties is essential for the owner-manager and even for the other family members so that they can take steps to prevent problems.

Over-reliance on the Founder.

Most family businesses remain highly dependent for their success on their leader, who is typically the founder of the business. Most have no contingency plan covering the disability or death of this person.

Higher Emotional Level.

Because of existing family relationships, some of the business decisions and evaluations may be more emotionally charged than they would be in a non-family setting. For example, the evaluation of performance or supervision affecting a family member employee may be biased positively or negatively because of the relationship. Family members often bring their personal feelings and stress to the business, which often precludes them from making objective decisions.

Blurring of Roles.

In many family-owned businesses, the personal and business roles of individual family members may become blurred. For example, the chief executive officer of the business may in practice not really be in control because of a subordinate role in the family. This often occurs when children have taken over the business, but their parents still exert informal control over both the children and the business. For example, Linda Hasenfratz, who succeeded her father as CEO of Ontario-based **Linamar Group**, recalls the conversation when her father first approached her about assuming the role of CEO. Her response was to ask him how his involvement in the business would change without the CEO title, and he replied it wouldn't change. Rather then leave the company, or operate without clarity in roles, the father and daughter team crafted a list of tasks he would handle as executive chairman, ultimately leaving the day-to-day management of the firm to Linda.[33] Linda has done exceptionally well. Since assuming the CEO title, she has increased revenue from $1.3 billion to $6.5 billion and has diversified Linamar from an auto-parts company to a global manufacturer of highly engineered products. Her accomplishments resulted in her being named Canada's Outstanding CEO of the Year by the *Financial Post* in 2018.[34]

Incompetence.

The problem of incompetence may arise in the family business in two areas. The first involves the relative who assumes the position of chief executive simply because of birthright. The experience, education, intelligence, and work ethic required to manage the business successfully may be lacking. The second situation involves hiring incompetent family members. Helping out an incompetent family member not only may lead to disappointment and damage to the business but can also have a disruptive effect on the non-family employees.

Non-family Employee Attitudes.

One common characteristic of family-owned businesses is high turnover of non-family employees. Many young employees see no chance for promotion to management in the company because they are not part of the family. As a result, they may gain experience in the business and then leave for other organizations that offer the opportunity for promotion.

Objectives of Family Owners.

In most family businesses, more than one member of the family owns shares or has an ownership interest in the business. Because these owners may be from different generations, have different levels of involvement in the business, and have various backgrounds and needs, differences of opinion regarding the operations of the business are common.

For example, owners who are actively involved in building up the business often want to reinvest more of the earnings in the business. The non-active owners or shareholders, however, may want their share of the profits to be distributed as dividends or payments to them.

Objectives regarding the growth of the business may also differ. Sometimes younger members of the family want to expand the business or make capital expenditures that older family owners are more conservative or cautious about making. Both situations can lead to conflicts that have a detrimental effect on the long-term progress of the business.

Principles of Success for Family Businesses.

The preceding section has demonstrated the many difficulties that can arise in a family business. As illustrated, these difficulties can be detrimental to the success of the business and damaging to family relationships. If the owner-manager is concerned about succession, planning for it should commence immediately rather than waiting until health or other circumstances force or prevent action. If you are involved in a family business or are contemplating bringing family members into the business, the practices discussed below may help prevent some of these difficulties from arising.

Recognize the Importance of Objectivity.

Evaluations and supervision involving family members should be done objectively. Even if tempted to do otherwise, the owner-manager must separate family discussions and emotions from business activities. Care should be taken to ensure that consistent policies are followed for both family and non-family employees. Many owner-managers have found it essential to separate their children physically and functionally from themselves and one another to prevent such difficulties from arising.

Create Clear Role Structures.

The solution to the problem of the blurring of roles may be difficult to implement, because much of the control may be exerted informally. A clear definition of the roles, objectives, and responsibilities of all associated family members may help solve the problem. Separation of business and family goals and systems has also been recommended to alleviate this concern.[35]

Ensure Competence.

Because an incompetent owner-manager can spell disaster for the business, providing the heir(s) with technical and practical training, along with increasing decision-making authority, is vital. Often family members are encouraged to work in the family business at a young age learning the business from the ground up. This is what happened in the Glowczewski family business, Tradition Fine Foods Ltd., which is based in Toronto. Both of the founder's children, Thomas and Catherine, started working in the company as teenagers. Catherine went to work in the office and Thomas, who eventually took over as President from his father Peter, started working on the factory floor. Thomas says, "We literally learned things from the ground up." Both children attribute their success to being involved in the company at a young age because that enabled them to better understand the business.[36] Often family member are encouraged to acquire some necessary skills outside the business at a college, a university, or another business before returning to become fully involved. Many potential inheritors of businesses appear to follow this route to the ownership of the family business.[37] For example, both Thomas and Catherine Glowczewski earned their MBAs from York University. If a competent family member is not available, the remaining family owners may be able to persuade the owner-manager to let a more capable individual run the day-to-day affairs of the company.

If training does not improve the performance of incompetent relatives, but for family reasons it is not possible to let the employee go, some owner-managers place such an employee in a position where they can do the least harm to the company.

Provide Incentives for Non-family Employees.

To maintain the loyalty of non-family employees and ensure that they stay with the company, the owner-manager will need to devise rewards and incentives. These incentives can be financial or may involve including employees in decision making and educational programs. It may still be impossible to retain an energetic young employee who wants to eventually rise to the top of the organization unless the owner-manager is prepared to give up some of the ownership of or authority in the business.

Clarify Objectives of Family Owners.

To prevent disharmony resulting from differing objectives of family members, it is important to formally clarify the long- and short-term objectives of the company. These might include objectives for such areas as expansion and distribution of profits. Some firms distribute a set percentage of profits in dividends or reinvest a specified amount back into the business annually.

Keep Communication Lines Open and Establish a Dispute Resolution Process.

Perhaps the most effective aspect of operating a family business successfully is open communication. Given many potential areas of conflict, differences of opinion must be communicated to the relevant parties before they develop into a serious problem. Formalized objectives, plans, roles, and procedures can accomplish this. Still, even with careful planning disputes will arise. Family business owners have noted that having a clear dispute resolution process in place is both prudent and effective in resolving conflict. Family business experts note that conflicts resolutions could include bringing the dispute to a to a family council, a board of advisors, or in some cases having a lawyer or mediator make a decision.

SELLING THE BUSINESS TO AN EMPLOYEE LO3

Another option for transferring the ownership of a firm is to sell the business to employees. Advance planning is still crucial for this type of succession, known as ESOP, or employee share ownership plan. Tomivino's, a Halifax pizzeria, recently went through a successful employee purchase where a couple working for the company bought the firm from its founder. The following steps should be a part of such a succession plan for an employee:

- Identify the time frame and exit strategy.
- Develop a plan to maximize the value of the business and minimize the tax effects before the transfer date.
- Choose the successor.
- Make yourself replaceable. Install the procedures that will allow the company to grow without you.
- Find a way to fund the transition, such as debt financing or subordinate financing.
- Introduce the successor to clients, suppliers, and other contacts.
- Make sure that the new owner's vision ensures the continuity of the business.
- Manage the possible financial, fiscal, legal, and other impacts of the transition process, drawing on the support of professionals.

SELLING THE BUSINESS TO OUTSIDERS

If owner-managers are not able or do not want to keep the business in the family, they may decide to sell all or part of the business to someone outside the family. This action, of course, could be taken at any time, not just when the owner-manager is ready to retire. Often owners sell the business as a way to maximize their return on their investment of time and capital. For example, Jonathan Latsky has sold two companies, including the recent sale of **Student Awards Inc.**, a Toronto-based scholarship-search website he co-owned. Latsky says selling a business is a way to exchange ownership or equity for money: "I'm always open to a discussion if I feel there's a good ROI for my investment, that might sound crass, but that's what it is."[38]

One possible outcome of selling the business may apply to a partner or other owner. As mentioned in **Chapter 4**, a buy/sell clause should be a part of the partnership agreement. This clause should be carefully worded to account for future differences in the value of the firm.

Sometimes small businesses are purchased by larger companies. The acquiring company is usually looking to expand or capitalize on some unique advantage or capability the small business has. For example, purchasing a small business may allow a company to capitalize on such strengths as a unique product, market access, or expertise it could not otherwise obtain. Dean Hartman, founder and president of Nubody's Fitness Centres Inc., recently sold his growing business to **GoodLife Fitness Clubs**. Hartman, who built Nubody's Fitness into the recognized leader in Atlantic Canadian exercise clubs, with 26 clubs, 750 employees, and 50,000 active members, sold to a national firm that was looking to grow. Through the purchase of Nubody's, Goodlife gets established exercise clubs and revenue from 50,000 members.[39] Similarly, Lori Van Opstal, owner of Cambridge-based Your Advantage Staffing Consultants Inc., an employment agency for truck drivers, became aware that a larger rival—Protrans Personnel of Mississauga—wanted to expand. Opstal contacted Protrans and negotiated a deal in less than one day to sell her firm.[40] In some situations, the owner-manager of the smaller business is retained in the organization. Sometimes this works well because the owner-manager can help the buyer run the firm, but in some cases, it does not work, because the entrepreneur has difficulty transitioning to an employee. For example, surfboard designer Corran Addison was successfully running his Montréal-based firm Imagine Surf, but he lacked the capital to fuel growth. When he was approached by Manhattan Beach, a California-based company, with a $2 million offer to buy the brand, invest in the company, and retain him as an employee, he jumped at the chance. He sold his controlling share in the business and moved to California where he assumed the role of an employee. Within a year, he started having some difficulties with Manhattan Beach's management, the relationship worsened, and Manhattan Beach eventually sold the company for slightly more than they paid for it.[41]

Dean Hartman, founder of Nubody's Fitness Centres Inc., Atlantic Canada's largest fitness club, sold his business to GoodLife fitness, a national chain that wanted to expand in the region.

Jeff Whyte/Shutterstock.com

Sometimes the owner-manager may want to sell only a part of the business. This is accomplished much more easily if the business is incorporated to allow a share transfer to take place. In such a case, the owner-manager may be able to retain control over the business while obtaining capital needed as payment for the shares.

GOING PUBLIC

Going public is another potential exit or harvesting strategy for an entrepreneur. Essentially the entrepreneur sells a percentage of their business to the public. This process is called an *initial public offering (IPO)* and the corporate status changes from a private to a public company. Entrepreneurs who successfully go public often maximize the value of their firm and get access to capital to pursue future growth. This is exactly what happened in the Canada Goose story in the **Small Business Profile** at the beginning of this chapter. Sometimes owners regret the move to go public rather than selling shares privately, as public companies face increased scrutiny and pressure from shareholders. For example, HomeAway co-founder and former CEO Brian Sharples noted in 2014 that his company needed to invest more in marketing as new competitors such as Airbnb had become the go-to website for finding home-sharing properties. Shareholders and investment firms almost immediately began criticizing the decision, and his company's share price declined. Sharples notes he spent considerable time explaining his decision to investors and his board. It was only after the marketing campaign began—and became successful—that Sharples was able to stop justifying his decision and redirect his energy.[42] Sharples went on to sell HomeAway to Expedia in late 2016 for $3.8 billion.[43] **Table 14-1** illustrates a comparison of public versus private placement. Going public may also allow control of the business to remain with the owner-manager if more than 50 percent of the shares are not sold.

The business should address the following issues if it is planning an IPO:[44]

- Improve the company's overall capital structure and financial performance.
- Review staff needs, including the need for a strong management team.
- Strengthen the organization through the purchase or sale of particular business units.
- Structure the board to include strong outside directors.
- Plan for effective distribution of earnings.

TABLE 14-1 Implications of Selling Shares

	GOING PUBLIC	PRIVATE PLACEMENT
Shareholders	Many new shareholders	Few investors
Importance of earnings	High	Low
Importance of stock performance	Short term	Long term
Investor communication required	Extensive	Limited
Board of directors	Independent members	Strategic members

One or more of the following characteristics may indicate that the small business is in a favourable position to go public:[45]

- The company is in a popular, specialized market.
- The company is in an above-average growth position.
- The business has a strong market niche and proven sales appeal in an emerging rather than a mature industry.
- The business can and does generate a return on equity of at least 20 to 25 percent.
- The company has at least $10 million in annual revenues.
- The company has strong management.
- The company has reached the point at which it needs a substantial amount of capital for growth and expansion.

If the owner-manager finds it necessary or wants the firm's shares to be offered to the public, the services of an investment dealer may be helpful. An investment dealer (or underwriter) will assist the owner by acting as the marketer for the stock. The investment dealer can use an over-the-counter market, one that includes securities that are not sold on the stock exchange. If this method is followed, a reputable investment dealer with substantial connections throughout the investment community should be selected.

CLOSING DOWN OR GOING BANKRUPT LO4

The third possible outcome for the business—generally a result of unsatisfactory performance—involves closing down, being placed into receivership, or going bankrupt. These are, of course, the least desirable outcomes for the small business. As discussed in **Chapter 2**, however, each year many small businesses end up in this situation because of lack of profitability. Closing down is much easier for an unincorporated business than for a limited company. In theory, the incorporated company is required to file dissolution forms and notify government agencies. Although this is the case if the company does not have a large debt load, the incorporated company has more protection in a debt situation because of its limited liability.

LEARNING OBJECTIVES SUMMARY

LO1 **Planning for the eventual transfer of the business is an important component of small business management and should be done five to ten years in advance of the transfer. Plans should include several scenarios, including the possibility of illness or death of the owner. Some of the more common methods of transferring ownership of a business to family members are through a will, a sale of the business to the heirs, a gifting program, a life estate, and joint ownership.**

LO2 **The unique problems of a family business are higher emotional levels, blurring of roles, incompetence, non-family employee turnover, differing objectives among family owners, and planning for succession.**

LO3 **There are different options for selling the business outside of the family. In some cases, a partner or employee may be in a position to purchase the business. Sometimes a small business that has been successful but needs a significant amount of capital may sell shares to the public to meet financial needs while retaining control of the company.**

LO4 **A business that cannot be transferred can be closed down, be placed in receivership, or file for bankruptcy.**

TIME TO TAKE ACTION

Although you may be only at the start-up stage of your company or business plan, it is a good idea to include a harvesting strategy, or at least to be aware of the options. As such, you may want to interview some entrepreneurs who have sold their businesses. Ask them about the pros and cons of the sale process and what motivated them to sell.

DISCUSSION QUESTIONS

1. Assume you owned a company that you wanted to keep in the family. One of your three children has been working in the business and is interested in taking over. However, the other two feel that they are entitled to their one-third share of the value of the business. What would you do?
2. Jim Duncan is the owner-manager of a local restaurant chain. In its earlier years, the three local family restaurants were very successful. Then a recession came, and the businesses did not do as well. Jim is 60 years old and is thinking about retirement or semi-retirement. He has a son who has managed one of the restaurants, but he is not sure Jim Jr. is ready for the problems of the whole operation. If you were Jim Sr., how would you transfer ownership? Explain your decision.
3. Your father has just made you president of the family sand and gravel company. You want to computerize the payroll and the accounts payable and receivable, but your father does not see the need for the extra expense when expenses are already too high. What two problems exist here? How would you resolve this conflict as the newly appointed president?
4. Your parents have just made you the manager of your family's grocery store. Since the transition, problems have seldom been brought to your attention, and you have received little feedback on your instructions. What problems might be evident? How would you solve these problems?
5. Hamilton Rogers is the owner-manager of a successful machine shop. In the last year, he has promoted his sons to floor managers. Recently, several employees have left the company. What factors could be responsible for the employees leaving their jobs? How could Hamilton have prevented this problem?

EXPERIENTIAL EXERCISES

1. Interview the manager of a family-owned-and-operated business. What unique problems are evident?
2. Interview someone who is a future heir of a family business and is now going to school or gaining business experience. What problems are evident from their perspective? Does this person want to go back to the business? Why or why not?
3. Pomaona Fastener Company has suffered several years of operating losses. Because of the unfavourable outlook for the firm, it filed for bankruptcy and was dissolved. On liquidation, $570,000 was received, to be split among the following creditors:

Accounts payable	$100,000
Secured loans from bank	400,000
Accrued wages	10,000
Rent due on building	20,000
Government loan	300,000
Trustee's fee	10,000

   What would be the priority of payment, and how much would each class of creditor receive?

4. Interview the owner-manager of a small business that recently went public, and find out what they learned through the experience.

CASES FOR PART 4

BAILEY'S OFFICE SUPPLY

In 1991, John Bailey left a major department store chain where he worked as the hardware department manager to open his own office supply store. John had worked for the chain for more than 15 years and was very knowledgeable about the business. He felt, however, that he could develop a successful business by offering more personalized customer service than the larger stores could. By 2006, the firm, Bailey's Office Supply, had become a large and well-known establishment in Toronto with three outlets. While the firm offered clients an extensive line of all basic office supplies and computers, its specialty was in office furniture. Its strength was, as John Bailey had intended, its superior customer service and knowledge about how to create efficient and effective work spaces. John was careful to properly train his employees to know not only their products but also their customers' needs. Bailey's Office Supplies would work with any business to ensure its office was properly furnished and set up in a way to maximize employee efficiency and customer service.

In 2015, John Bailey's son Marty was finishing college in business administration and decided to join his father in the business. Marty had worked for his father from time to time and thought that he might enjoy the business. John had told Marty, however, to get an education first. If he decided to work at Bailey's, he would have a job. Although John made this offer to Marty, he was concerned because he had a younger son and an older daughter and wondered how they would react to Marty being brought into the company.

Marty joined Bailey's as assistant sales manager with the understanding that he would be given the job of sales manager on the retirement of Kenneth Harker, due to take place in another three years. At the same time Marty's brother and sister, along with Marty, were placed on the board of directors for Bailey's. Although the board met only sporadically, it did have the authority to ratify major management decisions.

Since 2005, John Bailey had observed the phenomenal growth and development in ergonomic office furniture. Over the years Bailey's had lost some of its office supply and computer business to big box stores and online retailers, yet their personal touch and experience in layouts allowed them to build a fairly steady if not spectacular office furniture business. In addition, once Bailey's acquired a furniture client, they tended to order office supplies from them as they appreciated the same-day or next-day delivery service and the personal touch.

After some months of being involved in the business full time, Marty wants to make some major changes. He wants Bailey's to specialize in ergonomic office furniture; hire two occupational therapists to assist firms in creating safe workplaces for their employees; invest in employee training so they would understand the benefits and sales process of ergonomic furniture; invest in new innovative products, such as walking desks; and close two of the office supply stores. While all three stores were profitable, most of the profits came from office furniture sales which, Marty believed, could be sold from one location. Additionally, Marty thought that the company's knowledge of creating efficient and effective office layouts combined with new, enhanced knowledge in ergonomic furniture would ensure Bailey's could be sustainable for years to come. Marty painted a long-term picture of the remaining store as a showcase for Bailey's knowledge of office layouts and ergonomic furniture, showcasing innovative products, and eventually phasing out of the traditional office supply market. All of this would come with a sizeable investment in training for staff, new hires, and new inventory.

John Bailey, however, was fairly conservative and, having built the business to a success, was now looking forward to enjoying the fruits of his hard labour by playing more golf and travelling with his wife for a month or two every year. He still retained controlling interest in the business and was opposed to making any significant investments. Marty, on the other hand, was anxious to move the business in a new direction and felt strongly that his changes would increase sales and create a more sustainable business. He felt that Bailey's would have a difficult time competing with the office supply and furniture businesses if they did not make changes and invest in the business. As this would require a rather major reinvestment of earnings back into the firm, John and his other son and daughter were reluctant to move in this direction. These disagreements were a source of frustration for Marty and he contemplated leaving the family business and starting his own high-tech office furniture store.

By 2018, the effects of the competition had reduced the total income of business and the profit of Bailey's by some 20 percent. It was a sobering turn of events for a firm that had experienced slow and steady growth trajectory. After considering this, John Bailey feels that it might be wise to turn the management of the business over to Marty, along with some of his ownership interest. Under John's proposal he would retain majority ownership of the company and still come in to work part-time, but Marty would be responsible for the day-to-day operations. When John approaches Marty with the proposal, he is shocked to hear that Marty has decided to leave the firm. John feels that he has given Marty a tremendous opportunity to learn about and then take over the business that he has built into a success. He cannot understand why Marty is turning down such an offer.

Questions

1. Why would Marty want to leave the firm instead of accepting his father's offer?
2. What could be done now to salvage the situation and keep Marty with the company?
3. Assuming that Marty remained with the firm, what suggestions could be made to turn the business around?

BAKER HARDWARE LTD.

Baker Hardware Ltd. is a hardware store in the town of Souris, located in an agricultural area of southern Manitoba. Souris is 48 kilometres south of Brandon (population 55,000), which is the major trading centre for many smaller towns within a 100-kilometre radius.

Mr. Baker, the owner of Baker Hardware, is contemplating expanding his merchandise offering to include lumber and building supplies. Currently Baker's, in addition to a standard selection of hardware merchandise, carries paint and building tools; therefore, Mr. Baker thinks this new line would be fairly compatible.

Baker Hardware is a part of the Home Hardware network of dealers, a nationwide group of hardware stores and home centres located primarily in smaller towns and cities. For the past few years, Home Hardware has been encouraging its dealers to expand into building supplies. Concerned that there was another lumber yard in Souris (which happened to be next door to Baker Hardware), Mr. Baker has shown little interest in such a move in the past.

Recently, however, he became aware that this lumberyard, Banner Building Supplies, is for sale or will be closed down. Mr. Baker gathers information from both the owners of Banner and Home Hardware and is in the process of making a decision. As Mr. Baker sees it, he has three choices: (1) purchase Banner Building Supplies; (2) expand into building supplies through Home Hardware on his own premises; or (3) maintain current operations (not expanding into building materials).

The Market

As previously mentioned, Souris is a small town of about 2000 located 48 kilometres from Brandon. The estimated population of surrounding area farms is 500. Over the years, the retail communities in most of the small towns close to Brandon have deteriorated because of the strong competition of retailers there and the increased mobility of consumers. The building supply industry is no exception. Such chains as Canadian Tire and Beaver Lumber, which have outlets in Brandon, have attracted numerous customers from these rural communities.

The population of Souris consists mainly of farmers, commuters who work in Brandon, and professionals, such as teachers who work in the town. The town has experienced some growth in recent years because of its relaxed atmosphere and excellent recreational facilities. Projections indicate the population could reach 2500 by the year 2019.

Baker Hardware

Baker Hardware has operated successfully in Souris for many years. Mr. Baker purchased the store from his father and, with changes and modernizations, increased sales from $950,000 in 2000 to $1.8 million in 2019. Although sales show a significant increase, profits do not. The strong competition from hardware chains in Brandon in recent years has eroded Mr. Baker's profit margin. Baker Hardware's competitive strength has always been that it catered to the agricultural community. Unfortunately, farm incomes have experienced considerable volatility in recent years, and this trend directly affects Baker Hardware's profit performance.

Baker Hardware currently has 4000 square metres of selling space and a large (2700-square-metre) warehouse. Mr. Baker believes that if he goes into building supplies he could, with some renovations, free up about half of the warehouse space to house the new merchandise.

Baker Hardware's current financial situation, while not serious, is such that if a capital investment were made, Mr. Baker would have to borrow to finance it. At the current interest rate of 8 percent, this is a concern for Mr. Baker.

Home Hardware

Home Hardware Ltd. is a well-established franchise system of dealer-owners located across Canada. Originating in southern Ontario, it has expanded to become a dominant small-town retailer of hardware merchandise. Recently, Home Hardware moved into the building supply industry in an attempt to capitalize on the growth of the home centre concept. Home Hardware has been encouraging its dealers to branch into this area, and many have done so.

Mr. Baker obtains from Home Hardware a list of the recommended product assortment for a home building supply dealer. A summary of this list, along with space requirements and markups, appears in **Table 1**. Home Hardware also suggests that Mr. Baker needs a forklift (estimated cost $15,000, used), a delivery truck (estimated cost $10,000, used), and a shed of at least 5000 square feet (estimated cost $25,000).

Banner Building Supplies

Banner Building Supplies is a family-owned business that has operated in Souris for more than 40 years. It is owned by two brothers, both close to retirement age, who also own a window and door manufacturing plant. As the manufacturing plant is much larger in size and scope of operations, the Banners have devoted most of their time and energy to this business. The retail building supplies outlet has, over the years, taken second place in their business interests, although it provides a stable and needed outlet for the town.

TABLE 1 Recommended Home Building Supply Full Product Assortment

PRODUCT	COST	SUGGESTED MARKUP ON COST	ESTIMATED TURNOVER	SPACE REQUIREMENT
Insulation	$ 8,000	25%	4.0	600
Doors and mouldings (complete assortment)	9,000	35	2.5	900
Plywood (complete assortment, 2 pallets each)	30,000	15	5.5	2,100
Drywall (complete assortment, 2 pallets each)	15,000	15	4.5	600
Cement	2,000	30	5.0	180
Roofing materials	9,000	25	3.5	600
Nails	2,000	35	5.0	120
Siding, soffit, fascia	9,000	35	2.0	900
Dimensional lumber, 2 by 4, 2 by 6, etc. (complete assortment, 2 pallets each)	56,000	25	6.0	3,000
	$140,000			9,000

Interest in selling the retail outlet results from two major factors. First, both brothers want to cut back on their work responsibilities, as both are approaching retirement age and have no family members interested in taking over the business. However, one brother has a son-in-law who is interested in the manufacturing part of the business. Second, the profitability of the retail outlet has suffered in recent years because of strong competition from larger hardware chains and home centres in Brandon. Some of these competitors can sell certain types of lumber and other supplies at lower prices than Banner's costs. The estimated profit and loss statement Mr. Baker obtained from Banners for 2018 is shown in **Table 2**. Currently Banner Building Supplies has approximately $178,000 in inventory (see **Table 3**) and owns a large lot containing some sheds and a showroom next door to Baker Hardware. The estimated value of real estate and buildings is approximately $325,000. The company has no debt.

In looking at the merchandise requirements recommended by Home Hardware, Mr. Baker notes that Banner's inventory levels are somewhat different. Mr. Baker discusses this with the previous manager of Banner's and learns that some building supplies do not sell well in Souris. He informs Mr. Baker that the standard types of lumber

TABLE 2 Banner Building Supplies Estimated Income Statement For 2018

Sales	$930,000	
Cost of goods sold (75%)	697,500	
Gross profit		$232,500
Expenses:		
Wages	135,500	
Taxes and licences	15,000	
Insurance	5,000	
Professional fees and admin.	2,500	
Utilities	8,000	
Fuel (trucks, etc.)	6,200	
Bad debts	1,000	
Depreciation	8,000	
Repairs and maintenance	1,000	
Misc. supplies	$ 500	$ 182,700
Net income before taxes		$ 49,800

TABLE 3 **Banner Building Supplies Inventory Estimate**

Insulation	$ 20,000
Doors and mouldings	35,000
Plywood	37,000
Drywall	7,000
Cement	1,000
Roofing materials	6,000
Nails, etc.	3,200
Siding	12,000
Dimensional lumber	40,000
Paints	5,500
Tools and hardware	5,500
Carpet and linoleum	$ 5,800
	$178,000

(plywoods, 2-by-4s, etc.) are the steady sellers, although warpage causes considerable waste in dimensional lumber. He also mentions that it is very difficult to compete with the city building centres for the large contractors' business. The major market for Banner's has been the small contractor (renovators) and the do-it-yourself customer.

Armed with this information, Mr. Baker is determined to make a decision.

Questions

1. What other information should Mr. Baker obtain before he makes this decision?
2. Using the information provided, evaluate the alternatives Mr. Baker has identified. Be sure to evaluate the attractiveness of the proposed merchandise lines.
3. What other alternatives has Mr. Baker not explored?

BRIAN LUBORSKY—PREMIER SALONS INTERNATIONAL INC.

Brian Luborsky started out his business career as a chartered accountant with Coopers and Lybrand. It did not take long for him to realize, however, that he wanted to be part of something that was more growth-oriented and that allowed him to be more entrepreneurial. He still remembers the day he decided to quit. His boss wanted him to write a memo. Luborsky, who was building and buying houses on the side, was working to save $50,000 on a property to buy. "The deal was worth more than my annual salary," he laughs, "I wasn't doing myself any favours, and I wasn't being fair to the company, so I resigned."

Meanwhile he became interested in a new hair salon franchise called Magicuts. Magicuts was established in 1981 as a discount haircut chain that attempted to bring the McDonald's-style efficiency principles to hair salons. Luborsky joined Magicuts as a franchisee, purchasing four franchises in 2010. What lured him was the math: "There is such a high ratio of sales to assets in hair-cutting, it was hard to go wrong," he says. "Say it costs $150,000 to set up shop. I can do $450,000 in sales in a year out of that store. Now, say I make 10 percent on that: I'm getting a 50 percent return on investment over 5 years and 200 percent after 10 years, and that's hard to beat."

In 2015, Luborsky considered expansion to the United States. At this point he had eight Magicuts franchises. He felt that his company was in a position to grow and he became aware of a chain of hair salons that he felt could fit in with the system that he had developed for Magicuts. After difficult negotiations for financing, he was successful in acquiring a large but financially troubled Minneapolis-based chain of hair salons—MEI Salons. MEI had 24 outlets, three times as many as Magicuts, but was in need of financial and management stability, which Luborsky could provide.

Luborsky's goal for growth is now centred on three areas. First, he wants to continue to emphasize superior service to compete with the independent mom-and-pop salons that dominate the industry. Because of the size of the company, it can take advantage of economies of scale, and this allows investment in employees. As a result, Premier (as the salons were renamed) has invested heavily in extensive employee training. Premier's six trainers teach the latest styles and trends, as well as soft skills, such as dealing with clients. Luborsky's second push involves partnerships with retailers, which would be interested in the store-within a store concept. He is targeting small to mid-size, independent retailers who might be looking to earn additional funds to offset online competition. Luborsky's third growth strategy is to seek out compatible chains and purchase them, similar as he had done with MEI. Recently, Premier purchased six Boscov's salons in Pennsylvania.

Questions

1. What are some of the problems that Brian Luborsky will likely face with the expansion to the United States? What solutions can you suggest?
2. What questions should he have evaluated before the U.S. expansion?
3. Do you think Luborsky should pursue partnerships for store-within a store concept? Why or why not?

COMPANY'S COMING COOKBOOKS

Cooking has always been an important part of Jean Paré's life. In 1963, when her four children had all reached school age, Jean volunteered to cater the 50th anniversary of the Vermillion School of Agriculture, now Lakeland College. Working from her home, Jean prepared a dinner for more than 1000 people. The dinner was so successful that Jean decided to start a catering business. This business developed into a flourishing catering operation that continued for more than 18 years.

At first Jean single-handedly ran the business with part-time assistance from family members. It gave her an opportunity to try new recipes, and she soon wrote a cookbook that included some of her best ones. Jean also travelled across Alberta opening retail accounts to handle the book. As the business grew, Jean teamed up with her son Grant Lovig to form Company's Coming Publishing Limited. Between sales trips and publishing her second cookbook, she managed shipping and receiving, invoicing, and accounts receivable collections for her growing publishing venture.

Jean's first cookbook, entitled *150 Delicious Squares*, was very successful, and soon the company was publishing several cookbooks each year. By 2017, the company had published more than 200 titles and sold more than 30 million cookbooks worldwide, with annual sales in the millions. The head office is now a specially constructed building in Edmonton where Grant oversees business operations in his role as president.

Printed in both English and French, Company's Coming cookbooks are available in more than 6000 retail stores across Canada. The cookbooks are also distributed in the United States and various overseas markets. A Spanish-language edition of Jean Paré's familiar and trusted recipes can even be found in Mexico. Recipe developer Annabelle Waugh says that one of the reasons the cookbooks have done so well is the trust the brand has established with the reader. Her books resemble community recipes, not glossy books, and use simple instructions.[46]

Jean credits much of the company's success to the sales savvy of her son Grant, who developed the retail plan for the cookbooks. Grant feels the family connection is one of their great strengths. Although Jean is the primary creative force behind Company's Coming, she confides that some of her best material comes from yet another son, Brian, who lives in Kelowna, British Columbia. Her daughter Gail Lovig has also been a part of the company since its inception. Gail currently oversees all marketing and distribution efforts, leading a team that includes marketing personnel located in major cities across Canada.

Questions

1. Which success principles for operating a family business discussed in the text does Company's Coming appear to be following?
2. As Jean Paré looks to the future, what concerns might she have about family members being involved in the business? How could she address these concerns?

DIRECTORY OF SUPPLEMENTARY CASES

CASE TITLE	**APPROPRIATE PART**
THOMSON GREENHOUSE	PART 4 Looking to the Future
ROBINSON TEST PREP CO.	PART 1 The Decision to Start a Business AND PART 2 Preparing for Small Business Ownership
BEACH BUDDY	PART 1 The Decision to Start a Business AND PART 2 Preparing for Small Business Ownership
ORGANIC GOURMET EXPRESS	PART 2 Preparing for Small Business Ownership AND PART 3 Managing the Small Business
THE WINSLOW CLOCK COMPANY	PART 2 Preparing for Small Business Ownership AND PART 3 Managing the Small Business
WINDOW TECH INC.	PART 3 Managing the Small Business AND PART 4 Looking to the Future

CASE TITLE	APPROPRIATE PART
EDGE HOCKEY	PART 1 The Decision to Start a Business AND PART 2 Preparing for Small Business Ownership AND PART 3 Managing the Small Business
BEACH STAKE	PART 1 The Decision to Start a Business AND PART 2 Preparing for Small Business Ownership
THE FRAMEMAKERS	Comprehensive
TOP HUMAN TECHNOLOGY LIMITED	Comprehensive
CLOVIS JEWELLERS (On Connect)	PART 3 Managing the Small Business
BLAKE LOCK AND SECURITY SYSTEMS (On Connect)	PART 3 Managing the Small Business AND PART 2 Preparing for Small Business Ownership

THOMSON GREENHOUSE

BACKGROUND

Thomson Greenhouse is located just outside Sudbury, Ontario, and is owned by Earl and Lisa Thomson. It is a seasonal operation, offering many different types of bedding plants, vegetables, annuals, perennials, and specialty plants and arrangements. The business also has a one-hectare tree nursery and garden offering a wide range of trees from pines to fruit trees.

Earl and Lisa Thomson have been operating the business for 17 years after taking over the business from Lisa's parents. The original business was located on land on the outskirts of Sudbury that was annexed by the city. At that time, Earl and Lisa decided to move from the city to a small acreage so that they could continue the business and set up a new location. The structures were taken down and reassembled on the new acreage just northeast of Sudbury.

Much of the knowledge of the greenhouse business has been passed down from Lisa's parents, and as Earl and Lisa have three sons working in the business, it continues to be a solely family-run operation. Many of the aspects of the business have remained the same since it was established. Thomson Greenhouse has been serving the city of Sudbury and surrounding area for many years and has been fairly successful in establishing a name for quality products and good customer service.

Thomson Greenhouse is a form of second income to the Thomsons because of its seasonal nature and because Earl is the chief accountant for a local manufacturing company. It also has allowed the Thomsons' three sons to work in the business to help finance their schooling. The oldest son, Derek, is about to graduate with a bachelor's degree in business from the local university, while the other brothers, Ryan and Russell, are in Grades 10 and 12 respectively. Lisa's parents, Morris and Anna Slemko, also work in the business during the busy times.

Because of the success of the business and because their sons are getting to the age where they are about to leave home, the Thomsons are faced with some long-term decisions about the business.

ORGANIZATION

Thomson Greenhouse is a general partnership with the two partners being Earl and Lisa Thomson. Earl feels that although they have unlimited liability under this arrangement, the tax and flexibility advantages of a partnership outweigh this risk. Both partners own an equal share of the business, although Lisa spends more time working in the business because Earl has a full-time job in Sudbury.

Earl and Lisa have equal authority with regard to the employees. Both are knowledgeable regarding horticulture and care for trees and plants. Earl is more responsible for the accounting, advertising, deliveries, and seeding. Lisa handles orders, daily operations in the greenhouse, transplanting, sales, and customer service. Both Earl and Lisa know their strengths and weaknesses and tend to do the things they each do well. Overlap does occur, but this is advantageous in some ways because some operations are too big to handle by themselves.

Over the years there have been few conflicts in the management of the operation or with employees, as it has all been within the family. All three of the Thomson sons have worked in the business throughout the summer, as well as evenings and weekends, for a number of years. During the busy season Lisa's parents, from whom Earl and Lisa purchased the business, help out. Because the business is family owned and operated, no formal personnel policies or training programs have been developed. Management of the company has been carried out informally. The employees are paid on a straight salary, with considerable flexibility available for the sons as things come up that they need to do.

One of the major concerns that Earl and Lisa have is the future of the business when the children finish their high school and university studies. The business is not currently large enough to be a full-time occupation unless a considerable capital investment is made to expand the operation. Another difficulty is that the second-oldest son Ryan has expressed interest in becoming involved in the business, but the Thomsons are concerned about how to make this transition should it take place. They are wondering what effects such a move would have on their other two sons.

LOCATION AND PHYSICAL FACILITIES

Thomson Greenhouse is located just northeast of the city limits of Sudbury. The market area includes not only the city of Sudbury (population 90,000) but also many of the small communities around the city, which is estimated to have another 60,000 people. This location serves Thomson well because of its proximity to the city; as well, its rural location allows for plenty of space for production and expansion, if required. Distribution is carried out primarily by truck, and the highways and roads in the area are very well maintained.

Thomson Greenhouse is located on eight hectares, of which two are used for the greenhouse and the Thomsons' residence, and the other six are rented out to a local farmer. The greenhouse building covers approximately

800 square metres. Although most of the area is taken up with plants and could be referred to as selling space, a small area at the front is devoted to customer service and a cash counter. A small greenhouse at the back is used for personal items and the holding of special orders. The building's age is a concern, as it has begun deteriorating. The frame is made of wood and the aging process has damaged many of the wooden glass frames. Much of the material for this greenhouse came from the original greenhouse that was moved from the previous site.

Equipment owned by the business are a small front-end loader/garden tractor, a truck used to deliver plants to commercial customers, a rototiller, a dirt mixer, a dirt purifier, and other miscellaneous garden tools and greenhouse devices.

Purchasing for Thomson Greenhouse is carried out by both Earl and Lisa. They purchase their supply of inventory from various seed processors located primarily in Southern Ontario and the United States. Quality, dependability, and price are all used to evaluate suppliers. Lead times for ordering are about 30 days for most items. No formal inventory-ordering method is used as the business is small enough that Earl and Lisa are able to adjust their inventory levels from visual inspection and from previous experience.

MARKETING

The target market for Thomson Greenhouse consists of consumers who come to the greenhouse, as well as some large retail accounts to supermarkets, such as Superstore and Phillips. The consumer market tends to be older, those who have the resources and time to spend on their yards and gardens. The supermarket and commercial accounts purchase vegetables and some flowers, while those customers who come out to Thomson Greenhouse make greater purchases of bedding plants and trees. In terms of quality and price, the commercial accounts tend to be interested in low price. As a result, the margins that Thomson achieves with the commercial accounts are much lower than with the customer accounts. Those who come out to the greenhouse desire high quality and customer service, even if it means paying a slightly higher price. Earl Thomson realizes this and sets prices to meet these preferences and to ensure that the business is able to achieve a profit. The profit margin has to be high enough to include the discounts that inevitably occur at the end of the season because of the perishability of the product.

The busy time of year for bedding plants is during May and June as most people are preparing their yards and gardens. During the summer and fall, produce sales increase, and during the winter months very little business is done.

There are several other greenhouses in the Sudbury area, and many customers do price comparisons. Thomson Greenhouse has always prided itself on superior customer service and, despite the competitive nature of the industry, seems to retain a fairly loyal following. The commercial contracts also add to the stability of operations for Thomson. Earl has an informal idea of Thomson Greenhouse market share through the monitoring of sales of their various products.

One of the trends the Thomsons have noticed is the increasing market share that has been obtained in the gardening-nursery product category by department stores, such as Walmart and Canadian Tire. Thomson Greenhouse currently has contracts with only two supermarkets, and although these have provided steady volumes, purchases from these sources have not grown over the past few years. The Thomsons are considering attempting to obtain contracts with some of these department stores as a means of increasing sales. They realize that margins would be thin, however, and that price would be a major purchasing factor for the consumer. Many of the other greenhouses in the area are actively competing for the business of these stores. The Thomsons realize that they would have to be very competitive to be successful in obtaining a contract. If they were able to secure new purchasers, expansion of their current operation would seem to be necessary.

Thomson Greenhouse uses several forms of promotion. It places some ads in the local newspaper and uses some social media, focusing on Facebook to inform customers about store hours and some promotions. The company also purchases a booth at the Home and Garden Trade Show, which is held in Sudbury each spring. Occasionally, a direct mail promotion is used to highlight special sales or end-of-season discounts. Thomson uses business cards and has been actively involved in sponsoring minor hockey teams and karate schools as part of its public relations promotion. Earl and Lisa realize, however, that word of mouth is their most effective form of promotion, so they ensure that they and their sales staff are knowledgeable about the product and courteous to the customer.

FINANCIAL SITUATION

Thomson Greenhouse has been profitable since its establishment, earning about $40,000 per year on about $200,000 in sales. (See **Table 1** for the latest income statement.) Although sales haven't increased over the past five years, Earl and Lisa have not been concerned about this because there has been an increase in competition and they are currently operating at capacity with their present facilities. They have been using a one-book system for accounting but are currently switching over to an accounting software program in conjunction with their computer purchase.

TABLE 1 **Thomson Greenhouse: Financial Statements**

THOMSON GREENHOUSE INCOME STATEMENT
FOR THE YEAR ENDED DECEMBER 31, 2020

Revenue		$200,000
Expenses		
Cost of Goods Sold		
Seed and materials	$ 26,560	
Containers	23,150	
Fertilizer	4,290	
Water	2,305	
Soil	1,090	
Direct labour	23,000	$ 80,395
Occupancy and Selling Costs		
Building repairs	2,130	
Truck costs	12,300	
Office expenses	3,015	
Property taxes	6,560	
Heat and power	6,450	
Advertising	12,150	
Selling labour	28,150	
Depreciation	$ 7,800	$ 78,555
Profit before Income Taxes		$ 41,050

THOMSON GREENHOUSE BALANCE SHEET
AS AT DECEMBER 31, 2020

Current Assets		
Cash	$ 3,000	
Accounts receivable	1,500	
Inventory	25,000	
Fixed Assets		
Land	76,000	
Buildings	98,000	
Equipment	$ 41,000	
Total Assets		$244,500
Liabilities and Owner's Equity		
Liabilities		
Accounts Payable	23,500	
Owner's Equity	$221,000	

One of the concerns that Earl and Lisa have is the state of their current greenhouse, which is getting old. They are considering constructing a new one in addition to the current greenhouse. This would increase the capacity of the business and would allow for increased sales but would also increase the workload for the Thomsons, something that they are not sure they want. Alternatively, they could replace the existing greenhouse and maintain current operations, but at a more efficient level.

A new greenhouse of a similar size to the current one would cost approximately $75,000 and would last about 10 years. If the Thomsons decided to go ahead with this, they would finance $60,000 at the local bank at 8 percent interest. They estimate that the annual sales for a greenhouse of this size would be $60,000.

Discussion Questions

1. Discuss the implications of the Thomsons' attempt to obtain additional commercial contracts (the department stores) for their products.
2. Evaluate the decision to construct another greenhouse from a financial and an organizational point of view. (Use rate of return, payback, and break-even analysis in your evaluation.)
3. Comment on the financial health of Thomson Greenhouse through a review of the financial statements.
4. Discuss the implications for succession of the business if the decision were to pass the business to one of the sons sell the business to someone outside the family.

ROBINSON TEST PREP CO.

In the spring of 2019, Olivia Robinson felt that she had come to a crossroads with her business. As the founder and CEO of Robinson Test Prep, an Ontario company specializing in preparing people for the chartered professional accountant (CPA) exam, the Common Final Examination (CFE), she felt that she was not achieving market share and growing in the right direction. After three years of providing prep classes to both students and professionals, Robinson had about 5 percent of the market and was facing fierce competition from her primary rival, Canadian Assessment Centres. Uncertain with which growth direction to take, Olivia contemplated several options.

BACKGROUND

Olivia Robinson started Robinson Test Prep in the summer of 2016 after graduating with a master's degree in accounting. She began applying to accounting firms, such as Ernst & Young, KPMG, Grant Thornton, and PricewaterhouseCoopers. Frustrated after receiving several rejections, Olivia began to consider other employment options. Her undergraduate degree was in business, and after graduation, Olivia worked for several years in the business office of a small test prep company based in San Francisco. The company prepared students who wanted to take primarily the SAT, GRE, GMAT, MCAT, and LSAT. Although her job was to manage the company's business affairs, she also began teaching math to students several nights a week. Olivia received training from the company in teaching basic testing skills, and she applied those skills toward teaching the math portion of the exams. She received positive feedback from her students as a conscientious and innovative teacher. Olivia eventually was hired by KPMG and returned to Canada.

Olivia felt that her experience as a teacher for the test prep company helped her when she began studying for the CPA exam. She knew how to study efficiently, how to organize her notes, and how to practise for the various sections. Olivia was one of the 25 percent of students who passed all sections of the CPA exam on the first try.

When contemplating what to do next, Olivia was struck by the fact that so many of her colleagues were unable to pass the exam. Convinced that she was not only skilled in the accounting and finance principles but also in knowing how to study effectively, she decided to start her own test prep business teaching specifically for the CPA exam. She was confident that students and professionals wishing to become CPAs would benefit from a full-service program that gave students full classes and individualized attention.

Olivia put together a business plan and secured financing from a local angel investor who specializes in small start-ups. She decided to focus her business and marketing efforts in the Toronto area. Based on her research and the area's concentration of different types of businesses, Olivia estimated that there was a market of about 10,000 students a year.

CANADIAN ASSESSMENT CENTRES

Canadian Assessment Centres is Robinson's primary competition. CAC is a national test preparation company that has been in existence since 1962. The company teaches for virtually every standardized test that is offered and has programs for high school students, undergraduate students, and graduate students taking certification tests, such as the bar and CPA exams. In addition, the company has a program designed for international students taking the Test of English as a Foreign Language (TOEFL) exam.

CAC is a full-service program that offers a variety of options for students taking any of these exams. Most courses offer the opportunity to have classroom lectures, home-study videotapes, books, software, online tests, or a combination of any of these options.

The CPA course does not offer live classroom sessions but gives students the option of books, software, and online testing for one or all the areas covered on the exam. Students also have a toll-free number that they can call if they have questions, as well as access to online chats with CAC instructors. CAC offers students a free repeat course if they do not pass the CPA exam and boasted a 75 percent pass rate. The course is priced from $3000 to $4500, depending on which of the services the student chooses. Many of CAC's students are repeaters who initially chose to study on their own and use a book or software package. Such students are dedicated to passing the second time they take the exam and want the structure that the courses provide. CAC provides a study schedule, study techniques, and information about how to take the exam, which, it claims, cannot be found in any other course on the market.

Many of CAC's students have also taken a CAC course for a previous entrance exam. CAC has a higher overall pass rate for all its courses than any other test prep centre in the country. People who had taken a CAC course for another test and had passed, for example, felt confident that they would be equally prepared for passing the CPA exam. In a survey of undergraduate students who had taken CAC, 85 percent said they would take another CAC course to prepare them for a graduate school entrance exam.

THE ROBINSON TESTING ADVANTAGE

Despite CAC's success, Olivia knew that with a pass rate of only 25 percent for first-time takers, there was a need to provide a comprehensive program to students so that they could pass on their first try. She devised a full-service program that lasted for six weeks and was three to six hours per day. She worked with accounting, finance, and law professors to design a curriculum to give students a comprehensive approach to studying for the exam. She hired the professors at a rate of $300 an hour to give three live, one-hour lectures per day (five days a week), and she taught the test-taking techniques and organizing skills necessary to easily assimilate the mountains of information that students needed to know. Olivia also provided downloads for students so that they could review the lectures at home and suggested that they listen to them while commuting to and from work, thus maximizing the use of their time. The course also included several timed mini-tests for each topic and four practice essay questions, which Olivia and her professors graded. The responses to essays included many comments and much feedback to give students guidance on areas to improve.

Olivia also made herself completely available to her students. She felt that one-on-one attention was critical to their success, and she held biweekly meetings with each student to gauge progress and answer questions. In addition to the meetings, students could call Olivia or email her with questions, and she promised to get back to them within 24 hours.

Olivia held two sessions a year in March and September, allowing students to continue to study on their own before the exams. She also made herself available to students after the course to answer their questions and help them in any way she could. Pricing her course at $2500 per student, she felt that she was providing more of an advantage and better preparation than any of the CAC options. She also offered a guarantee, allowing students to repeat the course if they did not pass the exam.

Olivia had taken a year to develop the materials and create a marketing plan for her company. She decided to invest heavily in LinkedIn by creating a profile and using ads. She also invested considerable time reaching out to potential students individually. Olivia also placed ads in Toronto-area business schools to attract students contemplating taking the exam after graduation, and even created flyers to be placed in the schools. She introduced herself to local businesses and tried to alert them to her program so that up-and-coming accountants would be encouraged to take her class if they wanted to take the CPA exam.

The first year that she ran the program she had 10 students. Despite the small class size, students felt that they had been well prepared for the exam and appreciated the individual attention they received. All students passed the exam. The second course had 25 students, 70 percent of whom passed. The last session that she held had 50 students and 80 percent of those students passed. Olivia did not feel comfortable advertising her pass rate, however, because many of her students had taken the CPA exam one or two times before and failed. She was not sure whether they passed after taking her course because of the quality of the program or because they were bound to pass it at some point.

SPRING 2018

By the spring of 2019, Olivia had finished teaching the March course and was looking forward to the September class. Although she was pleased that the number of students in each session was rising, she felt concerned that she was not making enough of an impact in the market. With only 5 percent of the market tapped, Olivia knew she needed to gain market share. She also wondered if she needed to format the course differently to attract students who did not want to attend live lectures. She had initially believed that students would benefit from a structured program that kept them on track, but now she was not so sure. Many times students did not come to class but opted to download the lectures and listen at home. She wondered if a different course model would help grow her business. Finally, Olivia realized that in her zeal to get her business up and running she really didn't plan for marketing. Olivia is at a critical point in her business and has a lot to consider.

Discussion Questions

1. Although Olivia is confident about her share of the market in one-to-one test prep, but she sees potential for online course offerings to expand outside the region. How could she assess the demand to ensure the idea is worth pursuing?
2. What are the quantitative factors of this new business Olivia should consider? What about nonquantitive factors?
3. Olivia is already successful in her current business, but she recognizes she is weak in a few areas. Write a small business plan for Olivia, identifying what she is missing from her current business and why those aspects are important to include.
4. Reformatting the course and adjusting the work of the professors she has hired will mean recalculating her costs. Walk Olivia through her options for financing this new business venture.

BEACH BUDDY

Jack McDonald has a new product concept, the Beach Buddy, which he is ready to bring to market. McDonald is creative, optimistic, enthusiastic, flexible, and motivated. He is willing to put substantial time into developing and bringing the Beach Buddy to market. Although he lacks capital, McDonald is unwilling to license or sell the concept to a manufacturer; he is determined to maintain control and ownership of the product throughout the introduction and market penetration phases. McDonald believes there is a significant amount of money to be made and refuses to sell his product concept for a flat fee.

THE PRODUCT

The Beach Buddy is an extremely lightweight cooler that is large enough to carry everything needed for a day at the beach, including drinks, food, and more. What sets this product apart, however, is that it comes with a rechargeable battery, which allows the cooler to operate without ice, as well as a host of other features and attachments. The Buddy allows users to plug in any smart phone enabling them to listen to their music through the cooler's speakers. There is also a working blender that attaches to the top of the cooler, a plug-in mic, and four charging outlets for cell phones. The battery requires 24 hours to fully charge to operate all functions described above for up to eight hours.

COMPETITION

Currently there is one main competitor, the Coolest Cooler, which provides many of the same features as the Beach Buddy. The Coolest Cooler, however, requires ice to keep drinks and food cold, whereas the Beach Buddy operates like a rechargeable refrigerator. The Coolest Cooler retails for $249 and is available in a host of colours. Portable, rechargeable refrigerators are also sold on Amazon but most are priced in excess of $500 and are quite heavy. Of course, traditional coolers do exist but McDonald considers these to be more substitute products and not direct competitors.

MARKETING RESEARCH

McDonald had a group of college students do some preliminary research for the product, which included several focus groups, to determine potential consumer response. Results of the focus group indicated that several features should be modified. For example, the blender was too small for many of the participants and the speakers were not loud enough. On the plus side, the inside of the cooler was perceived as durable and of sufficient size; however, there was some small concern that the cooler would not be overly advantageous over coolers which relied on ice as ice would be needed for most drinks.

STRATEGY

McDonald investigated several methods of marketing the Beach Buddy, including selling it through retail stores in either upscale stores such as The Bay or discount stores such as Costco and Walmart. He also considered selling the product primarily online through a website and through Amazon. McDonald was also considering a crowdfunding campaign to raise some initial capital and prove his concept.

McDonald believes that online sales, while requiring the most effort, will provide higher margins, lower risk, and the overall best fit with McDonald's strengths and weaknesses, his market penetration objectives, and his limited financial resources. The Internet could also provide opportunities, but McDonald was unsure if he should pursue this option through crowdfunding or simply start to sell the product online and through Amazon.

PROMOTION

The product initially will be promoted heavily on social media. McDonald is planning to use Facebook advertising, create an Instagram account, and work with micro-influencers to promote the cooler. McDonald has been investing a fair bit of time learning about social media influencers and believes that working with micro-influencers will provide substantial returns on his investment. McDonald is also preparing to engage in some public relations with the product and hopes to generate some initial media buzz.

PRICING

The costs of manufacturing have been estimated at $150. McDonald hopes to charge $299 for the cooler, which is more than the Coolest Cooler but less than rechargeable refrigerators of similar size.

DISTRIBUTION

The product will be manufactured at a local factory, drop-shipped to a storage facility, and shipped via UPS or Canada Post to the consumer.

FINANCING

McDonald has substantial support from his family in starting the business, and his father will lend him $750,000, which will allow him to establish an initial inventory, engage in marketing, and hire some assistants.

GOING FORWARD

McDonald has reached a decision point. He needs to determine if he is going to move forward with his business. If he decides to pursue the opportunity, he needs to decide whether he will he sell the cooler online, through crowdfunding, or in retail locations. He also needs to finalize his sale price and target market. While McDonald initially thought college and university students would find the cooler appealing, he is concerned that the price point may be too high. He is also reconsidering the name because he wonders if the term *Beach Buddy* might be too limiting, but he does not want to compete in the portable refrigerator market.

ORGANIC GOURMET EXPRESS

Today many households have two incomes. At the end of the day the questions arise: "Who will cook?" or "What do I cook?" Time is limited. After a long day at work, few people want to face the lines at the grocery store. Often the choice is to eat out. But the expense of dining out or the boredom of fast food soon becomes unappealing. Pizza or fast-food delivery solves the problem of going out but does not always satisfy the need for nutritious, high-quality meals. Some people prefer a home-cooked meal, but don't like the hassle of grocery shopping, menu planning, and time-consuming preparation.

Jan Jones is one of those people. She is a hard-working professional in Durham Region, just east of Toronto, who would like to come home to a home-cooked meal. Jones is also concerned about the quality of ingredients she eats, choosing to eat only organic and ethically sourced food whenever possible. She also believes in supporting local farmers and frequently shops at farmers markets. Jones would not mind cooking herself, once at home, but making an extra trip to the store and frequenting farmers markets can be a major hassle. Jan thought it would be great to have the meal planned and all the ingredients at her fingertips. She thought of other people in her situation and realized there might be a market need for this kind of service. After thinking about the types of meals that could be marketed, the increased emphasis on organic and ethically sourced local food, Jan discussed the plan with her colleagues at work. The enthusiastic response led her to believe she had a good idea. While a number of meal delivery services have emerged, none have put a heavy emphasis on locally sourced, organic foods. After months of marketing research, menu planning, and financial projections, Jan was ready to launch her new business. The following is the business plan for Organic Gourmet Express.

EXECUTIVE SUMMARY

Organic Gourmet Express is a relatively new concept in grocery marketing. The product is a combination of menu planning and grocery delivery; a complete package of groceries and recipes for a week's meals is delivered to a customer's door. While grocery delivery and meal kit prep is not a new business, no one is currently focused on working with farmers and offering ethically sourced organic meals. The target market consists of young urban professionals living in two-income households in which individuals have limited leisure time, high disposable income, and a willingness to pay for services.

The objective is to develop a customer base of 400 households by the end of the third year after start-up. This level of operation will produce a new income of about $120,000 per year and provide a solid base for market penetration in the future.

The objective will be achieved by creating an awareness of the product through an intense promotional campaign at start-up and by providing customers with first-class service and premium-quality goods.

The capital required to achieve objectives is $258,000. Jan will invest $183,000 and will manage and own the business. The remainder of the capital will be financed through bank loans.

PRODUCT

The product consists of meal-planning and grocery-shopping services. It offers a limited selection of organic and ethically/locally sourced five-dinner packages delivered directly to the customer.

The criteria for the meal packages will be balanced nutrition, easy preparation, and premium quality. To ensure the nutritional requirements, the company will hire a nutritionist as a consultant. Nutritional information will be included with each order. The most efficient method for preparing the overall meal will be presented. Meals will be limited to recipes requiring no more than 20 minutes to prepare. Premium-quality, local and organic ingredients will be a selling feature. The customer should feel that he or she is getting better-quality ingredients than could be obtained from the grocery store.

MANUFACTURING AND PACKAGING

Since the customer will not be shopping on the premises, Gourmet Express will require only a warehouse-type space for the groceries. The store location or decor will be unimportant in attracting business. There will be fewer inventory expenses, since the customer will not be choosing among various brands. Only premium brands will be offered and ideally fresh food will only be stored for a limited amount of time.

It will be important to establish a reliable connection with farmers and organic suppliers for high-quality produce and to maintain freshness for delivery to the customer.

As orders are processed, the dinners will be assembled. All ingredients will be labelled according to the dinner to which they belong. The groceries will be sorted and bagged according to storage requirements: freezer, refrigerator, and shelf. Everything possible will be done to minimize the customer's task. Included in the packaging will be the nutritional information and preparation instructions.

Customers will be given the option of selecting their own meals from the monthly menu list or opting for a weekly selection from the company.

FUTURE GROWTH

Various options will be explored to expand the business. Some customers may prefer a three- or four-meal plan if they eat out more often or travel frequently. Another possibility might be the "last-minute gourmet"; that is, they can call any evening for one meal only.

Increasing the customer base will increase future sales. Expansion of Organic Gourmet Express can include branches in other locations or even franchising in other cities. With expansion and success, Organic Gourmet Express might be a prime target for a larger food delivery company to buy out.

INDUSTRY

The gourmet express concept is a relatively new idea with its own market niche. While several competitors exist none offer locally sourced organic foods.

A number of local restaurants will deliver food, yet few organic options exist.

SALES PREDICTION

The market segment will be households with an income of at least $65,000 per year. In the Oshawa region, this will cover an area including over 18,000 households that meet the target requirements of income, with an age range of 24 to 50 years. By the end of the third year, a customer base of 400 households will be developed (2.3 percent of the target market). At a growth rate of 2.73 percent a year, the target market of households should increase over three years to 19,000.

FINANCIAL

Various financial statements are included in **Table 1**, **Table 2**, **Table 3**, **Table 4**, **Table 5**, **Table 6**, **Table 7**, **Table 8**.

TABLE 1 **Start-Up Expenses**

Ad campaign		
Ad agency*	$3,000	
Social media & Online ads	7,000	
Radio spots‡	8,000	
Newspaper ads§	7,000	
Total		$25,000
Pre-start-up salaries**		16,000
Nutritionist consulting		6,000
Miscellaneous consulting (legal etc.)		1,500
Pre-start-up rent and deposits		4,000
Pre-start-up utilities and miscellaneous supplies		2,000
		$54,500

*40 hrs at $75/hr

†‡4 weeks intense campaign: 20 spots/week (30 seconds); $100/spot

§50 ads at an average of $100/ad

**Jan Jones at 3 months; clerks, two at 2 weeks

TABLE 2 **Capital Equipment List**

Computers:		
Apple, MacIntosh Office System		
3 Mac systems	$3,000	
Laser printer HP2300 series	1,000	
Networking	2,000	
Software	3,000	
Total		$ 9,000
Delivery vans		66,000
Food lockers and freezers		15,000
Phone system (Telus)		1,500
Furniture and fixtures		3,500
		$95,000

TABLE 3 Pro Forma Income Statement

	YEAR 1											
	MO. 1	MO. 2	MO. 3	MO. 4	MO. 5	MO. 6	MO. 7	MO. 8	MO. 9	MO. 10	MO. 11	MO. 12
Sales[1]	2,600	3,900	6,500	13,000	19,500	23,400	26,000	28,600	31,200	33,800	36,400	39,000
Less: Cost of goods sold[2]	1,700	2,550	4,250	8,500	12,750	15,300	17,000	18,700	20,400	22,100	23,800	25,500
Gross profit	900	1,350	2,250	4,500	6,750	8,100	9,000	9,900	10,800	11,700	12,600	13,500
Less: Operating expenses												
Salaries and wages[3]	7,400	7,400	7,400	7,400	7,400	7,400	9,800	9,800	9,800	9,800	9,800	9,800
Operating supplies	300	300	300	300	300	300	300	300	300	300	300	300
Repairs and maintenance	250	250	250	250	250	250	250	250	250	250	250	250
Advertising and promotion[4]	130	195	325	650	975	1,170	1,300	1,430	1,560	1,690	1,820	1,950
Bad debts	100	100	100	100	100	100	100	100	100	100	100	100
Rent[5]	1,667	1,667	1,667	1,667	1,667	1,667	1,667	1,667	1,667	1,667	1,667	1,667
Utilities	1,000	1,000	1,000	1,000	1,000	1,000	1,000	1,000	1,000	1,000	1,000	1,000
Insurance	600	600	600	600	600	600	600	600	600	600	600	600
General office	150	150	150	150	150	150	150	150	150	150	150	150
Licences	200	0	0	0	0	0	0	0	0	0	0	0
Interest[6]	310	310	310	310	310	310	530	530	530	530	530	530
Depreciation[7]	1,271	1,271	1,271	1,271	1,271	1,271	1,271	1,271	1,271	1,271	1,271	1,271
Total operating expenses	13,378	13,243	13,373	13,698	14,023	14,218	16,968	17,098	17,228	17,358	17,488	17,618
Profit (loss) before taxes	(12,478)	(11,893)	(11,123)	(9,198)	(7,273)	(6,118)	(7,968)	(7,198)	(6,428)	(5,658)	(4,888)	(4,118)
Less: Taxes	0	0	0	0	0	0	0	0	0	0	0	0
Net profit (loss)	(12,478)	(11,893)	(11,123)	(9,198)	(7,273)	(6,118)	(7,968)	(7,198)	(6,428)	(5,658)	(4,888)	(4,118)

(1)Sales—per Action Plan; see Table 8 for details.

(2)Cost of goods sold—80% of retail grocery price, or $40.00 per household per week ($170.00/month household). (80% is an average margin on groceries.)

(3)Salaries and wages—Jan's salary will be $5000/month. Order clerks will be paid $1300/month, and delivery clerks will be paid $1100/month. One additional order clerk and delivery clerk each will be added once sales reach 100 households, and again at 200 households. Salaries will escalate at 6%/year.

(4)Advertising and promotion—The grocery industry standard is 1% of sales. However, Organic Gourmet Express being a new business will require more than that level; 5% of sales is used in this plan. (Special pre-start-up advertising is covered with other start-up expenses.)

(5)Rent—2000/ft.^{2} @ $10.00/ft.^{2}; $1667/month; escalate at 6%/year.

(6)Interest—Loans on computer ($9000) and delivery vehicles ($22,000 ea.) at 12.0%/year. (Delivery vehicles will be added with delivery clerks.) (Debt service—based on three-year amortization of loans with payments of one-third at the end of each of three years.)

(7)Depreciation—All equipment will be depreciated per ACRS schedules: vehicles and computers—3 years; furniture and fixtures—10 years.

TABLE 4 Pro Forma Income Statement

	YEAR 2				YEAR 3			
	Q1	Q2	Q3	Q4	Q1	Q2	Q3	Q4
Sales[1]	136,500	156,000	194,698	234,000	253,500	273,000	292,500	312,000
Less: Cost of goods sold[2]	89,250	102,000	127,302	153,000	165,750	178,500	191,250	204,000
Gross profit	47,250	54,000	67,395	81,000	87,750	94,500	101,250	108,000
Less: Operating expenses								
Salaries and wages[3]	31,164	38,796	38,796	38,796	41,124	41,124	41,124	41,124
Operating supplies	900	900	900	900	900	900	900	900
Repairs and maintenance	750	750	750	750	750	750	750	750
Advertising and promotion[4]	6,825	7,800	9,735	11,700	12,675	13,650	14,625	15,600
Bad debts	300	300	300	300	300	300	300	300
Rent[5]	5,301	5,301	5,301	5,301	5,619	5,619	5,619	5,619
Utilities	3,000	3,000	3,000	3,000	3,000	3,000	3,000	3,000
Insurance	1,800	1,800	1,800	1,800	1,800	1,800	1,800	1,800
General office	450	450	450	450	450	450	450	450
Interest[6]	1,280	1,940	1,720	1,720	1,410	1,190	970	970
Depreciation[7]	6,910	6,910	6,910	6,910	7,493	7,493	7,493	7,493
Total operating expenses	58,680	67,947	69,662	71,627	75,520	76,275	77,030	78,005
Profit (loss) before taxes	(11,430)	(13,947)	(2,267)	9,373	12,230	18,225	24,220	29,995
Less: Taxes	0							
Net profit (loss)	(11,430)	(13,947)	(2,267)	9,373	12,230	18,225	24,220	29,995

(1)Sales—per Action Plan: see Table 8 for detail. Average unit sale is $40.00 for groceries plus $10.00 per week for delivery (Table 1), making the monthly unit sales per household (2 people) $215.00.

(2)Cost of goods sold—80% of retail grocery price, or $32.00 per household per week ($138.00/month household). (80% an average margin on groceries—*Progressive Grocer;* April 1984; p. 94.)

(3)Salaries and wages—Jan's salary will be $4500/month. Order clerks will be paid $1000/month, and delivery clerks will be paid $900/month. One additional order clerk and delivery clerk each will be added once sales reach 100 households, and again at 200 households. Salaries will escalate at 6%/year.

(4)Advertising and promotion—The grocery industry standard is 1% of sales. However, Organic Gourmet Express being a new business will require more than that level; 5% of sales is used in this plan. (Special pre-start-up advertising is covered with other start-up expenses.)

(5)Rent—2000/ft.^{2} @ $8.00/ft.^{2}; 1333 $1/month; escalate at 6%/year.

(6)Interest—Loans on computer ($10,000) and delivery vehicles ($12,000 ea.) at 12.5% year. (Delivery vehicles will be added with delivery clerks.) (Debt service-based on three-year amortization of loans with payments of one-third at the end of each of three years.)

(7)Depreciation—All equipment will be depreciated per ACRS schedules: vehicles and computers—3 years; furniture and fixtures—10 years.

TABLE 5 **Pro Forma Cash Flow Statement**

	YEAR 1												
	MO. 1	MO. 2	MO. 3	MO. 4	MO. 5	MO. 6	MO. 7	MO. 8	MO. 9	MO. 10	MO. 11	MO. 12	TOTAL
Cash receipts													
Sales	2,600	3,900	6,500	13,000	19,500	23,400	26,000	28,600	31,200	33,800	36,400	39,000	263,900
Other													
Total cash receipts	2,600	3,900	6,500	13,000	19,500	23,400	26,000	28,600	31,200	33,800	36,400	39,000	263,900
Cash disbursements													
Cost of goods sold	1,700	2,550	4,250	8,500	12,750	15,300	17,000	18,700	20,400	22,100	23,800	25,500	172,550
Salaries and wages	7,400	7,400	7,400	7,400	7,400	7,400	9,800	9,800	9,800	9,800	9,800	9,800	103,200
Operating supplies	300	300	300	300	300	300	300	300	300	300	300	300	3,600
Repairs and maintenance	250	250	250	250	250	250	250	250	250	250	250	250	3,000
Advertising and promotion	130	195	325	650	975	1,170	1,300	1,430	1,560	1,690	1,820	1,950	13,195
Bad debts	100	100	100	100	100	100	100	100	100	100	100	100	1,200
Rent	1,667	1,667	1,667	1,667	1,667	1,667	1,667	1,667	1,667	1,667	1,667	1,667	20,004
Utilities	1,000	1,000	1,000	1,000	1,000	1,000	1,000	1,000	1,000	1,000	1,000	1,000	12,000
Insurance	600	600	600	600	600	600	600	600	600	600	600	600	7,200
General office	150	150	150	150	150	150	150	150	150	150	150	150	1,800
Licences	200	0	0	0	0	0	0	0	0	0	0	0	200
Interest	310	310	310	310	310	310	530	530	530	530	530	530	5,040
Debt service (principal)												10,333	10,333
Total cash disbursements	13,807	14,522	16,352	20,927	25,502	28,247	32,697	34,527	36,357	38,187	40,017	52,180	353,322
Net cash flow	(11,207)	(10,622)	(9,852)	(7,927)	(6,002)	(4,847)	(6,697)	(5,927)	(5,157)	(4,387)	(3,617)	(13,180)	(89,422)

TABLE 6 Pro Forma Cash Flow Statement

	YEAR 2				YEAR 3			
	Q1	Q2	Q3	Q4	Q1	Q2	Q3	Q4
Cash receipts								
Sales	136,500	156,000	194,698	234,000	253,500	273,000	292,500	312,000
Other								
Total cash receipts	136,500	156,000	194,698	234,000	253,500	273,000	292,500	312,000
Cash disbursements								
Cost of goods sold	89,250	102,000	127,302	153,000	165,750	178,500	191,250	204,000
Salaries and wages	31,164	38,796	38,796	38,796	41,124	41,124	41,124	41,124
Operating supplies	900	900	900	900	900	900	900	900
Repairs and maintenance	750	750	750	750	750	750	750	750
Advertising and promotion	6,825	7,800	9,735	11,700	12,675	13,650	14,625	15,600
Bad debts	300	300	300	300	300	300	300	300
Rent	5,301	5,301	5,301	5,301	5,619	5,619	5,619	5,619
Utilities	3,000	3,000	3,000	3,000	3,000	3,000	3,000	3,000
Insurance	1,800	1,800	1,800	1,800	1,800	1,800	1,800	1,800
General office	450	450	450	450	450	450	450	450
Licences	0	0	0	0	0	0	0	0
Interest	1,280	1,940	1,720	1,720	1,410	1,190	970	970
Debt service (principal)		7,333		10,333	7,333	7,333		10,333
Total cash disbursements	141,020	170,370	190,054	228,050	241,111	254,616	260,788	284,846
Net cash flow	(4,520)	(14,370)	4,643	5,950	12,389	18,384	31,712	27,154

TABLE 7 Pro Forma Balance Sheets

END OF:	YEAR 1	YEAR 2	YEAR 3
Assets			
Current assets			
Cash	3,000	5,000	7,000
Accounts receivable	19,500	32,450	48,750
Inventory	12,750	21,217	31,875
Supplies	300	300	300
Prepaid expenses	1,667	1,767	1,873
Total current assets	37,217	60,734	89,798
Fixed assets			
Furniture and fixtures	18,000	16,000	14,000
Vehicles	33,000	32,780	8,140
Equipment	6,750	3,330	0
Total fixed assets	57,750	52,110	22,140
Total assets	94,967	112,844	111,938

	YEAR 1	YEAR 2	YEAR 3
Liabilities			
Accounts payable	12,750	21,217	31,875
Notes payable	0	0	0
Total current liabilities	12,750	21,217	31,875
Long-term liabilities			
Bank loans payable	42,667	47,000	22,000
Personal loans payable	0	0	0
Total long-term liabilities	42,667	47,000	22,000
Total liabilities	55,417	68,217	53,875
Owner's equity			
Paid-in capital	133,889	62,897	28,068
Retained earnings	(94,339)	(18,271)	29,995
Total owner's equity	39,550	44,627	58,063
Total liabilities and equity	94,967	112,844	111,938

TABLE 8 Sources and Uses of Funds

Sources of Funds	
Jan Jones (personal funds)	$182,913
Bank loans for computer and vehicles*	75,000
Total sources	$257,913
Uses of Funds	
Computer, peripherals, and software	$ 9,000
Food lockers and freezers	15,000
Delivery vehicles	66,000
Phone system	1,500
Miscellaneous furniture and fixtures	3,500
Start-up expenses†	54,600
Working capital	108,313
Total uses	$257,913

*Total for initial 3-year period. Computer and one delivery van will be acquired before start-up, one delivery van will be added 6 months after start-up, and another will be added 15 months after start-up. Financing will be handled simultaneously with procurement.

†To cover negative cash flow over first one and a half years of operation. (See pro forma cash flow statements.)

MARKETING

Distribution.

The product will be delivered directly to the customer.

Sales Strategy.

Advertising will include social media and online advertising, newspaper ads, radio spots, an Internet web page, and direct-mail brochures. All will be used during normal operations, but an intense online campaign will precede start-up. A series of "teaser" social media and newspaper ads will run before start-up, announcing a revolution in grocery shopping. At start-up, the social media and newspaper ads will have evolved into actually introducing the product, and radio spots will begin as well. A heavy advertising schedule will be used during the first four weeks of business. After start-up, social media and email will detail the description of the service and a menu plan.

Facebook, Pinterest, and Instagram will be the primary forms of social media used. Newspaper ads aimed at the target markets will be placed in entertainment and business sections. Radio spots will be geared to stations most appealing to the target market. Since the product is new, it may be possible to do interviews with newspapers and obtain free publicity.

Sales promotions will offer large discounts to first-time customers. These promotions will continue for the first six months of operations.

The service will be priced at $10 per week for delivery and planning, with the groceries priced at full retail level. According to the phone survey, most people who were interested in the service would be willing to pay the weekly service charge.

MANAGEMENT

The management will consist of the owner/manager. Other employees will be delivery clerks and order clerks. It is anticipated that after the business grows, an operations manager might be added to supervise the employees.

Discussion Questions

1. Based on the assessment of the business do you think Organic Gourmet Express will succeed? Why or why not?
2. What gaps were missed in the business analysis?
3. What recommendations would you make to Jan Jones?

THE WINSLOW CLOCK COMPANY

For the third time, Dr. Winslow sat up in bed, flipped on the light, and reached for The Winslow Clock Company business plan. Maybe reading through it again would calm his growing fears. As he flipped through the pages, he recalled again all the years of thinking, tinkering, and discovery that had gone into the development of his alarm clock. Could something he spent so much time and energy on be wrong? It was such a good idea, this "throwable" alarm clock: Millions of Canadians would want to get this kind of revenge on their daily call to the rat race. And, in its final design, it contained all kinds of computer-age technology. Surely, the investors tomorrow would love it!

What had happened to his confidence? He had been sure enough to invest all his savings in the clock's development. What a time to get second thoughts! Didn't he use the best technical help available to design the clock and plan the production and marketing? Maybe that was his problem—too much dependence on experts. Being a practising psychiatrist, he considered himself a good judge of character and motivation, but maybe his obsession with his clock had clouded his perception. Should he take more time to personally study the different production and marketing scenarios? He did not have any more time if he wanted to get production started to hit the Christmas season. Should he wait another year, or risk going to market at a slow time of year, or . . .?

The more he thought, the more the doubts and worries grew. He had to put a stop to this pointless mental exercise. The business plan he held in his hands was what he had to sell tomorrow at the meeting, so he had better have confidence in it. If things went badly, then he could think about changes. For now, he would read over the business plan for The Winslow Clock Company (which follows) just once more, concentrating on the favourable arguments his business experts had made.

SUMMARY

The attached five-year business plan for The Winslow Clock Company is based primarily on the estimated potential of the company's first product, an alarm clock designed and patented by Dr. Michael Winslow, a psychiatrist by profession. He expected the sales and the profits generated by this product to reach $8.5 million and $1.5 million, respectively, within three years, which would provide sufficient resources to enable the company to expand its line into related products now under consideration.

History of the Product.

Under development for 10 years, the concept for the clock stems from Dr. Winslow's thought that it would be fun to have the liberty to "get back at" the alarm that so readily awakens everyone each morning. The "fun" part—and what makes the alarm unique—is that you throw it to turn it off.

Development of the microchip and related technology in recent years has made the design of such a clock possible at a reasonable cost. The technical assistance on the clock was provided by students at Queen's University. The business and marketing planning for the clock was done with the help of Queen's Small Business Consulting (QSBC) under the direction of its faculty associate.

In addition, Dr. Winslow has contracted with a number of professional consultants in the areas of product design, product engineering, marketing and advertising, production, legal matters, and accounting.

Market Acceptance.

Early reaction from such major retailers as Canadian Tire has been very positive, thus supporting the belief that the targeted levels of sales are achievable.

Thus, in what might otherwise be considered a mature market, new design and technology are eagerly sought by retailers and customers anxious to provide or find a refreshing selection of alternatives. The company's projected level of sales in its first year represents less than 1 percent of this growing segment of the Canadian clock market.

Competition.

Although several major manufacturers account for most clock sales (with Japanese manufacturers dominating the sale of quartz movements), there is, nevertheless, a significant annual volume attributable to smaller specialty designers, most of whom purchase the clock movements on an OEM (original equipment manufacturer) basis from the larger producers and concentrate on unique housing designs.

Seiko, the company supplying the movement for Dr. Winslow's clock, has made impressive strides in Canada in the last four years by increasing its annual OEM business from 400,000 to 2 million units. Besides selling its own Seiko and Picco brands, it is developing a reputable supplier business. This strategy allows Seiko to enjoy some of the profit opportunity created by an expanded market without all the marketing costs and risks.

In addition, a number of large retailers contract with the major manufacturers for private-label production. This somewhat fragmented structure has created profitable opportunities for products designed for niches within the large clock market.

The question is: If the product is attractive enough to create a niche in the market, how soon will it have competition? The concept of a "throwable" alarm and several components designed specifically for the product are patented. In addition, it would require some time and expense for potential competitors to develop the impact switch and the microchip used in Dr. Winslow's clock.

Financial Projections: Opportunities and Risks.

Financial projections for the first five years of the company are summarized below. (Sales are based on only the first product, to be introduced in 2021.)

Since components and subassemblies would be purchased, rather than manufactured by the company, and then assembled and shipped by an outside contractor, the capital investment required is minimal, estimated at less than $50,000, the majority of which would be for tooling. Another $50,000 for start-up expenses, prototypes, and preproduction operating expenses would also be required in the first two months of 2021.

By March, however, the commitment increases. Because of the company's lack of credit history, all indications suggest that suppliers will require letters of credit to accompany the $814,000 in parts orders placed between March and September of 2021, when shipments are expected to begin. In addition, operating expenses between March and October are forecast at $176,000.

Given the projected level of sales in the first two years, the company is seeking equity capital of $600,000 as early as possible in 2021. An additional term loan of approximately $650,000 would be needed by June to carry financing and operating costs through year's end.

It should be emphasized that although this combined cash injection of $1.2 million is at apparent risk for at least the six to eight months before the beginning of shipments (and, of course, beyond), two factors diminish this risk. First, the initial selling effort in the spring of 2021 to secure orders for the Christmas season should provide a clear indication of market acceptance by the end of April. The long lead time required to order components then becomes a positive factor. Orders for 40,000 of the first season's production of 50,000 units could be cancelled without penalty a month in advance on standard items, such as the clock movement. This alone would save almost $730,000. In addition, many operating expenses could be curtailed accordingly and alternative marketing plans put into place. (Online sales, for example, is an approach that will be explored from the beginning anyway and, in a downside case, certainly would be a viable alternative.)

The second factor that diminishes the risk is that low fixed costs allow the break-even point to be projected at 16,000 units, which should be achieved in October, the second month of actual shipments.

According to its projected cash flow, the company should be able to repay its term loan in full within 18 months. From that point on, it can fund its continuing operations from the generated working capital.

The returns on investment are calculated at 19, 33, and 37 percent in the first three years, respectively, with returns on net worth at 34, 46, and 45 percent. Net present value for the original investors would be $1.7 million, based on five years of net cash flow and not including the salable value of the firm or its continuing earning power after that time. Payback is expected in one year, based on the forecast of sales and profits. Specific financial details are found in **Table 1**, **Table 2**, **Table 3**, **Table 4**, **Table 5**, and **Figure 1**. Note that the project is not without risks, as seen in **Figure 2**.

TABLE 1 The Winslow Clock Company Pro Forma Income Statements Five-Year Projection

	YEAR 1	YEAR 2	YEAR 3	YEAR 4	YEAR 5
Unit sales	50,000	150,000	200,000	150,000	125,000
Price	$ 42.50	$ 42.50	$ 42.50	$ 40.00	$ 40.00
Net sales (000s)	$ 2,125	$ 6,375	$ 8,500	$ 6,000	$ 5,000
Bad debt allowance (2%)	43	128	170	120	100
Adjusted net sales	2,082	6,247	8,330	5,880	4,900
Cost of goods sold	1,093	3,253	4,630	3,655	3,267
Gross margin	989	2,994	3,700	2,225	1,633
Operating costs	323	552	695	663	642
E.B.I.T.	666	2,442	3,005	1,562	991
Taxes (50%)	333	1,221	1,502	781	495
Net income	$ 333	$ 1,221	$ 1,503	$ 781	$ 496

TABLE 2 The Winslow Clock Company Pro Forma Balance Sheet as of December 31 ($000S)

	YEAR 1	YEAR 2	YEAR 3	YEAR 4	YEAR 5	YEAR 6
Assets						
Cash	5	203	256	1,019	2,722	3,539
Accounts receivable	–	1,345	2,044	2,726	1,924	1,283
Inventory						
Finished goods	–	73	44	48	53	58
Work-in-process	–	106	–	78	–	–
Raw materials	55	–	141	155	171	188
Net fixed assets	40	36	32	29	26	24
Total assets	100	1,763	2,517	4,055	4,896	5,092
Liabilities						
Accounts payable	40	50	141	155	171	181
Accrued liabilities	–	–	560	581	626	309
Est'd tax liability	–	70	–	–	–	–
Short-term debt	–	650	–	–	–	–
Long-term debt	–	–	–	–	–	–
Common stock	–	600	600	600	600	600
Paid-in capital (M. Winslow)	60	60	60	60	60	60
Retained earnings	–	333	1,156	2,659	3,439	3,935
Total liabilities	100	1,763	2,517	4,055	4,896	5,092

TABLE 3 The Winslow Clock Company Statement of Sources and Uses of Funds* Year Ended December 31 ($000S)

	YEAR 1	YEAR 2	YEAR 3	YEAR 4	YEAR 5
Sources					
Funds provided by operations					
Net income after taxes	333	823	1,503	780	496
Plus depreciation	4	4	3	3	2
Inc.–accounts payable	10	91	14	16	17
Inc.–accrued liabilities	–	560	21	45	–
Inc.–taxes payable	70	–	–	–	–
Inc.–common stock	600	–	–	–	–
Inc.–short-term debt	650				
Dec.–accounts receivable	–	–	–	802	641
Dec.–inventories	–	–	–	57	–
Total sources	1,667	1,478	1,541	1,703	1,156
Uses					
Inc.–cash	198	53	763	1,703	817
Inc.–accounts receivable	1,345	699	682	–	–
Inc.–inventories	124	6	96	–	22
Dec.–accrued liabilities	–	–	–	–	317
Dec.–taxes payable	–	70	–	–	–
Dec.–short-term debt	–	640	–	–	–
Total uses	1,667	1,478	1,541	1,703	1,156

*Based on pro forma balance sheets and income statements.

TABLE 4	Financial Data Backup
Unit sales, cost, margin analysis	
Retail suggested list	$85.00
Dealer margin	42.50
Mfr. selling price (dealer cost)	42.50
Cost of goods sold*	14.60
Gross margin	$27.90
Other variable costs*	
Warranty	.05
Quality control allowance	.29
Shipping & handling contribution	.20
Co-op advertising allowance	2.13
Selling commissions	4.25
Designer/developer fee	.17
Subtotal variable costs	7.09
Net margin	$20.81
Note: Total cost of goods	$21.69

*Backup detail provided.

TABLE 5	Financial Data Backup	
Cost of goods sold analysis		
Item		
Movement*	$2.77	$ 3.87
(and circuit board)	$1.10	
Chip (production model)		$ .79
Capacitors (3)		.30
Impact switch		1.03
Battery holder		.20
Photo transistor		.30
Ball		.87
Moulded sphere		.20
Velcro		.07
Molded cube (housing)		2.00
Batteries		.95
Face, crystal, hands, etc.		.60
Board		.40
Board assembly		1.00
Feet		.05
Speaker, lamp, socket		1.08
Assembly		.50
Product subtotal		$14.21
Package (inc. inside corrugated)		.24
Printed inserts		.05
Portion (1/6) master carton		.10
Package subtotal		$14.60

*Add $0.30 premium per unit for air shipments.

Note: Tooling not amortized in these calculations because first production run estimated to be 10K units; all other costs listed here based on runs of 100,000. Tooling at this point treated as a capital expenditure and listed under fixed costs.

FIGURE 1 Break-Even Quantity Calculation

1. Contribution margin per unit is estimated to be $20.81 in 2021 and 2022. (See unit sales, cost, margin analysis.)
2. Fixed costs for unit sales in the first year of 50,000 units are estimated to be $332,910, including $10,200 paid for prototype development in 2021. Break-even quantity would be $332,910/20.81 = 16,000 units.
3. Based on the expected seasonality of sales in the first year of selling, the break-even point should be reached in mid-October 2021, in the second full month of product shipments.

FIGURE 2 Critical Risks and Problems

Listed below are areas of particular concern and importance to the management.

1. *Timing* will play a critical role in the success of this venture. The key variables are
   - Product readiness
   - Financing
   - Approach to the marketplace
   - Production, from delivery of components to assembly, inventory, and shipping procedures
2. *Projections* used are best estimates, and all financial needs and operating costs have been based on what is considered to be the most likely volume of sales achievable. Because selling activities will begin early in 2021, reaction from the marketplace should be clear by late spring. Decisions can still be made to cut back—or to gear up—for the 2021 season.

   The first commitment to Seiko for 10,000 units (cost of $4.17 each) will have been made by mid-March, and estimates for the entire year will be in their production plan by then. While cutbacks can be made as late as a month in advance, increased production might be a problem since it would bump into Seiko's heaviest production season.
3. *Financing* would be another major consideration if sales were much in excess of expectations, particularly because we must assume that early orders are going to require an accompanying letter of credit. For this and other reasons, the marketing plan is meant to guard against some of these problems and is specifically geared to reach upscale stores and catalogues that will commit early to carry the "limited production" of the first year.
4. *Ironing out production* and assembly problems will be of major importance in June and July. Although the process is not complex, it will be totally new, and the production rate is currently scheduled at 5000 units in July and 10,000 in August to meet anticipated shipping requirements in September and to build minimal inventory requirements. For these reasons, selection of an experienced production manager will be critical.

INDUSTRY INFORMATION

The clock market in Canada has been growing at a rate of between 8 and 10 percent per year, with significantly higher growth (three times the industry average) recorded in the segments where innovative design or a technological change has been offered. The recent introduction of battery-operated quartz mechanisms combined with sleek styling to create lightweight, portable, wireless clocks has led to at least a 25 percent annual growth rate for decorative or kitchen wall clocks and to almost a 29 percent increase for alarm clocks.

Clocks are in most households and constitute an enduring and important retail gift category. As with many items that are so inherently useful that they might be considered a household necessity, the greater the opportunity to differentiate the product, the greater is the ability to segment the market by appealing to consumers through unique designs that are fashioned to suit a wide variety of tastes and income levels.

A handful of major competitors serve as the dominant force in the industry and often not only sell their own brands but make private-label brands for large retailers as well. (Seiko, for example, produces the private-label quartz alarm clocks for Walmart and Sears.) As a result, clock movements are inexpensive and readily available, which in turn spawns a significant opportunity for a number of smaller companies to specialize in unique designs that range from the very inexpensive to one-of-a-kind collector's items.

Clocks are sold through a variety of retail outlets that include mass merchandisers, department and specialty stores, furniture and interior design stores, jewellery stores, shops that deal exclusively in clocks, and museum gift stores.

Online and even traditional catalogue sales are also an important means of reaching the clock consumer. Furthermore, within a department store, clocks can be found in various departments that include gifts, luggage, electronics, fine collectibles, furniture, jewellery, and occasionally even in their own clock department.

This diversity of product and placement makes the clock market a natural arena in which independent sales representatives can operate. This fact simplifies, to some extent, the problems that the smaller producers face in trying to get their product to the national marketplace without incurring a disproportionate expense for the hiring, training, and support of a sales force.

It is apparent, then, that the market for clocks has ample room for product differentiation. Dr. Winslow's clock, we believe, presents an exciting opportunity to capitalize on a segment of this significant market.

THE PRODUCT: PRESENT AND FUTURE

The product will first be described and then discussed in terms of its future potential.

Product Description.

The battery-operated quartz alarm clock consists of two basic parts, the first of which is a lightweight black foam ball, approximately four inches in diameter, that contains the "brains" of the clock—a microchip, a circuit board, an impact switch, small batteries, and the audio device for the alarm. These are held inside a plastic capsule that is secured by a Velcro enclosure within the larger foam ball. The second part of the clock is the quartz movement that is housed in a handsomely styled cube of moulded plastic.

What makes the clock functionally unique is that throwing the ball turns off the alarm. Great care was taken to use materials that have virtually no chance of damaging the wall or any other object. The specifically designed impact switch is sensitive enough that even a light impact will stop the alarm. On the other hand, a throw of considerable force will not disturb the contents of the inner capsule. Two insurance companies specializing in product liability testing have been consulted. They both feel that the product is safe and free enough from liability risk that they have quoted the Winslow Clock Company the minimum premium for liability insurance.

Several achievements have made the clock technologically possible. There is no need for an electrical connection between the clock base and the ball because an ultrasound device signals the alarm to go off. A receiver in the inner capsule reads the signal and triggers the humorous crescendo of the alarm; on "advice" from the impact switch, a satisfying tone of demise is produced when the alarm hits the wall. In addition, a timing device has been built into the circuitry that automatically shuts off the alarm after one minute if the ball is not thrown.

The overall design and finish of the clock are clean and sophisticated to eliminate any sense of gimmickry that might lessen the perceived value of the clock. This elegant styling and the sophisticated electronics, combined with both the psychological satisfaction and the sense of fun and playfulness inherent in being able to throw one's alarm clock, should appeal to a significant cross section of consumers, from executives to athletes. The product has a strong appeal to retailers as well, who look for "something refreshing and new to pull people into the stores."

Technical specifications of the product are as follows:

Dimension: Base—12 cm × 12 cm × 12 cm; Ball—12 cm diameter

Colour: Model A—white clock housing with black face, charcoal ball, white, yellow, and red hands

Model B—black housing with other colours used for the same pieces as in Model A

Accuracy of movement: +/−20 seconds per month

Hands: Luminescent minute and hour hands

Foam ball: 35 ppi Crest Foam

Future Potential.

The new technological innovations that have emerged during the development of this first product have significance for the future of the company as well. First, extensions of the basic concept are possible in a variety of clocks with other features. Obvious examples are clock radios and snooze alarms. In addition, as production quantities increase, specialty designs for the premium market become possible at reasonable cost.

A family of related products, such as posters, a wall-mountable target, and other clocks—all dealing with the frustration people feel with time, alarm clocks, and schedules—are natural offshoots of the throwable alarm, and their development is currently being explored.

MARKETING PLAN AND STRATEGY

Given the clock's unique function, design, and appeal, the first year's marketing plan will focus on placing the clock in department stores, clock specialty stores, and using online sales and catalogues that reach upper-middle-income and upper-income executives and families. The early strategy is to keep the clock out of the lower-end mass market and discounters' trade, instead making it readily available to consumers more interested in its characteristics and uniqueness than its suggested list price of $85. The sales, cost, and margin analysis are based on the assumption that the suggested list price of $85 and dealer price of $42.50 will be held constant for three years. The goal is to introduce the product with a large enough margin for the dealer in the higher-end retail and catalogue business to make an adequate return and to allow the company to recapture its fixed costs as quickly as possible.

While the suggested list and dealer prices at this time are expected to remain the same in the second and third years, part of the strategy will be to refine the production and assembly costs, negotiate volume discounts with suppliers, and devise other cost-saving measures to offer more marketing support to the expanded dealer base without sacrificing profitability. If necessary, cost-saving measures will be adopted that will make it possible to lower the price dramatically as a means of defence against competitors in years 3 and 4 of the product's life.

Sales Tactics.

The principals of the firm will contact potential buyers directly at first, beginning in early 2021 when there are still budgets available for merchandise for the 2021 Christmas season. Sales in 2021 are planned at 50,000 units, on a first-come, first-served basis, unless a retailer will commit for a guaranteed order before June 1. A sales rep organization will also be retained to continue these early sales efforts and to expand distribution after the first season. A commission averaging 10 percent of the dealer price per unit has been incorporated into the cost of sales to cover the activities of these sales reps.

In addition, an experienced, full-time, in-house sales manager will coordinate the selling and promotional activities of the independent rep organization. Other responsibilities of the sales manager will include (1) making direct contact with buyers; (2) making direct contact with sales reps and evaluating their performance; (3) coordinating the marketing support and promotional activities of the sales rep force; and (4) developing other possible avenues for marketing the company's products. The direct marketing approach referred to earlier is an obvious example of this.

The company also plans to engage in some online sales but this will not be a focus for the company in the early years.

ADVERTISING AND PUBLICITY

A publicity campaign aimed at generating interest in the clock's development, its state-of-the-art technology, and its founder's concept of "functional fun" will be launched in early Fall 2021. This publicity and accompanying new product announcements will target the "executive toy" purchaser.

In addition, a print ad campaign slated for the 2021 Christmas retail market and a cooperative advertising plan to help participating dealers are expected to aid sell-through in the clock's first major season on the market.

Expanded advertising marketing support for the second season will include the following: attendance at trade shows (notably the EPTECH electronic trade show and at least one of the major gift shows); an in-store promotion plan highlighted by a 90-second video spot; continuation of the co-op advertising plan; and an overall advertising budget slated at 5 percent of anticipated sales for the year.

OPERATIONS MANAGEMENT

Since all assembly and subassembly operations will be handled by independent contractors, with final shipment emanating from the final point of assembly, the need for an office, a production staff, and overhead would be kept to a minimum.

Although Dr. Winslow will oversee all operations, his regular staff will supervise the critical functions of marketing and business development, administration (including office management, billing, and accounts receivable and payable), and production management (the control of all facets of outside assembly and vendor supplies and relations).

Marketing and business development (including sales in the initial stages) will be managed by Ms. Kristen Jones, who has 15 years of experience in marketing and finance in both domestic and international operations for Fuji Photo Film Canada. She has an MBA from the University of Toronto and a BA from Brock University.

The production management area (including product engineering) is currently handled in an advisory capacity by several consultants, including Mr. Steve Canon (see enclosed profile). As the company approaches actual production (now slated for June–July 2021 start-up), a full-time production manager will be hired. Several candidates are presently being considered for this position.

Strong relationships with highly responsible subcontractors have already been established. These include Seiko, for the precision quartz movement and related technology; Finproject N.A. Inc., Québec, QC, for the ball; Cocor Aero-Products Inc., Markham, ON, for the switch; and Bramcan Plastics Ltd., Brampton, ON, for the plastic moulding.

An outside contractor in the Toronto area will handle the assembly operation, which includes packaging and shipment to fulfill sales orders. Several companies are being considered and will be submitting quotes on the specifications early in 2021. A decision is expected to be made by the beginning of February. The possibility of an assembly operation outside Canada will be investigated as a cost-saving measure once production is being handled efficiently here.

The administrative position will have the responsibility of handling all office functions, including billing, receivables, credit, and payables. Two candidates are now being considered. It will be important to fill this function as soon as possible, even if it is on a part-time basis for the first few months. The candidates are available for such a schedule, if necessary.

Other critical areas that are now, and will continue to be, handled by consultants are advertising (including sales, promotion, and publicity)—Bill Barlow—and product design—John Edwards.

MANAGEMENT

Dr. Michael Winslow is the inventor of the clock and founder and president of the company. His profession is psychiatric medicine, and he is currently practising at the Kingston Regional Psychiatric Centre and is a lecturer in the Department of Psychiatry at Queen's University. He also maintains his own private practice. Dr. Winslow earned his undergraduate BSc degree at Dalhousie University and his medical degree at the University of Western Ontario.

It was while he was a resident in psychiatry that he conceived of the idea for the clock. He first pursued the concept as a hobby, trying to find a way to throw the clock without damaging either it or the surface it hit. Within the last two years, as it became apparent that it would be possible to create and produce such a clock at a reasonable cost, further development of the idea became another full-time occupation for Dr. Winslow.

Dr. Winslow is a man of great energy, but part of his success in bringing the product from the initial concept to the prototype stage lies in his effectiveness in finding and using the outside resources he has needed. He has also had enough confidence in, and received enough encouragement about, the ultimate marketability of the product that he has invested his own savings in development costs, a sum of approximately $60,000 to date.

Because his profession is very important to him, Dr. Winslow intends to continue his private medical practice. But he will also serve as president of the Winslow Clock Company, hiring professional managers to run the day-to-day operations for him and using consultants in those aspects of the business where a particular expertise is needed.

Kristen Jones joined Fuji Photo Film Canada, where her experience and responsibilities grew over a broad range of marketing and finance assignments.

During the years in which Fuji dramatically increased its market share, Jones was responsible for sales planning and forecasting for all its amateur photographic products. Later, as a financial analyst, her job was to assess the company's distributor markets around the world for potential as profitable wholly owned subsidiaries, as well as to carry out new product profitability analyses.

She then joined the domestic marketing division, where her assignments ranged from sales administration to marketing manager in charge of a test program to assess the potential of selling the company's Frontier System on a direct basis. In her last position as national merchandising manager, she created and managed the merchandising programs to support the national sales efforts for all consumer products.

In February 2020, she took advantage of the company's voluntary severance program to complete work on her master's degree in business administration at the University of Toronto. Jones earned her BA degree at Brock University in Ontario.

Steve Canon is a consultant, teacher, and businessman whose broad range of experience covers many aspects of new product design, development, and marketing. He presently has over 35 products of his own on the market and also teaches marketing and business law at the University of Western Ontario. In addition, he published a book in the spring of 2010 that deals with invention, product development, and marketing.

Among his numerous accomplishments, he has taught product design at Laval, University of Toronto, and Western. He has won awards for his contributions to the field, including two from Ford Motor Company for innovative product development. Canon has appeared on television talk shows, as both guest and host, discussing product marketing.

Although his primary contributions to the Winslow Clock Company are in the fields of product development and manufacturing/production, his knowledge of new product introductions has been very helpful in a number of other areas as well.

Bill Barlow has been president and creative director of Bill Barlow Advertising since 2008. Before establishing his own company, Barlow was director of advertising for Bose Canada, a national sales promotion manager and creative director at Polaroid Corporation, and a creative supervisor for Bell Canada.

In his years as an entrepreneur, Barlow has built an impressive list of clients and has won numerous awards and honours for excellence in advertising. Hewlett-Packard is his most noteworthy client.

He will be responsible for advertising, promotional support materials, and publicity for the Winslow Clock Company.

John Edwards is the founder of Edwards Design Associates, Inc., a firm that specializes in industrial design, product development, and graphic design. For the past seven years, this company has provided an integrated approach to the design of both products and the packaging and collateral materials to support the products.

His clients are primarily in the fields of consumer products and finance, and include Revlon, Chaps, and Hallmark.

Edwards has a BSc degree in mechanical engineering from École Polytechnique and an MSc degree in industrial design from the University of Ottawa.

In addition to designing Dr. Winslow's product, Edwards has also provided invaluable help in finding sources for the manufacture of several components, for injection moulding, and for packaging.

Discussion Questions

1. Based on the information here, do you think the Winslow Clock Company will succeed? Why or why not?
2. What gaps were missed in the business analysis?
3. What recommendations would you make to improve the business plan?
4. Is there a less-expensive market-entry strategy involving lower risk that should be considered? Why should Winslow consider such a strategy?

WINDOW TECH INC.

Ahmed Raj had been in the housing restoration business for 15 years when, in 2018, he designed a machine that could remove old windows from their frames without destroying the wooden panes known as muntins and mullions that surround the glass (see **Figure 1**). One of the big advantages of the tool is that it was built around a routing drill piece that moved on a three-dimensional plane. This allowed Raj to replace windows that, up until now, could not be serviced. Once the small panes were removed, they would be replaced by one large pane of double glass. The muntins and mullions would be inserted over the window to give it the same look as before.

FIGURE 1 **Window Design: Removing Windows and Keeping the Panes**

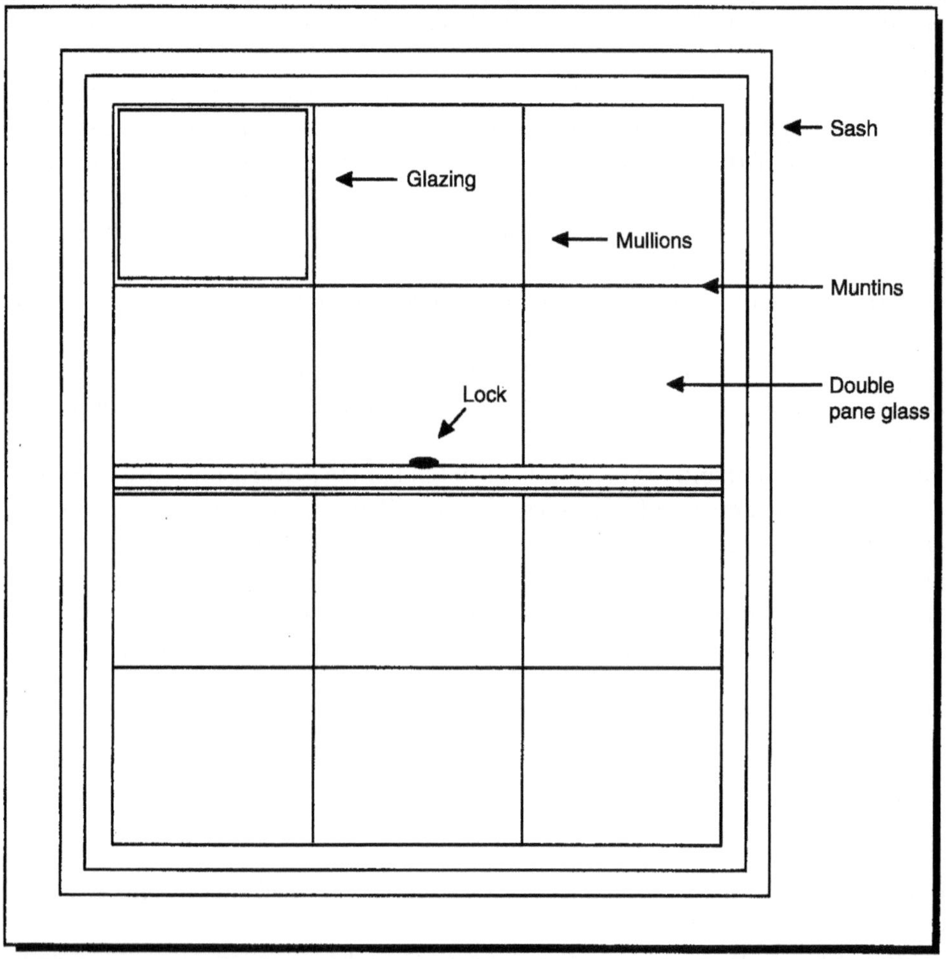

Raj applied for a patent as soon as he realized his machine was unique, and the patent was granted in August 2019. He has been operating the business since that time under the name of Window Tech Inc. He and his wife, Saira, are the sole owners and employees of the company. She oversees the advertising and promotional aspects, and Ahmed does the installation. They both engage in the selling process, particularly in the colder months when the installation business is slower. Their current geographic market is the Edmonton area, although they have done business outside it. They generally have concentrated on the residential market but have periodically completed commercial jobs.

The restoration market is affected by several factors that include the state of the overall economy, local employment levels, and the amount of a consumer's disposable income. Since the company began operations, the economy has been favourable. The GNP has been increasing, real disposable income has risen moderately, and there has been a decrease in unemployment in the Edmonton area. The restoration of windows is a relatively large expense, costing between $3000 and $7000, depending on the number of windows installed in a house. Home owners are more likely to invest in this type of restoration when their level of net disposable income is greater and when the economy is good. Today, there is a trend toward less saving on the part of many Canadians, and consumers are tending to borrow for expenditures, such as home renovations. Therefore, the level of interest rates affects Window Tech's business. Fortunately, interest rates have been low recently, so consumers have been able to afford such renovations.

Another factor that affects the renovation market is the cost of energy. In the late 1970s, the energy crisis forced many people to see energy as a limited resource. Since that time, people have generally tried to conserve energy. Consumers are faced with finding alternative sources of energy to heat and cool their homes and offices. This concern with conservation gives Window Tech an advantage in that it is replacing single-pane, non-insulated windows with energy-efficient dual-pane insulated windows.

Because of the favourable economy and Window Tech's unique method of installing double-pane glass, the Rajs have had more business than they can handle. They have advertised on Kijji, in the local paper, used social media, and have sent direct mail to the subscribers of a regional home improvement magazine. Their customers have referred their friends to the Rajs, so business has expanded considerably. Ahmed has two ideas on how to handle his growing business. He could hire and train a staff of salespeople and installers, or he could franchise his business. He enjoyed the selling and the actual installing of the windows, but neither he nor his wife was interested in managing a staff of workers. Therefore, franchising was more appealing to him. He felt that one of Window Tech's big advantages was the patented cutting tool, and he could bring the name Window Tech to more customers if he franchised the business. Several contractors he contacted had expressed an interest in the Window Tech machine and wondered if he was interested in franchising.

Ahmed decided that his goal was to franchise the business. There were three groups of people he could contact regarding franchising. First, he could sell the rights of the product to contractors who were in the business of restoring residential homes or commercial offices. He felt that their reach with consumers could help to broaden the exposure of the Window Tech name. He also thought that glass companies in the Edmonton area might be interested in a Window Tech franchise. Since his tool could cut odd-shaped glass, it had an advantage over existing methods, which glass companies would benefit from. Saira mentioned that individuals who wanted to get into the restoration business might also be potential targets for franchising.

Discussion Questions

1. Ahmed needs to know how to go about franchising the business. What kind of legalities would be involved?
2. He knew that he had patent protection on the machine, but what kind of procedures should Ahmed follow in terms of setting up guidelines for owning a Window Tech franchise?
3. Ahmed wants to sell his franchise to the group or groups that would give the Window Tech name the most exposure and continue to emphasize the quality of the work. Which group should he target for franchising?
4. How much should the franchise cost?
5. How should Ahmed proceed?

EDGE HOCKEY

Jack Supple was looking over his summer sales figures and was more than a little surprised. After starting to run summer hockey camps in the Moncton area four years ago the business had consistently experienced strong growth. Yet this year, sales were down. Jack was disappointed as his camps had previously always sold out. For example, if he expected 30 registrations he always received 30. This year he was likely going to operate at 75 percent capacity.

Additionally, the sales numbers had Jack seriously considering the future of his business. He had started the company, Edge Hockey, four years ago to supplement his income. Jack was a full-time school teacher but found the income was not enough to pay back his student loans as well as support his wife, who was still in school. Jack's long-term plans had been to teach during the school year and supplement his income by running hockey camps full time in the summer. While he had only recently started teaching, he found the pay after taxes and other deductions to be less than anticipated.

Jack had started Edge Hockey without any future plans. Jack had played university hockey and started to coach AAA minor hockey as a volunteer when he graduated. He coached much like he played – he was driven, and pushed himself and his players to be the best. While the top-end players and parents seemed to enjoy Jack's coaching style, some of the developing players and their parents found him to be too aggressive with his expectations for himself and his players.

Four years ago, Jack noticed the local rink had a week of free ice time, which was unusual. Without any concrete plans, he booked four hours of ice a day from Monday to Friday at a cost of $250 per hour and decided he would run a hockey camp. Jack recalled that in university he learned about the importance of supplementing his income, and he thought would give it a shot. Edge Hockey was born.

In the first year, Jack only had a week of ice time and decided he would price his camp much lower than any local competitors. While competitors were charging on average $500 a week for camps Jack opted to price his camp at $350. He figured if he was lucky he would break even and maybe make a few dollars. Jack had no real marketing plans and simply sent out the camp information through email to some parents he knew. Much to his surprise, he quickly had 36 registered players, all of whom played AAA hockey between the ages of 9 and 13. Jack realized he would need some help and hired six local university hockey players for 4.5 hours a day, at $25 an hour to help him run his camp.

While Jack didn't make a lot of money off his camp, he fell in love with the concept of Edge Hockey and quickly expanded. The next year he offered three camps, all of which sold out. The following year he provided four camps. Now, in year four, Jack was running five week-long hockey camps, that were operating at roughly 75 percent capacity. He is wondering if he will even make money this summer.

Edge Hockey camps were different. Unlike traditional summer camps, which often served as a babysitting service, Edge Hockey camps consisted of ice time as well as dry land, and were run over half days. Parents still needed to find childcare in the afternoons and had to interrupt their days to pick up the players after lunch. The camps themselves focused on pushing players to the maximum and in the first two years of business Jack had only top-end players register. His business was so successful that he did not even advertise. Jack relied solely on word of mouth to fill his registrations and he managed the business in the evening.

As Jack expanded his business, some AA, A, and even recreational players registered for his camps, and Jack was happy to have them. He found he enjoyed working with all calibers of players. He did start to receive some negative comments from some top-end AAA parents, who did not like to have their children share the ice with what they perceived to be lesser quality players. Jack would tell the AAA parents he grouped the players by skill and since his camps focused on individual skills that it did not matter who their children shared the ice with. Jack had started to notice a trend though, that more and more lower AA and A players were registering for his camps and the AAA players were opting to go elsewhere. While he still maintained some AAA players, they tended to shop around, always looking for the next big thing in player development, and some parents clearly did not want their players on the ice with what they thought were developing hockey players.

Jack had also started to raise the price of his camps, slowly at first, then more drastically bringing them in line with other local hockey camps. Unlike these camps though, Jack only ran half days, but he justified the price as his camps offered players much much more ice time. For example, all of Jack's camps offered 20 hours of ice a week. While his competitors who ran full day camps only offered 10 to 12 hours of ice a week. These camps filled in their days with movies, some dry land training, and fun activities. Jack felt this was the equivalent of offering a babysitting service which he did not want to do. He wanted to train hockey players. Yet as more AAA players gravitated away from his camps, Jack started to hear some feedback from his clientele that his camps were getting pricey. Jack was discovering that parents of AAA players were much less price sensitive than developing players.

Jack's financial plans for the camp were simple. He would rent the ice at $250 an hour and offer players four hours of ice a day and one session of dry land training. At the most he could accommodate 30 to 36 players who he now charged $450 a week (Monday to Friday) and for every 5 players registered he would hire a coach who he would pay between $25 and $35 an hour. He also paid $2500 a year for insurance and roughly $2000 a year for supplies. While not getting rich, the money was helpful, especially given that Jack and his wife had started a family and were expecting their daughter to be born later this year.

As Jack looked over his numbers again he wasn't sure what to think. He still was not advertising: He simply emailed camp information to previous campers and relied on word of mouth to fill remaining spots. There was very little formal competition in the area as the three local universities ran hockey and sports camps all summer. But Jack did not consider their on-ice development to be of the same quality. Jack also noticed that some local coaches were starting to run on-ice development sessions, which were the equivalent of hockey camps.

Jack thought he had three basic alternatives. First, he could simply close his camps. However, with a baby on the way, he wanted to continue supplementing his income, not make less money year over year. Next, he could expand his business. He could run numerous camps, including full-day camps, engage in some marketing, and become more professional in his overall approach. The final alternative would be to downsize his hockey camps. Jack thought he could run two to three camps a summer, just appeal to AAA players, raise his prices slightly, and focus on high-end development. With this option, he would make the same amount of money while possibly working less.

Discussion Questions

1. What are some of the advantages and disadvantages in running a supplementary business such as Edge Hockey for Jack?
2. Based on the information in the case what would you recommend to Jack? Why?
3. Complete a financial analysis of Jack's current business and determine if he will make money at 75 percent capacity?
4. If Jack is going to market his business more formally, how would you recommend he do this?

BEACH STAKE

Will Miller had just finished his first term at University and was excited about pursuing his entrepreneurial dream over the summer. Will had had used a 3D printer to perfect his Beach Stake toy, and thought he could be on to the next big thing in beach toys. Previous handcrafted versions of the toy had not worked as well, and, in Will's eyes, the 3D version was perfect.

The Beach Stake was a game where players could attach a bottle to a 5-foot-tall stake in the ground. Players would then throw balls at the object trying to knock the bottle off. Unlike homemade stakes, Will's Beach Stake had fasteners in place to firmly hold the bottle. The bottle could only be knocked off if it were hit with the ball directly and with enough force. The game could be played in very simple fashion where one player would throw a ball at the bottle on the stake. If he missed, the alternate player would catch the ball and throw it at that player's bottle. Generally, the players would select a score, say the first to knock the bottle off 10 times, to determine a winner. The game could also be played in groups, and Will and his friends played a version where they placed multiple stakes in the ground and could actively defend the stakes by jumping in front of the bottles and catching the balls. These games would often see multiple balls in play at the same time. While one-on-one play was fun, Will saw the multiple stake game as a much more enjoyable game.

While previous handmade versions had not always worked well, the new 3D printed stake looked like it would be durable when manufactured and tested in game play. Will had sent the plans and a prototype to a manufacturer in China, and was going to use almost all of his $50,000 savings to order 5000 pairs of Beach Stakes. Will was sure he could create enough online buzz with Instagram to quickly sell the stakes online at $20 a set, resulting in a nice profit.

Just as Will was going to place the order, his mother asked him to reconsider. She had been doing some research into the use of crowdfunding and thought that this might be a better approach for Will to use in starting his business.

Discussion Questions

1. What would be the advantages and disadvantages of crowdfunding for Will's business?
2. If Will opted to use crowdfunding, what would he have to do to create a successful crowdfunding campaign?
3. Has Will overlooked anything in completing his business analysis? If so, what did he not consider?
4. What recommendations would you make to Will?

THE FRAMEMAKERS

Robert and Teresa Norman are facing a big decision. They are contemplating Robert leaving his job managing his father's painting business to set up their own retail picture-framing store. As they think about this dilemma, their minds wander back to the events that led up to the impending decision.

Robert was raised in a small town about 32 kilometres south of Brandon, Manitoba. His father was a painter, and Robert worked in the painting business part-time for several years. After graduating from high school, he completed a two-year business administration in interior design course at a college in the United States. It was there that he met and married his wife, Teresa.

Teresa studied interior design at college. She came from a small farming community near Robert's hometown. One of her favourite pastimes when she was growing up was taking pictures of the beautiful scenery and making frames for them. Teresa, an only child, had always been very independent. Her parents, farmers, spent a lot of time tending to the farm. Teresa started helping them when she was very young by doing the bookkeeping and other administrative jobs.

Although Robert always thought he might come back to take over his father's painting business, he wanted to obtain some outside business experience first. As a result, he found a job in a Walmart store in Winnipeg after graduation. Robert enjoyed working with people in the retail setting but felt frustrated working for a large company. He wanted to be on his own and dreamed of someday running his own business. While Robert worked at Walmart, Teresa was developing her photography skills, working for local businesses helping them create online advertising and occasionally taking pictures at weddings. Though she was fairly busy with this, she did not feel as if she were being challenged.

Finally, after two years with Walmart, the Normans decided to leave Winnipeg and return to Brandon where they could begin to take over the painting business. Robert's father was pleased with their decision and, since he was approaching retirement age, allowed his son to assume a major role in the business. Norman managed the business for six years with Teresa doing the bookkeeping. But although it provided a steady income, he could see that the growth possibilities in terms of income and challenge were limited. In addition, he soon realized he did not like painting as much as he thought he would. As a result, he and Teresa started looking around for sideline opportunities to earn a little extra money. One they particularly enjoyed was assembling and selling picture frames.

One day, while in Winnipeg to obtain some water-seal paint, Robert ran across a small retail store called U-Frame-It. He went in to look around and talk to the manager about the business. He was impressed by the manager's enthusiasm and noticed that the store was extremely busy. Robert immediately began wondering about the possibility of starting his own picture-framing store.

Excited by what he had seen, Robert returned to Brandon without even buying his paint and told Teresa what had happened. She was extremely enthusiastic about the idea. Robert's father was skeptical and, as Robert had expected, disappointed that they wanted to leave the family business.

Robert and Teresa needed to make their decision quickly. The manager of the U-Frame-It store had indicated that the franchise chain was looking at Brandon as a possible site for another outlet sometime in the future.

After a few days of evaluating their small business decision, Robert and Teresa Norman decided to open the picture-framing retail outlet in Brandon. Robert had learned a great deal about the business from his visit with the U-Frame-It franchise in Winnipeg. He convinced his father that the opportunity had promise. Both were aware that many people were now becoming do-it-yourselfers in home decorating.

His college training had taught Robert the importance of thorough investigation before starting a business. He had realized he should do this even before deciding whether to start the business on his own or to become a franchisee. He contacted the Professional Picture Framers Association (PPFA) and learned that the average customer spends $32 per visit at a framing store. In checking framing costs with the U-Frame-It manager in Winnipeg, he confirmed this information. A typical per-customer profit statement for a framing shop was as follows:

Revenue	$32	(100%)
Materials	15	(47%)
Overhead (rent, utilities, wages, etc.)	9	(28%)
Profit per customer	8	(25%)

Robert knew there was one other framing store in Brandon, a city of 35,000. Using Winnipeg as an example, Robert calculated that a framing store could service a population of approximately 25,000 people and earn an acceptable profit.

While Robert was collecting his information, Teresa had conducted some of her own market research. She visited the only picture-framing store in Brandon and noted that the store was the busiest between the hours of 11 a.m. and 3 p.m. She also observed that many customers had some time to wait for available workstations and for the glue to dry. During this time, they browsed around the store looking at the merchandise.

Robert also attended an industry supplier seminar in Minneapolis. He was encouraged to learn that the do-it-yourself framing business was experiencing rapid growth throughout North America. While there, Robert learned about several online picture-framing trade magazines and bought subscriptions for them. He also made valuable contacts with suppliers and other dealers.

Things looked more positive each day, so Robert closed down the painting business, and he and Teresa began preparing to open their new store, which they would call The Framemakers.

Robert and Teresa Norman immediately went to work organizing their new business. They had contemplated signing a franchise contract with U-Frame-It but decided against it when they found out they would have to pay a $20,000 franchise fee and royalties of 10 percent of sales just for the name and set-up assistance. In addition, the franchisor required that the stores follow a set format and that all supplies be purchased from them.

Robert's college training had taught him the importance of drawing up a business plan, so they prepared the following outline for their business:

- *Target market.* We think the new store should cater to the price-conscious individual who wants to save a few dollars by doing his or her own framing. What we have learned about the do-it-yourself market seems particularly suitable for the new business. We judge that the target market is between the ages of 35 and 60, and customers could spend up to an hour in the store. This is based on our observations of the other framing store in Brandon.
- *Financial.* Based on data from the U-Frame-It franchise, we estimate start-up costs to be about $100,000. Since we are planning to lease space for the store, the capital requirements include only the purchase of shelves, fixtures, initial inventory, and tools. Because we have $25,000 in equity to put into the venture, we expect to be able to borrow the remaining $75,000 from a local bank.
- *Personnel.* We are hesitant to hire any employees until we are sure the business is successful. In addition, we want to be totally involved in the business to better learn about all aspects of framing. We will work full-time, each doing whatever needs to be done.

- *Regulations.* We know The Framemakers needs a business licence, which we will obtain from City Hall. We will operate the business as a proprietorship until the need to incorporate becomes evident.
- *Layout.* After looking at the U-Frame-It shop in Winnipeg, we have drawn up an interior layout plan we believe allows for efficiency and convenience in the store.
- *Location.* Although there are not many available locations in Brandon, we recognize the need to locate in a high-traffic area of the city. Not only will this be convenient for regular customers, but we hope it will attract some walk-in customers as well.

After developing this business plan, Robert and Teresa began making contacts to get the business going. Over the next month, Robert was busy negotiating with suppliers, landlords, the banker, and City Hall to get the business started as soon as possible.

After selecting their location, Robert and Teresa Norman began securing merchandise for their initial inventory in earnest. They soon learned, however, that suppliers wanted to be paid before making deliveries. Therefore, Robert approached his local bank's manager to obtain the money he needed to get started. He had known his banker for a long time, and he was surprised to find a less than positive reaction toward his proposal. Robert requested a $75,000 business loan, with he and Teresa contributing $25,000 of their own money to the estimated $100,000 cost of the venture.

The bank manager asked Robert to go home and prepare a detailed description of their needs and a projected operating statement for the first year's operations. The Normans were upset by this negative reaction and decided to visit other banks to obtain the funds. But they found out they would need to provide the requested information to obtain the money, no matter where they went. Robert and Teresa spent two days working feverishly and came up with the statements shown in **Table 1**.

TABLE 1

THE FRAMEMAKERS FINANCIAL REQUIREMENTS, YEAR 1

ITEM	AMOUNT	SOURCE OF INFORMATION
Inventory	$ 45,000	General estimate
Equipment and fixtures	35,000	Approximation
Opening promotion (trade show)	2,000	Price of booth
First month's rent	2,000	From landlord
Three months' salary (Robert and Teresa)	12,000	Estimated $4000/month
First three months' advertising	3,600	One ad on TV and radio, and in newspaper
Miscellaneous	400	Estimate
Total	$100,000	

THE FRAMEMAKERS PROJECTED INCOME STATEMENT, YEAR 1

	PER CUSTOMER (PROFESSIONAL PICTURE FRAMING ASSOCIATION FIGURES)		20 CUSTOMERS A DAY FOR 240 DAYS
Sales	$32	100%	$153,600
Expenses	24	75	115,200
Profit	8	25	38,400

When Robert took the proposals to the bank, the manager seemed impressed but still would not give approval for the loan. Some uncertainties about the statements still bothered the banker. Finally, after two weeks of collecting information—and pleading—the Normans' loan for $75,000 was approved only after Robert's father agreed to co-sign the document. A major reason for the approval was their past dealings with the bank, their good credit standing, and the addition of Robert's father as a co-signer as he had considerable assets. Now they could begin purchasing supplies to get started.

Before long, however, the Normans realized that they had underestimated many of their expenses. They also needed some additional supplies, even though they had overbought some unnecessary supplies from especially persistent salespeople. The landlord required the first and last months' rent before letting them move in. The equipment costs and inventory levels were higher than they had estimated. Finally, since the Normans had decided it would be better to incorporate their business, they faced additional legal costs for which they had not planned. The result of all these additions was that The Framemakers needed another $10,000—and the Normans had not even opened the doors!

Robert and Teresa did not know what to do. They were hesitant to go back to the bank and ask for more money because of the difficulty they had obtaining the first loan. However, they knew their chances of obtaining funding elsewhere were slim. On top of that, the time for the grand opening was rapidly approaching.

Discussion Questions

1. What aspects of Robert and Teresa Norman's backgrounds will contribute to their success with the picture-framing store?
2. What positive things have Robert and Teresa done in investigating the feasibility of the new store and what additional information might they have collected? From what sources could this information be obtained?
3. From the information provided, evaluate the business plan they have prepared for their new business.
4. Weigh the relevant pros and cons for the Normans of operating a U-Frame-It franchise instead of starting their business from scratch.
5. Evaluate the Normans' initial approach to obtaining financing for The Framemakers.
6. Assuming you are the banker, evaluate the financial requirements and projections Robert and Teresa prepared.

TOP HUMAN TECHNOLOGY LIMITED

Top Human Technology Limited (Top Human), an international organization offering diversified services in the development of human capital, is also the first professional company promoting coaching in Asia. "Realizing Potential, Inspiring Talent" is the mission statement of the company. Top Human believes that individual employees are the most important resource in an organization and that management should fully optimize the potential in human capital by maximizing each employee's individual qualities. Doing this enhances organizational productivity and improves corporate culture.

Founded by Eva Wong, Lawrence Leung, and others in 1995, Top Human, headquartered in Canada, has offices in Hong Kong, Macau, Guangzhou, Shenzhen, Shanghai, and Beijing. A pioneer of corporate coaching in Asia, Top Human created a unique business model based on "Training plus Coaching" and successfully expanded in various parts of China.

CORPORATE COACHING

Origin.

Coaching originally was a methodology used to train sports talent. Corporate coaching uses various tools and techniques to transfer the concept of sport coaching to the field of corporate management. In the 1970s, retired U.S. Navy veteran Tim Gallway developed an idea from playing tennis—the Art of Focus. He announced that he needed only 20 minutes to teach anyone who could not play tennis to be able to play a basic game. In a test in a televised demonstration, he taught a woman who had never played tennis before to focus her attention on the tennis ball and when the ball bounced up, shout "hit" and just wave the racket. Surprisingly, in 20 minutes, this woman could hit the ball with ease. Tim Gallway explained he did not teach her anything about the techniques in tennis but rather, he helped her overcome her existing attitude of "I cannot play." AT&T invited Tim Gallway to lecture its managers, which brought his concept of tennis coaching to the field of corporate management. Coaching was born. With the use of coaching by such companies as Coca-Cola, ExxonMobil, IBM, Ford, BP, and Honda, coaching occurred throughout Europe and America. One study indicated that while training alone increased productivity by 22.4 percent, Training plus Coaching increased productivity by 88 percent.

What Is Corporate Coaching?

According to Top Human, "Corporate Coaching is a management skill that facilitates the realization of an individual's full potential and enhances performance via improving mental models." Mental models refer to the set of beliefs and assumptions that influence the way people perceive the surrounding world and the actions they take. These beliefs and assumptions are often embedded deep in the minds of people; they can be invisible, be a subtle awareness, or be someone's beliefs and principles in life. Regardless of whether people are conscious of their mental models, the mental models are like mirrors: People intake information to conform with their mental models. They overlook or simply ignore other information, or use various means to deny or distort it. As such, mental models heavily influence an individual's cognition and behaviour, as well as his or her organizational environment and corporate culture. Furthermore, the concept of mental models plays a very important role in the theory of learning organizations, as is indicated in **Figure 1**.

FIGURE 1 **Mental Models and Their Relationship with the Other Four Essential Factors**

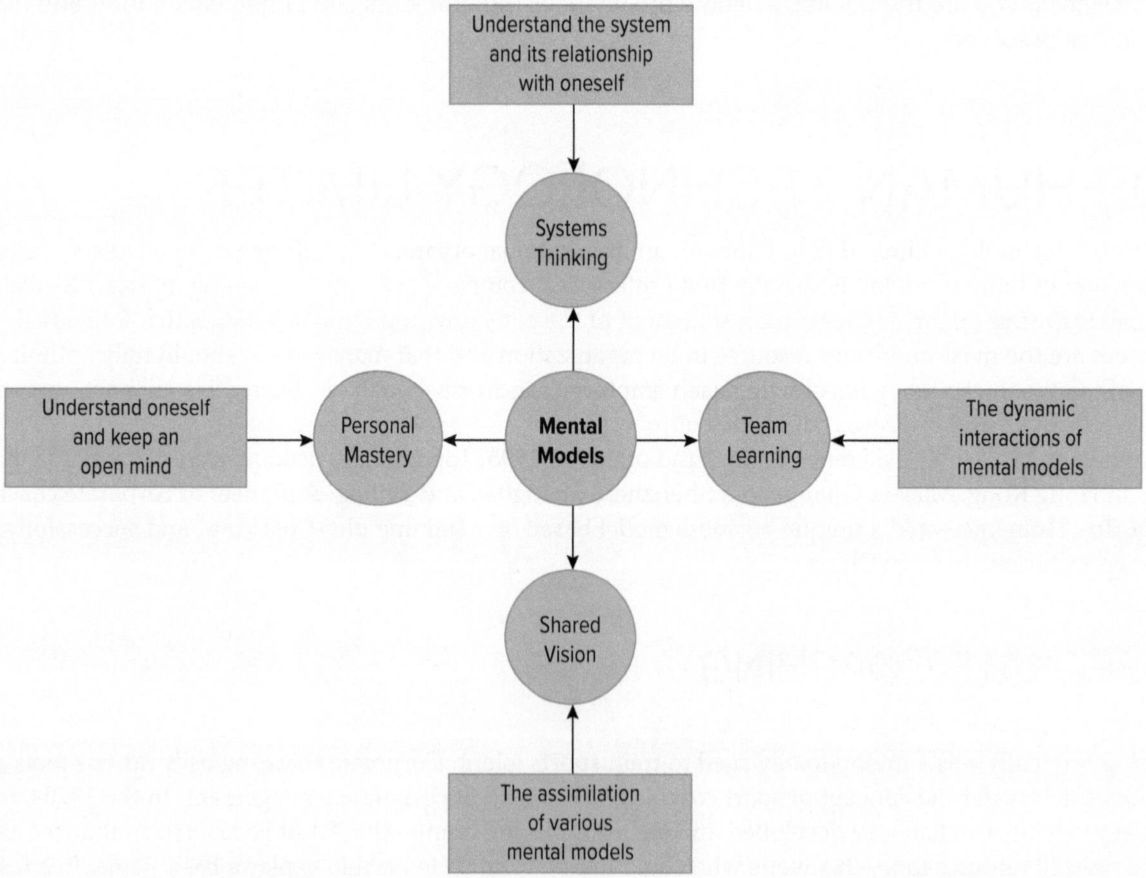

Distinction of Coaching versus Other Forms of Training.

The main distinction between coaching and other forms of training is that training mainly deals with the improvement of the ability of an individual or a group on a technical basis, such as personal skills training or management skills training. Coaching covers both the individual and organizational ability on a macro-societal level. Often the technical factors, which reflect the individual's ability and are the basis of organizational competitiveness, are not a match for the societal factors in the surrounding environment.

The essence of corporate coaching is to expand the corporation through respecting the individual's choice and facilitating the individual's development, similar to the concept of motivation. The traditional concept of motivation assumes that the goals of the corporation and its members are not the same, requiring that various management methods be used to help the members support the goals of the corporation. The traditional concept of motivation differentiates between the main subject and the objective targets, with the main subject being the investors or shareholders and the objects being the employees of the corporation. In corporate coaching, the main subject and the objects are the same. Corporate coaching is committed to helping every single member align his or her personal goals with those of the corporation, and through this process the corporation develops. Employees are no longer "worker bees" directed by management; they are "corporate citizens" with rights and opportunities.

Coaching Tools and Techniques and Experiential Learning.

In recent years, the coaching tools and techniques developed by Top Human have increased and now include Enneagram, Core Values, 360° Feedback, Cultural Differences, Body Consciousness and Tai Chi, Emotional Intelligence, and Meditation. Top Human uses the "Four-Step Coaching" process (clarifying goals, reflecting truth, shifting paradigms, and planning actions) and the "Four Coaching Abilities" (profound listening, precise questioning, perceptive distinction, and powerful feedback). Insight into body language, emotions, and language is also included.

As indicated in **Figure 2**, Top Human uses pre-training counselling, interactive and experiential learning in its training, and post-training follow-up and empowerment to achieve the final objective of behavioural change and enhancement of corporate performance; this is different from traditional training.

FIGURE 2 **Top Human Coaching Technology Training**

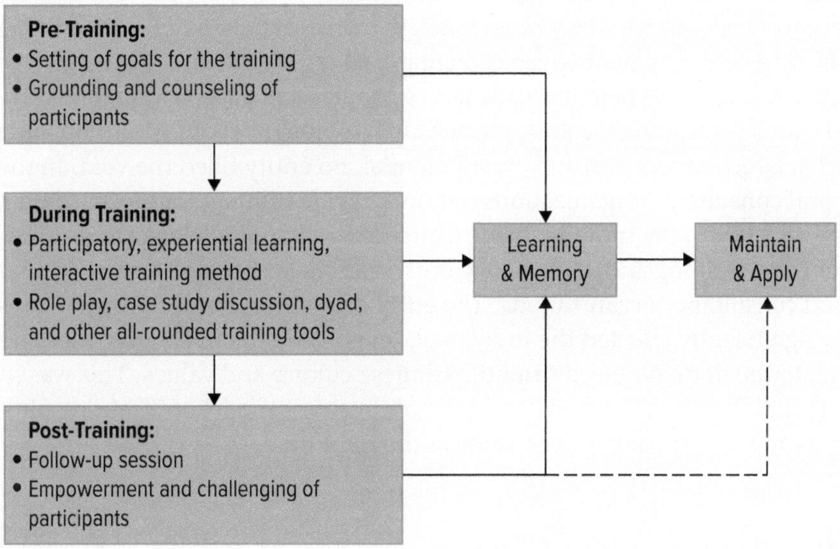

The emergence of corporate coaching reflects modern society's shift toward the development of human beings and the continual evolvement of organizations; it seeks to cover the sociocultural factors that technical skills training fails to cover. Coaching Technology, based on mental models as an entry point, facilitates the realization of one's potential and builds a corporate environment conducive for learning. Training and coaching are complementary and their synthesis helps harmonize the technical and societal factors in both individual and corporate ability.

THE DOMESTIC CHINESE MARKET FOR COACHING TECHNOLOGY

The reform of China and the opening of its economy allowed the creation of a large number of private enterprises. By the end of the twentieth century, these enterprises were responsible for a substantial portion of the country's economic output. In the early days of the developing economy, many owners of small and medium-sized enterprises relied on their spirit of risk-taking and hard work. The initial success of their companies was achieved through their personal perseverance and work; when their companies reached a certain size, problems started to occur.

At start-up, the entrepreneurs recruited their own relatives or friends. There was little staff, and the team knew each other well, so it was easy to coordinate and manage. As the number of employees grew, the company had to recruit and employ individuals beyond its personal relationship network; after 50 employees a company is beyond the ability of a single person. Doing everything oneself or refusing (or not knowing how) to delegate authority exhausts the entrepreneur and creates minimal return. As one entrepreneur stated: "In my corporation, I am the only, and also the most powerful, worker as I have to solve everything myself. The bigger my company becomes, the more tired I get. It is not that I am content with my present assets, but there is no point dying of exhaustion." Another entrepreneur stated: "In the corporation, my management style is to scold; I expect a lot from the staff but they always make mistakes. After attending Top Human training, I realize that the mediocre performance of my staff is largely my responsibility because the caliber of my staff is a reflection of my own caliber." One of Top Human's first clients, the owner of a handicraft company in Zhejiang, said, "I don't consider my company a small one as making several millions annually is very easy. I am the top entrepreneur in my district but all along I have been very fatigued, I do not know what I want to do after earning the money, I have no clue at all."

White-Collar Stratum.

The white-collar stratum, which started about the same time as private enterprises in China, is sensitive to its own surroundings and conditions. The rules and regulations in China's society are not at the level of people's expectations, yet the developmental changes in the Chinese society more often than not exceed their expectations. At the same time, each individual's development is also changing, making it difficult to maintain a balance in one's attitude; the uncertainty in change and choices usually leaves people feeling lost and helpless. The dramatic change in one's material life with a contrastingly blank spiritual life has brought about confusion and maladjustment.

Strangely, for such a large market with such vast potential, no entity filled the void. In the early 1990s in China, the training and consultancy organizations did not provide training that focused on shifting employees' attitudes. During the mid-1990s, the training inside China centred on knowledge and skills. Before the twenty-first century, most of these training and consultancy organizations were one-person organizations. There were few large training and consultancy organizations. The entry of American and European consultancy and training firms into China significantly affected the individual, one-person organizations; these new entrants still needed time to adjust to the domestic needs and the Chinese culture and values. This was the large, untapped market with vast potential that existed when Top Human's business model of "Training plus Coaching" appeared; the entrance of the company indeed came at the right time.

ESTABLISHING THE COMPANY

Training plus Coaching.

In 1991, Eva Wong left the Canadian Embassy in China, where she had worked for six years as a commercial officer. One of the reasons for her departure was her exposure to a lot of training courses in her work and her passion to become a trainer. Eva graduated from Hong Kong Polytechnic University with a degree in management.

Before her career at the Embassy, she had worked in accounting and administration. After leaving the Embassy, she worked as a trainer at several training companies in Hong Kong and as a professional trainer in the United States. After facilitating training in Hong Kong for several years, she found that there were some problems in the training content and organizational management of the companies. Eva began to think about solving these problems by starting her own company.

For a newly created training company to succeed, develop, and grow, it needs to have a unique training product. In the initial period, Eva and her then-boyfriend and now husband, Lawrence Leung, and other like-minded friends met frequently to brainstorm various aspects of the training industry and discuss various options for establishing a company.

This process of thorough planning and joint contributions, exploring all the possibilities and developing a strategy before taking actions, has become the practice in Top Human. This working style is closely related to the personalities of Eva and Lawrence. Eva has an open and straightforward personality and is willing to communicate and share her ideas with others. Her strength lies in her sound listening skills and the ability to express her ideas clearly. Lawrence prefers to keep a low profile and is humorous and direct and has keen insight. He is able to inspire others and is a very approachable person. Both Eva and Lawrence have worked for a long time in Hong Kong–the junction of Eastern and Western cultures–and both have a broad international view. They also understand Chinese culture and manners and the domestic market.

It was at this time Eva and the others came into contact with coaching on the international scene. They discovered that coaching can effectively adjust people's attitudes and empower and support people to success. In addition, the beliefs underlying coaching closely fit the Chinese traditional philosophy of Buddhism, Taoism, and Confucianism. It also is similar to the content of modern corporate management. They began to introduce coaching into Asia. Since there was no unified standard in the world for coaching, Eva, Lawrence, and others, together with a Russian friend, started to design Coaching Technology and its related training. They adopted the basic theories of international coaching and infused these with the Chinese culture, creating the unique "Training plus Coaching" approach which later became Top Human's main product and service. According to Lawrence, "In the past when China tried to connect with the world in various areas, it always had to adapt to overseas standards, but Coaching was a new profession and industry; there was room to play. In the future, everyone can be on equal footing and define the rules of the game together."

At the heart of the unique Coaching Technology, principally created by Eva and Lawrence, is building an environment–a special atmosphere where participants can see themselves clearly and their links with their surroundings, and in the process uncover their own potential. For example, during rope-course challenge training, there are individuals who discover their weaknesses in the process of climbing the pole while others discover their strengths. To individuals who succeed through personal endeavours, the team events at the Outdoor Challenge Center allow them to realize that teamwork can achieve things that are not attainable alone. "It is not about teaching them what to do, but rather their discovering and deciding for themselves what to do. Coaching only enables them [to] see a clear reflection of themselves." In the entire course of training, Eva regards herself as a mirror. She feels that modern corporations need more mirrors and that managers need to let their subordinates see their weaknesses and their potential.

The Establishment.

In July 1995, Eva, Lawrence, and two other partners jointly invested HKD750,000 to set up Top Human Technology Limited, with headquarters in Vancouver, Canada. The vision of Top Human was to re-engineer the talent of people and enhance the quality of life through "Training plus Coaching."

When Top Human started in Hong Kong, there was only Eva, a girl who handled the odd jobs, and other friends who frequently came to help Top Human as volunteers. To pursue personal interests, one of the partners withdrew from the company. The initial development of the company in Hong Kong was smooth and at the end of 1995, the company had three employees; there were seven employees at the end of 1996 and the company's revenue was more than HKD7 million. By mid-1997, the company staff reached 12 and that year, the revenue reached HKD11.5 million, mainly from Hong Kong. Top Human still had the goal to develop the China Mainland market. Although there is a large population in China, the market positioning of Top Human was based on the breadth of the training market as well as Eva's personal experience and understanding of China.

While Eva considered herself as a Hongkonger, after many experiences, she realized that she was actually Chinese. Following her deep understanding of China, she felt a fervent sense of responsibility to the land where she belonged and hoped to contribute something back to the country.

First Site—Guangzhou.

In March 1996, Top Human started in the Chinese market in Guangzhou. Guangzhou is not far from Hong Kong and is a large city with most of the people speaking Cantonese, not Mandarin. In addition, a member of the Top Human team, Catherine Ng, who used to be the operating manager for an American shipping company in the province of Guangdong, knew many people in Guangzhou.

Top Human priced its Performance Technology courses in Guangzhou in line with the prices charged in Hong Kong (about RMB20,000). In the beginning, not many people in Guangzhou understood Top Human's Coaching Technology. Finally, Top Human had its first course in Guangzhou with only one of the participants being local Chinese. The presence of Hong Kong's participants in these Guangzhou courses played a vital role in the development of the market in Guangzhou. One of Top Human's sales strategies was to find successful people, who are usually more comfortable with risk-taking and have a higher probability of having development problems. These successful people were usually at the heart of some network and their sharing of their experience helped Top Human create a market. For example, after one person from the advertising industry became Top Human's client, many in the industry followed. In addition, people who came in contact with these advertising individuals were generally from the management of their company, which further increased the development. This greatly shortened the market development time. By mid-1998, Top Human had four full-time staff in Guangzhou; at the end of 1998, this increased to six.

Some companies, such as Robust Group and TCL Computers, became clients and a few incorporated coaching into the management of their companies. For example, Fu Jie of Guangzhou Jiu Yi Advertising Ltd. applied corporate coaching in leading his team to create a television commercial themed, "The world is but a little place, after all" for China Mobile. This advertisement won a First Place Mobius Statuette in the Television Commercial Category in the 30th Mobius Advertising Awards held in Chicago.

Expansion to Shenzhen.

Top Human's business in Guangzhou continued to expand and people from around the vicinity came to Guangzhou for training. There were some Guangzhou-trained participants who volunteered to attract other participants and arranged training venues in places around Guangzhou, such as Shenzhen. To adapt to Shenzhen, where Mandarin is the main language, Top Human requested all its staff learn Mandarin and changed the language used in training to Mandarin. Top Human soon discovered not only was Shenzhen a substantial market for coaching, but it also had influence throughout China. Shenzhen has new industry and more high technology, companies, and most companies have a short history and rapid development. The population is young, highly educated, with contemporary ideas and a strong learning ability.

The development of business in Shenzhen shifted the emphasis of the company from Hong Kong to Shenzhen. To handle the business development in Shenzhen, Top Human transferred some key personnel to Shenzhen. In mid-1999, Top Human staff in Shenzhen reached six people, the same as Guangzhou. At the end of 1999, the staff was 12, exceeding the 8 people in Guangzhou. Top Human's number of employees in Shenzhen and Guangzhou (20 people) exceeded the number in the Hong Kong Office (19 people). In mid-2001, half the company staff was located in Shenzhen as was the management for the entire company. Hong Kong stayed the company's technical development base and Guangzhou became a local market office.

Moving into Shanghai.

In Shenzhen, Top Human wanted to develop a market with a vast area of geographical coverage. The early market exploration outside Shenzhen and Guangzhou was initiated by the clients. Top Human tried to start a coaching service in Kunming and Taiyuan, but the result was not good because the standard of economic development in the mid-western region was too low.

The coastal economic development zones consist of the Pearl River Delta, the Yangtze River Delta, and the Bohai Bay area. The interior of the Pearl River Delta region is closely linked, is accessible, and has a similar culture; the Shenzhen and Guangzhou branch offices can cover that entire region. Top Human began to consider entering Shanghai—the hub of the Yangtze River Delta region. To Zhejiang and others along the Yangtze River, Shanghai had a strong growing influence. Some people in Top Human felt that the company was not familiar with the culture of Eastern China and should stay and build its present base to avoid spreading the staff and resources too thin. Eva and Lawrence thought that the sooner they entered Shanghai, the better able Top Human would be to become a nationwide brand name. Eva also had personal ties with Shanghai. Top Human entered Shanghai in the beginning of 2001. "Since I was young under the influence of my mother, I've always had an indescribable yearning for my hometown Shanghai," Eva stated. Eva finds the people in Shanghai more diplomatic and more careful, and they take a long time to build trust.

The first step that Top Human took when it went into Shanghai was to employ six local people and send them to Shenzhen for comprehensive coaching training and to assimilate into the company's culture. Second, the company modified its existing Coaching case studies as the coaching examples that appeal to the people in Southern China would not be of interest to people in Shanghai. Third, when Top Human applied for a business licence in Shanghai, it found that the business scope of human capital development had no precedence in the past. After going through a lot of effort, Top Human finally got the first foreign enterprise business licence for human capital development in Shanghai.

The brand name of Top Human, very well known in Southern China, did not enjoy the same degree of recognition in Eastern China. To propel Top Human into a brand name in China, the company organized the Inaugural Coaching Forum in China. Top Human also got involved with various forums and seminars, such as the seminar "The Winning Way" jointly organized with Yang Cheng Wan Bao "Jobs Classified" in June 2000. After the Shanghai Forum, organizing large forums became a new area of company business.

Establishing the Corporate Technology Department and Its Restructuring.

In 1998, the Hong Kong telecommunication industry did not have favourable sales and China Motion was forced to adjust employees' salaries to cut costs; simultaneously the company introduced the CM Concept to meet the growing popularity of mobile phones. China Motion wanted to expand its retail arm, from simply retailing pagers to selling an entire series of telecommunication products. The company was afraid that the change from a system of fixed salary to an adjustable salary would decrease company morale and result in a major loss of staff. China Motion decided to use training to increase staff morale and help in the repositioning.

Even though there were many domestic and overseas training companies taking part in the bidding, China Motion selected Top Human. Top Human conducted a workshop, "Service from the Heart," for China Motion employees and sent three coaches to coach China Motion's more than 20 retail supervisors, with the support of two other senior coaches. Top Human senior coaches interacted with the senior management of China Motion every month. Top Human coaches also held meetings with China Motion staff on a regular basis. The close-knit cooperation between the two parties resulted in the successful repositioning of China Motion, and the CM Concept has been introduced in many cities in China. The managing director for China Motion then, Mr. Xiao Weidan, said, "The sales figures have increased twofold in a short period of three months. At the same time, our company supervisors have shown considerable improvement in their leadership ability, and the warmth displayed by our customer relations officers towards the clients has also greatly improved."

The use of Coaching for customized corporate training in the case of China Motion was a huge success, and Top Human set up a Corporate Technology Department that was independent of the Performance Technology Department. Staff was arranged in Hong Kong, Guangzhou, and Shenzhen to develop the business in corporate management. However, there was limited success in the Corporate Technology Department. By March 2000, the staff in the department went from eight to six people.

In the same year, Top Human restructured the Corporate Technology Department and put a full-time professional in charge. Second, the company had the department run the newly constructed Outdoor Challenge Center. Third, the staff in the department was increased to 20 people. Finally, the department would actively coordinate with the Performance Technology Department to make full use of the client network to develop its market. In a short time, the Top Human Corporate Technology Department had a big improvement and increased its customized workshop topics, including such new ones as Team Dynamics, Leadership Skills, Communication Skills, Sales Mastery, Creativity, and Innovation.

THE COMPANY CULTURE

Many people who come into contact with Top Human are very surprised that the company has been progressing rapidly and aggressively through exploring new activities and has not yet met any major hurdles. Why is it that with such a heavy workload, Top Human employees still maintain their high morale and commit to their job with passion?

Top Human's steady and rapid development and soaring morale are largely due to its use of Coaching in its own company management. At the same time that Top Human is helping other companies become learning organizations through Coaching, it is striving to ensure that Top Human itself has in place the various mechanisms needed to become a real learning organization (shared vision, equal partners, insightful discussion, and the ability to focus inwards).

Shared Vision.

Vision is the collective manifestation of the cultural values, interests, and ambitions of the members in an organization. Top Human uses vision in hiring its company employees. However, Top Human's vision is neither the vision of its top management nor one formed from a strategy. Rather, through Top Human associates expressing their dreams and listening to other people's dreams, the vision is the result of the true opinions and knowledge and the belief that faith generates from this exchange process. Eva and Lawrence are willing to communicate their thoughts and ideas with the staff, and seek their understanding and support while listening to and absorbing their views.

Not only is Top Human good at using vision to enroll and empower its employees, but it also places emphasis on breaking the vision down into qualitative goals and measurable targets to guide the effectiveness of the company's operations. The feedback mechanism linking such a corporate vision, quantification of goals, and actual means of operations allows the fine-tuning process to continually occur.

The Atmosphere for Learning.

The core of Top Human's Coaching Technology is to create an atmosphere where the participants can develop their own mental models to equip themselves and to adjust their attitudes. Top Human has been consciously developing an environment for learning inside its own organization. It expects every department manager to be able to take up the role of a coach and adjust the attitude of his or her department staff, to allow everyone to face their work with the correct attitude and to see the opportunities in their daily work where they can improve their own qualities and abilities. One of the primary roles of a manager is to be a coach for subordinates, with the responsibility of using coaching tools and techniques to help others improve their effectiveness, making the role of Top Human management more of a supporter than a controller. Correspondingly, the role of staff members has also switched from one of taking orders to taking responsibility.

Apart from focusing its attention on forming some integral mechanisms, Top Human took other measures to strengthen this relationship of equal partners. For example, people address each other by their English names, even top management. For instance, Eva Wong is "Eva" and Lawrence Leung is "Lawrence." The office layout of Top Human is based on an open concept. Eva Wong and Lawrence Leung did not give themselves extremely luxurious offices but rather go around to interact with other staff. To eliminate the boss-related complex and culture that are present in most companies, Eva and Lawrence started early to convert the ownership of Top Human into a shareholders' system and to lower themselves from the position of "bosses" to the position of company shareholders and management. Important decisions are made through the board of directors. The employees of Top Human have the opportunity to become company shareholders, and this greatly strengthens their sense of belonging. In company meetings, Eva and Lawrence seldom persist with their ideas or defend their position but carefully regulate the atmosphere of discussion, ensuring that the discussions end in more fruitful results.

Focusing Inward.

Shared vision, equal partners, insightful discussion, and other such components of a learning organization established a solid groundwork where members of the organization have the ability and attitude to focus inward, self-reflect, and self-improve. The management of Top Human, who are really concerned for the members in their organization, let the employees realize the difficulties encountered, actively ponder and find a solution, and make a difficult situation an opportunity for the employees to self-reflect, develop their abilities, and achieve personal growth. In a newly developed market, Eva will personally interview prospective employees. During the interview, she looks for their ability to be moulded, to express and to be distinct, their sense of mission toward their career, and their academic qualifications. Eva also frequently uses her own experience to coach the staff in overcoming their own limitations. After her divorce, Eva spent one year by herself traveling across Europe and the Middle East; the trip allowed her to see the world outside her original narrow social circle as a traditional career woman. She went through a very difficult adjustment process. Leaving behind her comfortable job as a commercial officer at the Canadian Embassy and stepping into the training line, Eva similarly experienced a long period of adjustment and exploration in her mind before she successfully established and developed Top Human.

Common Societal Model.

Top Human's shared vision, equal partners, insightful discussions, and the use of other such mechanisms is not just restricted to its employees. Top Human extends the use of such mechanisms to its clients and other relevant bodies, such as its franchise partners.

One unique feature in Top Human is its associate coaches, who are essential to the entire operation of Top Human. Top Human's associate coaches are all clients who have taken part in Top Human's training; the associate coaches dedicate their service and support to help new participants get into form faster. In this way, associate coaches can apply and practise their newly learned coaching techniques and tools and improve the core of their coaching ability—the ability to enroll and convince.

Top Human is also very concerned about the maintenance of the network among clients. For example, Top Human specially opened up chat rooms on the company's website to promote communication between the company and the participants and among the participants themselves. Top Human diligently monitors the progress of the client's development and continually seeks to expand the number of case studies from the successful individuals among its clients. Publicizing these successful figures and their success stories through various forms of media is a living testament to the effects of Coaching Technology.

Ever since Top Human entered the China market, it has not done any advertising to promote its business. Eva thinks that Coaching is a concept that can only be understood through personal experience, making it hard to accurately portray the essence of Coaching through advertisements. The dissemination by word-of-mouth from loyal, satisfied participants has become the main method of advertising for Top Human.

Organizational Design.

The organizational development of Top Human has gone through three stages. The first stage was before the expansion of business in Shenzhen, where Top Human's organizational structure centred around the development of the training business and the structure of the company was like a training department. The second stage was after Top Human set up its subsidiary company in Shenzhen and the company started to build a corporate management structure and the corresponding departments (see **Figure 3**). The third stage followed the company's expansion to various regions. Top Human implemented a series of adjustments that resulted in the organizational structure indicated in **Figure 4**.

ESTABLISHING THE KNOWLEDGE MANAGEMENT DEPARTMENT

Along with the gradual acceptance of the new concept of Coaching Technology by the market, some past participants started to enter the corporate coaching market. Two coaching companies emerged in Guangzhou. Top Human was concerned that these competitors might not be able to provide a high quality of service, which would affect the image of coaching and negatively impact the healthy development of the coaching industry.

Top Human felt that a fundamental strategy to ensure the company's competitive edge and to establish a good reputation for the coaching industry was to constantly innovate, making it difficult for competitors to copy. Top Human set up a knowledge management and product development department in Hong Kong and

FIGURE 3 **Top Human Organizational Structure (June 2001)**

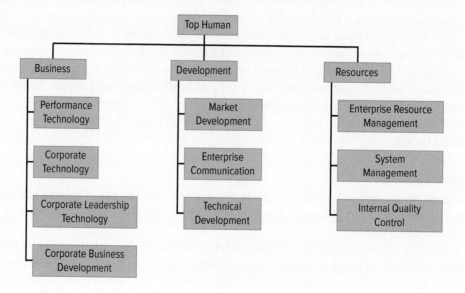

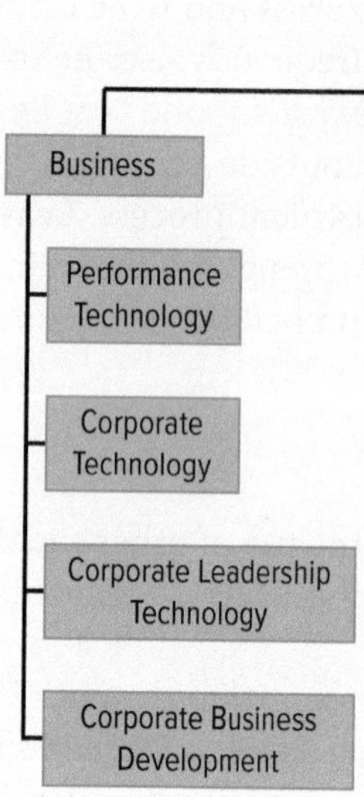

FIGURE 4 **Top Human Organizational Structure, January 2002 (excluding regional framework)**

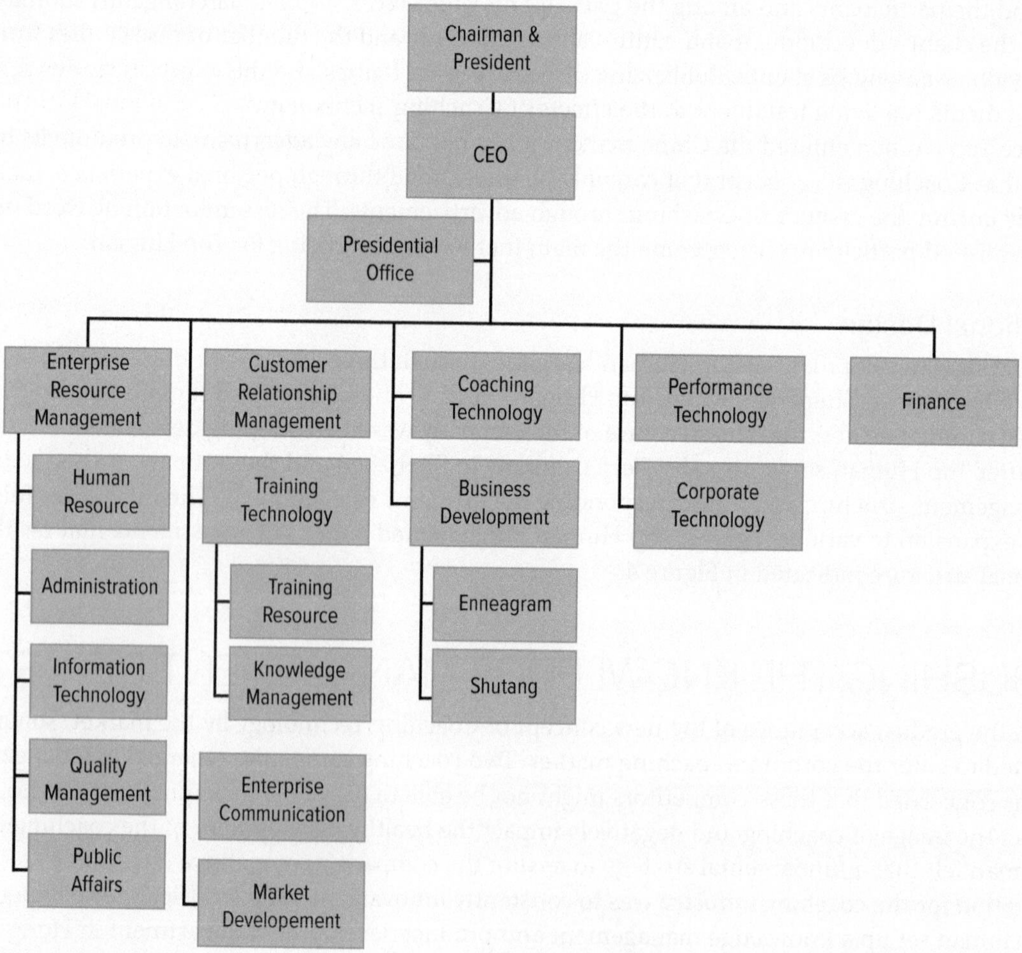

started planning for the establishment of the Coaching Technology Research Institute. The main objective of this technical development department was to innovate in the training content, to manage the flow of internal knowledge, and to develop new services for the company. The department was also responsible for training company employees to ensure that the standards of the company trainers were the highest in the industry. New services were developed, tested, and adjusted in the mature market of Hong Kong before being introduced in the mainland market.

The company also wants to establish the Coaching Technology Research Institute, the first one in the world, by partnering with reputable institutions throughout the country. The Institute would sponsor relevant scholastic research and nurture masters- and doctorate-level researchers.

ESTABLISHING SPECIALIZED DEPARTMENTS

To increase the image and business of Top Human, the company established an Enterprise Communication Department. The mission of Top Human's Enterprise Communication Department is to promote Top Human's image and make Coaching Technology better known through such things as organizing the international forum related to Coaching Technology; having "The Human Resource Journey" exhibition; and publishing coaching-related books.

Although the coaching business is still in the growth stage, Top Human will need to have new services and businesses if the company wants to grow in the future. To accomplish this, Top Human established the Strategic Market Development Department to develop the company's overall strategy and find new areas of business for the company.

Top Human also established the Enterprise Resource Management Department to control the use of funds and resources. Investment plans are carefully formulated before being presented to the board of directors, and the company is planning to become listed on a stock exchange, perhaps in the United States.

The Presidential Office.

Eva and Lawrence are coaches as well as company managers, and the growth of the company has significantly increased their workload. The initial objective of setting up the Presidential Office was to lighten this workload and enhance the communication inside and outside the company. However, the Presidential Office has become an incubator for training and new business development. Eva and Lawrence started to train some staff in the Presidential Office and share their management ideals and development goals.

DEVELOPMENT OF THE BRAND AND IMAGE

The brand name of Top Human has been developed through the Enterprise Communication Department and the choice of office locations through the organization of various charitable activities and by doing community work. Top Human continually establishes the coaching brand and portrays the company as the pioneer and the industry leader for corporate coaching in Asia. In March 2001, Top Human and the Zhongshan University MBA Centre signed a memorandum of understanding to train the university's MBAs and introduce Coaching Technology into the university system in China.

The company also introduced the Coaching Competency Certification Program (CCCP) to train corporate coaches. At the start of 1998, Top Human's board of directors decided to start the implementation of the ISO 9002 Quality Management System to improve its service quality to make the company's operations more systematic and scientific.

In February 2000, Top Human opened its newly constructed Outdoor Challenge Center at Shenzhen Xili Lake Holiday Resort, the first in the country that conformed to international standards. The obstacles at the challenge centre include the Pamper Pole, Dangle Duo, Climbing Wall, and Cat Walk among the 10 high elements, and its 17 low element activities include TP Shuffle, Amazon River, Electric Fence, and Initiative Wall. At present, the centre is one of the largest outdoor challenge centres in China with comprehensive facilities.

Outdoor challenge training allows the participants to participate in a series of interesting and challenging low and high elements in the outdoor environment to gain a deeper self-understanding, discover one's potential, break through one's existing thinking model, and learn to deal with fear. Outdoor challenge training is a form of experiential learning through interaction.

SALES AND EMPLOYEES

Top Human has steadily grown since 2001. In 2004, Top Human had turnover at HKD66 million, with an additional HKD12 million coming from franchisees. While the turnover was about the same for 2005, the revenue from franchisees increased to HKD15 million (see **Table 1**). The number of employees increased from 3 people in 1995 to 91 employees by 2001 (see **Table 2**).

TABLE 1 Top Human Annual Income (000 RMB)

			BRANCHES		
RMB' 000	**2001**	**2002**	**2003**	**2004**	**2005**
Coaching Technology 1	¥17,577	¥10,445	¥13,397	¥25,150	¥21,858
Coaching Technology 2	¥13,528	¥ 8,581	¥11,106	¥17,867	¥14,810
Technology in Action	¥ 4,404	¥ 2,480	¥ 4,314	¥ 7,727	¥ 7,989
Coaching Principal	¥ 3,949	¥ 4,960	¥ 5,309	¥11,031	¥12,453
Corporate Technology			¥ 5,190	¥ 4,529	¥ 9,373
Total	**¥39,457**	**¥26,465**	**¥39,316**	**¥66,305**	**¥66,483**
			FRANCHISEES		
RMB' 000	**2001**	**2002**	**2003**	**2004**	**2005**
Coaching Technology 1				¥ 4,405	¥ 5,314
Coaching Technology 2				¥ 3,528	¥ 4,025
Technology in Action				¥ 1,608	¥ 2,104
Coaching Principal				¥ 2,373	¥ 3,807
Total				**¥11,914**	**¥15,250**

TABLE 2 Top Human Employee Distribution by Geographic Region

	TOTAL	HONG KONG	%	GUANGZHOU	%	SHENZHEN	%	SHANGHAI	%	BEIJING	%
Dec 1995	3	3	100.0%	0	0.0%	0	0.0%	0	0.0%		
Jun 1996	5	5	100.0%	0	0.0%	0	0.0%	0	0.0%		
Dec 1996	7	7	100.0%	0	0.0%	0	0.0%	0	0.0%		
Jun 1997	12	12	100.0%	0	0.0%	0	0.0%	0	0.0%		
Dec 1997	13	13	100.0%	0	0.0%	0	0.0%	0	0.0%		
Jun 1998	21	17	81.0%	4	19.0%	0	0.0%	0	0.0%		
Dec 1998	20	14	70.0%	6	30.0%	0	0.0%	0	0.0%		
Jun 1999	28	16	57.1%	6	21.4%	6	21.4%	0	0.0%		
Dec 1999	39	19	48.7%	8	20.5%	12	30.8%	0	0.0%		
Jun 2000	62	26	41.9%	14	22.6%	22	35.5%	0	0.0%		
Dec 2000	83	27	32.5%	15	18.1%	35	42.2%	6	7.2%		
Jun 2001	91	16	17.6%	19	20.9%	48	52.7%	9	9.9%		
Dec 2001	109	14	12.8%	20	18.3%	56	51.4%	19	17.4%		
Jun 2002	107	16	15.0%	21	19.6%	48	44.9%	22	20.6%		
Dec 2002	115	20	17.4%	21	18.3%	45	39.1%	29	25.2%		
Jun 2003	133	21	15.8%	20	15.0%	59	44.4%	33	24.8%		
Dec 2003	147	3	2.0%	20	13.6%	78	53.1%	35	23.8%	11	7.5%
Jun 2004	172	2	1.2%	19	11.0%	82	47.7%	49	28.5%	20	11.6%
Dec 2004	212	2	0.9%	30	14.2%	88	41.5%	63	29.7%	29	13.7%
Jun 2005	282	2	0.7%	29	10.3%	121	42.9%	88	31.2%	42	14.9%
Nov 2005	285	2	0.7%	33	11.6%	121	42.5%	85	29.8%	44	15.4%

As is indicated in **Table 3**, in a short span of five years, Top Human has trained tens of thousands of people from such companies as Guangzhou Materials Group, Konka Group, Robust Group, China Motion Concept Limited, Legend Computers, TCL Computer Technology Co. Ltd., Cathay Pacific Airways, Shenzhen Party School of the Chinese Communist Party, Guangzhou Zhongshan University MBA Centre, American International Assurance Company, Conlia Limited, and Sun Microsystems.

TABLE 3 Number of People Attending Top Human Training

MAIN BRANCHES	2001	2002	2003	2004	2005
Coaching Technology 1	3,988	3,452	3,233	5,461	4,747
Coaching Technology 2	1,628	1,499	1,423	2,131	1,764
Technology in Action	1,099	951	889	1,337	1,258
Coaching Principal	512	816	726	1,389	1,473
Corporate Technology					
Total	**7,227**	**6,718**	**6,271**	**10,318**	**9,242**
SATELLITE OFFICES	**2001**	**2002**	**2003**	**2004**	**2005**
Coaching Technology 1				1,127	1,217
Coaching Technology 2				459	516
Technology in Action				329	348
Corporate Technology				338	481
Total				**2,253**	**2,562**

Endnotes

CHAPTER 1

1. Government of Canada, Business and Industry, "Key Small Business Statistics - January 2019," http://www.ic.gc.ca/eic/site/061.nsf/eng/h_03090.html.
2. Bruce Rothney, "To be Successful, Youth Need Entrepreneurial Skill and Experience," *Globe and Mail*, updated May 17, 2018, accessed August 6, 2019, https://www.theglobeandmail.com/business/careers/leadership/article-to-be-successful-youth-need-entrepreneurial-skills-and-experience/.
3. Jay Dingwall, interview by Peter Mombourquette: "On Entrepreneurship," June 1, 2019.
4. John Naisbitt, *Global Paradox* (New York: William Morrow and Company, 1994).
5. As reported in *Success*, February 1999, p. 12.
6. "Ideas, Business, and the True Key to Innovation with Arlene Dickinson," Media Planet, accessed August 2, 2019, http://www.industryandbusiness.ca/insight/ideas-business-and-the-true-key-to-innovation-with-arlene-dickinson.
7. "Self-Employment Rises with Joblessness, StatsCan Study Shows," CBC News, October 8, 2015, accessed August 2, 2019, www.cbc.ca/news/business/self-employment-study-1.3262831.
8. "Entrepreneurial Spirit Strong with a Majority of Canadians Thinking About Owning a Business: RBC Poll," RBC, September 20, 2018, accessed August 2, 2019, http://www.rbc.com/newsroom/news/2018/20180920-small-bus.html.
9. Hugh McKenna, "Nearly Half of Students Plan to Start Own Business: Survey," *Globe and Mail*, updated April 17, 2018, accessed August 2, 2019, www.theglobeandmail.com/report-on-business/small-business/startups/nearly-half-of-students-plan-to-start-own-business-survey/article14163719/.
10. "Entrepreneurship in Canada Ranks 2nd in World, Report Says," CBC News, updated May 29, 2015, accessed August 2, 2019, www.cbc.ca/news/business/entrepreneurship-in-canada-ranks-2nd-in-world-report-says-1.3093290.
11. Global Entrepreneurship Monitor, "GEM 2018/19 Global Report," uploaded January 21, 2019, accessed July 4, 2019, https://www.gemconsortium.org/report/gem-2018-2019-global-report.
12. *Small Business Quarterly*, Industry Canada, August 2006, p. 1.
13. As reported in GDSourcing.com, CIBC, October 2003.
14. "About," Genius Factor Games, www.geniusfactorgames.com/about; and Matthew Braga, "Was This a $4.8-Million Fraud?" *Globe and Mail*, updated April 30, 2018, accessed August 2, 2019, www.theglobeandmail.com/report-on-business/small-business/sb-tools/small-business-briefing/was-this-a-48-million-fraud/article4457675; and David Godsall, "Vancouver's Ailing Video Game Industry," BC Business, September 5, 2011, accessed September 13, 2019, https://www.bcbusiness.ca/vancouvers-ailing-video-game-industry.
15. "Social Impact," Lucky Iron Fish, accessed April 25, 2019, https://ca.luckyironfish.com; and Alina Bykova, "Burlington Native Wins Muhammad Ali Humanitarian Award," *Toronto Star*, July 27, 2017, https://www.thestar.com/news/gta/2017/07/27/burlington-native-wins-muhammad-ali-humanitarian-award.html.
16. Meghan McKenna, "5 Indigenous Entrepreneurs Creating Social Change in Their Communities," *Fashion*, June 21, 2018, accessed August 2, 2019, https://fashionmagazine.com/culture/indigenous-entrepreneurs-canada/.
17. Skoll Foundation, skoll.org/about/approach/.
18. "About Us," School for Social Entrepreneurs, 2019, www.the-sse.ca/about-us/.
19. Joe Castaldo, "Kick-Start a Radical New Funding Model," *Canadian Business*, March 21, 2013, accessed August 6, 2019, www.canadianbusiness.com/technology-news/kick-start-a-radical-new-funding-model/; and "Opportunity 2013: Social Financing," *Canadian Business*, January 9, 2013, accessed August 6, 2019, https://www.canadianbusiness.com/innovation/opportunity-2013-social-financing/.
20. Government of Canada, Business and Industry, "Key Small Business Statistics - January 2019," http://www.ic.gc.ca/eic/site/061.nsf/eng/h_03090.html.
21. Government of Canada, Business and Industry, "Key Small Business Statistics - January 2019," http://www.ic.gc.ca/eic/site/061.nsf/eng/h_03090.html.
22. Government of Canada, Business and Industry, "Key Small Business Statistics - January 2019," http://www.ic.gc.ca/eic/site/061.nsf/eng/h_03090.html.
23. Government of Canada, "Key Small Business Statistics-January 2019: Figure 6," Business and Industry Canada, http://www.ic.gc.ca/eic/site/061.nsf/eng/h_03090.html#point2-1.
24. Table 6 - Key Small Business Statistics - January 2019, accessed August 2, 2019, http://www.ic.gc.ca/eic/site/061.nsf/eng/h_03090.html#point2-2.
25. Treasury Board of Canada, "Red Tape Reduction Action Plan," accessed January 2, 2019, https://www.canada.ca/en/treasury-board-secretariat/services/federal-regulatory-management/red-tape-reduction-action-plan.html; Brian Pallister, "Red Tape and Your Government: How Cutting Bureaucracy Boosted Manitoba's Growth," *Financial Post*, January 21, 2019, https://business.financialpost.com/opinion/red-tape-and-your-government-how-cutting-bureaucracy-boosted-manitobas-growth; and Ellen Samek, "Doug Ford Gets an A- From the CFIB for Cutting Red Tape for Small Businesses," *Financial Post*, January 24, 2019, https://business.financialpost.com/entrepreneur/small-business/doug-ford-gets-a-for-cutting-regulations-from-cfib.

26. "Entrepreneurship Education," *Technological Entrepreneurship and Engineering in Canada, Canadian Academy of Engineering Report,* Chapter 9, Ottawa, 1997, pp. 149–160.
27. "Driving Wealth Creation & Social Development in Canada, 2015 Report" Global Entrepreneurship Monitor, accessed June 3, 2019, http://thecis.ca/wp-content/uploads/2016/04/GEM-Canada-Report-5.2015.pdf.
28. Thomas Peters and Robert H. Waterman, Jr., *In Search of Excellence* (New York: Harper and Row, 1982).
29. Thomas Peters and Robert H. Waterman, Jr., *In Search of Excellence* (New York: Harper and Row, 1982).
30. Stephanie Melita, "Small Talk," *Wall Street Journal,* May 21, 1998, pp. 28–29.
31. "Advocacy," Canadian Federation of Independent Business, accessed June 3, 2019, https://www.cfib-fcei.ca/; and "About Us," Canadian Federation of Independent Business, accessed June 3, 2019, https://www.cfib-fcei.ca/.
32. "Driving Wealth Creation & Social Development in Canada, 2017 Report," Global Entrepreneurship Monitor, accessed June 3, 2019, https://www.gemconsortium.org/report.
33. Jason Buckland, "How the Dragons' Den Effect Works," holycrap.com, accessed August 6, 2019, https://holycrap.com/blogs/news/16103181-how-the-dragons-den-effect-works.
34. "Defining Canadian Small Business," StrADegy, accessed August 6, 2019, https://www.stradegy.ca/article/canadian-small-business-defined.
35. "Table of Small Business Size Standards Matched to North American Industry Classification System Codes," U.S. Small Business Administration, October 2017, accessed August 30, 2019, https://www.sba.gov/sites/default/files/files/Size_Standards_Table_2017.pdf.
36. Canada Revenue Agency, "Small Business Deduction Rules," accessed May 1, 2019, https://www.canada.ca/en/revenue-agency/programs/about-canada-revenue-agency-cra/federal-government-budgets/budget-2018-equality-growth-strong-middle-class/passive-investment-income/small-business-deduction-rules.html.
37. R. Peterson, *Small Business—Building a Balanced Economy* (Erin, Ontario: Press Porcepic Ltd., 1977), p. 64.
38. Government of Canada, Business and Industry, "Key Small Business Statistics - January 2019," http://www.ic.gc.ca/eic/site/061.nsf/eng/h_03090.html.
39. "2017 GEM Canada Report on Youth Entrepreneurship," Global Entrepreneurship Monitor, accessed February 14, 2019, https://www.gemconsortium.org/report.
40. Frank Condron, "PROFIT Magazine Reveals Canada's Top Young Entrepreneurs, 2012," *Profit Magazine,* November 13, 2012, accessed August 6, 2019, https://www.canadianbusiness.com/innovation/profit-magazine-reveals-canadas-top-young-entrepreneurs-2012/.
41. Frank Condron, "PROFIT Magazine Reveals Canada's Top Young Entrepreneurs, 2012," *Profit Magazine,* November 13, 2012, accessed August 6, 2019, https://www.canadianbusiness.com/innovation/profit-magazine-reveals-canadas-top-young-entrepreneurs-2012/.
42. "The Young and the Restless," *Profit,* June 1993, p. 48.
43. As reported in *Costco Connection,* March–April 2005, p. 16.
44. Tracey Hanes, "The Secret to a Lasting Business: Create Something You Want for Yourself," Holy Crap Blog, accessed August 6, 2019, https://holycrap.com/blogs/news/16103193-the-secret-to-a-lasting-business-create-something-you-want-for-yourself; and "Holy Crap and Skinny B are the World's Most Amazing Breakfast Cereals," Holy Crap Blog, accessed August 6, 2019, https://holycrap.com/blogs/news/16103421-holy-crap-and-skinny-b-are-the-worlds-most-amazing-breakfast-cereals.
45. Susan Ward, "Statistics on Canadian Women in Business," The Balance, updated February 28, 2019, accessed August 6, 2019, https://www.thebalancesmb.com/statistics-on-canadian-women-in-business-2948029.
46. Leigh Mitchell, "Get Ready to Celebrate #Womensday: 12 Facts and Figures About Women Entrepreneurs in Canada," Women in Biz Network, February 9, 2015, accessed August 6, 2019, www.womeninbiznetwork.com/women-owned-business-statistics-in-canada/.
47. Susan Ward, "Statistics on Canadian Women in Business," The Balance, updated February 28, 2019, accessed August 6, 2019, https://www.thebalancesmb.com/statistics-on-canadian-women-in-business-2948029.
48. Leigh Mitchell, "Get Ready to Celebrate #Womensday: 12 Facts and Figures About Women Entrepreneurs in Canada," Women in Biz Network, February 9, 2015, accessed August 6, 2019, www.womeninbiznetwork.com/women-owned-business-statistics-in-canada/.
49. *Women in Management 9,* no. 2 (University of Western Ontario, December–January 1999), p. 2.
50. *Small Business Quarterly,* Industry Canada, February 2009, p. 1.
51. Elizabeth McMillan, "Peace by Chocolate Pledges to Hire 50 Refugees, and Mentor 10 Refugee Startups," CBC, February 15, 2019, https://www.cbc.ca/news/canada/nova-scotia/peace-by-chocolate-antigonish-employ-refugees-mentor-businesses-1.5019508.
52. CIBC World Markets, *Small Business in Canada, Trends & Prospects,* September 2006.
53. Alexandre Silberman, "Meet Canada's Young Entrepreneur of the Year," *The Brunswickan,* January 29, 2019, https://www.thebruns.ca/articles/meet-canadas-young-entrepreneur-of-the-year.
54. Government of Canada, Business and Industry, "Table 5 - Key Small Business Statistics - January 2019," accessed March 1, 2019, http://www.ic.gc.ca/eic/site/061.nsf/eng/h_03090.html#table5.
55. Government of Canada, Business and Industry, "Summary of the Survey on Financing and Growth of Small and Medium Enterprises - 2014," https://www.ic.gc.ca/eic/site/061.nsf/eng/02998.html.
56. "Future of Small Business Report (2009)," Intuit, accessed August 6,

2019, https://http-download.intuit.com/http.intuit/CMO/intuit/futureofsmallbusiness/intuit_fosb_report_march_2009.pdf.
57. "11 Questions for Ryan Holmes," Huffington Post, March 5, 2013, accessed August 6, 2019, www.huffingtonpost.ca/2013/03/05/11-questions-for-ryan-holmes-hootsuite_n_2793294.html.
58. Thomas Peters and Robert H. Waterman, Jr., *In Search of Excellence* (New York: Harper and Row, 1982).
59. Shannon Skinner, "Extraordinary Women: Kelsey Ramsden," Extraordinary Women TV, November 13, 2012, accessed August 9, 2019, www.extraordinarywomentv.com/topics/kelsey-ramsden/.
60. *Statistics on Foreign Ownership, Small versus Large* (Ottawa: Statistics Canada, Inter-Corporate Ownership, 1984), p. 252.
61. "Would You Want Your Son to Marry a Marketing Lady?" *Journal of Marketing,* January 1977, pp. 15–18.
62. Ivan I. Stefanovic, "Sidestepping Socialism in Yugoslavia," *Venture,* September 1984, p. 60.
63. *Global Entrepreneurship Monitor,* London Business School, Summer 2018.
64. Frank Condron, "Philanthropy: Small Business, Big Difference," *Canadian Business,* October 10, 2012, accessed August 6, 2019, https://www.canadianbusiness.com/innovation/philanthropy-small-business-big-difference/.
65. Ten Tree Apparel, www.tentree.org/about; and www.tentree.org/dragons-den.
66. Randall Litchfield, "Turn Change into Advantage," *Small Business,* June 1989, p. 19.
67. Ted Glendening, "How Technology Has Levelled the Playing Field for Small Business," Jungohr, April 21, 2017, accessed August 6, 2019, https://www.jungohr.ca/blog/how-technology-has-levelled-the-playing-field-for-small-businesses.
68. Robert D. Hisrich, Michael P. Peters, Dean A. Shepherd, and Peter Mombourquette, *Entrepreneurship,* 2nd Canadian edition (Toronto: McGraw-Hill Ryerson Ltd., 2009), p. 75.
69. "Opportunity 2013: Gen Y Enters Its Family Years," *Canadian Business,* December 14, 2012, accessed August 31, 2019, https://www.canadianbusiness.com/innovation/opportunity-2013-gen-y-enters-its-family-years/.
70. *North American Free Trade Agreement,* Chapter 10.
71. *North American Free Trade Agreement,* Chapter 3.
72. *North American Free Trade Agreement,* Articles 1202 and 1204.
73. Shannon Proudfoot and Jason Markusoff, "The USMCA Explained: Winners and Losers, What's In and What's Out," *Maclean's,* October 1, 2018, accessed August 30, 2019, https://www.macleans.ca/economy/the-usmca-explained-winners-and-losers-whats-in-and-whats-out/.
74. Bill Curry, "The ABCs of TTP," *Globe and Mail,* January 26, 2016, accessed August 30, 2019, www.theglobeandmail.com/report-on-business/international-business/what-is-tpp-understanding-the-new-pacific-tradedeal/article26648948/.
75. Joe Dangor, "Thriving on Change," *Small Business Magazine,* June 1989, p. 32.
76. Alain Hailley, *A Study of the Outsourcing Activities of Canadian Businesses: A Comparison of the Country's. Four Major Regions* (Montreal: École des Hautes Études Commerciales, 2000).
77. Michael Carmichael, "We're Getting a Look at the True State of Canada's Economy—and It's No World Beater," *Financial Post,* March 1, 2019, accessed August 30, 2019, https://business.financialpost.com/news/economy/were-getting-a-look-at-the-true-state-of-canadas-economy-and-its-no-world-beater.
78. Angus Reid Studies, June 2009.
79. Treasury Board of Canada Secretariat, "Red Tape Reduction Action Plan," Catalogue No. BT22-132/2012E-PDF, accessed January 2, 2019, https://www.canada.ca/en/treasury-board-secretariat/services/federal-regulatory-management/red-tape-reduction-action-plan.html.
80. GEM *Report in Business Research Newsletter,* February 28, 2005, p. 2.
81. World Bank, "Rankings and Ease of Doing Business," May 2018, accessed August 30, 2019, http://www.doingbusiness.org/en/rankings.
82. *Growing Small Business* (Ottawa: Industry Canada/Statistics Canada, February 1994), p. 1.
83. John Bulloch, "Policy Guidelines to Help Make Your Venture Work," *The Financial Post Special Report,* November 24, 1984, p. 53.
84. CFIB, "Prosperity Restricted by Red Tape," January 2010.
85. *Growing Small Business* (Ottawa: Industry Canada/Statistics Canada, February 1994).
86. "Nearly One Third of the $36 Billion Cost of Regulation in Canada is Unnecessary Red Tape," CFIB, January 22, 2018, accessed August 30, 2019, https://www.cfib-fcei.ca/en/media/nearly-one-third-36-billion-cost-regulation-canada-unnecessary-red-tape.
87. *Profits,* Business Development Bank of Canada, Winter 1999, p. 2.
88. "Canadian Small Business—A Growing Force," *CIBC World Markets,* September 2003, p. 2.

CHAPTER 2

1. "*Inc.* and *U.S.A. Today* Survey of 500 Fastest Growing Private Companies," *Inc.,* June 1986, p. 48.
2. Kenzie MacDonald, in-class presentation, "Small Business Management," Mount Saint Vincent University, May 2010, Halifax, Nova Scotia.
3. Frank Condron, "Bill Hennessey, 2012 Fuel Award Winner," Canadian Business, December 12, 2012, accessed August 9, 2019, https://www.canadianbusiness.com/innovation/qa-bill-hennessey-2012-fuel-award-winner/.
4. CIBC World Markets, January 2005, p. 4.
5. "Entrepreneurial Spirit Strong with Majority of Canadians Thinking About Owning a Business: RBC Poll," RBC, September 20, 2018, http://www.rbc.com/newsroom/news/2018/20180920-small-bus.html.
6. "Side Hustle Special," *Dragons'Den,* CBC, November 15, 2018, accessed August 7, 2019, https://www.cbc.ca/dragonsden/pitches/cobramask.
7. Pat Thompson, "Characteristics of the Small Business Entrepreneur in Canada," *Journal of Small Business and Entrepreneurship,* vol. 4, no. 3 (Winter 1986–87), p. 5.
8. *The Globe and Mail,* April 17, 1995, p. B4.

9. Heidi Fortes, "5 Things I Wish I knew Before Becoming an Entrepreneur," Lean In Canada, September 7, 2015, accessed August 9, 2019, http://leanincanada.com/5-things-i-wish-i-knew-before-becoming-an-entrepreneur/.
10. Frank Condron, "Ronald Richardson, 2012 Fuel Award Winner," *Canadian Business,* December 12, 2012, accessed August 9, 2019, www.profitguide.com/startup/success-stories/qa-ronald-richardson-2012-fuel-award-winner-45078.
11. "Steeped Tea," *The Canadian Business Journal,* April 16, 2018, http://www.cbj.ca/steeped-tea-fast-growing-tea-party-company/.
12. Karl Vesper, "Freedom and Power: What Every Entrepreneur Craves," *Success,* May 1988, p. 48.
13. "15 Success Stories of Inspiring Canadian Entrepreneurs," *Canadian Business,* September 21, 2017, https://www.canadianbusiness.com/innovation/canadian-entrepreneur-success-stories/image/15/.
14. Betsey Hiebert, interview by Gaebler: "Interview with My Care Necessities Founder Betsy Hiebert," Resources for Entrepreneurs, March 4, 2019, http://www.gaebler.com/My-Care-Necessities-Founder-Betsy-Hiebert.htm.
15. As reported in *Costco Connection,* September/October, 2003.
16. GEM Report as reported in *Business Research Newsletter,* February 2005, p. 6.
17. David P. Boyd and David E. Gumpert, "Coping with Entrepreneurial Stress," *Harvard Business Review,* March–April 1983, pp. 44–64.
18. Bryan Borzykowski, "Small Business Starting Out: Accidental Entrepreneurs Find Purpose and Success," *Globe and Mail,* updated May 11, 2018, accessed August 9, 2019, http://m.theglobeandmail.com/report-on-business/small-business/starting-out/accidental-entrepreneurs-find-purpose-and-success/article7509740/?service=mobile.
19. Public lecture, Mount Saint Vincent University, October 22, 2017.
20. RBC Study, as reported in *Business Research Newsletter,* February 2005, p. 5.
21. *Statistics Canada Survey of Employment,* July 2008, p. 10.
22. *Small Business Quarterly,* Statistics Canada, August 2010.
23. Frank Condron, "State of the Entrepreneur Nation," *Canadian Business,* October 10, 2012, accessed August 8, 2012, https://www.canadianbusiness.com/innovation/state-of-the-entrepreneur-nation/.
24. Heidi Fortes, "5 Things I Wish I knew Before Becoming an Entrepreneur," Lean In Canada, September 7, 2015, accessed August 9, 2019, http://leanincanada.com/5-things-i-wish-i-knew-before-becoming-an-entrepreneur/.
25. Brandon Turner, "Why I Quit My Own Business to Work with Someone Else," *Globe and Mail,* updated May 12, 2018, accessed August 8, 2019, www.theglobeandmail.com/report-on-business/small-business/sb-tools/sb-how-to/why-i-quit-my-own-busines-to-work-for-someone-else/article23210898/.
26. "*Inc.* and *U.S.A. Today* Survey of 500 Fastest Growing Private Companies," *Inc.,* June 1986, p. 48.
27. Government of Alberta, "2016 Alberta Self-Employment Profile," accessed March 15, 2019, https://work.alberta.ca/documents/labour-profile-self-employment.pdf.
28. *Small Business Quarterly,* vol. 5, no. 3, November 2008, p. 6.
29. Love, Mom, "How She Succeeds: Natalie Dusome of Poppies & Peonies," November 30, 2018, accessed August 8, 2019, http://lovemom.ca/how-she-succeeds-natalie-dusome-of-poppies-peonies/.
30. "Next Level Special," *Dragons'Den,* CBC, March 7, 2019, https://www.cbc.ca/dragonsden/pitches/poppy-peonies.
31. Ambareen Musa, "Six Things They Don't Tell You When You Start Your Own Business" *Globe and Mail,* updated May 12, 2018, accessed August 9, 2019, www.theglobeandmail.com/report-on-business/small-business/sb-tools/sb-how-to/six-things-they-dont-tell-you-when-you-leave-the-corporate-world-to-start-your-own-business/article22829151/.
32. Frank Condron, "State of the Entrepreneur Nation," *Canadian Business,* October 10, 2012, accessed August 8, 2019, https://www.canadianbusiness.com/innovation/state-of-the-entrepreneur-nation/.
33. Virginia Galt, "A Case Study on Luring Investment Angels," *Globe and Mail,* updated April 30, 2018, accessed August 9, 2019, www.theglobeandmail.com/report-on-business/small-business/sb-money/business-funding/a-case-study-on-luring-investment-angels/article555794/.
34. Virginia Galt, "A Case Study on Luring Investment Angels," *Globe and Mail,* updated April 30, 2018, accessed August 9, 2019, www.theglobeandmail.com/report-on-business/small-business/sb-money/business-funding/a-case-study-on-luring-investment-angels/article555794/.
35. *The Globe and Mail,* June 17, 1995, p. B5.
36. *Self-Employment in Canada—Trends and Prospects,* CIBC Economic Analysis, December 2000, p. 16.
37. *Small Business Quarterly,* Industry Canada, August 2008, p. 5.
38. *Small Business Quarterly,* Industry Canada, November 2009, p. 2.
39. *Small Business Quarterly,* Industry Canada, November 2009, p. 2; and Fondation de l'entrepreneurship,"Canadian Entrepreneurship Status, 2010," BDC, accessed August 8, 2019, www.bdc.ca/Resources%20Manager/misc/CES_2010_EN%20Final.pdf.
40. Terence Corcoran, "Entrepreneurial Drive and Innovation," *National Post,* December 1, 2009, p. 1.
41. Martin Studzinski, "Calgary Business Experts Encourage Risk Taking," IT Business, April 26, 2012, accessed August 9, 2019, www.itbusiness.ca/news/calgary-business-experts-encourage-risk-taking/17353.
42. "Ontario Entrepreneur of the Year: Risk Taker Has Midas Touch?" *Financial Post,* October 23, 2012, accessed August 9, 2019, http://business.financialpost.com/2012/10/23/ontario-entrepreneur-of-the-year-risk-taker-has-midas-touch/?__lsa=a1a9-eaec.

43. Amex, December 2005, as reported in GDSourcing.com, January 2006.
44. Charles A. Garfield, *Peak Performers* (New York: William Morrow, 1985).
45. "Networking and the Art of the Pitch," Futurpreneur, March 25, 2013, accessed August 8, 2019, https://www.futurpreneur.ca/en/press-media/networking-and-the-art-of-the-pitch/.
46. Mike Gettis, interview by Mike Morrison: "Getting in bed with a new career path," *I Quit*, podcast audio, August 2018, accessed August 8, 2019, https://soundcloud.com/user-376837011/ep-08-getting-in-bed-with-a-new-career-path-mike-gettis-i-quit-podcast-hosted-by-mike-morrison?in=user-376837011/sets/i-quit-the-podcast-hosted-by-mike-morrison.
47. Tara Deschamps, "Sleep Country Buys Endy for $88.7 Million, But the Two Will Operate Separately," *Financial Post*, November 30, 2018, accessed August 9, 2019, https://business.financialpost.com/pmn/business-pmn/sleep-country-buys-endy-for-88-7-million-but-the-two-will-operate-separately.
48. Pat Thompson, "Characteristics of the Small Business Entrepreneur in Canada," *Journal of Small Business and Entrepreneurship*, vol. 4, no. 3 (Winter 1986–87), p. 5.
49. Frank Condron, "Derrick Fung, 2012 Fuel Award Winner," December 12, 2012, accessed August 9, 2019, https://www.canadianbusiness.com/innovation/profile-derrick-fung-2012-fuel-award-winner/.
50. Lora Kolodny, "Drop, A Rewards App Start-Up, Snags Airbnb's Former Head of Engineering," CNBC, updated January 31, 2018, accessed August 9, 2019, https://www.cnbc.com/2018/01/30/drop-raises-21-million-for-mobile-rewards-app.html; Jessi Hempel, "LinkedIn Top 25 Startups 2019: The 25 Hottest Canadian Companies to Work for Now," September 4, 2019, https://www.linkedin.com/pulse/linkedin-top-startups-2019-25-hottest-canadian-companies-jessi-hempel/.
51. "A Nation of Entrepreneurs," *Report on Business Magazine*, October 1988.
52. "7 Key Leadership Skills for Entrepreneurs," BDC, accessed March 31, 2019, https://www.bdc.ca/en/articles-tools/entrepreneurial-skills/be-effective-leader/pages/7-key-leadership-skills-entrepreneurs.aspx.
53. *Self-Employment in Canada—Trends and Prospects*, CIBC Economic Analysis, December 2000, p. 16.
54. *Canadian Economic Observer*, November 1997, Statistics Canada, Catalogue #11-010-XPB, p. 19.
55. "Networking and the Art of the Pitch," Futurpreneur, March 25, 2013, accessed August 9, 2019, https://www.futurpreneur.ca/en/press-media/networking-and-the-art-of-the-pitch/.
56. Jayson DeMers, "Entrepreneurs Solve Problems Differently Than Other Professionals. Really! Here Are the 6 Ways," *Entrepreneur*, October 30, 2017, accessed August 9, 2019, https://www.entrepreneur.com/article/303407.
57. Jose Vasquez, "5 Ways Effective Entrepreneurs Solve Problems Differently," HuffPost, January 2, 2018, accessed August 9, 2019, https://www.huffpost.com/entry/5-key-ways-effective-entrepreneurs-solve-problems-differently_b_5a4bb8dce4b06cd2bd03e2a9.
58. Dan Ketchum, "Got a Problem? Turn It Into a Business Like These 15 Companies," GO Banking Rates, April 11, 2019, https://www.gobankingrates.com/net-worth/politicians/companies-that-solve-problems/#0.
59. Andrea Stairs, "5 Traits of Successful Online Entrepreneurs," Huffington Post, August 22, 2016, accessed August 9, 2019, https://www.huffingtonpost.ca/andrea-stairs/online-business-success_b_11612424.html.
60. Janet MacMillan, class presentation March 2018.
61. Carter Henderson, *Winners: The Successful Strategies Entrepreneurs Use to Build New Businesses* (New York: Holt, Rinehart and Winston, 1985), p. 178.
62. Ingrid Lunden, "Hootsuite Nabs $50M in Growth Capital for Its Social Media Management Platform, Passes 16M Customers," Tech Crunch, February 2018, accessed August 9, 2019, https://techcrunch.com/2018/03/15/hootsuite-raises-50m-more-for-its-social-media-management-platform-passes-16m-customers/; and Catherine Clifford, "From College Dropout to CEO of a Billion-Dollar Company: 3 Leadership Lessons from the Founder of Hootsuite," CNBC, October 5, 2017, accessed August 9, 2019, https://www.cnbc.com/2017/10/05/3-leadership-lessons-from-hootsuite-ceo-ryan-holmes.html.
63. John Lorinc, "Rethink Your Business Like It's Brand New," *Canadian Business*, October 22, 2012, accessed August 8, 2019, https://www.canadianbusiness.com/innovation/rethink-your-business-like-its-brand-new/.
64. John Lorinc, "Rethink Your Business Like It's Brand New," *Canadian Business*, October 22, 2012, accessed August 8, 2019, https://www.canadianbusiness.com/innovation/rethink-your-business-like-its-brand-new/.
65. Frank Condron, "Human Resources: The War for Better Workers," *Canadian Business*, October 10, 2012, accessed August 8, 2019, https://www.canadianbusiness.com/leadership/human-resources-the-war-for-better-workers/.
66. Andrew Hepburn, "How to Hire and Retain Talent like Canada's Fastest-Growing Companies," *Canadian Business*, November 23, 2017, accessed August 9, 2019, https://www.canadianbusiness.com/lists-and-rankings/profit-500/how-to-hire-and-retain-talent-like-canadas-fastest-growing-companies/.
67. Diane Jermyn, "Scientist Turned Entrepreneur Shares His Three Secrets to Success," *Globe and Mail*, October 27, 2015, accessed August 9, 2019, www.theglobeandmail.com/report-on-business/small-business/sb-growth/success-stories/scientist-turned-entrepreneur-shares-his-three-secrets-to-success/article23282094/.
68. Jason McCann, "How to Really Hear and Use Customer Feedback," *Entrepreneur*, June 27, 2018, accessed August 9, 2019, https://www.entrepreneur.com/article/315805.
69. Alex Turnball, "What 9 Successful Entrepreneurs Wish They Had Done

Differently," *Entrepreneur,* June 23, 2015, accessed September 3, 2019, https://www.entrepreneur.com/article/247598.
70. "X-Matik Self-Driving: Current Project Status," Lease Costs, January 23, 2019, https://www.leasecosts.ca/en/articles/x-matik-self-driving-current-project-status; "X-Matik," *Dragons' Den,* CBC, February 1, 2015, accessed August 30, 2019, https://www.cbc.ca/dragonsden/pitches/x-matik-inc.
71. "It's the End of the Line for Smokin' Tony's BBQ in Guelph," *CTV Kitchener News,* accessed March 31, 2019, https://kitchener.ctvnews.ca/video?clipId=1302554&binId=1.1147261&playlistPageNum=1, Television.
72. Lauren O'Neil, "One of Toronto's Favourite Italian Restaurants is Closing," BlogTO, February 14, 2018, accessed August 9, 2019, https://www.blogto.com/eat_drink/2018/02/lil-baci-italian-restaurant-closing-toronto/.
73. Jeffrey A. Timmons, Leonard E. Smollen, and Alexander L. M. Dingee, *New Venture Creation: A Guide to Entrepreneurship* (Homewood, Illinois: Richard D. Irwin, 1985), p. 28.
74. Jeffry Tannenbaum, "On Their Own," *Wall Street Journal,* May 21, 1998, p. R20.
75. Joel Corman and Robert Lussier, *Entrepreneurial New Ventures* (Cincinnati, Ohio: Thomson Learning, 2001), pp. 1–18.

CHAPTER 3

1. "Top 5 Most Successful Businesses Who Pitched on Dragons' Den," *Dragons' Den,* CBC, March 6, 2019, accessed August 30, 2019, https://www.cbc.ca/dragonsden/blog/top-successful-businesses.
2. Catherine Clifford, "From College Dropout to CEO of a Billion-Dollar Company: 3 Leadership Lessons from the Founder of Hootsuite," CNBC Make It, October 5, 2017, accessed August 31, 2019, https://www.cnbc.com/2017/10/05/3-leadership-lessons-from-hootsuite-ceo-ryan-holmes.html.
3. Danyal Hussain, "It's Just Like Play-Doh! Teenage Schoolgirl's Mesmerising Slime-Making Skills Wow Thousands as She Reaches Nearly a Million Followers on Instagram," *Daily Mail,* January 25, 2018, accessed August 9, 2019, https://www.dailymail.co.uk/news/article-5314069/Toronto-teen-girl-wows-thousands-slime-making-videos.html; and Alyssa Jagan, interview with Newsround - BBC: "Slime Star Reveals How She Makes Her Videos," video podcast, January 22, 2018, accessed August 9, 2019, https://www.bbc.co.uk/newsround/42781586.
4. Rose Behar, "Meet the Company that Teaches 24 Million Students Math through an RPG," Mobile Syrup, January 18, 2018, accessed August 9, 2019, https://mobilesyrup.com/2018/01/18/burlington-educational-game-prodigy-24-million-players/.
5. Steve MacNaull, "Fourth Time on *Dragons',*" *Daily Courier,* February 17, 2018, accessed August 9, 2019, http://www.kelownadailycourier.ca/business_news/article_5330b5a0-137e-11e8-b778-ff1cb9b6fe54.html.
6. Deborah Aarts, "Advice You Should Ignore," *Canadian Business,* April 1, 2013, accessed August 9, 2019, https://www.canadianbusiness.com/innovation/advice-you-should-ignore/.
7. Nicole Bogart, "Canadian Startup VarageSale Aims to Make Online Buying, Selling Safer for Families," Global News, July 27, 2015, accessed August 9, 2019, http://globalnews.ca/news/2129422/canadian-startup-varagesale-aims-to-make-online-buying-selling-safer-for-families/.
8. Shane Digman, "Fast Growing Canadian Startup VarageSale Raises 34 Million from Silicon Valley Investors," *Globe and Mail,* April 2, 2015, accessed August 9, 2019, www.theglobeandmail.com/report-on-business/small-business/sb-money/varagesale-app-raises-34-million-from-silicon-valley-investors/article23772596/.
9. Oded Shenkar, "Defend Your Research Imitation Is More Valuable Than Innovation," *Harvard Business Review,* April 2010, accessed August 9, 2019, https://hbr.org/2010/04/defend-your-research-imitation-is-more-valuable-than-innovation.
10. Joe Castaldo, "The Case for Stealing Your Success," *Canadian Business,* June 12, 2014, accessed August 9, 2019, https://www.canadianbusiness.com/innovation/the-case-for-stealing-your-success/.
11. "New Coffee Promises Restful Night's Sleep," Fox News, November 22, 2016, accessed August 9, 2019, https://www.foxnews.com/food-drink/new-coffee-promises-restful-nights-sleep; and Laura Robin, "Found: Coffee that will put you to sleep. Really," *Ottawa Citizen,* January 30, 2015, accessed August 9, 2019, https://ottawacitizen.com/life/food/found-coffee-that-will-put-you-to-sleep-really.
12. "The Story of Fox 40," About Us - Fox 40, accessed August 6, 2019, https://www.fox40world.com/the-story-of-fox-40.
13. "Events," Unstick, accessed August 9, 2019, http://www.unstick.ca/media/.
14. Frank Condron, "Michael Kaye, 2012 Fuel Award Winner," *Canadian Business,* December 12, 2012, accessed August 9, 2019, https://www.canadianbusiness.com/innovation/profile-michael-kaye-2012-fuel-award-winner/.
15. *Micro-Enterprises Survey 2000, A Progress Report.* Industry Canada, June 7, 2001, p. 10.
16. *Small Business Quarterly,* Industry Canada, August 2008, p. 2.
17. *The Financial Post,* October 29, 1994, p. S24.
18. Kevin J. Ryan, "The 1 Temptation Every Founder Needs to Resist," *Inc.,* March 12, 2019, https://www.inc.com/kevin-j-ryan/carey-smith-big-ass-solutions-founders-house-founders-project.html.
19. Frank Condron, "Growing Great Ideas," *Canadian Business,* June 28, 2012, accessed September 3, 2019, https://www.canadianbusiness.com/innovation/growing-great-ideas/.
20. Canadian Franchise Association website, 2010.
21. "About Us," Innovate Calgary, accessed August 9, 2019, https://www.innovatecalgary.com/about-us/; and Mario Toneguzzi, "Innovate Canada Sixth in World in University Business Incubator Rankings," *Calgary Herald,* updated November 27, 2015, accessed September 13, 2019,

https://calgaryherald.com/business/local-business/innovate-calgary-sixth-in-world-in-university-business-indicator-rankings.
22. Greg Bullock, "Eight Amazing Facts About Business Incubation," CEI, August 16, 2015, accessed May 1, 2019, https://www.ceigateway.com/blog/8-facts-business-incubation.
23. "National Business Incubator," *Inc.*, accessed August 9, 2019, https://www.inc.com/encyclopedia/national-business-incubation-association-nbia.html; Greg Bullock, "Eight Amazing Facts About Business Incubation," CEI, August 16, 2015, accessed May 1, 2019, https://www.ceigateway.com/blog/8-facts-business-incubation.
24. Cemre Kalender, "150 Accelerators And Incubators In Canada," Medium, October 11, 2017, accessed August 30, 2019, https://medium.com/mentornity-blog/150-accelerators-and-incubators-in-canada-6111e89e2fd8.
25. Canadian Association of Business Incubation website, 2010.
26. Ivor Tossel, "Awkward, Clunky and Just Plain Ugly: The Cane Gets a Much Needed Makeover," *Globe and Mail*, May 6, 2013, accessed August 9, 2019, https://www.theglobeandmail.com/report-on-business/small-business/startups/awkward-clunky-and-just-plain-ugly-the-cane-gets-a-much-needed-makeover/article11730586/.

CHAPTER 4

1. *Business Research Newsletter*, GDSourcing.com, vol. 3, no. 12, November, 2000, p. 9.
2. Angie Stocklin, "A Female Entrepreneur's Advice for Women Looking to Start Their Own Business," Ladders, March 20, 2019, accessed August 10, 2019, https://www.theladders.com/career-advice/a-female-entrepreneurs-advice-for-women-looking-to-start-their-own-business.
3. "1-800-Got-Junk?" Franchise Gator, accessed May 15, 2019, https://www.franchisegator.com/franchises/1-800-got-junk/.
4. The Young Entrepreneur Council, "10 Reasons Why You Should Write A Business Plan," Small Business Trends, updated December 22, 2018, accessed August 10, 2019, https://smallbiztrends.com/2013/01/10-reasons-write-business-plan.html.
5. Joe Mancuso, president of the Centre for Entrepreneurial Management.
6. The Young Entrepreneur Council, "10 Reasons Why You Should Write A Business Plan," Small Business Trends, updated December 22, 2018, accessed August 10, 2019, https://smallbiztrends.com/2013/01/10-reasons-write-business-plan.html.
7. "Secrets of Successful Business Planning," *Profit*, March 2007, p. 35.
8. Donald Rumball, *The Entrepreneurial Edge* (Toronto: Key Porter Books, 1989), pp. 225–33.
9. Adapted from "Success Story: Strategic Planning Sharpens Jonoke Software's Competitive Edge," *Business Development Bank of Canada newsletter*, March 2009, p. 1.
10. Stever Robbins, "Why You Must Have a Business Plan," *Entrepreneur*, accessed May 15, 2019, https://www.entrepreneur.com/article/74194.
11. Will Moniz, "Young Entrepreneur Profile: Notable TV's Julian Brass," Talent Egg, August 5, 2009, accessed August 10, 2019, http://talentegg.ca/incubator/2009/08/05/young-entrepreneur-profile-notabletvs-julian-brass/.
12. Mount Saint Vincent University Business and Tourism, March 8, 2013, accessed August 10, 2019, www.youtube.com/watch?v=rZAKSPogwYE.
13. Classroom presentation, Mount Saint Vincent University, October 2017.
14. "Secrets of Successful Business Planning," *Profit*, March 2007, p. 35.
15. Tracy MacKinnon, Class Presentation, Mount Saint Vincent University, October 2017.
16. C. Bart, "Words to Grow By," *Profit*, March 2006, p. 66.
17. Jerry White, "Canada's Free Trade Winners," *Small Business Magazine*, July–August 1990, p. 38.
18. Robert Morent, "Seven Principles of Admirable Business Ethics," About.com website, 2010.
19. Edmée Métivier, "Against the Grain," Business Development Bank of Canada website, 2010.
20. Paul Weber, "The Non-Risk Taker's Guide to Successful Entrepreneurship," Business.com, modified February 27, 2019, accessed September 13, 2019, https://www.business.com/articles/low-risk-guide-to-entrepreneurship/.
21. Trevor Cole, "Our Canadian CEO of the Year You've Probably Never Heard of," *Globe and Mail*, May 12, 2018, accessed September 13, 2019, https://www.theglobeandmail.com/report-on-business/rob-magazine/meet-our-ceo-of-the-year/article21734931/.
22. Sunday Steinkirchner, "The 4 Biggest Mistakes I've Made as an Entrepreneur," *Forbes*, September 4, 2014, accessed September 13, 2019, https://www.forbes.com/sites/sundaysteinkirchner/2014/09/04/the-4-biggest-mistakes-ive-made-as-an-entrepreneur/#25608794f95b.
23. "Facts and Stats You Need to Know About the 2018 Growth 500," *Canadian Business*, September 13, 2018, accessed September 13, 2019, https://www.canadianbusiness.com/lists-and-rankings/growth-500/facts-and-stats-you-need-to-know-about-the-2018-growth-500/.
24. Joanna Pachner, "Michele Romanow's Entrepreneurial Secret? Launch Now, Fix Later," *Canadian Business*, June 2, 2016, accessed September 13, 2019, https://www.canadianbusiness.com/leadership/michele-romanow/.
25. Robert Liwanag, "6 Brilliant Business Tips From One of Canada's Top Entrepreneurs," Reader's Digest Canada, accessed May 15, 2019, https://www.readersdigest.ca/home-garden/money/rajen-ruparell-success-secrets/.
26. "Canada's Fastest Growing Company Is Built for Growth," *Profit*, June 13, 2014.
27. *Small Business Quarterly*, Industry Canada, February 2009, p. 9.
28. *The Globe and Mail*, June 19, 1995, p. B7.
29. "About Us," Just Us! Coffee Roasters Co-op, accessed September 13, 2019, www.justuscoffee.com/our-co-op/beginnings.

30. "Secrets of Successful Business Planning," *Profit,* March 2007, p. 35.
31. Will Moniz, "Young Entrepreneur Profile: Notable TV's Julian Brass," Talent Egg, August 5, 2009, accessed August 10, 2019, http://talentegg.ca/incubator/2009/08/05/young-entrepreneur-profile-notabletvs-julian-brass/.

CHAPTER 5

1. Alison Anderson, "Six Reasons to Buy an Existing Business," CFIB, April 18, 2017, accessed September 13, 2019, https://www.cfib-fcei.ca/en/tools-resources/buy-existing-business.
2. "An Entrepreneur's Road to Success after Buying a Business," BDC, accessed May 15, 2019, https://www.bdc.ca/en/articles-tools/start-buy-business/buy-business/pages/road-success-after-buying-business.aspx?type=A&order=1.
3. Joanna Pachner, "Breakthrough: Dealmaker Slays His Competition with One Perfect Purchase," *Canadian Business,* February 21, 2013, accessed September 13, 2019, https://www.canadianbusiness.com/innovation/breakthrough-dealmaker-slays-his-competition-with-one-perfect-purchase/.
4. Chris Atchison, "How to Acquire Your Worst Enemy," *Canadian Business,* April 5, 2013, accessed September 13, 2019, https://www.canadianbusiness.com/innovation/breakthrough-dealmaker-slays-his-competition-with-one-perfect-purchase/.
5. Adapted from Cheryl Devoe Kim, "Takeover Helps Company Meet Its Target," *Globe and Mail,* March 24, 2009, pp. 1–3.
6. Chris Atchison, "How to Acquire Your Worst Enemy," *Canadian Business,* April 5, 2013, accessed September 13, 2019, https://www.canadianbusiness.com/innovation/breakthrough-dealmaker-slays-his-competition-with-one-perfect-purchase/.
7. Chris Atchison, "How to Acquire Your Worst Enemy," *Canadian Business,* April 5, 2013, accessed September 13, 2019, https://www.canadianbusiness.com/innovation/breakthrough-dealmaker-slays-his-competition-with-one-perfect-purchase/.
8. Chris Atchison, "What You Need to Know Before Making an Acquisition," *Canadian Business,* December 8, 2011, accessed September 13, 2019, https://www.canadianbusiness.com/leadership/what-you-need-to-know-before-making-an-acquisition/.
9. Chris Atchison, "What You Need to Know Before Making an Acquisition," *Canadian Business,* December 8, 2011, accessed September 13, 2019, https://www.canadianbusiness.com/leadership/what-you-need-to-know-before-making-an-acquisition/.
10. "Herjavec Group Announces Major Acquisition as Part of $250M Expansion," Herjavec Group (blog), August 10, 2014, accessed September 13, 2019, https://www.herjavecgroup.com/herjavec-group-announces-major-acquisition-part-250m-expansion/.
11. Brenda Bouw, "Buying an Established Business? There are Right Ways and Wrong Ways to Do a Deal," *Globe and Mail,* updated October 1, 2018, accessed September 13, 2019, https://www.theglobeandmail.com/business/article-buying-an-established-business-there-are-right-ways-and-wrong-ways-to/.
12. "Herjavec Group Announces Major Acquisition as Part of $250M Expansion," Herjavec Group (blog), August 10, 2014, accessed September 13, 2019, https://www.herjavecgroup.com/herjavec-group-announces-major-acquisition-part-250m-expansion/.
13. Chris Atchison, "How to Acquire Your Worst Enemy," *Canadian Business,* April 5, 2013, accessed September 13, 2019, https://www.canadianbusiness.com/innovation/breakthrough-dealmaker-slays-his-competition-with-one-perfect-purchase/.
14. Chris Atchison, "How to Acquire Your Worst Enemy," *Canadian Business,* April 5, 2013, accessed September 13, 2019, https://www.canadianbusiness.com/innovation/breakthrough-dealmaker-slays-his-competition-with-one-perfect-purchase/.
15. Brenda Bouw, "Buying an Established Business? There are Right Ways and Wrong Ways to Do a Deal," *Globe and Mail,* updated October 1, 2018, accessed September 13, 2019, https://www.theglobeandmail.com/business/article-buying-an-established-business-there-are-right-ways-and-wrong-ways-to/.
16. Grant Thornton LLP Study as reported on *About Small Business,* February, 2007.
17. Joanne Pachner, "Want to Buy a Business?" *Report on Business,* November 19, 2009, p. 2.
18. Peter Thomas, "Negotiate to Win," *Profit,* October 1991, p. 34.
19. Ian Portsmouth, "Ask the Legends: Mac Voisin," *Canadian Business,* February 16, 2011, accessed September 13, 2019, https://www.canadianbusiness.com/leadership/ask-the-legends-mac-voisin/.
20. Noemi LoPinto, "The Joy of Giving," *Alberta Venture,* July 2007, pp. 11–12; and Basket Boutique website, 2010.
21. *The Globe and Mail,* October 1995, p. B7.
22. "Canadian Franchise Statistics," Franchise 101, accessed May 15, 2019, http://www.franchise101.net/canadian-franchise-statistics.
23. Frank Zaid, "Mediation and Arbitration of Franchise Disputes—The Path of the Future," February 2012, accessed August 11, 2019, www.oba.org/en/pdf/sec_news_adr_feb12_Franchise_Art.pdf.
24. "2019 Franchising Trends Report," Franchise Canada, January 7, 2019, accessed September 13, 2019, https://www.cfa.ca/franchisecanada/2019-franchising-trends-report/.
25. "Canadian Franchise Statistics," Franchise 101, accessed May 15, 2019, http://www.franchise101.net/canadian-franchise-statistics.
26. "Canadian Franchises Abroad," Franchise Canada, October 27, 2017, accessed September 13, 2019, https://www.cfa.ca/franchisecanada/canadian-franchises-abroad/.
27. Gordon Brockhouse, "The Franchise Advantage," *Small Business Magazine,* July–August 1990, p. 48.
28. *Franchising in the Canadian Economy 1990–1992* (Toronto: Canadian Franchise Association and Price Waterhouse), p. 3.

29. "Franchise FAQs," Tim Hortons, accessed August 11, 2019, https://www.timhortons.com/ca/en/corporate/franchise-ca-faq.php.
30. Eve Lazarus, "Building the Perfect Franchise," *Canadian Business,* February 9, 2006, accessed August 13, 2019, https://www.canadianbusiness.com/leadership/building-the-perfect-franchise/.
31. Eve Lazarus, "Building the Perfect Franchise," *Canadian Business,* February 9, 2006, accessed August 13, 2019, https://www.canadianbusiness.com/leadership/building-the-perfect-franchise/.
32. Joanna Pachner, "Secrets of the Sunshine Girl," *Canadian Business,* February 18, 2010, accessed September 13, 2019, https://www.canadianbusiness.com/innovation/secrets-of-the-sunshine-girl/.
33. Tony Martin, "Love Thy Franchisees," *Canadian Business,* April 30, 2008, accessed September 13, 2019, https://www.canadianbusiness.com/leadership/love-thy-franchisees/.
34. Joanna Pachner, "Secrets of the Sunshine Girl," *Canadian Business,* February 18, 2010, accessed September 13, 2019, https://www.canadianbusiness.com/innovation/secrets-of-the-sunshine-girl/.
35. Faye Rice, "How to Succeed at Cloning a Small Business," *Fortune,* October 28, 1985, p. 60.
36. Elizabeth Sile, "Edible Arrangements in Legal Hot Water," *Inc.,* July 22, 2011, accessed September 3, 2019, https://www.inc.com/news/articles/201107/edible-arrangements-lawsuit.html.
37. Eve Lazarus, "Building the Perfect Franchise," *Canadian Business,* February 9, 2006, accessed August 13, 2019, https://www.canadianbusiness.com/leadership/building-the-perfect-franchise/.
38. David Joseph, "Why I Sold My Kumon Franchise," Franchise Publicity website, April 26, 2010, www.franchisepublicity.com/kumon-"why-i-sold-my-kumon-franchise.
39. "Reading the Fine Print," *CBC Venture,* February 2000.
40. U.S. Department of Commerce, *Franchising in the Economy, 1977–79* (Washington, D.C.: U.S. Government Printing Office, 1981), Table 3, p. 34.
41. John Southerst, "The Subway System Under Fire," WikiFranchise.org, November 28, 1995, accessed September 3, 2019, http://infofranpro.wikidot.com/19951128-the-subway.
42. John Southerst, "The Subway System Under Fire," WikiFranchise.org, November 28, 1995, accessed September 3, 2019, http://infofranpro.wikidot.com/19951128-the-subway.
43. Tim Devaney and Tom Stein, "Quiznos Settles Class-Action Lawsuit with Franchisees," All Business, accessed May 15, 2019, https://www.allbusiness.com/quiznos-settles-class-action-lawsuit-with-franchisees-13479172-1.html.
44. *Machias v. Mr. Submarine Ltd., April 2, 2002,* www.intelligentfranchising.com/case22.html; andMacchias v. Mr. Submarine, Superior Court of Justice of Ontario, CITE:[2002] O.T.C. 190 (SupCt), February 19, 2002, accessed September 3, 2019, https://ca.vlex.com/vid/machias-v-mr-submarine-680939393.
45. Jake Edmiston and Barbara Shecter, "Minnesota Franchisee Files Lawsuit Accusing Tim Hortons of Misrepresentation, Charging Excessive Markups," *Financial Post,* February 20, 2019, accessed September 3, 2019, https://business.financialpost.com/news/retail-marketing/minnesota-franchisee-files-lawsuit-accusing-tim-hortons-of-misrepresentation-charging-excessive-markups.
46. John Sotos, "Midas Class Actions," Sotos Class Actions, February 10, 2014, accessed September 3, 2019, https://sotosclassactions.com/cases/archived-class-actions/midas/.
47. Faye Rice, "How to Succeed at Cloning a Small Business," *Fortune,* October 28, 1985, p. 60.
48. Kenneth Barnes and Everett Banning, *Money Makers: The Secrets of Canada's Most Successful Entrepreneurs* (Toronto: McClelland and Stewart, 1985), p. 84.
49. Adapted from Derek Sankey, "Life's a Beach for High-Tech Spa Franchisee," *Financial Post,* February 23, 2009, pp. 1–2.
50. Kenneth Barnes and Everett Banning, *Money Makers: The Secrets of Canada's Most Successful Entrepreneurs* (Toronto: McClelland and Stewart, 1985), p. 84.
51. Kenneth Barnes and Everett Banning, *Money Makers: The Secrets of Canada's Most Successful Entrepreneurs* (Toronto: McClelland and Stewart, 1985), p. 84.
52. Eve Lazarus, "Building the Perfect Franchise," *Canadian Business,* February 9, 2006, accessed August 13, 2019, https://www.canadianbusiness.com/leadership/building-the-perfect-franchise/.
53. Eve Lazarus, "Building the Perfect Franchise," *Canadian Business,* February 9, 2006, accessed August 13, 2019, https://www.canadianbusiness.com/leadership/building-the-perfect-franchise/.
54. Joanna Pachner, "Secrets of the Sunshine Girl," *Canadian Business,* February 18, 2010, accessed September 13, 2019, https://www.canadianbusiness.com/innovation/secrets-of-the-sunshine-girl/.

CHAPTER 6

1. Hailey Salvian, "Elora Brothers Strike Dragons' Den deal for Pressa Bottle," February 2, 2018, https://www.cbc.ca/news/canada/kitchener-waterloo/elora-hambly-brothers-dragons-den-pressa-bottle-1.4516301.
2. *The Canadian Business Failure Record, 1999* (Toronto: Dun and Bradstreet Business Education Division, 1998).
3. Queenie Wong, "SME Financing Indicators," CFIB, October 2016, accessed August 20, 2019, https://www.cfib-fcei.ca/sites/default/files/article/documents/rr3412_0.pdf; Statistics Canada, "Survey on Financing and Growth of Small and Medium Enterprises, 2017," Revised March 21, 2019, https://www.ic.gc.ca/eic/site/061.nsf/vwapj/SFGSME-EFCPME_2017_eng_revised_March-21.pdf/$file/SFGSME-EFCPME_2017_eng_revised_March-21.pdf.
4. Saira Peesker, "B.C. sisters build startup on period products and straight talk,"

Globe and Mail, May 5, 2019, https://www.theglobeandmail.com/business/small-business/startups/article-bc-sisters-build-startup-on-period-products-and-straight-talk/.
5. Camilla Cornell, "She was Eight Months Behind on Her Rent. Instead of Kicking Her Out, The Landlord Issued a Challenge," *Globe and Mail,* November 13, 2018, https://www.theglobeandmail.com/business/small-business/startups/article-she-was-eight-months-behind-on-her-rent-instead-of-kicking-her-out/.
6. "Small and Medium Sized Enterprise Financing in Canada," Government of Canada Publication, 2003, p. 58.
7. Profit Staff Writer, "The Success Secrets of Gerry Schwartz," *Canadian Business,* May 16, 2011, accessed August 20, 2019, https://www.canadianbusiness.com/innovation/the-success-secrets-of-gerry-schwartz/.
8. Rebecca Gardiner, "PROFIT 100 Fundraising Secrets," *Canadian Business,* May 10, 2005, accessed August 20, 2019, www.profitguide.com/manage-grow/financing/profit-100-fundraising-secrets-28646.
9. Jessica Patterson, "Step by Step: Calgary Entrepreneur Dances her Way to Success," AVdance, 2010, accessed October 11, 2019, http://jessicapatterson.ca/wp-content/uploads/AVdance.pdf.
10. Elisa B., "Opportunity 2013: Gen Y Enters Its Family Years," *Canadian Business,* December 14, 2012, accessed August 20, 2019, https://www.canadianbusiness.com/innovation/opportunity-2013-gen-y-enters-its-family-years/; and R. Spence, "Stuck in the Middle," *Profit,* October 2007, p. 17.
11. "Kickstarter Stats," Kickstarter, accessed June 14, 2019, https://www.kickstarter.com/help/stats.
12. The Startups Team, "Key Crowdfunding Statistics," Startups, December 3, 2018, https://www.startups.com/library/expert-advice/key-crowdfunding-statistics.
13. Massolutions, "2015 CF The Crowdfunding Industry Report," Crowdsourcing, http://reports.crowdsourcing.org/index.php?route=product/product&path=0&product_id=54.
14. Paul Hayward, "New 'Start-up' Crowdfunding Exemptions Adopted in Some Canadian Jurisdictions," NCAC, June 5, 2015, accessed August 20, 2019, http://ncfacanada.org/new-start-up-crowdfunding-exemptions-adopted-in-some-canadian-jurisdictions/.
15. David Ebner, "Veteran Entrepreneur on Quest to Make Motorcycling Safer," *Globe and Mail,* April 7, 2019, https://www.theglobeandmail.com/business/small-business/startups/article-veteran-entrepreneur-on-a-quest-to-make-motorcycling-safer/; Janaki Jitchotvisut, "Our Mission to Cause A Paradigm Shift for Safer, Smarter, Motorcycling," RideApart, June 6, 2019, https://www.rideapart.com/articles/353423/damon-motorcycles-safe-motorcycle-tech-secures-funding/.
16. David Ebner, "Where's My Drone? A Crowdfunding Startup's Long Quest to Deliver," *Globe and Mail,* October 7, 2018, https://www.theglobeandmail.com/business/article-after-the-crowdfunding-four-years-later-backers-ask-toronto-startup/.
17. David Ebner, "Where's My Drone? A Crowdfunding Startup's Long Quest to Deliver," *Globe and Mail,* October 7, 2018, https://www.theglobeandmail.com/business/article-after-the-crowdfunding-four-years-later-backers-ask-toronto-startup/.
18. Yancey Strickler, Perry Chen, and Charles Adler, "Accountability on Kickstarter," The Kickstarter Blog, September 4, 2012, accessed June 1, 2019, https://www.kickstarter.com/blog/accountability-on-kickstarter.
19. "About NACO," NACO website, accessed July 3, 2019, https://www.nacocanada.com/cpages/about.
20. Colin Mason, "2018 Report on Angel Investing in Canada," June 2019, https://www.nacocanada.com/cpages/angel-activity-report.
21. Innovation, Science and Economic Development Canada, "Minister Ng Announces Funding for Angel Investment Network During the National Angel Capital Organization Summit," Cision, September 26, 2018, https://www.newswire.ca/news-releases/minister-ng-announces-funding-for-angel-investment-networks-during-the-national-angel-capital-organization-summit-694389431.html.
22. Kara Aaserud, "Private Investing: After the Handshake," April 30, 2008, accessed August 20, 2019, https://www.canadianbusiness.com/small-business/private-investing-after-the-handshake/.
23. Guy Dixon, "Ontario Entrepreneur's Gluten-Free Pasta Takes Off with Consumers," June 8, 2019, https://www.theglobeandmail.com/business/small-business/startups/article-ontario-entrepreneurs-gluten-free-pasta-takes-off-with-consumers/.
24. Sarah Niedoba, "How to Find the Best Angel Investor for Your Startup," September 13, 2018, *Canadian Business,* https://www.canadianbusiness.com/lists-and-rankings/growth-500/how-to-find-the-best-angel-investor-for-your-startup/.
25. Kara Aaserud, "Private Investing: After the Handshake."
26. Jim McElgunn, "Financing Strategies for Your Startup," *Canadian Business,* February 6, 2012, accessed August 20, 2019, https://www.canadianbusiness.com/innovation/financing-strategies-for-your-startup/.
27. Jim McElgunn, "Financing Strategies for Your Startup," *Canadian Business,* February 6, 2012, accessed August 20, 2019, https://www.canadianbusiness.com/innovation/financing-strategies-for-your-startup/.
28. Karen Geier, "Your Start-Up Business: How to Find an Angel Investor," HuffPost, January 10, 2013, accessed August 20, 2019, www.huffingtonpost.ca/karen-geier/angel-investor_b_2210768.html.
29. Sarah Niedoba, "How to Find the Best Angel Investor for Your Startup."
30. Kim Hart Macneill, "Pitching to an Angel," *Canadian Business,* July 25, 2012, accessed August 20, 2019, https://www.canadianbusiness.com/small-business/pitching-to-an-angel/.
31. Sarah Niedoba, "How to Find the Best Angel Investor for Your Startup."
32. Jim McElgunn, "Financing Strategies for Your Startup."
33. Kim Hart Macneill, "Pitching to an Angel."
34. "Venture Capital: More Money, Still Choosy," *The Magazine That's*

All about Small Business, May 1984, p. 49; Canadian Venture Capital Association website, October 2006.
35. Victoria Gibson, "Toronto Startup Second Closet Aims to 'Uber-ize' Self Storage," *Globe and Mail,* September 10, 2018, https://www.theglobeandmail.com/business/article-toronto-startup-second-closet-aims-to-uber-ize-self-storage/.
36. Canadian Venture Capital & Private Equity Association, "VC & PE Canadian Market Overview 2018," CVCA, https://central.cvca.ca/wp-content/uploads/2019/05/CVCA_EN_Canada_Q4-2018_Final2.pdf; PwC Management Services LP, "Venture Capital Funding in Canada Reaches an All Time High According to the MoneyTree Canada Report," Cision, January 24, 2018, https://www.newswire.ca/news-releases/venture-capital-funding-in-canada-reaches-an-all-time-high-according-to-the-moneytree-canada-report-670854763.html.
37. Canadian Venture Capital & Private Equity Association, "VC & PE Canadian Market Overview 2018."
38. "Recyc PHP: Of Vision and Volume," April 2008, www.butler-consultants.ca/news_profit.html.
39. Sarah Efron, "How the Tables Turned on Zane Caplansky, Toronto's Deli King," *Globe and Mail,* May 30, 2019, https://www.theglobeandmail.com/report-on-business/small-business/sb-managing/how-the-tables-turned-on-zane-caplansky-torontos-deliking/article38108377/.
40. *Statistics Canada,*"Survey on Financing of Small and Medium Business - Tables, 2017," Released November 2018.
41. *Small Business Quarterly,* Industry Canada, May 2009, p. 1.
42. "Venture Survey—Financing," *Venture,* October 1986, p. 24.
43. Peter Kenter, "How Snakes & Lattes Found a Better Way to Grow Their Business with Lending Loop," *Financial Post,* August 9, 2018, https://business.financialpost.com/sponsored/business-sponsored/how-snakes-lattes-found-a-better-way-to-grow-their-business-with-lending-loop.
44. Canadian Bankers Association, "Focus: Small and Medium Sized Lending Enterprises: Lending and More," CBA, October 3, 2018, https://cba.ca/small-and-medium-sized-enterprises.
45. *CFIB Banking Study,* October 7, 2003.
46. "Cozy Corner Saunas: The Relaxation Business That Almost Wasn't," http://s3images.coroflot.com/user_files/individual_files/337558_Dg7vsl2wkdC8BX7xODR6nhDJl.pdf.
47. "About Us," Futurpreneur Canada, accessed July 3, 2019, https://www.futurpreneur.ca/en/about/.
48. *Business Research Newsletter,* GDSourcing.com, vol. 4, no. 1, June 2001, p. 8.
49. Canadian Banker's Association Survey, CBA website, October 2009.

CHAPTER 7

1. Richard Carufel, "Half of Small Business Owners Lack a Marketing Strategy for 2019," Agility PR Solutions, April 26, 2019, https://www.agilitypr.com/pr-news/public-relations/half-of-small-business-owners-lack-a-marketing-strategy-for-2019/.
2. Harley Schachter, "20 Killer Examples of Influencer Marketing," Travel Mindset, accessed May 15, 2019, https://www.travelmindset.com/20-influencer-marketing-examples/.
3. "7 Sales Strategies of High-Growth Companies," June 3, 2013, accessed October 15, 2019, https://www.canadianbusiness.com/innovation/7-sales-strategies-of-high-growth-companies/.
4. Lisa Shepherd, "Why Your B2B Company Needs a Marketing Plan," Canadian Business, November 2, 2010, accessed August 21, 2019, https://www.canadianbusiness.com/innovation/why-your-b2b-company-needs-a-marketing-plan/.
5. Lisa Shepherd, "Why Your B2B Company Needs a Marketing Plan," *Canadian Business,* November 2, 2010, accessed August 21, 2019, https://www.canadianbusiness.com/innovation/why-your-b2b-company-needs-a-marketing-plan/.
6. "Success Stories," Canadian Centre for Aboriginal Entrepreneurship, accessed June 1, 2019, https://ccae.ca/success-stories/.
7. Marzena Czamecka, "Vets To Go is a Hit with Time-Starved Pet Owners (and Their Furry Friends)," *Canadian Business,* September 14, 2017, accessed August 21, 2019, https://www.canadianbusiness.com/lists-and-rankings/profit-500/2017-vets-to-go/.
8. P. Crescoe, *The Mavericks* (Toronto: McGraw-Hill Ryerson Ltd., 1999), pp. 311–312.
9. Kasey Kaplan, "How to Make Your Company's Brand Meaningful," *Forbes,* April 25, 2019, https://www.forbes.com/sites/theyec/2019/04/25/how-to-make-your-companys-brand-meaningful/#564d2d723608.
10. Alison Bowsher, "You Won't Believe How Much This Insane Playhouse Cost," The Loop, July 5, 2018, https://www.theloop.ca/pay-200000-playhouse/.
11. "Great Ideas: Smart Marketing for Startups," *Canadian Business,* October 17, 2010, accessed August 21, 2019, https://www.canadianbusiness.com/innovation/great-ideas-smart-marketing-for-startups/.
12. Catherine McIntyre, "How to Turn Your Brilliant Idea Into an Actual Business," September 14, 2017, https://www.canadianbusiness.com/lists-and-rankings/profit-500/2017-disruption-how-to/; and Elizabeth Segran, "Can Knix Win the $12 Billion Underwear Wars?" October 10, 2018, https://www.fastcompany.com/90249128/can-knix-win-the-12-billion-underwear-wars.
13. Michelle Strum, Class Presentation and Interview with Peter Mombourquette, 2018.
14. Caroline Forsey, "The Ultimate Guide to Relationship Marketing," Hubspot, updated June 26, 2019, https://blog.hubspot.com/marketing/relationship-marketing.
15. *Marketing,* Fourth Canadian Edition (Toronto: McGraw-Hill Ryerson, 1997).
16. "All in the Family," *BDC Success Stories,* p. 3, and the Olivier Soapery website, 2010.
17. Lawrence N. Stevenson, Joseph C. Shlesinger, and Michael R. Pierce,

Power Retail: Winning Strategies from Chapters and Other Leading Retailers in Canada (Toronto: McGraw-Hill Ryerson, 1999), p. 67.

CHAPTER 8

1. "Innovation - 34% of Canadians love it; 22% demonize it! (And the mechanical doll from Jacques Offenbach's Tales of Hoffmann)," Crop, May 28, 2017, accessed August 21, 2019, https://www.crop.ca/en/blog/2017/182/.
2. "About Us," TechPos, accessed June 1, 2019, https://techpos.ca/about-us/; and "TechPOS International," *Dragons' Den*, CBC, October 1, 2018, https://www.cbc.ca/player/play/1333793859576.
3. "Understanding Early Adopters and Customer Adoption Patterns," International Design Foundation, May 1, 2018, accessed August 22, 2019, https://www.interaction-design.org/literature/article/understanding-early-adopters-and-customer-adoption-patterns.
4. David Kates, "Unique Idea Strategy Fuel Game Cafe's Success," O Canada, April 17, 2012, accessed August 22, 2019, http://o.canada.com/life/unique-idea-strategy-fuel-game-cafes–success/.
5. John Zafris, Interview: With Author, February 14, 2019.
6. "Pet Peppy," *Dragons' Den*, CBC, accessed June 1, 2019, https://www.cbc.ca/dragonsden/pitches/pet-peppy; and "About Us," Pet Peppy, accessed June 1, 2019, https://petpeppy.com/pages/about.
7. Rimroller–Company website, www.rimroller.com.
8. *Fix Me Stick Blog*, "HowDragons' DenChanged Our Business," March 12, 2019, https://www.fixmestick.com/blog/6051-2/.
9. Deborah Aarts, "Canada's Fastest Growing Company Is Built for Growth," *Canadian Business*, June 13, 2014, accessed August 22, 2019, https://www.canadianbusiness.com/small-business/canadas-fastest-growing-company-is-built-for-growth/.
10. A. Holloway, "Try It! You'll Like It," *Profit*, November 2006, p. 65.
11. "Profit 100 Growth Strategies," *Profit*, November 2007, p. 17.
12. Lucy Hyslop, "Catching Up with Indochino Co-Founder Kyle Vucko," BC Business, June 27, 2016, https://www.bcbusiness.ca/catching-up-with-indochino-co-founder-kyle-vucko; Amanda Oleri, "The Best Suits for Men Under $1000," *Forbes*, April 29, 2019, https://www.forbes.com/sites/forbes-finds/2019/04/29/the-best-suits-for-men/#43f0e7ad5857.
13. "Life after Dragons' Den with Partner Vikram Vij," Quinta, September 14, 2016, accessed July 1, 2019, https://quinta.ca/2016/09/14/life-dragons-den-partner-vikram-vij/.
14. Rachel Beck, "Spin Master Toys Soars to Success with Air Hogs," *Los Angeles Times*, March 24, 1999, accessed August 22, 2019, http://articles.latimes.com/1999/mar/24/business/fi-20523.
15. "How She Succeeds: Natalie Dusome of Poppies & Peonies," Love, Mom,November 30, 2018, http://lovemom.ca/how-she-succeeds-natalie-dusome-of-poppies-peonies/; and "Steeped Tea," Canadian Business Journal, April 16, 2018, http://www.cbj.ca/steeped-tea-fast-growing-tea-party-company/.
16. "Industry Statistics and Research," Direct Sales Association, accessed June 11, 2019, https://www.dsa.ca/industry-statistics-and-research/.
17. "Dynamic Pricing Helps Keep Pace with Savvy Consumers," eMarketer, May 17, 2013, accessed August 22, 2019, www.emarketer.com/Article/Dynamic-Pricing-Helps-Keep-Pace-with-Savvy-Consumers/1009897.
18. Noel Hulsman, "Why Canada Goose Will Never Go on Sale," Yahoo! Finance, January 16, 2013, accessed August 22, 2019, http://ca.finance.yahoo.com/blogs/insight/why-canada-goose-never-sale-171840302.html.
19. John Lorinc, "Case Study: Sweet Tooth," Canadian Business, February 11, 2013, accessed August 22, 2019, https://www.canadianbusiness.com/leadership/case-study-sweet-tooth/.
20. Laura Pratt, "PROFIT Hot 50: Safer Passage," *Canadian Business*, August 31, 2009, accessed August 22, 2019, https://www.canadianbusiness.com/innovation/profit-hot-50-safer-passage/.
21. Jagoda Hruszko, "How to Develop a Successful Coupon Marketing Strategy and Increase Your Conversion Rates - The Ultimate Guide," Voucherify, March 18, 2019, https://www.voucherify.io/blog/coupon-marketing-strategy-ultimate-guide.
22. "Exhibitor Testimonials," The Canadian Gift and Tableware Association, accessed June 1, 2019, https://www.cangift.org/toronto-gift-fair/en/exhibitors/testimonials/.
23. Kim Shiffman, "3 Deadly Pricing Sins," *Canadian Business*, May 27, 2013, accessed August 22, 2019, https://www.canadianbusiness.com/innovation/3-deadly-pricing-sins/.
24. "Jordan Jolicoeur: Proud to be Working with Trans Mountain Pipeline, TransMountain," January 19, 2017, accessed August 22, 2019, https://www.transmountain.com/news/2017/jordan-jolicoeur-proud-to-be-working-with-trans-mountain-pipeline.
25. Lisa Evans, "The Growth of Calum McGuigan's Marketing Company," Canadian Immigrant, October 12, 2018, https://canadianimmigrant.ca/people/entrepreneur-immigrants/the-growth-of-calum-mcguigans-marketing-company.
26. *Community Futures Manitoba Blog*, "4 Unbeatable Marketing Strategies for Rural Small Businesses," January 25, 2018, https://cfmanitoba.ca/blog/4-unbeatable-marketing-strategies-for-rural-small-businesses.
27. Susanne Baillie, "How to Measure Your Marketing Effectiveness," *Canadian Business*, February 2, 2004, accessed August 22, 2019, https://www.canadianbusiness.com/innovation/how-to-measure-your-marketing-effectiveness/.
28. Hilary Bird, "Companies Seeing Success With Radio Ads," Duct Tape Marketing, accessed July 1, 2019, https://ducttapemarketing.com/success-with-radio-ads/.
29. *Finawear Blog*, "April 2019 Contest," April 6, 2019, https://finawear.ca/blogs/news.
30. "Young Entrepreneur: Calum McGuigan," Notable Life, June 28, 2011, accessed September 18, 2019, https://notablelife.com/

young-entrepreneur-calum-mcguigan/.
31. Ryan Lum, "Interview with Calum McGuigan," Brand Communications, June 28, 2011, http://brandcommunications.ca/news/.
32. "Community," Lululemon Athletica, accessed September 18, 2019, https://shop.lululemon.com/story/community?mnid=mn;en-CA;community.
33. Emily Wexler, "Brands of the Year: Lululemon Takes Local to the Next Level," Strategy, September 28, 2012, accessed August 22, 2019, http://strategyonline.ca/2012/09/28/brands-of-the-year-lululemon-takes-local-to-the-next-level/.
34. Graham F. Scott, "The Smart Way to Sell a Movement," June 12, 2014, accessed August 22, 2019, https://www.canadianbusiness.com/innovation/the-smart-way-to-sell-a-movement/.
35. Matt O'Grady, "Vancouver-Based Vega Sold for US$550 Million," BC Business, June 10, 2015, accessed August 22, 2019, www.bcbusiness.ca/retail/vancouver-based-vega-sold-for-us550-million.
36. Pamela Bartlett, "(Repost from smallbusinesspr.com) How Public Relations Can Help Your Small Business Grow," Red Dahlia Public Relations & Marketing, November 2, 2011, accessed September 18, 2019, https://rdprpressroom.blogspot.com/2011/11/repost-from-smallbusinessprcom-how.html.
37. Mia Wedgbury, "What Are They Saying about You?" *Globe and Mail,* June 17, 2008, accessed August 22, 2019, www.theglobeandmail.com/report-on-business/what-are-they-saying-about-you/article1056425/?page=all.
38. Marie Chevrier, "Ten New Marketing Concepts Your Company Needs to Understand Right Now," *Globe and Mail,* August 13, 2015, accessed August 22, 2019, www.theglobeandmail.com/report-on-business/small-business/sb-marketing/10-new-marketing-concepts-your-company-needs-to-understand-right-now/article25219912/.
39. Eleanor Beaton, "How to Sell More, More, More," *Canadian Business,* May 27, 2010, accessed August 22, 2019, https://www.canadianbusiness.com/innovation/how-to-sell-more-more-more/.
40. Ryan Pinkham, "3 Award Winning Small Business Marketing Campaigns," Constant Contact, 2015, accessed May 16, 2019, https://blogs.constantcontact.com/successful-marketing-campaigns/.
41. "Top Sites in Canada," Alexa, May 13, 2019, www.alexa.com/topsites/countries/CA.
42. Corinne Watson, "Your Brand's Guide to Facebook Marketplace: A New Channel for Growth," Big Commerce, accessed August 22, 2019, https://www.bigcommerce.com/blog/selling-on-facebook-marketplace/#what-is-facebook-marketplace.
43. Chris Neville, Interview with the Author, Halifax, Nova Scotia, May 1, 2019.
44. "Entrepreneur of the Year Awards - 2016 Entrepreneur of the Year," eBay, accessed July 1, 2019, https://pages.ebay.ca/eoy/.
45. Peter Kim, "Toronto Entrepreneur Sending Kids to College with eBay Sales," Global News, aired April 15, 2015, accessed May 31, 2019, https://globalnews.ca/news/1941080/toronto-entrepreneur-sending-kids-through-college-with-ebay-sales/.
46. "Entrepreneur of the Year Awards - 2017 Entrepreneur of the Year," eBay, accessed July 1, 2019, https://pages.ebay.ca/eoy/.
47. Fou Fou Dog—company website, www.foufoudog.com.
48. Steven Scheck, "6 Reasons Why Your Business Should Use Podcasting," Small Business Trends, June 8, 2018, https://smallbiztrends.com/2017/01/benefits-of-podcasting.html.
49. "41 Facebook Stats That Matter to Marketers in 2019," Hootsuite, November 13, 2018, https://blog.hootsuite.com/facebook-statistics/.
50. "Top Sites in Canada," Alexa.
51. "Measure for Measure, Facebook Ads Deliver," Facebook Business, January 28, 2016, accessed August 22, 2019, https://www.facebook.com/business/success/stratford-festival.
52. Becky Reuber, "How a Toronto Startup Is Changing the Product Sampling Game," *Globe and Mail,* January 6, 2016, www.theglobeandmail.com/report-on-business/small-business/sb-growth/day-to-day/how-a-toronto-startup-is-changing-the-product-sampling-game/article22291264/.
53. John Biggs, "Sampler Is Like Those People Who Give You Warm Cheeseballs at Costco but Only on the Internet," August 21, 2015, accessed August 22, 2019, http://techcrunch.com/2015/08/21/sampler-is-like-those-people-who-give-you-free-warm-cheeseballs-at-costco-but-only-on-the-internet/.
54. Randy Duermyer, "How to Use LinkedIn To Promote Your Home Business," The Balance Small Business, January 25, 2019, https://www.thebalancesmb.com/how-to-use-linkedin-to-promote-your-home-business-1794731.
55. Jennifer Goldberg, "How to Turn Social Media Engagement into Real Sales," *Canadian Business,* September 14, 2017, accessed August 22, 2019, https://www.canadianbusiness.com/lists-and-rankings/profit-500/2017-social-media-marketing/.
56. Susan Ward, "How and Why Your Small Business Should Use Twitter," The Balance Small Business," updated May 29, 2018, https://www.thebalancesmb.com/top-reasons-why-your-small-business-should-use-twitter-2948523.
57. Alan Smithson, "How I Used Twitter to Meet and Sell to DJs," *Globe and Mail,* October 9, 2013, accessed August 21, 2019, www.theglobeandmail.com/report-on-business/small-business/sb-managing/how-i-used-twitter-to-meet-famous-djs-in-ibiza/article14753084/.
58. Jim Estill, "Super Strategies for Small Guys," *Canadian Business,* November 30, 2008, accessed August 22, 2019, https://www.canadianbusiness.com/leadership/super-strategies-for-small-guys/.
59. Kara Aaserud, "Bonded by Blogging," Provident Security, October 1, 2006, accessed August 22, 2019, https://www.providentsecurity.ca/press/bonding-blogging/.
60. Eddie Shleyner, "Snapchat for Business: The Ultimate Marketing Guide," Hootsuite, February 13, 2019, https://blog.hootsuite.com/snapchat-for-business-guide/.

61. Todd Clarke, "22[+] Instagram Stats That Marketers Can't Ignore This Year," Hootsuite, March 5, 2019, https://blog.hootsuite.com/instagram-statistics/; and Ana Gotter, "Instagram Marketing 101: Using Hashtags, Stories, and More to Grow Your Business," Shopify, April 14, 2019, https://www.shopify.ca/blog/instagram-marketing.
62. Paige Cooper, "23 Pinterest Statistics That Matter to Marketers in 2019," Hootsuite, February 27, 2019, https://blog.hootsuite.com/pinterest-statistics-for-business/.
63. Alyssa Gregory, "7 Ways to Use Pinterest in Your Small Business," The Balance Small Business, March 25, 2018, https://www.thebalancesmb.com/pinterest-in-your-small-business-2951700.
64. "Top Sites in Canada," Alexa.
65. Jim McElgunn, "Make Your Business a YouTube Star," July 6, 2012, www.profitguide.com/manage-grow/sales-marketing/become-a-youtube-star-37951.
66. Fergus Baird, "The Complete Guide to YouTube Ads for Marketers," Hootsuite, March 12, 2019, https://blog.hootsuite.com/youtube-advertising/.
67. Heidi Cohen, "2016 Mobile Marketing Trends Every Marketer Needs," Actionable Marketing Guide, January 11, 2016, accessed August 22, 2019, http://heidicohen.com/2016-mobile-marketing-trends/.
68. Yoram Wurmser, "Mobile Time Spent 2018," eMarketer, January 18, 2018, https://www.emarketer.com/content/mobile-time-spent-2018.
69. Christene Dobby, "Checkout 51 App Lets You Shop Anywhere, Snap Pics of Receipt for Savings," *Financial Post,* December 14, 2012, accessed August 22, 2019, http://business.financialpost.com/entrepreneur/fp-startups/checkout-51-app-lets-you-shop-anywhere-snap-pics-of-receipt-for-savings?__lsa=6930-d566.
70. Derek Johnson, "10 Amazing Retail Mobile Marketing Examples," Tatango, February 18, 2014, accessed August 22, 2019, www.tatango.com/blog/10-amazing-retail-mobile-marketing-examples/.
71. Zach Bulygo, "How Mint Grew to 1.5M Users and Sold for over $170M in Just 2 Years," *Neil Patel Blog,* January 22, 2016, https://neilpatel.com/blog/how-mint-grew/.
72. Corina VanGerwen, "Startup Marketing Strategies: More of the Same—Only Better," February 14, 2013, accessed August 22, 2019, https://www.canadianbusiness.com/innovation/startup-marketing-strategies-more-of-the-same-only-better/.
73. James Cole, "Influencer Marketing – A Definitive Guide For 2019," Thought Catalogue, January 6, 2019, https://thoughtcatalog.com/james-cole/2018/09/influencer-marketing/.
74. Goldberg, "How to Turn Social Media Engagement into Real Sales."
75. Zameena Meja, "Kylie Jenner Reportedly Makes $1 Million per Paid Instagram Post—Here's How much Other Top Influencers Get," CNBC, updated August 1, 2018, https://www.cnbc.com/2018/07/31/kylie-jenner-makes-1-million-per-paid-instagram-post-hopper-hq-says.html; and BlakeDroesch, "Is Everyone on Instagram an Influencer?" eMarketer, March 5, 2019, https://www.emarketer.com/content/is-everyone-on-instagram-an-influencer.
76. Dinah Wisenberg Brin, "Small Businesses Find Micro-Influencers A Good Marketing Avenue," *Forbes,* July 31, 2018, https://www.forbes.com/sites/dinahwisenberg/2018/07/31/small-businesses-find-micro-influencers-a-good-marketing-avenue/#403072866f9f.
77. "Sneakertub," *Dragons' Den,* CBC, December 24, 2018, https://www.cbc.ca/dragonsden/pitches/sneakertub.
78. Cole, "Influencer Marketing – A Definitive Guide For 2019."

CHAPTER 9

1. "Small Business Magazine's First Annual Survey of Canada's Entrepreneurs," *Small Business,* June 1987, pp. 49–53.
2. Adam Sonnhalter, "Why Small Business Owners Must Understand Financial Statements," Small Business Trends, May 17, 2017, accessed August 23, 2019, https://smallbiztrends.com/2017/05/understand-financial-statements.html .
3. Rob MacDonald, interview by Peter Mombourquette: "Understanding Your Business' Finances: Key to Success," May 14, 2019.
4. Adam Sonnhalter, "Why Small Business Owners Must Understand Financial Statements," Small Business Trends, May 17, 2017, accessed August 23, 2019, https://smallbiztrends.com/2017/05/understand-financial-statements.html.
5. Rosemary Peavler, "The Importance of Cash Flow Management to Small Business Success," The Balance Small Business, updated August 20, 2019, https://www.thebalancesmb.com/cash-management-is-important-for-your-small-business-393118.
6. "Bonté Foods' Cash Flow Management Workout," BDC, accessed June 15, 2019, https://www.bdc.ca/en/articles-tools/money-finance/manage-finances/pages/cash-flow-management-tips-small-companies.aspx.
7. "Intuit Canada," as reported in GDSourcing.com, February 27, 2006.
8. Alika Cooper, "The Top Accounting Challenges Small Businesses Face," Business.com, updated June 12, 2018, https://www.business.com/articles/small-business-accounting-challenges/.
9. Kathy Yaka, "The Best Small Business Accounting Software for 2019," January 17, 2019, *PC Magazine,* https://www.pcmag.com/roundup/324120/the-best-small-business-accounting-software.
10. Matthew Baker, "The 7 Financial Habits of the Most Successful Small Business Owners," *Entrepreneur,* May 5, 2017, accessed August 23, 2019, https://www.entrepreneur.com/article/293662.
11. Richard Abbass, interview with Peter Mombourquette: "Growing Your Business through Financial Awareness," May 16, 2019.
12. Dana Flavelle, "Small Business Fights Visa's 'Smallenfreuden' Campaign," *The Star,* June 11, 2013, www.thestar.com/business/2013/06/11/small_business_fights_visas_smallenfreuden_campaign.html.

CHAPTER 10

1. *Profit*, December/January, 1999, p. 48.
2. Absar Saleh, "Benefits of ISO 9001 Implementation for Small Business," Advisera, September 17, 2018, https://advisera.com/9001academy/blog/2018/09/17/benefits-of-iso-9001-implementation-for-small-businesses/.
3. ISO website, www.iso.org/iso/home.html.
4. Chris Bardsley, "Importance of Window Displays," Unibox, August 21, 2017, https://www.unibox.co.uk/news-inspiration/types-importance-of-window-displays; Humayun Khan, "A Foolproof Guide to Creating Window Displays That Turn Heads and Drive Foot Traffic," Shopify, February 15, 2018, https://www.shopify.com/retail/120058947-a-fool-proof-guide-to-creating-window-displays-that-turn-heads-and-drive-foot-traffic; and Marjorie van Elven, "Window Displays Done Right: 7 Expert Tips to Get Shoppers to Come In," Fashion United, January 3, 2019, https://fashionunited.ca/news/retail/window-displays-done-right-7-expert-tips-to-get-shoppers-to-come-in/201901038495.
5. Humayun Khan, "How To Create Retail Store Interiors That Get People To Purchase Your Products," Shopify, February 28, 2018, accessed August 24, 2019, https://www.shopify.ca/retail/120057795-how-to-create-retail-store-interiors-that-get-people-to-purchase-your-products.
6. Tim Aldred, "Saving Money on Your Supplies," *Guardian*, March 18, 2013, accessed May 19, 2019, https://www.theguardian.com/small-business-network/2013/mar/18/saving-money-on-suppliers.
7. "About Us" Source for Sports, accessed June 1, 2019, https://www.sourceforsports.ca/en-CA/aboutus; https://www.sourceforsports.com/fr-CA/aboutus.
8. Brook Hayes, "The 6 Best Inventory Management Software for Small Business of 2019," Business.org, December 5, 2018, https://www.business.org/finance/cost-management/best-inventory-management-software/.
9. Kevin Kerridge, "Most Employee Theft Happens at Small Companies: The Warning Signs and 3 Ways to Stop It," *Inc.*, September 29, 2017, accessed August 24, 2019, https://www.inc.com/kevin-kerridge/most-employee-theft-happens-at-small-companies-warning-signs-3-ways-to-stop-it.html.
10. Naomi Levinson, "7 Steps to a Successful Relationship," *Canadian Retailer*, May/June 2000, p. 15.

CHAPTER 11

1. "Grant Thornton, L.L.P., October 2001," as reported in GDSourcing.com, April 2003.
2. Michael Wormstall-Cocolakis, "Labour Shortage: Here to Stay," BDC, September 2018, accessed September 8, 2019, https://www.bdc.ca/en/documents/analysis_research/labour-shortage.pdf.
3. Michael Wormstall-Cocolakis, "Labour Shortage: Here to Stay," BDC, September 2018, accessed September 8, 2019, https://www.bdc.ca/en/documents/analysis_research/labour-shortage.pdf.
4. "Broader Immigration and Credits Needed for Investment," CFIB, December 3, 2018, accessed September 4, 2019, https://www.cfib-fcei.ca/en/media/critical-atlantic-labour-shortages-forcing-small-businesses-do-more-less; Daniel Tencer, "Canada's Labour Shortage Is Actually Harming the Economy At This Point," HuffPost, January 17, 2019, https://www.huffingtonpost.ca/2019/01/17/labour-shortage-canada-economy_a_23645470/; and Greg Quinn, "Skilled Labour Shortages at Record Highs for Canadian Small Businesses," BNN Bloomberg, October 25, 2018, accessed October 2, 2019, https://www.bnnbloomberg.ca/skilled-labor-shortages-at-record-high-for-canada-small-business-1.1157970.
5. "Linda Duxbury and Christopher Higgins," as reported in *The Globe and Mail*, September 21, 1999, p. B1.
6. Sims et al, "Small Business, Big Investment: Improving Training for Tomorrow's Workforce, 2015," CFIB, accessed September 4, 2019, https://www.cfib-fcei.ca/sites/default/files/pdf/rr3361.pdf.
7. C. Lee Smith, "What I Learned After Making a Terrible Hiring Mistake," *Fast Company*, February 7, 2019, https://www.fastcompany.com/90371947/what-i-learned-after-making-a-terrible-hiring-mistake.
8. Canadian Federation of Independent Business, News Release, November 18, 2003.
9. "Hiring Tips from Canada's Fastest-Growing HR Firms," *Canadian Business*, September 15, 2014, accessed September 8, 2019, https://www.canadianbusiness.com/leadership/hot-hiring-tips-from-canadas-fastest-growing-hr-firms/.
10. "Achievers Publishes Guidelines for Successful Employee Referral Programs," Achievers, June 24, 2013, accessed September 8, 2019, https://www.achievers.com/press/achievers-publishes-guideline-successful-employee-referral-programs/.
11. Murad Hemmadi, "Master the Art of Hiring Right," *Canadian Business*, May 16, 2016, accessed September 8, 2019, https://www.canadianbusiness.com/leadership/master-the-art-of-hiring-right/.
12. Shannon Bowen-Smed, "3 Ways to Win the Best Employees," *Canadian Business*, February 8, 2013, accessed September 8, 2019, https://www.canadianbusiness.com/leadership/3-ways-to-win-the-best-employees/.
13. Deborah Aarts, "Social Media Recruiting," *Canadian Business*, December 6, 2010, accessed September 8, 2019, https://www.canadianbusiness.com/leadership/social-media-recruiting/.
14. Michael Wormstall-Cocolakis, "Labour Shortage: Here to Stay," BDC, September 2018, accessed September 8, 2019, https://www.bdc.ca/en/documents/analysis_research/labour-shortage.pdf.
15. Lisa MacNeil, "The Power of Perseverance," Mount Saint Vincent University, November 2017, accessed September 8, 2019, https://www.msvu.ca/en/home/programsdepartments/cooperativeeducation/coopwisdomprofilestips/thepowerofperseverance.aspx.

16. Michael Wormstall-Cocolakis, "Labour Shortage: Here to Stay," BDC, September 2018, accessed September 8, 2019, https://www.bdc.ca/en/documents/analysis_research/labour-shortage.pdf; and Jason Tchir, "Business Owners Turn to Syrian Refugees to Fill Job Vacancies," *Globe and Mail*, May 16, 2018, accessed September 8, 2019, https://www.theglobeandmail.com/report-on-business/small-business/talent/business-owners-turn-to-syrian-refugees-to-fill-job-vacancies/article29819925/.
17. Michael Wormstall-Cocolakis, "Labour Shortage: Here to Stay," BDC, September 2018, accessed September 8, 2019, https://www.bdc.ca/en/documents/analysis_research/labour-shortage.pdf.
18. Elizabeth McMillan, "Peace by Chocolate Pledged to Hire 50 Refugees, Mentor 10 Refugee Startups," CBC February 15, 2019, https://www.cbc.ca/news/canada/nova-scotia/peace-by-chocolate-antigonish-employ-refugees-mentor-businesses-1.5019508.
19. Murad Hemmadi, "Master the Art of Hiring Right", *Canadian Business*, May 16, 2016, accessed September 8, 2019, https://www.canadianbusiness.com/leadership/master-the-art-of-hiring-right/.
20. Kim Hart Macneill, "The Perfect Interview Formula," *Canadian Business*, May 17, 2013, accessed September 8, 2019, https://www.canadianbusiness.com/leadership/the-perfect-interview-formula/.
21. Kim Hart Macneill, "The Perfect Interview Formula," *Canadian Business*, May 17, 2013, accessed September 8, 2019, https://www.canadianbusiness.com/leadership/the-perfect-interview-formula/.
22. Sarah Niedoba, "Why It's So Important to Hire People Who Fit," *Canadian Business*, May 11, 2016, accessed September 8, 2019, https://www.canadianbusiness.com/leadership/why-its-so-important-to-hire-people-who-fit/.
23. Sarah Niedoba, "Why It's So Important to Hire People Who Fit," *Canadian Business*, May 11, 2016, accessed September 8, 2019, https://www.canadianbusiness.com/leadership/why-its-so-important-to-hire-people-who-fit/.
24. Robert D. Hisrich, Michael P. Peters, Dean A. Shepherd, and Peter Mombourquette, *Entrepreneurship*, 2nd Canadian edition (Toronto: McGraw-Hill Ryerson Ltd., 2009).
25. Michael Wormstall-Cocolakis, "Labour Shortage: Here to Stay," BDC, September 2018, accessed September 8, 2019, https://www.bdc.ca/en/documents/analysis_research/labour-shortage.pdf.
26. Robert Levering, Milton Moscowitz, and Michael Katz, *The 100 Best Companies to Work for in America, 1984* (Scarborough, New York: New American Library, 1985).
27. "How She Did It: Mandy Rennehan, Founder and Blue-Collar CEO of Freshco.ca," Women of Influence, October 8, 2018, https://www.womenofinfluence.ca/2018/10/08/how-she-did-it-mandy-rennehan-founder-and-blue-collar-ceo-of-freshco-ca/#.XS05K-hKiUk.
28. Saira Peesker, "The Latest Perk for Tech Companies Wooing Talent: On Site Career Coaching," *Globe and Mail*, April 29, 2019, https://www.theglobeandmail.com/business/small-business/talent/article-the-latest-perk-for-tech-companies-wooing-talent-on-site-career/.
29. Mike Kappel, "5 Tips for Successful Small Business Employee Training," *Forbes*, February 7, 2018, accessed September 8, 2019, https://www.forbes.com/sites/mikekappel/2018/02/07/5-tips-for-successful-small-business-employee-training/#1bb9aea85cc9.
30. Canadian Apprenticeship Forum, *Costco Connection*, July/August 2008, p. 11.
31. Cyberspace Industries 2000 Inc. website, 2007.
32. Jim Collins, *Good to Great* (New York: HarperCollins Publishers Inc., 2001).
33. Jim Kouzes and Barry Posner, *The Leadership Challenge* (San Francisco: Wiley, 2012).
34. Jim Kouzes and Barry Posner, *The Leadership Challenge* (San Francisco: Wiley, 2012).
35. For a complete discussion, see Donald Rumball, *The Entrepreneurial Edge* (Toronto: Key Porter Books, 1989), pp. 159–179.
36. Costa Elles, interview with Peter Mombourquette, Halifax, Nova Scotia, July 5, 2017.
37. David Pimentel, "To Find and to Keep: How to Recruit and Retain Good Employees," *Canadian Business*, December 8, 2011, accessed September 8, 2019, https://www.canadianbusiness.com/leadership/to-find-and-to-keep-how-to-recruit-and-retain-good-employees/.
38. Deborah Aarts, "The Real Reasons Your Staff Is Disengaged," *Canadian Business*, June 26, 2013, accessed September 8, 2019, https://www.canadianbusiness.com/smart-business-solutions-hr/the-real-reasons-your-staff-is-disengaged/.
39. "Canadians Top Job Satisfaction Survey," CBC News, updated November 18, 2013, accessed September 8, 2019, www.cbc.ca/news/business/canadians-top-job-satisfaction-survey-1.2430864.
40. Frederick Herzberg, *Motivation to Work* (New York: John Wiley and Sons, 1959).
41. *The Globe and Mail*, February 20, 1995, p. B6.
42. "Work Arrangements in the 1990s," Statistics Canada, May 1998, as reported in *Profit*, October 1998, p. 14.
43. Deborah Aarts, "The Business-Boosting Alternative to Snitch Lines," *Canadian Business*, July 24, 2013, https://www.canadianbusiness.com/leadership/the-business-boosting-alternative-to-snitch-lines/; and Megan Ip, "6 Innovative HR Tactics," *Canadian Business*, June 3, 2013, accessed September 4, 2019, https://www.canadianbusiness.com/smart-business-solutions-hr/6-innovative-hr-tactics/.
44. "Work Arrangements in the 1990s," Statistics Canada, May 1998, as reported in *Profit*, October 1998, p. 14.
45. "Work Arrangements in the 1990s," Statistics Canada, May 1998, as reported in *Profit*, October 1998, p. 14.
46. "Report: 65% of Employers Think Employees Are More Productive When They Work Remotely," Indeed Blog, November 14, 2018, accessed September 8, 2019, http://blog.indeed.ca/2018/11/14/remote-workers-survey/.
47. "Majority of Canadian Organizations Offer Flexible Working Options: Survey," Benefits Canada, May 30, 2018,

accessed September 8, 2019, https://www.benefitscanada.com/news/majority-of-canadian-organizations-offer-flexible-working-options-survey-115085.

48. "7 Sales Strategies of High-Growth Companies," *Canadian Business,* June 3, 2013, accessed September 8, 2019, https://www.canadianbusiness.com/innovation/7-sales-strategies-of-high-growth-companies/.
49. Susanne Ruder, "The Best Advice I Ever Got: Karen Flavelle," *Canadian Business,* October 25, 2005, accessed September 8, 2019, https://www.canadianbusiness.com/leadership/the-best-advice-i-ever-got-karen-flavelle/.
50. Hillary Bain Lindsay, "Just Us and Them?" Halifax Media Co-op, April 2, 2013, accessed September 8, 2019, http://halifax.mediacoop.ca/story/just-us-and-them/16963.

CHAPTER 12

1. Jennifer Warawa, "Nine Reasons Why Entrepreneurs Should Hire an Accountant," *Globe and Mail,* updated April 5, 2018, www.theglobeandmail.com/report-on-business/small-business/sb-money/nine-reasons-why-entrepreneurs-should-hire-an-accountant/article17023309/.
2. Kim Hart Macneill, "How to Find your Mentor," *Canadian Business,* July 31, 2012, accessed September 9, 2019, https://www.canadianbusiness.com/innovation/how-to-find-your-mentor/.
3. Brian Scudamore, "World's Greatest MBA," *Canadian Business,* June 1, 2006, accessed September 9, 2019, https://www.canadianbusiness.com/leadership/worlds-greatest-mba/.
4. Sheila Eugenio, "7 Reasons You Need a Mentor for Entrepreneurial Success," *Entrepreneur,* August 17, 2016, accessed September 9, 2019, https://www.entrepreneur.com/article/280134.
5. Kate Harrison, "New Study Reveals Entrepreneurs Need More Mentoring," *Forbes,* October 30, 2018, https://www.forbes.com/sites/kateharrison/2018/10/30/new-study-reveals-entrepreneurs-need-more-mentoring/#6d455e577819.
6. Sarah Niedoba, "How to Find the Best Angel Investor for Your Startup," *Canadian Business,* September 13, 2018, accessed September 9, 2019, https://www.canadianbusiness.com/lists-and-rankings/growth-500/how-to-find-the-best-angel-investor-for-your-startup/.
7. "The Importance of Mentorship," Futurpreneur, April 18, 2019, https://www.futurpreneur.ca/en/2019/the-importance-of-mentorship/.
8. Kate Harrison, "New Study Reveals Entrepreneurs Need More Mentoring," *Forbes,* October 30, 2018, https://www.forbes.com/sites/kateharrison/2018/10/30/new-study-reveals-entrepreneurs-need-more-mentoring/#6d455e577819.
9. Jay Dingwall, interview by Peter Mombourquette: "Interview with CEO of Famous Folks, Jay Dingwall," June 1, 2019.
10. "Mentor Spotlight: Sue Underhill," Futurpreneur, April 30, 2019, https://www.futurpreneur.ca/en/2019/mentor-spotlight-sue-underhill/.
11. Todd O'Keefe, interview with Peter Mombourquette, "O'Keefe on Planning a Small Business and Finding a Mentor," Halifax, Nova Scotia, June 1, 2013.
12. Adam Toren, "Mentors: A Young Entrepreneur's Secret Weapon," *Entrepreneur,* January 26, 2012, accessed September 9, 2019, www.entrepreneur.com/article/222694.
13. Rick Spence, "Bridging the Mentor Gap," *Canadian Business,* June 13, 2012, accessed September 9, 2019, https://www.canadianbusiness.com/leadership/bridging-the-mentoring-gap/.
14. Rahim Kanani, "Robin Chase, Founder & Former CEO of ZipCar, On Leadership and Innovation," *Forbes,* March 19, 2012, accessed September 9, 2019, www.forbes.com/sites/rahimkanani/2012/03/19/robin-chase-founder-former-ceo-of-zipcar-on-leadership-and-innovation/.
15. "How to Assemble an Effective Advisory Board," *Canadian Business,* August 31, 2015, accessed September 9, 2019, https://www.canadianbusiness.com/small-business/how-to-assemble-an-effective-advisory-board/.
16. Robert D. Hisrich, Michael P. Peters, Dean A. Shepherd, and Peter Mombourquette, *Entrepreneurship,* 2nd Canadian ed. (Toronto: McGraw-Hill Ryerson Ltd., 2009).
17. "How an Advisory Board Can Boost Your Business," BDC, accessed May 18, 2019, https://www.bdc.ca/en/articles-tools/business-strategy-planning/manage-business/pages/can-advisory-board-help-grow.aspx.
18. Sarah Efron, "Entrepreneurs, Watch Out for These Four New Tax Traps," *Globe and Mail,* updated May 25, 2019, https://www.theglobeandmail.com/business/small-business/money/article-entrepreneurs-watch-out-for-these-four-new-tax-traps/.
19. Canada Revenue Agency, "T2 Corporation– Income Tax Guide—Chapter 4: Page 4 of the T2 Return," Government of Canada, accessed September 9, 2019, https://www.canada.ca/en/revenue-agency/services/forms-publications/publications/t4012/t2-corporation-income-tax-guide-chapter-4-page-4-t2-return.html#P2862_208254.
20. Canada Revenue Agency, "Corporation Tax Rates," Government of Canada, accessed September 9, 2019, https://www.canada.ca/en/revenue-agency/services/tax/businesses/topics/corporations/corporation-tax-rates.html.
21. "Lifetime Capital Gain Exemption," Tax Tips, accessed September 9, 2019, https://www.taxtips.ca/smallbusiness/capitalgainsdeduction.htm.

CHAPTER 13

1. Kim Shiffman, "Profit W100 Overview: Big Is Beautiful," *Canadian Business,* July 11, 2007, accessed September 10, 2019, https://www.canadianbusiness.com/innovation/profit-w100-overview-big-is-beautiful/.
2. Kim Shiffman, "Profit W100 Overview: Big Is Beautiful," *Canadian Business,* July 11, 2007, accessed September 10, 2019, https://www.canadianbusiness.

com/innovation/profit-w100-overview-big-is-beautiful/.
3. Brenda Bouw, "More than a Fad? Home-grown Cannabis Equipment Companies See Strong Sales," *Globe and Mail,* July 7, 2019, https://www.theglobeandmail.com/robcannabispro/article-more-than-a-fad-home-grow-cannabis-equipment-companies-see-strong/.
4. Matt Linder, "E-tailor Beyond the Rack Files for Credit Protection," Digital Commerce 360, April 8, 2016, accessed September 10, 2019, https://www.digitalcommerce360.com/2016/04/08/e-retailer-beyond-rack-files-creditor-protection/.
5. Richard Abbas, interview with Peter Mombourquette, "On Managing a Mature Business," Halifax, Nova Scotia, July 7, 2019.
6. Chris Atchison, "Middle Managers' Engagement Key to Company Success," *Canadian Business,* February 8, 2012, accessed September 10, 2019, https://www.canadianbusiness.com/leadership/middle-managers-engagement-key-to-company-success/.
7. Stephen Haynes, in-class presentation, "Small Business Management," Mount Saint Vincent University, May 2013, Halifax, NS.
8. Jerry Langton, "Did You Know This Shopping Website Is Canadian?" *Globe and Mail,* updated May 9, 2018, www.theglobeandmail.com/report-on-business/economy/canada-competes/did-you-know-this-shopping-website-is-canadian/article5061065/.
9. Tony Martin, "Financing Solutions: Crossing the Cash Chasm," *Canadian Business*, May 31, 2008, accessed September 10, 2019, https://www.canadianbusiness.com/small-business/financing-solutions-crossing-the-cash-chasm/.
10. Ian Portsmouth, "Canada's Fastest-Growing Companies," *Canadian Business,* June 3, 2013, accessed September 10, 2019, https://www.canadianbusiness.com/innovation/canadas-fastest-growing-companies/.
11. Kristene Quan, "The 7 Obstacles Standing in the Way of Your Growth," *Canadian Business,* March 19, 2015, accessed September 10, 2019, https://www.canadianbusiness.com/leadership/the-7-obstacles-standing-in-the-way-of-your-growth/.
12. Cailynn Klingbeil, "Clean Start: Syrian Refugee Rebuilds His Fourth-Generation Soap Business in Canada," *Globe and Mail,* January 13, 2019, https://www.theglobeandmail.com/business/small-business/growth/article-a-clean-slate-syrian-refugee-rebuilds-his-fourth-generation-soap/.
13. Camilla Cornell, "Five Key Lessons from the 2018 Globe and Mail Small Business Summit," *Globe and Mail,* May 9, 2018, accessed September 10, 2019, https://www.theglobeandmail.com/business/small-business/growth/article-five-key-lessons-from-the-2018-globe-and-mail-small-business-summit/.
14. Adam McDowell, "Canadian Companies Sticking with Chinese Growth Plans Despite Trade Tensions," *Globe and Mail,* April 14, 2019, https://www.theglobeandmail.com/business/small-business/growth/article-canadian-companies-sticking-with-chinese-growth-plans-despite-trade/.
15. Salmaan Farooqui, "As Millenials Take up Film Photography, Darkrooms See a Bright Future," *Globe and Mail,* October 9, 2018, accessed September 10, 2019, https://www.theglobeandmail.com/business/small-business/growth/article-as-millennials-take-up-film-photography-darkrooms-see-a-bright-future/.
16. Amy Jo Ehman, "Innovative Products Don't Happen by Fluke," *Canadian Business,* September 13, 2018, accessed September 10, 2019, https://www.canadianbusiness.com/lists-and-rankings/growth-500/innovative-products-dont-happen-by-fluke/.
17. Tracey Lindeman, "Vegetable Growers Convert to Cannabis to Help Boost Margins," *Globe and Mail,* January 21, 2018, accessed September 10, 2019, https://www.theglobeandmail.com/report-on-business/small-business/sb-growth/vegetable-growers-convert-to-cannabis-to-help-boost-margins/article37677955/.
18. Sarah Treleaven, "How to Grow Your Exports Beyond the Usual-Suspect Countries," *Canadian Business,* September 14, 2017, accessed September 10, 2019, https://www.canadianbusiness.com/lists-and-rankings/profit-500/2017-exporting-how-to/.
19. Rick Spence, "The 5 Winning Strategies of High-Growth Companies," *Canadian Business,* June 1, 2011, accessed September 10, 2019, https://www.canadianbusiness.com/innovation/the-5-winning-strategies-of-high-growth-companies/.
20. Tara Deschamps, "Want to Sell to the U.S.? Better Do Your Homework," *Globe and Mail,* updated July 7, 2019, https://www.theglobeandmail.com/business/small-business/article-want-to-sell-to-the-us-better-do-your-homework/.
21. David Ebner, "East Vancouver's JJ Bean Cafe Takes on Toronto," *Globe and Mail,* January 8, 2018, accessed September 10, 2019, https://www.theglobeandmail.com/report-on-business/small-business/sb-growth/east-vancouvers-jj-bean-cafe-takes-on-torontos-coffeescene/article37521247/.
22. Richard M. Hodgetts, *Effective Small Business Management.* Reproduced by permission of Academic Press Inc., 1982, p. 197.
23. Rick Spence, "The 5 Winning Strategies of High-Growth Companies," *Canadian Business,* June 1, 2011, accessed September 10, 2019, https://www.canadianbusiness.com/innovation/the-5-winning-strategies-of-high-growth-companies/.
24. David Ebner, "Meal-kit Company Fresh Prep Faces Hefty Competition as it Gears Up for Expansion," *Globe and Mail,* November 18, 2018, accessed September 10, 2019, https://www.theglobeandmail.com/business/small-business/growth/article-meal-kit-company-fresh-prep-faces-hefty-competition-as-it-gears-up-for/.
25. Chris Albrecht, "Canadian Meal Kit Company Fresh Prep Raises $3.3M," The Spoon, December 12, 2018, accessed September 10, 2019, https://thespoon.tech/canadian-meal-kit-company-fresh-prep-raises-3-3m/.
26. Michael Gerber, *The E-Myth Revisited: Why Most Small*

Businesses Don't Work and What to Do About It (New York: HarperCollins Publishers, 1995); "Start a Franchise," 1-800-GOT-JUNK website, accessed October 2, 2019, https://www.1800gotjunk.com/ca_en/franchise/business-opportunity.
27. *The Globe and Mail,* October 12, 2005, B13.
28. *Profits* (Business Development Bank of Canada, Winter 1999), p. 4.

CHAPTER 14

1. "3 Common Exit Strategies for Small Business," BDC, accessed September 11, 2019, https://www.bdc.ca/en/articles-tools/change-ownership/plan-succession/pages/3-common-exit-strategies.aspx?it=business-planning/succession-planning/; "Getting the Transition Right," Canadian Federation of Independent Business, November 2018, accessed October 8, 2019, https://www.cfib-fcei.ca/sites/default/files/2018-11/Getting-the-transition-right-succession-planning-report.pdf.
2. Tom Corner and Sylvie Ratté, "The Coming Wave of Business Transitions in Canada," Government of Canada, September 2017, accessed September 11, 2019, http://publications.gc.ca/collections/collection_2017/bdc/Iu134-1-4-2017-eng.pdf.
3. Rick Spence, "Tsunami Warning," *Canadian Business,* September 17, 2012, accessed September 11, 2019, https://www.canadianbusiness.com/innovation/tsunami-warning/.
4. Pierre Somers, "The Succession Planning Crisis: How to Transfer your Legacy to Millennials," *Globe and Mail,* updated May 16, 2018, accessed September 11, 2019, www.theglobeandmail.com/report-on-business/careers/leadership-lab/the-succession-planning-crisis-how-to-transfer-your-legacy-to-millennials/article29289353/.
5. Jim McElgunn, "Why It's a Lousy Time to Sell Your Business," *Canadian Business,* July 31, 2013, accessed September 11, 2019, https://www.canadianbusiness.com/small-business/why-its-a-lousy-time-to-sell-your-business/.
6. Rick Spence, "Tsunami Warning," *Canadian Business,* September 17, 2012, accessed September 11, 2019, https://www.canadianbusiness.com/innovation/tsunami-warning/.
7. Rick Spence, "Tsunami Warning," *Canadian Business,* September 17, 2012, accessed September 11, 2019, https://www.canadianbusiness.com/innovation/tsunami-warning/.
8. Mark Groulx, "Selling Your Business 101," *Canadian Business,* August 16, 2011, accessed September 11, 2019, https://www.canadianbusiness.com/innovation/selling-your-business-101/.
9. Rick Spence, "Tsunami Warning," *Canadian Business,* September 17, 2012, accessed September 11, 2019, https://www.canadianbusiness.com/innovation/tsunami-warning/.
10. "Keeping It in the Family: Succession Planning Tips and Insights from a CPA," CPA Canada, February 23, 2018, accessed September 11, 2019, https://www.cpacanada.ca/en/connecting-and-news/blogs/leadership-innovation/2018/february/succession-planning-tips-and-insight.
11. Susanne Baillie, "Eight Steps to a Profitable Exit," *Canadian Business,* September 30, 2004, accessed September 11, 2019, https://www.canadianbusiness.com/innovation/eight-steps-to-a-profitable-exit/.
12. Rick Spence, "Tsunami Warning," *Canadian Business,* September 17, 2012, accessed September 11, 2019, https://www.canadianbusiness.com/innovation/tsunami-warning/.
13. "Too Many Family Businesses Have No Succession Plan," *Canadian Business,* September 19, 2014, accessed September 11, 2019, https://www.canadianbusiness.com/leadership/too-many-family-businesses-have-no-succession-plan/.
14. Chris Neville, interview with Peter Mombourquette, "On Investing in a Business While Preparing to Sell," December 01, 2018.
15. Jim McElgunn, "Selling Your Baby," *Canadian Business,* January 31, 2009, accessed September 11, 2019, https://www.canadianbusiness.com/innovation/selling-your-baby/.
16. "2016 Global Family Business Survey: The 'Missing Middle' - Canadian Results," PwC Canada, accessed September 11, 2019, https://www.pwc.com/ca/en/private-company/family-business.html.
17. John Lorinc, "Don't Let Your Family Ruin Your Business," *Canadian Business,* January 22, 2015, accessed September 11, 2019, https://www.canadianbusiness.com/innovation/dont-let-your-family-destroy-your-business/.
18. P. C. Rosenblatt, L. deMik, R. M. Anderson, and P. A. Johnson, *The Family in Business* (San Francisco: Jossey-Bass, 1985), p. 5.
19. Samantha Garner, "6 Facts about Canadian Family Business," Go Forth Institute, August 15, 2015, accessed September 11, 2019, http://canadianentrepreneurtraining.com/6-facts-about-canadian-family-businesses/
20. S. I. Lansberg, "Managing Human Resources in Family Firms: The Problem of Institutional Overlap," *Organizational Dynamics,* Summer 1983, pp. 39–46.
21. *Canadian Business,* May–June, 2005, p. 55.
22. Curtis Hartman, "Main Street Inc.," *Inc.,* June 1986, pp. 49–54.
23. "Too Many Family Businesses Have No Succession Plan," *Canadian Business,* September 19, 2014, accessed September 11, 2019, https://www.canadianbusiness.com/leadership/too-many-family-businesses-have-no-succession-plan/.
24. *The Globe and Mail,* October 9, 1995, p. B7.
25. Ralph Douglas and Costello How, *K.C.: The Biography of K.C. Irving* (Toronto: Key Porter Books, 1993).
26. Erin Anderssen, "Irving Family's Fortunate Son Explains How He Fell into a Dark Depression, and Rose Again," *Globe and Mail,* November 12, 2017, accessed September 11, 2019, https://www.theglobeandmail.com/report-on-business/kenneth-irving/article33791019/.
27. Marshall Paisner, "Myths about Succession," *Inc.,* October 1986, p. 146.
28. Joanna Pachner, "When Kids Run the Family Business," *Canadian Business,* April 11, 2010, accessed September 11, 2019, https://www.canadianbusiness.com/leadership/when-kids-run-the-family-business/.

29. Josh O'Kane, "Canada Goose CEO's 'Aha' Moment: I Realized the Brand Was Real," *Globe and Mail,* updated May 7, 2018, accessed September 11, 2019, www.theglobeandmail.com/report-on-business/small-business/sb-growth/day-to-day/canada-goose-ceos-aha-moment-i-realized-the-brand-was-real/article10982951/.
30. Robert D. Hisrich, Michael P. Peters, Dean A. Shepherd, and Peter Mombourquette, *Entrepreneurship,* 2nd Canadian ed. (Toronto: McGraw-Hill Ryerson Ltd., 2009).
31. "How to Start Your Family Business Succession Planning" BDC, accessed October 8, 2019, https://www.bdc.ca/en/articles-tools/change-ownership/plan-succession/pages/family-business-succession-overcoming-barriers.aspx.
32. "How to Start Your Family Business Succession Planning" BDC, accessed October 8, 2019, https://www.bdc.ca/en/articles-tools/change-ownership/plan-succession/pages/family-business-succession-overcoming-barriers.aspx.
33. Joanna Pachner, "A Second Generation Success Story: Linda Hasenfratz at Linamar," *Canadian Business,* January 15, 2015, accessed September 11, 2019, https://www.canadianbusiness.com/leadership/a-second-generation-success-story-linda-hasenfratz-at-linamar/.
34. Andy Holloway, "Canada's Outstanding CEO Of the Year: Linda Hasenfratz," *Financial Post,* November 8, 2018, https://business.financialpost.com/feature/canadas-outstanding-ceo-of-the-year-linda-hasenfratz.
35. Rosenblatt, deMik, Anderson, and Johnson, *The Family in Business,* p. 274.
36. "Succession Planning: Secrets of a Smooth Transition in a Family Business," BDC, accessed December 01, 2018, https://www.bdc.ca/en/articles-tools/change-ownership/plan-succession/pages/succession-planning-secrets-family-business.aspx?type=A&order=1.
37. Sue Birley, "Succession in the Family Firm: The Inheritor's View," *Journal of Small Business Management,* vol. 24, no. 3 (July 1986), p. 36.
38. Jim McElgunn, "Selling Your Baby," *Canadian Business,* January 31, 2009, accessed September 11, 2019, https://www.canadianbusiness.com/innovation/selling-your-baby/.
39. Jeff Beer, "The Sweat Smell of Success," Canadian Business, July 14, 2011, accessed September 11, 2019, https://www.canadianbusiness.com/business-strategy/the-sweat-smell-of-success/.
40. Kim Shiffman, "Business Exit Strategy: Company Sold in One Day," *Canadian Business,* February 8, 2012, accessed September 11, 2019, https://www.canadianbusiness.com/leadership/business-exit-strategy-company-sold-in-one-day/.
41. Tenille Bonoguore, "Surfboard Designer Finds Buyout a Rough Ride," *Globe and Mail,* updated April 30, 2018, accessed September 11, 2019, www.theglobeandmail.com/report-on-business/small-business/sb-money/valuation/surfboard-designer-finds-buyout-a-rough-ride/article4216665/.
42. Tom Foster, "Do You Really Want Your Business to Go Public?" *Inc.,* October 2015, accessed September 11, 2019, https://www.inc.com/magazine/201510/tom-foster/do-you-really-want-to-go-public.html.
43. Riley McDermid, "With HomeAway Growing like Crazy, Expedia Closes in on Airbnb for Market Share," Austin Business Journal, July 25, 2017, accessed September 11, 2019, https://www.bizjournals.com/austin/news/2017/07/25/with-homeaway-growing-like-crazy-expedia-closes-in.html.
44. "You're Going Public Checklist," *Profit,* November 1998, p. 47.
45. Mark Stevens, "When to Take Your Company Public," *Entrepreneurial Manager's Newsletter,* vol. 7, no. 4 (1986), p. 4.
46. Kristy Woudstra, "How Jean Paré Taught Canada to Cook," *The Walrus,* updated January 29, 2018, accessed September 11, 2019, https://thewalrus.ca/how-jean-pare-taught-canada-to-cook/.

Chapter Sources

CHAPTER 1

- **Small Business Profile** - Jay Dingwall, interview by Peter Mombourquette: "On Entrepreneurship," June 1, 2019; "Our Story—Famous Folks," accessed June 11, 2019, http://famousfolks.ca/our-story/.
- **Figure 1-1** - Industry Canada, Small Business Research and Policy, April 2016, accessed September 14, 2019, Data from: http://www.statcan.gc.ca/daily-quotidien/160205/t002a-eng.htm.
- **Small Business in Action 1-1** - Mat Boiselle, "Jesse and Luke Hambly - Pressa Water Bottle," accessed March 31, 2019, https://soundcloud.com/itzmatb/pressawater; "From 3D Printing to Dragons' Den," accessed May 11, 2019, https://www.pressabottle.com/pages/about-us; "Pressa Bottle - Experience Pressed Water," accessed May 24, 2019, https://www.kickstarter.com/projects/1082826199/pressa-bottle-experience-pressed-water; and Hailey Salvian, "Elora Brothers Strike *Dragons' Den* Deal for their Pressa Bottle," CBC, February 2, 2018, https://www.cbc.ca/news/canada/kitchener-waterloo/elora-hambly-brothers-dragons-den-pressa-bottle-1.4516301.
- **Small Business in Action 1-2** - Frank Condron, "Profile: Greg Overholt, 2012 FuEL Award Winner," *Canadian Business,* December 12, 2012, https://www.canadianbusiness.com/innovation/profile-greg-overholt-2012-fuel-award-winner/; "About Us," Students Offering Support, accessed August 2, 2019, https://studentsofferingsupport.ca/our-impact/; and Textbooks for Change, accessed August 2, 2019, https://textbooksforchange.com/our-impact/#our-story.
- **Figure 1-2** - "Key Small Business Statics - January 2019," Business and Industry Canada, accessed January 31, 2019, https://www.ic.gc.ca/eic/site/061.nsf/eng/h_03018.html#point2-3.
- **Figure 1-3** - Based on data from Susan Ward, "Statistics on Canadian Women in Business," February 28, 2019, accessed September 12, 2019, https://www.thebalancesmb.com/statistics-on-canadian-women-in-business-2948029; "Women Entrepreneurs a Big Part of Canadian Economy," *Calgary Herald,* updated March 4, 2012, accessed September 12, 2019, https://calgaryherald.com/business/women-entrepreneurs-a-big-part-of-canadian-economy; and Key Small Business Statistics, Statistics Canada 2018.
- **Small Business in Action 1-3** - "BDC Chic Marie," CBC, accessed June 1, 2019, https://www.cbc.ca/dragonsden/bdc/chic-marie; Guy Dixon, "Female-Led Start-Ups Face a Funding Hurdle," *Globe and Mail,* May 17, 2018, https://www.theglobeandmail.com/report-on-business/careers/business-education/female-led-startups-face-a-funding-hurdle/article34321970/; Jessica Dostie, "Chic Marie En Mode Expansion," Global News, *Journal Métro,* April 19, 2017, accessed September 12, 2019, https://journalmetro.com/opinions/tendances-etc/1120569/chic-marie-en-mode-expansion/; and Felicia Parrillo, "Chic Marie: A New Way to Shop," *Global News,* December 30, 2016, accessed August 6, 2019, https://globalnews.ca/news/3093414/chic-marie-a-new-way-to-shop/.
- **Small Business in Action 1-4** - Gerrit De Vynck, "Canadian Tech Unicorn Hootsuite Gets Written Down by Fidelity," *Globe and Mail,* March 2, 2016, accessed September 12, 2019, www.theglobeandmail.com/technology/canadian-tech-unicorn-hootsuite-gets-written-down-by-fidelity/article29004492/; "Hootsuite Surpasses 15 Million Users, Hosts World's Largest Online Social Media Conference, for Free," Hootsuite Press Release, October 20, 2016, accessed March 13, 2019, https://hootsuite.com/newsroom/press-releases/hootsuite-surpasses-15-million-users-hosts-worlds-largest-online-social-media-conference-for-free; Kurt Wagner, "Hootsuite Reaches $1 Billion in Valuation in Latest Funding Round," Vox, September 25, 2014, accessed August 6, 2019, http://recode.net/2014/09/25/85062/; and *CFIB Small Business Profile,* December 2009, p. 2.
- **Small Business in Action 1-5** - Jean-Rene Halde, Business Development Bank of Canada, Special Supplement to *The Lethbridge Herald,* October 19, 2009, p. 2.
- **Small Business Beginnings** - David Burke, "'You Can Do Anything': Syrian Chocolatier's Success Inspires Antigonish," CBC, September 10, 2017, accessed September 12, 2019, https://www.cbc.ca/news/canada/nova-scotia/peace-by-chocolate-antigonish-hadhad-syrian-refugees-business-1.4283023; CTV News Staff, "Syrian Refugee Chocolatier's Treats are Literally Going Out of This World," CTV News, September 21, 2018, accessed September 12, 2019, https://www.ctvnews.ca/canada/syrian-refugee-chocolatier-s-treats-are-literally-going-out-of-this-world-1.4103643; David Israelson, "Small-Town Hiring No Piece of Cake, Chocolate Maker Says," *Globe and Mail,* October 16, 2018, accessed September 12, 2019, https://www.theglobeandmail.com/business/article-small-town-hiring-no-piece-of-cake-chocolate-maker-says/; Cynthia Martin, "Tareq Hadhad on Building a Successful Business in Canada as a Refugee," *Globe and Mail,* February 12, 2018, accessed September 12, 2019, https://www.theglobeandmail.com/report-on-business/careers/tareq-hadhad-on-building-a-successful-business-in-canada-as-a-refugee/article37933851/; and Holly McKenzie-Sutter, "Nova Scotia Chocolatier Peace by Chocolate Pledges To Hire 50 Refugees By 2022," Huffington Post, February 16, 2019, https://www.huffingtonpost.ca/2019/02/16/nova-scotia-chocolatier-peace-by-chocolate-pledges-to-hire-50-refugees-by-2022_a_23671164/.

CHAPTER 2

- **Small Business Profile** - T'Cha Dunlevy, "SmartHalo the 'future of biking'," *Montreal Gazette,* October 27, 2017, accessed June 1, 2019, https://montrealgazette.com/business/local-business/more-than-a-gps-creators-call-smarthalo-the-future-of-biking; Jan Lee, "SmartHalo Exceeds Kickstarter Goal on Day One," TriplePundit, August 27, 2015, accessed August 7, 2019, https://www.triplepundit.com/story/2015/smarthalo-exceeds-kickstarter-goal-day-one/32306; Nick Lucchesi, "Xavier Peich is the Best Kind of Shit Disturber," Inverse, June 14, 2019, accessed August 30, 2019, https://www.inverse.com/article/56628-xavier-peich-ceo-of-smarthalo;
- **Small Business in Action 2-1** - Linsey Knerl, "5 Successful 'Mompreneurs'," January 11, 2011,www.nbcnews.com/id/40969268/ns/business-small_business/t/successful-mompreneurs/; The Mompreneur website, www.themompreneur.com; "Sarah Davis, Founder and Chief Creative Officer Fashionphile," ideamensch.com, April 11, 2018, https://ideamensch.com/sarah-davis/; and FashionPhile.Com Company Overview, March 4, 2019, https://www.crunchbase.com/organization/fashionphile#section-overview.
- **Small Business in Action 2-2** - *Small Business Quarterly,* vol. 5, no. 3, November 2003, p. 6; *Small Business Statistics,* Statistics Canada, July 2008; Peter Carbonara, "Tulip Retailer Thinks It Can Save Brick-And-Mortar and Become a $100 Billion Business. Really." *Forbes,* November 14, 2017, accessed August 9, 2019, https://www.forbes.com/sites/forbestreptalks/2017/11/14/tulip-retail-

thinks-it-can-save-brick-and-mortar-and-become-a-100-billion-business-really/#65db042963ac; "Tulip Raises $40 Million to Accelerate Retail Transformation with Leading Mobile Platform for Store Workers," Cision, August 22, 2017, accessed August 9, 2019, https://www.prnewswire.com/news-releases/tulip-raises-40-million-to-accelerate-retail-transformation-with-leading-mobile-platform-for-store-workers-300506187.html; "Tulip Retail Overview," Crunchbase.com, accessed March 1, 2019, https://www.crunchbase.com/organization/tulip-retail; and Craig Daniels, "Ali Asaria: The Tech CEO Who Gave Away His Money," *Communitech News,* February 26, 2018, accessed August 9, 2019, http://news.communitech.ca/ali-asaria-the-tech-ceo-who-gave-away-his-money/.

- **Figure 2-2** - Innovation, Science and Economic Development Canada, SME Research and Statistics, Accessed March 4, 2016, https://www.ic.gc.ca/eic/site/061.nsf/eng/02826.html.
- **Small Business Beginnings 2-1** - "How She Succeeds: Natalie Dusome of Poppies & Peonies," Love, Mom, November 30, 2018, http://lovemom.ca/how-she-succeeds-natalie-dusome-of-poppies-peonies/; Alex Brown, "Pristine Poppies – Natalie Dusome of Poppy & Peonies," City Life, April 6, 2018, https://mycitylife.ca/people/success-story/natalie-dusome-poppy-peonies-handbag/; Aleesha Harris, "Style Q&A: Natalie Dusome, Founder of Poppy & Peonies, Turns Passion into Handbag Brand," *Vancouver Sun,* updated November 14, 2017, https://vancouversun.com/life/fashion-beauty/style-qa-natalie-dusome-founder-of-poppy-peonies-turns-passion-into-handbag-brand; and "Next Level Special," *Dragons' Den,* CBC, March 7, 2019, https://www.cbc.ca/dragonsden/pitches/poppy-peonies.
- **Small Business in Action 2-3** - Rob Lewis, "Canadian Entrepreneur on Raising Venture Capital at Age 17," Techvibes, January 16, 2013, accessed September 26, 2019, www.techvibes.com/blog/canadian-entrepreneur-on-raising-venture-capital-at-age-17-2013-01-16; Sarah Perez, "AppHero Raises $1.8 Million for App Recommendation Service Which Learns Your Interests from Facebook," Tech Crunch, July 5, 2012, accessed September 26, 2019, http://techcrunch.com/2012/07/05/apphero-raises-1-8-million-for-app-recommendation-service-which-learns-your-interests-from-facebook/; and Darrell Etherington, "AppHero Acquired by Mobile App Publishing Firm Fuse Powered, Will Turn Its Attention to Ads," Tech Crunch, June 14, 2014, accessed September 26, 2019, http://techcrunch.com/2013/12/02/apphero-acquired-by-mobile-app-publishing-firm-fuse-powered-will-turn-its-attention-to-ads/.
- **Table 2-2** - Julia Geller, "Failure Factors—Seven Signs Your Business Is Sinking," *Profit,* December/January 2003, pp. 31–33.
- **Table 2-4** - An extensively modified version of a table in G. Pinchot, *Intrapreneuring* (New York: Harper & Row, 1985), pp. 54–56.

CHAPTER 3

- **Small Business Profile** - Amara McLaughlin, "Forget Your Key Combination? This Toronto Engineer Revolutionized the Padlock with One Touch," *CBC News,* updated April 1, 2018, accessed August 9, 2019, https://www.cbc.ca/news/canada/toronto/tapplock-fingerprint-padlock-1.4600551; and "Tapplock Corp.," *Dragons' Den,* CBC, accessed August 9, 2019, https://www.cbc.ca/dragonsden/pitches/tapplock-corp.
- **Small Business in Action 3-1** - Canada Drives CEO Cody Green, interview by Nick Zulovich, Auto Remarketing Canada, podcast audio, August 9, 2018, accessed August 1, 2019 **https://www.autoremarketing.com/arcanada/podcast-canada-drives-ceo-cody-green**; "About Us," Canada Drives, accessed August 30, 2019, https://www.canadadrives.ca/about-us/newsroom/articles; Parry, Jacob, "Entrepreneur of the Year 2016: Fintech," September 30, 2016, accessed May 18, 2019, https://www.bcbusiness.ca/entrepreneur-of-the-year-2016-fintech; V.I.A. Custom Content, "5 to 500 Employees in 5 Years: Secrets of One of Vancouver's Fastest Growing Companies," Vancouver Is Awesome, May 30, 2019, accessed July 2, 2019, https://www.vancouverisawesome.com/2019/05/30/canada-drives-vancouver/.
- **Small Business in Action 3-3** - Luc Rinaldi, "A Canadian CPA is Transforming America's Game," CPA Canada, January 2, 2019, accessed August 10, 2019, https://www.cpacanada.ca/en/news/pivot-magazine/2019-01-02-vivek-jain-transforming-football; and "What Makes the FCFL Different?" FCFL News, December 31, 2017, accessed August 10, 2019, https://news.fcfl.io/what-makes-the-fcfl-different-part-one/.
- **Small Business in Action 3-4** - "Gord Dickie: Sometimes You Don't Have to Talk," www.-bluteaudevenney.com/business-insights/gord-dickie-sometimes-you-dont-have-to-talk.html; and "Blade Runner on Ice," www.-progressmedia.ca/article/2011/11/small-business-blade-runner-ice; and "Blue Star Sports Acquires Goalline," BusinessWire, March 16, 2016, accessed August 9, 2019, https://www.businesswire.com/news/home/20160516005868/en/Blue-Star-Sports-Acquires-Goalline.
- **Small Business in Action 3-5** - Brenda Bouw, "Here's a Twist: Developers Ask Residents What Stores They Want," *Globe and Mail,* April 15, 2013, accessed August 25, 2019, www.theglobeandmail.com/report-on-business/small-business/starting-out/heres-a-twist-developers-ask-residents-what-stores-they-want/article11165548/; Jeff Quipp, "Adapt or Die: The Revolution in Marketing," *Canadian Business,* February 26, 2013, accessed August 25, 2019, https://www.canadianbusiness.com/innovation/adapt-or-die-the-revolution-in-marketing/; Lyndsie Bourgon, "The No-Money Startup Miracle," January 3, 2013, https://www.canadianbusiness.com/innovation/the-no-money-startup-miracle/; and Kim Hart McNeill, "A New Way to Kickstart a Business," *Canadian Business,* September 5, 2012, accessed August 25, 2019, https://www.canadianbusiness.com/innovation/a-new-way-to-kickstart-a-business/.
- **Table 3-1** - *Market Research Handbook,* 2009, Statistics Canada; Metro Toronto Information, 2009; and *Average Household Expenditures,* 2009.
- **Small Business in Action 3-6** - Peter Kenter, "Why Small Businesses Have One—and Only One—Advantage Over the Competition," *Financial Post,* updated December 17, 2018, accessed August 25, 2019, https://business.financialpost.com/sponsored/business-sponsored/why-small-businesses-have-one-and-only-one-advantage-over-the-competition; "Embracing The Lean Startup Approach In Crowdfunding," Arikovani (blog), February 21, 2017, accessed August 25, 2019, https://blog.arikovani.com/en/embracing-the-lean-startup-approach-in-crowdfunding/; Tim Metz, "9 Common Crowdfunding Mistakes People Make (and How to Avoid Them)," Indiegogo, accessed May 15, 2019, https://entrepreneur.indiegogo.com/education/article/9-common-crowdfunding-mistakes-people-make-avoid-2/; and Charlie Gentles, "Read This Before You Even Think About Crowdfunding," Medium, August 6, 2018, accessed August 25, 2019, https://medium.com/swlh/read-this-before-you-even-think-about-crowdfunding-9dede644cf09.
- **Small Business Beginnings 3-1** Adapted from Lee Oliver, "Appetite for Resurrection," *Profit,* November 2003, pp. 19–20, and Crazy Plates website, 2013.

CHAPTER 4

- **Small Business Profile** - Kia Kokalitcheva, "A Venture Capital May Not be a One-Size Fits All System," Axios, December 18, 2019, accessed August 10, 2019, https://www.axios.com/

venture-capital-finding-e-commerce-companies--d137c4a7-1425-45ad-a544-d04d2dfcbd8b.html; Kristen Marano, "What I Know Now: Michele Romanow, Co-Founder Clearbanc," You, Inc., August 23, 2018, accessed August 10, 2019, https://youinc.com/content/leadership/the-real-deal-what-i-know-now-with-michele-romanow.

- **Small Business in Action 4-1** - Steve Blank, "Why the Lean Start-Up Changes Everything," *Harvard Business Review,* May 2013, accessed September 14, 2019, https://hbr.org/2013/05/why-the-lean-start-up-changes-everything; Steve Blank, interview by Curt Nickisch: "When Startups Scrapped the Business Plan," *HBR Ideacast,* podcast audio, August 3, 2017, accessed August 10, 2019, https://hbr.org/ideacast/2017/08/when-startups-scrapped-the-business-plan.html; Bruce Hakutizwi, "After 10 Years, How Has the Lean Startup Fared," Business, updated December 4, 2018, accessed September 14, 2019, https://www.business.com/articles/lean-startup-principles/; Nistha Tripathi, "5 Reasons Not to Follow the Lean Startup Process for Your Next Idea," *Entrepreneur,* October 5, 2018, accessed September 14, 2019, https://www.entrepreneur.com/article/320508; Innov8rs Team, "Let's Get Real: Why Lean Startup is NOT Right For Everyone," Innov8rs, February 12, 2018, accessed September 14, 2019, https://innov8rs.co/news/lets-get-real-lean-startup-not-right-everyone/; and Howard Tullman, "Busting the Lean-Startup Myth," *Inc.,* accessed May 15, 2019, https://www.inc.com/howard-tullman/busting-the-lean-startup-myth.html.
- **Small Business in Action 4-2** - Will Moniz, "Young Entrepreneur Profile: Notable TV's Julian Brass," Talent Egg, August 5, 2009, accessed September 14, 2019, http://talentegg.ca/incubator/2009/08/05/young-entrepreneur-profile-notabletvs-julian-brass/; Teresa Kruze, "Noteable.ca's Julian Brass—From Living in Dad's Basement to Success," *Metro News,* November 18, 2012, www.metronews.ca/views/the-incredibility-factor/2012/11/18/notabe-cas-julian-brass-from-living-in-dads-basement-to-success.html; and "Profile: Noteable's Julian Brass" *VV Magazine,* December 2, 2014, accessed September 14, 2019, http://viewthe-vibe.com/profile-notable-julian-brass/; and Noteable Awards, 2015, http://notableawards.com/.
- **Small Business in Action 4-3** - "Shockbox," *Dragon's Den,* CBC, November 25, 2012, accessed September 14, 2019, https://www.cbc.ca/dragonsden/pitches/shockbox; Russ Bitely, "Making Sensor Out of Concussions," *Examiner;* Diane Jermyn, "Concussion Sensor Gets a Cool Reception from Sports Helmet Firms," *Globe and Mail,* updated May 12, 2018, accessed September 14, 2019, https://www.theglobeandmail.com/report-on-business/small-business/sb-growth/the-challenge/concussion-sensor-gets-a-cool-reception-from-helmet-makers/article20110577/; Paul Attfield, "Maker of Helmet Sensors Finds a Buyer, and Running Room," *Globe and Mail,* April 12, 2017, accessed September 14, 2019, https://www.theglobeandmail.com/report-on-business/small-business/sb-growth/the-challenge/maker-of-helmet-sensors-finds-a-buyer-and-running-room/article34664176/; and "i1 Biometrics Introduces the Athlete Intelligence Brand," Athlete Intelligence (blog), March 10, 2017, accessed September 14, 2019, http://blog.athleteintelligence.com/i1-biometrics-introduces-the-athlete-intelligence-brand.
- **Small Business in Action 4-4** - "Quicksnap," *Dragons' Den,* CBC, 2008, accessed September 14, 2019, https://www.cbc.ca/dragonsden/pitches/quicksnap; and Daryl-Lynn Carlson, "Quicksnap Invention Clicks with Investors," *Calgary Herald,* January 12, 2009, accessed September 14, 2019, http://www.calgaryherald.com/news/Episode+QuickSnap+invention+clicks+with+investors/1067682/story.html.
- **Small Business Beginnings 4-1** - Derek Sankey, "Good Partnership Juices Up Profits," *Financial Post,* August 25, 2009, pp. 1–2.
- **Small Business in Action 4-6** - "Ratehub," *Dragons' Den,* CBC, October 2016, accessed September 14, 2019, https://www.cbc.ca/dragonsden/pitches/ratehub; David Ebner, "Ratehub Taps $12-Million in Venture Funding from Boston-Based Elephant Partners LP," *Globe and Mail,* January 15, 2018, accessed September 14, 2019, https://www.theglobeandmail.com/report-on-business/small-business/sb-money/ratehub-taps-12-million-in-venture-funding-from-boston-based-elephant-partners-lp/article37600612/; "Ratehub CEO Talks Taking Risks While On Top," *MaRS Discovery District,* webcast, September 5, 2018; and "Alyssa Furtado: Breaking Out of the Plateau," Gore Mutual, November 28, 2018, accessed September 14, 2019, https://www.goremutual.ca/alyssa-furtado-breaking-out-of-the-plateau/?fbclid=IwAR37mV68zFiErJuP6TXbpl7l6SiBRAixJPBB23Z_I-zw6QA2YlztMWNfTXU.

CHAPTER 5

- **Small Business Profile** - "Hope Restored for Nova Scotian Crystal," CBC News, updated March 14, 2013, accessed September 14, 2019, https://www.cbc.ca/news/canada/nova-scotia/hope-restored-for-nova-scotian-crystal-1.1402840; Tom Mason, "A Clear Future," *Halifax Magazine,* June 12, 2013, accessed September 14, 2019, http://halifaxmag.com/style/a-clear-future/; and Stephanie vanKampen, "Nova Scotian Crystal Bounces Back from Receivership," *CBC News,* December 23, 2015, accessed September 14, 2019, https://www.cbc.ca/amp/1.3378415.
- **Small Business in Action 5-1** - Judith Lam Tang, "Rocky Mountain Soap Company at WEM: Totally Toxin Free," Juicy Green Mom, November 5, 2015, accessed September 14, 2019, http://juicygreenmom.ca/rocky-mountain-soap-company-at-wem-totally-toxin-free/; and Esha Chhabra, "This Canadian Company has $11 Million in Annual Sales While Putting the Environment First," *Forbes,* January 23, 2017, accessed September 14, 2019, https://www.forbes.com/sites/eshachhabra/2017/01/23/how-this-canadian-company-has-11-million-in-annual-sales-while-putting-the-environment-first/#67ec70735085.
- **Small Business in Action 5-2** - Cheryl Devoe Kim, "Takeover Helps Company Meet Its Target," *Globe and Mail,* updated April 29, 2018, accessed September 14, 2019, www.theglobeandmail.com/report-on-business/small-business/sb-money/takeover-helps-company-meet-its-target/article4258993/; and Chris Atchison, "Acquisitions: Buying a Business," *Profit,* December 8, 2011, www.profitguide.com/manage-grow/strategy-operations/acquisitions-buying-a-business-30314.
- **Small Business in Action 5-3** - Melanie Patten, "Buyer Steps Forward for NovaScotian Crystal," *Metro News,* March 14, 2013; Roger Taylor, "New Owner May Revive Beloved NovaScotian Crystal," *Chronicle Herald,* February 21, 2013; and Chris Lambie, "NovaScotian Crystal to Go Into Receivership," *Chronicle Herald,* February 15, 2013.
- **Table 5-2** - Adapted from Paul Harmon, *Small Business Management–A Practical Approach* (New York: D. Van Nostrand), p. 76. Figures updated from Dun and Bradstreet, *Key Business Ratios.*
- **Small Business in Action 5-4** - Adapted from Laura Bogomolny, "Smoothie Chain Booster Juice Finds Expanding Globally Is Not Always Smooth," *Canadian Business,* January 30, 2006, accessed August 11, 2019, 2019, https://www.canadianbusiness.com/business-strategy/smoothie-chain-booster-juice-finds-expanding-globally-is-not-always-smooth/; Mark Sutcliffe, "Booster Juice Founder," *Ottawa Citizen,* September 12, 2007; and "Our Story," Booster Juice website, accessed August 11, 2019, https://www.boosterjuice.com/our-story/about-booster-juice/.
- **Small Business in Action 5-5** - The Canadian Press, "Tim Hortons, Franchisee Group Close to Settling Two Class-Action

Lawsuits," *Canadian Business,* February 6, 2019, accessed September 14, 2019, https://www.canadianbusiness.com/business-news/tim-hortons-franchisee-group-close-to-settling-two-class-action-lawsuits/.

- **Table 5-5** - "2018 Top Newest Franchises," *Entrepreneur,* accessed August 11, 2019, https://www.entrepreneur.com/franchises/topnew; and "2019 Franchising Trends Report," CFA, accessed August 11, 2019, https://www.cfa.ca/franchisecanada/2019-franchising-trends-report/.
- **Small Business in Action 5-6** - Mary Teresa Bitti, "How a $300,000 *Dragons' Den* Deal is Setting Velofix on the Road to Growth," *Financial Post,* updated November 30, 2014, accessed September 3, 2019, https://business.financialpost.com/entrepreneur/deal-with-dragon-sets-mobile-repair-shop-on-road-to-growth-2; Mary Teresa Bitti, "*Dragons' Den* Alumnus Velofix Well on the Road to Dominating the Bicycle Repair Market," *Financial Post,* updated July 5, 2016, accessed September 3, 2019, https://business.financialpost.com/entrepreneur/fp-startups/dragons-den-alumnus-velofix-well-on-the-road-to-dominating-the-bicycle-repair-market; Pawel Dwulit, "Mobile Bike Shop Expands in High Gear," *Globe and Mail,* April 5, 2017, accessed September 14, 2019, https://www.theglobeandmail.com/report-on-business/small-business/sb-growth/the-challenge/mobile-bike-shop-expands-in-high-gear-across-n-america/article34576123/; and "Velofix Continues Growth with New Locations and Offers a $500 Signing Bonus for Ex-Performance Staff," Bicycle Retailer, February 28, 2019, accessed September 14, 2019, https://www.bicycleretailer.com/announcements/2019/02/28/velofix-continues-growth-new-locations-and-offers-500-signing-bonus-ex#.XIaR6YhKiUk.
- **Small Business in Action 5-7** - A&W Franchise Disclosure Documents (FDDs); "A&W CEO Kevin Bazner Responds to Unhappyfranchisee.com," August 15, 2012, www.unhappyfranchisee.com/category/franchisor/aw-restaurants-franchise/.
- **Table 5-6** - "2019 Franchise 500 Ranking," *Entrepreneur,* accessed August 11, 2019, https://www.entrepreneur.com/franchise500/2019; Olivia Minnock, "Top 10 franchises in Canada," Business Chief, accessed August 16, 2019, https://canada.businesschief.com/top10/2172/Top-10-franchises-in-Canada; "Canadian Franchise Association Announces Winners of 2019 Awards for Excellence in Franchising," Cision, accessed August 1, 2019, https://www.newswire.ca/news-releases/canadian-franchise-association-announces-winners-of-the-2019-awards-of-excellence-in-franchising-854201074.html; "Franchise Canada Awards of Excellence 2018," Canadian Franchise Association, accessed August 1, 2019, https://www.cfa.ca/lookforafranchise/top-franchises/2018-cfa-awards-of-excellence-in-franchising/.
- **Small Business Beginnings 5-2** - Mary Teresa Bitti, "Dragons' Den: Why This Spray-Paint Franchisor Didn't Need Jim Treliving's Deal After All," *Financial Post,* February 4, 2016, accessed September 14, 2019, https://business.financialpost.com/entrepreneur/fp-startups/dragons-den-why-this-spray-paint-franchisor-didnt-need-jim-trelivings-deal-after-all; Deirdre Kelly, "'Problem with Authority' Fuels Founder of House-Painting Franchise," *Globe and Mail,* updated May 15, 2018, accessed September 14, 2019, https://www.theglobeandmail.com/report-on-business/small-business/sb-growth/the-challenge/the-best-kind-of-entrepreneur-i-have-a-problem-with-authority/article25500334/; and Mei Mei Fox, "Why Franchising Was The Key To Success For These 6 Young Entrepreneurs," *Forbes,* August 24, 2017, accessed September 14, 2019, https://www.forbes.com/sites/meimeifox/2017/08/24/why-franchising-was-the-key-to-success-for-these-6-young-entrepreneurs/#4a0951ff5603.

CHAPTER 6

- **Small Business Profile** - Kim Girard, "Razor Suleman, CEO of I Love Rewards, on Engaging Employees," March 4, 2011, http://digitalpuck.ca/the-digital-puck/razor-suleman-ceo-of-i-love-rewards-on-engaging-employees/; "I Love Rewards Is Now Achievers," Achievers, September 19, 2011, www.achievers.com/about-us/press-release/i-love-rewards-now-achievers; "Razor Suleman's Achievers Acquired for $137 Million" TechVibes, July 1, 2015, accessed August 20, 2019, www.techvibes.com/blog/torontos-achievers-acquired-for-137-million-2015-07-01; Maya Kosoff, "Why a Founder on Track to Take His Company Public Sold It for $110 Million in Cash Instead," Business Insider, July 2, 2015, accessed August 20, 2019, www.businessinsider.com/how-achievers-founder-razor-suleman-sold-his-company-for-110-million-2015-7.
- **Table 6-1** - Statistics Canada, "Survey on Small and Medium Business Financing 2017," Revised March 21, 2019, https://www.ic.gc.ca/eic/site/061.nsf/vwapj/SFGSME-EFCPME_2017_eng_revised_March-21.pdf/$file/SFGSME-EFCPME_2017_eng_revised_March-21.pdf.
- **Small Business Beginnings 6-1** - "Coolest Cooler: 21st Century Cooler that's Actually Cooler," Kickstarter, accessed June 24, 2019, https://www.kickstarter.com/projects/ryangrepper/coolest-cooler-21st-century-cooler-thats-actually; Elise Moreau, "Kickstarter vs. Indiegogo: Which One Should You Choose," LifeWire, April 24, 2019, https://www.lifewire.com/kickstarter-vs-indiegogo-3485780; Michael Mayer, "5 Things I Wish I Knew Before Launching My First Crowdfunding Campaign," *Forbes,* May 8, 2018, https://www.forbes.com/sites/ventureforamerica/2018/05/08/5-things-i-wish-i-knew-before-launching-my-first-crowdfunding-campaign/#18d746ff5009; Josh Kraus, "8 Successful Crowdfunding Campaigns and the Apps Behind Them," Zapier, August 2, 2018, https://zapier.com/blog/successful-crowdfunding-donation-app-campaigns/; The Scientific Approach to Crowdfunding, part 2/8: Use Your Friends and Family," Symbid, posted 2013, accessed May 11, 2019, https://www.symbid.com/articles/152-the-scientific-approach-to-crowdfunding-part-2-8-use-your-friends-family.
- **Small Business Beginnings 6-2** - Annie Pilon, "What If Your Crowdfunding Campaign Doesn't Raise Enough Money," updated November 1, 2017, accessed August 20, 2019, https://smallbiztrends.com/2014/10/double-fine-productions-crowdfunding-campaign.html; Jessica Leeder, "When Kickstarter Isn't Enough," *Globe and Mail,* October 19, 2017, accessed August 20, 2019, https://www.theglobeandmail.com/report-on-business/small-business/when-kickstarter-isnt-enough/article36641454/.
- **Small Business Beginnings 6-3** - Deborah Aarts, "Financing Foreign Sales," December 7, 2011, *Canadian Business,* accessed September 17, 2019, https://www.canadianbusiness.com/small-business/financing-foreign-sales/.
- **Table 6-7** - Colin Mason, "2018 Report on Angel Investing in Canada," NACO, June 2019, accessed September 20, 2019, https://www.nacocanada.com/cpages/angel-activity-report.
- **Small Business Beginnings 6-4** - Repshift website, accessed July 11, 2019, https://repshift.com/; Qasim Mohammad, "After Working in Venture Capital, I Vowed to Build My Own Company without Outside Investors," *Globe and Mail,* February 4, 2019, https://www.theglobeandmail.com/business/small-business/money/article-after-working-in-venture-capital-i-vowed-to-build-my-company-without/.
- **Small Business Beginnings 6-5** - Doron Telem, "The Canadian FinTech Landscape, 2018," KPMG, accessed August 20, 2019, https://

assets.kpmg/content/dam/kpmg/ca/pdf/2018/10/the-canadian-fintech-landscape.pdf; David Nault, "Status of the Canadian Fintech Landscape," Medium, October 30, 2018, https://medium.com/luge-capital/status-of-the-canadian-fintech-landscape-830ea5d-b4aae; "Total Value of Fintech Investments Worldwide from 2008 to 2018," Statista, accessed March 23, 2019, https://www.statista.com/statistics/502378/value-of-fintech-investments-globally/; Sarah Efron, "Does This Dragons' Den Star's Financing Startup Clearbanc Live Up to Its Lofty Promises?" *Globe and Mail,* May 25, 2019, https://www.theglobeandmail.com/business/small-business/money/article-does-this-dragons-den-stars-financing-startup-clearbanc-live-up-to/.

- **Small Business in Action 6-3** - Peter Kenter, "How Snakes & Lattes Found a Better Way to Grow Their Business with Lending Loop," *Financial Post,* August 9, 2018, https://business.financialpost.com/sponsored/business-sponsored/how-snakes-lattes-found-a-better-way-to-grow-their-business-with-lending-loop; Loop Financial Inc., "Lending Loop Launches Online Business Lending Marketplace on Back of Seed Funding," Cision, June 11, 2015, accessed August 20, 2019, https://www.newswire.ca/news-releases/lending-loop-launches-online-business-lending-marketplace-on-back-of-seed-funding-517922901.html.
- **Small Business in Action 6-4** - Canadian Bankers Association, "Focus: Small and Medium Sized Lending Enterprises: Lending and More," CBA, October 3, 2018, https://cba.ca/small-and-medium-sized-enterprises; Queenie Wong, "Battle of the Banks, 2017," CFIB; "Credit Unions Rated Best by Small Business; Scotiabank Tops List Among Big Five," CFIB, October 20, 2016, accessed August 20, 2019, https://www.cfib-fcei.ca/en/media/credit-unions-rated-best-small-business-scotiabank-tops-list-among-big-five; Queenie Wong, "SME Financing Indicators," CFIB, October 2016, accessed August 20, 2019, https://www.cfib-fcei.ca/sites/default/files/article/documents/rr3412_0.pdf; Michael Duck, Class Presentation - Mount Saint Vincent University, 2018; Deborah Aarts, "Canada's Fastest Growing Company Is Built for Growth," *Canadian Business,* June 12, 2014, accessed August 23, 20 19, https://www.canadianbusiness.com/small-business/canadas-fastest-growing-company-is-built-for-growth/; Kevin Carmichael, "Innovation Nation: How Canada's Banks are Holding Back the Knowledge Economy," *Financial Post,* March 27, 2019, last updated April 16, 2019, https://business.financialpost.com/technology/innovation-nation-how-canadas-banks-are-holding-back-the-knowledge-economy.
- **Small Business Beginnings 6-6** - Adapted from Alexandra Lopez-Pacheco, "Good Palate and Tenacity," *Financial Post,* September 21, 2009, pp. 1–2.
- **Appendix 6A - Adapted from:** "Provincial Venture Capital Corporations: A Comparative Analysis," *Journal of Small Business and Entrepreneurship—Canada,* vol. 4, no. 5 (Fall 1986), p. 22.

CHAPTER 7

- **Small Business Profile** - "Our Story," Spin Master, accessed August 21, 2019, http://www.spinmaster.com/our-story.php?userLoc=us; Dawn Calleja, "How Spin Master Got Its Mojo Back," *Globe and Mail,* July 2, 2015, accessed August 21, 2019, www.theglobeandmail.com/report-on-business/rob-magazine/how-spin-master-got-its-mojo-back/article22639332/; Courtney Shea, "How Spin Master Conquered the Lucrative International Toy Market," *Canadian Business,* September 13, 2018, https://www.canadianbusiness.com/lists-and-rankings/growth-500/how-spin-master-conquered-the-lucrative-international-toy-market/; and "Spin Master Reports Q4 and Full Year 2018 Financial Results," Cision, March 6, 2019, https://www.newswire.ca/news-releases/spin-master-reports-q4-and-full-year-2018-financial-results-865227414.html; Hollie Shaw, "Spin Master Joins Digital Gaming Ranks," *Financial Post,* December 21, 2012, accessed August 21, 2019, http://business.financialpost.com/2012/12/21/spin-master-joins-digital-gaming-ranks/; Clark Shultz, "Spin Master IPO Launches in Canada," Seeking Alpha, July 30, 2015, accessed August 21, 2019, http://seekingalpha.com/news/2676695-spin-master-ipo-launches-in-canada; "Spin Master Corp Shares Rise in First Day as Public Company," *Financial Post,* July 30, 2015, accessed August 21, 2019, http://business.financialpost.com/investing/spin-master-corp-shares-rise-in-first-day-as-a-public-company; and "Spin Master Introduces Explosive Entertainment and Innovative Play with 2019 Product Portfolio," Spin Master, February 15, 2019, https://www.spinmaster.com/news-releases-view.php?id=122786.
- **Small Business in Action 7-3** - Meghan McKenna, "5 Indigenous Entrepreneurs Creating Social Change in Their Communities," *Fashion,* June 21, 2018, accessed August 2, 2019, https://fashionmagazine.com/culture/indigenous-entrepreneurs-canada/; Mark Marsolais-Nahwegahbow, Interview by ELMNT FM Ottawa: "Birch Bark Coffee," November 9, 2018, https://www.youtube.com/watch?v=s_d3roFqE40; and "Founder," Birch Bark Coffee Company, accessed May 18, 2019, https://birchbarkcoffeecompany.com/pages/founder.
- **Small Business Beginnings 7-1** - Adapted from *Profit Magazine,* "Entrepreneur's Diversification Strategy Takes Off," Business Development Bank of Canada, Fall 2009, pp. 12–13.
- **Small Business in Action 7-4** - Susan Krashinsky, "Facebook Using More Personal Data to Deliver Targeted Ads," *Globe and Mail,* November 14, 2014, accessed August 21, 2010, www.theglobeandmail.com/report-on-business/industry-news/marketing/facebook-using-more-personal-data-to-deliver-targeted-ads/article21570316/; Bruce Rogers, "Neil Patel's KISSMETRICS Brings Big Data to Small Companies to Optimize the Customer Experience," *Forbes,* January 9, 2013, accessed September 19, 2019, https://www.forbes.com/sites/brucerogers/2013/01/09/neil-patels-kissmetrics-brings-big-data-to-small-companies-to-optimize-the-customer-experience/#7b08fe24a359; and Brett Nuckles, "5 Location-Based Mobile Marketing Tools for Small Businesses," Business News Daily, January 10, 2014, accessed August 21, 2019, www.businessnewsdaily.com/5753-location-based-mobile-marketing-tools-small-businesses.html.
- **Small Business in Action 7-5** - Adapted from Rhona Macinnes, "The Loyalty Puzzle," *Grocer Today,* January–February 2008, pp. 10–12.

CHAPTER 8

- **Small Business Profile** - Mary Theresa Bitti, "Dragons' Den: Why Popular Music Streaming App Musi Ended Up Being Too Risky a Play," *Financial Post,* March 3, 2016, accessed October 1, 2019, https://business.financialpost.com/entrepreneur/small-business/dragons-den-why-popular-music-streaming-app-musi-ended-up-being-too-risky-a-play; "Musi," *Dragons' Den,* CBC, accessed February 1, 2019, https://www.cbc.ca/dragonsden/pitches/musi; "Musi – Simple Music Streaming," Daily Sales Data, Thinking Game, accessed May 8, 2019, https://thinkgaming.com/app-sales-data/110741/musi-unlimited-free-musiyoutube/c-for-; "MoPub Publisher Spotlight: Aaron Wojnowski & Christian Lunny, Musi," MoPub, March 26, 2018, accessed October 1, 2019, https://www.youtube.com/watch?v=xxTGJpzHC_A; and Aaron Wojnowski, "How I Hacked App Store Ratings for a Consistently Perfect Five Stars," Medium, January 2, 2015, accessed October 1,

2019, https://medium.com/@awojnowski/how-i-hacked-app-store-ratings-for-a-consistently-perfect-5-stars-3de17d40ca1f.

- **Small Business in Action 8-1** - Karen Kwan, "From Home Remedy to Worldwide Organic Skincare Success," StartUp HERE Toronto, February 19, 2019, https://startupheretoronto.com/type/profiles/from-home-remedy-to-worldwide-organic-skincare-success/; Jennifer Kolbuc, "From Crockpots to Whole Foods: The Launch of Satya Organic Skincare," The Mompreneur, October 17, 2018, https://medium.com/the-mompreneur/from-crockpots-to-whole-foods-the-launch-of-satya-organic-skin-care-cbff28f5ca1e; and Rick Spence, "Fire Up the Crock Pot – The Baby Has Eczema and Mom Has the Answer," January 12, 2018, accessed October 1, 2019, https://business.financialpost.com/entrepreneur/1219-biz-rs-satya-fpe.
- **Small Business Beginnings 8-1** - Robb Mandelbaum, "Is Amazon Good or Bad for Small Business," *Forbes,* March 31, 2018, https://www.forbes.com/sites/robbmandelbaum/2018/03/31/is-amazon-good-or-bad-for-small-business-yes/#7e83e2b74467; Ali Montag, "The Instant Pot is Selling Like Crazy on Amazon—and Its PhD Inventor Says He's Read All 39,000 reviews," CNBC, November 24, 2017, accessed October 1, 2019, https://www.cnbc.com/2017/11/24/why-robert-wangs-instant-pot-is-a-bestseller-on-amazon.html; TJ McCue, "Amazon Report Cites More Than 1 Million Small Business Sellers on Platform," *Forbes,* July 24, 2018, accessed October 1, 2019, https://www.forbes.com/sites/tjmccue/2018/07/24/amazon-report-cites-more-than-1-million-small-business-sellers-on-platform/#151966833e83; Serenity Gibbons, "How Small Business Can Master The Art of Selling on Amazon," *Forbes,* March 19, 2019, https://www.forbes.com/sites/serenitygibbons/2019/03/19/how-small-businesses-can-master-the-art-of-selling-on-amazon/#32bbd97b1a46; and Pilar Newman, "How to Successfully Sell Products on Amazon," A Better Lemonade Stand, January 4, 2019, https://www.abetterlemonadestand.com/how-to-sell-on-amazon/.
- **Small Business in Action 8-2** - Rick Spence, "The 5 Winning Strategies of High-Growth Companies," *Canadian Business,* June 1, 2011, accessed October 1, 2019, https://www.canadianbusiness.com/innovation/the-5-winning-strategies-of-high-growth-companies/; "Daily Deal Toronto," Groupon, accessed May 4, 2019, https://www.groupon.com/browse/greater-toronto-area?category=things-to-do&category2=tickets-and-events&rating=%5B4..5%5D; Jessica McDiarmid, "5. Get Creative with Price Tags," *Canadian Business,* October 19, 2015, accessed August 22, 2019, https://www.canadianbusiness.com/small-business/5-get-creative-with-price-tags/.
- **Small Business in Action 8-3** - "The Dirty Secrets of Stealth Online Marketing," CBC News, May 16, 2011, accessed August 22, 2019, https://www.cbc.ca/news/technology/the-dirty-secrets-of-stealth-online-marketing-1.1096797; Tracy Blanchard, 10 Best Stealth Marketing Campaigns," *Delnext Blog,* accessed June 1, 2019, https://www.delnext.com/blog/en/stealth-marketing-campaigns/; Jeff Scanlon and Bill Hearn, "Stealth Marketing: To Disclose or Not To Disclose - That is the (Legal) Question," Mondaq, last updated August 14, 2006, accessed September 27, 2019, http://www.mondaq.com/canada/x/42078/advertising+marketing+branding/Stealth+Marketing+To+Disclose+Or+Not+To+Disclose+That+Is+The+Legal+Question.
- **Small Business in Action 8-4** - Brett Nelson, "Bang for Your Marketing Buck," *Forbes,* June 9, 2005, www.forbes.com/2005/09/06/marketing-advertising-entrepreneurs-cx_bn_0906marketing.html; "Dragons' Den Effect," Stilt Guys, October 27, 2012, accessed August 22, 2019, http://stiltguys.com/2012/10/27/dragons-den-effect/; Emily Kathryn Rudow, "What Actually Happened After Dragons' Den?" January 31, 2017, accessed August 22, 2019, https://medium.com/@emilykathrynrudow/what-actually-happened-after-dragons-den-5411b6808cbc; and *Holy Crap Blog,* Jason Buckland, "How the *Dragons' Den* Effect Works," April 19, 2012, accessed August 22, 2019, https://holycrap.com/blogs/news/16103181-how-the-dragons-den-effect-works.
- **Small Business Beginnings 8-2** - Trevor Melanson, "Is HootSuite Canada's Next Billion-Dollar Tech Titan?" *Canadian Business,* January 9, 2013, accessed August 22, 2019, https://www.canadianbusiness.com/technology-news/is-hootsuite-canadas-next-tech-titan/; Ingrid Lunden, "HootSuite Gets Creative, Now Integrates Vimeo for Video, WordPress for Blogs, and Pinterest Tracking," TechCrunch, December 6, 2012, accessed August 22, 2019, http://techcrunch.com/2012/12/06/hootsuite-gets-creative-now-integrates-vimeo-for-video-wordpress-for-blogs-and-pinterest-tracking/; and "10 Interesting Hootsuite Facts and Statistics (2019) By the Numbers," Expanded Ramblings, updated June 26, 2019, https://expandedramblings.com/index.php/hootsuite-facts-statistics/.
- **Small Business in Action 8-5** - Ilyse Liffreing, "Jagermeister Turns to Snapchat for Halloween Push," Digiday UK, October 22, 2018, https://digiday.com/marketing/jagermeister-turns-snapchat-halloween-push/; Brandon Doyle, "24 Creative Snapchat Campaigns from Brands to Inspire Your Snap Strategy," Wallaroo Media, April 7, 2019, https://wallaroomedia.com/blog/snapchat/25-snapchat-campaigns-to-inspire-snap-strategy/; Vikas Agrawal, "Swipe Right: How Brands Are Using Tinder for Marketing," Relevance, July, 2017, https://www.relevance.com/swipe-right-how-brands-are-using-tinder-for-marketing/; Sarah McDermott, "Domino's Can Help You Find Love with Cheesy Tinder Chat-Up Lines", February 13, 2018, https://www.cnet.com/news/dominos-can-help-you-find-love-with-cheesy-tinder-chat-up-lines/; "Use Tinder to Attract New Customers, Not Bad Dates," *Forbes,* January 26, 2017, https://www.forbes.com/sites/under30network/2017/01/26/use-tinder-to-attract-new-customers-not-bad-dates/#21d71c8eb117.

CHAPTER 9

- **Small Business in Action 9-1** - Annette Bourdeau, "Cash Flow," *Profit,* June 2009, p. 23; also, Annette Bourdeau, "PROFIT 100: Growth Solutions," *Canadian Business,* accessed September 19, 2019, https://www.canadianbusiness.com/leadership/profit-100-growth-solutions/.
- **Small Business Beginnings 9-1** - "Meet the 2018 Food and Agribusiness Convergent Innovation Prize Winner," McGill University, April 27, 2019, https://www.mcgill.ca/desautels/channels/news/meet-2018-food-and-agribusiness-convergent-innovation-prize-winner-286886; Linda Sutherland, "Student Entrepreneurs Go Up Against The Dragons," McGill University, January 11, 2019, https://www.mcgill.ca/giving/why-giving-matters/2019/01/11/student-entrepreneurs-go-against-dragons.
- **Small Business in Action 9-2** - "The Freshbooks Story," Freshbooks, accessed June 1, 2019, https://www.freshbooks.com/about/ourstory; and Becky Reuber, "From His Parents' Basement, Entrepreneur Builds Accounting Powerhouse," *Globe and Mail,* updated May 10, 2018, accessed August 23, 2019, www.theglobeandmail.com/report-on-business/small-business/sb-digital/biz-categories-technology/from-his-parents-basement-entrepreneur-builds-accounting-powerhouse/article6230133/.
- **Small Business in Action 9-3** - Randall Litchfield, "The Accounting Skills You Really Need to Grow," *Canadian Business,* June 1, 2011, accessed August 23, 2019, https://www.canadianbusiness.com/small-business/the-accounting-skills-you-really-need-to-grow/.

- **Small Business in Action 9-4** - Chris Atchison, "Running as a Lean as a Greyhound," *Profit,* May 2009, p. 23; also, Chris Atchison, "Discipline 4–Running As Lean As a Greyhound," *Canadian Business,* August 2, 2012, accessed September 20, 2019, https://www.canadianbusiness.com/leadership/discipline-4-running-as-lean-as-a-greyhound/.
- **Small Business in Action 9-6** - Dave O'Connor, interview by Peter Mombourquette, "Managing Cash Flow at Glow Promotions," May 17, 2019.
- **Small Business in Action 9-7** - Tijana Martin, "Merchants Hit Hard by Premium Credit Card Fees, Round Table Participants Say," The Record, April 28, 2013, accessed September 20, 2019, www.therecord.com/news-story/2629115-merchants-hit-hard-by-premium-credit-card-fees-round-table-participan/; and Tracy Sherlock, "Merchants Up in Arms Over Credit Card Fees," *Vancouver Sun,* November 22, 2012, accessed September 20, 2019, www.vancouversun.com/business/Merchants+arms+over+credit+card+fees/7597414/story.html.

CHAPTER 10

- **Small Business Profile** - Costa Elles, interview by Peter Mombourquette, "About Ela! Greek Taverna," October 23, 2013.
- **Small Business in Action 10-1** - Adapted from Eleanore Beaton, "Launch and Learn," *Profit,* October 2008, pp. 45–47; see also, "Launch and Learn: Management Lessons from the PROFIT Hot 50," *Canadian Business,* September 15, 2008, accessed September 20, 2019, https://www.canadianbusiness.com/innovation/launch-and-learn-management-lessons-from-the-profit-hot-50-2/.
- **Table 10-1** - Adapted from Curtis E. Tage, Jr., Leon C. Megginson, Charles R. Scott, Jr., and Lyle R. Trueblood, *Successful Small Business Management,* 3rd ed. (Georgetown, Ont.: Irwin-Dorsey of Canada, 1982), p. 244.
- **Small Business in Action 10-2** - "Simplifying Godin Guitars' Supply Chain to Become a Global Leader," EDC, November 21, 2017, accessed September 20, 2019, https://www.edc.ca/en/article/godin-guitars-become-global-export-leader.html; Guy Dixon, "How Montreal's Godin Guitars Strummed Its Way to the Top," *Globe and Mail,* March 25, 2019, accessed September 20, 2019, https://www.theglobeandmail.com/business/article-how-montreals-godin-guitars-strummed-its-way-to-the-top/#comments; Luke Michielsen, "Godin Factory Tour," Brickhouse Guitars, May 27, 2017, accessed September 20, 2019, https://brickhouseguitars.com/godin-factory-tour/.
- **Table 10-2** - John B. Kline, Donald P. Stegall, and Lawrence L. Steinmetz, *Managing the Small Business,* (Homewood, Ill.: Richard D. Irwin, 1968).
- **Small Business in Action 10-3** - Scott Shpak, "Lean Manufacturing Pros and Cons," Chron, accessed August 24, 2019, https://smallbusiness.chron.com/lean-manufacturing-pros-cons-44749.html; adapted from BDC, "Get the Edge," *Profit,* (Fall 2009), accessed September 20, 2019, http://publications.gc.ca/collections/collection_2009/bdc/CC142-1-29-2E.pdf.
- **Small Business in Action 10-4** - Carolyn Thomas, "Four Marketing Tricks that IKEA Used to Seduce Us," *The Ethical Blog,* September 5, 2010; James Tozer, "Why Shoppers Find It So Hard to Escape from Ikea: Flatpack Furniture Stores Are 'Designed Just Like a Maze'," *Daily Mail,* January 24, 2011, accessed August 24, 2019, www.dailymail.co.uk/femail/article-1349831/Ikea-design-stores-mazes-stop-shoppers-leaving-end-buying-more.html; Marina Strauss, "How Ikea Seduces Us," *Globe and Mail,* updated April 30, 2018, accessed August 24, 2019, https://www.theglobeandmail.com/report-on-business/rob-magazine/how-ikea-seduces-us/article4328972/; and "Annual Revenue of the IKEA Group Worldwide from 2001 to 2018 (in billion euros)," Statista, accessed August 24, 2019, www.statista.com/statistics/264433/annual-sales-of-ikea-worldwide/.
- **Table 10-3**- Sang Lee and Marc Schniederjams, *Operations Management* (Houghton Mifflin, Boston, 1994), p. 256.

CHAPTER 11

- **Small Business Profile** - Jason Tafler, "I Was a Corporate Executive Addicted to Work. But an Unexpected Crisis Made Me Realize I Was on the Wrong Path," *Globe and Mail,* January 23, 2019, https://www.theglobeandmail.com/business/small-business/startups/article-i-was-a-corporate-executive-addicted-to-work-but-an-unexpected-crisis/#comments; "Manage Stress and Thrive in Everyday Life," Unyte, accessed July 11, 2019, https://unyte.com; "Unyte: Interactive Meditation," Kickstarter, accessed July 1, 2019, https://www.kickstarter.com/projects/190163941/unyte-interactive-meditation; "Unyte: Interactive Meditation," Indiegogo, accessed July 4, 2019, https://www.indiegogo.com/projects/unyte-interactive-meditation#/; Audrey Carleton, "Self Care and Productivity are Not Mutually Exclusive," *Globe and Mail,* March 29, 2019, https://www.theglobeandmail.com/business/careers/workplace-award/article-self-care-and-productivity-are-not-mutually-exclusive/; "Careers," Unyte, accessed July 3, 2019, https://unyte.com/pages/careers.
- **Small Business in Action 11-1** - Max Greenwood, "The Real Estate Agents's Agent: Avenue HQ's Rebecca Troelstra," Tech Vibes, December 19, 2018, https://techvibes.com/2018/12/19/the-real-estate-agents-agent-avenuehqs-rebecca-troelstra; "A Flexible Work Environment Helps this Tech Star Find and Keep Staff," BDC, accessed July 1, 2019, https://www.bdc.ca/en/articles-tools/employees/recruit/pages/a-flexible-work-environment-helps-this-tech-find-keep-staff.aspx; Michael Wormstall-Cocolakis, "Labour Shortage: Here to Stay," BDC, September 2018, https://www.bdc.ca/en/documents/analysis_research/labour-shortage.pdf.
- **Small Business in Action 11-2** - Gregory Lewis, "How Small Business Can Use LinkedIn to Recruit," *LinkedIn Blog,* November 28, 2017, accessed September 4, 2019, https://business.linkedin.com/talent-solutions/blog/small-business/2017/how-small-businesse-can-use-linkedin-to-recruit; Susan Heathfield, "Use LinkedIn for Recruiting Employees," The Balance, updated May 30 2019, http://humanresources.about.com/od/recruiting/a/recruit_linked.htm.
- **Small Business in Action 11-3** - Mandy Rennehan, "Does the Colour of Your Collar Define Success?" TEDx Talks, April 8, 2019, https://www.youtube.com/watch?v=B5-7EvXuaUg; "How She Did It: Mandy Rennehan, Founder and Blue-Collar CEO of Freshco.ca," Women of Influence, October 8, 2018, accessed September 8, 2019, https://www.womenofinfluence.ca/2018/10/08/how-she-did-it-mandy-rennehan-founder-and-blue-collar-ceo-of-freshco-ca/#.XS05K-hKiUk; Katie Underwood, "Freshco Brought Fresh Talent to An Industry that Needs It," *Canadian Business,* September 13, 2018, https://www.canadianbusiness.com/lists-and-rankings/growth-500/freshco-brought-fresh-talent-to-an-industry-that-needs-it/.
- **Small Business in Action 11-4** - Jacquelyn Smith, "How Social Media Can Help (or Hurt) You in Your Job Search," *Forbes,* April 16, 2013, accessed September 4, 2019, www.forbes.com/sites/jacquelynsmith/2013/04/16/how-social-media-can-help-or-hurt-your-job-search/; Dr. Amy Thurlow, interview with Peter Mombourquette, "On the Acceptable Use of Online Information in Hiring Practices," Mount Saint Vincent University, Halifax, Nova Scotia, June 5, 2013.

- **Small Business in Action 11-5** - "Nikolai Bratkovski of OpenCare Presents It's A Talent War," Tech Toronto YouTube Channel, November 23, 2016, accessed September 4, 2019, https://www.youtube.com/watch?v=AfVzd9PgZiI; and "TechTO Exclusive: Scaling a Toronto Startup with Silicon Valley Venture Capital," Tech Toronto YouTube Channel, February 12, 2019, https://www.youtube.com/watch?v=QYebKeA8X3U; Jessi Hempel, "LinkedIn Top Startups 2019: The 25 Hottest Canadian Companies to Work for Now," LinkedIn, September 4, 2019, accessed October 3, 2019, https://www.linkedin.com/pulse/linkedin-top-startups-2019-25-hottest-canadian-companies-jessi-hempel/.
- **Small Business Beginnings 11-1** - Jim Collins, *Good to Great* (New York: HarperCollins Publishers Inc., 2001).
- **Small Business in Action 11-6** - Adapted from Eleanor Beaton, "Pay for Profit," *Profit,* May 2008, pp. 39–41.
- **Small Business in Action 11-7** - Liz Palika and Jennifer Fearing, *Dogs at Work: A Practical Guide to Creating Dog-Friendly Workplaces* (New York: Humane Society Press, 2008); Rhonda Abrams, "Dogs in the Workplace: Good for You, Your Employees, and Your Bottom Line," *USA Today,* June 21, 2017, accessed September 8, 2019, https://www.usatoday.com/story/money/columnist/abrams/2017/06/21/dogs-workplace-good-you-your-employees-your-bottom-line/414653001/; and Lisa Evans, "Your Best New (Furry) Employee," *Canadian Business,* June 21, 2013, accessed September 8, 2019, https://www.canadianbusiness.com/leadership/your-best-new-furry-employee/.
- **Table 11-4** - "Employee Benefits—What's Hot and Not in Workplace Perks," *Canada News Wire Service,* September 5, 2008.
- **Small Business in Action 11-8** - *Small Business in Canada,* 1990, p. 61.

CHAPTER 12

- **Small Business Profile** - S. VanHeuvelen, "Fab 30: Devon Brooks, Co-Founder, Blo Blow Dry Bar," *Canadian Business,* July 18, 2012, accessed September 9, 2019, https://www.canadianbusiness.com/innovation/fab-30-devon-brooks-co-founder-blo-blow-dry-bar/; Frances Bula, "Blow-Dry Bar Concept Heats Up," *Globe and Mail,* updated May 8, 2018, accessed October 1, 2019, www.theglobeandmail.com/report-on-business/small-business/sb-growth/success-stories/blow-dry-bar-concept-heats-up/article4180474/; Anthony Reinhart, "Branding Blow-by-Blow: Q&A with Devon Brooks," Canadian Digital Media Network, May 25, 2012; David Ebner, "Serial Entrepreneur Devon Brooks Taps into the Popularity of Coaching for Her New Venture," *Globe and Mail,* March 12, 2019, https://www.theglobeandmail.com/business/small-business/startups/article-serial-entrepreneur-devon-brooks-taps-into-the-popularity-of-coaching/; "About Us," Sphere, accessed May 18, 2019, https://www.sphereishere.com/about-us; and "Leader Spotlight: Devon Brooks, Sphere," Futurpreneur, December 4, 2018, accessed September 9, 2019, https://www.futurpreneur.ca/en/2018/leader-spotlight-devon-brooks-sphere/.
- **Small Business in Action 12-1** - Avi Savar, "3 Things Every Entrepreneur Needs to Know About Advisory Boards," *Inc.,* accessed June 17, 2019, https://www.inc.com/avi-savar/how-to-find-and-leverage-a-killer-advisory-board.html.
- **Figure 12-1** - "Total Tax Burden Remains Top SME Concern, 2015" Canadian Federation of Independent Business, accessed January 30, 2016, http://www.cfib-fcei.ca/cfib-documents/res-OMO76-1506-AGG-Nat.pdf.
- **Small Business in Action 12-2** - Adapted from Sasha Nagy, "The Little Shoebox of Horrors," *Globe and Mail Update,* March 21, 2006; www.theglobeandmail.com; Ronald L. Johnson C.A., 2010.
- **Small Business Beginnings 12-1** - Stephanie Whittaker, "Childcare for Career Set," Canwest News Service, June 2008; Rick Spence, "New Twist On An Old Business," *Profit,* June 2008, pp. 57–58; and "Press and Awards," Kids & Company, accessed September 9, 2019, https://kidsandcompany.com/about-us/press-awards/

CHAPTER 13

- **Small Business Profile** - Halifax Business Awards, "PAVIA – Business of the Year," Christopher Webb Youtube Channel, April 9, 2018, accessed September 10, 2019, https://www.youtube.com/watch?v=IBhh6xnaal8; Christopher Webb and Victoria Foulger, interview with Peter Mombourquette: "Interview with PAVIA Gallery - Espresso Bar & Café Co-founders Chris Webb & Victoria Foulger," May 2019; Allison Saunders, "Pavia wins a spot in the new library," The Coast, April 16, 2014, accessed September 10, 2019, https://www.thecoast.ca/RestaurantandBarNews/archives/2014/04/16/pavia-wins-a-spot-in-the-new-library; Carol Moreira, "Pavia: A Model Ethical Coffee Shop," Entrevestor, November 2, 2017, accessed September 10, 2019, http://entrevestor.com/ac/blog/pavia-a-model-ethical-coffee-shop.
- **Small Business Beginnings 13-1** - Becky Reuber, "Mabel's Label's Social Media Strategy Sticks," *Globe and Mail,* updated April 30, 2018, accessed October 2, 2019, http://m.theglobeandmail.com/report-on-business/small-business/sb-marketing/mabels-labels-social-media-strategy-sticks/article600065/?service=mobile; Francine Kopun, "Mabel's Labels at Walmart Canada," *Toronto Star,* June 25, 2012, accessed September 10, 2019, www.thestar.com/business/2012/06/25/mabels_labels_at_walmart_canada.html; Deborah Aarts, "Why We Sold Our Company," *Canadian Business,* January 12, 2016, accessed September 10, 2019, https://www.canadianbusiness.com/innovation/why-we-sold-our-company-mabels-labels/amp/.
- **Small Business in Action 13-1** - Jerry Langton, "Did You Know This Shopping Website Is Canadian?" *Globe and Mail,* updated May 9, 2018, www.theglobeandmail.com/report-on-business/economy/canada-competes/did-you-know-this-shopping-website-is-canadian/article5061065/; James Berkow, "Montreal's Beyond The Rack Closes US$37M Funding Round," *Financial Post,* November 9, 2011, accessed September 10, 2019, http://business.financialpost.com/entrepreneur/montreals-beyond-the-rack-closes-us37m-funding-round?__lsa=4df7-4abf; "Flash Events," Beyond the Rack, accessed July 4, 2019, www.btr.com; Eva Friede, "What Went Wrong with Montreal's Beyond the Rack?" *Montreal Gazette,* updated April 18, 2016, accessed September 10, 2019, https://montrealgazette.com/business/local-business/what-went-wrong-with-montreals-beyond-the-rack.
- **Table 13-1** - Ronald W. Torrence. *In the Owner's Chair: Proven Techniques for Taking Your Business from Zero to $10 Million,* © 1986, p. 259.
- **Table 13-2** - Adapted from Norm Brodsky, *Paying for Growth: How Much Cash You Need to Carry New Sales,* Inc. Online Tools & Apps: Worksheet, October 2008.
- **Small Business in Action 13-2** - Grant Buckler, "Tiny Tech Firm Scores One for Universal Passwords," *Globe and Mail,* updated May 9, 2018, accessed September 10, 2019, https://www.theglobeandmail.com/report-on-business/small-business/sb-managing/tiny-tech-firm-scores-one-for-universal-passwords/article5610227/; and "Secure Key Concierge," Secure Key Technologies, accessed September 10, 2019, https://securekeyconcierge.com/.
- **Small Business in Action 13-3** - Solana Cain, "Franchisee pushes eco-friendly paving option," Sudbury Star, April 21, 2014, accessed October 6, 2019, https://www.thesudburystar.com/2014/04/21/franchisee-pushes-eco-friendly-pavement-option/wcm/3f526841-620f-74d2-0c1d-9bcb6d77545d; Enviro Paving Corp. "What are we

going to do about all these tires?" Facebook, June 27, 2017, accessed October 6, 2019, https://www.facebook.com/enviropaving/videos/enviropaving-100-recycled-tire-rubber-paving-since-2009/1776939509002350/.

CHAPTER 14

- **Small Business Profile** - John Lorinc, "The Golden Goose," *Canadian Business,* October 17, 2012, accessed September 11, 2019, https://www.canadianbusiness.com/innovation/the-golden-goose/; Hollie Shaw, "Canada Goose's Made-in-Canada Marketing Strategy Translates into Success," *Financial Post,* May 18, 2012, accessed September 11, 2019, http://business.financialpost.com/2012/05/18/canada-gooses-made-in-canada-marketing-strategy-translates-into-success/; Josh O'Kane, "Canada Goose CEO's 'Aha' Moment: I Realized the Brand Was Real," *Globe and Mail,* updated May 7, 2018, accessed September 11, 2019, www.theglobeandmail.com/report-on-business/small-business/sb-growth/day-to-day/canada-goose-ceos-aha-moment-i-realized-the-brand-was-real/article10982951/; "Canada Goose Stock Goes Public Today on Toronto, New York Stock Exchanges," *Canadian Business,* March 16, 2017, accessed September 11, 2019, https://www.canadianbusiness.com/business-news/canada-goose-ipo-toronto-new-york/.
- **Small Business in Action 14-1** - Statistics Canada, *Small Business Quarterly,* January 2001; S. Birley, "Succession in the Family Firm: The Inheritor's View," *Journal of Small Business Management,* vol. 24, no. 3 (July 1986), p. 36; Brenda Dalglish, "Family Feud," *Maclean's,* September 3, 1993, accessed October 3, 2019, https://archive.macleans.ca/article/1993/9/6/family-feud; John Lorinc, "The Golden Goose," *Canadian Business,* October 17, 2012, accessed October 8, 2019, https://www.canadianbusiness.com/innovation/the-golden-goose/; Jennifer Low, "Dad, When Are You Going to Let Go?" *Profit,* October 1991, p. 28.
- **Small Business in Action 14-2** - Adapted from "Success Story: Family Succession Know-how," *Business Development Bank of Canada Newsletter,* November 2008, p. 2.
- **Figure 14-1** - "Mom and Pop Quiz: How Succession-Ready Is Your Company?" *Success,* December 1998, p. 80.
- **Small Business in Action 14-3** - Julienne Isaacs, "Cottonwood Holsteins: Being the Ultimate Partner in Succession Planning," Family Farm Succession, June 09, 2017, accessed October 6, 2019, https://www.familyfarmsuccession.ca/success-stories/cottonwood-holsteins-being-the-ultimate-partner-in-succession-planning-17; Jennifer Paige, "Transitioning the Poultry Farm to the Fourth Generation," Family Farm Succession, June 09, 2017, accessed October 6, 2019, https://www.familyfarmsuccession.ca/success-stories/transitioning-the-poultry-farm-to-the-fourth-generation-18.
- **Table 14-1** - *The Globe and Mail,* June 12, 1996, p. B7.

Index

B

C

D

E

F

G

H

I

J

K

L

M

N

O

P

Q

R

S

T

U

V

W

X

Y

Z